TAB KEY

For Ann and Betty—
without whom . . .

Canadian Cataloguing in Publication Data

Messenger, William E., 1931–
   The Canadian writer's handbook

Includes index.
ISBN 0-13-113259-8

1. English language – Grammar – 1950– 2. English
language – Composition and exercises. I. De Bruyn,
Jan, 1918– II. Title.

PE1408.M48 1985   808'.042   C85-099348-2

©1986 by Prentice-Hall Canada Inc.
Scarborough, Ontario

Prentice-Hall, Inc., Englewood Cliffs, New Jersey
Prentice-Hall International, Inc., London
Prentice-Hall of Australia, Pty., Ltd., Sydney
Prentice-Hall of India Pvt., Ltd., New Delhi
Prentice-Hall of Japan, Inc., Tokyo
Prentice-Hall of Southeast Asia (Pte.) Ltd., Singapore
Editora Prentice-Hall do Brasil Ltda., Rio de Janeiro
Prentice-Hall Hispanoamericana, S.A., Mexico

ISBN 0-13-113259-8

Production editors: Mary Land, Maureen Chill
Designer: Steven Boyle
Production co-ordinator: Joanne Matthews
Typesetter: Q Composition Inc.
Printed and bound in Canada by Alger Press Ltd.

3 4 5 6 AP 91 90 89

THE CANADIAN WRITER'S HANDBOOK

SECOND EDITION

WILLIAM E. MESSENGER
Department of English
University of British Columbia

JAN DE BRUYN
Department of English
University of British Columbia

Prentice-Hall Canada Inc.
Scarborough, Ontario

CONTENTS

PART TWO
MECHANICS   241

VI SPELLING 258

PREFACE:
How to Use This Book

The second edition of *The Canadian Writer's Handbook*, like the first, is intended to help you improve your use of English, especially to help you write correctly and effectively. To that end, it covers even more thoroughly than before the conventions of grammar and syntax, punctuation, mechanics, spelling, and usage that prevail in Canada today; and in new or greatly expanded sections it covers such matters as clarity and emphasis, effective sentences and paragraphs, argument, and the entire writing process, including planning and organization. Along with the many other improvements, this new edition offers twice as many exercises for you to practise on. Though it remains a handbook—a reference text—it is also a text that can be taught and, above all, a text that can be studied.

The first thing to do with this book is to familiarize yourself with its contents: what it has to offer, how the material is arranged, what the table of contents and index and cross-referencing enable you to find. Useful advice won't help you if you never discover that it is there.

Some writers will want to begin at the beginning and proceed carefully through the book. Many points in the later chapters will not be fully clear to you unless you understand the material in the early chapters. If you understand basic grammar—the parts of speech and their functions, and the syntactic principles governing English sentences—you may need no more than a quick review of the first three chapters. The obvious way to find out if you know the material is to test yourself with the exercises that appear with each section.

If you know or find out that you are weak on specific points, concentrate on them; do all the pertinent exercises and have them checked by an instructor or someone similarly knowledgeable. An instructor who considers a student weak in some particular matter may assign the relevant section and its exercises for special study or review. Or an instructor may assign one or more sections to a whole class for study and discussion.

When you finish a piece of writing, check your work by going through the *Omnibus Checklist* (Chapter XII). If you come across something about which you feel less than confident, follow the cross-references to the sections that will give you the help you need.

When an essay is returned to you with marks and comments, first consult Chapter XI, "The Correction Symbols Explained." The information it contains may be enough to enable you to understand and correct your errors. But if you need more than a reminder about a specific kind of error or weakness — if you don't understand the fundamental principles the error violates — simply follow the cross-references provided and study the sections that discuss and illustrate those principles in greater detail. You should then be able to make the necessary corrections and revisions with understanding and confidence.

An important feature of this book is that various kinds of errors and weaknesses are discussed and illustrated in several places: in the main discussions themselves, in the exercises that accompany those discussions, in the review exercises at the ends of major chapters, in the sample essays, and in the chapter explaining the correction symbols. If one or another of these is not sufficient to clarify a point, remember that you have not yet exhausted the available resources: consult the other relevant parts of the book as well. If necessary use the index to find them (it lists even the exercises).

The book is divided into sections and subsections that are numbered consecutively throughout, without regard to chapters. Cross-references in the text are to section and subsection numbers, or occasionally to chapter numbers (Roman numerals); in the index, references are to page numbers. Most instructors prefer to use the correction symbols to indicate errors or weaknesses, but some may wish to use these section numbers instead. Or an instructor may use a correction symbol, such as *p* (for punctuation) and require a student to provide, as part of the correction, the precise number relevant to a particular error, such as 37a (restrictive and nonrestrictive relative clauses).

The exercises are not numbered consecutively but according to the sections or subsections they appear in. For example Exercise 24 deals with dangling modifiers, the subject of section 24. (Not all sections include exercises.) A particular exercise may be assigned for written submission, for discussion in conference with the instructor, or for oral presentation or group discussion in class. But you needn't wait for exercises to be assigned: if a particular matter interests you or troubles you, do the exercise that covers it; most instructors will be happy to look over the work you do on your own.

The first time or two an important term occurs in the book, it appears in **boldface type**, like that. Pay attention to these terms, for they make up the basic vocabulary necessary for the intelligent discussion of grammar, syntax, and style. If you don't know the terms, much of what this book is telling you won't mean much or help much, nor will a good deal of what your instructor tells you, whether in class or in comments on your papers.

If you use it conscientiously and carefully, this book will be a trustworthy and helpful authority and guide as you work to improve your writing.

Acknowledgments: Over many years of teaching and being taught, one absorbs much from one's teachers, colleagues, and students. Further, a book such as this must by its nature owe much to its predecessors, each of which, like this one, builds upon the work of others. In preparing this second edition, we have also been aided by the criticisms and suggestions of teachers and students who used the first edition. Such indebtedness is too broad and manifold to be detailed here. But we wish particularly to thank several friends and colleagues for their spiritual and material contributions, whether to the first or second edition or both: Moira Farrow, Lilita Rodman, Hilda L. Thomas, Professors Raymond E. Parshall and Peter A. Taylor, and especially Margaret New and Professors Ann P. Messenger and W.H. New, who scrutinized the entire manuscript and made many valuable suggestions for its improvement. We are also grateful to others who reviewed the manuscripts for the first and second editions of this book and offered helpful suggestions and criticisms: they were, for the first edition, L.W. Connolly (University of Guelph), Victor A. Neufeldt (University of Victoria), Margot Northey (University of Toronto), and Andrew Parkin (University of British Columbia); and for the second edition, Gloria Dalton (Crescent Heights Senior High School, Calgary), Judith Rice Henderson (University of Saskatchewan), Bruce Lundgren (University of Western Ontario), and John Moss (University of Ottawa). With the kind permission of The Certified General Accountants' Association of British Columbia, we have incorporated some material from *Writing Effective English* (1957) and *Effective Writing in Business* (1963), both by Jan de Bruyn. For their encouragement and editorial assistance we remain grateful to Marta Tomins and the late Frank Hintenberger, and to their names we now add those of Clifford J. Newman, Mary Land, Maureen Chill, and especially our project editor, Elynor Kagan. Finally—reserving the position of emphasis and honour for them—we want to express our deep appreciation to all our students over the years, especially to the many who have let us use their sentences, paragraphs, and essays as illustrations and exercises throughout this book.

INTRODUCTION:
The Conventions of Language

Words are the building-blocks with which people put together language structures that enable them to communicate with each other. Combinations of words produce sentences; combinations of sentences produce paragraphs; combinations of paragraphs can form stories, detailed expositions, descriptions, arguments. When we write we represent speech sounds with symbols called letters which combine to form the units of sound called words. People who share familiarity with a language are able to communicate because each person knows the meaning of the sounds. If you said "Look" when you meant to convey the meaning of "Listen," you would fail to communicate. The success of the process depends upon the universal acceptance of the **convention**.

The combining of words into sentences is equally subject to conventions which help to ensure that the process of communication will be successful. Hence, words are arranged in certain orders, and certain ways of indicating relations between words have become standard; and in symbolizing speech in writing, some visual conventions have been introduced that clarify meaning and make unambiguous communication easier. The conventions governing the arrangement of words and the relations between words constitute the **grammar** of a language. The visual non-verbal conventions necessitated by writing as opposed to speaking are called **punctuation**. In these first four chapters we describe and illustrate these conventions and ways of avoiding common errors in their use.

Don't be intimidated or otherwise made uncomfortable by the thought that you're studying "grammar." You are doing so primarily as a means to an end: to find out how to control your writing, how to avoid weaknesses in it, and thus how to write more effectively. And look at it this way: if you are reading these words and sentences and understanding what we are saying, you already *know* a great deal of grammar; chances are you learned it, unconsciously, early in life. All you need do now is raise some of that unconscious understanding into consciousness so that you can use it—when you need to—to help you control the effectiveness of your writing. Most often you probably won't need to, for you will be able to trust your unconscious grasp of the way English words and sentences work. But if English is not your first language, you may have to make much more frequent and conscious use of the principles you learn from this book.

The term *grammar* as we are using it here refers less to the systematic study of everything pertaining to language than to the description of how the elements of English words and sentences work. In large part the term *grammar* is virtually equivalent to the term *syntax*, which refers to the relations among and the order of words in individual sentences. We have for the most part retained the vocabulary of "traditional grammar," because for many it still has the virtue of simplicity and familiarity and, as well, of being the vocabulary most likely to be useful whenever you undertake to learn another language. It is also the vocabulary used by dictionaries in their definitions and in their discussions of usage.

Learning these terms and their meanings should not be difficult. Many people learn the basic details presented in this and other such books in a matter of only a few days. If you find the task difficult, you may well be making it unnecessarily difficult for yourself. If you fight the material, it will fight back. But if you approach it with interest and a genuine desire to learn, you'll find that it will co-operate with you and that the quality of your writing will improve as you increase your mastery of the conventions. Further, a great deal of what your knowledge will enable you to do is less a matter of following "rules" in order to produce "correct" sentences than a matter of knowing how to *choose* one form or usage or order rather than another. Good writing is often a result of being able to make intelligent choices from the alternatives available to you.

SENTENCES:
Their Elements and Basic Patterns

The first four chapters of this book are about sentences, the primary units of communication: how they work, what goes into them, what their varieties are, how they are arranged, how they are punctuated. This chapter introduces the basic elements and patterns of English sentences and defines and classifies different kinds of sentences. Understanding the material in this chapter is essential to an understanding of the discussions and advice in succeeding chapters.

1 The Conventions of Sentences

Perhaps the most obvious fact about sentences is that they have a purpose, namely to communicate ideas or feelings. And there are certain *conventional* ways of communicating certain things. For example, if someone says to you,

> I didn't finish my homework last night.

you know that you are to understand the sentence as stating a fact, or a supposed fact. If the same person then says,

> Did you get your history report written?

you know that you are being asked a question and that you are expected to give an answer. If your friend then says,

> Leave me alone for a while.

you know that you are being told to do something, that you are being given a mild command. And when your fellow-student says

What a tough assignment!

you know that you are hearing an emphatic expression of strong feeling.

We all know how to take these different kinds of utterances because we all understand and accept the *conventions* of the way sentences communicate. That is, we can classify sentences according to the kind of purpose each has. Sentences that *make statements* we call **declarative**:

> Canada is a large country.
> Crime doesn't pay.
> The police-officer asked me a question.
> There will be a quiz on this material at the beginning of Wednesday's class.

Sentences that *ask questions* we call **interrogative**; in writing, they end with a **question mark**:

> Was John A. Macdonald an effective leader?
> Are you going to the concert?
> Have you been drinking?
> Who will speak first?
> What do you think?
> When?
> What for?

Sentences that *give commands* or *make requests*, that expect action or compliance, we call **imperative**:

> Please close the door.
> Be sure to get to class on time tomorrow.
> Proofread carefully.

And there are also **exclamatory** sentences, sentences that exclaim, that express strong feeling with particular vigour or emphasis; these customarily end with an **exclamation point**:

> Wow!
> That was quite a day!
> Not if I can help it!

Like many other traditional categories, however, these classifications aren't always so simple or obvious. For example, a sentence may include both *interrogative* and *declarative* elements:

> "Have you been drinking?" the police-officer asked.

or both *imperative* and *declarative* elements:

> Be sure to get to class on time tomorrow: there's going to be a quiz.

A sentence may easily be both *imperative* and *exclamatory*:

> Stop that!

And many *imperative* sentences, especially those that make requests, are at least implicitly *interrogative* even though they don't end with a question mark:

> Take these books back to the library for me. (Will you please take these books back to the library for me?)

Sometimes the same basic sense can be expressed in all four ways:

> I need your help.
> Will you help me?
> Help me with this.
> Help!

Nevertheless, you're seldom in doubt about the purpose of sentences you hear or read, and you're seldom if ever in doubt about the purpose or purposes of any particular sentence you speak or write. Your unconscious awareness of the *conventions* guides you: you know instinctively how you must frame a sentence in order to make it do what you want it to do.

But an improved grasp of sentences and the way they work will help you frame your sentences even more effectively than you now do; it will help you at those moments when you are in doubt; and it will help you not only to avoid weaknesses and errors but also to revise and correct them when they do occur. Since the vast majority of sentences are *declarative* sentences, their patterns are the ones you need to understand first. Most of the rest of this chapter, then, deals with the basic patterns and elements of declarative sentences.

1a Subject and Predicate, Noun and Verb

A standard declarative sentence consists of two parts, a **subject** and a **predicate**. The subject is what acts or is talked about; the predicate is what the subject does or what is said about it.

For example:

Subject	Predicate
Grass	grows.
Cats	scratch.
They	purr.
I	paint.

The essential element of the subject part of a sentence is a **noun** (*Grass, Cats*) or a **pronoun** (*They, I*) (see **2** and **3**); the essential element of the predicate part of a sentence is a **verb** (*grows, scratch, purr, paint*) (see **6**).

Exercise 1a

Compose ten two-word sentences similar to those given above. Each must have a single-word noun or a pronoun as its subject and a single-word verb as its predicate.

1b   Articles and Other Modifiers

Few sentences, however, consist of only a one-word subject and a one-word predicate. Frequently, for example, nouns are preceded by **articles** (*a, an, the*) (see **8c**):

Subject	Predicate
The grass	grew.

And both the subject and the predicate parts of sentences often include **modifiers,** words that change or limit the meaning of nouns and verbs. Nouns, for example, are modified by **adjectives** (see **8**):

Subject	Predicate
The *green* grass	grew.
An *angry* cat	will scratch.

And verbs are modified by **adverbs** (see **9**):

Subject	Predicate
The green grass	grew *profusely.*
They	purr *contentedly.*

Exercise 1b

Rewrite at least five of the sentences you wrote for Exercise 1a, adding articles and single-word adjectives and adverbs to them as you think appropriate.

1c-k   Basic Sentence Patterns

Such single-word modifiers as those above, however, account for only part of the richness of many sentences, with their array of modifying phrases and clauses (see for example the sentences discussed in section **15**). Yet complicated as they may often seem, almost all English sentences use only a few basic patterns. If you can recognize and understand these half-dozen simple patterns, you are well on your way to being able to analyze any sentence you read—or write.

1c   Sentence Pattern 1

This is the pattern you've already looked at and imitated. The subject consists of a noun (with its modifiers) or a pronoun; the predicate consists of a verb (with its modifiers):

Subject	Predicate
The Siamese cat	scratched fiercely.
Birds	fly.
These large, ungainly birds	can fly surprisingly fast.
They	soar majestically.

Exercise 1c

Return to the sentences you wrote for Exercise 1b, or compose new ones, this time adding a few more modifiers to the nouns and the verbs.

1d   Sentence Pattern 2A

In this pattern you expand the basic sentence core by adding a **direct object** to the predicate. A direct object, like a subject, must be either a noun or a pronoun, and the verb must be a **transitive verb** (see **6a**):

Subject	Predicate	
noun or pronoun	*transitive verb*	*direct object*
I	paint	pictures.
John	threw	the ball.
Sandra	hates	television.
It	always annoys	her.
Pierre	was picking	flowers.
Farmers	grow	nutritious vegetables.
Nervous cats	scratch	careless children.

In this pattern the subject acts, the verb indicates the action, and the direct object is what the action produces (*pictures*) or is directed toward (*television, children*). Note that nouns serving as direct objects can, like subject-nouns, be modified by adjectives (*nutritious, careless*).

Exercise 1d

Compose five sentences following Pattern 2A, some with modifiers and some without modifiers.

1e   Sentence Pattern 2B

This pattern reverses the order of the main elements of Pattern 2A. That is, the former direct object becomes the subject of the sentence, and the former subject moves to the end after the **preposition** *by* (see **11**). The verb stays in the middle, but changes its form to that of the **passive voice**—a form of the verb *be* followed by a **past participle** (see

10c). Usually you will want to avoid the passive voice, for it is weak and wordy compared to the **active voice**. But occasionally the passive voice is preferable. For example, a detective might say, using Pattern 2A,

> Poison killed him. (active voice)

But in the circumstances it would be more natural to say that

> He was killed by poison. (passive voice)

Similarly, you can write some of the sentences under Pattern 2A, above, according to Pattern 2B, as follows:

Subject	Predicate	
noun	*verb*	*prepositional phrase*
Pictures	are painted	by me.
Television	is hated	by Sandra.
Flowers	were being picked	by Pierre.
Nutritious vegetables	are grown	by farmers.
The ball	was thrown	by John.

But you can see that such alternative sentences would be preferable only in unusual circumstances, for example if you wanted special emphasis on *Flowers*, or *The ball*. Note that in this pattern the *by*-phrase is often omitted as unnecessary or unimportant:

He	has been poisoned	(by someone).

See also **6m-n** and **18f**.

Exercise 1e

Convert each of the sentences you wrote for Exercise 1d into Pattern 2B. How many of them now seem to be sentences you could use in normal discourse? Try to include them in contexts where they would be preferable to the versions you wrote using Pattern 2A.

1f   Sentence Pattern 3

A sentence with a direct object sometimes includes an **indirect object**, which must also be a noun or a pronoun. In this pattern, the verb that has a direct object has another object as well:

Subject	Predicate		
noun	*transitive verb*	*indirect object*	*direct object*
John	threw	me	the ball.
He	told	his friend	a story.
Some teachers	don't give	students	enough homework.

1f *sentence pattern 3*

Note that you can usually vary this pattern, and still say essentially the same thing, by changing the indirect object to a prepositional phrase:

Subject	Predicate		
noun	*transitive verb*	*direct object*	*prepositional phrase*
John	threw	the ball	to me.
Some teachers	don't give	enough homework	to their students.

The prepositional phrase in such a sentence functions as an adverb, modifying the verb (see **9**).

Exercise 1f

Compose five sentences in Pattern 3. Then rewrite two of them so that you use a prepositional phrase, with *to*, instead of an indirect object. Note that in these second versions you change the order of the elements.

1g   Sentence Pattern 4A

Some verbs—called **linking** verbs (see **6a**)—require that something other than an object follow them in the predicate part of the sentence in order to *complete* the idea—something that is therefore called a **complement**. And since it is linked to the subject, it is sometimes called a **subjective** complement. The principal linking verb is the common verb *be* in its various forms (see **6f**). In Pattern 4A, such a verb links the subject to an adjectival modifier in the predicate part of the sentence; the modifier is therefore called a **predicate adjective**. Here are some examples of Pattern 4A:

Subject	Predicate	
noun	*linking verb*	*subjective complement (predicate adjective)*
Sharon	is	rich.
John	isn't	tired.
Computers	are becoming	ubiquitous.
Anchovies	taste	salty.
Tame cats	are	relatively safe.

Exercise 1g

Compose three sentences on the model of Pattern 4A.

1h **Sentence Pattern 4B**

Again in this pattern a subject is followed by a linking verb that begins the predicate. But instead of being completed by an adjective, as in Pattern 4A, in Pattern 4B the predicate is completed by a noun or pronoun; this complement is therefore called a **predicate noun**:

Subject	Predicate	
noun	*linking verb*	*subjective complement (predicate noun)*
Anna	is	a lawyer.
This	is	it.
The most popular boy	was	an athlete.
Margaret Atwood	is	a well-known poet.
She	is	also a novelist.
Computers	are	useful tools.
Irving	remains	a Montrealer.
Some good cooks	are	men.

See also **6a**.

Exercise 1h

Compose three sentences on the model of Pattern 4B.

1i **Sentence Pattern 5A**

Another useful pattern—though not a common one—forms itself around verbs such as *appoint, believe, call, consider, declare, designate, elect, find, judge, make, name, nominate, select,* and *think,* which are sometimes followed not only by a direct object but also by what is called an **objective complement**—that is, a complement that describes the object rather than the subject. In Pattern 5A, a direct object is described by an *adjective,* just as the subject is in Pattern 4A:

Subject	Predicate		
noun	*transitive verb*	*direct object*	*objective complement (adjective)*
The members	considered	Walter	incompetent.
The jury	found	her	guilty.
They	made	themselves	obnoxious.

Exercise 1i

Compose three sentences on the model of Pattern 5A.

1j   Sentence Pattern 5B

In this variation, the objective complement completes the meaning of the object with another *noun*, just as a noun links with the subject in Pattern 4B:

Subject	Predicate		
	transitive		*objective complement*
noun	*verb*	*direct object*	*(noun)*
The members	elected	Herbert	treasurer.
I	call	that idea	a winner.
Sandra	thinks	television	a waste of time.

Exercise 1j

Compose three sentences on the model of Pattern 5B.

1k   Sentence Pattern 6

This final pattern is another one that, like Pattern 2A (the passive voice), you should not use often: the **expletive** pattern. In this pattern the word *there* or *it* appears at the beginning, in the place usually occupied by the subject; then comes a linking verb, usually a form of the verb *be* (see **6f**); and then comes the subject. The words *there* and *it* serve as structural aids, enabling you to make certain kinds of statements in a more natural way or with a different emphasis than you could otherwise. For example, instead of having to say

Subject	Predicate
That life begins at forty	may be true.
No answers	existed.
No plumbing	was in the cabin.

you can, using Pattern 6, say

Expletive	Linking Verb	Complement	Subject
It	may be	true	that life begins at forty.
There	were		no answers.
There	was		no plumbing in the cabin.

Here are some further examples of Pattern 6:

There were fifteen people at the hearing.
It was difficult to believe him.
It is not easy to succeed.
There are no excuses.
There wasn't a cloud in the sky.
It's delightful the way she can imitate her brother.

See also **7e, 18f,** and **59a.**

Exercise 1k (1)

Try converting the example sentences above into a different pattern (for example, *Fifteen people were at the hearing*). In what kinds of contexts might the alternative—and more direct—versions be preferable?

Exercise 1k (2)

Convert the following sentences into Pattern 6:

1. Ten books are on the table.
2. No way around the obstacle exists.
3. To look directly at a solar eclipse is dangerous.
4. A magnificent occasion occurred.
5. People were everywhere!
6. A fly is in my soup.

Do some of these sentences seem better in the expletive form? Why? How might context determine one's choice?

Exercise 1c-k: Identifying sentence elements and patterns

Identify the pattern of each of the following sentences. Label each subject-noun or -pronoun *s* and each predicate-verb *v*. Then, where appropriate, label each direct object *do*, indirect object *io*, subjective complement *sc*, and objective complement *oc*. If you wish, also label any articles and other modifiers.

1. Food nourishes.
2. Sandra finds television stupid.
3. The Schmidts are amateur cooks.
4. I love spaghetti.
5. There are nine major planets.
6. Poor Stephen was hit by a bus.
7. Jacques brought me luck.
8. Good music can affect one's emotions.
9. The chairman appointed Maya secretary.
10. Most people are generous.

1-1 Other Elements: Structure-Words

Most declarative sentences, then, use one or more of the above patterns. And the elements in those patterns—subjects, verbs, modifiers, objects, and complements—make up the substance of all sentences. In most sentences, however, these elements occur with words like *and, but, for, of, under, with*: words that have little or no denotative meaning by themselves but that are important because they serve to connect the other elements in various ways and thus to establish meaningful relations between them. Such words are sometimes called **structure-words** or **function-words**; most of them belong to two other classes of words, or "parts of speech," **conjunctions** (see **12**) and **prepositions** (see **11**). All these elements are discussed and illustrated at greater length in Chapter II.

1m-r **Phrases and Clauses**

But before you go on to Chapter II, you need to understand the difference between **phrases** and **clauses** and how they function in sentences. Phrases and clauses are groups of words that function as grammatical units or elements *within* sentences but that—with the exception of independent clauses (see **1n**)—cannot stand alone *as* sentences.

1m **Phrases**

A **phrase** is a group of words that does not contain a subject and a predicate but that functions as a grammatical unit in a sentence. For example, a **verb phrase** (see **6g**) acts as the verb in this sentence:

> Most of our guests *will be leaving* in the morning. (Pattern 1)

A **prepositional phrase** (see **11**) can be an adjectival modifier:

> Most *of our guests* will be leaving in the morning.

or an adverbial modifier:

> Most of our guests will be leaving *in the morning*.

The words *Most of our guests*—the pronoun *Most* along with its modifying prepositional phrase—themselves constitute a **noun phrase** functioning as the subject of the sentence. Any noun or pronoun along with its modifiers—so long as the group does not contain a subject-predicate combination—can be thought of as a noun phrase. Similarly, a **gerund phrase** (see **10d**) can function as a subject:

> *Losing weight* can be difficult. (Pattern 4A)

or as a direct object:

> They tried *losing weight*. (Pattern 2A)

A **participial phrase**—always adjectival (see **10c**)—can modify a subject:

> *Obeying his catcher's signal*, Enrique threw the batter a low curve ball. (Pattern 3)

or a direct object:

> The car hit the man *standing on the corner*. (Pattern 2A)

An **infinitive phrase** (see **10a**) can function as a direct object (noun):

> They tried *to lose weight*. (Pattern 2A)

or as a subject (noun):

> It is difficult *to lose weight*. (Pattern 6)

but it can also function as an adjective, for example one modifying the subject:

His failure *to lose weight* was predictable. (Pattern 4A)

or as an adverb, for example one modifying the verb:

He arranged the furniture *to suit his own taste*. (Pattern 2A)

Adverbial phrases, or even single-word adverbs, can also act as **sentence modifiers**, modifying not the verb or any other word alone but rather all the rest of the sentence:

Luckily,
In fact,   the fundamentals of grammar are easily mastered.
To be sure,

1n Independent Clauses

A **clause** is a group of words that, like the sentences discussed in the preceding sections, contains both a *subject* and a *predicate*. If it is an **independent clause**, it can, as the term indicates, stand by itself as a sentence. Each of the sample sentences in the preceding sections is an independent clause, since each contains the minimum requirement: a noun as subject and a verb functioning in the predicate; each is a **simple sentence** (see **1z**).

But an independent clause need not be treated as a sentence by itself; it can also function as only part of a sentence. For example, if you start with two separate independent clauses—that is, two separate sentences—like these:

Tuition fees went up.
Students complained.

you can put them together to form a **compound sentence** (see **1z**):

Tuition fees went up; students complained.
Tuition fees went up, and students complained.
Tuition fees went up; therefore students complained.

Each of the two halves of these sentences is an independent clause; each could stand alone as a sentence.

1o Subordinate Clauses

A **subordinate clause**, on the other hand, usually cannot stand by itself. Even though, as a clause, it contains a subject and a predicate, it is by definition *subordinate, dependent* on another clause—an *independent* one—for its meaning. It therefore must be treated as only part of a sentence, as in the following examples (the subordinate clauses are in italics); these are called **complex sentences** (see **1z**):

When tuition fees went up, students complained.
Students complained *because tuition fees went up*.
Students complained *that tuition fees had gone up two years in a row*.
Tuition fees went up, *which angered many students*.

Note that subordinate clauses often begin with such words as *when*, *because*, *that*, and *which*; such words are then called **subordinators**, and often clearly signal the presence of a subordinate clause as opposed to an independent clause (see **12c**).

(Of course some subordinate clauses could be used separately, for example in dialogue or as answers to questions, where the context would be clear: Why are students complaining? *Because tuition fees went up*. Except in such special circumstances, however, a subordinate clause should not be allowed to stand by itself as if it were a sentence. See **1x** and **1y**.)

1p   Functions of Subordinate Clauses

Like a phrase, a subordinate clause functions as a grammatical unit in its sentence. That is, subordinate clauses can occupy several of the slots in the sentence patterns illustrated above. For example, a **noun clause** can serve as the subject of a sentence.

That hummingbirds can fly is astonishing. (Pattern 4A)

as a direct object:

Jill knows *what she is doing*. (Pattern 2A)

or as a predicate noun:

The question is *where the money is going to come from*. (Pattern 4B)

Adjectival clauses (also called relative clauses) modify nouns or pronouns, such as a direct object:

The principal congratulated the student *who had won the prize*. (Pattern 2A)

or a subject:

The horse *that she had bet on* won easily. (Pattern 1)

Adverbial clauses usually modify main verbs:

He wept *because he was deeply moved*. (Pattern 1)

Exercise 1 m-p: Recognizing phrases and clauses

After each of the following groups of words, indicate whether it is an independent clause, a subordinate clause, or a phrase. Label the subject (*s*) and verb (*v*) of each clause.

1. not only Lily but Joan as well
2. never had he seen such a storm

3. for the first time in her life she was happy
4. since no one was looking
5. around the corner from our house
6. but the minister was not in his office
7. while she was on the telephone
8. the boat sank
9. after the party was over
10. according to the elaborately printed instructions in the guidebook

---

1q Appositives

Two other kinds of phrases you should be familiar with are the *appositive* and the *absolute*.

An **appositive phrase** is a group of words that renames or restates, in other terms, the meaning of a neighbouring word. For example if you start with two simple sentences,

Marvin is our gardener. He looks after the flowers.

you can reduce the first and combine it with the second:

Marvin, *our gardener*, looks after the flowers.

Most appositives are nouns or noun phrases that redefine, usually in more specific terms, the nouns they follow. Occasionally, however, the appositive precedes the other noun:

A fine gardener, Marvin deserves our gratitude.

And occasionally another part of speech can function as an appositive, for example a participial (adjective) phrase:

Studying assiduously, *reviewing every page of the text*, they prepared for the exam.

or a verb:

Parse (*analyze grammatically*) some of these sentences.

An appositive can also consist of a single word, often a name:

Our gardener, *Marvin*, looks after the flowers.

And, rarely, even a subordinate clause can function as an appositive:

How I got here—*whether I paid my own way or not*—is none of your business.

Note that an appositive is grammatically equivalent to the term it defines, and could replace it in the sentence:

Our gardener looks after the flowers.
A fine gardener deserves our gratitude.
Reviewing every page of the text, they prepared for the exam.

Analyze some of these sentences grammatically.

Marvin looks after the flowers.

Whether I paid my own way or not is none of your business.

(For the punctuation of appositives, see **37b** and **44g.**)

Exercise 1q (1): Writing appositives

By reducing one of each pair to an appositive, combine each of the following pairs of sentences into a single sentence. Construct one or two of them so that the appositive comes first.

1. Fido is a lazy mutt. He sleeps most of the day.
2. The manager is a stickler for accuracy. She insists that we triple-check every set of figures.
3. I must thank my uncle for putting me through school. He is a wealthy man.
4. The mayor believes in ghosts. He attends séances at least once a month.
5. You can save time by preparing carefully. That is, you can take careful notes and draw up a preliminary outline.

Exercise 1q (2): Using appositives

Combine each of the following pairs of sentences into a single sentence by reducing all or part of one of them to an appositive. You will be able to drop some words, and you may want to change and rearrange others, but don't change the essential meaning. For practice, try doing some of the sentences in more than one way; then decide which version you prefer, and why.

Example: Hong Kong is a British Crown Colony. It is a major Pacific commercial centre.

Hong Kong, a British Crown Colony, is a major Pacific commercial centre.

Hong Kong, a major Pacific commercial centre, is a British Crown Colony.

A British Crown Colony, Hong Kong, is a major Pacific commercial centre.

A British Crown Colony, Hong Kong is a major Pacific commercial centre.

1. The book I read last weekend is *The Jewel in the Crown*. It is the first volume of Paul Scott's *The Raj Quartet*.
2. To become a good doctor is not easy. It takes many years of study and hard work.
3. I always look forward to September. It is the month when the new academic year begins.
4. My hobbies more than occupy my spare time. I collect stamps, play chess, listen to classical music, and eat.
5. Tabloid newspapers seem to go in for sensationalism. They are the smaller, easier-to-hold newspapers.
6. Canada has a larger land mass than any other country, except the Soviet Union. It is a country with a relatively small population.

7. She was relaxed and confident when she began the race. She was sure she could win.
8. The word *hamburger* is one of the common words we take for granted. It comes from the name of a German city.
9. Dr. Snyder is our family physician. He is a dedicated man who works long hours.
10. Running marathons is not something everyone should try. It is a potentially dangerous sport.

1r   Absolute Phrases

Like appositives, **absolute phrases** have no direct grammatical link with what they modify; they depend simply on juxtaposition, in effect modifying the rest of the sentence by hovering over it like an umbrella. Most absolute phrases amount to a sentence with the verb changed to a participle (see **10c**). Instead of using two sentences,

> The sky had cleared. The game could finally begin.

you can reduce the first to an absolute phrase modifying the second:

> *The sky having cleared,* the game could finally begin.

If the original verb is a form of *be,* the participle can often be omitted:

> *Her last exam (being) over,* Elana relaxed for the rest of the day.
> In the heavy seas the ship pitched wildly, *its bows (being) sometimes entirely awash.*

Sometimes, especially with certain more-or-less idiomatic expressions, the participle is not preceded by a noun:

> There were a few rough spots, but *generally speaking* the rehearsal was a success.
> *Judging by the results,* it was not a good campaign.

And sometimes infinitives (*to*-phrases) function as absolutes:

> *To say the least,* the campaign was not a success.

You can also think of many absolutes as *with*-phrases (prepositional) from which the preposition has been dropped:

> *(With) Her last exam finished,* Elana could relax.
> The ship pitched wildly, *(with) its bows sometimes awash.*

And you can think of most absolutes as functioning much like an adverb modifying the whole of the sentence it's attached to (see **9**):

> absolute: *All things considered,* it was a fair examination.
> adverb: *Unfortunately,* I hadn't studied hard enough.

See also **10f** and Exercise 10 (5).

Exercise 1r: Writing absolute phrases

Compose five sentences using absolute phrases. You may want to start with pairs of sentences or with sentences containing a *with*-phrase.

The foregoing examples are not meant to be exhaustive. Rather they illustrate some of the great variety of ways you can use phrases and subordinate clauses as elements in different kinds of sentences. (Chapters II and III further discuss and illustrate these and several other kinds of elements as they combine to make up sentences.) You may be able to write well enough without consciously knowing all, or any, of these grammatical principles. But if you have any difficulty writing correct and effective sentences—and nearly all writers do—you will find it much easier to overcome your difficulties if you know how sentences work. More positively, the greater your understanding of how sentences work, the greater will be your ability to control your writing, to make intelligent choices among the syntactical and stylistic alternatives available to you. You will find an understanding of sentence grammar especially useful in helping you improve both the correctness and the effectiveness of your punctuation (see Chapter IV). And basic to such an understanding are your awareness of the various sentence patterns and your ability to recognize phrases and clauses.

1s **Order of Essential Elements in Declarative Sentences**

You probably recognized some or all of the basic patterns as standard ways of putting words together to make statements. Even if you don't—or didn't—know the names of all the bits and pieces, chances are you felt the sample sentences to be natural ones, the kinds you use every day without even thinking about their structure. Note that the natural order of the elements in almost all the patterns for these declarative sentences is the same:

> subject–verb
> subject–transitive verb–object(s)–(objective complement)
> subject–linking verb–subjective complement

The only exception is Pattern 6, the expletive, in which the subject follows the verb (see **1k**).

This conventional order of *subject–verb–object or complement* has proved itself to be the most direct and forceful pattern of expression:

> A stitch in time saves nine.
> Beggars can't be choosers.
> Humpty Dumpty had a great fall.
> Mariposa is not a real town.
> When I go into a bank I get rattled.

I mix a good deal with Millionaires. I like them.
We are such stuff as dreams are made on.
We shall defend every village, every town, and every city.
This was their finest hour.
These are the times that try men's souls.

But this conventional order can be altered to create special stylistic effects, to achieve special emphasis, and to introduce occasional pleasing variations:

direct object	subject	transitive verb	
The dessert, however,	we	ate	with gusto.

subjective complement	linking verb	subject
Evil	was	the day that I first met that man.

Such inversions are not wrong, for conventions (or rules) are made to be broken as well as followed; but their very unconventionality demands that we use them sparingly. Such variations are rare outside of poetry or highly poetic prose:

Such thoughts to Lucy I will give. . . .
No motion has she now. . . .
Thirty days hath September. . . .
And now abideth faith, hope, charity, these three; but the greatest of these is charity.
Never in the field of human conflict was so much owed by so many to so few.

Any pattern that departs from the usual one almost automatically calls attention to itself; for that reason, such variations are seldom appropriate in everyday prose. But used occasionally, and appropriately, they can be highly effective.

Exercise 1s: Using alternative word-orders

Try composing four or five declarative sentences that vary the standard order of elements in one way or another. Then choose one of your sentences and use it in a paragraph that you think justifies the unorthodox order.

1t Order of Elements in Interrogative Sentences (**Questions**)

The conventional order for **interrogative sentences** is usually different from that for declarative sentences. It is of course possible to use the declarative order for a question—for example in speaking, when one can use stress and end with the rising or falling intonation that usually indicates a question:

> The man bit the dog?

thereby conveying a meaning something like

> What?! Do you mean to tell me that the *man* actually bit the *dog*, instead of the other way around?

But except in recording dialogue, it is difficult to use this technique effectively in writing.

Usually, an interrogative sentence, besides ending with the conventional question mark, will take one of the following patterns. If the verb is a single-word form of *be*, it precedes the subject:

verb	subject	subjective complement
Was	Macdonald	an effective leader?

With all other single-word verbs, it is necessary to supply a form of the auxiliary verb *do* before the subject; the main part of the verb then follows the subject in the normal way:

auxiliary verb	subject	main verb
Did	Macdonald	lead effectively?

If the verb is already a verb phrase, the first auxiliary comes before the subject:

auxiliary verb	subject	second auxiliary verb	main verb
Are	you		going?
Will	Max		speak first?
Have	you	been	drinking?

If the question includes a negative, the *not* goes before or after the subject, depending on whether one uses the less formal, contracted form:

> Aren't you going?
> Are you not going?

With questions using expletives (Pattern 6), the expletive and the verb are reversed:

> Were there many people at the hearing?
> Was it difficult to believe him?

With so-called "tag" questions, a statement is followed by a verb-pronoun question; note also that a *not* appears in one or the other of the two parts:

> Mark has been drinking, hasn't he?
> Mark hasn't been drinking, has he?

All the above questions invite a *yes* or *no* answer, perhaps extended by a short clause made up of the appropriate pronoun (or expletive) and auxiliary, such as

> *Yes, he was. Yes, I am. No, I haven't. Yes, there were. No, it wasn't. No, he has not.*

Note that the negative answers include a *not*.

The only other common form of question begins with a *question-word*, one of the interrogative pronouns or adverbs; these invite answers beyond a mere *yes* or *no*. If an interrogative *pronoun* (see **3c**) functions as the *subject*, the sentence retains standard declarative word order:

> Who will speak first?

If the pronoun functions as the *object* of the verb or of a preposition, it will come first; then will come the added auxiliary *do* or the first part of a verb phrase, then the subject, and then the rest of the verb, just as in the *yes or no* pattern:

> Whom did you ask?
> What will the speaker deal with? (*or* With what will the speaker deal?)

The same sort of reversal occurs when an interrogative pronoun functions as a possessive or other adjective (see **8a**):

> Whose (Which, What) explanation did you favour?
> To what (which, whose) problems will the speaker address himself?

(See also **11b**, on the placement of prepositions in questions.) When a question begins with an interrogative *adverb* (see **9a**), again a form of *do* or another already-present auxiliary comes before the subject:

> Where (When) are you going?
> Why did he say that?

Exercise 1t: Constructing interrogative sentences

Select a representative variety of ten or twenty sentences from those you've written for earlier exercises in this chapter and rewrite them as questions. Try using two or more different forms of question for some of the sentences.

1t interrogative order

1u   The Structure of Imperative Sentences (Commands)

Although it is possible, especially with emphatic commands, to use the full structure of a declarative sentence:

Subject	Predicate
You	take that back!
You two in the corner	please stop your chattering.

the conventional form of **imperative sentences** uses only the *predicate* part of the sentence; the *subject* (an understood *you*) is omitted entirely:

> Come into the garden, Maud. (*Maud* is not the subject, but a noun of address; see **2b**).
> Look before you leap.
> Stop that noise.
> Close the door.
> Take two aspirins and go to bed.
> Proofread carefully.
> Hush.

Sometimes, especially in dialogue or informal contexts, even the verb can be omitted; a complement alone does the job:

> Careful. Easy, now. Steady.

You may think that you will have little use for imperative sentences. But if you ever want to write a set of instructions, you will need to use a great many of them. And they can provide useful variety in other contexts as well, just as questions can. *Declarative* sentences are unquestionably the mainstay of expression; but *interrogative* and *imperative* sentences are also necessary. Use them.

Now for a different kind of look at these groups of words called "sentences" that we have been arranging and rearranging:

1v   What Is a Sentence?

The sentence has been variously defined, but most definitions are unsatisfactory and unrealistic. For example, one definition asserts that a sentence is a group of words containing a subject and a finite verb. But here are some sentences which have neither subject nor verb:

> Yes. No. Now or never. Oh my goodness! Wow!

Here are some with a "subject," or a noun or pronoun that could serve as a subject, but no verb:

> Who, me? Well, I never! John. Spaghetti.

Here are some with finite verbs but no stated subjects:

> Come here. Never mind. Call me Ishmael. Sink or swim.

Out of context, these sentences do not tell us very much, but no one will dispute the fact that they are acceptable units. Moreover, there are groups of words which do contain subjects and finite verbs and yet are not sentences. Starting a subordinate clause with a capital letter and ending it with a period does not make it an acceptable sentence:

> I decided to make a list. Before I went shopping.
> He bought me the bicycle. That I had stared at in the store the week before.

The second clause in each of these examples remains a *fragment*. (See **1y**.)

Another common definition claims that a sentence is a complete thought. But there is nothing complete about *Yes* unless we know what precedes it. The same is true of *Oh my goodness! Spaghetti, Never mind*, and the other examples. Moreover, there is nothing necessarily *incomplete* about the thoughts expressed by such words as *dog, hand, chair, liberty, love*; yet these words are not normally thought of as sentences.

Remember that language is speech sound, and you will find that a more realistic definition of a sentence is the following: *A sentence is a satisfyingly complete pattern of intonation or expression*: i.e., a complete utterance. Your voice and natural tone should soon tell you whether or not a certain group of words is a sentence. Get into the habit of reading your written work aloud whenever possible, or at least sound it over in your mind's ear. This practice will help you to avoid serious errors.

1w-y Major Sentences, Minor Sentences, and Fragments

Sentences—that is, acceptable patterns of expression—are of two kinds, which we call **major** and **minor**. Though most of what this and similar books have to say about sentences pertains to *major* sentences, and though you are not likely to have much use for *minor* sentences in formal writing, you should understand what minor sentences are if only so that you can use them occasionally for emphasis or other rhetorical effects or in a piece of dialogue. It is also important that you be able to distinguish between the minor sentence, which is acceptable, and the fragmentary expression, which is not.

1w Major Sentences

A **major sentence** is a grammatically independent group of words that contains at least two essential structural elements: a subject and a finite verb (see **1a** and **6d**).

1x Minor Sentences

A **minor sentence** is an acceptable pattern of expression that nevertheless lacks either a subject or a finite verb, or both. There is no difficulty, however, in supplying the missing element or elements from context, for whereas *major* sentences can usually stand by themselves, most *minor* sentences need a context of one or more nearby major sentences in order to make sense—most obviously, for example, as answers to questions. The minor sentence, however, like the major, is grammatically independent.

An expression which we call a minor sentence is usually one of four kinds:

1. Exclamations: Oh! Well, I never! Heavens!

2. Questions or responses to questions: When? Tomorrow. How many? Seven. Why? What for? How come? What else? Yes. No. Please. Perhaps. Certainly.

3. Proverbial or idiomatic expressions or aphorisms that are so much a part of the language as to be universally understood: Easy come, easy go. Now or never. In a pig's eye! Better late than never.

4. Minor sentences used for rhetorical or stylistic effect by writers who know how to handle them. They are more common in narrative and descriptive writing, but they can be effective in other contexts as well. Here for example is how Dickens begins *Bleak House*:

> London. Michaelmas Term lately over, and the Lord Chancellor sitting in Lincoln's Inn Hall. Implacable November weather. As much mud in the streets, as if the waters had but newly retired from the face of the earth, and it would not be wonderful to meet a Megalosaurus, forty feet long or so, waddling like an elephantine lizard up Holborn Hill.

And so on for three fairly long paragraphs. Here is how William Zinsser begins his essay "Nobody Here but Us Dead Sheep" (1969):

> Nerve gas in Okinawa. Nuclear explosions in Nevada. Chemical Mace in the eyes. Every day it's something else in American life which strikes me as outlandish.

One student began an essay this way:

> Money, money, money. It makes the world go round.

And here is a paragraph from another student's essay:

> One of my favourite distractions is my junk drawer. You know, that drawer in the kitchen overflowing with miscellaneous tidbits of memorabilia. The treasure chest of hastily tossed-in articles which may include anything from letters, coupons long past their expiry date, junk mail, and old photos, to the odd sock you thought the washing-machine ate.

1y ▌ Fragments
frag

Be careful to distinguish between acceptable minor sentences and unacceptable **fragments**.

> *frag:* I did not attend the meeting. Because I felt that it would be a waste of time.

The "because" clause is a fragment; the period after *meeting* should be changed to a comma so that the subordinate clause can take its rightful place in the sentence. (Note, however, that "Because I felt that it would be a waste of time," like many other fragments, would be acceptable in a different context, for example if it were the answer to an immediately preceding question: Why didn't I go to the meeting? Because I felt that it would be a waste of time.)

> *frag:* It was a terrible scene. One that I will never forget.

The clause beginning with *one* should be linked to the preceding independent clause with a comma, not separated from it by a period; it can then take its rightful place as a noun clause in apposition to *scene*.

> *frag:* She gave me back the ring. Being of a forgiving nature.

The participial phrase beginning with *being* is not a separate sentence but an adjective modifying *She*; it should be introduced by a comma, or even moved to the beginning of the sentence:

> Being of a forgiving nature, she gave me back the ring.

The fragments in these examples (which tend to come after the independent clauses with which they should be joined) are not satisfyingly complete patterns of intonation, and therefore should not be treated as minor sentences.

Exercise 1xy: Recognizing minor sentences and fragments

Indicate whether the second group of words in each of the following is a minor sentence or a fragment.

1. He stayed in the parking place. Until the time on the meter had run out.
2. Just look at the way she's dressed. Good heavens!
3. You say you've never seen this man? Never?
4. He decided to stay in bed until eleven. It being a Sunday, after all.
5. How much wood can a woodchuck chuck? Plenty.

1z ▌ Kinds of Major Sentences

Sentences are usually classified as simple, compound, complex, and compound-complex.

Simple sentences have one subject and one finite verb, and therefore contain only one clause, an independent clause:

> Denis works.
> The boat leaks.
> The dilapidated old building collapsed during the night.

The subject or the verb, or both, can be compound—that is, consist of more than one part—but the sentence containing them will still be simple:

> *Jules and Kim* left early. (compound subject)
> He *watched and waited*. (compound verb)
> The *sergeant and his men moved* down the hill *and crossed* the river. (compound subject, compound verb)

Compound sentences in effect consist of two or more simple sentences—that is, independent clauses—linked by co-ordinating conjunctions (see **12a**), by punctuation, or by both:

> The starter's flag fell and the race began.
> The clouds massed thickly against the hills; soon the rain fell in torrents.
> He wanted to go by plane, but she insisted on taking a ship.
> Gabriel's patience and persistence worked: he not only won the prize but also earned his competitors' respect. (compound subject in the first clause, compound verb in the second)
> The day was warm, the breeze was mild, and everyone had a a good time.

Complex sentences consist of one independent clause and one or more subordinate clauses; in the following examples, the subordinate clauses are italicized:

> He claimed *that he was innocent*. (noun clause as direct object)
> She left *before the party was over*. (adverbial clause modifying *left*)
> Ivan is the one *who is most likely to win*. (adjectival clause modifying *one*)
> Anita, *who is the most intelligent*, scored highest. (adjectival clause modifying *Anita*)
> *When the time came*, he put his belongings in the suitcase *which he was carrying*. (adverbial clause modifying *put*; adjectival clause modifying *suitcase*)
> *Although it was late*, they decided to start anyway. (adverbial clause of concession, in effect modifying the rest of the sentence)

Note that subordinate clauses are most often introduced by some subordinating word, such as a relative pronoun (*who, which*) or a subordinating conjunction (*before, when, although*) (see **12c**). But note that, when the meaning is clear, the conjunction *that* introducing the noun clause, or the relative pronouns *that* or *which*, can be omitted:

> He claimed *he was innocent.*
> . . . the suitcase *he was carrying.*

The clauses in question nevertheless remain subordinate.

Compound-complex sentences consist of two or more independent clauses and one or more subordinate clauses:

> Because he knew that the job was important, he began very carefully, but as time passed he grew impatient and therefore he failed to obtain the results he had hoped for.

Analyzing this example:

> Because he knew (adverbial clause)
> that the job was important (noun clause)
> he began very carefully (independent clause)
> but (co-ordinating conjunction)
> as time passed (adverbial clause)
> he grew impatient (independent clause)
> and (co-ordinating conjunction)
> therefore (conjunctive adverb)
> he failed to obtain the results (independent clause)
> [that] he had hoped for (adjective clause)

Exercise 1z (1): Recognizing kinds of sentences

Label each of the following sentences as simple, compound, complex, or compound-complex.

1. Although Canada has a vast territory, its population is relatively small.
2. Nobody is going to give you something for nothing.
3. The man who fixed my car yesterday is the same one I took it to last year.
4. The rains came and the river rose.
5. Few things are more pleasant than a lovingly prepared and carefully served elegant meal consisting of several courses, consumed in good company, with soft background music, and accompanied by noble wines.
6. He saw the book he wanted on the top shelf, but he couldn't reach it.
7. Josephine decided against going for a ride in his flying machine.
8. A philosophy major may learn to think clearly and may even acquire a sense of cultural history, but when he graduates he will probably have difficulty finding a job that makes use of his training.
9. Whether violence on television is responsible for violent behaviour in children, or even in adults, is debatable.
10. Northern oil and gas deposits have created a mixture of benefits and problems for Canadians and Americans alike.

1z   major sentences

1z   major sentences

Exercise 1z (2): Constructing different kinds of sentences

(a) Compose three simple sentences.

(b) Compose three compound sentences, each with two independent clauses.

(c) Compose three complex sentences, each containing one independent and one subordinate clause.

(d) Compose three compound-complex sentences, each containing two independent clauses and one or more subordinate clauses.

Try recycling one or more of your original simple sentences as you go on to the more complicated sentences. Use as many other modifiers—words and phrases—as you want.

THE PARTS OF SPEECH AND HOW THEY WORK IN SENTENCES

Introduction: Word Order, Inflection, and the Parts of Speech

As you saw in Chapter I, *word order* is important in English, for it helps determine whether a sentence is asking a question or making a statement. But the standard word order of sentences is important in another and even more basic way. The order of elements in Pattern 2A, for example—subject, verb, direct object—determines *meaning*. Take for example this sentence:

> Cats dislike dogs.

Clear enough, for we know, from standard English word order, that *Cats* is the subject, *dislike* the verb, and *dogs* the direct object. If we reverse the order, the meaning too is reversed:

> Dogs dislike cats.

Now we know that *Dogs* are doing the disliking and that *cats* are the objects of the dislike. If you know a language like German or Latin, you know how different—and in some ways more difficult—they can be; for in such languages it is the *form* of the words, rather than their order, that determines meaning. For example the sentence

> Dogs cats dislike.

would, in English, not only sound awkward but also be equally capable of two interpretations. But the same three words in Latin, for example, would be clear because the forms of the two nouns, *dogs* and *cats*, would show which was subject and which was object, in effect saying either

> Dogs (subject)–cats (object)–dislike.

(that is, *Dogs dislike cats*) or

> Dogs (object)–cats (subject)–dislike.

(that is, *Cats dislike dogs*).

The change in a word's form is called **inflection**; that is, a word's form is changed, or **inflected**, to fit particular circumstances. A language like Latin or German, in which inflection is the primary key to grammatical or syntactical relations, is called *synthetic*; a language like English, whose grammar is predominantly expressed by word order rather than by inflection, is called *analytic*. But English is not a purely analytic language, for it retains some features of its synthetic ancestor, Anglo-Saxon: some words in modern English must be inflected in order for sentences to communicate clearly. If for example you want the word *boy* to denote more than one male youngster, you change it— inflect it—by adding an *s* to give it the meaning of more than one: *boys*. If you want to use the verb *see* to denote the act of seeing in some past time, you change its form so that you can say, for example, *I saw* or *I have seen* or *I was seeing*.

Words in the English language fall traditionally into eight categories called **parts of speech**. Five of these can be inflected in one or more ways:

> Noun, Pronoun, Verb, Adjective, Adverb

The other three parts of speech are almost never inflected:

> Preposition, Conjunction, Interjection

For example the word *in* is always *in*; the word *but* is always *but*. (The only exceptions to this principle occur when words are referred to *as words*, as in "There are too many *and*'s in that sentence," or in unusual usages such as "I don't want to hear any *ifs, ands,* or *buts*" and "He knows all the *ins* and *outs* of the process," where such words are in fact functioning as nouns rather than as prepositions and conjunctions.)

Note that the term *inflection* applies only to the change of a word's form *within its part of speech*. That is, when the noun *boy* is inflected for the plural, the new form—*boys*—is still a noun; when the pronoun *they* is inflected to *them* or *theirs*, the new forms are still pronouns. (Again there is an exception: when you inflect a noun or pronoun for the possessive case in front of a noun—the *boy's* coat, *their* idea—you turn it into an adjective, although some people, thinking of *form* rather than of *function*, prefer to call these "possessive nouns" and "possessive pronouns.")

Obviously many words can be changed in other ways so that they function as different parts of speech. For example the noun *centre* can be made into the adjective *central*, or the noun *meaning* into the adjective *meaningful*, or the verb *vacate* into the noun *vacation*. Such changes are not inflections, however, but *derivations*; a word can be *derived* from a word of a different part of speech, often by the addition of one or more suffixes: *trust, trustful, trustfully, trustfulness*. In fact, as you work your way through this chapter you will see that many words, even without being changed, can serve as more than one "part of speech." For example:

> Have you no *trust* in me? (noun)
> I *trust* you. (verb)
> She works for a *trust* company. (adjective)

The word *word* itself can be a noun ("Use this *word* correctly"), a verb ("How will you *word* your reply?"), or an adjective ("*Word* games are fun"). The word *right* can be a noun (his legal *right*), an adjective (the *right* stuff), an adverb (turn *right*, do it *right*), or a verb ("Let's *right* the overturned canoe"). Or consider the versatility of the common little word *over*:

> At least we have a roof *over* our heads. (preposition)
> The game is *over*. (adjective)
> Write that page *over*. (adverb)
> How many balls are pitched during an *over* in cricket? (noun)
> "Roger. Message received. *Over*." (interjection)

Shakespeare even has a character say "I'll *over* then to England"—a rare use of the word *over* as a verb. The *form* of a word, then, does not always determine its function. What part of speech a word is depends on its *function* in a particular sentence.

The rest of this chapter discusses the eight parts of speech—their inflections (if any) and other grammatical properties, their subcategories, some of their important derivatives (verbals), and the way they work with other words in sentences—and calls attention to some of their potential trouble-spots, such as *agreement* and verb *tenses*.

2 ▮ Nouns

A **noun** (from the Latin *nomen*, meaning *name*) is a word that names or stands for a thing, class, concept, quality, or action: *boy, garden, machine, silence, vegetable, road, liberty, beauty, river, spring, investi-*

gation. **Proper nouns** are names of specific persons, places, or things and begin with a capital letter: *Winnipeg, Dorothy, England*, the *Lusitania.* All the others, called **common nouns**, are usually capitalized only if they begin a sentence:

> *Liberty* is a precious commodity.
> *Spring* is my favourite season.

or form part of a proper noun:

> Spring Garden Road, Statue of Liberty, Ottawa River

or are personified or otherwise emphasized, for example in poetry:

> Let there be light! said Liberty,
> And like sunrise from the sea,
> Athens arose!
> > (Shelley)

> Our noisy years seem moments in the being
> Of the eternal Silence. . . .
> > (Wordsworth)

(See **47**, on capitalization.)

One can also classify nouns as either **concrete**, names of tangible objects (*girl, book, utensil, barn*), or **abstract**, names of intangible things or ideas (*liberty, honour, happiness, history*). (See **54**.)

Collective nouns are names of collections or groups considered as units: *army, committee, family, herd, flock.* (See **7f**.)

2a   Inflection of Nouns

Nouns can be inflected in only two simple ways: for *number* and for *possessive case.*

Number: Nouns that stand for *countable* things are either **singular** (naming a single thing) or **plural** (naming more than one thing). Most singular nouns are inflected to indicate the plural by the addition of *s* or *es*; for example: *boy, boys; box, boxes.* But some nouns are inflected for the plural in other ways; for example: *child, children; stimulus, stimuli.* (For more on the formation of plurals, see **51t**).

Some nouns, called **mass** or **noncountable** nouns, stand for things or qualities not usually considered countable, such as *gold, oxygen, journalism, honour* (abstract nouns are always noncountable). Such nouns are therefore usually not inflected for plural number. Some nouns, however, can be either countable or noncountable, depending on context; for example:

> The butcher sells *meat.* (noncountable)
> The delicatessen offers several delicious smoked *meats.* (countable, equivalent to *kinds of smoked meat*)

Many *honours* were heaped upon the returning hero. (countable, since *honours* here is not abstract, but designates specific things like medals, citations, the key to the city, etc.)

(See **7g** and **8c/6**.)

Possessive Case: *Case* is a term designating the syntactical relation of a noun or pronoun to other words in a sentence. Because English depends more on word order than synthetic languages do, case is relatively unimportant; whether a noun is serving as a *subject* (**subjective** case) or as an *object* (**objective** case) is shown by word order rather than by inflection. Nouns are inflected only for **possessive** case. By adding an apostrophe and an *s*, or occasionally only an apostrophe, you inflect a noun so that it shows possession or ownership: *my father's job, the children's toys, the students' programs*. (For more on the inflection of nouns for possessive case, see **51w**).

2b Grammatical Function of Nouns

Nouns function in sentences in the following ways:
Subject of a verb:

> *Students* work hard. (See **1a**.)

Direct object of a verb:

> Our team won the *championship*. (See **1e**.)

Indirect object of a verb:

> We awarded *Beverly* the prize. (See **1g**.)

Object of a preposition:

> We gave the prize to *Beverly*. It was a book about *mountain-climbing*. (See **1g** and **11**.)

Predicate noun (subjective complement) after a linking verb:

> Harold is an *accountant*. (See **1i**.)

Objective complement:

> The judges declared Beverly the *winner*. (See **1k**.)

An appositive to any other noun:

> André, the *policeman*, spotted Roger, the *thief*.
> We gave Beverly the prize, a *book* about mountain-climbing.
> Dr. Davis, our family *physician*, advised us to get flu shots.
> My brother *Henry* graduated last year.

(See **1s**. For the punctuation of appositives, see **37b** and **44g**.)

When nouns in the *possessive case* come just before other nouns

2b function of nouns

(their usual position), they function as adjectives; they modify the nouns that immediately follow them (See **8a**):

> *Maria's* coat (Which coat? Maria's.)
> a *month's* work (How much work? A month's.)

Even without being inflected for possessive case, many nouns also function as adjectives: the *school* paper, the *automobile* industry, the *dessert* course, *police* procedure, and so on (but see **59g** for a warning about the "noun disease").

A noun (or pronoun) referring to someone being directly addressed, as in dialogue or in a letter, is called a "noun of address." Such nouns, usually proper names, are not directly related to the syntax of the rest of the sentence:

> *Judith*, are you all right?
> Soon, *Steve*, you'll see what I mean.
> Hey *you*—give me a hand here!

Exercise 2b: Recognizing nouns

Identify each noun or noun phrase in the following sentences and determine whether it is functioning as a subject, a direct object, an indirect object, an object of a preposition, a subjective complement (predicate noun), an objective complement, an appositive, or a possessive adjective.

1. Canada's youngest province, Newfoundland, joined Confederation in 1949.
2. The Queen was given a twenty-one-gun salute.
3. Halifax's mayor gave the visiting dignitary the key to the city.
4. The book calls Vancouver a major city.
5. July was a month to remember: Marsha had never had such a rewarding holiday.
6. Shakespeare wrote many plays, but *Hamlet*, a tragedy, is his best-known work.
7. Too much work makes Jack a dull boy.

---

3 Pronouns

A **pronoun**, as its name indicates, is a word that stands for (*pro*) or in place of a noun, or at least functions like a noun in a sentence. Most pronouns refer to nouns that appear earlier, their **antecedents** (from the Latin for "coming before"):

> Jack offered an interpretation, but he didn't feel confident about it. (*Jack* is the antecedent of the pronoun *he*; *interpretation* is the antecedent of the pronoun *it*.)

Occasionally an "antecedent" can come after the pronoun that refers to it, especially if the pronoun is in a subordinate clause and if the context is clear—that is, if the pronoun couldn't refer to some other noun:

> Although *he* offered an interpretation, *Jack* didn't feel confident about it.

There are eight kinds of pronoun: *personal, impersonal, interrogative, relative, demonstrative, indefinite, reflexive,* and *reciprocal.* Generally, pronouns perform the same functions in sentences as nouns do: they are most often subjects of verbs, direct and indirect objects, and objects of prepositions. Some of them can also function as appositives and predicate nouns. Some pronouns are inflected much more than nouns, and some require particular care in their use.

The following sections discuss the different kinds of pronoun—their inflections and their grammatical functions in phrases, clauses, and sentences—and focus on the special problems of case (**3e**), agreement (**4-4f**) and reference (**5-5e**).

3a   Personal Pronouns

Personal pronouns refer to specific persons or things. They are inflected in four ways:

For **person**:

first-person pronouns (*I, we,* etc.) refer to the person or persons doing the speaking;

second-person pronouns (*you, yours*) refer to the person or persons being spoken to;

third-person pronouns (*he, she, it,* etc.) refer to the person(s) or thing(s) being spoken about.

For **number**:

singular: *I* am writing. *She* is writing.

plural: *We* are writing. *They* are writing.

(The second-person pronoun *you* can be either singular or plural.)

For **gender**:

masculine pronouns (*he, him, his*) refer to males;

feminine pronouns (*she, her, hers*) refer to females;

neuter pronouns (*it, its*) refer to things or to creatures—such as animals and sometimes babies—whose gender is unknown or irrelevant to the context.

(In the plural forms—*we, you, they,* etc.—there is no indication of gender.)

For **case**:

Pronouns that function as subjects must be in the **subjective** case:

> *I* paint. *She* paints. *They* are painting.

3b impersonal pronouns

Pronouns that function as objects must be in the **objective** case:

The car hit *them.* Give *me* the book. Give it to *me.*

Pronouns that indicate possession or ownership must be in the **possessive** case.

The red book is *mine.* Where is *yours?*

The possessive forms *my, your, his, her, its, our,* and *their* always precede nouns and function as adjectives, called **possessive adjectives** or **pronominal adjectives**: *my* book, *your* book, *his* book, *their* books.

The following chart shows all the inflections of personal pronouns:

		subject	object	possessive pronoun	possessive adjective
Singular	1st person	I	me	mine	my
	2nd person	you	you	yours	your
	3rd person	he	him	his	his
		she	her	hers	her
		it	it		its
Plural	1st person	we	us	ours	our
	2nd person	you	you	yours	your
	3rd person	they	them	theirs	their

(Note that the forms *you* and *it* are inflected only for possessive case. And note that the form *his* serves as both possessive pronoun and possessive adjective, and that *her* serves as both objective case and possessive adjective.)

Caution: Never use apostrophes to indicate the possessive case of pronouns. The correct form is *hers,* not *her's; theirs,* not *their's.* The most common error of this sort is to write *it's* (contraction of *it is*) when what is meant is *its* (possessive form of *it*). The word *it's* always means *it is.*

3b Impersonal Pronouns

The **impersonal pronoun** *one,* especially in relatively formal contexts, serves in place of a first-, second-, or third-person pronoun:

One must be careful when crossing the street.

The pronoun *it* is also used as an impersonal pronoun in such sentences as the following; note that *it* almost always occurs as the subject of some form of the verb *be* (see **6f**) and that it almost always refers to time, distance, weather, and the like:

It is getting late.

It's cold outside.
It feels colder today than *it* did yesterday.
It was just one of those things.
It is a mile and a half from here to the station.

3c Interrogative Pronouns

Interrogative pronouns are *question-words* used usually at or near the beginning of *interrogative sentences* (see **1t**). *Who* is inflected for objective and possessive case, and *which* for possessive case:

Subjective	Objective	Possessive
who	whom	whose
which	which	whose
what	what	

Who refers to persons, *which* and *what* to things; *which* sometimes also refers to persons, as in *Which of you is going?* The compound forms *whoever* and *whatever*, and sometimes even *whichever* and *whomever*, can also function as interrogative pronouns. Here are some sentences showing the interrogative pronouns functioning in different ways:
As subject:

> Who said that? Which of these books is best? What is the baby's name? Whoever told you that?

As direct object of verb:

> Whom do you recommend for the job? What did you give Aunt Jane for Christmas?

As object of a preposition (see also **11**):

> To whom did you give the book? To what do I owe this honour?

As objective complement:

> What did you call me? You've named the baby *what?*

When one of these interrogative words comes before a noun it functions as an **interrogative adjective**:

> Whose book is this? Which car shall we take?

For more on *who* and *whom*, see **3e**.

3d Relative Pronouns

A **relative pronoun** usually introduces an *adjective clause*—called a **relative clause**—in which it functions as a subject, a direct object, or an object of a preposition. The pronoun links, or *relates*, the clause to an antecedent in the same sentence, a noun or pronoun that the whole clause modifies. The relative pronouns are *who, which,* and *that* (and sometimes *what*). *Who* and *which* are inflected for case:

Subjective	Objective	Possessive
who	whom	whose
which	which	whose
that	that	

Who refers to persons (or sometimes to animals thought of as persons), *which* refers to things, and *that* refers to either persons or things. Compounds with *ever* (*whoever, whomever, whichever, whatever*) can also function as relative pronouns. Here are some sentences illustrating how relative pronouns function:

> Tom, who is leaving in the morning, will call us later tonight. (*who* as subject of verb *is*; clause modifies *Tom*)
> Margaret tried to describe the man whom she had met at the party. (*whom* as object of verb *had met*; clause modifies *man*)
> At midnight Jerry began to revise his descriptive essay, which was due in the morning. (*which* as subject of verb *was*; clause modifies *essay*)
> He postponed working on the essay that he was having trouble with. (*that* as object of preposition *with*; clause modifies *essay*)

A relative clause is either *restrictive* and unpunctuated, or *nonrestrictive* and set off with punctuation (see **37**). If the relative pronoun in a *restrictive* clause is the *object* of either a verb or a preposition, it can usually be omitted:

> Margaret tried to describe the man [*whom* or *that*] she had met at the party.
> He postponed working on the essay [*that*] he was having trouble with.

But note that if the second example is written in this form:

> He postponed working on the essay with which he was having trouble.

the relative pronoun can be dropped only if *with* is moved to the end.

The word *whose* often precedes and modifies a noun in a relative clause; *whose* is then functioning as what is called a **relative adjective**:

> His mother was the person whose experience he most valued.

And sometimes an adverb introduces a relative clause; *when* and *where* often function as such *relative adverbs*:

> Here's an aerial photo of the town where I live. (The clause *where I live* modifes the noun *town*.)
> My parents warned me of a time when I'd regret my decision. (The *when*-clause modifies the noun *time*.)

For more on *who* and *whom*, see **3e**. For more on adjective clauses, see **8** and **15a**.

3e Case

Few if any people have difficulty choosing the correct *number* or *person* of a pronoun. But sometimes people have trouble deciding upon the correct **case** of personal, interrogative, and relative pronouns. The main problems are limited to choosing between *subjective* and *objective* forms, and the problems arise with only a few kinds of sentences, and then only in formal writing. Many educated as well as uneducated speakers commonly say things like "*Who* did you lend the book to?" and "It's *me*" and "That's *her*"; if you were writing realistic dialogue in a story or an essay, chances are those would be the appropriate forms to use. But in other kinds of writing, certainly in formal writing (and in strictly formal speech), you should be careful to use what are considered the correct grammatical forms.

If you understand how a pronoun is functioning grammatically, you will know which form to use. Here are the few kinds of sentences that sometimes cause problems, along with advice on how to avoid the problems.

1. A pronoun functioning as the *subject* of a verb should be in the *subjective* case.

   Error sometimes occurs when a pronoun is only part of a subject. Someone who wouldn't dream of saying something like "*Me* am going to the store" could slip and say or write something faulty like "Susan and *me* studied hard for the examination." Whenever you use a pronoun as part of a *compound subject* (see **1z**), make sure it's in the *subjective* case:

   > Susan and *I* studied hard for the examination.

   The simple test is to remove the other part of the subject; then you will know which pronoun sounds right:

   > *I* studied hard for the examination.

   But even one-part subjects can lead someone astray:

   > *faulty*:   Us students should stand up for our rights.
   > *revised*: We students should stand up for our rights.

   The pronoun *We* is the subject; the word *students* is an appositive (see **1s**) further identifying it, as if saying "We, the students, should. . . ."

2. A pronoun functioning as the *object* of a verb should be in the *objective* case.

   Again, error most often occurs with a two-part structure—here, a *compound object* (see **1z**). Someone who would never say "The club asked *I* for my opinion" could slip and say "They asked Ingrid and *I* to take part in the play." When you use a pronoun as part of a compound object, make sure it's in the *objective* case; again, test by removing the other part to find out how the pronoun sounds by itself:

> They asked [Ingrid and] *me* to take part in the play.

Caution: Don't fall victim to what is called "hypercorrection." Since many people say incorrect things like "Jake and me went camping," others—not understanding the grammar but wishing to seem correct—use the " . . . and I" form even when it is an object, and therefore should be " . . . and me."

3. A pronoun functioning as the *object* of a preposition should be in the *objective* case:

> *faulty*: The administration sometimes forgets about the needs of we students.
>
> *revised*: The administration sometimes forgets about the needs of *us* students.

Again, since the objective *us* sounds suspect (because it is followed by a noun, *students*, as if at the beginning of a sentence like "We students should. . . ."), unthinking speakers and writers sometimes overcorrect and use the subjective *we*; but the objective *us* is correct, for it is the object of the preposition *of*. Check your pronoun by leaving off the appositive noun; *us* will then sound right.

4. A pronoun functioning as a *subjective complement* (see **1i** and **14d**) after a linking verb should be in the *subjective* case:

> It is *they* who must decide, not *we*.
> The girl who won the prize is *she*, over there by the pool.
> It is *I* who will carry the greater burden.

If such usages sound stuffy and artificial to you—as they do to many people—simply find another way to phrase your sentences; for example:

> They, not we, must decide.
> The girl over by the pool is the one who took first prize.
> First prize went to that girl, over there by the pool.
> I will be the one carrying the greater burden.
> I, myself, will be carrying the greater burden. (In writing, when you can't use speech rhythms and stress for a desired emphasis, an extra word, such as an intensive pronoun like *myself*, often works. See **3h**.)

Again, watch out for compound structures:

> *faulty*: The nominees are Arnold and me.
> *revised*: The nominees are Arnold and *I*.

5. In formal usage, *as* and *than* are still considered conjunctions, not prepositions; pronouns following them in statements of comparison should therefore be in the *subjective* case, since they are functioning as subjects—even if their verbs are not expressed (the verbs are then said to be "understood"):

> Roberta is brighter than *they* (are).
> Aaron has learned less than *I* (have).
> He hasn't learned as much as *I* (have).
> Claude is as tall as *I* (am).

See also *so . . . as* in **60**.

6. Use the appropriate case of the interrogative and relative pronouns *who* and *whom*, *whoever* and *whomever*. Although *who* is often used instead of *whom* in speech and informal writing, you should know how to use the two correctly when you want to write or speak more formally.

a. Use the *subjective* case for the subject of a verb in a question:

> *Who* is going?

and for the subject of a verb in a relative clause:

> Dickens was a novelist *who* entertained his readers in many ways.

Don't let an intervening parenthetical clause like *you think* or *they believe* mislead you into thinking the objective *whom* is correct:

> Who do you think will win?
> She is the one who most people say will win.

In these examples *who* is the subject of the verb *will win*. Note that you can remove the intervening clause without destroying the sense of the relative clause with *who* as its subject:

> Who will win?
> She is the one who will win.

And don't be fooled by a verb in the passive voice (see **1f** and **6n**):

> He is a public servant who will be long remembered.

The relative pronoun *who* is the subject of the passive-voice verb *will be . . . remembered*. If you feel tempted to try *whom* there, as if it were the object of *remembered*, ask yourself what you could then think of as the *subject* of the verb. Or try substituting a more familiar objective pronoun to find out what it sounds like; it is unlikely that you would be satisfied with sentences like *Him will be long remembered* or *Me will be long remembered*. So use *who*, not *whom*.

b. Use the *objective* case for the object of a verb:

> *Whom* do you prefer in that role?
> He is the actor *whom* I admire most.

and for the object of a preposition:

> To *whom* do you intend to award the prize?
> She is the manager for *whom* the employees have the most respect.

Again, if such usages with *whom* strike you as unnatural and stuffy, avoid them by rephrasing your sentences:

> Who is going to get the prize?
> Which student are you going to award the prize to?
> The employees have more respect for her than for the other managers.
> She is the manager that the employees respect most.

c. The interrogative words *who, whoever, whom,* and *whomever* can also function in *noun clauses* that contain implicit questions; think of these subordinate clauses as derivations or transformations of questions. For example, the question *Who wishes to repeat the quiz?* could turn up as a noun clause in a declarative sentence:

> Whoever wishes to can repeat the quiz next week.

Whoever is the subject of the verb *wishes*; the noun clause *Whoever wishes to* is the subject of the main verb, *can repeat*. Here are some other examples:

> I can't tell who will win. (*Who* is the subject of the verb *will win*; the noun clause *who will win* is the direct object of the verb *can't tell*.)
> How can you tell who won?
> I'll give the prize to whomever the judges declare the winner. (*Whomever* is the direct object of the verb *declare*; the whole noun clause, with its objective complement, *the winner*, is the object of the preposition *to*.)
> The instructor planned to award a book-prize to whoever wrote the best essay.

In this last example some people would automatically use the objective *whomever*; but *whoever* is correct because it is the subject of the verb *wrote* in the noun clause *whoever wrote the best essay*, and it is the function of a relative pronoun *in its clause* that determines its case. Here the entire subordinate clause, not just the pronoun that begins it, is the object of the preposition *to*.

For the possessive case of pronouns with *gerunds*, see **10e**.

Exercise 3e(1): Using correct pronouns

In the following sentences, underline the correct pronoun in each of the pairs in parentheses.

1. (She, Her) and (I, me) will work on the problem tonight.
2. There stood Eva, (who, whom) we had just said goodbye to.
3. The judge released the two men (who, whom) had been incorrectly charged.
4. Is Genevieve the person (who, whom) you think will do the best job?
5. This gift will please (whoever, whomever) receives it.
6. The coach advised Anwar and (I, me) not to miss any more practice.
7. (Who, Whom) do you wish to see?

Exercise 3e(2): Problem pronouns

Make up five sentences that use a personal pronoun in the subjective case (*I, he, she, they*) after a form of the verb *be*, and five sentences using the pronoun *whom* or *whomever* in a correct, formal way. Then rewrite each of your sentences, keeping them acceptably formal, but avoiding the possible stuffiness of these usages.

3f Demonstrative Pronouns

Demonstrative pronouns, which can be thought of as accompanied by a demonstrative gesture, namely pointing, are inflected for *number* only:

Singular:	this	that
Plural:	these	those

This and *these* usually refer to something nearby, *that* and *those* to something farther away:

> Would you like to try some of this?
> Surely you don't want any of those.

This and *these* also often refer to something that has just been said or that is about to be said, *that* and *those* to something more remote in time or longer in duration:

> These are the main reasons for my objection to the proposal.
> That was the story he told us the next morning.

Avoid the nonstandard *this here* and *that there*: the pronoun conveys the meaning without the adverbial intensifier.

These pronouns also often occur in prepositional phrases with *like* and *such as*:

> Would you go out with someone who dresses like that?
> I'd like to have more friends like those!
> An alibi such as this will not stand up in court.
> You can't get out of it with such an excuse as that.

3f demonstrative pronouns

When they are used in the same way as *this* and *that*, the words *such* and *so* can also function as demonstrative pronouns:

> Such was the story he told them.
> He didn't like their decision and he told them so.

Useful as demonstrative pronouns can be, however, you should use them as little as possible, for they can all too easily be vague in their reference. When followed by nouns, these words function as **demonstrative adjectives**, and there is no risk of vagueness: *this* belief, *that* statement, *these* buildings, *those* arguments. (See **5c**, **28**, and **ref** in Chapter XI.)

3g   Indefinite Pronouns

Indefinite pronouns refer to *indefinite* or unknown persons or things, or to indefinite or unknown quantities of persons or things. The only major difficulty with these words stems from whether they are *singular* or *plural*. Think of indefinite pronouns as falling into four groups. Group 1 consists of compounds with *body*, *one*, and *thing*; these words function like nouns—that is, they need no antecedents—and they are almost always considered *singular*:

anybody	everybody	nobody	somebody
anyone	everyone	no one	someone
anything	everything	nothing	something

Group 2 comprises other indefinite pronouns that are almost always *singular*:

| another | each | either | much | neither | one | other |

Group 3 includes indefinite pronouns that are always *plural*:

| both | few | many | several |

Group 4 includes indefinite pronouns that can be either *singular* or *plural*, depending on context and intended meaning:

| all | any | more | most | none | some |

For discussions of the important matter of grammatical *agreement* with indefinite pronouns, and examples of their use in sentences, see **4c** and **7d**.

Of all the indefinite pronouns, only *one* and *other* can be inflected for number, by adding *s* to make them plural: *ones*, *others* (the words *somebodies* and *nobodies* are nouns, not pronouns). Several indefinite pronouns can be inflected for possessive case; unlike personal pronouns, they take *'s*, just as nouns do:

anybody's	anyone's	everybody's	everyone's
nobody's	no one's	somebody's	someone's
one's	other's	another's	

(The plural form of *other* takes only an apostrophe: *others'*.)

The rest must use *of* to show possession; for example:

That was the belief *of many* who were present.

When in the possessive case, of course, these words function as adjectives. Further, all the words in Groups 2, 3, and 4, except *none*, can also function as adjectives (see **8a**):

any boat	*some* people	*few* people
more money	*each* day	*either* direction

The adjective expressing the meaning of *none* is *no*:

Send *no* flowers.

Sometimes the cardinal and ordinal numbers (*one, two, three*, etc., and *first, second, third*, etc.) are also classed as indefinite pronouns, for they often function similarly, both as pronouns:

How many ducks are on the pond? I see *several*. I see *many*. I see *seven*. I see *ten*.
Do you like these stories? I like *some*, but not *others*. I like the *first* and the *third*.

and as adjectives:

He owns *two* boats.
Tune in for the *second* thrilling episode.

▌3h▐ Reflexive and Intensive Pronouns

These pronouns are formed by adding *self* or the plural *selves* to the possessive form of the first- and second-person personal pronouns, to the objective form of third-person personal pronouns, and to the impersonal pronoun *one* (see **3a** and **3b**):

Singular	*Plural*
myself	ourselves
yourself	yourselves
himself	
herself	themselves
itself	
oneself	

A **reflexive pronoun** is used as an object to *reflect* or refer back to the subject of a sentence when the object is the same person or thing as that subject:

He treated *himself* to a candy-bar. (direct object)
He gave *himself* a treat. (indirect object)
We kept the information to *ourselves*. (object of preposition)
One should pamper *oneself* a little now and then. (direct object)

These pronouns are also used as **intensive pronouns** to emphasize a subject or object. An intensive pronoun comes either right after the noun it emphasizes or at the end of the sentence:

> Although he let the others choose their positions, Angelo *himself* is going to pitch.
> The professor told us to count up our scores *ourselves*.

They are also used in prepositional phrases with *by* to mean *alone* or *without help*:

> I can do the job by *myself*.

Do not use this form of pronoun as a substitute for a personal pronoun:

> The boss talked Hank and *me* [not *myself*] into doing the job.

3i   Reciprocal Pronouns

Like reflexive pronouns, **reciprocal pronouns** refer back to the subject of a sentence; this time, however, the subject is always plural. The two reciprocal pronouns are singular, and consist of two words each:

> each other   one another

They can be inflected for possessive case by adding *'s:*

> each other's   one another's

These pronouns express some kind of mutual interaction between or among the parts of a plural subject:

> The President and the Prime Minister praised each other's policies.
> The members congratulated one another.

See also *each other, one another,* in the usage checklist, **60**.

4   Agreement of Pronouns with Their Antecedents
agr

Any pronoun that refers to or stands for an *antecedent* (see **3**) must **agree** with (that is, be the same as) that antecedent in **person** (1st, 2nd, or 3rd), **number** (singular or plural), and **gender** (masculine, feminine, or neuter). For example:

> *Joanne* wants to go to university so that *she* will be trained to take *her* place in the world.

Since the proper noun *Joanne,* the antecedent, is third person, singular, and feminine, any pronouns that refer to it must also be third person, singular, and feminine: *she* and *her* thus "agree" grammatically with their antecedent.

The following sections (**4a-f**) point out the most common sources of error in pronoun agreement. Note that most of these potentially troublesome circumstances are similar to some of those affecting subject-verb agreement (see **7**). Note also that these errors all have to do with *number*—whether a pronoun should be *singular* or *plural*. Mistakes in *gender* are highly unlikely, and mistakes in *person* are infrequent (but see **26**, on Shifts).

4a   Antecedents Joined by *and*

When two or more singular antecedents are joined by *and*, use a *plural* pronoun:

> The manager and the accountant compared *their* estimates.
> Both Jennifer and Timothy contributed *their* know-how.

If such a compound antecedent is preceded by *each* or *every*, however, the pronoun should be *singular*:

> Each book and magazine in the library has *its* own number.

4b   Antecedents Joined by *or* or *nor*

When two or more antecedents are joined by *or* or *nor*, use a *singular* pronoun if the antecedents are singular:

> The dog or the cat is sure to make *itself* heard.
> Either David or Jonathan will bring *his* car.
> Neither Doris nor her mother gave *her* consent.

a *plural* pronoun if the antecedents are plural:

> Neither the players nor the coaches did *their* jobs properly.

If the antecedents are mixed singular and plural, a pronoun should agree with the antecedent nearest to it; but if you start with a plural antecedent and end with a singular one, the sentence will almost inevitably be awkward:

> *Awkward:* Neither the actors nor *the director* could control *his* temper.

Note that the possible awkwardness here extends to gender: if the actors included both men and women, then neither *his* nor *her* would be appropriate as a pronoun (see **4d**). Therefore always construct such sentences so that the last antecedent is plural:

> *Revised:* Neither the director nor *the actors* could control *their* tempers.

4c   Antecedent an Indefinite Pronoun

If the antecedent is an *indefinite pronoun* (see **3g**), you will most often want to use a *singular* pronoun to refer to it. The indefinite pronouns in Group 1 (the compounds with *body*, *one*, and *thing*) are singular, as are those in Group 2 (*another, each, either, much, neither, one, other*):

> *Each* of the boys worked on *his* own project.
> *Either* of these women is likely to buy that sportscar for *herself*.
> *Everything* has *its* proper place.

Occasionally, however, the indefinite pronoun *everyone* or *everybody* can have an obviously plural sense; a pronoun referring to it should then be *plural*:

> When the hat had been passed to *everyone* in the room, Stephen counted up *their* contributions.

Indefinite pronouns from Group 3 (*both, few, many, several*) present no difficulty; use *plural* pronouns to refer to them:

> Only a *few* sent *their* condolences.

The indefinite pronouns in Group 4 (*all, any, more, most, none, some*), though they can be either singular or plural, seldom cause trouble; the intended meaning is usually clearly either singular or plural:

> *Some* of the food could be criticized for *its* tastelessness.
> *Some* of the ships had been restored to *their* original beauty.

Here the mass noun *food* demands the singular sense for *some*, and the countable noun *ships*, in the plural, demands the plural sense (see **3a**). But confusion about number sometimes arises with the indefinite pronoun *none*. Although *none* began by meaning *no one* or *not one*, it is now also common in the plural sense of *not any*:

> *None* of the men removed *their* hats.

But if the intended meaning is *not one*, *not a single one*, it is correct to treat *none* as singular:

> *None* of the men removed *his* hat.

Whenever you are uncertain, treat *none* as *singular*; that usage is more formal, and will usually be correct.

When any of these words function as adjectives, the same principles apply:

> *Each* boy worked on *his* own project.
> *Either* woman may buy the car for *herself*.
> Only a *few* people sent *their* condolences.
> *Some* food could be criticized for *its* tastelessness.
> *Some* ships had been restored to *their* original beauty.

The word *every* used as an adjective requires a *singular* pronoun:

> *Every* boy has *his* own project.

4d **The Problem of the Generic** *he*

Several of the indefinite pronouns, indefinite nouns like *person* or *individual*, and many other nouns used in a generalizing way, give rise to an additional pronoun problem. When a *singular antecedent* has no grammatical gender, but can refer to either male or female, it has long been conventional to use the masculine pronoun *he* (*him, his, himself*) in a generic sense, meaning any person, male or female:

> *Everyone* present raised *his* hand.
> *Anyone* who doesn't pay *his* taxes is asking for trouble.
> If a *person* is considerate of others' feelings, *he* will get along better.
> A *writer* should be careful about *his* diction.

But nowadays this practice is increasingly frowned upon as unfair and unrealistic since it implies, for example, that no women were present, that only men pay taxes, that all persons are males, that there are no women writers.

But you can usually avoid this problem of sexist language. Colloquially and informally, many people simply use a plural pronoun:

> *agr:*   Anyone who doesn't pay *their* taxes is asking for trouble.

But this fosters bad habits; it is unacceptable to most people who care about language, for it is grammatically awkward. (Note for example the clash in that sentence between the plural pronoun *their* and the singular verb *is*.) Even though a plural pronoun sometimes sounds all right with the antecedent *everyone*:

> Everyone present raised *their* hands.

don't adopt it as a general practice. There are better solutions. Here is what we recommend:

1. If you are referring to a group or class consisting entirely of either men or women, it is only logical to use the appropriate pronoun, whether masculine or feminine (this is not a matter of grammar so much as of common sense):

> Everyone in the room raised *his* hand.
> Everyone in the room raised *her* hand.

Or avoid gender entirely by using the indefinite article:

> Everyone raised *a* hand.

2. Often the simplest technique is to make the antecedent itself plural: then the plural pronoun referring to it is grammatically appropriate, and no problem of gender arises:

> *Those* who don't pay *their* taxes are asking for trouble.
> *Writers* should be careful about *their* diction.

4d generic he

3. If your purpose and the formality of the context permit, you can use the impersonal pronoun *one*:

> If *one* is considerate of others' feelings, *one* will get along better.

But if this sounds stuffy, consider using the less formal second-person pronoun *you*:

> If *you* are considerate of others' feelings, *you* will get along better.

4. Or you can revise a sentence so that no pronoun is necessary:

> Everyone's hand went up.
> In order to get along better, be considerate of others' feelings.

Sometimes the pronoun can simply be omitted:

> A writer should be careful about diction.

5. But if a sentence doesn't lend itself to such changes, or if you want to keep its original structure for a particular emphasis or rhythm, you can still manage. Don't resort to the awkward and unsightly *he/she, him/her, his/her, him/herself.* But an *occasional* use of *he or she* or *she or he* and the like is acceptable:

> Each man and woman has *his or her* special assignment.
> A writer should be careful about *his or her* diction.

But do this only occasionally; used often, such terms become tedious and cluttering.

4e   Antecedent a Collective Noun

If the antecedent is a *collective noun* (see **2**), a pronoun referring to it can be either singular or plural, depending on context and desired meaning. If the collective noun stands for the group seen as a unit, use a *singular* pronoun:

> The *team* did *its* job well.
> The *committee* announced *its* decision.

If the collective noun stands for the members of the group seen as separate individuals, use a *plural* pronoun:

> The *team* took up *their* starting positions.
> The *committee* had no sooner taken *their* seats than *they* began arguing among *themselves*.

4f   Agreement with Demonstrative Adjectives

Demonstrative pronouns cause little or no agreement trouble, but demonstrative *adjectives* may pose a problem, especially when followed by *kind* or *kinds* (or *sort* or *sorts*). Demonstrative adjectives must agree in number with the nouns they modify:

> *Wrong*: *These kind* of doctors work especially hard.
> *Right*: *This kind* of doctor works especially hard.
> *These kinds* of doctors work especially hard.

If "these kinds" or "those kinds" sounds stuffy or awkward in a particular context (as it does here), take a moment to rephrase; for example:

> Doctors such as these work especially hard.

Exercise 4: Correcting agreement errors

In the following sentences, correct any lack of agreement between pronouns and their antecedents. Revise sentences as necessary to avoid possibly sexist use of the generic masculine pronoun.

1. Everybody is free to express their own opinion.
2. Una or Gwendolyn will lend you their textbook.
3. Anyone who doesn't think for themselves can be deceived by advertising.
4. His arguments cannot alter my opinion, for it seems to me illogical.
5. After studying his statements for over an hour, I still couldn't understand it.
6. It is usually a bad sign when a person stops caring about their appearance.
7. Everyone who wants to play the game will be provided with a pencil to write their answers with.
8. All the boys arrived on time, each with their books carried proudly in both hands.
9. In order to make sure each sentence is correct, check them carefully during revision and proofreading.
10. None of the women agreed to those proposals that would limit their rights.

▆ 5 ▆ Reference of Pronouns
ref

A pronoun's **reference** to an antecedent must be clear. If the antecedent is remote, ambiguous, vague, or missing, the meaning of the pronoun, and of the statement it appears in, will not be clear.

▆ 5a ▆ Remote Reference

Make sure the antecedent is close enough to the pronoun to be unmistakable; your reader should not have to pause and search for it. An antecedent should seldom be more than one sentence back. For example:

> People who expect to experience happiness in material things alone may well discover that the life of the mind is more important than

the life of the physical senses. Material prosperity may seem fine at a given moment, but in the long run its delights have a way of
ref: fading into inconsequential tedium and emptiness. *They* then realize, too late, where true happiness lies.

The word *People* is too far back, too remote, to serve as a clear antecedent for the pronoun *They* that begins the last sentence. If the second sentence had also begun with *They*, the connection might have been clear enough. Or the third sentence might have used, instead of the weak pronoun, a more particularizing phrase, like "Such people . . . ."

5b   Ambiguous Reference

Make sure that a pronoun refers clearly to only one antecedent; if a pronoun has more than one possible antecedent, revision will be necessary:

Ambig ref: When Donna's mother told her that *she* needed an operation, *she* was obviously upset.

Each of the *she's* could refer either to Donna (that is, to the word *her*) or to Donna's mother. When revising such a sentence, don't try to clear it up by inserting explanatory parentheses; rephrase the sentence:

Weak: When Donna's mother told her that she (her mother) needed an operation, she (Donna) was obviously upset.

Clear: Donna was obviously upset when her mother told her about needing an operation.

Clear: Donna's mother needed an operation, and she was obviously upset when she told Donna about it.

Clear: Donna was obviously upset when her mother told her, "I must have an operation."

Another example:

Ambig ref: His second novel was far different from his first. *It* was an adventure story set in Australia.

A pronoun like *it* in this example often has as its antecedent the subject of the preceding independent clause, here "second novel"; but the *it* is also pulled toward the closest noun or pronoun, here "first." The resulting ambiguity needs revising:

Clear: His second novel, an adventure story set in Australia, was far different from his first.

Clear: His second novel was far different from his first, which was an adventure story set in Australia.

Note that the problem is easily solved by *combining* the two sentences, reducing the second to either an appositive phrase or an adjective clause.

5c Vague Reference

Vague reference is particularly likely to occur with the demonstrative pronouns *this* and *that* and the relative pronoun *which*.

> *Vague ref:* There were three isolated people leaning against the wall, and it was very dark. *This* made Shelagh wary as she approached the bus stop.

(*This* could easily be changed, after a comma, to *which*, which would be just as bad.) *This* (or *which*) seems to refer to the entire content of the preceding sentence, but it also seems to refer specifically to the fact that it was dark. Revision is necessary:

> *Clear:* The extreme darkness and the three isolated people leaning against the wall made Shelagh wary as she approached the bus stop.
>
> *Clear:* Three isolated people were leaning against the wall, and it was very dark. These circumstances [facts] made Shelagh wary as she approached the bus stop.
>
> *Clear:* Three isolated people leaned against the wall, and it was very dark, facts which taken together made Shelagh wary as she approached the bus stop.

A *this* (or *which*) can be adequate if the phrasing (and meaning) are appropriate—that is, if the reference of the pronoun is not ambiguous:

> *Clear:* Three separate people were leaning against the nearby building, but this did not worry Shelagh, for she was a judo expert. But it was also getting very dark, which did make her a little wary as she approached the bus stop.

Here is another example:

> *Vague ref:* Othello states many times that he loves Iago and that he thinks he is a very honest man; Iago uses *this* to his advantage.

The third *he* is possibly ambiguous, but more serious is the vague reference of *this*. Changing *this* to *this opinion, these feelings, this attitude, these mistakes, this blindness of Othello's* or even *Othello's blindness*, makes the reference clearer. Even the *his* is slightly ambiguous: "Iago takes advantage of" is better—or just omit the *his*.

In particular, avoid catching the "this" disease; sufferers from the "this" plague are driven to begin a large proportion of their sentences with *This*. Whenever you catch yourself beginning a sentence (or a clause) with *This*, look very carefully to see

1. if the reference to the preceding clause or sentence or paragraph is indeed as clear on paper as it may be in your mind;
2. if the *This* could be replaced by a specific noun or noun phrase, or otherwise avoided, for example by rephrasing or subordinating;

5c vague reference

3. whether, if you finally decide to retain the *This*, it is a mere demonstrative pronoun; if it is, you can probably make it clearer by turning it into a **demonstrative adjective**, giving it a noun to modify—even if the noun is no more specific than something like "This *idea*," "This *fact*," or "This *argument*." (See **3f** and **28**.)

And always check to see if an opening *This* refers back to a noun that is in fact singular, for it may be that *These* ideas, facts, or arguments would be more appropriate.

5d Missing Antecedent

Sometimes an antecedent may be only implicit; the writer may have had an antecedent in mind but failed to write it down.

> *ref:* In the early seventeenth century the Renaissance had concentrated mainly on the arts rather than on developing the scientific part of *their* minds.

The pronoun *their* has no antecedent; the writer was probably thinking of "the people of the Renaissance," but did not write it down. Simply changing *their* to *people's* would clear up the difficulty.

> *ref:* After the senator's speech *he* agreed to answer questions from the audience.

The pronoun *he* has no real antecedent. The implied antecedent is of course *senator*, but it is not there, for *senator's* is in the possessive case and therefore functions as an adjective rather than as a noun. Several revisions are possible:

> *Clear:* When the senator finished his speech, he agreed to answer questions from the audience.
>
> *Clear:* After speaking, the senator agreed to answer questions from the audience.
>
> *Clear:* At the end of his speech the senator agreed to answer questions from the audience.

Note that in this last version *his* comes before its supposed "antecedent," *senator*—an unusual pattern, but acceptable if the context is clear (for example, if no other possible antecedent occurred in the preceding sentence) and when the two are close together.

> *ref:* Whenever a student assembly is called, *they* are required to attend.

Since *student* here functions as an adjective, it is necessary to replace *they* with *students*—and then probably one would want to omit the original *student*. Or one could refer to "an assembly of students" and retain the *they*.

ref: Over half the cars were derailed, but *it* did not injure anyone seriously.

Again, no antecedent for the *it*. Change *it* to "the accident" or "the derailment," or use the passive voice: "but no one was seriously injured." (For the passive voice, see **1e, 6n,** and **18f.**)

5e Indefinite *you, they,* and *it*

In formal writing, avoid the pronouns *you* and *they* when they are indefinite:

> *Informal:* In order to graduate, *you* must have at least sixty units of credit.
>
> *Formal:* In order to graduate, a student must have at least sixty units of credit.

(The impersonal pronoun *one* would be all right, but less good because less specific—and stuffier.)

> *Informal:* In some cities *they* do not have enough police protection.
>
> *Formal:* Some cities do not have enough police protection.
>
> *Formal:* Some city police forces are understaffed.

Although it is correct to use the expletive or impersonal *it* (see **1k** and **18f**) and say "*It* is raining," "*It* is difficult to get up in the morning," "*It* is seven o'clock," etc., one should avoid the indefinite use of *it* in such expressions as the following:

> *Informal:* *It* says in our textbook that we should be careful how we use the pronoun *it.*
>
> *Formal:* Our textbook says that we should be careful how we use the pronoun *it.*

Exercise 5: Correcting faulty pronoun reference

Correct any faulty pronoun reference in the following sentences.

1. Schools were of high quality—for those who could afford it.
2. If it rains on Maui it is soon evaporated into thin air.
3. Huck, the protagonist, is the narrator of the novel. Twain does this to let us see society through the eyes of a boy.
4. Many people believe that success is necessary for happiness, and they work hard to attain it.
5. You cannot suppress truth, for it is morally wrong.
6. Othello swore she was faithful and true and would have bet his life that she would not betray him, but he ends by taking her life for this very reason.
7. The deadline was a month away, but I failed to meet it, for something happened that prevented it.
8. The tone of the poem is such that it creates an atmosphere of romance.

9. In Shakespeare's Sonnet 65, it points out the differences between love and time.
10. Television usually shows regular commercial movies but this is sometimes supplanted by made-for-TV films.

---

6 Verbs

Verbs are the most important part of speech because they are the most important elements in the grammatical patterns of English sentences. A verb acts as the focal point of a sentence or a clause. As you saw in Chapter I, standard sentences consist of a subject and a predicate: every subject must have a predicate, and the heart of every predicate is its **verb.**

Verbs are often said to be the "action" words in sentences; yet many verbs express little or no action. It is more sensible to think of verbs as expressing not only *action* but also *occurrence, process,* and *condition* or *state of being.* All verbs *assert* or *ask* something about the nouns that are their subjects, sometimes by *linking* the subject with a necessary complement in the predicate. Some verbs are single words; others are verb phrases consisting of two or more words. Here are some sentences with the verbs italicized:

> He *throws* curves.
> She *flew* in space.
> I *thought* for a while.
> Gershom *is* a lawyer.
> Something *happened* last night.
> I *am cooking* spaghetti.
> By this time next week I *will have driven* two thousand kilometres.
> *Are* you *listening?*
> The two columns of figures *came out* even.
> *Will* you *be needing* this book later?
> The fresh bread *smells* delicious.
> They *will set out* for the pole in June.

(For a discussion of such two-part verbs as *come out* and *set out,* see **11d.**)

6a Kinds of Verbs: Transitive, Intransitive, and Linking

Verbs are commonly grouped in three categories according to the way they function in sentences. You have already met these in Chapter I; now consider them in more detail.

A verb that has a *direct object* is called a **transitive** verb. *Transitive* means "effecting transition": a transitive verb makes a transition, conveys a movement, from its subject to its object. A verb that has no direct object is called **intransitive**. Verbs that normally have direct objects are considered *transitive*; for example:

> She *has* good taste.
> He *introduced* me to his uncle.
> Greg never *neglects* his homework.
> She *expresses* her ideas eloquently.
> He *stuffed* himself with pizza.
> Where *did* you *lay* that book?

A direct object answers the question consisting of the verb and *what* or *whom*: Introduced whom? Me. Neglects what? Homework. Stuffed whom? Himself.

Some other verbs normally occur without direct objects and are considered *intransitive*; for example:

> When *will* you *arrive*?
> She *cringed*.
> You *should lie* low for a while.
> He *lied* to his roommate.
> Please *go*.

Many verbs, however, can be either transitive or intransitive, depending on how they function in particular sentences. Such a verb is *transitive* when it has a direct object, *intransitive* when it does not have a direct object; for example:

> I *ran* to the store. (no object; intransitive)
> I *ran* the business effectively. (object is *business*; transitive)
>
> He *paints* for a living. (no object; intransitive)
> He *paints* pictures. (object is *pictures*; transitive)
>
> I can *see* well enough from here. (no object; intransitive)
> I can *see* the parade better from the balcony. (object is *parade*; transitive)
>
> She *wished* upon a star. (no object; intransitive)
> He *wished* that he were home in bed. (object is the noun clause *that he were home in bed*; transitive)

In fact, very few verbs are exclusively either transitive or intransitive. Verbs felt to be clearly transitive can also be used intransitively:

> He leaned back in the chair and *remembered*.

And verbs felt to be clearly intransitive can be used transitively, especially when the object is the noun form of the same word:

> She *slept* the sleep of the just.

A third kind of verb is called a **linking** or copulative verb. The main one is the verb *be* in its various forms. Some other common verbs in this class are *become, seem, get, remain, feel, act, look, appear, smell, sound,* and *taste.*

6a kinds of verbs

The distinguishing feature of linking verbs is that they do not have objects, but are yet incomplete, requiring a **subjective complement**. Linking verbs are like equal signs in mathematical equations: something must come at the right-hand (predicate) end to balance what is at the left-hand (subject) end. A complement with a linking verb will be either a noun or an adjective; because complements occur in the predicate, they are called *predicate nouns* or *predicate adjectives*. (See also **1g** and **1h**.) Here are some examples:

Angela *is* a lawyer. (*Lawyer* is a predicate *noun*.)
Angela *is* not well. (*Well* is a predicate *adjective*.)
Martin *became* a pilot. (*Pilot* is a predicate *noun*.)
Martin *became* uneasy. (*Uneasy* is a predicate *adjective*.)
Irma *remains* a strong woman. (*Woman* is a predicate *noun*.)
Irma *remains* strong. (*Strong* is a predicate *adjective*.)
The winner *is* Nathan. (*Nathan* is a predicate *noun*.)

The complement usually follows the linking verb, though it can precede it, for example in a question or in a sentence or clause inverted for emphasis:

How *sick* are you?
However *angry* he may have been, he did not let it show.

Like an object, a complement answers the question consisting of the verb and *what* or *whom*: Is what? A lawyer. Is what? Strong. Is whom? Nathan. It differs from an object in that it is the equivalent of, or says something about, the subject.

With linking verbs other than *be* or *become*, the complement is usually an adjective:

He looks *well*.
She seems *stubborn*.
The music sounds *loud*.
He feels *fit*.
The surface felt *sticky*.
The steak tastes *good*.
The garbage smells *terrible*.

Such verbs as *act, sound, taste, smell*, and *feel* can also of course function as transitive verbs: She *acted* the part. He *sounded* his horn. He *smelled* the hydrogen sulphide. I *tasted* the steak. He *felt* the bump on his head.

Similarly, many of these verbs can also function as regular intransitive verbs, usually accompanied by *adverbial* modifiers (see **9**): The all-clear *sounded*. The garbage *smelled*. We *looked* at the painting. Gerald *is* on the roof. Teresa *is* at home. We *are* here.

But whenever one of these verbs is accompanied by a predicate noun or a predicate adjective, it is *functioning* as a **linking verb**.

6a kinds of verbs

Exercise 6a(1): Using transitive and intransitive verbs

After each transitive verb in the following, supply an object; after each intransitive verb, supply an adverb (or adverbial phrase) or a period. If a particular verb can be either transitive or intransitive, do both.

Examples: Moira *wants* money. (tr.)
Moira *waited* (intr.) patiently. (intr.)
Moira *speaks* loudly, (intr.)
with authority (intr.)
her mind (tr.)

1. Lisa *drinks*
2. Murray *talks*
3. Adriana *expects*
4. The company *ordered*
5. Yukio *learned*
6. Olivier *performed*
7. Monty *responded*
8. Sonya *planted*
9. Ricardo *bought*
10. Tony *washed*
11. Kamala *knelt*
12. Yvonne *believed*
13. Jonathan *flew*
14. Pierre *repaired*
15. The council *vetoed*
16. Everybody *breathed*
17. Donald *opened*
18. They *liberated*
19. Claudia *relaxes*
20. Matilda *teaches*
21. Bianca *attempted*
22. Colin *sold*
23. Fawad *selected*
24. Hilda *drove*
25. Horace *sang*

Exercise 6a(2): Recognizing subjective complements

Underline the complement of each italicized linking verb in the following sentences and indicate whether it is a predicate adjective or a predicate noun.

1. She *was* sorry he *felt* so ill.
2. Since he *was* an experienced seaman, he *was* confident that he could handle the crisis.
3. The book *became* a best-seller even though it *was* critical of most people's beliefs.
4. Since the house *was* well insulated, it *stayed* warm throughout the severe winter.
5. Incredible as it *seems*, the mixture *tasted* as good as it *looked* odd.

Exercise 6a(3): Using subjective complements

After each linking verb, supply (a) a predicate noun, then (b) a predicate adjective.

Example: Kevin *was* (a) an engineer. (b) exhausted.

1. Erika *is*
2. Priscilla *became*
3. Luigi *remained*
4. They *were*
5. Lorne *had been*

Exercise 6a(4): Using verbs

Compose sentences using some of the common linking verbs listed above, other than *be* or *become*. Then compose other sentences using the same verbs as either transitive or intransitive verbs, without complements. Can any of the verbs function as all three kinds? Try *smell*, for example, or *act*.

▄▄ 6b ▄▄ Inflection of Verbs; Principal Parts

Verbs are not only the most important of the parts of speech but also the most complex, the most highly inflected. Verbs are inflected

1. for **person** and **number** in order to agree with a subject (see **6d**);
2. for **aspect** in order to show the character of an action—whether an action is indefinite in duration, completed, or continuing (see **6g**);
3. for **tense** in order to show the time of an action—present, past, or future (see **6g**);
4. for **mood** in order to show whether a verb is being used as part of a direct statement (indicative), in a conditional or other unusual way (subjunctive), or in a command (imperative) (see **6j** and **6k**); and
5. for **voice** (active or passive) to show whether a subject is performing an action or being acted upon (see **6m-n**).

Every verb (except some auxiliaries; see **6e**) has what are called its **principal parts**: its **basic** form (the form under which the dictionary lists it), its **past-tense** form, its **past participle**, and its **present participle.** Verbs regularly form both the past tense and the past participle simply by adding *ed* to the basic form; for example:

Basic Form	*Past-Tense Form*	*Past Participle*
push	pushed	pushed
cook	cooked	cooked

If the basic form already ends in *e*, however, only a *d* is added:

move	moved	moved
agree	agreed	agreed

Present participles are regularly formed by adding *ing* to the basic form of the verb:

Basic Form	*Present Participle*
push	pushing
cook	cooking
agree	agreeing

But verbs ending in an unpronounced *e* will usually drop it before adding *ing*:

move	moving
skate	skating

And some verbs double a final consonant before adding *ed* or *ing*:

grin	grinned	grinning
stop	stopped	stopping

To check on these irregularities, see for example **51c** and **51e** in the chapter on *spelling*. Further, good dictionaries list any principal parts not formed by simply adding *ed* or *ing* to a basic form of a verb; whenever you aren't sure, check your dictionary.

It is from these four parts—the basic form and the three principal inflections of it—that all other inflected forms of a verb are made.

Note: The *basic* form of a verb is sometimes called the *infinitive* form, meaning that it can be preceded by the word *to* to form the verbal derivative called an *infinitive: to be, to push, to agree.* Infinitives, along with participles and gerunds, are called **non-finite** verbs; they *function* as other parts of speech (see **10**). **Finite** verbs, unlike non-finite verb forms, are so-called because they are restricted or limited by person, number, tense, mood, and voice; they function as the main verbs in predicates; non-finite verbs, or verbals, cannot function that way.

6c | Irregular Verbs

Some of the most common verbs are irregular in the way they are inflected for their past-tense forms and their past participles. These **irregular verbs** seldom cause trouble for native speakers of English, though occasionally even they might slip and say something like "He *sweared* that he had *took* all the necessary courses" rather than "He *swore* that he had *taken* all the necessary courses." Whenever you are uncertain about the principal parts of a verb—for whatever reason—check your dictionary. And here is a list of most of the common irregular verbs with their past-tense forms and their past participles; if necessary, practise by composing sets of sentences using each form (for example: "*Choose* the one you want. I *chose* mine yesterday. Haven't you *chosen* your topic yet?"):

Basic or Present Form	Past-Tense Form	Past Participle
arise	arose	arisen
awake	awoke or awaked	awaked (sometimes *awoken* or *awoke*)
bear	bore	borne (passive *born* for "given birth to")★
beat	beat	beaten or beat
become	became	become
begin	began	begun
bet	bet (sometimes *betted*)	bet (sometimes *betted*)
bid (offer)	bid	bid
bid (order, invite)	bade	bidden
bind	bound	bound
bite	bit	bitten or bit
bleed	bled	bled
blow	blew	blown
break	broke	broken

breed	bred	bred
bring	brought	brought
burst	burst	burst
buy	bought	bought
cast	cast	cast
catch	caught	caught
choose	chose	chosen
cling	clung	clung
come	came	come
cost	cost	cost
creep	crept	crept
cut	cut	cut
deal	dealt	dealt
dig	dug	dug
dive	dived or dove	dived
draw	drew	drawn
dream	dreamed or dreamt	dreamed or dreamt
drink	drank	drunk
drive	drove	driven
eat	ate	eaten
fall	fell	fallen
feed	fed	fed
feel	felt	felt
fight	fought	fought
find	found	found
flee	fled	fled
fly	flew	flown
forbid	forbade or forbad	forbidden
forget	forgot	forgotten or forgot
forsake	forsook	forsaken
freeze	froze	frozen
get	got	got or gotten
give	gave	given
go	went	gone
grind	ground	ground
grow	grew	grown
hang	hung	hung
hang (execute)	hanged	hanged
hear	heard	heard
hide	hid	hidden or hid
hit	hit	hit
hold	held	held
hurt	hurt	hurt
keep	kept	kept
kneel	knelt or kneeled	knelt or kneeled
knit	knitted or knit	knitted or knit
know	knew	known
lay	laid	laid

lead	led	led
leap	leaped or leapt	leaped or leapt
leave	left	left
lend	lent	lent
let	let	let
lie	lay	lain
light	lighted or lit	lighted or lit*
lose	lost	lost
make	made	made
mean	meant	meant
meet	met	met
mistake	mistook	mistaken
mow	mowed	mown
overcome	overcame	overcome
pay	paid	paid
prove	proved	proved or proven
put	put	put
quit	quit (sometimes *quitted*)	quit (sometimes *quitted*)
read	read (changes pronunciation)	read (changes pronunciation)
ride	rode	ridden
ring	rang	rung
rise	rose	risen
run	ran	run
say	said	said
see	saw	seen
seek	sought	sought
sell	sold	sold
send	sent	sent
set	set	set
shake	shook	shaken
shed	shed	shed
shoot	shot	shot
shrink	shrank or shrunk	shrunk
shut	shut	shut
sing	sang	sung
sink	sank	sunk
sit	sat	sat
slay	slew	slain
sleep	slept	slept
slide	slid	slid
sling	slung	slung
slink	slunk	slunk
speak	spoke	spoken
speed	sped or speeded	sped or speeded
spend	spent	spent
spin	spun	spun

finite verbs **6d**

spit	spit (sometimes *spat*)	spit (sometimes *spat*)
split	split	split
spread	spread	spread
spring	sprang or sprung	sprung
stand	stood	stood
steal	stole	stolen
stick	stuck	stuck
sting	stung	stung
stink	stank or stunk	stunk
strew	strewed	strewn
stride	strode	stridden
strike	struck	struck (or *stricken* for "ill" or "afflicted")★
string	strung	strung
strive	strove or strived	striven or strived
swear	swore	sworn
sweep	swept	swept
swell	swelled	swelled or swollen
swim	swam	swum
swing	swung	swung
take	took	taken
teach	taught	taught
tear	tore	torn
tell	told	told
think	thought	thought
thrive	throve or thrived	thrived or thriven
throw	threw	thrown
thrust	thrust	thrust
wake	woke or waked	waked (sometimes *woken* or *woke*)
wear	wore	worn
weep	wept	wept
win	won	won
wind	wound	wound
write	wrote	written

★ For verbs marked with an asterisk, check your dictionary for information about usages and definitions.

6d   Finite Verbs: Inflection for Person and Number

In order to agree grammatically with a subject, a verb is inflected for *person* and *number*. To illustrate, here are the forms for four verbs as they are inflected for person and number in the *present tense*, using as subjects the personal pronouns (see **4a**):

Singular

1st person	I walk	I move	I push	I fly
2nd person	you walk	you move	you push	you fly
3rd person	he walks	he moves	he pushes	he flies
	she walks	she moves	she pushes	she flies
	it walks	it moves	it pushes	it flies

Plural

1st person	we walk	we move	we push	we fly
2nd person	you walk	you move	you push	you fly
3rd person	they walk	they move	they push	they fly

Note that the inflection occurs *only in the third-person singular* and that it consists simply of adding *s* or *es* to the basic form of the verb (if necessary, first changing a final *y* to *i*; see **51d**).

6e   Auxiliary Verbs

English uses what are called **auxiliary** or **helping verbs** that go with other verbs to form verb phrases indicating tense, aspect, voice, and mood.

One auxiliary, *do*, you have already encountered in Chapter I as an aid in constructing questions (see **1t**):

> *Did* you arrive in time?

It also helps in constructing negative sentences:

> I *did not* arrive in time.
> She *doesn't* care for asparagus.

and in expressing emphasis:

> I *did* wash my face!
> I *do* admire that man.

(The auxiliary *do* works only in the simple present and the simple past tenses; see **6g**.)

The principal **modal auxiliaries** are *can, could, may, might, must, should,* and *would*. These auxiliaries combine with main verbs and other auxiliaries to express such meanings as ability, possibility, obligation, and necessity; for example:

> I *can* understand that.
> There *could* be thunderstorms tomorrow.
> I *would* tell you the answer if I *could*.
> The general *may* decide to call off the attack.
> I *might* attend, but then again I *might* not.
> You *should* have received the letter by now.
> That man *should* lose some weight.
> *Must* we listen to that song again?

Caution: To use *would have* in a conditional *if*-clause in the past tense is incorrect: "If I *would have* known you were coming, I would have baked a cake." In the independent clause *would have* is correct; in the *if*-clause the auxiliary should be *had*. In the present tense, *would* in both clauses is less objectionable ("If I would study harder, I would get better grades"), though even there the first clause could be less informally phrased as "If I studied harder."

Could and *might* also serve as the past-tense forms of *can* and *may*, for example if demanded by the sequence of tenses after a verb in the past tense (see **6i/1**):

> He was sure that I *could* handle the project.
> She said that I *might* watch the rehearsal if I promised to behave myself.

When not part of a sequence of tenses, *might* sometimes serves interchangeably with *may* to express possibility:

> She *may* (*might*) challenge the committee's decision.
> He *may* (*might*) have finished the job by now.

But often there is a difference in meaning, with *may* indicating a strong possibility, *might* a less likely one:

> Since more rain is forecast, the flood *may* (i.e., *may well*) get worse overnight.
> The weather report says the worst is over, though the river *might* (i.e., *could*, but probably won't) rise still further.

To express a condition contrary to fact (see **6k/2**, on the subjunctive), *might* is the right word:

> If you had studied more systematically, you *might* (not *may*) have passed the course.

The equivalent phrases *able to* (*can*), *ought to* (*should*), and *have to* (*must*) also function as modal auxiliaries, as sometimes do verbs like *let*, *dare*, and *need* ("*Let* me go!" "*Dare* I ask?" "*Need* you shout so?"). Unlike other verbs (see **6d**), modal auxiliaries are not inflected for third-person singular:

> I can go. You can go. He or she or it can go.

Like forms of *do*, they can join with the contraction *n't*, or, in the case of *can*, with the uncontracted word *not* itself: *cannot*, *can't*, *couldn't*, *shouldn't*, *wouldn't*, *mustn't*. (One is not likely nowadays to encounter *mayn't*, though *mightn't* still occurs.) Nor do these verbs have any participial forms, or an infinitive form (one cannot say *to can*, but must use another verb: *to be able*). But they can work as parts of perfect tenses as well as of simple present and simple past tenses (see **6g**). (For more on modal auxiliaries, see **6-l**. For *should* and *would* as past-tense forms, see **6h/3**. For the distinction between *can* and *may*, see **60**.)

The principal auxiliary verbs, however, are *be, have, will,* and *shall*. They enable us to form tenses beyond the simple present and the simple past, as illustrated in section **6g**. *Be* and *have* go with main verbs and with each other to form the perfect tenses and the various progressive tenses. *Will,* and sometimes *shall,* help form the various future tenses (see **6h**).

6f Inflection of *do, be,* and *have*

The auxiliary verbs *do, be,* and *have* are different from the other auxiliaries in that they can function also as main or substantive verbs: they have lexical meanings of their own. (So of course do *can* and *will*—but those actually constitute different words from the auxiliaries *can* and *will*.) As a substantive verb *do* generally has the sense of *perform, accomplish* (see your dictionary):

> I *do* my job. He *did* what I asked. She *does* her best.

Have as a substantive verb generally means *own, possess, contain* (see your dictionary):

> I *have* enough money. July *has* thirty-one days.

And *be* as a substantive can mean *exist* or *live* (a sense seldom used: "I think; therefore I *am*," "Shakespeare *is* in his works," "All that *is* and *shall be* . . . "), but most often means *occur, remain, occupy a place* (see your dictionary):

> The exam *is* today. I won't *be* more than an hour. The car *is* in the garage.

Even when functioning as auxiliaries, these verbs are fully inflected. Here are the inflections for *do* and *have*, which are, as you can see, *irregular*:

Singular	*1st person*	I do	I have
	2nd person	you do	you have
	3rd person	he does	he has
		she does	she has
		it does	it has
Plural	*1st person*	we do	we have
	2nd person	you do	you have
	3rd person	they do	they have
Past-tense form		did	had
Past participle		done	had
Present participle		doing	having

The most common verb of all, *be,* is also, because of its origins and history, the most irregular. Here are its inflections:

		present tense	*past tense*
Singular	*1st person*	I am	I was
	2nd person	you are	you were
	3rd person	he is	he was
		she is	she was
		it is	it was
Plural	*1st person*	we are	we were
	2nd person	you are	you were
	3rd person	they are	they were

Past participle: been
Present participle: being

For a fuller discussion of tense, see the next section.

6g   Time and the Verb: Inflection of Verbs for Aspect and Tense

Although verbs must conform with their subjects in person and number (see **6d** and **7-7j**), they nevertheless are the most powerful elements in sentences because they not only indicate action but also control *time*. The verb is the part of speech that by its inflection indicates the *time* of an action, event, or condition.

There are two ways of looking at an action, event, or condition with respect to time, and verbs commonly indicate both. First, there is the matter of *when*: does an action occur in the past, the present, or the future? A verb shows *when* through its **tense**:

Past tense: Yesterday I *saw*.
Present tense: Today I *see*.
Future tense: Tomorrow I *will see*.

Here we have used adverbs (*yesterday, today, tomorrow*) to emphasize the *when* of the action, but the meanings are clear without them:

I *saw*.   I *see*.   I *will see*.

Second, there is the matter of the *character* or *nature* of an action. Whether it takes place in the past, the present, or the future, it may have any one of three **aspects**: If it is *indefinite*, the time when it starts or stops is unknown or unimportant. If it is *completed*, it has a definite stopping time. If it is *continuing*, it is going on during a given time.

The **indefinite** aspect comprises what are called the **simple** tenses: *simple present, simple past,* and *simple future*. Verbs in these tenses describe actions that occur at or during a given time, without being precise about when they begin or end:

I *painted* a picture yesterday. (simple past tense of *paint*)

They can also describe actions that are *habitual, repeated*—again without being precise about starting or stopping times:

I *painted* pictures last year. (past)
I *paint* pictures for a living. (present)
I *will paint* pictures next year. (future)

The **completed** aspect comprises what are called the **perfect** tenses (from the Latin *perfectus*, "completed"). Verbs in these tenses describe actions that are complete in the *present*:

> I *have painted* a picture; take a look at it. (simple present of *have* plus past participle of *paint*)

in the *past* before some specific time:

> I *had painted* a picture just before you arrived. (past-tense form of *have* plus past participle of *paint*)

or in the *future*, again before some specific time referred to or understood:

> By this time next week I *will have painted* a picture. (*will* plus basic form of *have* plus past participle of *paint*)

The third aspect, which we call **continuing**, comprises the **progressive** tenses. There is a corresponding progressive tense for each of the other six tenses. For example, to describe a *continuing* action in the *simple present* tense—one going on, in progress at the present, with no specific time of beginning or ending—you would use the *present progressive* tense:

> I *am painting* a picture, so go away and don't bother me. (simple present of *be* plus present participle of *paint*)

To describe a *continuing* action in the *past perfect* tense—an action going on in the past, and completed before some specific time—you would use the *past perfect progressive* tense:

> I *had been painting* pictures for three years before I finally sold one. (past-tense form of *have* plus past participle of *be* plus present participle of *paint*)

To describe a *continuing* action in the *simple future* tense—an action that will be going on and that has no definite time of completion—you would use the *future progressive* tense:

> I *will be painting* pictures as long as I can hold a brush. (*will* plus basic form of *be* plus present participle of *paint*)

To describe a *continuing* action in the *future perfect* tense—an action that will be completed at or before some specific time in the future—you would use the *future perfect progressive* tense:

> When my retirement cheques finally begin to arrive, I *will have been painting* pictures for thirty-five years. (*will* plus simple present of *have* plus past participle of *be* plus present participle of *paint*)

Aspect	Tense		Verb Form
Indefinite (duration of action not specified; may be once only or repeated)	Simple Present	I, you	paint
		he, she, it	paints
		we, you, they	paint
	Simple Past	I, you, he, she, it, we, you, they	painted
	Simple Future	I, you, he, she, it, we, you, they	will paint
Completed (add the past participle of the main verb to the indefinite inflection of *have*)	Present Perfect	I, you, he, she, it, we, you, they	have painted
	Past Perfect	I, you, he, she, it, we, you, they	had painted
	Future Perfect	I, you, he, she, it, we, you, they	will have painted
Continuing: Simple (add the present participle of the main verb to the indefinite inflection of *be*)	Present Progressive	I	am painting
		you	are painting
		he, she, it	is painting
		we, you, they	are painting
	Past Progressive	I	was painting
		you	were painting
		he, she, it	was painting
		we, you, they	were painting
	Future Progressive	I, you, he, she, it, we, you, they	will be painting
Continuing: Perfect (add the present participle of the main verb to the indefinite inflection of *have* and the past participle of *be*)	Present Perfect Progressive	I, you	have been painting
		he, she, it	has been painting
		we, you, they	have been painting
	Past Perfect Progressive	I, you, he, she, it, we, you, they	had been painting
	Future Perfect Progressive	I, you, he, she, it, we, you, they	will have been painting

And so on. From these examples you can at least begin to see how the auxiliary verbs—especially *be* and *have*—combine with other verbs to indicate both the *duration* of an action in time and the *time* at which it occurs: *aspect* and *tense*.

On the preceding page is a chart showing all the standard *aspects* and *tenses* of a verb.

·6h· The Functions of the Different Tenses

The tenses of English verbs are generally clear and straightforward. Most people, especially if their native language is English, have little or no trouble with them. But there are some peculiarities that you may need to watch. Although the points that follow are sometimes over-simplifications of very complex matters, and although there are other exceptions and variations than those listed, these guidelines should help you to use the tenses properly and to take advantage of the possibilities they offer for clear expression. Following are brief descriptions and illustrations of the main functions of each tense.

1. *Simple present:* Generally, use this tense to describe an action or condition that is happening now, at the time of the utterance:

   The pitcher *throws* the ball. The batter *swings*. It *is* a high fly ball . . . .
   The day *is* very warm. I *am* uncomfortable. *Are* you all right? I *can manage*.

   But the simple present tense also has several other common uses. It can be used to indicate a general truth or belief:

   The Grand Banks *are* a major fishing ground.
   Everest *is* earth's highest mountain.
   Cheetahs *can outrun* any other animal.

   to describe a customary or habitual or repeated action or condition:

   Anne *spells* her name with an *e* at the end.
   I *love* to go to the movies.
   I always *eat* breakfast before going to work.

   to describe the characters or events in a literary or other work of art, or the acts of the author in such a work (see also **6i/5**):

   Oedipus *searches* for the truth almost like a modern detective.
   The Seven Dwarfs *whistle* while they work.
   Chaucer *begins* by introducing his characters.

   and even to express future time, especially with the help of an adverbial modifier (see also number 7 below):

   He *arrives* tomorrow.
   We *leave* for England next Sunday.

2. *Simple past:* Use this tense to describe a single or repeated action or condition that began and ended in the past (compare number 4 below):

> I *earned* a lot of money last summer.
> I *was* out in the field before six every morning.
> The Battle of Hastings *took place* in 1066.
> The weather *was* unusually warm last week.
> *Did* the Romantic Period *end* with the accession of Victoria?
> I *visited* Greece in 1975, 1980, and 1984.

3. *Simple future:* Although there are other ways to indicate future time (see for example number 1 above and number 7 below), the most common and straightforward is to use the simple future tense, putting *will* or *shall* before the basic form of the verb:

> He *will arrive* tomorrow morning.
> I *will paint* your portrait next week.
> We'*ll have* a nice picnic if it doesn't rain.

Shall, once considered the correct auxiliary for use with a first-person subject (*I*, *we*), is now restricted largely to expressing emphasis or determination:

> I *shall* never *give in*.

or to unusually formal or polite contexts:

> *Shall* you *be attending* the luncheon?
> We *shall expect* you at one, then.

or to *first-person questions* asking for agreement or permission or advice, where *will* would sound unidiomatic:

> *Shall* we *go*?
> *Shall* I *take* the wheel now?
> What *shall* I *do* now?
> What *shall* we *give* Bertram for Christmas?

Other questions about the future, in whatever person, asking simply for information, use *will*:

> Where *will* you *be* at this time tomorrow?
> *Will* we *arrive* in time?

In less formal contexts, one can often use the contractions *I'll*, *we'll*, etc., and the question of choosing between *will* and *shall* doesn't arise. With negative statements or questions, the contracted forms of *will not* and *shall not* are *won't* and *shan't*:

> *Won't* we *arrive* on time?
> No, I *shan't be able* to attend.

(After another verb in the past, *would* and *should* serve as the past-tense forms of *will* and *shall*:

> He told me he *would arrive* at ten in the morning.

See **6i**, on sequence of tenses.)

4. *Present perfect:* Use this tense to indicate an action or condition that began in the past and that continues to the present (compare number 2 above):

> I *have earned* a lot of money this summer.
> The Prime Minister *has* just *entered* the room.
> The weather *has been* unusually warm lately.
> Her illness *has lasted* for two months.

Even if what you are referring to occurred entirely in the past, you can use the present perfect tense if you don't specify just when it occurred and if you feel it as somehow impinging on the present—that is, if you intend to imply the sense of "before now" or "so far" or "already":

> The instructor *has told* us how she wants us to handle our assignments.
> I *have visited* Greece three times.
> We *have beaten* them seven out of ten times.

5. *Past perfect:* Use this tense to indicate an action completed in the past before a specific past time:

> Though I *had seen* the movie twice before, I went again last week.
> They got to the station only a minute late, but the train *had* already *left*.
> I *had hoped* for an A, but I didn't do quite well enough on the exam.
> After jogging for two hours, she felt that she *had had* enough exercise to last a week.

6. *Future perfect:* Use this tense to indicate an action or condition that will be completed before a specific future time:

> When I finish this lap, I *will have run* seventy-five miles this week.
> Some biologists predict that by the year 2000 they *will have found* a cure for cancer.
> I *will* already *have eaten* by the time you arrive.

Sometimes the simple future tense will work as well as the future perfect; for example *will find* serves just as well as *will have found* in the second example above.

7. *Present progressive:* Use this tense for an action or condition that began at some past time and that is continuing now, in the present:

I *am writing* my rough draft.
The drought on the Prairies *is getting* worse.

Sometimes the simple and the progressive forms of a particular verb say much the same thing:

We *hope* for good weather. We're *hoping* for good weather.
I *feel* sick. I *am feeling* sick.

But usually the progressive form emphasizes—if only slightly— an activity, or the singleness or continuing nature of an action, rather than a larger condition or general truth:

Inflation *hurts* many people. Inflation *is hurting* many people.
I *go* to university. I *am going* to university.
I *wonder* how he'll explain. I *am wondering* how he'll explain.
I *assume* they know the answer. I *am assuming* they know the answer.

Like the present tense (see number 1 above), the present progressive tense can also express future time, especially with the help of adverbial modifiers:

They *are arriving* early tomorrow morning.
We're *taking* our vacation earlier this year than last; we leave next week.

You can also express future time with a form of the verb *be* and the phrase *going to* before the basic form of a main verb:

They *are going to appeal* the verdict.
Isn't the officer *going to lay* charges?

8. *Past progressive:* Use this tense for an action that was in progress during some past time, especially if you want to emphasize the action or its continuing nature:

He *was driving* very fast.
They *were protesting* the council's decision.

Sometimes the past progressive tense suggests an interrupted action or an action during which something else happens:

When the telephone rang I *was shampooing* my hair.
Just as he *was stepping* off the curb, the bus roared by.

9. *Future progressive:* Use this tense for a continuing action in the future or for an action that will be occurring at some specific time in the future:

You *will be learning* things for the rest of your life.
They *will be arriving* on the midnight plane.
Next week I *will be studying* for final exams.

10. *Present perfect progressive:* Use this tense to emphasize the continuing nature of a single or repeated action that began in the past and that has continued at least up to the present:

> I *have been working* on this paragraph for two hours.
> The dollar *has been declining* in value.
> Our study-group *has been meeting* once a week since January.

11. *Past perfect progressive:* Use this tense to emphasize the continuing nature of a single or repeated past action that was completed before some other past action occurred or that was interrupted by a second past action:

> We *had* all *been expecting* something quite different.
> The candidates *had been planning* their strategies for months before the campaign began.
> She *had been corresponding* with him for years before she met him.
> I *had been pondering* the problem for over an hour when suddenly the solution popped into my head.

12. *Future perfect progressive:* This tense is seldom used. Use it only when you want to emphasize the continuing nature of a future action before a specific time in the future or before a second future action:

> If she continues to paint, by 1995 she *will have been working* at it for over half her life.
> You *will* already *have been driving* for about nine hours before you even get to the border.

Exercise 6h(1): Using verb tenses

If you are a native speaker of English, verbs and their tenses probably come naturally to you. But if English is not your first language, verbs and their tenses may be causing you some trouble. In either event, you can not only learn something but also have some fun by practising with them. Choose a few fairly standard verbs—say, three regular verbs and three from the list of irregular verbs (**6c**)—and run them through their paces. That is, compose sentences using them in all the tenses illustrated in the chart (**6g**) and the examples above (**6h**).

Exercise 6h(2): Using auxiliary verbs

Select ten or so of the sentences you wrote for the preceding exercise and try using *do* and some of the *modal auxiliaries* (see **6e**) with them to produce different meanings. For example:

> I do paint pictures. I did paint pictures. Didn't you paint pictures? I may have painted pictures. Can you paint? I should be painting the garage. I should have been painting pictures. I shouldn't have been painting pictures. Could I have been painting pictures? They must have been painting pictures.

6i sequence of tenses

6i **Sequence of Tenses**

When two or more verbs occur in the same sentence, they will sometimes be of the same tense, but often they will be of different tenses. In a compound sentence, made up of two or more independent clauses (see **1z**), the verbs can be equally independent; use whatever tenses the sense requires:

> I *am leaving* (present progressive) now, but she *will leave* (future) in the morning.
> The polls *have closed* (present perfect) and the clerks *will* soon *be counting* (future progressive) the ballots.
> He *had made* (past perfect) his promise, and the committee *decided* (past) to hold him to it; therefore they *expect* (present) his cooperation.

1. *Past tense in main clause*

In complex or compound-complex sentences, if the verb in the main or independent clause is in any of the past tenses, the verbs in any subordinate clauses will usually also be in one of the past tenses. For example:

> I *told* him that I *was* sorry.
> I *had told* him about the man who *would succeed* him.

Refer to a time *earlier* than that of a past main verb by using the *past perfect* tense:

> I *told* him that I *had seen* her the day before.
> I *was telling* him about what I *had done*.

But there are exceptions. When the verb in the subordinate clause states a general or timeless truth or belief, or something characteristic or habitual, it stays in the present tense:

> Columbus set out to demonstrate that the earth *is* round.
> They found out the hard way that money *doesn't guarantee* happiness.
> She reminded him that London Bridge *is* now in Arizona.

And common sense sometimes dictates that other kinds of verbs in subordinate clauses should retain their original tenses rather than be attracted into a past tense; if you feel that a tense other than the past would be clearer or more accurate, use it; for example:

> I *learned* this morning that I *will* be able to get into the new program in the fall.

In that sentence, the rule calls for *would* rather than *will*, but *will* is logical and clear.

> In an interview yesterday, Smith *said* that he *is* determined to complete the investigation.

To use *was* rather than *is* in that sentence would at best be ambiguous, implying that Smith's determination was a thing of the past; if it definitely *was* past, then *had been* would be the clearer verb.

> I *had* already *told* him about the man who *will succeed* him next month.

Here the adverb *next month* makes it clear that the succession has not yet occurred; hence the future tense is the logical one. And here is one more example of a sentence in which the "sequence of tenses" rule is best ignored:

> The secretary *told* me this morning that Professor Barnes *is* ill and *will not be holding* class this afternoon.

But unless you firmly believe that another tense is better, use past with past.

2. *Infinitives after a finite verb* (see **10a**)

Generally, use the *present tense* of an infinitive (a verb's basic form preceded by *to*) after a finite verb, even one in a past tense. The infinitive then indicates the same or a later time than that of the verb:

> I am pleased *to meet* you.
> I was pleased *to meet* you.
> I would have liked *to meet* [not *to have met*] you earlier.

But if the infinitive indicates an action that occurred *before* the time indicated by the verb, use the *present perfect* tense (a verb's past participle preceded by *to have*):

> I was lucky *to have met* the manager before the interview.

3. *The tense of participles* (see **10c**)

As with infinitives, use a *present* participle to indicate the same or a later time than that of a verb:

> *Knowing* computer language, Doreen easily held her own with the technicians.

To indicate a time *earlier* than that of a verb, use a *past* or a *perfect* participle (the past participle preceded by *having*):

> *Trained* in computer programming, she spotted the weakness quickly.
> *Having studied* computers for several months, she understood them better than her colleagues did.

4. *Verb phrases in compound predicates*

When a compound predicate consists of two verb phrases in different tenses, don't carelessly omit part of one of them:

6j *mood*

> *wrong*:   The party has never and will never practise nepotism.

Rather, spell each of them out completely or rephrase the sentence:

> *revised*:   The party has never practised and will never practise nepotism.
> *revised*:   The party has never practised nepotism and will never do so.

5. *Tenses in writing about literature*
When discussing or describing the events in a literary work, it is customary to use what is called the "historical present" tense (see also **6h/1**):

> When Hamlet *returns* to Denmark he *meets* Horatio and they *observe* Ophelia's burial.

Other tenses can occur in such a context to indicate times before or after the "now" of the historical present being discussed:

> While he *was* away, Hamlet *had arranged* to have Rosencrantz and Guildenstern put to death. Now he *holds* Yorick's skull and *watches* Ophelia being buried. And later he *will meet* his own death in the duel with Laertes. Clearly death *is* one of the principal themes with which Shakespeare *is concerned* in the play.

Note that it is customary to speak even of a long-dead author in the present tense when one is discussing a particular work. Here is another example of that:

> In *Moby-Dick* Melville *tells* of mad Ahab's pursuit of the great white whale.

6j   Mood

English verbs are usually considered to have three moods: *indicative, imperative,* and *subjunctive.* The **mood** of a verb (related to *mode*) has to do with the nature of the expression it's being used in. The ordinary mood is the **indicative**, used for statements of fact or opinion and for questions:

> The weather forecast for tomorrow *sounds* promising.
> Shall we *proceed* with our plans?

The **imperative** mood is used for most commands and instructions (see **1** and **1u**):

> *Put* the picnic hamper in the trunk.
> *Don't forget* the mustard.
> *Be sure* to lock the door.

These offer no difficulty. Only the **subjunctive** mood causes any problems, and those only rarely.

6k   **Using the Subjunctive**

The subjunctive has almost disappeared from modern English. It survives in some standard expressions or idioms such as "*be* that as it may," "long *live* the Queen," "heaven *forbid*," and "*come* what may." Other than such expressions, which most people use without even thinking about the subjunctive, you need know about only two kinds of instances where the subjunctive still functions.

1. Use the subjunctive—usually in *that* clauses—after verbs expressing demands, obligations, requirements, recommendations, suggestions, wishes, and the like. Here are some examples:

> It is necessary that we *be* there before noon.
> The judge recommended that Ralph *attend* the meeting.
> Ruth asked that the door *be* left open.
> I wish [that] I *were* in Paris.

2. Use the subjunctive to express conditions contrary to fact, conditions that are hypothetical or impossible or not real—often in *if* clauses or their equivalents. Some examples:

> He looked as if he *were* going to explode. [But of course he didn't explode.]
> If Diane *were* here she would back me up. [But she *isn't* here.]
> If he *weren't* so stubborn, he'd be easier to get along with. [But he *is* stubborn.]

An *as if* or *as though* clause almost always expresses a condition contrary to fact, but not all *if* clauses do; don't be misled into using a subjunctive where the ordinary indicative form would be correct:

> *Wrong*:   He said that if there *were* another complaint he would resign.

The verb should be *was*, for the condition could turn out to be true: there may be another complaint.

Since only a few subjunctive forms differ from those of the indicative, they are easy to learn and remember. The third-person singular form loses its *s*:

> *Indicative*:   I like the way she *paints*.
> *Subjunctive*:   I suggested that she *paint* my picture.

The subjunctive forms of the verb *be* are *be* and *were*:

> *Indicative*:   He *is* my friend. (I *am*, you *are*, we *are*, they *are*)
> *Subjunctive*:   I asked that he *be* my attorney. (that I *be*, that you *be*, that we *be*, that they *be*)

6k subjunctives

6-1 subjunctives

> *Indicative*:   I know that I *am* in Edmonton.
> *Subjunctive*: I wish that I *were* in Florence.
>
> *Indicative*:   They *are* not particularly prominent people.
> *Subjunctive*: They behave as if they *were* royalty.

Note that both *be* and *were* function with either singular or plural subjects. Note also that the past-tense form *were* functions in present-tense expressions of wishes and contrary-to-fact conditions. Other verbs also use their past tense as subjunctives after a present-tense wish:

> I wish that I *painted* better.

After a past-tense wish, use the standard past-perfect form:

> He wished that he *had been* more attentive.
> She wished that she *had played* better.

Although it is not unusual to hear and read informal expressions like "I wish I *was* in Paris" and "If Diane *was* here," the subjunctive form is still preferable in formal writing and is used and expected by many educated writers and readers. It isn't dead yet. But if subjunctives worry you, see the next section.

6-1   Using Modal Auxiliaries and Infinitives Instead of Subjunctives

The *modal auxiliaries* (see **6e**) offer common alternatives for many sentences using subjunctive forms; they express several of the same moods, or modes:

> We *must* be there before noon.
> The judge said that Ralph *should* (*ought to, might want to*) attend the hearing.
> I wish that I *could* be in Paris.
> He looked as if he *might* explode.
> If Diane *could have been* here, she would back me up.
> If he *would be* less stubborn, he'd be easier to get along with.
> I asked if she *would* paint my portrait.
> I asked him if he *would* be my attorney.
> I wish that I *could* paint better.

Yet another alternative uses the *infinitive* (see **10a**):

> It is necessary for us *to be* there before noon.
> The judge advised Ralph *to attend* the hearing.
> Ruth asked us *to leave* the door open.
> He seemed about *to explode*.
> I told her I wanted her *to paint* my portrait.
> I asked him *to be* my attorney.
> I would like *to be* in Florence.

Exercise 6k1: Using subjunctives

Compose ten sentences using a variety of the subjunctive forms illustrated above. Then try to revise each so that it uses a modal auxiliary or an infinitive instead of a subjunctive; you should be able to change at least half of them, if not all.

6m　**Voice**

There are two voices, **active** and **passive**. The active voice is direct statement: *I made this boat.* The passive voice reverses the normal subject–verb–object pattern: *This boat was made by me.* Passive voice is easily recognized; the verb uses some form of the verb *be* followed by a past participle: *was made.* What in active voice would be a direct object, in passive voice becomes the subject of the verb (*boat*). (Usually, then, only transitive verbs can be put in the passive voice; see **6a**.)

6n　**The Passive Voice**

pas

Although the passive voice has its uses, only in certain circumstances is it preferable to the active voice. Rhetorically, passive constructions are frequently weak because they are indirect and obscure; often the agent of the action or state they describe disappears from the scene. That is why politicians and civil servants are so fond of the passive voice: it enables people to make assertions which promise action without committing themselves to perform it, and makes possible the admission of error without anyone having to accept responsibility. For example:

> *Passive*:　Be assured (by whom?) that action will be taken (by whom?).
> *Active*:　I assure you that I will act.
> *Passive*:　It is to be regretted (by whom?) that an error has been made (by whom?) in your account. The matter will be investigated (by whom?).
> *Active*:　I am sorry we made an error in your account. I will look into the matter and correct it immediately.

The passive voice tends to be impersonal and lacks the vigour of directness. It often leads to fuzziness, wordiness, awkwardness, and even grammatical error. Therefore if you find yourself inclined to overuse the passive voice, foster a counter-tendency; make your assertions in the bolder and more lively active voice. Here are some examples from students' papers:

> *Passive*:　All of this *is communicated* by Tolkien by means of a poem rather than prose. The poetry *is shown* as a tool which Tolkien

employs in order to foreshadow events and establish ideas which otherwise *could* not *be* easily *communicated* to us.

The wordiness and general cotton-woolly consistency of this passage result largely from the passive voice. A change to active voice reduces the length, clarifies the sense, and produces a crisper, more vital style. Begin by making the agent of the action the subject of the verb; the rest then follows naturally and logically:

> *Active:*   Tolkien *communicates* all this in poetry rather than prose be-
> cause with poetry he can foreshadow events and establish ideas
> that would otherwise be difficult to convey.

Other examples:

> *Passive:*   And as I stood admiring the small hills, rich grass, and tall
> poplars, as I had often done before, they *were* now *being com-*
> *pared* with the landscape at home.

The passive voice here serves only to confuse the reader. Clearly the *I* is the only possible agent:

> *Active:*   And as I stood admiring the small hills, rich grass, and tall
> poplars, as I had often done before, I was now comparing them
> with the landscape at home.

Here is one more example:

> *Passive:*   By weeding out the errors in one's writing, good habits *are*
> also *learned*.

Here the passive voice has resulted not only in awkwardness and weakness, but also in a grammatical error: a dangling modifier (see **24**). The frequency of this kind of error is in itself a sufficient reason to be careful with the passive voice. Change the passive to the active and the dangling modifier disappears.

> *Active:*   By weeding out the errors in one's writing, one also *learns* good
> habits.

The passive voice should be used only when the active voice is impossible or unnecessarily awkward, or when the passive is for some other reason clearly preferable or demanded by the context. In the preceding sentence, for example, we began with a passive construction (*should be used*) in order to be able to begin the sentence emphatically with *The passive voice*; in addition, the agent in this instance—i.e., all writers—is less important than *The passive voice* itself, which we have emphasized by making it the subject of the sentence. Here are some good reasons for using the passive voice:

1. When the agent, or doer of the act, is indefinite or not known.
2. When the agent is not as important as the act itself.

3. When you want to emphasize either the agent or the act by putting it at the beginning or end of the sentence.

For example:

It *was reported* that there were two survivors.

Here the writer does not know who did the reporting. To avoid the passive by saying "Someone reported that there were two survivors" would be to strain the point by seeming to emphasize the mysterious "someone." And the fact that someone did the reporting is, in this instance, less important than the content of the report.

The accident *was witnessed* by more than thirty people.

Here the writer wishes to emphasize the large number of witnesses. One could say "More than thirty people witnessed the accident," but the emphasis is clearly greater at the end of the sentence than at the beginning. There will surely be other occasions when you will want to use the passive, but if you make it a habit never to use it unwittingly and uncritically, your writing will inevitably be better.

Remember, a verb in the passive voice consists of some form of the verb *be* followed by a past participle (*to be accompanied, was given, had been given, will be charged, is shown, are legalized, is being removed*). Whenever you find yourself forming such verbs in your writing, stop to consider whether an active structure might not be more effective.

Note: Like *mood* and *aspect*, *voice* operates regardless of *tense*; do not confuse *passive* with *past*. Passive constructions can occur in any of the tenses. See also **1e** and **18f**.

Exercise 6n: Revising passive voice

Revise the following sentences, changing any verbs that are in the passive voice to the active voice if you think the change improves the sentence. Leave in the passive voice any verbs that you think should remain passive.

1. The house was broken into during the night, but only some loose change was taken.
2. After some packing boxes were found, the tedious process of individually wrapping my valuables began.
3. Once all the packing was completed I had to start cleaning up the apartment.
4. The car was driven by Denise, while Anton acted as map-reader.
5. Another factor that makes Whistler's ski resort so popular is the diversity of entertainment that can be found.
6. Some went swimming, some went on short hikes, some just lay around, and baseball was played by others.
7. Although a daily routine was followed, there was enough variety to keep us from becoming bored.

8. The solution to the problem was worked out by our resident efficiency expert.
9. According to the planning committee, it is hoped that visitors to the province during the exposition will be treated fairly and hospitably wherever they go.
10. We were informed by our guide that the cathedral was built in the thirteenth century.

---

7 Agreement Between Subject and Verb
agr

A finite verb should agree with its subject in **number** and **person**. A finite verb is "limited" (made finite) in its form by the number and person of its subject; the subject governs the form of the inflected part of the verb. We say *I see*, not *I sees*, and *he sees*, not *he see*. Most English speakers automatically use the correct form of the verb to go with the *person* of the subject, but they sometimes have trouble making verbs agree with their subjects in *number*. Here are the main points to watch out for.

7a Something Intervening Between Subject and Verb

Errors sometimes occur when something comes between a singular subject and its verb, for example a prepositional phrase in which the object of the preposition is plural, or an appositive consisting of a plural or of several parts. The verb in such a sentence must agree with the singular subject; don't let the intervening plural mislead you:

> Far below, a *landscape* of rolling brown hills and small trees *lies* in disharmony with the grim structures of steel and cement.
> *Each* of the poems *has* certain striking qualities.
> *Neither* of the men *was* willing to volunteer.
> The whole *experience*—the decision to go, the planning, the ocean voyage, and especially all the places we went and things we saw—*was* consistently exciting.

Nor of course should you let an intervening singular noun affect the agreement between a plural subject and its verb.

7b Compound Subject: Singular Nouns Joined by *and*

A compound subject made up of two or more singular nouns joined by *and* is usually plural:

> Careful thought and close attention to detail *are* essential for effective writing.
> Coffee and tea *were* served on the balcony.

Exceptions can occur, however. If the two nouns name or identify the same person or thing, or if the two nouns taken together are thought of as a unit, then the verb will be singular:

> A husband and father *has* an obligation to share the domestic responsibilities.
> Bacon and eggs *is* a popular breakfast combination.

Nevertheless, if you find yourself wanting to use a singular verb after a subject consisting of two singular nouns joined by *and*, look again: you may have used two nouns that mean virtually the same thing and that are therefore *redundant* (see **59c**); for example:

> *faulty:*   The *strength* and *power* of his argument is undeniable.

Get rid of one or the other, or find a single word to replace them both (*force?*).

Caution: Phrases such as *as well as, in addition to, together with,* and *along with* are prepositions, not conjunctions like *and*. A singular subject followed by one of them still takes a singular verb:

> The cat as well as the dog *comes* when I whistle.
> Mrs. Hondiak, along with her daughters, *is* attending college this year.

Compound subjects preceded by *each, every,* or *many a* take a singular verb:

> Each dog and cat *has* its own supper-dish.

7c   **Compound Subject: Parts Joined by *or* or a Correlative**
When the parts of a compound subject are joined by the co-ordinating conjunction *or* (see **12a**) or by the correlative conjunctions *either . . . or, neither . . . nor, not . . . but, not only . . . but also,* or *whether . . . or* (see **12b**), the part of the subject nearest to the verb determines whether the verb is singular or plural:

> One or the other of you *has* the key. (both parts singular: verb singular)
> Neither the men nor the women *like* the proposal. (both parts plural: verb plural)
> Neither the mainland nor the islands *are* being served. (first part singular, second part plural: verb plural)
> Neither my parents nor I *was* to blame. (first part plural, second part singular: verb singular)

Since the construction used in the last example usually sounds awkward, it should be avoided if possible; it can easily be rephrased; for example:

> Neither I nor my parents were to blame.
> My parents were not to blame, nor was I.

7c compound subjects

7d   Agreement with Indefinite Pronouns

In formal usage, most of the indefinite pronouns are considered singular and should take the singular form of a verb: *another, anybody, anyone, anything, each, either, everybody, everyone, everything, much, neither, nobody, no one, one, other, somebody, someone, something.* A few, however—*all, any, more, most, none,* and *some*—can be either singular or plural, depending on whether they refer to a single quantity or to a number of units within a group—that is, whether they stand for a singular or plural noun or pronoun. (See also **3g** and **4c**). For example:

> *Some* of the money *is* missing. (a single sum; *money* is singular)
> *Some* of the men *are* missing. (a number of men; *men* is plural)
> *All* of this novel *is* good. (a whole novel; *novel* is singular)
> *All* of his novels *are* well written. (a number of novels; *novels* is plural)
> *Most* of the beef *is* grain-fed. (a single mass; *beef* is singular)
> *Most* of the cattle *are* grain-fed. (a number of animals; *cattle* is plural)
> *None* of the work *is* done. (a single unit; *work* is singular)
> *None* of the papers *are* ready. (a number of items; *papers* is plural)

None, however, is still considered by some people as always singular. But you will be safe enough if you simply ask yourself what you mean by the word *none* in a particular context. For example:

> *None* of the runners *is* tired yet. (none = *not one*)
> *None* but the fainthearted *are* staying behind. (none but = *only they*)

The meaning of the phrase *more than one* is obviously plural, but the force of the word *one* usually dictates a singular verb; if the phrase is broken up, however, a plural verb usually sounds idiomatic:

> Of the five answers, more than one *is* probably correct.
> More answers than one *are* probably correct.

7e   Subject Following Verb

When the subject for one reason or another *follows* the verb, be sure to make the verb agree with the real subject and not some word that happens to precede it:

> There *is* only one *answer* to this question.
> There *are* several possible *solutions* to the problem.
> Here *comes* the *punch line.*
> Here *come* the *clowns.*
> Thirty days *has* September.
> Charging about all over the landscape *were* the *group* of scouts *and* their *leader.*

When compounded singular nouns follow an opening *there* or *here,* the verb will normally be plural:

> There *were* a *computer and* a *copier* in the next room.

Sometimes, however, especially when the compound subject consists of noun phrases or clauses, a plural verb sounds unnatural; then a singular verb is more idiomatic:

> There *was* still an *essay* to be revised *and* a *play* to be studied before he could think about sleep.

Some writers claim that such a verb should agree with the part of the subject nearest to it, regardless of what comes next:

> There *was* still the *play* to be read *and* his *lines* to be memorized.

But this is risky; it is sure to strike some readers as wrong or awkward. Since opinion is divided, clearly the best and easiest solution is simply to avoid the issue by rephrasing your sentences:

> A computer and a copier were in the next room.
> He still had an essay to revise and a play to study before he could think about sleep.
> He still had to read the play and memorize his lines.

An expletive *it* always takes a singular verb—usually a linking verb:

> It *is* questions like these that give her the most trouble.

For more on the expletives *it* and *there*, see **1k** and **59a**.

Caution: Don't let a predicate noun determine the number of the verb; the verb must agree with the subject of the sentence, not the complement:

> The last *word* in style that year *was* [not *were*] suede shoes and broad lapels.

7f   Agreement with Collective Nouns

Some nouns—called **collective nouns** (see **2**)—are names of groups and may be considered either singular or plural, depending on whether they refer to something as a whole, a unit, or to the individual persons or things that make up the whole:

> The faculty has made its decision regarding student representation. (singular)
> The faculty have not yet made up their minds about student representation. (plural)
> His family comes from Iceland. (singular)
> His family come from Jamaica, India, and Southern Europe. (plural)
> The audience was composed and attentive. (singular)
> The audience were sneezing, coughing, blowing their noses, and chatting with each other. (plural)

Words like *number, half,* and *majority* can also be considered collective nouns and can be either singular or plural:

A number of lumps of coal *are* missing. (*a*: plural)
The number of people here *is* quite large. (*the*: singular)
Half of the team *is* here. OR Half of the team *are* here.
Half of the women *are* going.

(See also *amount, number* in **60.**)

Other terms of quantity, like some of the indefinite pronouns (see **7d**), can be either singular or plural:

Five pieces of candy *is* quite enough for one day.
Five of us *are* going to the play.
Eggs cost too much.
A *dozen eggs costs* too much.
A *dozen* of them *do* not have to take the final examination.
That *quartet plays* very well.
The *quartet pick* up *their* instruments and the room grows quiet.

7g   Nouns Always Either Singular or Plural

Some nouns, because of their meaning, cannot be inflected for number and will always be either singular or plural. For example:

The *gold comes* from the Yukon. (always singular)
Oxygen is essential to human life. (always singular)
Mathematics is difficult for some people. (always singular)
Good *news is* always welcome. (always singular)
The *scissors are* in the kitchen. (always plural)
His *trousers are* soaking wet. (always plural)
Her *clothes are* very stylish. (always plural)

For more on *mass* nouns and *countable* nouns, see **2a**; see also **8c/6.**

7h   Titles of Literary Works

Titles of literary and other works, and words referred to as words, should be construed as *singular* even if they are plural in themselves:

The Two Gentlemen of Verona **is** one of Shakespeare's lesser comedies.
The Seasons **is** probably Vivaldi's best-known work.
Heebie-jeebies **is** an out-of-date slang term.

7i   Agreement with Relative Pronouns

Whether a relative pronoun is singular or plural is determined by its antecedent (see **4** and **4c**). Therefore when a relative clause has *who,* *which,* or *that* as its subject, the verb must agree in number with the pronoun's antecedent:

His success is due to his intelligence and perseverance, which *have overcome* all obstacles. (The antecedent of *which* is *intelligence and perseverance;* therefore *which* is plural and needs the plural form of the auxiliary verb.)

Errors most often occur with the phrases *one of those . . . who* and *one of the . . . who*:

> He is one of those people who *have* difficulty reading aloud.
> He is one of the few people I know who *have* difficulty reading aloud.

The plural *have* is correct, since the antecedent of *who* is the plural *people*, not the singular *one*. Just remember that this construction always takes a plural verb unless *one* is preceded by *the only*; that changes the syntax so that the word *one* is the antecedent of *who*, and a singular verb is correct:

> He is the only one of those attending who *has* difficulty reading aloud.

If you find such constructions troublesome, try simplifying, for they are often wordy and unnecessarily cumbersome to begin with:

> He has difficulty reading aloud.
> Of those attending, he alone has difficulty reading aloud.

7j ▊ **Plurals: *criteria, data, media,* etc.**

The following words are *plural*; don't use them with singular verbs (see **51t**):

> criteria　　data　　media　　trivia　　phenomena　　strata

Exercise 7(1): Choosing correct verbs

In the following sentences, underline the correct form of each of the pairs of verbs in parentheses.

1. Both the chairman and the secretary (has, have) asked for volunteers, but neither Richard nor Lisette (is, are) likely to stand up.
2. There (is, are) root beer and ice cream in the refrigerator.
3. The army (resents, resent) having to adopt a new style of uniform.
4. Linda and her sisters (is, are) going, but neither John nor his brothers (plans, plan) to attend.
5. It (was, were) three months later that they met again.
6. The book as well as the magazines (contains, contain) useful information.
7. Aphra Behn is one of the many early women writers who (is, are) underrated.
8. What data (is, are) available on the topic?
9. Each of the generals (wants, want) to take command of the operation.
10. There (is, are) only ten people present.
11. Most critics agree that T. S. Eliot's *Four Quartets* (is, are) important in modern literature.
12. The number of pages assigned (was, were) reduced by half, but a large number of students (was, were) still unhappy.
13. Wood chips (makes, make) good ground-cover.
14. All work and no play (makes, make) Jack a dull boy.
15. She is the only one of those who (was, were) present who (thinks, think) that the bulk of our taxes (goes, go) for military spending.

7j criteria, data, media

8 adjectives

Exercise 7(2): Correcting faulty agreement

Revise each of the following sentences as necessary to correct any lack of agreement between subject and verb.

1. Recent discoveries about the weather reveals that there are more than one kind of cycle.
2. Hamlet's intellect and word mastery is evident in this speech.
3. Baroque sculpture in Germany and Austria were very imaginative.
4. Day after day, the media is feeding us advertisements.
5. Germaine Greer speaks of exploitation of the female in the past and present, but it seems to me that she, along with most other feminists, are the exploiters of the intellects of both females and males.
6. Everything in this speech, the metre, the repetition of vowels and consonants, and the vibrant imagery, lead us to believe that this is the high point of Othello's love—and, as far as we know from this play, of his life.
7. The use of subliminal messages are known to all advertising experts.
8. Power and the desire for wealth is just as strong now as it was then.
9. If you smile a second time your flair and charm is bound to catch someone's attention.
10. Indeed, the exercise of careful thought and careful planning seem to be necessary for the successful completion of the project.
11. But scandal, unfair politics, and the "big business" of politics has led to the corruption of the system.
12. The poet's use of words and alliteration help maintain the quiet, consoling, yet cheerful mood of the poem.
13. There appears to be four different ways of approaching such a problem.
14. My faith and trust in him was complete.
15. The number of jobs available to students under sixteen are very few.

---

8   Adjectives

An **adjective** modifies—limits or qualifies or particularizes—a noun or pronoun. Adjectives generally answer the questions *Which? What kind of? How many? How much?*

> The *black* cat ate *five* sardines and drank *some* milk; he was *hungry*.

Which cat? *The black* cat. What kind of cat? *Hungry* (modifying the pronoun *he*). How many sardines? *Five*. How much milk? *Some*.

8a   Kinds of Adjectives

There are two classes of adjective. First, there are several kinds of **non-descriptive** adjectives, some of which are basically *structure-words* (see **1-l**). These include the following:

The **articles**: *a, an,* and *the* (see **8c**)
The **demonstrative** adjectives (see also **3f**):

> *this* hat, *that* problem, *these* women, *those* books

The **interrogative** and **relative** adjectives (see also **3c** and **3d**):

> *Which* book do you want? *What* time is it? *Whose* opinion do you trust?
> She is the one *whose* opinion I trust.

Possessive adjectives, consisting of the possessive forms of personal and impersonal pronouns (see **3a** and **3b**); for example:

> *my* book, *her* car, *its* trajectory, *their* luck, *one's* beliefs

and possessive forms of nouns (see **2b**):

> a *man's* coat, the *river's* mouth, the *car's* engine, *Shirley's* job, *Hamlet's* ego, *Pearson's* cabinet

Indefinite and **numerical** adjectives (see also **3g**):

> *some* money, *any* time, *more* fuel, *several* people, *three* ducks, *thirty* ships, the *fourth* episode, etc.

Descriptive adjectives, the other major class, give information about such matters as the size, shape, colour, nature, and quality of whatever a noun or pronoun names:

> a *fast* car; a *delicate* balance; a *large, impressive three-storey gray Victorian* house; a *beautiful* painting; a *brave* man; a *tempting* dessert; a *well-done* steak; a *once-in-a-lifetime* opportunity; *Canadian* literature; a *Shakespearean* play; *composted* leaves; a *fascinating* place *to visit*; *kitchen* towels; a *dictionary* definition; *looking tired and discouraged*, he . . . ; the book *to beat all other books;* the woman *of the hour*; the rabbits *who caused all the trouble*

As these few examples illustrate, adjectival modifiers can be single (*fast, delicate, beautiful*, etc.), in groups or series (*large, impressive three-storey gray Victorian*), or in compounds (*three-storey, well-done, once-in-a-lifetime*); they can be *proper* adjectives, formed from proper nouns (*Victorian, Canadian, Shakespearean*); they can be words that are adjectives only (*delicate, beautiful*) or words that can also function as other parts of speech (*fast, brave, tempting*, etc.), including nouns functioning as adjectives (*kitchen, dictionary*); they can be present participles (*tempting, fascinating*), past participles (*composted*), or infinitives (*to visit*); they can be participial phrases (*looking tired and discouraged*), infinitive phrases (*to beat all other books*), or prepositional phrases (*of the hour*); or they can be relative clauses (*who caused all the trouble*). On the punctuation of nouns in series, see **38**; on the overuse of nouns as modifiers, see **59f**; on participles and infinitives, see **10a** and **10c**.

8b **Comparison of Descriptive Adjectives**

Most descriptive adjectives can be inflected or supplemented in order to express *degree* or to make *comparisons*:

I am *taller* than she is, but she is *more graceful.*
Al ordered the *most expensive* dish on the menu.
He is the *calmest* and *least pretentious* person I know.

The basic or dictionary form of a descriptive adjective is called its **positive** form: *high, difficult.* By adding *er* to the basic form or by putting *more* (or *less*) in front of it, you make the **comparative** form: *higher, more difficult, less difficult.* By adding *est* to the basic form or by putting *most* (or *least*) in front of it, you make the **superlative** form: *highest, most difficult, least difficult.*

It is impossible to set rules for when to add *er* and *est* and when to use *more* and *most,* but you can follow these guidelines: For adjectives of *one* syllable, generally add *er* and *est:*

Positive	Comparative	Superlative
short	shorter	shortest
low	lower	lowest
rough	rougher	roughest
dry	drier	driest
grim	grimmer	grimmest
brave	braver	bravest

(Note the spelling changes in the last three examples: final *y* after a consonant changes to *i*; a final consonant after a vowel is doubled; a final *e* is dropped. See Chapter VI.) For adjectives of *three or more* syllables, use *more* and *most* (or *less* and *least*):

beautiful	more beautiful	most beautiful
troublesome	more troublesome	most troublesome
acerbic	more acerbic	most acerbic
ridiculous	more ridiculous	most ridiculous

For most adjectives of *two* syllables ending in *ect, ed, ent, ful, ic, id, ing, ish, ive, ous* (and any others where an added *er* or *est* would simply *sound* wrong), generally use *more* and *most:*

direct	more direct	most direct
quoted	more quoted	most quoted
potent	more potent	most potent
bashful	more bashful	most bashful
manic	more manic	most manic
candid	more candid	most candid
pleasing	more pleasing	most pleasing
churlish	more churlish	most churlish
restive	more restive	most restive
conscious	more conscious	most conscious

For other adjectives of two syllables, you usually have a choice; for example:

gentle	gentler, more gentle	gentlest, most gentle
bitter	bitterer, more bitter	bitterest, most bitter
lively	livelier, more lively	liveliest, most lively
silly	sillier, more silly	silliest, most silly

When there is a choice, the forms with *more* and *most* will usually sound more formal and more emphatic than those with *er* and *est*. And sometimes you will choose according to the rhythm of a sentence. In fact, you can use *more* and *most* (or *less* and *least*) with almost any descriptive adjective, even one-syllable ones, if you want the little extra emphasis or the different rhythm:

> Of all the grim statistics I have seen, these are by far the most grim.

But the converse isn't true: adjectives of three or more syllables, and even shorter ones ending in *ous* and *ful* and so on, must use *more* and *most*—unless you want to represent slangy or uneducated dialogue, or to create a humorous effect, as when Alice finds things in Wonderland to be growing "curiouser and curiouser."

Caution: The one thing you should not do is double up the comparative or superlative forms and write things like *more better* or *most prettiest*. If you want to emphasize a comparative or superlative, you can use the adverbial intensifiers *much* or *far* or *by far*:

> much livelier, much more lively, far livelier, far more lively, livelier by far, much the livelier of the two, much the liveliest, by far the liveliest

Further, beware the potential and all-too-likely ambiguity of expressions like

> more intelligent people

You can instead say something like

> smarter people
> people with higher intelligence
> increasingly intelligent people

or

> more people who are intelligent
> a greater number of intelligent people

whichever would sound best and make your meaning clearest.

Notes:

(1) A few common adjectives form their comparative and superlative degrees irregularly:

good	better	best
bad	worse	worst

8b comparison of adjectives

| little | littler, less, lesser | littlest, least |
| much, many | more | most |

Your dictionary should list all irregular forms after the basic entry, including those in which a spelling change occurs.

(2) Because of their meanings, some adjectives should not be compared: see *unique* in the usage checklist, **60**. There is also an old rule that the *comparative* form should be used for two things, the *superlative* only for three or more:

> She is the *better* chess player. [of the two]
> Alaska is the *largest* of the fifty American states.

This is a principle usually worth adhering to, but there can be exceptions to it ("May the best man [of the two] win!"). See also **28**, on faulty comparison, and **comp** in Chapter XI.

Exercise 8b: Comparing adjectives

Try to come up with some adjectives that don't fit neatly into the guidelines about degree. For example, would you use *er* and *est* with one-syllable adjectives like *pat, chic, prone,* and *lost*? Or with two-syllable adjectives like *sudden, thorough, malign,* and *sanguine*? Can you think of any three-syllable ones that sound all right with *er* and *est*? What about *slippery*? Do some longer adjectives take *est* comfortably, but not *er*? Can you think of any descriptive adjectives that for some reason don't lend themselves to use in comparisons at all? Try some past-participial forms, for example, or words that function primarily as nouns or other parts of speech.

8c Articles

art

Articles—sometimes considered separately from parts of speech—are most conveniently thought of as kinds of adjectives. Like adjectives, they modify the nouns or noun-equivalents that they precede. They are also sometimes called *markers* or *determiners* because an article always indicates that a noun is to follow (though of course other modifiers may intervene); in this they are like the other relatively non-inflected adjectives, such as demonstratives and possessives.

The definite article *the* and the indefinite article *a* (or *an*) are used idiomatically (see *Idiom*, **58**). They are sometimes baffling to those whose native language is not English—and no wonder, for it is almost impossible to set down rules for their use. We nevertheless include here a few principles for your guidance.

1. The easiest thing to remember about articles is that the form *a* of the indefinite article is used before words beginning with a consonant (*a dog, a building, a wish, a yellow orchid*), including words beginning with *h* when the *h* is pronounced (*a horse, a historical event, a hotel, a hypothesis*) and words beginning with *u* or *o* whose initial sound is that of *y* or *w* (*a useful book, a one-sided contest*). The form *an* is used before words beginning with a vowel sound (*an opinion, an underdog, an ugly duckling, an honour*). Similarly, the pronunciation of *the* changes from "thuh" to "thee" before a word beginning with a vowel sound.

2. Generally, the definite article designates one or more particular persons or things whose identity is established by context or a modifier:

   The black horse is in *the* barn.
   The building is on *the* corner.
   The teacher stands in front of *the* class.
   The town is near *the* city.
   The cars are at *the* starting line.

   whereas a person or thing designated by the indefinite article generally is not specific:

   He wants to buy *a* horse.
   The company needs *a* new building.
   Each class has *a* teacher.
   She prefers living in *a* city to living in *a* small town.

   The indefinite article should be considered as equivalent to *one*; it can be used only before singular nouns. Sometimes it is even used to mean *one*:

   I thought I would like the job, but I lasted only *a* week.
   This will take *an* hour or two.

   Here are some further illustrations comparing *a* and *the*:

   He gave me *a* gift. (unspecified)
   He gave me *the* gift I had hoped for. (particularized by the modifying clause *I had hoped for*)

   Give me *a* book. (any book that's handy)
   Give me *the* book. (a particular book, one already identified or otherwise clear from the context)

   Look up the word *schism* in *a* dictionary. (Any dictionary will do.)
   Look up the word *schism* in *the* dictionary. (This also means *any*, but considers all dictionaries as a class; or it implies "the particular dictionary you customarily use.")
   Look up the word *schism* in *your* dictionary. (the one you own)

8c articles

3. Articles can also be used generically: *The horse is a beautiful animal;* this emphasizes the *class* "horse" (and is not, here, equivalent to *That horse, standing over there by the fence, is a beautiful animal).* *A horse is a beautiful animal;* this means the same thing, but using the indefinite article emphasizes an individual member of the class. If no article is used—*Horses are beautiful animals*—the plural *Horses* causes the emphasis to fall on all the individual horses.

4. The definite article is used with some proper nouns but not with others.

We say:		but:	
Canada			the Dominion of Canada
Russia			the Soviet Union, the USSR
Great Britain			the United Kingdom
America			the United States, the States
Vancouver Island			the Leeward Islands
Mount Garibaldi			the Rocky Mountains, the Rockies
Great Slave Lake			the Great Lakes
Hudson Bay			the Bay of Fundy
Dalhousie University			the University of Manitoba

Notice that *the* is usually used with plurals, names containing *of* phrases, and names consisting of a modified common noun (the United *Kingdom*) as opposed to a modified proper noun (Great *Britain*).

5. The definite article can also be used to indicate exclusiveness; *the* is then equivalent to *the only* or *the best* (in both speech and writing, such a *the* is sometimes emphasized):

He was *the* man for the job.

But if such exclusiveness is not intended, *the* should not be used:

Wrong: He soon becomes *the* good friend of each of the main characters.

If *good* were changed to the superlative *best* (there can be only one *best*), the definite article would be correct; otherwise, *a* is correct:

He soon becomes *a* good friend of each of the main characters.

6. *Mass* nouns—i.e., nouns standing for something which cannot be counted, something which normally has no plural—and *abstract*

nouns are not preceded by articles if the mass or abstract sense is the governing one:

> *Wrong*:   The poem is *a* direct, simple *praise* of God.

Here the *a* must be removed. But notice the difference if a concrete noun is inserted; then the article is correct:

> The poem is *a* direct, simple *hymn* of praise.

If such a noun is used to specify a particular part of the totality, the definite article is used:

> *The praise* that she bestowed upon him made him blush.
> Look at *the gold* that I panned.

Thus it is correct to say:

> He lacks humility.
> He lacks *the* humility necessary for that position.
>
> Give me liberty, or give me death.
> Give me *the* liberty to know, to utter, and to argue freely according
>   to conscience, above all liberties.
> The disclosure meant *the* death of his dreams.
>
> Orange juice is good for you.
> Drink *the* orange juice I gave you.

It sometimes helps to think of each *the* in such instances as similar to a demonstrative or possessive adjective:

> *Her* praise was generous.
> Look at *my* gold.
> Give me *that* liberty above all others.
> Drink *your* orange juice.
> Drink *that* orange juice sitting in front of you.

If an abstract noun is used in a concrete but not particularized sense, the indefinite article precedes it; if used in a particularized way, the definite article:

> That horse is *a* beauty. He is *the* beauty I was telling you about.
> This is *an* honour. He did me *the* honour of inviting me.
> Hers is *a* very special honesty. She has *the* honesty of a saint.

See also **2**, **2a**, and **7g**.

7. The definite article usually precedes an adjective used as a noun (see **8f**):

> Only *the* strong will survive.
> *The* poor will always be with us.
> *The* French oppose independence for Brittany.
> This is *the* most I can do.

But not always:

> More is sure to come.
> Most will arrive on time.

Caution: A common error is to put *the* before *most* when *most* is adverbial:

> *Wrong*:   What people want *the* most is security.
> *Wrong*:   That is what they want *the* most of all.

8. Titles of artistic works are not usually preceded by articles, but, with the normal inconsistency characterizing the realities of usage, some titles can be and sometimes are preceded by the definite article. It would never be correct to say this:

> *Wrong*:   Donne's poetic power is evident in *the* Sonnet X.

And one would not say "the *Alice in Wonderland*" or "the *Paradise Lost*." But one is more likely to say "in the *Areopagitica*" than "in *Areopagitica*," or "in the *Adventures of Huckleberry Finn*" than "in *Adventures of Huckleberry Finn*." (Of course if *A* or *The* is itself a part of a title, it must be included: *A Midsummer Night's Dream*, *The Portrait of a Lady*.) Yet if a possessive form of the author's name precedes, no article would be used: "in Milton's *Areopagitica*." One might well speak of one of Michelangelo's great sculptures as "the *David*" (but "In Florence we saw Michelangelo's *David*"), whereas one would never use the article before the title of Earle Birney's poem, *David*.

9. With the names of academic fields and courses, whether proper nouns or abstract common nouns, no article is used:

> She is enrolled in Psychology 301.
> He reads books on psychology.
> He is majoring in English.
> This is a program in English Language and Literature.

But if such terms are particularized common nouns or used adjectivally, the definite article is used:

> She studies *the* psychology of animal behaviour.
> You are learning more about *the* English language.

Yet it would be incorrect to speak of "*the* English literature," unless particularized as *the* English literature of, say, Uganda or India.

10. The definite article is used before the names of ships:

the *Golden Hind*, the *Titanic*, the *St. Roch*

and trains:

the *Super Chief*, the *Orient Express*

11. In some instances the indefinite article is used to identify something in a general sense; but once the context has been clearly established, the definite article takes over:

> Tonight I wish to discuss *a* problem that has arisen recently, for I think it is *an* important one. *The* problem to which I refer is that of . . .

The idiomatic use of articles can be learned only through intimate familiarity with usage. When in doubt about a particular instance consult a good dictionary, which will outline briefly the various uses of articles. (See also *Idiom*, 58.)

Exercise 8c: Using articles

In each blank, place either *a*, *an*, or *the*; or put *0* if no article is needed. If an article could be used, but need not, place the article in parentheses, thus: (the) (an) (a). Some of the answers will be debatable, and we hope that you will debate them.

1. In _____ Canadian society, everyone is considered _____ equal.
2. After two years in _____ college, I decided to go to _____ business school.
3. My sister got _____ Honours degree for her work in _____ chemistry.
4. _____ weather report said we could expect _____ storms.
5. _____ hospital is prepared for _____ union walkout.
6. There was _____ uninterrupted movie on _____ television last night.
7. It was _____ lucky day when I bought _____ ticket in _____ lottery.
8. I think you should put _____ onion in _____ stew.
9. This is _____ picture of _____ amoeba, and notice that _____ picture is magnified _____ thousand times so that we can see _____ amoeba's structure.
10. If you belong to _____ union you must be prepared to honour _____ picket lines.

8d　Placement of Adjectives

Most adjectival modifiers come just before or just after the word or words they modify. *Articles* and other determiners almost always precede the nouns they modify, usually with either no intervening words or only one or two (usually other adjectives):

> Trying to save *some* money, *the* manager decided to let *his* clerk go.
> *The angry* manager decided to sack *his clumsy* and *forgetful* clerk.

Predicate adjectives (see **1g**) almost always follow the subject and a linking verb:

> This pensioner is very *poor* and *lonely*.
> Shortly after his operation he again became *sick*.

Adjectives serving as *objective complements* follow the direct object (see **1i**):

> I thought the suggestion *preposterous*.

Most other single-word adjectives, and many compound adjectives, precede the nouns they modify:

> The *tall, dark,* and *handsome* hero lives on in *romantic* fiction.
> The *weather* map shows a *cold* front moving into the *northern* Prairies.

Phrases like "the map weather" or "a front cold" or "the Prairies northern" are obviously unidiomatic. (Note that the pattern, or order, can determine the meaning of a word, how it is functioning; for example a *cold head* is not the same thing as a *head cold*: in this instance, adjective and noun reverse their functions as they reverse their positions.)

But deviations from the standard patterns are possible. In poetry, for example, one often finds inversions for purposes of emphasis and rhythm and rhyme:

> *Fled* is that music . . . .
> *Red* as a rose is she . . . .
> This Hermit *good* lives in that wood . . . .
> And he called for his fiddlers *three*.

Such inversions also occur in non-poetic, even non-literary, contexts—though you should not indulge in them often, for when the unusual ceases to be unusual it loses much of its power. But if you want a certain emphasis or rhythm, you can put a predicate adjective before a noun (see also **6a**):

> *Frustrated* I may have been, but I hadn't lost my wits.

or a regular adjective after a noun:

> He had faith *extraordinary*.
> She did the only thing *possible*.
> There was food *enough* for everyone.

(And note such standard terms as *Governor General* and *court-martial*.) Compound adjectives and adjectives that are in phrases are especially easy to place after a noun:

> His friend, always *faithful and kind*, came at once to his aid.
> Elfrida, *radiant and delighted*, left the room, *secure* in her victory.

Other kinds of adjectival modifiers—relative clauses and various kinds of phrases—customarily follow the nouns they modify:

> He is one inspector *who believes in being thorough.* (relative clause, modifies *inspector*)
>
> The president *of the company* will retire next month. (adjectival preposi-tional phrase, modifies *president*)
>
> The time *to build* is now! (infinitive, modifies *time*)

The only kind of adjectival modifier not generally restricted in its position is the participial phrase (see **10c**):

> It was a proposal *welcomed by everyone.*
>
> *Welcomed by everyone*, the proposal was soon adopted unanimously.
>
> *Having had abundant experience*, Kenneth applied for the job.
>
> Kenneth, *having had abundant experience*, applied for the job.
>
> Kenneth applied for the job, *having had abundant experience*.

Such a variety of possible positions enables you to choose, guided by your taste and by stylistic appropriateness. This movability of the participial phrase makes it a popular device for introducing variety into writing and for controlling emphasis, but it is not without its dangers. For example, inexperienced writers sometimes lean too heav-ily on *ing* phrases to begin sentences with. And one must be careful not to place such phrases in a way that creates awkward or ambiguous reference to some noun other than the intended one. Such awkwardness usually takes the form of a *dangling modifier*:

> *dm*: Having had abundant experience, the job was applied for by Ken-neth.
>
> *dm*: Having had abundant experience, the job seemed just right for Kenneth.

See **24** for ways to recognize and avoid such errors; and see **23**, on misplaced modifiers.

8e Order of Adjectives

When two or more adjectives come before a noun, they usually follow an order that is idiomatic in English: an article or possessive or dem-onstrative comes first; then numbers, if any; then descriptive adjec-tives, usually in an order moving toward the more specific. Any adjectives indicating such things as size, age, and colour usually come in that order. For example:

> the three big old black bears
>
> my two favourite hiking companions
>
> that well-known Canadian free-style swimming champion

(Note that such pairs as *hiking companions, free-style swimming,* and *swimming champion* are virtually inseparable; they thus partly determine the order.) But such ordering principles are not sacrosanct. Occasionally, for a slightly different emphasis or meaning, you can change the order a little; for example:

> my favourite two hiking companions

8f   Adjectives Functioning as Nouns

If preceded by the definite article (*the*) or a possessive, many words normally thought of as adjectives can function as *nouns,* usually referring to people, and most often in a plural sense; for example:

> the Swedish, the British, the French, the Lebanese
> the free, the brave, the sick and dying, society's poor, the more fortunate, the powerful, the big and the small, the high and the mighty, the wealthy, the starving
> the enslaved, the badly injured, their wounded, the uneducated, the unemployed, the underprivileged
> her beloved, my dearest, the deceased
> the abstract, the metaphysical, the good, the true

(See **8c/7**.)

9   Adverbs

The category or part of speech known as **adverbs** is in some ways the trickiest of all; it is sometimes called the "catch-all" or "garbage" category, since any word that can't be neatly accounted for in some other way is almost automatically assumed to be an adverb. Yet basically, and as far as most of our needs go, adverbs are similar to and only a little more complicated than adjectives.

9a   Kinds and Functions of Adverbs

Whereas adjectives can modify only nouns and pronouns, adverbs can modify *verbs* (and *verbals,* see **11**), *adjectives,* other *adverbs,* and whole *sentences* or independent clauses. Adverbial modifiers generally answer such questions as *How? When? Where? Why?* and *To what degree?* That is, they express such things as *manner* (How?), *time* (When? How often? How long?), *place* and *direction* (Where? In what direction?), *cause, result,* and *purpose* (Why? To what effect?), and *degree* (To what degree? How much?). They also express such things as affirmation and negation (*yes, no*), conditions (*if*), concessions (*although*), and comparisons. Here are some examples:

Fully expecting to fail, he slumped *disconsolately in his seat* and began the examination.

To what degree expecting? *Fully.* The adverb of degree modifies the participial (verbal) phrase *expecting to fail.* Slumped how? *Disconsolately.* The adverb of manner modifies the verb *slumped.* Slumped where? *In his seat.* The prepositional phrase functions as an adverb of place or location modifying the verb *slumped.*

For many years they lived *very happily together in Australia.*

Lived how? *Happily* and *together.* The adverbs of manner modify the verb *lived.* To what degree happily? *Very.* The intensifying adverb modifies the adverb *happily.* Lived where? *In Australia.* The adverbial prepositional phrase modifies the verb *lived.* How long? *For many years.* The prepositional phrase functions as an adverb of time or duration modifying the verb—or it can be thought of as modifying the whole clause *they lived happily together.*

Fortunately, the cut was *not* deep.

To what effect? *Fortunately.* The word is a sentence adverb or sentence modifier: rather than modifying any single word, its meaning hovers over the whole sentence. To what degree deep? *Not* (at all). The negating adverb modifies the adjective *deep*.

Because their budget was tight, they *eventually* decided *not* to buy a new car.

Why? *Because their budget was tight.* The adverbial clause of cause modifies the verb *decided*—or in a way the rest of the sentence. Decided when? *Eventually.* The adverb of time modifies the verb *decided.* The negating *not* modifies the infinitive (verbal) *to buy.*

Their budget was *so* tight *that they couldn't afford a new car.*

The adverbial clause of result modifies the adjective *tight*; or you can think of it as answering the question To what degree tight?

Last November the sun *seldom* shone.

Shone when? *Last November.* The noun phrase functions as an adverb of time modifying the verb *shone.* Shone how often? *Seldom.* The adverb of time or frequency modifies the verb *shone.*

Driving *fast* is *often* dangerous.

Driving how? *Fast.* The adverb of manner modifies the gerund (verbal) *driving.* Dangerous when? *Often.* The adverb of time or frequency modifies the adjective *dangerous.*

She was *better* prepared *than I was.*

The adverb *better* modifies the adjective *prepared*; it and the clause *than I was* express comparison or contrast.

> *Although she dislikes Los Angeles intensely*, she agreed to go *there in order to keep peace in the family*.

Intensely (degree) modifies the verb *dislikes*. *There* (place) modifies the infinitive *to go*. The clause *Although she dislikes Los Angeles intensely* is an adverbial clause of concession. The prepositional phrase *in order to keep peace in the family* is an adverb of purpose modifying the verb *agreed*. The smaller adverbial prepositional phrase *in the family* modifies the infinitive phrase *to keep peace*, answering the question Where?

> *If you're tired*, I'll wash the dishes.

The conditional clause modifies the verb (*'ll wash*).

Adverbs as condensed clauses

Obviously, some single-word adverbs and adverbial phrases—especially sentence modifiers—can be thought of as reduced forms of clauses:

> *Fortunately* [It is fortunate that], the cut was not deep.
> *Unfortunately* [I think it is unfortunate that], she muffed her opening lines.
> *When possible* [When it is possible], let your writing cool off *before proofreading it* [before you proofread it].

Other kinds of adverbs

There are also the *relative* adverbs *where* and *when*, used to introduce adjective clauses:

> He returned to the town *where he had been born*. (modifies *town*)
> He did not look forward to the moment *when it would be his turn*. (modifies *moment*)

The *interrogative* adverbs (*where*, *when*, *why*, and *how*) are used in questions:

> *Where* are you going? *Why? How* soon? *When* will you return?

And there are *conjunctive* adverbs, which usually join whole clauses or sentences to each other and indicate the nature of the connection:

> It was an important question; *therefore* they took their time over it.
> Only fifteen people showed up. *Nevertheless*, the candidate didn't show any disappointment.
> The tornado almost flattened the town; no one, *however*, was seriously injured.

For more on conjunctive adverbs, see **33h**.

Forms of Adverbs; Adjectives and Adverbs

Adverbs ending in *ly*

Many adverbs are formed by adding *ly* to descriptive adjectives, for example *roughly, happily, fundamentally, curiously.* Don't carelessly use an adjectival form where an adverbial form is needed:

> She is a *careful* driver. (adjective modifying *driver*)
> She drives *carefully* [not *careful*] in heavy traffic. (adverb modifying *drives*)

Adverbs not ending in *ly*

Some adverbs have no *ly* ending—for example *ahead, almost, alone, down, however, long, now, often, quite, since, soon, then, there, therefore, when, where.* Others without the *ly* are identical to adjectives—for example *far, fast, little, low, more, much, well*:

> He owns a *fast* car. (adjective)
> In it he drives *fast.* (adverb)
> She has a *low* opinion of him. (adjective)
> She flew *low* over the lake. (adverb)

Well as an adjective means *healthy* (I am quite *well,* thank you.) or sometimes *satisfactory, right,* or *advisable* (All is *well.* It is *well* you came when you did. It is *well* to prepare carefully.). Otherwise *well* is an adverb, and should be used instead of the frequently misused *good,* which is an adjective. Similarly, *bad* is an adjective, *badly* an adverb. Be careful with these often misused forms:

> She did a *good* job. The team played *well* today.
> They felt *bad* about the child. (*Felt* is a linking verb here.)
> The child had played *badly* in the game.

See also *good, bad, badly, well* in the usage checklist, **60.**

Adverbs with short and long forms

Some common adverbs have two forms, one with *ly* and one without it. The form without the *ly* is identical to the adjective. With a few of these, especially if you are not fully attuned to English idiom, you must be particularly careful, for the two members of the pair do not mean the same thing. Check your dictionary if you are not sure of the meanings of such pairs as these:

> hard–hardly, high–highly, just–justly, late–lately, near–nearly, right–rightly, even–evenly, fair–fairly

With some of the others, the short form is a true and idiomatic equivalent of, even occasionally preferable to, the longer form; for example:

Don't talk so *loud*. Look *deep* into my eyes.
They travelled far and *wide*. Come *straight* home.

But for the rest (words such as *cheap, clear, close, direct, loose, quick, quiet, sharp, smooth, strong, tight, wrong*), even though you may often hear and see them used as adverbs, in formal contexts you should use the *ly* form. Regardless of what the road-signs may say, drive *slowly*, not *slow*.

But if you find yourself writing a set of instructions, such as a recipe, don't get trapped into the opposite error—one made in many cookbooks. It's correct to tell your readers to "stir the sauce *slowly*," but it's not correct to tell them, for example, to "slice the meat *thinly*." You wouldn't tell someone to "hammer the copper *smoothly*" or to "sand the wood *smoothly*," but *smooth*—that is, until it is smooth; so slice the meat [so that it is] *thin*, and chop the nuts [until they are] *fine*. In these examples the modifier goes with the noun, not the verb.

Real and *really*, *sure* and *surely*

Don't use the adjectival form (*real, sure*) when the adverbial is called for:

> I found her suggestion exciting: it was *really* [not *real*] different.
> He *surely* [not *sure*] was right about the weather.

But the second example probably sounds odd to you; most people would stick with *sure* in a colloquial context and substitute *certainly* in a formal context. And the intensifier *really* is seldom needed at all: see *very* in the usage checklist, **60**.

Adjectives ending in *ly*

Finally, there is the problem caused by the fact that some adjectives themselves end in *ly*, among them *burly, curly, daily, early, friendly, holy, homely, hourly, kindly, leisurely, likely, lively, lovely, lowly, monthly, orderly, silly, surly, ugly, weekly*, and *yearly*. Whatever some dictionaries may say, it is usually best not to try to form adverbs by adding another *ly* to such adjectives; the result is inevitably awkward in sound (*livelily, friendlily, uglily*) and therefore in reading also. And though dictionaries often label such adjectives as legitimate adverbs as well (He walked *leisurely* toward the door. She behaved *friendly* toward the strangers.), most people find such usages awkward, and easily avoid the problem by spending a few more words:

> He walked toward the door in a leisurely manner.
> She behaved in a friendly way toward the strangers.
> (or simply: She was friendly toward the strangers.)

In a few instances, however, the *ly* adjectives serve idiomatically as adverbs as well; for example:

> He spoke *kindly* of you. *Kindly* shut the window. She rises *early*. He exercises *daily*. The tour leaves *hourly*. The paper is published *weekly* [or *monthly*].

But there's no need for *yearly* as an adverb since we have *annually*. (And don't fall into the jargon of *on a daily* [weekly, monthly, yearly] *basis*: see *basis* in the usage checklist, **60**.)

9c   Comparison of Adverbs

Like descriptive adjectives, most adverbs that are similarly descriptive can be inflected or supplemented for degree (see **8b**). Some short adverbs without the *ly* ending form their comparative and superlative degrees with *er* and *est*; for example:

Positive	Comparative	Superlative
fast	faster	fastest
hard	harder	hardest
high	higher	highest
late	later	latest
low	lower	lowest
soon	sooner	soonest
straight	straighter	straightest

Less and *least* can also sometimes be used with these; for example:

> She flew *less straight* than she had intended.
> They ran *least hard* during the second mile.
> They still ran fast, but *less fast* than they had the day before.

Adverbs of three or more syllables ending in *ly* use *more* and *most* or *less* and *least*; for example:

happily	more happily	most happily
disconsolately	more disconsolately	most disconsolately
stridently	less stridently	least stridently

Most two-syllable adverbs, whether or not they end in *ly*, also use *more* and *most* or *less* and *least*, though a few can also be inflected with *er* and *est*; for example:

slowly	more slowly	most slowly
loudly	more loudly	most loudly
fully	more fully	most fully
grimly	more grimly	most grimly
kindly	kindlier, more kindly	kindliest, most kindly
often	oftener, more often	oftenest, most often

Some adverbs form their comparative and superlative degrees irregularly:

badly	worse	worst
well	better	best
much	more	most
little	less	least
far	farther, further	farthest, furthest

(See *farther, further*, in the usage checklist, **60**). A few adverbs of place or direction use *farther* and *farthest* (or *further* and *furthest*):

down	farther down	farthest down
north	farther north	farthest north

As with adjectives (see **8b**), the adverbs *much* and *far* and *by far* serve as intensifiers in comparisons:

> They live *much* more comfortably than they used to.
> He practises harder *by far* than anyone else on the team.

9d Placement of Adverbs

Adverbs modifying adjectives or other adverbs

An intensifying or qualifying adverb almost always goes just before the adjective or adverb being modified:

> *almost* always, *very* hot, *very* quickly, *very* often, *only* two, *strongly* confident, *most* surely

Only for unusual emphasis or in representing dialogue can such adverbs be wrenched out of their normal position:

> "As you can see, I am tired—very—and I would like to be left alone for a while."

Modifiers of verbs

Whether single words, phrases, or clauses, most modifiers of verbs are more flexible in their position than any other part of speech. Often they can be placed almost anywhere in a sentence and still function clearly:

> *Quickly* he jumped sideways.
> He *quickly* jumped sideways.
> He jumped sideways *quickly*.

But note that the emphasis—and therefore the overall effect, or meaning—changes slightly. It is therefore important that you know precisely what you want to say before you decide where to place an adverbial modifier. Don't just stick it in anywhere, assuming that it will do the job you want it to. Here is another example; note how much you can control the emphasis:

> *Because she likes drama*, Sue *often* goes to the theatre.
> Sue, *because she likes drama*, *often* goes to the theatre.
> Sue *often* goes to the theatre, *because she likes drama.*

And in each version, the adverb *often* could also effectively be placed after *goes* or after *theatre*. Try it.

Adverbs of place

The above example also illustrates the only major restriction on adverbial modifiers of the verb. You have virtually no option but to put a phrase like *to the theatre* right after the verb it modifies. Sometimes an adverb of place or direction can come first if a sentence's usual word order is reversed for emphasis or some other reason:

> *Off to market* we shall go.
> *There* she stood, staring out to sea.
> *Where* are you going? (but: Are you going *there?*)
> *Downward* he plummetted, waiting until the last moment to pull the ripcord.

Sentence modifiers

Sentence modifiers usually come at the beginnings of sentences (or independent clauses), but they too can be placed elsewhere for purposes of emphasis or rhythm:

> *Fortunately*, the cut was not deep.
> The cut, *fortunately*, was not deep.
> The cut was, *fortunately*, not deep.
> The cut was not deep, *fortunately.*

With longer or more involved sentences, however, a sentence modifier at the end loses much of its force and point, obviously; obviously it works better if placed earlier.

See also **33h**, on the placement and punctuation of conjunctive adverbs, and **23**, on misplaced modifiers.

Exercise 8-9(1): Recognizing adjectives and adverbs

Underline all the single-word adverbs and circle all the single-word adjectives (including articles) in the following sentences.

1. The hot weather continued unabated; it was the fifth consecutive sweltering day.
2. Although he felt bad, he decided, reluctantly, to stay very quiet in his little corner.
3. The fireplace screen was too hot to touch.
4. When he was fully recovered, he returned eagerly to the scene of his grisly accident.
5. Surely we can find some way to leave this benighted area quietly.

9d placement of adverbs

Exercise 8-9(2): Correcting misused adjectives and adverbs

Correct any errors in the use of adjectives and adverbs in the following sentences.

1. She concentrated so hardly that she got a headache.
2. The prize usually goes to the talentedest and beautifullest contestant.
3. His condition had improved considerable overnight.
4. Jake seemed to me to be a real bright fellow.
5. He preferred to wear his corduroy brown old jacket.
6. The quarterback isn't passing as good as he usually does.
7. Temperatures were more closer to our average this month than they were last.
8. The slowlier you drive, the less fuel you use.
9. He treats his closest friends poorest of all.
10. Which member of the quartet is the better musician?

Exercise 8-9(3): Using adjectival and adverbial modifiers

Enrich and elaborate each of the following basic sentences by adding a variety of adjectival and adverbial modifiers. Use phrases and clauses as well as single words. And try several versions of each sentence. (Change tenses of verbs if you wish, and add auxiliaries.)

1. Children play.
2. Women write novels.
3. The camper was bitten by a snake.
4. Hiking gives one an appetite.
5. Travel is broadening.
6. Computers are tools.
7. There are lessons in history.

Exercise 8-9(4): Using adjectives and adverbs

Make a list of ten adjectives (*other* than those listed or discussed above) that can also serve as or be changed into adverbs. Use each adjective in a sentence; then make each an adverb and use those in sentences. Then choose two and compose sentences using them in their comparative and superlative forms as both adjectives and adverbs.

10   Verbals: Infinitives, Participles, and Gerunds

Verbals is the name given to *infinitives, participles*, and *gerunds*—forms that are derived from verbs but that cannot function as the main or finite verbs of sentences. Verbals are **non-finite** forms—that is, *unfinished*, not restricted by person and number as finite verbs are (see **6d**). They function in sentences as *other parts of speech*, but at the same time they retain some of the characteristics of verbs: they can have objects, they can be modified by adverbs, and they can show differences in tense and voice. Verbals frequently introduce *verbal phrases*, groups of words which themselves function as other parts of speech (see **1m**).

Verbals are well worth cultivating and practising with, for they enable people to inject much of the strength and liveliness of verbs into their writing even though the words are functioning as adjectives, adverbs, and nouns.

10a Infinitives

When discussing verbs, people sometimes use a form called the **infinitive** to identify particular verbs. They speak of "the verb *to be*" or "the verb *to live*" (In this book we use the basic or dictionary form, *be, live*.) An infinitive usually consists of the word *to* (often called "the sign of the infinitive") followed by the basic form: *to be, to live*. Infinitives can function as *nouns, adjectives*, and *adverbs*.

Infinitives as nouns:

> *To save* the horses was his primary intention.

The infinitive phrase *To save the horses* is the subject of the verb *was*. The noun *horses* is the direct object of the infinitive *To save*: To save what? The horses.

> She wanted *to end* the game quickly.

The infinitive phrase *to end the game quickly* is the direct object of the verb *wanted*. The infinitive *to end* is modified by the adverb *quickly* and has the noun *game* as its own direct object. The subject pronoun *She* is also the subject of the infinitive.

> She wanted me *to stop* the game.

In this instance, the phrase *me to stop the game* is the object of the verb *wanted*; the pronoun *me*, although in the objective case, functions as the "subject" of the infinitive *to stop*.

Infinitives as adjectives:

> His strong desire *to be* the winner was his undoing.

The infinitive phrase *to be the winner* modifies the noun *desire*. Since *be* is a linking verb, the infinitive is here followed by the predicate noun *winner*.

> The green coupons are the ones *to save*.

The infinitive *to save* modifies the pronoun *ones*.

Infinitives as adverbs:

> He was lucky *to have* such a friend.

The infinitive phrase *to have such a friend* modifies the predicate adjective *lucky*. The noun phrase *such a friend* is the direct object of the infinitive *to have*.

> He went to Calgary *to see* his sister.

The infinitive phrase *to see his sister* modifies the verb *went; his sister* is the direct object of the infinitive *to see*.

Tense and voice of infinitives (see **6g-h, 6i/2,** and **6m**)
Infinitives may be either *present* (to indicate a time the same as or later than that of the main verb):

> He wanted me *to go* to South America with him.

or *present perfect* (to indicate a time prior to that of the main verb); the sign of the infinitive—*to*—then goes with the auxiliary verb *have*:

> He is lucky *to have inherited* so much money.

Each of these may also take the *progressive* form, using the auxiliaries *be* and *have*:

> I expect *to be travelling* abroad this summer.
> He was thought *to have been planning* the coup for months.

Infinitives may also be in the passive voice, again putting *to* with the appropriate auxiliaries, then adding a past participle:

> The children wanted *to be taken* to the circus.
> He was thought *to have been motivated* by sheer greed.

Note: After some verbs, an infinitive can occur without the customary *to*; for example:

> Let sleeping dogs *lie*.
> We saw the man *jump*.
> He felt the house *shake*.
> I helped her *decide*.

10b Split Infinitives
split

The reason it is usually considered wrong to split an infinitive is that an infinitive is felt to be a unit; separating its parts can weaken it, and often results in awkwardness—the more intruding words, the more awkward the split:

> He wanted *to* quickly *conclude* the business of the meeting.
> She claimed that it was too difficult *to* very accurately or confidently *solve* such a problem in the time allowed.

It is usually possible to avoid or repair such splits by rephrasing or rearranging a sentence so that adverbial modifiers don't interrupt the infinitive:

> He wanted *to conclude* the business of the meeting quickly.
> She claimed that it was too difficult, in the time allowed, *to solve* such a problem with any degree of accuracy or confidence.

But some writers argue that there is nothing wrong with splitting an infinitive. Certainly it is better to split one than to sound awkward or over-refined:

> The yellow car swerved way over and contrived *to* narrowly *miss* the car that was near the edge of the track.

This is clearly better than *to miss narrowly* or *narrowly to miss*—and *narrowly* can't be moved elsewhere, away from the infinitive it modifies. Again:

> It is impossible *to* more than *guess* at her intentions.

The adverbial *more than* cannot be moved, though a conscientious writer might insert *do* after *to*, thereby avoiding the problem. If the infinitive includes a form of *be* or *have* as an auxiliary, an adverb coming before the last part is less likely to sound out of place:

> The demonstration was thought *to have been* carefully *planned*.
> We seem *to have* finally *found* the right road.

Our advice: Try never to *unnecessarily* or *unintentionally* split an infinitive.

10c Participles

A verb's **past participle** and **present participle** work with various auxiliaries to form the verb's several *perfect* and *progressive* tenses. These finite verb forms then function as the main verbs in sentences. (See **6g** and **6h**.) But without all the necessary auxiliary verbs (specifically those indicating person and number), the participles are non-finite, incomplete, and cannot function as finite verbs. Instead they then function as *adjectives*, modifying nouns and pronouns:

> *Soaking* himself in the bath, Sidney suddenly noticed his *reddened* and *swollen* ankle.

Present participles always end in *ing*, regular past participles in *ed* or *d*; irregular past participles end variously: *made, mown, broken*, etc. (See **6b** and **6c**.) Of course a regularly formed past participle is identical to the *past-tense* form of a verb; but you can easily see which a given word is by examining its *function* in a sentence. In the above example, the past-tense form *noticed* clearly has *Sidney* as its subject; the past participle *reddened* has no subject but functions as an adjective modifying the noun *ankle*. Some more examples:

> *Painted* houses require more care than brick ones.

The past participle *Painted* modifies the noun *houses*: What kind of houses? *Painted* houses.

> *Impressed*, she recounted the film's more *thrilling* episodes.

The past participle *Impressed* modifies the subject, *she*; the present participle *thrilling* modifies the noun *episodes* and is itself modified by the adverb *more*.

> The subject *discussed* most often was unemployment.

The past participle *discussed* modifies the noun *subject*. The adverbial *most often* modifies *discussed*.

> Suddenly *finding* himself alone, he became very *frightened*.

Here the present participle *finding* introduces the participial phrase *finding himself alone*, which modifies the subject pronoun *he*; *finding*, as a verbal, has as its direct object the pronoun *himself* and is modified by the adverb *suddenly*. The past participle *frightened* functions as a predicate adjective after the linking verb *became*; it modifies *he* and is itself modified by the adverb *very*.

Tense and voice of participles (see **6g-h, 6i/3,** and **6m**)
The standard present or past participle indicates a time the same as or later than that of the main verb:

> *Being* the tallest, Juliet played centre.

Strictly speaking, a past participle by itself amounts to passive voice:

> *Worried* by what he'd heard, Joe picked up the phone.

With the *ing* attached to one or another of the auxiliaries *be* and *have*, participles—like infinitives—can also be in the perfect or perfect-progressive tense, indicating a time prior to that of the main verb:

> *Having painted* himself into a corner, George climbed out the window.
> *Having been painting* for over two hours, Herb decided to take a break.

Participles in the present-progressive and the perfect tenses can also be in the passive voice:

> The subject *being discussed* was unemployment.
> *Having been warned*, she knew better than to accept the offer.

Caution: It is particularly important that you know a present participle when you write one. If you use a present participle and think it's functioning as a finite verb, you may well produce a **fragment** (see **1y**).

<hr>

Exercise 10c: Using participles

Write down the *present participle* and the *past participle* of each verb listed below. Then compose sentences using each as a *single-word* adjective modifying a noun or pronoun (predicate adjectives are permissible). (You might also want to try adding one or more auxiliaries to each so that you can use them as finite verbs in sentences.)

Example: *stun–stunning–stunned*
She looked *stunning*. It was a *stunning* blow. The *stunned* boxer hit the mat. He lay there, *stunned*.
(He *was stunning* us with his revelations. He *has stunned* others before us. One *can be stunned* by a jolt of electricity.)

| care | drive | cut | sleep | trouble |
| dry | grow | boil | change | rejuvenate |

<hr>

10d   Gerunds

When the *ing* form of a verb functions as an adjective, it is called a *present participle* (see **10c**). When the same form functions as a *noun*, however, it is called a **gerund**. Present participles and gerunds are identical in form; they are differentiated only by the way they function in sentences:

> It was a very *moving* experience.

Here *moving* is a present participle, an adjective modifying the noun *experience*: What kind of experience? A *moving* experience.

> *Moving* furniture can be hard work.

Here *Moving* is a gerund, a noun; it is the subject of the sentence and has as its complement the predicate noun *work*; it also, as a verbal, has *furniture* as its direct object: Moving what? Furniture.

> Because he knew it was good exercise, Boris took up *swimming*.

Here the gerund *swimming* is the direct object of the verb *took up*.

> Sylvester has a profound fear of *flying*.

Here *flying* is the object of the preposition *of*.

> Careful preparation—*brainstorming* and *organizing* and *outlining*—helps produce good essays.

Here the three gerunds constitute an appositive of the subject noun *preparation* (see **1q**).

Tense and voice of gerunds (see **6g-h** and **6m**)
As with infinitives and participles, the *perfect* form of a gerund indicates a time prior to that of the main verb:

> His *having built* the boat himself caused him to boast a little.

Perfect-progressive tense is possible, though often unwieldy; usually another way of expressing an idea will prove better:

> My *having been feeling* unwell caused me to stay home.
> (Since I had been feeling unwell, I decided to stay home.)

And a gerund can be in the passive voice, though again a different phrasing will usually be preferable:

> Her *having been told* the rules meant that she had no excuse for doing it wrong.
> His *being praised* by the boss gave him a big lift.

10e   Possessives with Gerunds

In formal usage, a noun or a personal pronoun preceding a gerund will usually be in the possessive case; that is, it functions as a possessive adjective before a noun:

> *His* driving left much to be desired.
> The trouble was caused by *our* not knowing what to do.
> She approved of *Bob's* cooking the dinner.
> I can't understand the *minister's* always refusing to reveal the source of his information.
> Can you explain the *engine's* not starting?

But as with many other points about style, the desired intonation should help you determine whether or not to use the possessive. For example if you mean to emphasize the noun or pronoun, you'll probably not use the possessive:

> She approved of *Bob* cooking the dinner rather than Jim.
> Can you imagine the *minister* refusing to reveal his sources?
> The trouble was caused by *us* not knowing what to do, not *them*.

Further, in order to avoid awkward-sounding constructions, you usually won't use a possessive form when a noun is (a) abstract, (b) plural, (c) multiple, or (d) separated from the gerund by modifiers (other than adverbs like *not* or *always* when they sound almost like part of the verbal):

> (a) He couldn't bear the thought of *disaster striking* again.
> (b) The possibility of the *thieves returning* to their hide-out was slim.
> (c) There is little likelihood of *Alberto and Henry agreeing* to your proposal.
> (d) One might well wonder at a *man* with such a record *claiming* to be honest.

Note: A gerund followed immediately by another noun will sometimes (but not always) sound awkward or ambiguous unless you put *of* or *the* or some similar term between them to keep the gerund from sounding like a participle: his building (of) boats, your organizing (of the) material, his revealing (of) sources, my practising (the) piano.

10f   **Verbals in Absolute Phrases**

Infinitives and participles (but not gerunds) can function in **absolute** phrases (see **1r**). An absolute phrase acts like a sentence modifier; it modifies the rest of the sentence without being grammatically connected with it:

> *To say the least,* the day was not a success.
> They drew up rough plans, *the finer details to be worked out later.*
> *Strictly speaking,* their actions were not legal.
> *The day being hot,* she decided to go for a swim.
> *All things considered,* the meeting was a success.

Exercise 10(1) Recognizing verbals

Underline all the verbals in the following sentences and label each as an infinitive, a past or present participle, or a gerund. Identify any syntactical features (objects, modifiers) that reveal the *verbal* character of these elements.

1. Coming as he did from the prairies, he found the coastal scenery to be stunning.
2. She wanted to fly, and learning was easier than she had expected.
3. My answering service had promised to buzz me if anything startling were to arise.
4. The celebrated performers got top billing for the first showing of the winning film.
5. Trying to study hard with a splitting headache is usually not very rewarding.
6. The party was certain to last until midnight, permitting everyone to eat and drink too much.
7. Turning table legs on a spinning lathe is one way to spend a pleasant and relaxed evening.
8. Sent as he had been from one office to another, Sherman was tired of running back and forth and up and down; he was now resolved to go straight to the top.
9. When doing one's daily exercising, one should be careful not to overstrain already taxed muscles.
10. The contrived plot of the currently running play is enough to make the audience get up and leave the theatre without worrying about the author's supposed talent or his past record of charming tired city-dwellers with rural high jinks.

Exercise 10(2): Using verbals

Because they come from verbs, verbals are useful components of a vigorous, lively, and economical style. Here is a series of exercises to help you to get the feel of verbals and to recognize, consciously, what you can do with them.

a. Write down five infinitives. Then use each one, if possible by itself, in a *short* sentence, first as a noun, then as an adjective, then as an adverb (if possible; they are less common).

Example: *to sit*
        noun: To sit is restful. (subject) I like to sit. (object) A good way to relax is to sit. (predicate noun)
   adjective: I need a place to sit. I have a strong urge to sit.

        adverb: He was determined to sit. She cleared a space in order
                to sit.

Then use each one in three longer sentences—again once each as noun, adjective, and adverb—this time expanded into an infinitive *phrase*, and with as much elaboration in the rest of the sentence as you want.

Example: (of the first one only):
             To sit, feet up, before a quietly crackling fire on a cold winter
             night, reading a moderately engrossing detective story, is one of
             the most relaxing pleasures available to modern civilized human
             beings.

You need not simply build on one of the shorter sentences, as we have done here; but you may.

b. Starting with three basic verbs, make three present participles and three past participles. Then compose sentences using each to modify nouns that are functioning in at least three different ways (subjects, direct objects, indirect objects, objects of prepositions, predicate nouns, objective complements, appositives); make it a point to put some of them in participial *phrases*. Some verbs won't work (*sit*, for example); try verbs whose participles lend themselves more to descriptive or narrative purposes, like *disguise, remember, burn,* and *study*. But find some of your own.

c. Make *ing* forms of five verbs and use them as gerunds—that is, *nouns*—in sentences. Use at least one as a subject, one as a direct object, one as a predicate noun, and one as an object of a preposition. Use each one first in a short sentence, and then in a longer one with the gerund as part of a gerund *phrase*.

If you haven't already done so, try varying the tenses of some of your verbals. Have you put any in the passive voice? If so, can you improve your sentence by getting rid of the passive voice—even if you have to get rid of the verbal as well?

Exercise 10(3): Reducing clauses to infinitive phrases

By reducing clauses to phrases, one can often get rid of unnecessary stylistic heaviness and also cut down on wordiness. For practice, reduce each italicized clause in the following sentences to an infinitive phrase that conveys the same meaning. Change or rearrange words as necessary.

Example: We wondered *what we should do next.*
              We wondered *what to do next.*

1. He claimed *that he was invincible.*
2. She said *that I should study harder.*
3. Remember *that you should use a new typewriter ribbon.*
4. *If you want a good grade,* you must work hard.
5. Sherrill thought *that I had given up.*
6. The quarterback's problem was *that he had to decide* what play *he should use next.*
7. She was so confident *that she entered every race.*
8. The policeman said *that we should follow him to the station.*
9. The time *that you should worry about* is the hour before the race.
10. It is said *that break-dancing originated* during street-fights in New York City.

Do any of these strike you as preferable with the clauses left intact rather than changed to phrases? Might one's choice depend on context?

Exercise 10(4): Reducing clauses

As in the preceding exercise, reduce the italicized clauses in the following sentences to phrases, but this time reduce each clause to the kind of phrase specified in parentheses after each sentence.

Example: *As she changed her mind*, she suddenly felt much better. (present participial)
Changing her mind, she suddenly felt much better.

1. The whistle blew *when it was noon*. (prepositional)
2. Sometimes the best part of a vacation is *when you plan it*. (gerund)
3. Getting high grades is something *that you can be proud of*. (infinitive)
4. *Because he felt queasy*, he decided to forgo dinner. (present participial)
5. *Because there were only two minutes left in the game*, the coach knew they couldn't win. (absolute)
6. *The fact that she had won the contest* came as something of a shock to her. (gerund)
7. *Because repeated failures had discouraged them*, they gave up and went home. (past participial)
8. The clown *who had on the funny hat* started turning somersaults. (prepositional; also present participial)
9. *As he slammed the door behind him*, he realized he'd left his keys inside. (present participial)
10. *When I had run* for only half a mile, I felt nearly exhausted. (prepositional, with gerund)

Exercise 10(5): Using absolute phrases

Absolute phrases are particularly useful for expressing cause-effect relations or for providing vivid descriptive details. Since absolute phrases constitute a considerable heightening of style, you should not use them often. But do use them sometimes. For practice, combine each of the following pairs of sentences into a single sentence by reducing one of them (usually the first) to an absolute phrase consisting of a noun followed by a participle (along with any modifiers). Remember that if the participle is the word *being* (from the linking verb *be*), it can sometimes, but not always, be omitted (see **1r**).

Examples: Dinner was over and the dishes were washed. They sat down to watch a movie on television.
Dinner (being) over and the dishes (being) washed, they sat down to watch a movie on television.
Everyone present agreed. The motion passed unanimously.
Everyone present agreeing, the motion passed unanimously.

1. The little boy was very dirty. His mother hauled him upstairs for a bath.
2. The car refused to start. They had no choice but to hoof it.
3. His voice was cracking and his eyes were watering. He sat down, hoping he had made his point.
4. The flags waved and the band played. The parade turned the last corner and disappeared.
5. The day was breezy yet warm. They decided to go for a sail on the lake.
6. She smiled and accepted the judgment. Protest, she knew, was futile.
7. His theory was in ruins. He sheepishly retreated to his study.
8. Extra money was hard to come by. He was forced to curtail his extracurricular activities.
9. The lie in the bushes was unplayable. He dropped the ball in the clear

and took a one-stroke penalty.
10. He smiled at the audience and sat down. The effect he wanted had already been sufficiently achieved.

---

11   Prepositions

Prepositions are *structure-words* (see **1-l**); they never change their form. Usually a preposition introduces a **prepositional phrase**; as its name indicates, a preposition usually *pre*cedes in *position* the rest of the phrase, which always includes a *noun* or *pronoun* (or a group of words functioning as a noun) which is the **object** of the preposition:

> This is a book *about* writing.
> She sent the letter *to* her brother.

A question consisting of the preposition and the word *what* or *whom* will always produce as its answer the object of the preposition: About what? Writing. To whom? Her brother.

11a   Functions of Prepositions

A preposition *links* its object to some other word in the sentence; the prepositional phrase then functions as either an *adjectival* or an *adverbial* modifier:

> He laid the book *on the table.*

Here the preposition *on* links its object, *table*, to the verb *laid*; the prepositional phrase *on the table* therefore functions as an *adverb* describing *where* the book was laid.

> It was a time *for celebration.*

Here the preposition *for* links its object, *celebration*, to the noun *time*; the prepositional phrase then functions as an *adjective* indicating *what kind of* time.

Note: Occasionally a prepositional phrase can function as a noun, for instance as the subject of a sentence:

> *After class* is a good time to talk to the instructor.

11b   Placement of Prepositions

Prepositions usually come before their objects. In fact they are sometimes classed, like articles, as "determiners" or "markers" because they signal that a noun or pronoun is to follow. But a preposition can also come at the end of its clause or sentence, well after its object, for example in a question, for emphasis, or to avoid awkwardness or stiffness:

Which house do you want to look *at?*
Whom are you buying the book *for?*
She is the one I want to give the book *to.*
They had several problems to contend *with.*
This is the restaurant I was telling you *about.*
The problem he was dealing *with* seemed insoluble.

Some would prefer to say "The problem with which he was dealing . . . ," especially in a formal context. It is not inherently wrong to end a sentence or clause with a preposition, in spite of what many people have been taught; the point is that you should not do it when it is unnecessarily awkward, or so often that it calls attention to itself.

> This is the page the quotation comes from.

is just as good as, though a little less formal (or stiff) than,

> This is the page from which the quotation comes.

11c   Common Prepositions

Most prepositions indicate, either literally or figuratively, a spatial or temporal relation, or such things as purpose, concession, comparison, manner, and agency. Here is a list of most of the prepositions you are likely to encounter or need:

about	beneath	in front of	over
above	beside	in order to	past
according to	besides	in place of	regarding
across	between	in relation to	regardless of
across from	beyond	inside	round
after	but	in spite of	since
against	by	into	such as
ahead of	by way of	like	through
along	concerning	near	throughout
alongside	considering	next to	till
among	contrary to	notwithstanding	to
apart from	despite	of	toward(s)
around	down	off	under
as	during	on	underneath
as far as	except	on account of	unlike
at	except for	onto	until
away from	excepting	on top of	up
because of	for	opposite	upon
before	from	out	with
behind	in	out of	within
below	in addition to	outside	without

Note that prepositions can consist of more than one word.

Exercise 11a-c(1): Recognizing prepositional phrases

Underline each prepositional phrase in the following sentences and label it as either adverbial (adv.) or adjectival (adj.).

1. He went into town to buy some bacon for his breakfast.
2. There stood a man of about forty, in the hot sunshine, wearing a heavy sweater with the collar turned up.
3. In the morning the president called his secretary on the telephone and told her to come to the office without delay.
4. The bulk of the material was sent ahead in trunks.
5. Louis looked under the table for the ball of yarn that had fallen from his lap.

Exercise 11a-c(2): Using prepositional phrases

Prepositional phrases are essential components of writing, but they can be overdone. This three-part exercise gives you practice both in using them and in avoiding their overuse.

a. Reducing clauses to prepositional phrases: Prepositional phrases will occur in your writing without your conscious effort, but sometimes you should consciously try to tighten and lighten your style by reducing various kinds of clauses to prepositional phrases that do virtually the same job. Reduce the italicized clauses in the following sentences to equivalent prepositional phrases. Revise in other ways as well if you wish to, but don't change the essential meaning.

Example: The cold front *that is over the coast* will move inland overnight.
The cold front *over the coast* will move inland overnight.

1. *If you have enough stamina,* you can take part in all the athletic events.
2. *I am afraid of flying,* so I travel mostly by train and ship.
3. *Because she was so confident,* she entered every race.
4. Students *who have part-time jobs* must budget their time carefully.
5. We need the advice *that an expert can give us.*

b. Reducing clauses to prepositional phrases using gerunds: Gerunds (the *ing*-nouns formed from verbs) are often used as objects of prepositions. Convert the italicized clauses in the following sentences to prepositional phrases with gerunds.

Example: *Although he trained rigorously,* he didn't get past the preliminaries.
In spite of his rigorous training, he didn't get past the preliminaries.

1. *Before she submitted the essay,* she proofread it carefully.
2. *It is sometimes difficult to write,* but the difficulty can challenge one to produce better work.
3. You can't hope to pass *unless you do all the assignments.*
4. *They checked letters carefully,* and caught several spies.
5. He deserves some credit *because he tried so hard.*

c. Getting rid of excessive prepositional phrases: When prepositional phrases come in bunches, they can contribute to wordiness and awkwardness. Practise getting rid of unnecessary clutter by revising the following sentences so as to reduce the number of prepositional phrases in each by at least half. (The number of prepositional phrases present is shown in parentheses after each sentence.)

Example: Some of the players on the football team are in danger of losing their eligibility because of the poor quality of their work for classes and on examinations. (8)

Because they are doing so poorly academically, some football players may lose their right to play. (reduced to zero)

1. He got to the top of the moutain first by using several trails unknown to his competitors in the race, which was held during the celebration of the centennial of the province's entry into confederation. (9)
2. The feeling of most of the people at the meeting was that the candidate spoke in strident tones for too long about things about which he knew little. (7)
3. The man at the top of the stairs of the old house shouted at me to get away from his door in a hurry. (6)
4. One of the most respected of modern historians has some odd ideas about the beginning of the war between European nations that broke out, with such devastating consequences, in early August of 1914. (8)
5. Economists' predictions about the rise and fall of interest rates seem to be accurate for the most part, but only within the limits of a period of about three or four weeks, at most, and even at that you have to take them with a grain of salt. (10)

11d   two-part verbs

11d   Two-part Verbs

English is generous, even profligate, with **two-part** (and sometimes three-part) verbs consisting of a simple verb in combination with another word or words, such as *cool off, act up, blow up, find out, hold up, carry on, get on with, stick up for.* It doesn't matter whether you think of the added words—*off, up, on,* etc.—as prepositions, adverbs, or some indefinable sort of "particle." Indeed, sometimes it is difficult to say whether a word like *down* in *sit down* is functioning as part of the verb or as an adverb describing how one can sit; but the *down* and *up* in "sit down to a good meal" and "sit up in your chair" seem more like parts of the verbs than, say, the preposition *at* in "He sat at his desk." Usually you can sense a difference in sound: in "He *took over* the operation" both parts are stressed when said aloud, whereas in "He *took* over three hours to get here" only the *took* is stressed: *over* functions separately. Often, too, the parts of a verb can be separated and still mean the same, whereas the verb and preposition or adverb cannot:

The hecklers were *won over* by his reply.
He *won* the hecklers *over* with his reply.
He *won* over his nearest opponent by three strokes.

They *blew up* the plane.
They *blew* the plane *up*.
The wind *blew* up the chimney.

But that is not a sure test, for some two-part verbs cannot be separated;

for example:

> see to, look after, run across, sit up, turn in (go to bed)

Some simple verbs can add two or more different words to form new verbs; for example:

> try out, try on; think out, think up; fill up, fill in, fill out; fall out, fall in, fall off

Some can use several different words:

> let alone, let down, let go, let loose, let off, let on, let out, let up
> turn against, turn down, turn in, turn loose, turn off, turn on, turn out, turn over, turn to, turn up
> bring about, bring around, bring down, bring forth, bring forward, bring in, bring off, bring on, bring out, bring over, bring to, bring up

Using Two-part Verbs: Informality and Formality

We bring these verbs to your attention so that you will be able consciously to use them or avoid them to the degree appropriate to any particular piece of writing you do. Although most such verbs are standard and idiomatic, some are clearly informal or colloquial or even have a touch of slanginess about them, for example *let up on, trip up, shake up* (see also **52**). Many even of the standard ones are relatively informal—that is, they have more formal equivalents. Consider the following, for example:

> give away————bestow; reveal, betray
> give back————return
> give in————yield, concede
> give off————discharge, emit
> give out————emit; distribute; become exhausted
> give over————relinquish, abandon; cease
> give up————despair; renounce; surrender; deliver
> give way————withdraw, retreat; make room for; collapse

By consulting your dictionary and your own sense of style and tone, you can go a long way toward controlling the formality or informality of a piece of writing. If you choose *buy* as more appropriate to your context than *purchase*, for example, you'll probably also want to use some two-part verbs rather than their more formal, often Latinate, equivalents; you'd choose for example to say *put up with* rather than *tolerate*. Or vice versa: If you're writing a strictly formal piece, you may want to avoid the informal terms, or allow in only a couple for contrast or spice. You're probably aware that much writing nowadays, including academic writing, is becoming increasingly informal; anything that eschewed the kind of vigour these two-part verbs can impart would risk sounding insufferably pompous and stiff.

Exercise 11d: Using two-part verbs

---

a. Draw up a good-sized list of two-part (and three-part) verbs and their formal equivalents. Draw upon those listed above and add as many more as you can think of. Think about such common verbs as *come, go, put, take, get,* and *set,* and try combining them with as many as possible of such common prepositions or adverbs as *about, at, away, back, down, in, off, out, over, through, to, up, upon,* and *with.* Consult your dictionary. If you don't find many listed (usually under the entry for the basic verb itself), look in a bigger dictionary. You shouldn't have to go as far as the *Oxford English Dictionary* to come up with a substantial number.

b. Compose several sentences—or better yet compose two or three separate paragraphs on different kinds of topics—using as many verbs from your list as you can squeeze in. Read them over—aloud—to see how they sound.

c. Rewrite your paragraphs or sentences, wherever possible substituting more formal verbs for your originals. Now how do they sound?

d. Go back and judiciously mix the two kinds of verbs. Which version of each paragraph do you now like best? Does it depend on your subject? Would it depend at all on your intended audience?

---

12 Conjunctions

Conjunctions are another kind of function word (see 1-l). As their name indicates, *conjunctions* are words that "join together." There are three kinds of conjunction: *co-ordinating, correlative,* and *subordinating.*

12a Co-ordinating Conjunctions

There are only seven **co-ordinating** conjunctions; you should memorize them:

> and, but, or, nor, for, yet, so

When you use a co-ordinating conjunction, choose the appropriate one; they're not interchangeable (see 28, on faulty co-ordination). *And* indicates addition, *nor* indicates negative addition (equivalent to *also not*), *but* and *yet* indicate contrast or opposition, *or* indicates choice, *for* indicates cause or reason, and *so* indicates effect or result. Co-ordinating conjunctions remain grammatically independent of the elements they join, like a spot of glue connecting two things without being a part of either one.

Some of the co-ordinating conjunctions can also be other parts of speech, though you shouldn't have any trouble telling which is which: *yet* can be an adverb (It's not *yet* ten o'clock); *so* can be an adverb (It was *so* dark that . . .), an adjective (That is *so*), a demonstrative pronoun (I liked him, and I told him *so*), and an interjection (*So!*);

for is also a common preposition (*for* a while, *for* me); even *but* can be a preposition, meaning *excepting* (all *but* two).

For *punctuation* with co-ordinating conjunctions, see Chapter IV, especially **33a-c** and **44d**.

Joining words, phrases, and subordinate clauses

The conjunctions *and, but, or,* and *yet* join co-ordinate elements— words, phrases, or subordinate clauses—within sentences. The elements joined by a co-ordinating conjunction should usually be of equal importance and of similar or parallel grammatical structure and function; when joined, they are sometimes called *compounds* of various kinds (see **1z**, under *simple sentences*). When there are three or more elements being compounded, the conjunction usually appears only between the last two, though *and* and *or* can appear between each two, for purposes of rhythm or emphasis:

> There was a tug-of-war and a sack race and an egg race and a three-legged race and . . . well, there was just about any kind of game anyone could want at a picnic.

Here are examples of the compounding of various kinds of sentence elements:

> I saw *Jean* and *Ralph.* (two direct objects)
> *Jean* and *Ralph* saw me. (two subjects)
> The driver was *short, fat,* and *ugly.* (three predicate adjectives)
> He ate *fast* and *noisily.* (two adverbs)
> The bird flew *in the door* and *out the window.* (two adverbial prepositional phrases)
> *Tired* but *determined,* she plodded on. (two past participles)
> Give *Jerry* or *me* your answer by tomorrow. (two indirect objects)
> The dessert was *sweet* yet *tart.* (two predicate adjectives)
> The children *cooked the dinner* and *washed the dishes.* (two verbs with direct objects)
> People *who invest wisely* and *who spend carefully* can weather a recession. (two adjective clauses)
> I travel *when I have the time and money* and *when I can find someone pleasant to accompany me.* (two adverbial clauses)
> The lawyer told him *what he should wear* and *how he should speak.* (two noun clauses)

Obviously the elements being joined won't always be *identical* in structure, but you shouldn't risk disappointing a reader's natural expectation that compound elements will be reasonably parallel. For example it would be weaker to write

> The lawyer told him *what he should wear* and *how to speak*

for even though both elements are functioning as nouns (direct objects of *told*), one is a clause and the other is an infinitive phrase. (See **27**, on faulty parallelism.)

Joining independent clauses

All seven co-ordinating conjunctions can be used to join independent clauses to make compound (or compound-complex) sentences (see **1z**). The clauses will be grammatically equivalent because they are *independent*; but they need not be grammatically parallel or even of similar length—though they often are both, for parallelism is a strong stylistic force. Here are some examples:

> The players fought, the umpires shouted, *and* the fans booed.
> The kestrel flew higher and higher, in ever-wider circles, *and* soon it was but a speck in the sky overhead.
> Jean saw me, *but* Ralph didn't.
> Will you answer her letter, *or* shall I ask Violet to?
> I will not do it, *nor* will she. (With *nor*, there must be some kind of negative in the first clause. Note that after *nor* the normal subject-verb order is reversed.)
> He began to drive more slowly, *for* it was getting dark.
> The economy seemed in good shape, *yet* the market went into a slump.
> There was no way to avoid it, *so* I decided to get as much out of the experience as I could.

Notes:

(1) The co-ordinating conjunction *so* is considered informal; in formal writing, you can almost always indicate the cause-effect relation with a *because* or *since* clause instead:

> Since there was no way to avoid it, I decided to get as much out of the experience as I could.

And so, however, is acceptable, but shouldn't be used often.

(2) Although the conjunction *for* is often identical in meaning to *because*, and could then just as easily be thought of as a subordinator, it remains classified with the *co-ordinating* conjunctions for two reasons. First, like the other co-ordinators, it can be placed only *between* the two clauses it joins; it and the clause that follows it cannot be moved to the beginning of a sentence, the way a *because* clause can. Second, there is a semantic distinction—albeit a decreasing one—between *for* and *because*. *Because* introduces a direct, factual reason:

> She went back to college because she wanted to improve her mind.
> Because it was getting dark, he began to drive more slowly.

For tends to be less direct, less blunt, more subtle. Always preceded by a comma, it and the clause it introduces seem more like a parenthetical afterthought, as if offering the writer's own interpretation or explanation rather than the hard, objective fact:

> She went back to college, for she wanted to improve her mind.

Further, the conjunction *for* is distinctly formal; it seldom occurs in speech, where it usually sounds stilted. In colloquial contexts terms like *since* and *seeing that* convey a similar sense. (Most good dictionaries discuss these terms in a usage note under *because*.)

Joining sentences with co-ordinating conjunctions

In spite of what you may have been taught, it is not wrong to begin a sentence with *And* or *But*, or for that matter any of the other co-ordinating conjunctions. However, since *for* is so similar in meaning to *because*, it often sounds awkward at the beginning of a sentence, as if it were introducing a fragmentary subordinate clause (see **12c**); and *so* often sounds colloquial, even immature ("So then I said to him . . . ."). But the rest, especially *and* and *but*, make good sentence-openers; it's just that you shouldn't overdo them. An opening *But* or *Yet* can nicely emphasize a contrast or other turn of thought (as in the preceding sentence). An opening *And* can also be emphatic:

> He told the judge he was sorry. And he meant it.

Both *and* and *but* as sentence-openers can contribute to paragraph coherence (see **69d**). And, especially in a narrative, a succession of opening *And*'s can impart a feeling of rapid pace, even a sense of breathless excitement. Used too often, they can become tedious, but used carefully and when they feel natural, they can be effective.

Note: Many quite respectable sentences use co-ordinating conjunctions that don't seem to connect equivalent or parallel elements; for example:

> I'll drop by to see you this afternoon, *but* only for a few minutes.
> Continuing economic growth—*and* the speaker emphasized this—is not
>   something we should take for granted.
> The new party already has a thousand members, *or* about that many.

What is happening in such sentences is either that part of the meaning is "understood" but left unstated, or that the parts of the sentence have been rearranged in an unusual way, probably for emphasis. The above sentences, for example, could be rewritten as follows:

> I'll drop by to see you this afternoon, *but* I'll be able to stay only a few
>   minutes.
> The speaker said that continuing economic growth is not something we
>   should take for granted, *and* he emphasized this point.
> The new party already has a thousand—*or* about that many—members.

These versions seem less natural and more wordy, but the co-ordinating conjunctions can now be seen to be doing their proper job: connecting grammatically equivalent elements.

Exercise 12a: Using co-ordinating conjunctions

Put an appropriate co-ordinating conjunction in each blank. If more than one is possible, say so.

1. Vernon got home late, _____ he had a good excuse.
2. There is only one solution to this problem, _____ I know what it is.
3. You can sign up for the club today, _____ you can wait until next week.
4. No one likes pollution, _____ some people insist that we have to live with it.
5. I cannot give you an answer tonight, _____ should you expect me to give one tomorrow.
6. It was an extremely well-written novel, _____ I enjoyed it very much.
7. Ernest decided not to skip class, _____ there was to be a quiz that day.
8. My mother arrives tomorrow morning, _____ she expects to be met at the airport.
9. The fishing season is postponed two weeks this year, _____ Arthur is somehow controlling his impatience.
10. Keep a bandage on that cut, _____ it will take weeks to heal.

12b   Correlative Conjunctions

Correlative conjunctions always come in pairs. They *correlate* ("relate together") two parallel parts of a sentence. Since they too produce compounds, they are also a kind of co-ordinating conjunction. The principal correlative conjunctions are *either . . . or, whether . . . or, neither . . . nor, both . . . and, not . . . but,* and *not only . . . but also.* (The *only* in the last one is sometimes replaced by such words as *just* and *merely;* the *also* is sometimes omitted or replaced by *as well, in addition, too,* and the like.) Correlative conjunctions enable you to write sentences containing forcefully balanced elements. But like most good things, they shouldn't be overdone. They are also more at home in formal than in informal writing. Here are some examples:

> *Either* Rodney *or* Elliott is going to drive.
> You can put the suitcase *either* on the bed *or* on the chair.
> *Whether* by accident *or* by design, the number turned out to be exactly right.
> She accepted *neither* the first *nor* the second offer.
> *Both* the administration *and* the student body are pleased with the new plan.
> He was worried *not* about his money *but* about his reputation.
> She *not only* plays well *but also* sings well.
> *Not only* does she play well, *but* she *also* sings well.
> He was worried *not only* about his money *but* about his reputation *as well.*

In the first part of the next-to-last example, note how the idiomatic use of the auxiliary verb *does* alters the strict parallel; and note in both the last two examples how some constructions permit the *also* or its equivalent to be moved away from the *but*. Except for these variations, make what follows one term exactly *parallel* to what follows the other term: *by accident/by design, the first/the second, plays well/sings well;* that is, write "either *on the bed* or *on the chair*" or "on either *the bed* or *the chair*," but not "either *on the bed* or *the chair*." (See **27,** on faulty parallelism.)

Further, with the *not only . . . but also* pair, you should usually make the *also* (or some equivalent) explicit. Although it is sometimes omitted, many readers feel its absence as an unsatisfactory incompleteness.

> *Incomplete*: He was *not only* tired, *but* hungry.
> *Complete*: He was *not only* tired, *but also* hungry.
> *Complete*: He was *not only* tired, *but* hungry *as well*.

This is a simple example. The longer and more complicated a sentence is, the easier it is to forget the *also*. Note, however, that if the second part doesn't *add to* or *complete* the first part but merely *intensifies* it, no *also* should be included:

> As predicted, the day was not only hot, but downright stifling.

See **7c** for *agreement of verbs* with subjects joined by some of the correlatives.

12c   Subordinating Conjunctions

A **subordinating** conjunction introduces a *subordinate* (or *dependent*) clause and links it to the *independent* (or *main* or *principal*) clause to which it is grammatically related:

> I will not attend class, *because* I have a severe headache.

The subordinating conjunction *because* introduces the *adverbial* clause *because I have a severe headache* and links it to the independent clause whose verb, *will not attend,* it modifies. The *because* clause is *subordinate* because it cannot stand by itself: by itself it would be a *fragment* (see **1y**). It *depends* on the other clause for its legitimate existence. It is less important than the clause to which it is attached; it is merely a modifier of part of the other clause. Note that a subordinate clause can also come first in a sentence:

> *Because* I have a severe headache, I will not attend class.

Even though *Because* does not occur between the two unequal clauses, it still links them grammatically.

That she will win the prize is a foregone conclusion.

Here *That* introduces the *noun* clause *That she will win the prize,* which functions as the subject of the sentence. Note that whereas a *co-ordinating* conjunction is like a spot of glue between two things and not a part of either, a *subordinating* conjunction is an integral part of the clause it introduces. In the following sentence, for example, the subordinating conjunction *whenever* is a part of the clause *whenever you feel like it,* the whole of which modifies the imperative verb *leave:*

Leave *whenever you feel like it.*

Here is a list of the principal subordinating conjunctions:

after	however	than	when
although	if	that	whenever
as	if only	though	where
as though	in case	till	whereas
because	lest	unless	wherever
before	once	until	whether
even though	since	what	while
ever since	rather than	whatever	why

There are also many terms consisting of two or more words ending in *as, if,* and *that* which serve as subordinating conjunctions; for example: *inasmuch as, insofar as, as long as, as soon as, as far as, as if, even if, only if, but that, except that, now that, in that, provided that, in order that.*

Note that some of these subordinating conjunctions can also serve as adverbs, prepositions, and relative pronouns. But don't worry about parts of speech. It will be easier if you think of all these terms simply as **subordinators**—including the relative pronouns and relative adverbs (*who, which, that, where,* and *when*) that introduce adjective clauses. (Strictly speaking, subordinating conjunctions can introduce only adverbial and noun clauses.) What is important is that you understand the *subordinating* function that they all perform, so that you can understand the syntax of complex and compound-complex sentences (see **1z**) and, most important, avoid *fragments* (see **1y**).

Exercise 12c(1): Recognizing subordinate clauses

Underline each subordinate clause in the following passage and indicate how each one is functioning in its sentence: as an adjective, an adverb, or a noun. (Remember that sometimes relative pronouns are omitted from relative clauses; see **3d** and **37**.) Show what each clause is doing; that is, what word or words does each adjectival or adverbial clause modify? And is a noun clause functioning as a subject, an object, or what? (You might begin by identifying all

12c subord. conjunctions

the *independent* clauses; and you might also want to mark the subject and verb of each clause, of whatever kind.)

Once upon a time, when he was only seven years old, Jean-Paul decided that he wanted to be a musician. He especially liked drums, the toy ones his parents had foolishly bought for him to play with. As he grew older, he discovered that there were other kinds of percussion instruments—the piano, for example, and the xylophone. But whenever he asked for a piano, or a xylophone, his parents, who were not well off, had to say no. That he kept on playing with drums, therefore, is not surprising. Eventually he even bought some drums for himself, out of the money he earned delivering papers. When the noise he made became too much, his father set aside a room in the cellar for him to practise in. Then Jean-Paul was happy. And only a few years later (though the time passed rapidly for all of them), Jean-Paul became a regular member of a band that played in local clubs. But his parents, who still thought the noise was awful, never went to hear him. But Jean-Paul was one of those who struck it lucky. And when he suddenly (it was all quite different from what they'd expected) blossomed as a video star—one who had his own band—they didn't know whether they should celebrate or disown him. But since he made lots of money, he felt so generous that he paid off their mortgage and even let them invite him home for holidays. They hope that someday soon he'll even get married, and perhaps settle near them, with his drums and his wife; if he does, then maybe they'll all be able to live more or less happily ever after.

Exercise 12c(2): Writing subordinate clauses

Combine each of the following pairs of simple sentences (independent clauses) into a single sentence by subordinating one clause and attaching it to the other with one of the subordinators listed above. You may need to change or delete or add some words. You may also want to reverse the order of the two clauses, or otherwise rearrange words. Try using two or three different subordinators with each pair of sentences.

Example: The computer revolution has affected many business and professional people. Its largest impact may prove to have been on the young.
(Though, Although) the computer revolution has affected many business and professional people, its . . . .
The computer revolution has affected many business and professional people, (though, even though) its . . . .

1. The art gallery won't open until next week. The leak in the roof hasn't been repaired yet.
2. I will finish my exams next week. Then I am going to look for a summer job.
3. See that old house on the corner? I used to live there.
4. Canada's election campaigns are much shorter than those in the United States. We should be thankful for this.
5. Some of the workers have a legitimate grievance. They will probably vote in favour of a strike.
6. Some students may not have paid all their fees. They would not yet be considered officially registered.
7. The Prairies are very dry this year. They haven't been this dry for several years.
8. First you should master the simple sentence. Then you can work on complex sentences.
9. Shouting protesters surrounded the limousine. Nevertheless, there was no violence.
10. The election campaign drew nearer its end. The number of undecided voters decreased.

---

13 Interjections

An **interjection** is a word or group of words *interjected* into (i.e., "thrown into") a sentence in order to express emotion, whether strong:

> But—*good heavens!*—what did you expect?
> *Oh,* what fun!
> *Well,* aren't you the sly one!
> *My goodness,* it's been a long day.

or relatively mild:

> It was, *well,* a bit of a disappointment.

Strictly speaking, interjections have no grammatical function. They are simply thrust into sentences and play no part in their syntax. But you can think of them—especially the mild ones—as in effect modifying the whole sentence, like this sentence adverb:

> *No,* the government had no choice but to act as it did.

Mild interjections are usually set off with commas. Strong interjections are sometimes set off with dashes and are often accompanied by exclamation points (see **39** and **42c**). An interjection may also be a minor sentence by itself:

> *Ouch!* That hurt!
> *Well.* So much for the preliminaries. Now comes the hard part.

Review Exercises: Chapter II

(1) Recognizing parts of speech
To test yourself, see if you can identify the *part of speech* of each word in the following sentences. Can you say how each is functioning grammatically? What kinds of sentences are they?

1. The skyline of modern Toronto provides a striking example of what modern architecture can do.
2. Students with carefully planned programs can begin a new academic year relatively confident that they know what they're doing.
3. Waiter, there's a fly in my soup!
4. Well, to tell the truth, I just did not have the necessary patience.
5. Why should anyone be unhappy about paying a fair tax?
6. Neither the captain nor his men could be blamed for the terribly costly accident.
7. Forestry is one of the principal industries of British Columbia.
8. The terminally ill are now getting increasingly considerate attention in our hospitals.
9. The elevator business has been said to have its ups and downs.
10. Pamela, please put back the chocolate cake.
11. The minister should pressure the committee to release its data.
12. While abroad I learned to make do with only a bath towel.
13. In a few seconds, the computer told us much more than we needed to know.
14. The game was, unfortunately, little more than a brawl, a knock-down-drag-out fight, almost from beginning to end.
15. Help!

(2) Using different parts of speech
For fun, write some sentences using the following words as different parts of speech—as many different ones as you can. Each is good for at least two.

shed	plant	still	wrong	round	cross
best	before	train	last	set	near
left	study	cover	fine	rose	down

WRITING EFFECTIVE SENTENCES:

Basic Elements and Modifiers; Length, Variety, and Emphasis; Analyzing Sentences; Common Errors and Weaknesses

Writing effective sentences means putting words together in ways that will best convey your ideas to your readers. After studying the basic elements and patterns of sentences (Chapter I) and the parts of speech that make up those elements and patterns (Chapter II), you should be able to choose your words more carefully and decide how to arrange them in the kinds of sentences you want to write. In this chapter we provide a brief overview of the basic structural elements of sentences and the forms they can take, and how various forms of modifiers can work with them. Then we offer three methods of analysis that will help you understand how sentences work. Finally we discuss and illustrate the more common errors and weaknesses that writers need to guard against. If you have difficulty understanding any of the terms and concepts discussed below, you may need to review parts of the first two chapters; use the cross-references and the index to locate the parts you need to study further.

14-15 Basic Sentence Elements and Their Modifiers

14 Subject, Verb, Object, Complement

Consider again the bare bones of a sentence. The two essential elements are a *subject* and a *finite verb* (see **1a**).

14a   Subject

The *subject*, as the word suggests, is that which is talked about. More precisely, it is the source of the action indicated by the finite verb, or the person or thing experiencing the state of being or possessing the condition indicated by the verb and its complement:

> *Rosa* watched the performance. (*Rosa* is the source of the action of watching.)
>
> *We* are happy about the outcome. (*We* indicates those experiencing the state of being happy.)
>
> *Education* is important. (*Education* indicates what possesses the condition of being important.)

If in doubt, ask the question *Who?* or *What?* followed by the finite verb (and complement); the answer will be the subject of the sentence:

> Who watched? *Rosa* watched. Who is happy? *We* are. What is important? *Education* is.

The subject of a sentence will ordinarily be one of the following: a noun, a pronoun, a gerund or gerund phrase, an infinitive or infinitive phrase, or a noun clause. For example:

> The *cow* chewed slowly. (noun; see **2**)
>
> *He* likes to discuss politics. (pronoun; see **3**)
>
> *Swimming* is an excellent exercise. (gerund; see **10d**)
>
> *Throwing frisbees* used to be popular. (gerund phrase)
>
> It was necessary *to leave*. (infinitive; see **10a**)
>
> *To study a text closely* is the only way to appreciate it fully. (infinitive phrase)
>
> *That the firm is solvent* is obvious from these records. (noun clause; see **1o**)

14b   Finite Verb

The **finite verb** is the focal point of the sentence. It indicates the nature and time of the action (see **6g**):

> The teacher *will describe* the examination. (The action is that of describing; the time when the action will occur is the future.)
>
> We *rested* halfway up the mountain. (The action is that of resting; the time of the action is the past: it has already occurred.)

The verb answers the question formed by the subject and *what?* or *did what?*

> The teacher what? The teacher *will describe*. We did what? We *rested*.

For discussions of the various forms verbs may take (tenses, moods, voices, etc.), see **6**.

14c Direct Object

If a verb is *transitive* (see **6a**), there will be a **direct object** to complete the pattern (see **1d**). The direct object answers the question formed by the verb and *what?*

> Will describe what? Will describe the *examination*.

Like the subject, the direct object may be a noun, a pronoun, a gerund or gerund phrase, an infinitive or infinitive phrase, or a noun clause:

> Ferdinand likes *flowers*. (noun)
> The dog accepted *him* as master. (pronoun)
> She enjoys *hiking*. (gerund)
> He enjoys *playing golf*. (gerund phrase)
> They decided *to attend*. (infinitive)
> They want *to learn French well*. (infinitive phrase)
> The supervisor knew *that Marie was a good worker*. (noun clause)

(There may also be an indirect object or an objective complement; see **1f**, **1i**, and **1j**.)

14d Subjective Complement

Similarly, after a *linking* verb (see **6a**), a **subjective complement** is necessary to complete the pattern. This complement will be either a *predicate noun* or a *predicate adjective* (see **1g** and **1h**):

> She is a *doctor*. (predicate noun)
> He remained a *student* for three more years. (predicate noun)
> The class-president is my *brother*. (predicate noun)
> She is very *intelligent*. (predicate adjective)
> He became *impatient*. (predicate adjective)

A question formed by the verb and *what?* or *whom?* will yield the subjective complement as its answer:

> Is what? A *doctor*. Is whom? My *brother*. Is what? *Intelligent*.

A predicate adjective will ordinarily be a standard adjective, a participle, or an idiomatic prepositional phrase:

> I am *happy*. (standard adjective)
> The regulations are *annoying*. (present participle)
> We were *annoyed*. (past participle)
> The phone is *out of order*. (prepositional phrase)

A predicate noun may be a noun, a pronoun, a gerund or gerund phrase, an infinitive or infinitive phrase, or a noun clause:

> It's a *girl*! (noun)
> Is this the *one*? (pronoun)

15 modifiers

> Her favourite pastime is *skiing*. (gerund)
> The next job is *bathing the dog*. (gerund phrase)
> My first thought was *to run*. (infinitive)
> His ambition was *to drive a fire engine*. (infinitive phrase)
> Is he *what he claims to be*? (noun clause)

These elements—subject, finite verb, and object or complement—are the bare bones of the structure of major sentences. They are closely linked in the ways indicated above, with the verb as the focal and uniting element. (For a discussion of the *order* in which these basic elements occur, see **1s**, **1t**, and **1u**.)

15   Modifiers

Other grammatical elements put flesh on the bones. Such elements are called **modifiers** because they limit or describe other elements so as to modify—that is, change—a listener's or reader's idea of them. The two principal kinds of modifiers are *adjectives* (see **8**) and *adverbs* (see **9**). Also useful, but less frequent, are *appositives* (see **1q**) and *absolute phrases* (see **1r** and **10f**). An adjectival modifier, of course, may even be part of the bare bones of a sentence if it completes the predicate after a linking verb (Education is *important*). Similarly, an adverbial modifier may be an essential part of a sentence if it modifies a linking verb (Peter is *home*) or an intransitive verb whose meaning might otherwise seem incomplete (Peter lives *in an apartment*). But generally modifiers do their work by adding to, enriching, a central core of thought.

15a   Adjectival Modifiers (see 8)

Adjectival modifiers modify nouns, pronouns, and phrases or clauses functioning as nouns. They commonly answer the questions Which? What kind of? How many? How much? An adjectival modifier may be a single-word adjective, a series, a participle or participial phrase, an infinitive or infinitive phrase, a prepositional phrase, or a relative clause. For example:

> *Serious* athletes keep *their* bodies in *good* condition. (single words modifying the nouns immediately following)
> They are usually *healthy*. (single word, predicate adjective modifying pronoun *They*)
> What you're asking me to do is *ridiculous*. (predicate adjective modifying noun clause *What you're asking me to do*)
> *Three muscular young* men showed up. (series modifying *men*)
> Stan jogs around the *football* field. (noun functioning as adjective, modifying *field*)
> *Sweating*, he runs around and around. (present participle modifying *he*)

The team pressed on, *undaunted*. (past participle modifying *team*)
Finally convincing himself, he went on a diet. (present participial phrase modifying *he*)
Geraldine could relax, *having been thoroughly checked by a doctor*. (participial phrase, perfect tense, modifying *Geraldine*)
Tuesday was a day *to remember*. (infinitive modifying *day*)
Her ability *to pass up dessert* impressed us. (infinitive phrase modifying *ability*)
The books *on the shelves* are mine. (prepositional phrase modifying *books*)
The salesman, *who by now had his foot in the door*, wouldn't let me interrupt. (relative clause modifying *salesman*)

For a discussion of the *placement* of adjectival modifiers, see **8d**.

15b   Adverbial Modifiers (see 9)

Adverbial modifiers modify verbs, adjectives, other adverbs, and whole clauses or sentences. They commonly answer the questions How? When? Where? Why? To what degree? Like adjectival modifiers, adverbial modifiers may be single words, phrases, or clauses; specifically, an adverbial modifier may be a single word, a series, an infinitive or infinitive phrase, a prepositional phrase, or an adverbial clause:

He drove *slowly*. (single word modifying the verb *drove*)
The fog was *exceedingly* thick. (single word modifying the adjective *thick*)
He drove *very* slowly. (single word modifying the adverb *slowly*)
She *soon* moved. (single word modifying the verb *moved*)
Obviously, he's not sticking to his diet. (single word modifying the rest of the sentence)
Slowly, carefully, even tediously, he described his experience. (series modifying the verb *described*)
To relax, she listens to music. (infinitive modifying the verb *listens*)
He was lucky *to have survived the fall*. (infinitive phrase modifying the predicate adjective *lucky*)
She moved *to the suburbs*. (prepositional phrase modifying the verb *moved*)
They arrived *before noon*. (prepositional phrase modifying the verb *arrived*)
He joined *because he believed in their principles*. (clause modifying the verb *joined*)
He drove slowly *because the fog was exceedingly thick*. (clause modifying the verb *drove*, or the verb with its adverb: *drove slowly*)
Turn out the light *when you're finished*. (clause modifying preceding independent clause)

For a discussion of the *placement* of adverbial modifiers, see **9d**.

15c   Overlapping Modifiers

The examples above are meant to illustrate each kind of adjectival and adverbial modifier separately, in tidy isolation from the other kinds. And of course such sentences are not uncommon, for relative simplicity of sentence structure can be a stylistic strength. But many sentences, both written and spoken, are more complicated, for a great deal of overlap among modifiers is possible, even normal. Modifiers occur as parts of other modifiers: single-word modifiers occur as parts of phrases and clauses, phrases occur as parts of other phrases and as parts of clauses, and subordinate clauses occur as parts of phrases and as parts of other clauses. That's the way many sentences get built. Here are examples to illustrate some of the possible structural variety (you may wish to check back to sections **1c-k** in order to match up these sentences and their clauses with the various patterns that go to make them up).

They gazed languidly at the setting sun.

languidly—adverb modifying finite verb *gazed*
at the setting sun—adverbial prepositional phrase modifying *gazed*
setting—participial adjective modifying *sun*

Most of his off-the-cuff remarks fell flat.

of his off-the-cuff remarks—adjectival prepositional phrase modifying *Most*
off-the-cuff—hyphenated prepositional phrase, adjective modifying *re-marks*

Desiring to learn to speak French well, they spent a year in Paris.

Desiring to learn to speak French well—participial phrase modifying *they*
to learn to speak French well—infinitive phrase, object of the participle *Desiring*
to speak French well—infinitive phrase, object of infinitive *to learn*
well—adverb modifying the infinitive *to speak*
in Paris—adverbial prepositional phrase modifying the finite verb *spent*

It was daunting to think of the consequences that might ensue.

to think of the consequences that might ensue—infinitive phrase, delayed subject of sentence
of the consequences—adverbial prepositional phrase modifying the infinitive *to think*
that might ensue—relative clause modifying *consequences*
daunting—participle, predicate adjective modifying the subject (If you have difficulty understanding this structure, try converting the sentence from pattern 6 to pattern 4A.)

They cherished the thought, a recurring one for them, that they might someday be out of debt.

a recurring one for them—appositive phrase further defining *thought*
for them—adverbial prepositional phrase modifying *recurring*
recurring—participle modifying *one*
that they might someday be out of debt—relative clause modifying *thought*

out of debt—prepositional phrase, predicate adjective after the linking verb *might be*
someday—adverb modifying *might be*

With the bonus money, he bought what he had dreamed about for years: a computer to play with.

With the bonus money—adverbial prepositional phrase modifying *bought*
bonus—adjective modifying *money*
what he had dreamed about for years—noun clause, direct object of *bought*
about [what]—adverbial prepositional phrase modifying *dreamed*
for years—adverbial prepositional phrase modifying *dreamed*
a computer to play with—appositive phrase modifying the noun clause
to play with—adjectival infinitive phrase modifying *computer*

Because she wanted to become better educated, she enrolled in night school.

Because she wanted to become better educated—adverbial clause modifying the independent clause *she enrolled in night school*
to become better educated—infinitive phrase, direct object of *wanted*
better—adverb modifying *educated*, the predicate adjective after *to become*
in night school—adverbial prepositional phrase modifying *enrolled*
night—noun functioning adjectivally to modify *school*

He was a man who, being well versed in the finer things of life, knew bad music when he heard it.

who . . . knew bad music when he heard it—relative clause modifying the predicate noun *man*
when he heard it—adverbial clause modifying *knew*
being well versed in the finer things of life—participial phrase modifying the relative pronoun *who*
versed—past participle, predicate adjective after *being*
well—adverb modifying *versed*
in the finer things of life—adverbial prepositional phrase modifying *versed*
of life—adjectival prepositional phrase modifying *things*

The book being one of the kind that puts you to sleep, she laid it aside and dozed off.

The book being one of the kind that puts you to sleep—absolute phrase
of the kind that puts you to sleep—adjectival prepositional phrase modifying *one*
that puts you to sleep—relative clause modifying *kind*
to sleep—adverbial prepositional phrase modifying *puts*

He is the man who knows what must be done when an oil well blows.

who knows what must be done when an oil well blows—relative clause modifying *man*

15c overlapping modifiers

> *what must be done when an oil well blows*—noun clause, direct object of
> *knows*
> *when an oil well blows*—adverbial clause modifying the verb *must be done*

These examples at least suggest the kind of richness that is possible, the kind you undoubtedly create at least some of the time without even thinking about it. But think about it. Try concocting some sentences with the sorts of syntactical complications illustrated above. You may be surprised at the kinds of sentences you can turn out when you set your mind to it. You might also discover that working—or playing— with sentences in this way will help you generate material for developing your paragraphs and essays.

15d   Using Modifiers

Suppose you were assigned an essay on the kinds of recreational reading you do. In getting your ideas together and taking notes, you might draft a bare-bones sentence such as this:

> I like novels. (subject, transitive verb, object)

It's a start, but you soon realize that the sentence isn't exactly true to your thoughts. It needs qualification. So you begin *modifying* its elements to make it represent your feelings more accurately:

> I like *modern* novels.

The adjective limits the meaning of the word *novels*—you don't care for older novels so much. Then you remember that you haven't much liked some recent novels about princesses or the rich or heroes and heroines of high romance and adventure, so you add an adjectival prepositional phrase to further limit the word *novels*:

> I like modern novels *about everyday people.*

(The adjective *everyday* modifies *people*, which wouldn't make much sense here by itself.) Then you recall a couple of novels that were both modern and about ordinary people but that were pretty bad; therefore you insert yet another adjective to further qualify, or rather quantify, the noun *novels*:

> I like *most* modern novels about everyday people.

Then you have an attack of logic and realize that the word *most* implies that you are familiar with *all* such modern novels; otherwise how could you know that you liked *most* of them? But you quickly see a way to revise the sentence so as to convey your thoughts accurately; you take out the adjective *most* and put the adverb *usually* in front of the verb:

> I *usually* like modern novels about everyday people.

So far so good. But the sentence somehow doesn't impress you; you suspect that a reader might well appreciate a little more information about these "everyday people." Of course you could go on to explain in another sentence or two, but you'd like to try getting a little more meat into this sentence. Then you have a flash of inspiration: you can help clarify your point and at the same time inject some rhythm and parallelism into your sentence by adding a participial phrase to modify the noun *people*:

> I usually like modern novels about everyday people *having everyday problems*.

Then you almost automatically add another prepositional phrase—not because it adds anything important about the kind of problems but because it seems to round off the sentence nicely:

> I usually like modern novels about everyday people having everyday problems *with their lives*.

You rather like it. But working at this one sentence has got your brain going, so before you leave it you think about your reasons for liking such novels. You like them, you decide, because they're about people like yourself, and because their problems aren't so much those caused by outside pressures as they are home-grown problems, problems like your own. You feel the words beginning to come, and you consider your options: you can put the explanation in a separate sentence; you can join it to your present sentence with a semicolon or a colon or a co-ordinating conjunction like *for*, creating a compound sentence; or you can integrate it more closely by making it a subordinate clause, turning the whole into a complex sentence. You decide on the third method, and put the new material in the form of an adverbial *because* clause modifying the verb *like*. And while you're thinking about it, you begin to feel that, given the way your sentence has developed, the word *like* now sounds rather pallid, weak because relatively common; you decide to change it to the more vigorous verb *enjoy*. Now your sentence is finished, at least for the time being:

> I usually enjoy modern novels about everyday people having everyday problems with their lives, because I can identify with the characters and share their troubles—and their triumphs.

By adding modifiers, a writer can enlarge the reader's knowledge of the material being presented and impart precision and clarity to a sentence, as well as improve its style and vary its intonation. Minimal or bare-bones sentences can themselves be effective and emphatic; you should use them when they are appropriate. But most of your sentences will be longer. And it is in elaborating and enriching your sentences with modifiers that you as author and stylist exercise much of your

15d   using modifiers

15d   using modifiers

control: you take charge of what your readers will learn and how they will learn it.

Here is another core sentence:

The house was sturdy. (subject, linking verb, complement)

And here is how it might be filled out with various kinds of modifiers:

Constructed of stone and cedar, the large house that the Smiths built on the brow of Murphy's Bluff—an exposed promontory—was so sturdy that even the icy blasts of the continual north wind in December and January made no impression on it.

Breaking this sentence up, you can see how its various elements work:

Constructed of stone and cedar (participial phrase modifying *house*)
the (definite article specifying a particular house)
large (adjective describing the house)
house (noun as essential element: the subject)
that the Smiths built on the brow of Murphy's Bluff (adjectival clause further modifying *house*)
an exposed promontory (appositive phrase further characterizing *Murphy's Bluff*)
was (linking verb as essential element)
sturdy (predicate adjective modifying *house*; essential element—complement—after linking verb)
so . . . that even the icy blasts of the continual north wind in December and January made no impression on it. (adverbial clause modifying *sturdy*, answering the question How sturdy?)

Note that you can also break the phrases and clauses up into their components: The opening phrase contains the adverbial prepositional phrase *of stone and cedar* modifying the participial adjective *Constructed*; the adjectival clause contains two prepositional phrases (*on the brow*, adverbial modifying the verb *built*, and *of Murphy's Bluff*, adjectival modifying the noun *brow*); the appositive contains the adjective *exposed* modifying the noun *promontory*; the long adverbial clause contains three prepositional phrases (*of the continual north wind, in December and January*, and *on it*) and several single-word modifiers, some within the first phrase (*even, icy, continual, north, no*). And of course the two subordinate clauses have their own subjects (*Smiths, blasts*), finite verbs (*built, made*), and direct objects (*that, impression*).

Exercise 15: Using modifiers

Here are some bare-bones sentences. For practice, choose at least ten of them and flesh them out with various kinds of modifiers; compose at least five expanded sentences for each. Use some single-word modifiers if you wish, but work mainly with phrases and clauses. Include some noun clauses. Identify each modifier you use. Keep the sentences simple or complex, not compound or compound-complex (see **1z**). (If you don't like our core sentences, make up some of your own.)

Example: The ship sank.
The old ship sank in a storm.
When the ship sank I was very sad.
Why the ship sank no one could tell.
The ship at the tail of the convoy sank after being hit by a torpedo.
The once proud ship sank like a stone to the bottom of the sea.
The ship that many thought to be unsinkable sank after hitting an iceberg.
That the ship sank surprised almost everyone.

Education is important.
I enjoy my hobby.
Movies entertain.
I travelled to _____ .
People annoy me.
I use the library.
Children play games.
Free trade might work.
I read a novel.
Advertising works.
Are you going?
It's not funny.
Unemployment is a problem.
I passed the course.
Spring is coming.

Athletes train.
_____ is a politician.
The river meandered.
People buy lottery tickets.
Can you explain?
The soldiers fought.
Save money.
Nothing can be done.
The music continued.
The sun shone.
Writing is difficult.
The birds chattered.
Think of Quebec.
Manners matter.
Stop.

16   *sentence length*

16   Sentence Length

How long should a sentence be? Long enough. A sentence may consist of one word (for example a question, command, or exclamation) or it may go on for a hundred words or more. There are no arbitrary criteria. If you're curious, do some research to determine the average sentence length in several different published works you have handy—for example this book, other texts, a recent novel, newspapers, magazines. You'll probably find that the overall average is somewhere between 15 and 25 words per sentence, that longer sentences are more common in formal and specialized writing, and that shorter sentences are more at home in informal writing, popular writing, and narrative and dialogue. There are, then, some general guidelines, and you'll probably fit your own writing to them automatically. But it might pay you to check your own writing to see how you're faring, for if you're far off what seems to be the appropriate average, you can do something about it.

16a   Short Sentences

If you find that you're writing an excessive number of short sentences—
if your prose sounds like something put together by a child—try (1)
building on them, elaborating their elements with modifiers, including
various kinds of phrases and clauses; (2) combining some of them to
form compound subjects, predicates, and objects or complements; (3)
combining two or more of them—especially if they are simple sentences—into one or another kind of complex sentence. (Note that
compound sentences, made up as they are of two or more simple sentences joined with punctuation or co-ordinating conjunctions or both,
will read like a series of shorter, simple sentences.)

16b   Long Sentences

If you find yourself writing too many long sentences, check them for
two possible dangers: (1) You may be rambling or trying to pack too
much into a single sentence, possibly destroying its unity (see **28**) but
certainly making it unnecessarily difficult to read; try breaking it up
into more unified or more easily manageable chunks. (2) You may
simply be using too many words to make your point; try cutting out
any deadwood (see **59**). In either of these kinds of unwieldly sentence,
check that you haven't slipped into what is called "excessive subordination"—too many loosely related details obscuring the main idea,
or confusing strings of subordinate clauses modifying each other; try
removing some of the clutter, and try reducing clauses to phrases (see
Exercises 10/3, 10/4, and 11a-c/2 [parts a and b]) and reducing phrases
to single-word modifiers (see Exercise 11a-c/2 [part c]).

For more on sentence length, see the next two sections, **17** and
18.

17   Sentence Variety

Both for emphasis (see **18**) and for ease of reading—that is, to avoid
monotony—vary both the lengths of your sentences and the kinds of
sentences you use. Examine closely some pieces of prose that you
particularly enjoy or that you find unusually clear and easy to read:
you will likely discover that they contain both a pleasing mixture of
short, medium, and long sentences and a similar variety of kinds and
structures.

17a   Variety of Lengths

You shouldn't have any difficulty varying the length of your sentences.
A string of short sentences will sound choppy and fragmented; reduce

the staccato effect by interweaving some longer ones. A succession of long sentences will make your ideas hard to follow; give your readers a break—and your prose some sparkle—by inserting a few short, emphatic sentences here and there. Even a string of medium-length sentences may bore your readers into inattention. Impart some rhythm, some shape, to your paragraphs by varying sentence length. Especially consider using a short, snappy sentence to open or close a paragraph, and perhaps an uncommonly long sentence to end a paragraph. They can be effective.

17b Variety of Kinds

A string of simple and compound sentences risks coming across as simple-minded. In a narrative, successive simple and compound sentences may be appropriate for recounting a sequence of events, but when you're writing reasoned prose, let some of the complexity of your ideas be reflected in complex and compound-complex sentences. On the other hand, a string of complex and compound-complex sentences may become oppressive, just as a long string of monumental floats in a parade soon becomes tiresome unless relieved by an occasional clown or tumbler. Give your readers a breather now and then.

17c Variety of Structures

Try to avoid an unduly long string of sentences that use the same syntactical structure. For example, although the standard order of elements in declarative sentences is subject–verb–object or –complement, consider the possibility of varying that order occasionally for the purpose of emphasis (see **1s** and **18c**). Perhaps use an occasional interrogative sentence (see **1t**), whether a rhetorical question (a question that does not expect an answer) or a question that you proceed to answer as you develop a paragraph. Even an occasional expletive pattern or passive voice can be refreshing—*if you can justify them on other grounds as well* (see **1e**, **1k**, **6n**, and **18f**). That is, introducing such variety purely for variety's sake is dangerous.

Especially, don't *begin* a string of sentences with the same kind of word or phrase or clause—unless you are purposely setting up a controlled succession of parallel structures for emphasis or coherence (see **69a**). Imagine the effect of several sentences beginning with such words as *Similarly . . . . Especially . . . . Consequently . . . . Nevertheless . . . . Fortunately . . . .* Whatever was in the rest of the sentences, the monotony would be stultifying. Or imagine a series of sentences all starting with a subject-noun, or with a present-participial phrase. To avoid such undesirable sameness, take advantage of the way modifiers of various kinds can be moved around in sentences (see **1q**, **1r**, **8d**, **9d**, **11b**, and **18d**).

18 Emphasis in Sentences

In order to communicate clearly and effectively, you need to ensure that your readers perceive the relative importance of your ideas the same way you do. You need to make sure not only that what you want emphasized gets emphasized, but also that what gets emphasized is what you want emphasized.

You can emphasize whole sentences in several ways. You can set a sentence off by itself, as a short paragraph. You can place an important sentence at the beginning or the end of a paragraph, the two most emphatic positions. You can put an important point into a short sentence following several long ones, or into a long sentence among several shorter ones. Or you can shift the style or structure of a sentence to make it stand out from others around it. (See **70**.)

In similar ways you can emphasize appropriate parts of individual sentences themselves. The principal devices for achieving appropriate emphasis *within* sentences are position and word order, repetition, stylistic contrast, syntax, and punctuation.

18a-f Emphasis by Position and Word Order

18a Endings and Beginnings

The most emphatic position in a sentence is its ending; the second most emphatic position is its beginning. Consider these two sentences:

> The flood killed seven people.
> Seven people died in the flood.

Each sentence emphasizes both the *flood* and the *seven people*, but the first emphasizes the *seven people* a little more, while the second emphasizes the *flood* a little more. The longer the sentence, the more pronounced the effect of emphasis by position. Compare the different emphases in the following versions of the same basic idea:

1. The best teacher I've ever had was my high-school history teacher, a lively woman in her early sixties.
2. A lively woman in her early sixties, my high-school history teacher was the best teacher I've ever had.
3. My high-school history teacher, a lively woman in her early sixties, was the best teacher I've ever had.
4. The best teacher I've ever had was a lively woman in her early sixties who taught me history in high school.

Each of these sentences is made up of the same three ideas, but each distributes the emphasis differently and would therefore be appropriate for a different purpose. In each the last part receives the greatest emphasis, the first part the next highest emphasis, and the middle part the least emphasis. Number 1 could introduce a paragraph focussing on the quality of the teacher but emphasizing her character, her age, and the fact that she was a woman. Number 2 could introduce a similar paragraph, but one focussing more on the quality of her teaching than on her age, gender, and character. Number 3 could lead into a paragraph stressing the quality of the teaching and the nature and level of the subject; the details of the teacher's age, gender, and character would be only incidental. Number 4 may seem the flattest, the least emphatic and least likely of the four, yet it could easily introduce a mainly narrative paragraph focussing on the writer's good experience in the high-school class. Note that the part referring to "the best teacher I've ever had" almost has to be placed either first or last: the superlative *best* conveys an inherent emphasis which would make it sound unnatural in the unemphatic middle position—unless its inherent emphasis is acknowledged in some other way, for example by the appositive's being set off with a pair of dashes (see **39b**):

> My high-school history teacher—the best teacher I've ever had—was a lively woman in her early sixties.

Then the sentence could work much the same as number 1.

18b   Loose Sentences and Periodic Sentences

Loose is not a pejorative term in this context. A so-called *loose* or *cumulative* sentence is one that makes its main point in an independent clause relatively early and then goes on adding modifying subordinate elements:

> The day began ominously, with the sun trying in vain to peek between the horizon and the dark clouds that had built up during the night, and the wind leaning heavily on our tent.

Such sentences are common, for they are "loose" and comfortable, easy-going, natural. At the other extreme is the *periodic* sentence, one in which the main point, the independent clause, is partly or wholly delayed until the end, just before the period:

> With the wind leaning heavily on our tent and the sun trying in vain to peek between the horizon and the night's build-up of dark clouds, the day was off to an ominous start.

Full periodic sentences are not likely to come about without careful thought and planning; they sound contrived, less natural, and therefore should not be used often. But they can be dramatic and emphatic, creating suspense as the reader waits for the meaning to fall into place at the end. But if you try for such suspense, don't separate subject and predicate too widely, as a student did in this awkward sentence:

> *awk:* The abrupt change from one moment when the air is alive with laughing and shouting, to the next when the atmosphere resembles that of a morgue, is dramatic.

18b loose, periodic

Many sentences, of course, delay completion of the main clause only until somewhere in the middle rather than all the way to the end. To the degree that they do delay it, they are partly periodic, like this one.

18c   The Importance of the Final Position

Because the final position in a sentence is naturally so emphatic, readers expect something important to occur there; don't disappoint their expectations by letting an incidental or merely qualifying word or phrase fall at the end, for then the sentence itself will fall: its energy will be dissipated and wasted, its essential meaning distorted. For example:

emph: That was the fastest I've ever driven a car, I think.

The uncertain *I think* should go at the beginning or, even less emphatically, after *That* or *was.*

emph: Cramming for exams can be counterproductive, sometimes.

The qualifying *sometimes* could go at the beginning; but its best place would be after *can,* letting the emphasis fall where it belongs, on *cramming* and *counterproductive.*

18d   Changing Word Order

Several earlier sections point out certain standard patterns: the major elements of a sentence usually line up as subject–verb–object or –complement (**1c-j**), and single-word adjectives usually precede—or, if predicate adjectives, follow—the nouns they modify (**8d**). But variations from these patterns are possible, and because these patterns are so strongly recognized as standard, any departure from them will automatically stand out (see **1s** and **8d** for examples). But be careful, for if the inverted order calls attention to itself at the expense of clear meaning, the attempt may backfire. Consider the following sentence, for example; did the writer strain a little too hard for emphasis?

It is from imagination that have come all the world's great literature, music, architecture, and works of art.

Can you find some less risky way to achieve the emphasis the writer evidently desired?

18e   Movable Modifiers

Many modifiers are movable, enabling you to shift them or other words to the positions you want them to occupy in a sentence. Appositives can sometimes be transposed (see **1q**). You can move participial phrases, if you do so carefully (see **8d**). Absolute phrases (see **1r**), since they function as sentence modifiers, can usually occupy the beginning, the middle, or the end of a sentence, whichever gives you the effect you prefer; for example:

The computer being down, we were forced to do all the layouts by hand.
We were forced, *the computer being down*, to do all the layouts by hand.
We were forced to do all the layouts by hand, *the computer being down*.

But adverbial modifiers are the most movable of all (see **9d**). As you compose, and especially as you revise your drafts, consider the possible placements of any adverbial modifiers you've used. Take advantage of their flexibility in order to exercise maximum control over the rhythms of your sentences and, most important, to get the emphases that will best serve your purpose. Consider the following examples:

We inched our way *slowly and painfully* along the narrow tunnel.

Would the adverbs be more emphatic at the end? Try it:

We inched our way along the narrow tunnel *slowly and painfully*.

A little better. Now try them at the beginning, and maybe leave out the *and* and use punctuation to emphasize the slowness:

Slowly, painfully, we inched our way along the narrow tunnel.

Or take the following, from a student's draft:

> *draft:* When I entered university I naturally expected it to be different from high school, but I wasn't prepared for the impact it would have on the way I lived my day-to-day life.

Clear enough. But the writer decided to try separating the independent clauses and using a conjunctive adverb to get a little more of the emphasis he felt he needed:

> *revised:* When I entered university I naturally expected it to be different from high school. *However*, I wasn't prepared for the impact it would have on the way I lived my day-to-day life.

But that sounded too stiff (as *However* often does at the beginning of a sentence). After some further fiddling with the adverbs, he came up with this:

> *revised:* When I entered university I expected it to be different from high school—naturally. I was not, however, prepared for the impact it would have on the way I lived my day-to-day life.

He decided that putting *naturally* at the end of the first sentence, and setting it off with a dash, not only emphasized his naïveté but also added a desirable touch of self-mockery. And moving *however* a few words into the sentence not only got rid of the stiffness but also, because of the pause forced by its commas, added a useful emphasis to the word *not*, spelled out in full. (For more on *however*, see **33h**.)

Caution: When shifting modifiers about, be careful to avoid creating danglers. See **24**.

18e movable modifiers

18f   Using the Expletive and the Passive Voice for Emphasis

Two of the basic sentence patterns, the *expletive* (**1k**) and the *passive voice* (**1e, 6n**), are in themselves often weak and unemphatic. Keep them to a minimum and your writing will be clearer and more vigorous. Sometimes, however, they are useful in enabling writers to avoid a misleading emphasis or an otherwise awkward or even absurd construction. For example:

> Three desks are in the office.

Using the expletive pattern produces a more natural sentence by delaying the subject and thus getting rid of the unwanted emphasis on it:

> There are three desks in the office.

Here is another possibly awkward sentence rendered more natural by an expletive construction:

> The time to go had come. (It was time to go.)

The passive voice can be similarly useful. The emphasis in the following sentence, for example, sounds awry:

> His victory at the polls rewarded him for his efforts during the campaign.

Switching to the passive voice gets rid of the problem:

> He was rewarded for his efforts during the campaign by his victory at the polls.

The subject of a sentence, especially when it begins the sentence, automatically receives a good deal of emphasis:

> The legal system—judge, jury, lawyers, witnesses, etc.—convicted him of murder.

Not only is the emphasis on the subject undesirable, but even the very presence of the subject is distracting. The passive voice enables one to omit it, clarifying the emphasis:

> He was convicted of murder.

Again:

> Someone has rescued the trapped child.

Who is this mysterious "someone"? In a passive construction the partly misleading word can disappear:

> The trapped child has been rescued.

When for purposes of emphasis and clarity you need to delay or delete the subject of a sentence, an expletive or a passive construction will often enable you to do it. Nevertheless, avoid these patterns when possible. Use them only when you have good reason to.

18g Emphasis by Repetition

You too can do what advertising jingles and slogans do: repeat an important word or idea in order to emphasize it, make it stick in your readers' minds. Careless, unintentional repetition can be wordy and tedious (see **59b**), but intentional, controlled repetition can be highly effective, especially in sentences with balanced or parallel structures:

> I especially admired her hands, her long, elegant, piano-playing hands.
> If you want to understand another country you should travel to that country.
> If you have the strength to face the facts, the facts can sometimes give you strength.
> If it's a fight they want, it's a fight they'll get.
> She liked to read sentimental romances, and she tried to turn her own life into a sentimental romance.
> People and their ideas seldom change; society and its ideas do.
> Many North-American homes are littered with antiques: antique books, antique silver, antique weapons, antique furniture, and antique junk.

Note that the items in a parallel series normally move toward the most important, which then occupies the emphatic final position. But you can also use the natural emphasis of that final position for an ironic or humorous effect, as in the last example above.

18h Emphasis by Stylistic Contrast

A stylistically heightened sentence—for example a periodic sentence (**18b**), a sentence with parallelism or a balanced structure (**27, 18g**), or a richly metaphorical or allusive sentence (**53**)—stands out beside relatively everyday sentences; for that reason such a sentence often appears at the end of a paragraph (see **68**). In the same way, though usually less strikingly, a word or phrase may stand out from its surroundings:

> She attempted to convince me in the most eloquent terms that I should scram.
> The unprecedented increase in the cost of living has rendered everyday life for many citizens a tough fight.
> He was an irrationally scared child.
> It appears that somewhere in the corridors of power lurks a resident *éminence grise*.

(Terms from other languages naturally stand out, but don't make the mistake of using them showily, for many readers are unimpressed by them; use one only when there is no satisfactory English equivalent.) Note that such stylistically contrasting terms often gravitate toward that position of natural emphasis, the end of the sentence.

18i   Emphasis by Syntax

Put important points in independent clauses; put lesser matter in subordinate clauses and phrases. Sometimes it can go either way, depending on what you want to emphasize:

> Accepting the booby prize, he grinned fatuously.
> Grinning fatuously, he accepted the booby prize.

But at other times the choice is determined by the content:

> *emph:* I strolled into the biology laboratory, when my attention was attracted by the pitter-pattering of a little white rat in a cage at the back.
>
> *revised:* When I strolled into the biology laboratory, my attention was attracted by the pitter-pattering of a little white rat in a cage at the back.
>
> *emph:* Choosing my courses carefully, I wanted to get a well-rounded education.
>
> *revised:* Because I wanted to get a well-rounded education, I chose my courses carefully.
>
> *emph:* I had almost reached the top of the ladder when I missed my footing and fell.
>
> *revised:* When I had almost reached the top of the ladder, I missed my footing and fell.
>
> *emph:* She felt perfectly well, although she decided to follow her doctor's advice.
>
> *revised:* Although she felt perfectly well, she decided to follow her doctor's advice.

Granted, the original versions of the last two examples could be appropriate in a particular context; but unless you have a good contextual reason, don't distort apparently logical emphasis by subordinating main ideas.

See also **28** and **12c**.

18j   Emphasis by Punctuation

Obviously an exclamation point (!) denotes emphasis. But using exclamation points is not the only way, and usually not the best way, to achieve emphasis with punctuation. Try to make your sentences appropriately emphatic without resorting to this sometimes lame and artificial device. Arrange your words so that commas and other marks fall where you want a pause for emphasis (see **18e**). Use dashes, colons, and even parentheses judiciously to set off important ideas (see **18a**). Occasionally use a semicolon instead of a comma in order to get a more emphatic pause (but only in a series or between independent clauses). Study Chapter IV carefully, especially the following sections: **32c, 32d, 33b, 33h, 33i, 35a, 36, 38c, 38d, 38e, 39b, 39c, 42c, 43g**, and **44d**.

Note: As much as possible, avoid emphasizing words and sentences with such mechanical devices as underlining and capitalization. See **47s** and **49d**.

Exercise 16-18: Sentence length, variety, and emphasis

Below are five paragraphs from draft versions of student essays. For practice, revise each one to improve the effectiveness of sentence length, variety, and emphasis. Try not to change the basic sense in any important way, but change whatever you need to in order to make the paragraphs effective.

(a) My father drove up to the campsite and chose an empty spot close to the lake, up against the thickly covered mountainside. We had just unpacked our equipment and set up our tent when an elderly man walked up our path. He introduced himself and told us that he was camped farther up the mountain, about a hundred yards away. He told us that only an hour before, as he walked toward his campsite, he saw a huge black bear running away from it. He said he then drew closer and saw that his tent was knocked down and his food scattered all over the ground. He suggested that we might want to move our camp to a safer place, not so close to this bear's haunts.

(b) The sky promised hot and sunny weather as we quickly finished closing side-pockets and adjusting straps on our packs in preparation for our hike up Black Tusk, which is in Garibaldi Park, a hike which, because it was to be on a trail I had never been on before, I had been looking forward to with great enthusiasm, which is what I felt now as we set off in the early morning light on the first leg of the journey which would take us to the top in a few hours.

(c) The way time passes can be odd. The mind's sense of time can be changed. I remember an experience which will illustrate this. It happened when I was nine. I rode my bike in front of a car and got hit. I don't remember much about this experience. However, a few details do come to mind. These include the way the car's brakes sounded suddenly from my right. I never even saw the car that hit me. And I remember flying through the air. It was a peculiar feeling. The ground seemed to come up slowly as I floated along. Time seemed almost to have stopped. But then I hit the ground. And then time speeded up. A neighbour ran up and asked if I was all right. My parents pulled our car up. They carefully put me in it. And all of a sudden I was at the hospital, it seemed. It all must have taken twenty or thirty minutes. To me it seemed that only a minute or two had passed since I had hit the ground.

(d) It's not so difficult to repot a houseplant, although many plant-owners procrastinate about doing this because they think it's too messy and time-consuming, when actually repotting takes very little time and effort if you follow a simple set of instructions such as I'm about to give you, and you'll find that when you've done the repotting both you and your plant will benefit from the process because the plant will then be able to receive fresh minerals and oxygen from the new soil which will make it grow into a healthier plant that will give you increased pleasure and enjoyment.

(e) I believe that we should all do volunteer work in our communities. I know that there isn't always a lot of extra time available. But we should make the extra time. Instead of sitting down to watch television, we should do something useful. We could spend two hours with a handicapped child. We could take a fatherless young boy to a ball-game. We can help even if we can't find time to leave home. We can volunteer our services from inside our homes. For example we can make telephone calls and type letters. Or we can simply stuff envelopes and put stamps on them. There are hundreds of ways we can volunteer our services to the community. Let's share some happiness with someone else. Let's volunteer our services today.

19   Analyzing Sentences

One way to acquire greater confidence and facility in writing effectively—as well as to increase your ability both to avoid committing errors and to catch those committed inadvertently—is to analyze your own and others' sentences. The more thoroughly you understand how sentences work, the better able you will be to write sentences that are both effective and correct.

It should be possible to see the grammatical links that tie together all the parts of a sentence (words, phrases, clauses) into a coherent and unified pattern. You should be able to account for each word: no essential element should be missing, nothing should be left over, and the grammatical relations among all the parts should be clear. If these conditions are not met, the sentence in question is likely to be incorrect or in some way misleading or ambiguous. If the words, phrases, and clauses fit the roles they are being asked to play, the sentence should be all right.

The first step in analyzing a sentence is to establish the basic or elemental structure: the *subject*, the *finite verb*, and the *object* or *complement*, if any. (If the sentence is other than a simple sentence, of course there will be more than one set of these essential parts.) Then proceed to the modifiers of these elements, and then to modifiers of modifiers. Finally, if any of the modifiers are themselves phrases or clauses, break them down as well.

19a   The Chart Method

Here is a convenient arrangement for analyzing the structure of relatively uncomplicated sentences:

The angry coach severely punished the wayward goalie.

Subject	Finite Verb	Object or Complement	Adjectival Modifier	Adverbial Modifier
coach	punished	goalie (direct object of verb *punished*)	The (modifies *coach*) angry (modifies *coach*) the (modifies *goalie*) wayward (modifies *goalie*)	severely (modifies verb *punished*: "how?")

This most beautiful summer is now almost gone.

Subject	Finite Verb	Object or Complement	Adjectival Modifier	Adverbial Modifier
summer	is (linking verb)	gone (predicate adjective as complement)	this (demonstrative adj. modifies *summer*) beautiful (adj. modifies *summer*)	most (modifies adj. *beautiful*: "to what degree?") now (modifies verb *is*: "when?") almost (modifies adj. *gone*: "to what degree?")

The very befuddled Roger realized that driving a car was not easy.

Subject	Finite Verb	Object or Complement	Adjectival Modifier	Adverbial Modifier	Other
Roger	realized	that . . . easy (noun clause as direct obj.)	The (modifies *Roger*) befuddled (modifies *Roger*)	very (modifies adj. *befuddled*)	
driving (gerund)	was (linking verb)	easy (predicate adj. as complement) a car (obj. of gerund *driving*)		not (modifies adj. *easy*)	that (in the noun clause, a subordinating conjunction)

In the last example, the items below the dotted line belong to the subordinate clause in this complex sentence.

19b　The Vertical Method

For more complicated sentences, you may find that a different scheme of analysis is more convenient, one such as the following, for example, where the sentence is written out vertically:

When the canoe trip ended, Philip finally realized that the end of his happy summer was almost upon him.

		word	part	function
complex sentence	ind. cl. → sub. cl. (adv.)	When	conj.	subordinating / intro. sub. cl.
		the	art.	mod. *trip*
		canoe	adj.	mod. *trip*
		trip	noun	subj. of ended
		ended	verb	finite v. of cl. / intrans.
		Philip	noun (proper)	subj. of ind. cl.
		finally	adv.	mod. *realized*
		realized	verb	finite v. of cl. / trans.
	sub. cl. (n.) dir. obj. of verb	that	conj.	subordinating / intro. noun cl.
		the	art.	mod. *end*
		end	noun	subj. of *was*
		of	prep.	mod. *summer* — prep. phrase, adj., mod. *end*
		his	adj. (pron.)	mod. *summer*
		happy	adj.	mod. *summer*
		summer	noun	obj. of prep.
		was	verb (linking)	finite v. of clause
		almost	adv.	mod. adj. phr. *upon him*
		upon	prep.	obj. of prep — prep. phr. / adj., compl. after linking verb
		him	pron.	

As you can see, this method virtually forces you to account for the grammatical function of every word in the sentence.

19c　The Diagramming Method

Another way to analyze sentences is to use the old but still serviceable diagramming method. This method does have its drawbacks: there is no way to distinguish between adjective and adverb, for example, unless you label each one; and it also requires learning a separate and sometimes complicated system. Nevertheless, it can be usefully graphic in revealing the workings of a sentence. Here are sample diagrams of the most common kinds of sentences:

1. Simple Sentences

Subject | verb   Birds | chirp

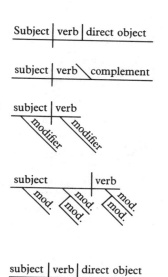

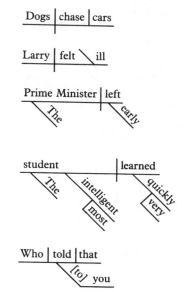

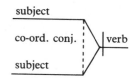

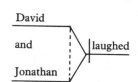

Compound Subject:

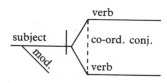

Compound Verb:

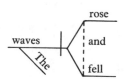

Compound Object:

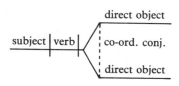

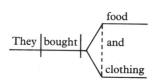

Prepositional Phrases:

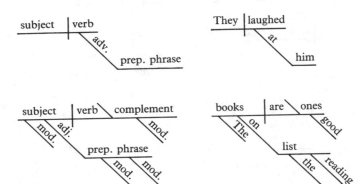

Participial Phrase:

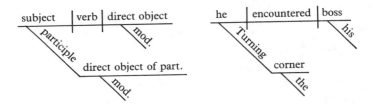

Gerund Phrase as Subject:

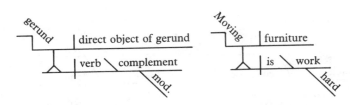

Infinitive Phrase as Noun:

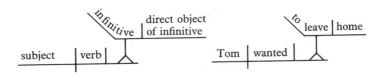

Infinitive Phrase as Adjective:

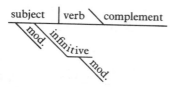

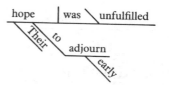

Infinitive Phrase as Adverb:

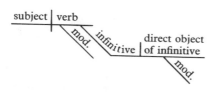

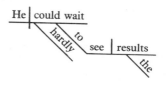

19c diagramming method

2. Complex Sentences

Noun Clause as Direct Object:

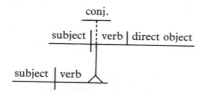

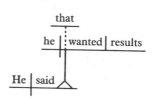

Noun Clause as Object of Preposition:

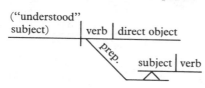

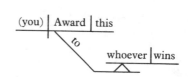

Relative Clause Modifying the Subject:

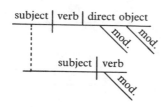

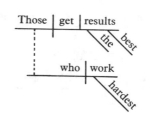

19c diagramming method

Relative Clause Modifying a Direct Object:

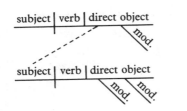

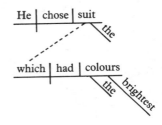

Relative Clause Modifying a Complement:

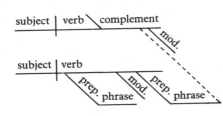

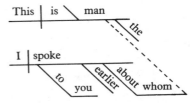

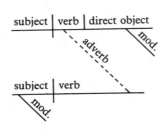

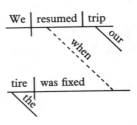

Adverbial Clause:

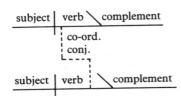

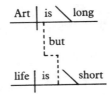

3. Compound Sentences

4. Compound-complex sentences are diagrammed following similar patterns.

Grammatical analysis, by whatever method, is not an end in itself. Its purpose is to give you insight into the accepted structures of the basic unit of communication, the sentence, and to enable you to construct sound sentences and to discover and eliminate errors in your writing. As you become more familiar with the analytic process and with the demands of correct sentence structure, you should find the process becoming automatic and the elimination of errors easier.

Exercise 19: Analyzing sentences

Try analyzing the following sentences by each of the three methods suggested above. Doing so should give you a sense of the advantages and disadvantages of each; then you can use or adapt the one you prefer, or use different methods for different kinds of sentences. You may even want to invent your own method.

1. Police rushed to the scene of the accident.
2. A chinook is a warm wind blowing eastward off the Rocky Mountains.
3. Many potentially good films are spoiled by sensationalism.
4. Both the beaver and the maple leaf are Canadian emblems.
5. Although he was discouraged, Joel persevered, and after a few more tries he succeeded in clearing the two-metre bar.

20-31 **Common Sentence Errors and Weaknesses**

20-22 **Fragments, Comma Splices, and Run-on (Fused) Sentences**

The three most serious sentence errors are the *fragment*, the *comma splice*, and the *run-on* sentence. Many readers consider the members of this unholy trinity to be signs of illiteracy; if you care about the quality of your writing, you must assiduously avoid them.

20 **Fragment**
frag

A **fragment** is a group of words that is not an acceptable sentence, either major or minor, but that is punctuated as if it were a sentence (that is, started with a capital letter and ended with a period). The fragment is discussed along with the minor sentence, which it sometimes resembles: see **1x** and **1y**. See also **frag** in Chapter XI.

21 Comma Splice

cs

A **comma splice** is the joining of two independent clauses with only a comma. Although the error stems from a failure to understand sentence structure, it is nevertheless discussed under *punctuation*, since it requires attention to punctuation marks: see **33e-g**. See also **cs** in Chapter XI.

22 Run-on (Fused) Sentence

run-on

A **run-on** sentence, sometimes called a *fused* sentence, is in fact not a single sentence but *two* sentences that have been run together with neither a period to mark the end of the first nor a capital letter to mark the beginning of the second. It is so bizarre a gaffe that it is usually attributed to extreme carelessness or typographical haste—or both. But such attribution may be too generous, for the error sometimes occurs, like the comma splice, as the result of a genuine failure to understand how sentences work. And since a run-on sentence occurs with the same kind of sentence structure as does the comma splice, and like it requires some attention to punctuation, it is discussed alongside the other error: see **33j**. See also **run-on** in Chapter XI.

Other sentence errors, less serious but nonetheless worth avoiding, are analyzed and illustrated in the sections that follow. For further discussion of these errors, see the relevant entries in Chapter XI.

23 Misplaced Modifiers

23a Movability and Poor Placement

mm

As already noted, much of the meaning in English sentences is conveyed by the position of words in relation to each other (see the introduction to Chapter II). And though there are some standard or conventional arrangements for the parts of a sentence, a good deal of flexibility is possible (see **1s, 1t, 8d, 11b,** and **15**). Adverbial modifiers are especially movable (see **9d**). Because of this flexibility, writers sometimes unthinkingly put a modifier where it conveys an unintended or ambiguous meaning, or where it is linked by juxtaposition to a word it can't logically modify. Note the changes in meaning that result from the different placement of the little word *only* in the following sentences:

Only his son works in Halifax. (No other members of his family work there.)
His only son works in Halifax. (He has no other sons.)
His son only works in Halifax. (He does not live in Halifax, but commutes.)
His son works only in Halifax. (He works in no other place.)

In order to say precisely what you mean, then, you have to be careful in placing your modifiers—especially adverbs. The following sentence demonstrates how misplacement can result in absurdity:

> *mm:* He watched the sun set at the beach.

Obviously the sun does not set at the beach. In this sentence, the adverbial phrase *at the beach* can logically modify the finite verb *watched* but not the finite verb *set*. The error can be corrected by changing the clause *the sun set* to a noun—*the sunset*—or by moving the phrase *at the beach* to the beginning of the sentence, nearer the verb it modifies and away from the verb it cannot logically modify:

> *clear:* He watched the sunset at the beach.
> *clear:* At the beach he watched the sun set.

Here then is one instance where an adverbial modifier can occupy only one position. Here is another example:

> *mm:* A man soon learns not to scatter his clothes about after he is married in the bathroom.

The distortion in meaning here is obvious: the adverbial prepositional phrase *in the bathroom* has been so placed that it seems to modify the finite verb *is married* instead of the infinitive *to scatter*. Revising the sentence makes the intended meaning come through clearly:

> *clear:* After he is married, a man soon learns not to scatter his clothes about in the bathroom.

It is best to keep modifiers and the words they modify as close together as possible. Note that in this example the adverbial clause *after he is married* could also be placed—between commas—following *learns*, still leaving the adverbial phrase and the infinitive it modifies next to each other. Here is another example of carelessly placed adverbial modifiers causing ambiguity and conveying an unintended meaning:

> *mm:* We visited the cottage *in Stratford* where Will Shakespeare courted Anne Hathaway *last summer*.

Does the writer mean to convey that Will courted Anne last summer? Obviously not—yet that is what the sentence says. Further, are we meant to think of Stratford or of the cottage as the place where the courtship took place? As the sentence stands the point is ambiguous.

Revised, the sentence states precisely what the writer intended:

> *clear:* Last summer in Stratford we visited the cottage where Will Shakespeare courted Anne Hathaway.

Here is an example of an adjective awkwardly out of place:

> *mm:* Love is a *difficult* emotion to express in words.
> *clear:* Love is an emotion (that is) difficult to express.

and an example of a misplaced relative clause:

> *mm:* In 1683, the first St. Cecilia's Day festival was held in London, which is a festival of the performing arts.

London is a festival? Perhaps—especially to those trying to lure tourists. But what the writer of this sentence meant was something else:

> *clear:* In 1683, the first St. Cecilia's Day festival, (which is) a festival of the performing arts, was held in London.

23b   Only, almost, etc.

Be particularly careful with such adverbs as *only, almost, just, merely,* and *even*. Colloquially we toss these around like tiddlywinks, but in formal writing we should put them where they clearly mean what we want them to:

> *mm:* Hardy *only* wrote novels as a sideline; his main interest was poetry.
> *clear:* Hardy wrote novels *only* as a sideline; his main interest was poetry.
> *mm:* The students *almost* washed thirty cars last Saturday.
> *clear:* The students washed *almost* thirty cars last Saturday.

23c   Squinting Modifiers

One particular kind of misplaced modifier is what is called a **squinting modifier**. This error occurs when a word or phrase occupies a position between two elements either of which it could modify—but the reader cannot be sure which one was intended. That is, a modifier "squints" so that one cannot tell which way it is looking, resulting in awkward ambiguity.

> *squinting:* It was so hot *for a week* we did hardly any work at all.

Which clause does the adverbial phrase modify? Although the meaning would be about the same either way, no reader should be subjected to such ambiguity. Sometimes one is tempted to mend the flaw by putting a comma before or after the squinting modifier, but that is like putting a band-aid on a serious wound: very seldom can a comma be effective; in fact, it usually makes the problem worse because it makes the sentence sound awkward. It is much better to revise in some other way. Here, simply inserting a *that* removes the ambiguity at once:

> *clear:* It was so hot that for a week we did hardly any work at all.
> *clear:* It was so hot for a week that we did hardly any work at all.

Part of the reason for the problem, of course, is the absence of a speaking *voice* which could impart clarifying emphasis to such a sentence. Written language requires the removal or avoidance of ambiguity that would likely not appear if such a sentence were spoken aloud. A writer must substitute words or structures for the missing vocal emphasis. Another example:

> *squinting:* My father advised me *now and then* to invest in stocks.

With this kind of squinting modifier, rearrangement is necessary:

> *clear:* My father now and then advised me to invest in stocks.
> *clear:* My father advised me to invest now and then in stocks.

Even a modifier at the end of a sentence can in effect "squint," be ambiguous. When rearrangement does not work, substantial revision will be necessary:

> *ambiguous:* He was upset when she left for more reasons than one.
> *clear:* He was upset for more reasons than one when she left.
> *clear:* He had more than one reason to be upset when she left.
> *clear:* He was upset because she had more than one reason for leaving.

Note: An awkwardly split infinitive is also caused by a kind of misplaced modifier; see **10b**.

Exercise 23: Correcting misplaced modifiers

Revise the following sentences to eliminate awkwardness resulting from misplaced modifiers.

1. His outbursts were only viewed as signs of bad temper.
2. I vowed to never discriminate against children when I became an adult.
3. He decided that on this day he would skip dinner entirely in the morning.
4. I could see my grandfather coming through the window.
5. He was naturally upset by her remark.
6. They discussed rebuilding the hotel for three days but decided against it.
7. Another reason why David lives a barren emotional and social life more pertinent to the theme of this essay is his thwarted love for Judith.
8. A piano stands in the centre of the stage with its outline only visible to the audience in the darkness.
9. Farmer Jones only plowed three acres yesterday.
10. It merely seemed a few days before they were back again.

24 Dangling Modifiers
dm

A **dangling modifier** is one that has no logical word in the rest of the sentence to hook on to, but only an implied or obviously incorrect one (it is similar to a pronoun without an antecedent); it is therefore said to "dangle," to be left hanging there, grammatically unattached. Most dangling modifiers are verbal phrases; be particularly careful with them when you write.

24a Dangling Participial Phrases (*see* 10c)

> *dm:* *Striding* aggressively into the room, my eyes fell upon the figure cowering in the corner.

The participial phrase *striding aggressively into the room* is adjectival, and therefore it wants a noun to modify; it usually picks the subject of the adjacent clause, here *eyes*. One's eyes may be said, figuratively, to "fall" on something, but they can scarcely be said to "stride." If one were to say, "Striding aggressively into the room, my eyes tripped over the edge of the carpet," the absurdity would be immediately obvious. To avoid the unintentionally humorous dangler, simply change the participial phrase to a subordinate clause:

> *revised:* *As I strode aggressively into the room*, my eyes fell upon the figure cowering in the corner.

Or, if you wish to keep the effect of the opening participial phrase, merely rework the following clause so that its subject is the logical word to be modified:

> *revised:* *Striding* aggressively into the room, *I* at once directed my gaze toward the figure cowering in the corner.

Here is another example:

> *dm:* *Living* in a small town, there wasn't much to do for entertainment.

The participle *living*, along with the rest of its phrase, is left dangling because it has no noun to modify; "there" is an expletive, not a real subject. Something must be provided for the participle and its phrase to modify, in a logical way, or the sentence must be revised in some other way.

> *revised:* *Living* in a small town, *we* had little to do for entertainment.
> *revised:* Since we lived in a small town, there wasn't much to do for entertainment.

The first correction provides a true subject, *we*, for the participle to modify. The second correction changes the participial phrase to a subordinate clause with its own subject. Another example; the passive voice got this writer into trouble (see **6n**):

> *dm:*   *Looking* up to the open sky, not a cloud could be seen.
> *revised:*   *Looking* up to the open sky, *I* could not see a cloud.
> *revised:*   There was not a cloud to be seen in the open sky.

24b   Dangling Gerund Phrases (see 10d)

> *dm:*   After *being* informed of the correct procedure, our attention was directed to the next steps.

The verbal phrase has no proper subject to modify, since obviously it is not "our attention" that was "informed." Again the lapse into the passive voice is at least partly to blame.

> *revised:*   After *being* informed of the correct procedure, *we* were directed to attend to the next steps.

But this is still passive and awkward. Such a sentence can be better revised this way:

> *revised:*   After informing us of the correct procedure, the instructor directed our attention to the next steps.

24c   Dangling Infinitive Phrases (*see* 10a)

> *dm:*   *To follow* Freud's procedure, the speaker's thoughts must be fully known.

Passive voice is again the culprit, depriving the infinitive of a logical word to modify.

> *revised:*   *To follow* Freud's procedure, *one* most know the speaker's thoughts fully.

Another example:

> *dm:*   *To make* the mayor's plan work, it requires the people's cooperation.

The error in this example is more complicated, since the pronoun *it*, to which the infinitive phrase seems to be attached, has no antecedent (see **5d**). The infinitive phrase can be treated as a noun phrase, or the sentence can be revised in some other way:

> *revised:*   To make the mayor's plan work will require the people's cooperation.
> *revised:*   If the mayor's plan is to work, the people will have to cooperate.

24d Dangling Elliptical Clauses

An **elliptical clause** is an adverbial clause that has been abridged so that its subject and verb are only "understood" or implied rather than stated; the subject of the independent clause then automatically serves also as the subject of the subordinate clause. If the implied subject is different from the subject of the independent clause, the subordinate element will dangle, sometimes ludicrously:

> *dm:* Once in the army, a person's life is totally regimented.

It is not *a person's life* that is in the army, but a person himself. One can correct such a sentence by supplying a subject for the elliptical clause and making the subject of the independent clause agree logically with it:

> *revised:* Once *one* is in the army, *one* finds that his life is totally regimented.
>
> *revised:* Once *you* are in the army, *your life* is totally regimented.

or by retaining the elliptical clause and making the subject of the independent clause conform to it:

> *revised:* Once in the army, a *person* finds that his life is totally regimented.

Another example:

> *dm:* When well oiled, put the parts of the rifle back together.

Here the understood subject is *the parts*, but the understood subject of the independent clause of this imperative sentence is *you*. Supply a subject for the elliptical clause and it will no longer dangle:

> *revised:* When the parts of the rifle are well oiled, put them back together.

24e Dangling Prepositional Phrases and Appositives (see 11 and 1q)

Prepositional phrases and appositives can also dangle. For example:

> *dm:* Like a child in a toy-shop, *it* is all she can bear not to touch everything.
>
> *revised:* Like a child in a toy-shop, she can hardly bear not to touch everything.

The dangerous indefinite *it* (see **5e**) is again the troublemaker.

> *dm:* A superb racing car, the engine of a Ferrari is a masterpiece of engineering.

"A superb racing car" seems to be in apposition with "engine"; but since it is illogical to equate an engine with an entire car, revision is necessary:

revised: A superb racing car, a Ferrari has an engine that is a masterpiece of engineering.

Note that one could not say "a Ferrari's engine," since the possessive form is adjectival and cannot serve as a noun to be modified (see **2b** and **3a**).

Exercise 24: Correcting dangling modifiers

Revise the following sentences to eliminate dangling modifiers.

1. Feeling carefree and nonchalant, all my problems were forgotten.
2. By using Huck as the narrator we are drawn into his centre of consciousness.
3. In order to ski one must be outdoors, thereby being good for physical and mental health.
4. Looked at in this light, one has to find Hamlet very much like other people.
5. Réamur introduced the idea of testing small sample rods and then studying their structure when fractured.
6. Being the youngest sibling in my family, it is easier for me to understand children.
7. When not going to school or working, my hobbies range from athletics to automobiles.
8. By using this style it added more flair to the story.
9. The colonel began to send groups of reinforcements to the weakened position only to be ambushed along the jungle trails.
10. After seeing a few more trials, another case attracted my attention.

▆ 25 ▆ Mixed Constructions
mix

A writer may occasionally begin a sentence with one construction and then absent-mindedly shift to a different construction. It is at least as awkward as changing horses in midstream. Such a lapse can easily occur in the heat of composition and rapid thought—though even then it argues a weak sentence sense and a failure to think clearly. If you find yourself apt to commit mixed constructions, some practice with sentence analysis may help (see **19**).

mix: Physical education can be enjoyable for both the noncompetitive student as well as the competitive one.

In the latter part of this sentence the writer set up a *both . . . and* pattern, but then shifted to *as well as* instead of following through with the *and*. Remedy: change *as well as* to *and*, or omit the *both*.

mix: Since Spain was a devout Catholic country, therefore most of its art was on religious themes.

This writer began with a subordinating *since*, but then used *therefore* to introduce the second clause, which would be correct only if the first clause had been independent. Remedy: drop either the *since* or the *therefore* (if you drop *since*, the comma must become a semicolon; see **33e**).

Exercise 25: Correcting mixed constructions

Revise the following sentences to eliminate mixed constructions.

1. Piranesi worked on a colossal scale, putting more emphasis on density and texture rather than on outline.
2. The reason for the drop in production was due to labour troubles.
3. It wasn't until five years later before he returned to the place.
4. I found that the introductory part of the book to be very helpful.
5. The new styles were popular with both men and women alike.
6. Since, for most of us, our earliest recollections are mere fragments of things that made up our childhoods, we therefore must rely on the objects or ideas around us to trigger the past.
7. Just because people like to watch television doesn't mean our society is in a state of decay.

---

26 Point of View—Shift in Perspective
pv shift

Be consistent in your point of view within a sentence—and usually from one sentence to the next, as well. Avoid awkward or illogical shifts in the tense, mood, or voice of verbs, and in the person and number of pronouns.

26a Shift in Tense (see **6g** and **6h**)

> *pv:* The professor *told* us what he expected of us and then he *leans* against the desk and *smirks*.

Change *leans* to *leaned*, and *smirks* to *smirked*, past tenses like *told*.

26b Shift in Mood (see **6j**, **6k**, and **6-l**)

> *pv:* If it *were* Sunday and I *was* through with my homework, I would go skiing with you.

The awkward shift from subjunctive to indicative can be corrected by changing *was* to *were*.

> *pv:* First *put* tab A in slot B; next *you will put* tab C in slot D.

Omit the *you will* to correct the shift from imperative to indicative.

26c   Shift in Voice (see 6m and 6n)

pv: Readers should not have to read a second time before some sense can be made of the passage.

pv: We drove thirty miles to the end of the road, after which five more miles were covered on foot.

Such awkward shifts from active to passive could also be marked **pas** (see **6n**). (Note that such shifts also cause an awkward shift of subject from one clause to the next.) These wobbly sentences can easily be restored to health and vigour by retaining the active voice:

revised: Readers should not have to read a passage a second time before they can make sense of it.

revised: We drove thirty miles to the end of the road and then covered another five miles on foot.

26d   Shift in Person of Pronoun (see 3a and 3b)

pv: If *one* wants to learn about trees, *you* should study forestry.

The shift from third to second person can be corrected by changing *you* to *one* or *he*. (This and the following pronoun errors could also be marked **agr**: see **4**.)

26e   Shift in Number of Pronoun (see 3a)

pv: If the committee wants *its* recommendations followed, *they* should have written *their* report more carefully.

The committee changed from a collective unit (*it*) to a collection of individuals (*they, their*); the committee should have been either singular or plural throughout. See also collective nouns, **7f**.

27   Faulty Parallelism
fp, //

Parallelism is one of the strongest stylistic techniques available to you. Not only does it make for vigorous, balanced, and rhythmical sentences, but it can also help develop and help tie together paragraphs (see **69a**). Like any other good thing, parallelism can be overdone, but a more common weakness is an insufficient use of it. Of course, if you're writing an especially sober piece, like a letter of condolence, you won't want to use lively devices like parallelism and metaphor. But in most writing a good dose of parallel structure is healthful. Build parallel elements into your sentences, and now and then build two or three successive sentences so that they are parallel with each other.

27 faulty parallelism

Here for example is a sentence from a student's paper on computer crime; note how parallelism (along with alliteration) strengthens the first part of it, thereby helping to set up the last part:

> Although one can distinguish the malicious from the mischievous or the harmless hacker from the more dangerous computer criminal, security officials take a dim view of anyone who romps through company files.

But you need to be careful, for it is all too easy to slip, to set up a parallel and then muff it. Study the following examples carefully. (See also **12a** and **12b**.)

27a   With Co-ordinate Elements

Co-ordinate elements in a sentence should have the same grammatical form. If they differ from each other grammatically, the sentence will lack parallelism and therefore be awkward at best.

> *fp:*   Mario is wealthy, handsome, and a bachelor.

Here the three elements following the verb *is* are co-ordinate in that they constitute a series of complements. But the first two are predicate adjectives (*wealthy, handsome*) and the third a predicate noun (*bachelor*). Here revision is easy: simply change the noun to an equivalent adjective:

> *revised:*   Mario is wealthy, handsome, and unmarried.

Sometimes the problem is more complicated:

> *fp:*   Trolls were very large, ugly, hoarded treasure, killed for pleasure, and ate raw flesh.

Again a series of attributes follows a linking verb, *were*. But after the first two, which are adjectives (*large, ugly*), the writer switched to verb phrases (*hoarded . . . killed . . . ate*). One cannot logically say "Trolls were hoarded treasure" or "Trolls were ate raw flesh," and note that "Trolls were killed for pleasure" completely changes the meaning. The writer no doubt intended to co-ordinate the verbs *hoarded, killed,* and *ate* with the verb *were*, but the second adjective, *ugly*, occurring as it does before those verbs, leads to a breakdown of parallel structure and creates confusion. Here is a possible correction:

> *revised:*   Trolls were large and ugly; they hoarded treasure, killed for pleasure, and ate raw flesh.

The co-ordinate parts of compound subjects, verbs, objects, and modifiers—whether or not these parts are joined by co-ordinating conjunctions—should also be parallel in form.

> *fp:*   Eating huge meals, too many sweets, and snacking beween meals can lead to obesity.

This sentence can be corrected either by making all three parts of the subject into gerunds:

> *revised:* Eating large meals, eating too many sweets, and snacking between meals can lead to obesity.

or by using only the first gerund and following it with three parallel objects:

> *revised:* Eating large meals, too many sweets, and between-meal snacks can lead to obesity.

Here is another example:

> *fp:* He described the computer in terms suggesting a deep affection for it and that also demonstrated a thoroughgoing knowledge of it.

Here the compound adjectival modifier has a participial phrase (*suggesting* . . .) for its first part and a relative clause (*that demonstrated* . . .) for its second part. The best way to revise it would be to change the first part to a relative clause (*that suggested* . . .) to match the second part.

It is particularly easy for a careless writer to omit a second *that*:

> *fp:* Rachel of course has to tell Nick *that* her mother will be worrying about her and therefore she should get home as soon as possible.

Another *that* is needed before *therefore*. Here is another example:

> *fp:* Marvin was convinced *that* the argument was unsound and he could profitably spend some time analyzing it.

A second *that*, before *he*, corrects the error. In effect this error is not only a breakdown in parallelism but also an implied shift in point of view (see the preceding section); it could be marked **pv** as well as **fp**; it could also be marked **ambig**. In the second sentence, for example, the lack of a second *that* invites or at least allows the reader to take "he could profitably spend some time analyzing it" as an independent clause—expressing the writer's own opinion about what Marvin should do—rather than what the writer intended, a second subordinate clause expressing a part of Marvin's opinion. The same point applies to the sentence about Rachel. (See also **pv** in Chapter XI.)

27b With Correlative Conjunctions

One must be especially careful when using correlative conjunctions (see **12b**):

> *fp:* Whether for teaching a child the alphabet or in educating an adult about the latest political development, television is the best device we have.

The constructions following the *whether* and the *or* should be parallel; change the *in* to *for*.

27b correlatives

27c parallelism in series

The correlative pair *not only . . . but also* can be particularly troublesome:

> *fp:* She not only corrected my grammar but also my spelling.

Such an error can be corrected either by repeating the verb *corrected* (or by adding some other appropriate verb, such as *criticized* or *repaired*) after *but also*:

> *revised:* She not only corrected my grammar but also corrected my spelling.

or by moving *corrected* so that it occurs before *not only* rather than after it:

> *revised:* She corrected not only my grammar but also my spelling.

Either method makes what follows the *not only* parallel in form to what follows the *but also*. Obviously the second version is more economical.

27c With a Series

In any series of three or more parallel elements, make sure that little beginning words like prepositions, pronouns, and signs of the infinitive (*to*) precede either the first element alone, or each of the elements, and that necessary articles aren't omitted:

> *fp:* The car was equipped with a CB radio, stereo tape deck, an AM-FM receiver, and a miniature television receiver.

The missing *a* before the second item breaks the parallelism.

> *fp:* He exhorted his followers to obey the rules, to think positively, and ignore criticism.

Since the *to* occurs in the first two phrases, it must either lead off the third as well or be omitted from the second. If necessary, you can test such sentences by arranging the series in a list after the word which introduces it.

The car was equipped with	a CB radio,
	stereo tape deck,
	an AF-FM receiver, and
	a miniature television receiver.
He exhorted his followers	to obey the rules,
	to think positively, and
	ignore criticism.
He exhorted his followers to	obey the rules,
	to think positively, and
	ignore criticism.

The slips in parallelism become glaringly obvious.

Exercise 27: Correcting faulty parallelism

Revise the following sentences in order to repair faulty parallelism.

1. Disagreements were not only apparent between clergy and scientists, but between various elements of the church as well.
2. People adopt roles in life which they are most comfortable with, or will benefit them the most.
3. Not only was our black Snowball like a baby but also very much like a dog.
4. It is necessary that we tighten our belts and to try to control our spending.
5. Part of the scene is not only concerned with the present situation but also prepares the way for the important scene that follows.
6. We are told that we should eat more protein, less fat, and exercise regularly.
7. The elderly are an important part of our society, and our own lives.
8. About 1750, it became clear to the French that the arrival of the few English traders was only the beginning and soon masses of settlers would follow and destroy the French empire in North America.
9. When she grows up she wants to be a teacher, a homeowner, and travel.
10. A pet not only gives an elderly person something to care for, but also a sense of usefulness.
11. Perhaps even the daily newspaper may someday be delivered by co-axial cable rather than the paper-boy.
12. Soldiers have to cope with obsolete or too few pieces of new equipment.
13. The speaker narrates the poem as if he has walked along the streets at night more than once before and that he is acquainted with what goes on around him during his walks.
14. There are many kinds of smiles. For example there are smiles of pleasure, compassion, humour, contempt, winning, competitive, shared secrets, idiotic grins, leers, gloating, sneers, recognition, friendliness, greeting, social, professional, gratification, spontaneous, contagious, deliberate, suppressed, courtesy, anger, humility, rebellion, embarrassment, and surprise.
15. Everything the fortuneteller told me was happy and exciting: I would marry a rich man, have two children, one who will become a famous hockey player, and the other will be a doctor, travel all over the world, and live until I'm ninety-five, healthy as a baby.

28 faulty co-ordination

---

28 Faulty Co-ordination: Logic, Emphasis, and Unity
fc log emph u sub

If unrelated or unequal elements—usually clauses—are presented as co-ordinate, the result is faulty **co-ordination**. Similarly, if two elements are joined by an inappropriate co-ordinating conjunction, the result is again faulty co-ordination—sometimes referred to as "loose" co-ordination. Here is an example of the first kind:

fc: Watches are usually water-resistant *and* some models have the ability to glow in the dark.

There is no logical connection between the two clauses—other than that they both say something about watches. The ideas would be better expressed in two separate sentences. Note also that co-ordinating two such clauses produces a sentence with little or no **unity**. Here is another example of faulty co-ordination—from a description of a particular jar—in which the resultant lack of unity is even more glaring:

> *fc:* One might find this kind of jar in a small junk shop *and* it can be used for anything from cotton balls to rings and things, or just to stand as a decoration.

Since there is no logical connection between the jar's location and its possible uses, the suggestion about the junk shop should either be in another sentence or be subordinated.

The second kind of faulty co-ordination is a more common weakness:

> *fc:* Nationalism can affect the relations between nations by creating a distrustful atmosphere *and* an ambassador's innocent remark can be turned into an insult by a suspicious listener.

The *and* joining these two clauses misrepresents the relation between them; the second clause is not an additional fact, as the *and* implies, but rather an example or result of the fact stated in the first clause. Simply joining the two clauses with a semicolon would be preferable. Note that this compound sentence could also be changed to a complex one by changing the first independent clause to a **subordinate** clause:

> *revised:* Because nationalism can affect the relations between nations by creating a distrustful atmosphere, an ambassador's innocent remark can be turned into an insult by a suspicious listener.

Such a version, however, probably does not reflect the **emphasis** the writer intended; if anything, the first clause appears more important than the second (see **18i**). Here is a clearer example, from a student's description of how a particular scene in *Hamlet* should be staged:

> *fc:* In this scene Rosencrantz is the main speaker of the two courtiers; therefore he should stand closer to Hamlet.

This sentence could be marked **sub** or **emph** as well as **fc**, indicating that its logical emphasis would be more accurately expressed by subordinating one of the independent clauses. Since the positioning of the characters is clearly the main point, that idea should be expressed in an independent clause, the rest in a subordinate clause:

> *revised:* Because in this scene Rosencrantz is the main speaker of the two courtiers, he should stand closer to Hamlet.

Granted that the *therefore* in the original sentence does express this relation, the sentence was nonetheless a compound one, tacitly equating the two clauses. Emphasis and clarity are much better served by ac-knowledging, by means of the syntax, the logically subordinate nature of the first clause. The original sentence, then, could also have been marked **log**, for **logic**, though that would not have been a very precise indication of its weakness. Sometimes, however, **fc** and **log** are about equally applicable to an offending sentence. Consider this example:

> *fc, log:* Alliteration is a very effective poetic device when used sparingly but appropriately.

The meaning expressed by the conjunction *but* in this sentence is entirely illogical, for it implies an opposition; it "says" that if one uses alliteration sparingly, one is then very likely to use it inappropriately—but just the opposite is more likely true: a poet who uses it sparingly will also probably be careful to use it appropriately. In this instance the writer should have used a simple and neutral *and* for a co-ordinating conjunction.

A particularly weak form of loose co-ordination overlaps with the "this" disease (see **5c**, and Chapter XI under **ref**):

> *fc:* The poem's tone is light and cheery, *and this* is reinforced by the mainly one-syllable words and the regular rhythm and rhyme.

Whenever you find such an *and this* in your draft, try to revise it out, for not only is the co-ordination weak, but the demonstrative pronoun *this* is weak as well, since it has no antecedent.

> *revised:* The poem's light and cheery tone is reinforced by the mainly one-syllable words and the regular rhythm and rhyme.

Another kind of faulty co-ordination is that which links several short independent clauses with co-ordinating conjunctions, mostly *and*'s; the result is a loose string of seemingly unrelated parts. Such sentences tend to ramble on and on, emphasizing nothing:

> *rambling:* The ferry rates were increased and the bigger commercial ve-hicles had to pay more to use the ferry service and so the cost of transporting goods rose and the consumers who bought those goods had to pay more for them but they had to pay higher fares on the ferries as well and naturally most people were unhappy about it.

The data needed to make the point are here, but the ineffective syntax of the sentence leaves the poor reader floundering, trying to decipher the connections and the thought behind the whole thing. The *but* seems to be used less for logic than for variety, and the vague *it* at the end effectively dissipates any emphasis the sentence might have had. A little judicious tinkering sorts out and rearranges the facts, shortens the sentence by half, reduces the five co-ordinating conjunctions to a pair of correlative conjunctions, reduces the six independent clauses

28 *faulty co-ordination*

to two independent and one subordinate, and achieves at least some emphasis at the end:

> *revised:* The increased ferry rates not only cost travellers more, but, since the commercial vehicles also had to pay more, the cost of transported goods rose as well, affecting all consumers.

See also **18i** and **16b**.

28 faulty co-ordination

Exercise 28(1): Using subordination

Convert each of the following pairs of sentences into one sentence, subordinating one or the other with an appropriate subordinating conjunction. When possible, subordinate each part of a pair in turn.

1. The book was very well written. I did not find it rewarding.
2. The wind was very cold. He wore a heavy sweater.
3. It stopped snowing. He shovelled the driveway.
4. She read a good book. He played solitaire.
5. The meeting was contentious. A consensus was reached.

Exercise 28(2): Correcting faulty co-ordination

Revise the following sentences to eliminate faulty or loose co-ordination; keep in mind good subordination, unity, emphasis, and logic. You may also find that you can reduce wordiness.

1. There are no windows in the room, and all lighting is from fluorescent fixtures.
2. At this point Ophelia becomes confused, and this becomes evident when she speaks her next line.
3. Rachel is afraid of God and when Calla takes her to the Tabernacle service she goes crazy.
4. The last appearance of the ghost is in the "closet" scene and the purpose of its appearance is to prevent Hamlet from diverging from his "blunted purpose."
5. We want more than our neighbours and then buy the most ridiculous things.
6. Her experiments with chimpanzees were unusual but they were interesting.
7. Older people have already been through what others are experiencing, and this enables them to help.
8. Experts are not always right, and they are seldom wrong.
9. The city's streets are well paved and some of them badly need repair.
10. He is a genius; some people claim that he is an imposter.
11. The stores are usually the first to remind us that Christmas is coming and set the mood with decorations, music, and advertising.
12. The activity of milking a cow becomes very commonplace to the farmer, but it is fun to do and fascinating to watch.
13. Texans are noted for their chauvinism and they often brag unreasonably about their state's virtues.
14. She prepared diligently for the examination and failed it twice, and then passed it with flying colours the third time.
15. Unemployment is unusually high and one should not expect to be hired at the first place one tries.

■ 29 ■ Logic
log

Clear and logical thinking is essential to clear and effective writing. For example, writers must be careful not to make sweeping statements unsupported by specific evidence: over-generalization is one of the most common weaknesses in student writing. Writers must also make sure that the evidence they use is sound and that the authorities they cite are reliable. Such matters are particularly important in writing arguments (and in a sense all writing is argument, for every essay tries to convince a reader of something—even if it is only the accuracy of the point of view being expressed). A writer must also avoid bad reasoning; such logical missteps as begging the question, reasoning in a circle, jumping to conclusions, and leaning on false analogies can mar the effectiveness of an essay (see **74h**).

There are many ways in which logic is important even in something so small as a sentence. The problems discussed in the preceding sections, from *Misplaced Modifiers* on, have in part been problems in logic, as we have noted. (We discuss one other category in the next section, *Alignment*.) Here are some examples of other ways in which sentences can be illogical. (Some of these are also discussed and illustrated elsewhere in the book, as noted below.)

Unsound reasoning leads to sentences like this:

> *log:* James's father was proud of him, for he had the boy's picture on his desk.

The conclusion may at first seem reasonable, but it would at least have to be qualified with a *probably*, or more evidence would have to be provided, for there are other possible reasons for the picture's being on the desk. James's mother could have put it there, for example, and the father just not bothered to remove it; perhaps he lacks the courage to do so. Or he could feel love for a lazy son, and therefore display the picture, without feeling pride. Or he could use it to feign love and pride, knowing inside that he does not feel those emotions.

> *log:* Wordsworth is *perhaps* the first English Romantic poet, *for* his major themes—man, nature, human life—are characteristic of the Romantic style of poetry.

To begin with, the word *perhaps* is pointless, for either the writer is making a point of Wordsworth's primacy and there is no "perhaps" about it, or there is no point to be made and the whole clause is superfluous. Even more important is the inadequate evidence given to substantiate the statement. If Wordsworth's use of themes common to Romanticism makes him first, then all Romantic poets are first. The writer probably meant something like this:

> *revised:* Wordsworth is the first English Romantic poet to develop the major themes of the Romantic movement: man, nature, human life.

In the preceding example, muddy thinking was reflected by muddy writing. But even if writers know what they want to say they must be careful that the words they choose and the ways they use them actually communicate what they intend. For example:

> *log:* The town is surrounded on one side by the ocean.

Of course *surrounded* is illogical here; if the place were indeed surrounded, it would be an island. The correct word here is *bounded*. This error might equally well be designated an error in diction: see **ww** (*Wrong Word*) in Chapter XI.

> *log:* Having a car with bad spark plugs or points or a dirty carburetor causes it to run poorly and to use too much gas.

Here the sentence structure wins, the writer loses. The intention is clear enough, but the verb, *causes*, has as its subject the gerund *having*; consequently the sentence implies that mere possession of the car is what causes it to run poorly—as if one could borrow a similar car and it would run well. The plugs and points and carburetor—clearly the real cause—are mere objects of the preposition *with*, and are therefore unable to do the syntactic job expected of them. A logical revision:

> *revised:* Bad spark plugs or bad points or a dirty carburetor cause a car to run poorly and to use too much gas.

The parallelism was also faulty, for *points* alone would not have caused trouble (see **27**).

> *log:* Throughout history man has been discussing and proposing theories about his purpose on earth, and thus far they can be divided into three general camps.

Here the pronoun *they*, being plural, has only one possible antecedent, *theories*. But one divides not theories, but men, into *camps*. To correct this, either change *camps* to *groups*, *classes* or *categories*, or change *man* to *men* or, better, *people*, which would avoid the generically unfair use of *man*.

> *log:* The mood and theme play a very significant part in this poem.

This might be called an empty sentence; it would be illogical for the very *theme* of a poem to play other than a significant part in it.

> *log:* For the next five years my memory is quite vague.

This sentence, taken from a student's autobiographical narrative, should have been caught during revision or proofreading. Obviously what was intended was this:

> *revised:* My memory of the next five years is quite vague.

Sometimes a writer will let an extra word creep in and ruin an otherwise logical sentence:

> *log:* Alexander Graham Bell is known as the modern inventor of the telephone.

The writer was probably—perhaps subconsciously—thinking of the telephone as a *modern* invention, and the word just popped into the sentence. If we took the statement at face value, it would have to mean that there was also another, earlier, perhaps ancient, inventor of the telephone. The word *modern* must go.

> *log:* Captain Beard appears as more heroic, while MacWhirr is more stupid, but both would face anything just for duty's sake. So as skippers both are respected highly by their crews.

In this passage comparing the captains in two of Joseph Conrad's sea stories ("Youth" and "Typhoon"), the second sentence is a *non sequitur* (Latin for "it does not follow"), because the word *so*—meaning *therefore*—tells us that MacWhirr's crew respect him because he is *more stupid*, which is unlikely. The writer clearly intended the *so* to hinge on the two captains' adherence to *duty*, which is reasonable; for that meaning to prevail, the first clause should have been subordinated:

> *revised:* Although Captain Beard is heroic and MacWhirr stupid, they both would face anything for duty's sake; therefore they are highly respected by their crews.

Now the emphasis is clear and the logic no longer faulty. Nevertheless, you will notice that we have changed the first part of the sentence in another way: the comparisons using *more* were removed because they were illogical and incomplete. *Heroic* and *stupid* are not logical opposites; in fact, some heroes are heroic simply because they are stupid. But the original statements were also examples of incomplete comparison (see **comp** in Chapter XI). That is, to be logically complete, one would have to say that Beard is more heroic *than MacWhirr*, and MacWhirr more stupid *than Beard*. (Even if one reads between the lines and assumes that the two skippers are being compared, the implied contrast breaks down on the logical grounds already mentioned.) Here is an example of another kind of incomplete comparison that causes problems:

> *log, comp:* French painting did not follow the wild and exciting forms of Baroque art as closely as most European countries.

Again the meaning is apparent but the syntax faulty. A reader should not have to read between the lines—or the words—in order to understand a sentence clearly. As stated, the sentence says either that "European countries followed the wild and exciting forms of Baroque art" to some degree or that "French painting followed most European countries more closely than they followed the wild and exciting forms of Baroque art," neither of which makes logical sense. Completing the comparison straightens out the syntax and permits the intended meaning to come through unambiguously:

> *revised:*   French painting did not follow the wild and exciting forms of Baroque art as closely as *did that of* most European countries.

Another kind of ambiguity appears in this sentence:

> *log:*   Numerous scientific societies were founded in every developed country.

Once again the intended meaning is fairly clear, but the sentence could mean that each developed country had "numerous scientific societies," when the more probable and logical meaning is that "Numerous scientific societies were founded, at least one in every developed country." See **ambig** (*Ambiguous*) and **cl** (*Clarity*) in Chapter XI. Be sure that your words and sentences say what you want them to say.

> *log:*   His lack of knowledge of the subject was visible on every page.

This example illustrates another way in which a sentence can be illogical. Once more the meaning is clear, but it is odd to think of a *lack* being *visible*. It would be preferable to say something like this:

> *revised:*   Every page revealed his ignorance of the subject.

Finally, make sure that nouns are inflected to agree logically with the context:

> *log:*   All the students suffered mental stiffness as a result of the unusual exercise involved in using their brain.

Brain obviously must be changed to *brains* in order to conform logically to the sense.

Exercise 29: Improving logic

Analyze the errors in logic in the following sentences; then eliminate them by revising the sentences.

1. As he approached the shore, he felt a challenge between himself and the sea.
2. Milton's influence on other subsequent poets was very great.
3. Some auto accidents are unavoidable, but can be prevented by proper maintenance.

4. Shakespeare fashioned *A Midsummer Night's Dream* around the theme of love and created the characters and situations to illustrate it in the best possible way. Thus he freely used a variety of comic devices in developing the theme.

5. By the use of imagery, diction, symbolism, and sound, we may also see the structure of the plot.

6. It employed the technique of using projected images on a screen and a corresponding taped conversation which visually enforced the lesson.

7. Its shape is a rectangle about three times as long as it is wide or high.

8. Through the use of too much abstract language, jargon, and clichés the clarity and effectiveness of this article have been destroyed.

9. As I think back to the days when we were in our early teens, we had a lot of fun together.

10. After his wife died, his paintings of excited forms changed to quiet ones.

▌30▐ Alignment
al

Another kind of illogical sentence results when a writer tries to make words do work that their meanings will not permit. We call this error **alignment**, meaning that two or more elements of a sentence are illogically or incongruously aligned with each other. Such errors often take the form of a verb saying something illogical about its subject. This is sometimes called faulty **predication**; that is, what is predicated about the subject is an impossibility. For example:

> *al:*   Many new inventions and techniques occurred during this period.

An invention could, with some strain, be said to *occur*, but *techniques* do not *occur*. The sentence needs to be revised; one way is to use the passive voice:

> *revised:*   During this period there were many new inventions, and many new techniques were developed [or *discovered*].

Another example; here the verb repeats the meaning of the subject:

> *al:*   The setting of the play takes place in Denmark.
> *revised:*   The play takes place in Denmark.
> *better:*   The play is set in Denmark.

Usually errors in predication involve a form of the verb *be*:

> *al:*   The amount of gear to take along is the first step to consider when planning a long hike.

But an *amount* cannot be a *step*; again, drastic revision is needed:

> *revised:*   The first step in planning a hike is to decide how much gear to take along.

Note that this also removes the other illogicality: one does not *consider* a *step*; rather the considering, or deciding, *is* the *step*.

> *al:* The value of good literature is priceless.

It is not the *value* that is priceless, but the *literature* itself.

> *al:* The cost of my used car was relatively inexpensive.
> *revised:* The cost of my used car was relatively low.
> *revised:* My used car was relatively inexpensive.

Other errors in alignment are not errors in predication, but are similar to them in using words illogically:

> *al:* In narrative, the author describes the occurrences, environment, and thoughts of the characters.

It is logical to speak of characters having thoughts and an environment, but not *occurrences*; substitute the word *experiences*.

> *al:* Its fine texture was as smooth and hard as a waterworn rock.

This, which illogically equates *texture* and *rock*, is also one form of incomplete comparison (see **comp** in Chapter XI); insert *that of* after *hard as*.

> *al:* Physical Education is one of the many things students can do to keep healthy.

But one does not *do* Physical Education; *take part in* or *engage in* would suffice, though the sentence could be revised in other ways as well.

> *al:* Beliefs such as being a Christian or a Jew or a Moslem or even an atheist should not cause anyone to be denied a job.

But *being* a Christian, etc., is not a *belief*. One could begin the sentence with *Being*, or one could recast it completely:

> *revised:* People should not be denied jobs because of their religious beliefs, be they Christian . . . or anything else.

Exercise 30: Improving alignment

Revise the following sentences to remove illogical or incongruous alignments.

1. I decided not to buy it, for the price was too expensive.
2. Even religious principles were being enlightened, giving people the freedom they should have.
3. It is clear that this general conception of his ability is greatly underestimated.
4. The only source of light in the house came through the windows.
5. By taking Physical Education, students can learn what activities they can do in their leisure time.

6. The poem expresses the meaningless and useless achievements of war.
7. The character of the speaker in the poem seems weary and tired.
8. The need for such great effort on the part of the reader represents serious weakness in the writing.
9. Life and death was a constant idea in the back of the pioneers' minds.
10. He started university at a very young age.

31 Sentence Coherence
coh

Although the word *coherence* is usually used to refer to the connection between sentences and between paragraphs, the parts of a sentence must also cohere, stick together. Each sentence fault discussed in the preceding sections is capable of making a sentence incoherent (the dictionary meanings *disjointed, illogical, confused, loose, inconsistent, disorganized* all apply). If a sentence lacks coherence, the fault probably lies in one or more of the following: faulty arrangement (word order, misplaced modifier), unclear or missing or illogical connections and relations between parts (faulty reference, lack of agreement, dangling modifier, faulty co-ordination, faulty logic, incongruous alignment), syntactic shift from one part to another (mixed construction, shift in point of view, faulty parallelism); or the weakness may be due to something that can only be labelled *awkward* or *unclear* (see **awk** and **cl** in Chapter XI). Consult these specific sections, as necessary, to ensure that your sentences are coherent within themselves.

Review Exercise: Chapters I, II, and III

The following sentences contain various kinds of errors and weaknesses discussed in the preceding chapters. Decide what is wrong with each sentence, label it with the appropriate correction symbol, and then revise the sentence in order to eliminate the problem. Note that some sentences have more than one thing wrong with them.

1. Our coach is overweight, Hungarian, overpaid, and over forty.
2. One receives this impression when the colour of the picture is considered.
3. Many organic diseases present symptoms that are very similar to autism.
4. Great distances now separate he and his father.
5. The writer's skill was very good.
6. It's true that love and romance come when you least expect it.
7. No player in our school has ever scored as highly as Schmidt did this year.
8. The poem is separated into two parts. The first being his memories and an account of how he reacted to his father's death.
9. Its shape is rounded slightly resembling a keyhole.
10. I pulled over to the side of the road in a green truck I had borrowed from my roommate, and because the weather was warm I was dressed only in shorts and a bandana, which I had tied around my head.

11. Borelli supposed that there was a tendency for celestial bodies to attract each other but a fluid pressure prevented this.
12. Shakespeare's *Othello* is a brilliant but tragic story of the betrayal of the Moor of Venice by his most trusted friend, Iago.
13. The whole meaning of Housman's poem is that it is better to die young with honour and glory intact than to have someone take it away from you.
14. The forefinger along with the other digits of the hand have enabled us to evolve to the position of being the ruler of the world.
15. He says he would like to have another chance at being premier; but if he couldn't run the government right the first time, how can anyone think he's about to do it right again?
16. Smitty is so eager about Michael's friendship, and this is easy to understand.
17. Those who are actually involved in this Christmas frenzy may find themselves feeling like getting in touch with old friends, making peace with people they haven't been getting along with, giving to their loved ones and even to strangers, decorating, and enjoying each other's company.
18. They preferred to go out with friends to movies and parties than to stay home and watch TV with their families.
19. By creating an atmosphere of concern for the main character we are more open to the message of the story.
20. What a university stands for more than anything else is an institution where one furthers his education.
21. He has an old worn coat which is far too big for him, but alterations are something he has neither money for nor feels the need to get done.
22. At the beginning, he played things very cautious.
23. Her success is credited to her slyness and wit which always prevails over her daughter's weaknesses.
24. Physical activity of any kind is always beneficial for the individual.
25. At present the fees are already very expensive.
26. Many people think of themselves as a well-educated person when they really are not.
27. The poet suggests that our lives are but a speck in time and there is nothing we can do about it.
28. Good nutrition need not be expensive, for junk food often costs more.
29. The cost of computers are now starting to drop.
30. Ask the average television viewer how many programs he saw more than a few days before he can remember.
31. He had been given instructions on how to repair the engine, but it did not do much good.
32. Old buildings should not be thoughtlessly destroyed and replaced with modern architecture without admiring their quality and detail.
33. Being the youngest of four children, old clothing is something I know a good deal about.
34. The main contrast is between the attitudes of the older children to that of the younger children.
35. Often the cafeteria foods will have sauces and gravies available if people wish, which adds flavour.
36. There are also several phrases in the story that seem to have a dual meaning. One meaning being commonplace and the other having to do with ancient mythology.
37. The poem is about the loss that a child feels when his father dies at a young age.

38. Always look both to the left and the right before you cross a busy street.
39. Unlike many of his contemporaries whose humorous writings quickly faded, Twain's masterpiece has become a classic and will continue to entertain readers for a long time.
40. The man whom they believed was the cause of the trouble left the country.
41. The author uses characterization to develop her characters.
42. Someone who is sensible can judge their own impulses and emotions accurately.
43. Don't give up an aspiring career just to please someone else.
44. Vico's theories omitted many countries because they did not have the highly evolved pattern of civilization as Greece and Rome did.
45. One of the first things that the audience feels towards Hamlet is sympathy for the recent death of his father.
46. Belief in witchcraft and witch-tests declined in later years, but were never completely forgotten.
47. It is not the characters themselves that is important but what they represent.
48. There are several courses that I know I don't want to do.
49. We want to know why Hamlet behaves as he does, and until one is satisfied that one knows, he will always remain a mystery.
50. One rarely throws anything out, because you never know when it might be needed.

exercises

PUNCTUATION

There are two common misconceptions about punctuation: one is that punctuation is of little consequence, that it has little to do with the effectiveness of written English; the other is that good punctuation is somehow arcane, a mystery whose secrets are available only to those with a special, instinctive gift. Those who labour under one or both of these delusions usually approach the task of punctuating with a combination of fear and abandon: some omit necessary punctuation for fear of making mistakes; others strain so hard to find the right mark that they make mistakes; still others punctuate with slapdash unconcern, as if they were playing Pin the Tail on the Donkey, sticking in various punctuation marks here and there in the hope that somehow it will come out all right.

The first assumption could not be further from the truth: good punctuation is essential to clear and effective writing. It helps a writer to clarify meaning and establish tone, and consequently it helps a reader to understand what the writer wishes to communicate. In addition, punctuation in itself can have meaning. Like words, some punctuation marks are symbols: they enable a writer to indicate meaning that would, in spoken language, be indicated by pauses and by pitch and tone and stress. In effect, correct punctuation enables a reader to *hear* a sentence the way the writer intended. Marks like the comma, the semicolon, and the colon also help to clarify the internal structure of sentences; often the very meaning of a sentence depends on how it is punctuated. The word *punctuation* is etymologically related to the word *pointing*; when you are *punctuating* you are in a sense *pointing to* meaning and tone and emphasis, *pointing out* just what it is you want a reader to understand. Punctuation marks are like signposts to help guide the reader through your sentences. Even people who are poor at punctuating must depend on punctuation in order to understand what they read; such people need to raise their unconscious habits to a conscious level so that they can control punctuation and use it effectively.

As for the second misconception, the principles of good punctuation are not mysterious or remote; a command of them should not be difficult to attain. And here yet another common misconception should be corrected at once: what are often called the "rules" of punctuation are not really rules but conventions. For example, English-speaking people have agreed upon the convention that the word for a feline animal, especially the small domestic feline, is *cat*: if you wish to write something about this animal, you will almost surely use that word to identify it. If you spelled it *kat* you would probably be understood, though readers would wonder why you had strayed from the conventional spelling—and to that extent you would have lost touch with them, disturbed the quality of their understanding of the meaning you intended. However, if you chose to call the small domestic feline you were writing about a *zyb*, you would not just have strayed slightly from the convention; you would have completely departed from it. And you would have lost your readers entirely, for they could have no idea of what you meant. The "rule" that *cat* is spelled c-a-t is of course not a moral or legal restraint on behaviour; no one is going to sue you or put you in jail if you choose to spell it z-y-b. But you will have exercised that degree of your freedom of choice only by defeating your purpose: clear and effective communication.

The conventions of punctuation are similar: they have come to be agreed upon by writers and readers of English for the purposes of clear and effective communication. To be sure, good writers will often stray from the conventions of punctuation, but they usually do so not out of ignorance but rather because they have a sufficient command of the conventions to break a "rule" in order to achieve a desired effect. One of the best ways to improve your own punctuation is to become more aware of other people's punctuation. Look not only for good things but also for bad things, for weaknesses as well as strengths. If you do this consciously and conscientiously as you read, you will soon acquire a better sense of what punctuation does and how it does it—a sense which you can then apply to your own writing, and which will soon become instinctive.

The following explanations of the conventions are intended for your guidance. They cover the most common circumstances, and even some relatively uncommon ones; if you understand them, they will help you to punctuate your writing correctly and effectively. Note that a clear understanding of many of these principles depends on a clear understanding of the syntax of the sentences in question; if you find that you can't grasp the principles clearly, review the appropriate sections on grammar and sentence sense. Note also that, far from being like straitjackets, repressing and limiting your individuality and freedom, many of the principles that follow not only allow but actually invite you to exercise a considerable amount of choice.

32-41 Internal Punctuation: Using Commas, Semicolons, Colons, and Dashes

32 The Marks Defined

32a The Comma **,**

The **comma** is a light or mild separator. It is the most neutral or least obtrusive punctuation mark. It is also the most frequently used mark. It is used to separate words, phrases, and clauses from each other when no heavier or more expressive mark is required or desired. A comma makes a reader *pause* slightly.

Main Functions of Commas

Basically commas are used in only three ways; if you know and follow these rules, you'll seldom have any trouble with commas:

1. Generally, use a comma between independent clauses joined by a co-ordinating conjunction (*and, but, or, nor, for, yet, so*; see **12a**):

   > We watched the changing of the guard at Buckingham Palace, and then we walked across Hyde Park.
   > Most of us went back to college in the fall, but Dorothy Wang was tempted by an opportunity to travel, so she took off for Italy.

   See **33**.

2. Generally, use commas to separate items in a series of three or more:

   > It is said that early to bed and early to rise will make one healthy, wealthy, and wise.
   > Theocritus, Bion, and Moschus were three early pastoral poets.

   and to separate two or more parallel adjectives before a noun:

   > The room was full of happy, carefree people.

   See **38**. And see **44c** on a common error with such constructions.

3. Generally, use commas to set off parenthetical or interruptive elements such as introductory words, phrases, or clauses and nonrestrictive appositives or relative clauses:

There are, however, some exceptions.
Hearing her flight number called, she began to run.
E.M. Forster's last novel, *A Passage to India*, is both serious and humorous.
The Beatles, who were so popular in the 60's, are little known to today's younger generation.

See **34, 35, 37**, and **39**.

Other Conventional Uses of the Comma

1. Use a comma between elements of an emphatic contrast:

   This is a practical lesson, not a theoretical one.

2. Use commas to indicate a pause where a word has been acceptably omitted:

   Ron is a conservative; Sally, a socialist.
   To err is human; to forgive, divine.

3. Use commas to set off a noun of address (see **2b**):

   Simon, please write home more often.
   Tell me, sir, how you think I should handle this.

4. Generally, use commas with a verb of speaking before or after a quotation (see also **43d**):

   Then Hilda remarked, "I think the project stinks."
   "It doesn't matter to me," said Rominder laughingly.

5. Use commas after the salutation of informal letters (Dear Gail,) and after the complimentary close of all letters (Yours truly,). In formal letters, it is conventional to use a colon after the salutation (Dear Sir:).

6. Use commas correctly with dates. Different forms are possible:

   He left on January 11, 1984, and was gone a month. (Note the comma *after* the year.)
   On 11 January 1984 he left for a month's holiday.

   With only month and year, you can use a comma or not—but be consistent:

   The book was published in March, 1984, in Canada.
   It was published in March 1984 in Canada.

7. Use commas to set off geographical names and addresses:

   He left Fredericton, New Brunswick, and moved to Windsor, Ontario,

in hopes of finding a better-paying job. (Note the commas *after* the
names of the provinces.)

Her summer address will be 11 Bishop's Place, Lewes, Sussex, England.

For some common errors with commas, see **44**.

32b   The Semicolon   **;**

The **semicolon** is a heavy separator, often almost equivalent to a period
or "full stop." It makes a reader pause much longer than a comma
does. And compared with the comma, it is used sparingly. Basically,
semicolons have only two functions:

1. Generally, use a semicolon between closely related independent
   clauses that are *not* joined by one of the co-ordinating conjunctions
   (see **12a**):

   > The caffeine in coffee can be harmful; the caffeine in tea usually is
   > not harmful.
   > There were seventy-five people but room for only fifty; therefore twenty-
   > five had to wait for a second bus.

   See **33**. And see **44i** on how to avoid misusing the semicolon.

2. You can also use a semicolon where a comma would ordinarily go,
   but only if a comma for some reason would not be heavy enough—
   for example if clauses or the elements in a series had internal commas
   of their own (see **33b** and **38c**).

32c   The Colon   **:**

The **colon** is a punctuation mark often avoided by beginning writers
because they do not understand its expressive function. It is commonly
used to precede lists (for example, after "the following:" or "as follows:") or to introduce long or formal quotations, but its possibilities
in more everyday sentences are often overlooked. Put most simply,
the colon looks forward or anticipates: it gives readers an extra push
toward the next part of the sentence. In the preceding sentence, for
example, the colon is intended to give readers a little extra impetus,
to set up a sense of expectation about what is coming. Another mark
that could have been used in that spot, a semicolon, would in contrast
have brought readers to a screeching halt, leaving them to make, entirely on their own, the necessary connection between the two parts
of the sentence. With the colon, however, the relation between the
two parts (here, a relation in which the second part restates and further
clarifies, with emphasis, what the first part said) is pointed out, even
emphasized, making it easier for readers to understand the writer's
intention. (To be fully accurate, we should point out that a semicolon

in that spot would not only be separating the two clauses; it would also be acting as a joiner, informing readers that the two clauses were closely related to each other. Only a full stop, a period, would act as a complete separator.) Here is another example, a more common kind, where the anticipatory function of the colon can be seen more clearly:

> The garden contained only four kinds of flowers: roses, tulips, geraniums, and chrysanthemums.

Here are some further illustrations of how the colon can be used effectively:

> He wanted only one thing from life: happiness. (Note that, even with this common use of the colon, what follows it need not be an extended list.)
> It was a warm day: we soon removed our jackets and sweaters.
> Let me add just this: anyone who expects to achieve excellence must be prepared to work hard.
> His shortcomings were several: laziness, slovenliness, lack of talent, and a short temper.
> It was a lovely time of year: the trees were in blossom, garden flowers bloomed all around, the sky was clear and bright, and the temperature was just right.

Ms note: Practice varies regarding spacing with colons. Many writers insist on following a typed colon with *two* spaces, instead of only one, to mark it as special and to keep it from being mistaken for a semicolon. Whichever practice you adopt, be consistent. In any event, when a colon is used in a footnote or a bibliographical entry, or to precede the subtitle of a written work, only *one* space follows it.

See **44j** on how to avoid a common misuse of the colon.

32d The Dash ——

The **dash** is a much-abused punctuation mark. Careless writers often use it as a hasty substitute for a comma, or where a colon would be better—probably because they feel insecure about colons. The best way to avoid inappropriate or sloppy use of the dash is to be sure that when you use it you have a definite reason for doing so. Like the colon, a dash in a sentence is a signal to the reader; like the colon, it sets up expectations in the reader's mind. The dash differs from the colon, however, in that the expectation it sets up is not simply an expectation that what is to follow will somehow explain, summarize, define, or otherwise comment on what has gone before. Rather, the expectation evoked by a dash is that what follows will be either emphatic or somehow surprising, involving some sort of twist or irony, or at least a complete break in syntax. The dash is an abrupt break, and induces a slightly prolonged pause; the colon, on the other hand, although it induces a similar pause, at the same time impels the reader onward. Consider the following sentence:

32d *dash*

> What he wanted—and he wanted it very badly indeed—was to be well liked by everyone.

To set off that parenthetical clause with commas instead of dashes would not be "incorrect," but it would certainly be weak, for the content of the clause is clearly emphatic, and only dashes have the power to signal that emphasis; the dashes, therefore, are appropriate, whereas commas would not be, since they would be contradicting what the clause says. Here is another sentence:

> The teacher praised my wit, my intelligence, my organization, and my research—and failed the paper for its lousy spelling and punctuation.

Here the dash clearly adds to the punch of what follows it. Its signal prepares the reader for the unexpectedness, even the irony, of the last part of the sentence. A comma, being a very light and neutral mark, could not do this; if a comma were used instead of the dash, the sentence would lose most of its force, and even sound odd, since the resulting matter-of-fact **tone** would not be in harmony with the substance. Only the dash can convey the appropriate tone (see introduction to Chapter VII).

The dash is also used to attach a summarizing clause to a long and involved sentence, for example a sentence with a long series as its "subject":

> The laws of supply and demand, the health of the stock market, the strength of our currency, the world money market, the balance of payments, inflation, unemployment—all these and more go to shape our everyday economic lives, often in ways unseen or little understood.

Note that even here the emphasizing quality of the dash serves the meaning, though its principal function in such a sentence is to mark the abrupt and unusual syntactic break.

Ms note: A typewritten dash is composed of two hyphens, and is not preceded, followed, or interrupted by a space.

33-38 How to Use Commas, Semicolons, Colons, and Dashes

33 Between Independent Clauses

33a Comma and Co-ordinating Conjunction

Generally, use a *comma* between independent clauses that are joined by one of the co-ordinating conjunctions (*and, but, or, nor, for, yet,* and sometimes *so*):

> The course proved very difficult, and she found herself burning a lot of midnight oil.

It was a serious speech, but he included many jokes along the way, and the audience loved it.

Jared could go into debt for the sports car, or he could buy the much cheaper economy car.

He knew what he should do, yet he could not bring himself to take the first step.

If the clauses are short, or if only one of a pair of clauses is short, the comma or commas may be omitted:

The road was smooth and the car was running well and the weather was perfect.

The walls were crumbling and the roof was full of holes.

But sometimes even with a short clause a comma is advisable when a natural pause would make the sentence read more smoothly and clearly:

The building was old, and the ivy had climbed nearly to the top of its three storeys.

When the clauses are parallel in structure the comma may often be omitted:

Art is long and life is short.

He stood up and she sat down.

When the subjects of two clauses are the same, a comma is less likely to be needed between them:

It was windy and it was wet. (Note also the parallel structure.)

The play was well produced and it impressed everyone who saw it.

Caution: Independent clauses joined by the co-ordinating conjunctions *but* and *yet*, since they explicitly mark a contrast, will almost always need a comma between them. And when the co-ordinating conjunction *for* joins two clauses, it should always be preceded by a comma in order to prevent its being misread as a preposition:

He was eager to leave early, for the restaurant was sure to be crowded.

33b Semicolon and Co-ordinating Conjunction

You will sometimes want to use a *semicolon* between independent clauses, even though they are joined by a co-ordinating conjunction, when one or more of the clauses have other punctuation marks within them:

Old as he was, my uncle, Abner, the best farmer in the district, easily won the ploughing contest; and no one who knew him—or even had only heard of him—was in the least surprised.

or when at least one of the clauses is unusually long:

A politician may make long-winded speeches full of clichés and generalities and the sort of things it is obvious everyone wants to hear; but people will still vote for him because they like his face.

or when you want the extra emphasis provided by a stronger pause:

> He protested that he was sorry for all his mistakes; but he went right on making them.

33c Dash and Co-ordinating Conjunction

Note that in the preceding example a similar and even better effect could be achieved by using a dash:

> He protested that he was sorry for all his mistakes—but he went right on making them.

If the conjunction were changed to the more neutral *and*, a rhetorically different effect could be achieved, the dash taking over the contrasting function of the word *but*:

> He protested that he was sorry for all his mistakes—and he went right on making them.

Similarly, notice the slightly different effects of these two versions of the same sentence:

> It may not be the best way, but it's the only way we know.
> It may not be the best way—but it's the only way we know.

Of course, even a period could be used to separate such clauses. (There is nothing inherently wrong with using an *And* or a *But* to begin a sentence. It's just that because they are co-ordinating conjunctions, one expects them to join internally rather than begin. But even as the first word of a sentence, an *And* or a *But* is in fact still performing its joining function. See **12a**.)

Reminder: The co-ordinating conjunction *so* is considered informal. See **12a**.

33d Semicolon Without Co-ordinating Conjunction

Generally, use a semicolon between independent clauses that you don't join with one of the co-ordinating conjunctions (*and, but, or, nor, for, yet, so*):

> When Hamlet begins trying to kill Claudius the audience is with him all the way; they believe Claudius deserves it.

33e Comma Splice

cs

Using only a comma between independent clauses that are not joined with a co-ordinating conjunction results in a **comma splice**:

cs: When Hamlet begins trying to kill Claudius the audience is with him all the way, they believe Claudius deserves it.

cs: Being a mere child I didn't fully understand what I had witnessed, I just knew it was wrong.

A semicolon signals that what comes next is an independent clause; with only a comma in place, readers would be led to expect some kind of subordinate sentence element, and if they encountered an independent clause instead, their train of thought would be derailed. A comma *with a co-ordinating conjunction* is enough:

When Hamlet begins trying to kill Claudius the audience is with him all the way, *for* they believe Claudius deserves it.

A comma *without* a co-ordinating conjunction is not enough. In most such sentences, then, in order to avoid seriously distracting your readers, you should use semicolons:

Being a mere child I didn't fully understand what I had witnessed; I just knew it was wrong.

Students who work will gain their reward; students who shirk will also gain theirs.

The President of the United States is elected; the members of his cabinet are not.

Vancouver, the largest city in British Columbia, is not the capital; Victoria has that distinction.

For a discussion of ways to correct comma splices, see the entry **cs** in Chapter XI.

33f-g **Exceptions: Using Commas Alone Between Independent Clauses**

33f **Commas with Short and Parallel Clauses**

If the clauses are short, and especially if they are parallel in structure, commas rather than semicolons may be sufficient:

She cooked, he ate.
I came, I saw, I conquered.

33g **Commas with Series of Clauses**

Also, relatively short independent clauses in a *series* of three or more, especially if they are grammatically parallel, may be separated by commas rather than semicolons:

The water was calm, our luck was good, and the fish were biting.

If you want to do well you must pay attention, you must read carefully, you must work diligently, you must write correctly, and you must keep your fingers crossed.

(Here a dash would work nicely in place of the last comma.) Sentences such as these should be the only exceptions you permit, the only instances where you even consider using a comma to splice together independent clauses in the absence of a co-ordinating conjunction. In other sentences, the strength of a semicolon is needed to splice such clauses together.

33h Caution: Use Semicolons with Conjunctive Adverbs and Transitional Phrases

Be sure to use a semicolon between independent clauses that you join with a conjunctive adverb. Here are most of the common ones:

accordingly	hence	next
afterward	however	nonetheless
also	indeed	otherwise
besides	instead	similarly
certainly	later	still
consequently	likewise	subsequently
conversely	meanwhile	then
finally	moreover	therefore
further	namely	thus
furthermore	nevertheless	undoubtedly

The same caution applies to such common transitional phrases as these:

as a result	in addition	on the contrary
for example	in fact	on the other hand
if not	in the meantime	that is

Conjunctive adverbs often have the *feel* of subordinating or co-ordinating conjunctions, but they are not conjunctions; rather they are adverbs doing a joining or "conjunctive" job:

> The book's print was very small; therefore she got a headache.

In this example, *therefore* works very much like *so*; but it is a *therefore* and not a *so*, and consequently a semicolon must be used, rather than a comma, which would result in a comma splice.

> He felt well enough to go; however, his doctor ordered him to stay in bed.

Here *however* works very much like *but*; nevertheless, it is a conjunctive adverb, not a conjunction, and must therefore be preceded by a semicolon. (Note also that *however*, in this usage, must be followed by a comma; other conjunctive adverbs may on occasion be followed by commas, but *however* must be, in order to prevent its being misread as a regular adverb—meaning "in whatever way"—rather than a conjunctive adverb.) Note that conjunctive adverbs can be shifted around within a clause; you may find it helpful to apply that test if you are not sure whether a particular word is a conjunctive adverb or a conjunction.

Style Note: *However* often sounds stiff and awkward at the beginning of a sentence or a clause. Unless you want special emphasis on the word, equivalent to underlining it, it is better to place it at some appropriate place within the clause; delaying it just one or two words into the clause often works best:

> His doctor, however, ordered him to stay in bed.

33i Dashes and Colons Without Co-ordinating Conjunctions

Dashes and colons may also be used between independent clauses not joined by co-ordinating conjunctions: use a dash when you want stronger emphasis on the second clause; use a colon when you want its anticipatory effect—when the second clause explains or enlarges upon the first clause. For example:

> He was a bounder from head to toe: gentlemanly behaviour was the last thing one could expect from him.
> The proposal horrified him—it was unthinkable.
> He took the obvious way out: he turned and ran.
> It was a unique occasion—everyone at the meeting agreed on what should be done.

In most such sentences either a dash or a colon would be appropriate; the choice depends on the particular tone or emphasis one wishes to convey. Note also that in none of these examples would a comma be correct. A semicolon could be used, but it would be very weak and usually inappropriate (except perhaps in the first example). But note that a crisp and emphatic effect could be achieved, especially in the second and third examples, by using a period, turning each into two separate sentences.

33j Run-on Sentences
run-on fs

Failure to put any punctuation between independent clauses where there is also no co-ordinating conjunction results in a **run-on** or fused sentence:

> *Run-on:* Philosophers' views did not always meet with the approval of the authorities therefore there was constant conflict between writers and the church or state.

A semicolon after *authorities* corrects this serious error.

See **run-on** in Chapter XI.

exercises

Exercise 33(1): Punctuating between independent clauses

Insert whatever punctuation mark (other than a period) you consider desirable or necessary between the independent clauses in the following sentences. You may decide that some need no punctuation. Be prepared to explain your decisions.

1. The Beatles phenomenon swept the 1960's the four hirsute Liverpudlians took the world by storm.
2. Lori needed some answers and she thought she knew where she could find them.
3. Parades aren't just for children many adults enjoy them as well.
4. Some people eat to live others live to eat.
5. It was a fascinating hypothesis but no one seemed eager to support it.
6. She laughed she cried she tore her hair.
7. The hurricane warning went up and most people began heading inland.
8. Easy come easy go.
9. The wolves came closer that winter than ever before it broke all records for low temperature.
10. The strike was over people were delighted.

Exercise 33(2): Correcting comma splices and run-ons

Correct any comma splices and run-on sentences in the following.

1. I had not been back since my childhood therefore I was very surprised at all the changes that had taken place.
2. The actual value of the reward is unimportant it is the relative value that matters.
3. We started to unpack our things, pretty soon clothes were strewn all over the place.
4. Throughout the poem Frost uses various techniques to get his point across, however, the literal sense is sufficiently clear.
5. But I heard nothing, everything around me was still and peaceful.
6. Estragon doesn't remember things he can't even remember what day it is.
7. The rest of the syllables do not flow easily together, therefore the line slows.
8. Life in those days was a gruelling chore, but that was what made it satisfying.
9. Industry was not very developed at this time, however, the world of commerce was hectic.
10. At last we pushed off from the shore , the canoes were buffeted by the rolling waves caused by the tidal flow.
11. Sometimes there are too many projects to be accomplished in one day, therefore, some have to be put off until the next free day.
12. It was a feeble attempt the defendant made no impression on the jury.
13. Its lines are symmetrical and clear, its colour is off-white.
14. The cost of the computer was higher than I had anticipated, however, it is an investment that will pay for itself.
15. Be careful with punctuation, otherwise you'll distract your readers.

34 Between Independent Clauses and Adverbial Clauses

34a Commas with Introductory Clauses

Generally, use a comma between an introductory adverbial clause and an independent (main) clause:

> If you think you can learn to write well without hard work, you are mistaken.
> After I had selected all the things I wanted, I discovered that I had left my wallet at home.
> Since he was elected by a large majority, he felt that he had a strong mandate for his policies.
> When the party was over, I went straight home.

When the introductory clause is short and when there would be no pause if the sentence were spoken aloud, you may often omit the comma:

> When the party was over I went straight home.
> While you are out you can pick up a loaf of bread.
> Since he felt ill he decided to stay home.

But if omitting the comma could cause misreading, it must be retained:

> Whenever I wanted, someone would bring me something to eat.
> Long before the sun rose, high above the mountains I could see a jet's con-trail streaking the sky.

Whenever you aren't sure, use a comma; it will always be acceptable.

34b Commas with Concluding Clauses

When an adverbial clause follows an independent clause, a comma may or may not be needed between them. If the subordinate clause is essential to the meaning of the sentence, it is called *restrictive* and should not be set off with a comma; if it is not essential, but contains only additional information or comment, it is called *nonrestrictive* and should be set off with a comma. (See the discussion of *restrictive* and *nonrestrictive* modifiers below, **37**.) Consider the following examples:

> I went straight home when the party was over.
> You are mistaken if you think you can learn to write well without hard work.
> He felt that he had a strong mandate for his policies because he was elected by a large majority.
> He simply could not succeed, however hard he may have tried.
> She did an excellent job on her second essay, although the first one was a disaster.

34b concluding clauses

Most such concluding adverbial clauses will be restrictive, necessary to the meaning of the sentence, and won't need a comma. If you are in doubt, try omitting the adverbial clause to see if the sentence still says essentially what you want it to. Consider the following pair of sentences:

> The conference was a success even though it began in wild confusion.
> The conference was a success, even though it began in wild confusion.

The meanings are different, depending on whether or not there is a comma.

Exercise 34: Punctuating complex sentences

Insert commas where you think necessary in the following sentences. Indicate any places where you think a comma would be optional.

1. Although the hour was late he knew he had to stay up and finish the paper.
2. You can leave now if you want to.
3. You can leave whenever you wish.
4. The fruit crop is especially good this year because there was such a warm spring.
5. Because spring was so warm this year the fruit crop is unusually heavy.
6. Before you go to Greece you should read this book about the islands.
7. Travel by airplane is certainly fast though it is also very expensive.
8. You can often tell where commas are required by reading your sentence aloud and listening for the natural pauses.
9. After she had won the race she seemed oddly less confident than she had before the race began.
10. However you look at the problem you cannot find a simple answer.

---

35   **Between Introductory and Concluding Words and Phrases and the Rest of the Sentence**

The principles governing the punctuation of introductory and concluding words and phrases are similar to those governing the punctuation of adverbial clauses. Studying these modifiers separately, however, will help you understand the principles more clearly. In addition, there are special points pertaining to certain kinds of words and phrases.

35a   **Adverbial Phrases**

Generally, set off a long introductory adverbial phrase with a comma:

> After many years as leader of the party, he retired gracefully.
> In order to get the best results from your computer, you must follow the instruction manual carefully.
> Just like all the other long-time employees, she felt loyal to the company.

Single-word adverbs and short phrases do not need to be set off if the sentence flows smoothly without a comma:

> Unfortunately the weather didn't co-operate.
> Slowly they crept closer to the fire.
> With a mighty heave they hoisted the beam into place.
> In order to punctuate well you have to feel a sentence's rhythm.
> In 1971 they moved to Calgary.
> Toward the end of the year he began to act rather strange.

There is nothing wrong with these sentences, although in the past such openers would have been set off, and even today many people think they should be. Generally, however, you need to set off an introductory adverb or adverbial phrase only if you want a distinct pause, for example for emphasis or qualification or to prevent misreading:

> Unfortunately, the weather didn't co-operate.
> Generally, follow our advice about punctuation.
> Normally, I walk to work.
> With a shrug, he said he'd accept their decision.
> Usually, quiet people are easier to work with.

Of the conjunctive adverbs, only *however* must always be set off, although the others frequently are as well (see **33h** and **44f**).

When such words and phrases follow the independent clause, most—but not all—will be restrictive and therefore not set off with commas:

> He retired gracefully after many years as leader of the party.
> You must follow the instruction manual carefully in order to get the best results from your computer.
> She felt loyal to the company, just like all the other long-time employees.
> The weather didn't co-operate, unfortunately.

If you intend the concluding element to complete the sense of the main clause, it should not be set off; if you don't intend it as essential to the meaning of the main clause but merely to provide additional information or comment, it should be set off with a comma.

35b   Participial Phrases

Always set off an introductory participle or participial phrase with a comma (see **10c**):

> Finding the course unexpectedly difficult, she began to worry.
> Feeling victorious, he left the room.
> Having been in prison so long, he scarcely recognized the world when he emerged.
> Puzzled, she turned back to the beginning of the chapter.

Closing participles and participial phrases almost always need to be set off as well; if you feel a distinct pause, use a comma:

She began to worry, finding the course unexpectedly difficult.
Higher prices result in increased wage demands, contributing to the inflationary spiral.

Occasionally a sentence will flow clearly and smoothly without a comma, especially if the modifier is in effect restrictive, essential to the meaning:

He left the room feeling victorious.
She sat there looking puzzled.
We spent all afternoon window-shopping.

If the closing participle modifies a predicate noun or a direct object, there usually should not be a comma:

He was a man lacking in courage.
I left him feeling bewildered.

But if the participle in such a sentence as the last modifies the subject rather than the object, a comma is necessary:

I left him, feeling bewildered.

Only the presence or absence of the comma tells a reader how to understand such a sentence.

Caution: Don't mistake a *gerund* for a *participle* (see **10c** and **10d**). A gerund or gerund phrase functioning as the subject of a sentence should not be followed by a comma (see **44a**):

participle: Singing in the rain, we happily walked all the way home.
gerund: Singing in the rain kept us from feeling gloomy.

Similarly, don't mistake a long infinitive phrase functioning as a noun for one functioning as an adverb (see **10a**):

adverb: To put together a large jigsaw puzzle in one day without help, you need to be either gifted or very lucky.
noun: To put together a large jigsaw puzzle in one day without help is a remarkable feat.

35c   Absolute Phrases

Always set off absolute phrases with commas (see **1r**):

The doors locked and bolted, she went to bed feeling secure.
Timmy went to his room, head bowed, a tear coursing down his cheek.

Exercise 35: Punctuating opening and closing words and phrases

Insert commas in the following sentences wherever you think they are necessary. Indicate any places where you think a comma would be optional.

1. Unnoticed I entered the house by the side door.

(margin:) **35c** *absolute phrases*

2. We walked slowly soaking up the sights and sounds along the waterfront.
3. At the end of the lecture I had no clearer understanding of the subject than I had when I came in.
4. The dishes washed and put away I decided to relax with a good book.
5. The brain regulates and integrates our senses allowing us to experience our environment.
6. Raising prices results in increased wage demands adding to inflation.
7. Following the instructions I poured the second ingredient into the beaker with the first and shook them shutting my eyes in expectation of something unpleasant.
8. Before going to bed I fixed myself a light snack naturally.
9. To make a long story short I found my aunt looking healthier than I'd ever seen her before.
10. Looking strained and furious the coach stared back at the referee without saying a word.

---

36 Dashes and Colons with Concluding Summaries and Appositives

Either dashes or colons may be used to set off concluding summaries or appositives in a sentence. Some say that a dash should be used to set off a short summary or appositive and a colon to set off a long one. But in fact either a colon or a dash may effectively be used in either instance: the length of the concluding element is unimportant; what matters is its relation to the preceding part of the sentence. If its relation is straightforward, use a colon; if it is in some way emphatic or un-expected, use a dash. Consider one of the sentences used earlier to illustrate a use of the colon:

He wanted only one thing from life: happiness.

A dash could be used there instead of a colon, but only if the writer wants to impart a special emphasis to the word *happiness*. But note that the nature of the whole sentence, and the colon followed by the single word *happiness*, already convey a good deal of emphasis; it could be argued that any greater emphasis, such as that provided by a dash, would be unnecessary, even inappropriate to the ordinariness of the sentiment. But if we change the final word, the *tone* also is altered:

He wanted only one thing from life—money.

Here too a colon would be acceptable, and would convey a certain emphasis, as in the original version. But the idea of *money* as someone's single desideratum, because it is less expected, introduces more vigour into the expression than did the idea of happiness. The resultant tone of the sentence would not be as well served by the quietness of a colon as by the dash of a dash. The same principles apply to setting off longer

36 concluding summaries

concluding appositives and summaries, though colons are more common; use a dash only when you wish to take advantage of its special flavour.

Note: Sometimes you will find a comma used instead of a colon or a dash in such instances. But a comma is unlikely to be as effective as the other marks, and can even be temporarily misleading.

37 Between Nonrestrictive Elements and the Rest of the Sentence

A word or phrase or clause is **nonrestrictive** when it is not essential to the principal meaning of a sentence; it should be set off from the rest of the sentence, usually with commas, though dashes and parentheses can also be used (see **39**). A **restrictive** modifier is essential to the meaning and should not be set off by punctuation:

> *restrictive:*   Anyone wanting a refund should see the manager.
> *nonrestrictive:* Edna, wanting a refund, asked to see the manager.

The participial phrase *wanting a refund* explains why Edna asked to see the manager, but the sentence is clear without it: "Edna asked to see the manager." The phrase is therefore nonrestrictive. In the first sentence the phrase is essential, for without it the sentence wouldn't make sense: "Anyone should see the manager." The phrase is therefore restrictive and not set apart with commas. The question most often arises with relative clauses. Appositives, though usually nonrestrictive, can also be restrictive. And some other elements can also be either restrictive or nonrestrictive (see **34b, 35a,** and **35b**).

37a Restrictive and Nonrestrictive Relative Clauses

Always set off a nonrestrictive relative clause from the rest of the sentence; do not set off restrictive relative clauses:

> She is a girl who likes to travel.

Clearly the relative clause "who likes to travel" is essential to complete the meaning of the sentence; it is therefore restrictive and not set off with a comma.

> Viola, who likes to travel, is going to Greece this summer.

In this sentence, the relative clause "who likes to travel" is merely additional—though explanatory—information: it is not essential to the identification of Viola, who has been explicitly named, nor is it essential to the meaning of the main clause. Being nonrestrictive, then, it must be set off by commas, as above, or by dashes or parentheses.

> Students, who are lazy, should not expect much from their education.

Punctuated as a nonrestrictive clause, the relative clause here applies to all students, and the sentence borders on the libelous. Punctuated as a restrictive clause, it applies only to those students who are in fact lazy, and the sentence becomes a statement of truth:

> Students who are lazy should not expect much from their education.

Now the relative clause *who are lazy* restricts the meaning of *students who . . . should not expect much* to those who are in fact lazy.

> The chair, which I admired, was badly damaged in the fire.

The relative clause *which I admired* is here punctuated as nonrestrictive. The chair being referred to is clearly the subject of discussion: there was only one chair in the room, or else the particular chair meant has already been identified.

> The chair which I admired was badly damaged in the fire.

With the commas removed, the clause becomes restrictive; it would then distinguish that chair from other chairs, as for example would be necessary if there were three chairs in the room, but the only one damaged was the one the speaker particularly admired.

> The book, which I so badly wanted to read, was not in the library.

The book, we must assume, has been clearly identified in a preceding sentence.

> The book which I so badly wanted to read was not in the library.

Punctuated thus, as restrictive, the relative clause must be seen as essential to the identification of the particular book meant: other books the library had in abundance, but the particular one the speaker wanted very much to read was not there.

Note: When the relative pronoun *that* is used, the clause is almost invariably restrictive:

> The book that I so badly wanted to read was not in the library.

Further, the relative pronoun *that* can often be omitted, in which case the clause is definitely restrictive:

> The book I so badly wanted to read was not in the library.

Similarly, if the relative pronoun *whom* can be omitted, the relative clause in question is, again, clearly restrictive and not set off by punctuation:

37a relative clauses

The person [whom] I most admire is the one who works hard and plays hard.

See also **3d.**

Caution: Do not carelessly omit the relative pronoun *that* when it is necessary to prevent misreading:

cl: Examples of the quality of art commercials contain can be found in almost any magazine.

cl: After reading through the draft again, he concluded it was too long and set about cutting it.

A *that* is needed after *art* and after *concluded* in order to prevent the reader from momentarily misreading the sequences as "art commercials" and "he concluded it."

Note: Some writers prefer to use *which* only in nonrestrictive clauses, leaving *that* exclusively for restrictive clauses. In a better world such a tidy distinction might make linguistic life simpler. Unfortunately, however, the use of *which* in restrictive clauses is so common—so natural and idiomatic—that it is absurd to insist on the distinction. And sometimes *which* simply sounds better, for example in a sentence which already contains one or two *that*'s. Nevertheless it is true that *that* is much more common than *which* in restrictive clauses. But when for some reason *which* just sounds or feels better than *that*, there is no good reason why you shouldn't use it.

37b   **Restrictive and Nonrestrictive Appositives**

Always set off a nonrestrictive appositive from the rest of the sentence; do not set off a restrictive appositive:

Gus, our gardener, keeps the lawn mowed all summer.

Karl—the man I intend to marry—is tops in all categories.

Milton's *Paradise Lost* is a noble work of literature, one that will live in men's minds for all time.

Hugh is going to bring his sister, Eileen.

In the last sentence, punctuating the appositive as nonrestrictive indicates that Hugh has only one sister. Without the comma it becomes restrictive, indicating that Hugh has more than one sister, and that the particular one he is going to bring is the one whose name is Eileen:

Hugh is going to bring his sister Eileen.

Some appositives have become parts of names or titles and are not set off:

William the Conqueror won the Battle of Hastings in 1066.

The Apostle Paul wrote several books of the New Testament.

Ivan the Terrible was the first czar of Russia.

Caution: Avoid awkwardly setting off titles of literary works and the like as nonrestrictive appositives. It's *the good ship "Lollipop,"* NOT *the good ship, "Lollipop."* There is, after all, more than one good ship.

> *wrong:*   In his poem, *Paradise Lost,* Milton tells of the fall of man.
> *wrong:*   In the novel, *Great Expectations,* Dickens's theme is that of growing up.

This punctuation makes it sound as if Milton wrote only this one poem and that Dickens's novel is the only novel in existence. Omit at least the first comma; after so short an introductory phrase, the second could also be omitted. If the context is clear, the explanatory words are often not necessary at all:

> In *Paradise Lost* Milton tells. . . .
> In *Great Expectations* Dickens's theme. . . .

The urge to punctuate before titles of literary works leads to the even worse error of putting a comma between a possessive form of an author's name and a title:

> *wrong:*   I remember enjoying Thurber's, "The Secret Life of Walter Mitty."

Don't do that.

See also **44g**.

37c   *Because* Clauses and Phrases

Caution: Adverbial clauses or phrases beginning with *because* (or sometimes *since* or *for*) can present a special problem.

> They don't trust him, because he is a foreigner.

The comma is probably necessary (in spite of what we have just said about not setting off restrictive elements) since the intended meaning is that the reason they don't trust the man is that he is a foreigner. If we remove the comma—or the pause in speech—the meaning changes:

> They don't trust him because he is a foreigner.

The sentence now says that they do trust him, but for some reason other than his being a foreigner, so that we are inclined to ask, "Well, then why *do* they trust him?" The problem is caused by the explicit negative (*not*) in the independent clause preceding the *because* clause. If we remove the negative, but still retain the essential meaning of the sentence, the comma is no longer necessary:

> They distrust him because he is a foreigner.

Whenever you have a negative statement followed by a *because* clause or phrase, be sure to punctuate it so that it means what you intend it to mean:

> Mary didn't pass the exam, because she had stayed up all night studying for it: she was so sleepy she couldn't even read the questions correctly.
> Mary didn't pass the exam because she had stayed up all night studying for it. That no doubt helped, but her thorough grasp of the material would have enabled her to pass it without the extra work.
> He didn't like the man, because of his face.
> He didn't like the man because of his face. Rather he liked and respected him for his intelligence.

Exercise 37: Punctuating nonrestrictive elements

Decide whether the italicized elements in the following sentences are restrictive or nonrestrictive and insert punctuation as required.

1. The student *who takes studying seriously* is the one *who is most likely to succeed.*
2. The novels *I like best* are those *that tell a good story.*
3. This movie *which was produced on a very low budget* was a popular success.
4. Whitehorse *the capital of the Yukon* is a cold place to spend the winter.
5. Cato *the Elder* was one of the principal Stoic philosophers.
6. Sentence interrupters *not essential to the meaning* should be set off with commas.
7. Academics *who cannot write good prose* should not be given tenure.
8. The London *which is in Ontario* was named after the London *which is the capital of England.*
9. Raymond Massey *the actor* is the brother of one of Canada's governors general.
10. In the view of small-town newspaper editor *John Smith* the storm was nothing to get excited about.

38   Between Items in a Series

38a   Commas

Generally, use commas between words, phrases, or clauses in a series of three or more:

> He sells books, magazines, candy, and tobacco.
> He promised the voters to cut taxes, to limit government spending, and to improve transportation.
> Carmen explained that she had visited the art gallery, that she had walked in the park, and that eventually she had gone to a movie.
> He stirred the sauce frequently, carefully, and hungrily.

38b   Comma Before Final Item in a Series

Some writers omit the final comma, the one before the conjunction, especially when the items in the series are short; but they then trap themselves into being inconsistent, for sometimes it is necessary to include the comma before the *and* in order to prevent awkwardness or misreading. Consider the following sentences:

> For breakfast I like toast, coffee, ham and eggs.

Clearly this sentence needs either a comma after *ham* or, if "ham and eggs" is meant as a unit, an *and* before *ham* as well as after it.

> Besides good ideas, your teacher wants your essays to have good diction, good sentences, good paragraphs, good punctuation and mechanics, and good organization.

The comma after *mechanics* helps prevent confusion.

> They prided themselves on having a large and bright kitchen, a productive vegetable garden, a large recreation room with a huge fireplace and two fifty-foot cedar trees.

One might well be proud of a room that could contain huge trees. The ambiguity and the unintended humour are removed when a comma is inserted after *fireplace*. Look what the omission of the comma before *and* does to this sentence:

> The Speech from the Throne discussed foreign trade, improvements in transportation, slowing down the economy and the postal service.

It is more prudent always to include the comma before the *and*, for not only will your sentences then have a smoother rhythm (punctuate a sentence the way you want it to be heard), but also you will be able to be consistent, and you will never need to worry about awkwardness or ambiguity.

38c   Semicolons

If the phrases or clauses in a series are long or contain internal punctuation, you will probably want to separate them with semicolons rather than commas:

> How wonderful it is to awaken in the morning when the birds are clamouring in the trees; to see the bright light of a summer's morning streaming into the room; to realize, with a sudden illuminating flash of joy, that it is Sunday and that this perfect morning is completely yours; and then to loaf in the sun without a thought of tomorrow.

> Saint John, New Brunswick; Victoria, British Columbia; and Kingston, Ontario, are all about the same size.

If you want to create emphasis and a slower rhythm, you can separate even short items in a series with semicolons:

> There are certain qualities we expect in our leaders: honesty; integrity; intelligence; understanding.

(The omission of the customary *and* before the final item stylistically heightens the effect, reinforcing the emphasis gained by using semicolons.)

38d   Dashes

One can also emphasize items in a series by using dashes to separate them; but this device should be used only very rarely and with great circumspection. The sharpness of the breaks provided by the dashes can considerably heighten the rhetorical effect of a sentence:

> Rising taxes—rising insurance rates—rising transportation costs—skyrocketing food prices: it is becoming more and more difficult to live decently and still keep within a budget.

Here again the omission of the customary *and* contributes, as does the repetition and the parallel structure, to the almost stridently emphatic tone of the first part of the sentence. Even the colon that ends the series adds its touch to the effect. But such dashes can also be used effectively in a quieter context:

> Upon rounding the bend we were confronted with a breathtaking panorama of lush valleys with meandering streams—flower-covered slopes—great rocks and trees—and, overtopping all, the mighty peaks with their hoods of snow.

38e   Colons

Even colons can be used between items in a series, but even more rarely than dashes. Colons too provide a certain emphasis, partly because they are so unusual in such instances, but the distinguishing feature is rather that they assist in producing a cumulative effect; hence they are appropriate only in those rare circumstances where each item in the series leads to the next (again, the anticipatory function of the colon), building to at least a mild climax:

> He held on: he persevered: he fought back: and eventually he won out, regardless of the seemingly overwhelming obstacles.
> It blew: it rained: it hailed: it sleeted: it even snowed—it was a most unusual month of June.

(Notice how the dash sets one up for the final clause in the last example.)

38f   Series of Adjectives

Use commas to separate two or more adjectives in a series preceding a noun if they are parallel, each modifying the noun itself; do not separate adjectives in a series before a noun if they are not parallel—that is, if each in effect modifies the group of words, consisting of adjective(s) and noun, following it.

> He is an intelligent, efficient, ambitious officer.

Here each of the three adjectives modifies the noun, *officer*.

> She is a tall young woman.

Here *tall* modifies *young woman*, not just *woman*. It is a *young woman* who is *tall*, not a *woman* who is *tall* and *young*.

> She wore a new black felt hat and a long red dress with many gold, silver, and black sequins on it.

Here *new* modifies *black felt hat*, *black* modifies *felt hat*, and *long* modifies *red dress*; hence no separating commas are needed. *Gold, silver,* and *black* all separately modify *sequins*, and must be separated by commas. But it is not always easy to decide whether adjectives in a series are parallel. There is one rule of thumb that will often help in difficult instances. Try putting the co-ordinating conjunction *and* between the adjectives. If it seems to work comfortably there, then the adjectives are probably parallel and should be separated by commas; if *and* does not sound right, no commas are needed. Applying this to the last example, one would quickly realize that to say "a new and black and felt hat" or "a long and red dress" would be absurd, whereas to say "gold and silver and black sequins" would be quite natural; where an *and* will not go, a comma should not go—and the problem is solved.

It is partly also a matter of word order. We naturally say

> He was a tired old man.

and no comma is needed, since *tired* modifies *old man*. But if one wanted to depart from the natural order and say

> He was an old, tired man.

then a comma would be necessary. The *and* test verifies the punctuation of these two versions as well. But the natural word order is not always amenable to such changes. For example, it is natural to speak of a *new brick house*, but who would even consider referring to a *brick new house*, with or without a comma? Another hint to remember: it is usually correct to omit commas after numbers (*three blind mice*), and after common adjectives designating size or age (*long red dress; new brick house*). This is not foolproof, however, as *old, tired man* demonstrates; the matter of word order apparently takes precedence over this general rule.

There will no doubt be occasions when neither logic nor rules of thumb will seem to help. You must then rely on instinct or common sense, or both. For example, no hint or rule will help one to decide if commas are needed in a series of adjectives such as these:

> There was an ominous wry tone in her voice.
> What caught our eye in the antique shop was a comfortable-looking tattered old upholstered leather chair.

On such occasions, one can only try different arrangements and punctuations and settle on the one that sounds best or that seems best to fit one's intentions—or one can give up and rewrite the sentence.

Exercise 38: Punctuating series

Punctuate the following sentences as necessary.

1. The things I expected from my education were better self-discipline a broader outlook on life and the arts and preparation for a possible career.
2. April May and June are my favourite months.
3. The handsome young man wore gray plaid slacks a yellow turtleneck sweater and a smartly tailored blue blazer with square brass buttons.
4. The nice cute little baby soon began to crawl fall and squall.
5. The recital was over the audience began to cheer and applaud loudly and the pianist who was obviously pleased stood up and bowed.

■ 39 ■ Punctuating "Sentence Interrupters" with Commas, Dashes, and Parentheses: The Punctuation Marks that Come in Pairs

Sentence interrupters are parenthetical elements—words, phrases, or clauses—that interrupt the syntax of a sentence. They can be of several different kinds, some of which have already been discussed under other headings. We isolate interrupters here, however, in order to stress two points: (1) interrupters must be set off at *both* ends; (2) you can choose among three kinds of punctuation marks to set them off: a pair of commas, a pair of dashes, or a pair of parentheses.

■ 39a ■ Set Off with Commas

Set off light, ordinary interrupters with a pair of commas:

> Boswell, the biographer of Samuel Johnson, was a keen observer. (nonrestrictive appositive phrase)
> This document, the lawyer says, will complete the contract. (parenthetical clause of explanation)
> Thank you, David, for your good advice. (noun of direct address)
> Mr. Hao, feeling elated, left the judge's office. (participial phrase)
> At least one science course, such as botany or astronomy, is required of all students. (prepositional phrase of example)
> You may, on the other hand, wish to concentrate on the final examination. (transitional prepositional phrase)
> Could you be persuaded to consider this money as, well, a loan? (mild interjection)
> Grandparents, who are often far too indulgent, should not be allowed to spoil their grandchildren. (nonrestrictive relative clause)
> But the canned tuna, it now occurs to me, may after all be responsible

for our upset stomachs. (clause expressing afterthought)
It was, all things considered, a successful concert. (absolute phrase)

39b   Set Off with Dashes

Use a pair of dashes to set off abrupt interrupters or other interrupters that you wish to emphasize. An interrupter that sharply breaks the syntax of a sentence will often be emphatic for that very reason, and dashes will be appropriate to set it off:

> This document—so says the lawyer, anyway—will complete the contract.
> The stockholders who voted for him—a quite considerable group, by the way—were obviously dissatisfied with our recent conduct of the business.
> He told me—believe this or not!—that he would never drink again.
> Samuel Johnson—the eighteenth century's most eminent man of letters—is the subject of James Boswell's great biography.

In this last example the appositive phrase could be set off with commas, but dashes seem more appropriate because of both the length and the content of the appositive; further, an appositive of that length coming so soon in the sentence, after only a proper name, does amount to an abrupt interruption, further justifying the dashes. In other instances where you want emphasis or a different tone, dashes can be used where commas would ordinarily serve:

> The best student—Roger Lefebvre—was elected class president.
> The modern age—as we all know—is a technology-ridden age.
> But since the steak was well done, he—of course—ate the whole thing.

In the last example, the interrupter *of course* could have been left unpunctuated; therefore the exaggerated pauses caused by the dashes produce a considerable tonal effect, namely of sarcasm. Dashes are also useful to set off an interrupter consisting of a series with its own internal commas, such as the appositive in our first sentence in this section. Set off with commas, it would be confusing; set off with dashes, it is clear:

> *confusing:* Sentence interrupters are parenthetical elements, words, phrases, or clauses, that interrupt the syntax of a sentence.
> *clear:* Sentence interrupters are parenthetical elements—words, phrases, or clauses—that interrupt the syntax of a sentence.

39c   Set Off with Parentheses

Use parentheses ( ) to set off abrupt interrupters or other interrupters that you wish to de-emphasize:

> The stockholders who voted for him (a quite considerable group, by the way) were obviously dissatisfied with our recent conduct of the business.
> The best student (his name is Roger Lefebvre) was elected class president.

In these examples, interrupters that could be emphatic (see the preceding section) have been de-emphasized in order to emphasize the main parts of the sentences.

Dashes call attention to the intrusion; parentheses normally play down the intrusion.

> But since the steak was well done, he (of course) ate the whole thing.

Here, by de-emphasizing the slight interrupter, an effect is achieved similar to that achieved by emphasizing it with dashes, but this time by an ironic rather than an insistent tone. Here are some further examples of parentheses used to enclose explanations, qualifications, and examples whose syntax is not related to the syntax of the sentences in which they occur:

> It is not possible at this time (it is far too early in the growing season) to predict with any confidence just what the crop yield will be.
>
> Speculation (I mean this in its pejorative sense) is not a safe foundation for a business enterprise.
>
> Some modern sports activities (hang-gliding for example) involve an unusually high element of danger.

Could a pair of dashes be used in any of these?

Remember, punctuation marks that set off sentence interrupters come in pairs. If you have put down an opening parenthesis, you are not likely to omit the closing parenthesis (unless you are very careless!). It is just as wrong to omit the closing comma or dash. Of course, if one of these "interrupters" does not really interrupt, that is, if it comes at the beginning or end of a sentence, only one comma or dash is required (but two parentheses, of course—like this).

(left margin) 39c *parentheses*

Exercise 39: Punctuating sentence interrupters

Set off the italicized sentence interrupters with commas, dashes, or parentheses. Be prepared to defend your choices.

1. It was seven o'clock in the evening *a mild autumn evening* and the crickets were beginning to chirp.
2. No one *at least no one who was present* wanted to disagree with the speaker's position.
3. One Sunday morning *a morning I will never forget* the phone rang clamorously.
4. Since it was only a mild interjection *no more than a barely audible snort from the back of the room* he went on with scarcely a pause *but with a slightly raised eyebrow* and finished his speech.
5. And then suddenly *out of the blue and into my head* came the only possible answer.

▆ 40 ▆   Parentheses   ( )

Parentheses have three principal functions in nontechnical writing: (1) to set off certain kinds of interrupters (see **39c** above), (2) to enclose cross-reference information within a sentence, as we just did and as we do throughout this book, and (3) to enclose numerals or letters setting up a list or series, as we do with the numerals *1, 2,* and *3* in this sentence. Note that if a complete sentence is enclosed in parentheses within another sentence (here is an example of such an insertion), it needs neither an opening capital letter nor a closing period. Note also that if a comma or other mark is called for by the sentence (as in the preceding sentence, and in this one), it comes *after* the parenthesis, not before it. And don't make the mistake of assuming that the parenthesis itself, since it requires a kind of pause, takes the place of such a comma; it does not.

Other punctuation marks go inside the parentheses only if they are a part of what is enclosed, as with the exclamation point in the paragraph just before Exercise 39. (When an entire sentence or more is enclosed, the terminal mark of course comes inside the parentheses—as does this period right here.)

▆ 41 ▆   Brackets   **[ ]**

Brackets (often referred to as "square brackets," since some people think "brackets" means "parentheses") are used primarily to enclose anything you find it necessary to insert in a direct quotation: see **43j**, and paragraphs 19 and 21 in the sample research paper, **84**. If you have to put parentheses inside parentheses, change the inner ones to brackets. If you are careful, this should never be necessary, unless perhaps in a footnote or a bibliographical entry, where parentheses have particular uses (see **84**, footnote 3).

▆ 42 ▆   End Punctuation: The Period, the Question Mark, and the Exclamation Point

The end of every sentence must be marked with a period, a question mark, or an exclamation point. The **period** is the most common terminal punctuation; it ends the vast majority of sentences. The **question mark** is used to end direct questions or seeming statements that are intended interrogatively. The **exclamation point** is used to end sentences that express strong emotion, emphatic surprise, or even emphatic query. Usually the appropriate choice of mark will be obvious, but sometimes you will want to consider just what effect you want to achieve. Note for example the different effects—provided entirely by the end punctuation—in the following sentences:

> You said that you didn't understand me. (simple statement of fact)
> You said that you didn't understand me! (emphatic assertion of speaker's belief)
> You said that you didn't understand me? (expression of speaker's disbelief)

In each instance, the end punctuation would dictate the necessary tone of voice and distribution of emphasis and pitch with which the sentence would be said aloud. Again:

> He succeeded. (matter-of-fact)
> He succeeded! (surprised or emphatic)
> He succeeded? (sceptical or surprised)

42a The Period •

Use a period to mark the end of statements and unemphatic commands:

> It is much colder this winter than it was last winter.
> Geoffrey Chaucer, the author of *The Canterbury Tales*, died in 1400.
> Close the door on your way out, please.
> Do not let yourself be fooled by advertising claims.

A period can also be used after a polite question that is not meant interrogatively:

> You'll write to us soon, won't you.
> Why don't you come over here and sit by me.

Use a period after most abbreviations:

> abbr., Mr., Ph.D., Dr., Jr., B.A., Mt., Nfld., P.E.I., etc.

(Note: In England it is conventional to omit the period after abbreviations that include the first and last letter of the abbreviated word: Mr, Mrs, Dr, Bart, ft, Jr, St, etc.) Periods are not used after metric and other symbols (unless they occur at the end of a sentence):

> km, cm, kg, C, Hz, Au, Zr

Periods are often omitted with initials, especially of groups or organizations, and especially if the initials are acronyms or thought of as a name and written in capital letters:

> UN, UNESCO, NATO, RCMP, RAF, NDP, TV, MLA, MP, STOL, CNR

If you are in doubt, consult a good dictionary. If there is more than one acceptable usage, be sure to be consistent: stick with the one you choose.

Note: Required punctuation marks follow the periods of abbreviations except when the abbreviation ends the sentence; in such an instance the abbreviation's period also marks the end of the sentence:

> He gets up at 8 a.m., breakfasts at 9 a.m., and goes riding promptly at 10 a.m.

42b **The Question Mark ?**

Use a question mark at the end of direct questions:

> Who is the greatest philosopher of all time?
> How many tons can you deliver?

Note that a question mark is necessary—and even more important—after questions that are not phrased in the usual interrogative way:

> You are going? (instead of "Are you going?")
> You want him to accompany you? (instead of "Do you want him to accompany you?")

A question may also appear as a sentence interrupter; it will still need a question mark at its end:

> I went back to the beginning—what else could I do?—and tried to get it right the second time through.
> The gentleman in the mackintosh (what was his name again?) took a rear seat.

Note that since these interrogative interrupters are necessarily abrupt, dashes or parentheses will be the appropriate marks with which to enclose them.

42c **The Exclamation Point !**

Use exclamation points after emphatic statements and after expressions of emphatic surprise, emphatic query, and strong emotion—that is, after exclamations:

> He came in first, yet it was only his second time in professional competition!
> What a fine actor!
> You don't say so!
> Isn't it beautiful today!
> Be careful! You might fall!
> Wow!

Caution: An exclamation point will seldom turn an otherwise ordinary sentence into an exclamation. The sentence should already *be* emphatic in order for the exclamation point to be appropriate. Of course there are exceptions to this: some sentences that a writer wishes to be read as exclamations will not in themselves appear emphatic, but rather than change a desirable wording the writer will simply settle for a final exclamation point to mark his intention.

Note: There are two other ways to end sentences, ways which occur occasionally in narrative fiction but rarely elsewhere. Dashes, or more commonly the three dots of ellipsis—sometimes called suspension points—are sometimes used at the ends of sentences, especially in dialogue or at the end of a paragraph or a chapter, to suggest "and so on," a fading away, or an interruption, or to create mild suspense, so that the reader wonders what's going to happen next. . . . (See **43i**.)

43 Punctuation with Quotations;   " "
Q   Using Quotation Marks

There are two kinds of **quotation**: dialogue or **direct speech**, as in a story, novel, or nonfiction narrative, or even in an essay that is not primarily a narrative; and verbatim quotation from a published work or other **source**.

43a   Direct Speech

Enclose all direct speech in quotation marks:

> "Henry, get your feet off the coffee table."

In dialogue, where there are two or more speakers, it is conventional to begin a new paragraph each time the speaker changes:

> "Henry," she said, a note of exasperation in her voice, "please get your feet off the coffee table."
> "Oh, yes," he replied. "Sorry, dear, I keep forgetting."
> She examined it for scratches. "Well, no harm done this time, I guess. But please try to remember."

Even when speeches are not complete, the part that is verbatim still must be enclosed in quotation marks:

> After only two weeks, he said he was "tired of it all" and that he was "going to look for a more interesting job."

43b   Direct Quotation from a Source

Enclose in quotation marks all direct quotation from other sources when you run the quotation into your own text:

> According to Francis Bacon, "No pleasure is comparable to standing upon

the vantage-ground of truth."

If a prose quotation extends to four or five lines or more, it is customary to indent it and single-space it; in a manuscript this represents what in a printed work would be an excerpt set in reduced type:

> As Milton puts it, in one of those ringing passages that make his *Areopagitica* so memorable:
>
>> I cannot praise a fugitive and cloistered virtue, unexercised and un-breathed, that never sallies out and seeks her adversary, but slinks out of the race where that immortal garland is to be run for, not without dust and heat.

Similarly, quotations of more than two or three lines of poetry are usually indented and single-spaced:

> In poetry, "The sound must seem an echo to the sense," as Pope says in his *Essay on Criticism*. He then goes on to say, demonstrating the while, that
>
>> Soft is the strain when zephyr gently blows,
>> And the smooth stream in smoother numbers flows;
>> But when loud surges lash the sounding shore,
>> The hoarse rough verse should like the torrent roar.

And there should be a *triple* line-space before and after such an inset quotation, for if you were quoting a single line of poetry, ordinary double spacing would make it look like the beginning of a new paragraph. For the same reason it is advisable to indent such quotations more than the customary five-space paragraph indention—say eight or ten spaces.

Notes:

(1) The act of indenting and single-spacing is tantamount to using quotation marks; therefore no quotation marks are added. If, however, the original passage is itself in quotation marks, then these must be reproduced in your quotation of it:

> Budgets can be important. As Dickens had Mr. Micawber say in *David Copperfield,*
>
>> "Annual income twenty pounds, annual expenditure nineteen nineteen six, result happiness. Annual income twenty pounds, annual expenditure twenty pounds ought and six, result misery."

(2) If you quote a single paragraph or part of a paragraph and set it off from your text, do not include the paragraph indention. If your

quotation takes in more than one paragraph, include the paragraph indentions. If you are quoting two or more paragraphs that are in quotation marks in the original, put quotation marks at the beginning of each paragraph, but put them at the end of the final paragraph only.

(3) A quotation of less than four or so lines may be indented and single-spaced if you want it to receive special notice, to be slightly emphasized. A quotation of two lines or even a single line of poetry is often treated this way. If you wish to quote more than one line of poetry and to run it into your own text rather than set it off with indention and single spacing, then the end of each line should be marked with a diagonal line, called a *slash* or *virgule*, with a space before and after it:

> Wordsworth's comment in one of his sonnets almost two hundred years
>
> ago could well be applied to the way we live today: "The world is too
>
> much with us; late and soon, / Getting and spending, we lay waste our
>
> powers: / Little we see in Nature that is ours."

(In formal writing, avoid using the slash to form pairs of alternative terms such as *and/or* and *he/she*. See **4d** and entries in **60**.)

43c Single Quotation Marks: Quotation within Quotation

Use **single quotation marks** (' ') to enclose a quotation that occurs within something that is already enclosed in quotation marks:

> "Well," said Noel, "when I got there I found a sign on the door that said 'Out to lunch.' "
>
> In Conrad's *Heart of Darkness*, after a leisurely setting of the scene by the unnamed narrator, the drama begins when the man who is to be the principal narrator first speaks: " 'And this also,' said Marlow suddenly, 'has been one of the dark places of the earth.' "

This is the only way single quotation marks should be used.

43d With Verbs of Speaking Before Quotations

When verbs of speaking or their equivalent precede a quotation, they are usually followed by commas:

> Adriana looked up and asked, "What time is it?"
> Helen said, "He will do exactly as I tell him."

If the quotation is short, however, a comma may not be necessary:

> He said "Not yet," so we waited a little longer.

Again, punctuate the sentence the way you want it to be heard; your sense of its rhythm should help you decide. On the other hand, if the quotation is long—especially if it consists of more than one sentence—or if the context is formal, a colon will probably be more appropriate:

When dinner was over Oscar turned to his hostess and said: "Seldom have I enjoyed a meal more, my dear. The balance of courses was superb, and the wines were the perfect accompaniment."

If the introductory element is itself an independent clause, then a colon or a period must be used:

Oscar turned to her and spoke: "A delicious repast, my dear."

Spoke, unlike *said*, is here an intransitive verb.

43e **With Long or Formal Quotations**

Colons are conventionally used to introduce long and formal quotations that are set off by indention and single-spacing. If the quotation is worked into the syntax of your own sentence, however, it can be punctuated accordingly:

In one of his *Devotions*, John Donne wrote that

No man is an island, entire of itself; every man is a piece of the continent, a part of the main; if a clod be washed away by the sea, Europe is the less, as well as if a promontory were, as well as if a manor of thy friends or of thine own were; any man's death diminishes me, because I am involved in mankind; and therefore never send to know for whom the bell tolls; it tolls for thee.

The word *that* makes all the difference; if it were removed, a colon would be needed. The same applies to shorter quotations worked into your own syntax:

It is often said that "Sticks and stones may break my bones, but words will never hurt me"—a singularly inaccurate notion.

No punctuation—not even a comma—should follow the introductory *that*.

43f **With Verbs of Speaking After Quotations**

If verbs of speaking or other such elements follow a quotation, they are usually set off by commas (or on occasion, as in the preceding example, by a dash):

"The Great Lakes are extremely important to the commerce of the area," he said.
"I think there's a fly in my soup," she muttered.

But if the quotation ends with a question mark or an exclamation point, no other punctuation should be added:

"Have you read Margaret Laurence's latest novel?" she asked.
"Mr. Chairman! I insist that I be heard!" he shouted.

43f verbs of speaking

Similarly, if a quotation is at the end of a sentence, its own terminal punctuation, whether period, question mark, or exclamation point, is also the terminal punctuation for the whole sentence; no extra period should be added.

If the phrase with the verb of speaking interrupts the quotation, it should be preceded by a comma and followed by whatever mark is called for by the syntax and the sense:

> "Since it's such a long drive," he said, "we'd better get an early start."
> "It's a long drive," he argued; "therefore I think we should start early."
> "It's a very long way," he insisted. "We should start as early as possible."

43g   Words Used in a Special Sense

Put quotation marks around words used in a special sense or words for which you wish to indicate some qualification:

> What he calls a "ramble" I would call a twenty-mile hike.
> He had been up in the woods so long he was "bushed," as the saying is.
> "Competent" is hardly the word for it; I would call it magnificent!

Note: Some writers put quotation marks around words referred to as words, but it is better practice to italicize them (i.e., in a manuscript, underline them):

> The dictionary defines fulsome as "distastefully excessive in an oily or insincere way."
> The word aggravate is commonly misused.

(See **49c**.)

Caution: Do not put quotation marks around slang terms, clichés, and the like; if the word or phrase is so weak that you have to apologize for it, you should not be using it in the first place. Setting off such a word or phrase also calls attention to it, which is the last thing it needs. Moreover, this practice implicitly insults readers by presuming that they will not recognize a bit of slang when they see it. Similarly, try to resist the temptation to use quotation marks for effects of comic irony:

> The "girl" behind the counter was forty if she was a day!

It is a cheap effect at best, and the snide tone often backfires upon the writer. One final point: do not use quotation marks for emphasis; they do not work that way.

43h   Other Marks with Quotation Marks

Put *periods* and *commas* inside closing quotation marks; put *semicolons* and *colons* outside them:

"Knowing how to write well," he said, "can be a source of great pleasure"; and then he added that it had "one other important quality": he identified it simply as "hard work."

This is simply a printer's convention; the sample sentence exemplifies the dominant Canadian practice. Since it is also the standard practice in the United States, it could be called a North American convention. In England, however, it is conventional to place all four of these punctuation marks outside quotation marks. Some Canadians follow one method, some the other, and sometimes the two are mixed. In the interest of consistency, we recommend following the dominant North American practice.

Question marks, exclamation points, and *dashes* are put either inside or outside closing quotation marks, depending on whether they apply to the quotation or to the whole sentence:

"What time is it?" he asked.
Who said, "To be or not to be, that is the question"?
Did you find out who shouted "God save the Queen!"?

43i   **Ellipses for Omissions**   **. . .**

Indicate any omission from quoted material with three *spaced* periods (**ellipsis**); if the omission includes the end of a sentence, add a fourth period. For example, if you wanted to quote only certain parts of the passage from Donne's *Devotions* quoted at length earlier (**43e**), you might do it like this:

As John Donne wrote: "No man is an island, entire of itself . . . any man's death diminishes me, because I am involved in mankind . . . ."

If the omission is from the beginning of the following sentence, do not leave a space before the first of the four periods, for it serves as the sentence period. If you omit an entire paragraph or more of prose or one or more lines of poetry, indicate the omission with a whole line of spaced periods. You need not indicate an ellipsis at the *beginning* of a quotation unless it could be mistaken for a complete sentence—for example, if the quoted portion of a sentence began with *I* or some other capital letter:

One could say, echoing Donne, ". . . I am involved in mankind . . . ."

You need not use the dots at either end if your quotation is a mere word or phrase that could in no way be mistaken for a complete sentence.

Caution: Be careful not to omit material from a quotation in such a way that you distort what the author is saying, or destroy the integrity of the syntax. Similarly, do not quote unfairly "out of context"; that is, if an author qualifies a statement in some way, do not quote the statement bare, as if it were unqualified. If what you are quoting is a fragmentary part of a sentence, make sure that it conforms to the syntax of your own sentence.

43j Brackets for Additions, Changes, and Comments [ ]

Enclose in brackets any editorial addition you make within a quotation. The passage from Milton's *Aeropagitica* quoted earlier (**43b**), for example, would be clearer with an added piece of information:

> As Milton put it:
>
> I cannot praise a fugitive and cloistered virtue . . . that never sallies out and seeks her adversary, but slinks out of the race where that immortal garland [truth] is to be run for . . . .

The word *truth*, taken from a nearby sentence, identifies what "that immortal garland" refers to. Use this method also when it is necessary to change a word to make it conform to your syntax or tense:

> One of my friends wrote me that his "feelings about the subject [were] similar to" mine.

Similarly, use the word *sic* (Latin for *thus*) in brackets to indicate that an error in the quotation occurs in the original:

> One of my friends wrote me: "My feelings about the subject are similiar [sic] to yours."

(For the use of quotation marks around titles, see **48** below.)

44 Some Common Errors in Punctuation to Guard Against

44a

Do not put a comma between a subject and its verb unless some intervening element calls for punctuation:

> *no p:* His enthusiasm for the project and his desire to be of help, led him to add his name to the list of volunteers.

The comma after *help* intrudes between the compound subject ("enthusiasm . . . and . . . desire") and its verb, *led*. It is just as wrong as the comma in this sentence:

> *no p:* Edna, went to class.

But if some other element, for example an appositive or a participial phrase, intervenes between subject and verb, it must be set off:

(margin) **43j** *brackets*

His enthusiasm for the project and his desire to be of help, both strongly felt, led him to add his name to the list of volunteers.

Edna, the star student, went to class.

Here the sentence interrupters are properly set off by *pairs* of commas (see **38a**).

Occasionally, however, if a subject is unusually long or complicated or heavily punctuated, a comma after it and before the verb may be useful:

> Students who come to university looking not for an education but for a good time, to whom classes are a necessary evil and the weekend parties the really important occasions, and who feel that teachers and libraries are things to be avoided as much as possible, are not only likely to perform miserably but are also fundamentally wasting their own and everyone else's time and money.

The comma after *possible*, while not essential, does make the sentence easier to read. Sometimes such a comma is required simply to prevent misreading:

> The spirit of adventure and the openness to the unexpected sights, sounds, tastes, and people, give independent travellers a familiarity with a place that those on package tours could never have.

The last comma prevents *people* from being even momentarily mistaken for the subject of the verb *give*.

44b Do not put a comma between a verb and its object or complement unless some intervening element calls for punctuation:

> *no p:* Jeremy found, that he could no longer keep his eyes open.

Here the noun clause beginning with *that* is the direct object of the verb *found* and should not be separated from it. Only if an interrupter requires setting off should there be any punctuation:

> Jeremy found, moreover, that he could no longer keep his eyes open.

> Jeremy found, as he tried once again to read the paragraph, that he could no longer keep his eyes open.

Another example:

> *no p:* Ottawa's principal claim to fame is, that it is the national capital.

Here the comma intrudes between the linking verb *is* and its complement, the predicate noun consisting of a clause beginning with *that*. If there were an interrupter that required setting off, then a pair of commas (or dashes or parentheses) would be necessary:

> Ottawa's principal claim to fame is, according to many, that it is the national capital.

44c   Do not put a comma between the last adjective of a series and the noun it modifies:

> How could anyone fail to be impressed by such an intelligent, outspoken, resourceful, fellow as Jonathan has proved himself to be?

The comma after *resourceful* is wrong, though it may momentarily sound right because a certain rhythm has been established and because there is no *and* before the last of the three adjectives; don't let yourself be trapped into this error. Similarly, do not put a comma after the last noun of a series.

44d   Generally, do not put a comma between words and phrases joined by a co-ordinating conjunction; use a comma only when the co-ordinate elements are clauses:

> *unnecessary:*   The dog and cat circled each other warily, and then went off in opposite directions.
>
> *unnecessary:*   I was a long way from home, and didn't know how to get there.
>
> *unnecessary:*   He was not only intelligent, but also very industrious.

All the commas in these examples are unnecessary. Sometimes a writer will use such a comma to achieve a mild emphasis, but if you want an emphatic pause, a dash will probably work better:

> The dog and cat circled each other warily—and then went off in opposite directions.

Or the sentence can be slightly revised in order to gain the emphasis:

> He was not only intelligent; he was also very industrious.
> I was a long way from home, and I had no idea how to get there.

In the last example the comma is better, for the sentence now consists of two independent clauses; in this example, even though the subject remains the same, a comma is preferable to no punctuation.

There are occasions, however, when it is appropriate to use commas between co-ordinate elements other than clauses, times when one desires a slight pause, or a mild emphasis, but yet does not want to call attention to it with a dash. (We have used two such commas in the preceding sentence.) When you do use such a comma, do so as the result of a conscious decision; mere instinct or a vague sense of rhythm can all too easily lead you into over-punctuation.

44e   If the two elements joined by a conjunction involve an emphatic repetition, a comma is sometimes optional:

> I wanted not only to win, but to win overwhelmingly.

This sentence would be equally correct and effective without the comma. In the following sentence, however, the comma is necessary:

> It was an object of beauty, and of beauty most spectacular.

Again, sounding the sentence over to yourself should enable you to decide.

44f Generally, do not set off introductory elements or interrupters that are very short, that are not really parenthetical, or that are so slightly parenthetical that you feel no pause when reading them:

no p: Perhaps, she was trying to tell us something.
no p: But, it was not a case of mistaken identity.
no p: We were asked to try it out, for a week, to see if we really liked it.
no p: Therefore, he put on his raincoat.

When the pause is strong, however, be sure to set off the phrase:

> It was only then, after dinner, that we could all relax.

Often such commas are optional. Writers who are insecure about their punctuation will often insert commas where they are not needed. Here are a few sentences in which a comma is optional, depending on the pattern of intonation the writer wants:

> In Canada (,) the progress of the seasons is sharply evident.
> In Canada (,) as elsewhere, money talks.
> Last year (,) there was a record wheat crop.
> In order to keep dry (,) therefore, he put on his raincoat.
> It was one of those lovely days (,) in June (,) when everything seems perfect. (either two commas or none)
> After dinner (,) we all went for a walk.
> As she walked (,) she thought of her childhood on the farm.

Sometimes a comma is necessary simply to prevent misreading:

> After eating, the dog Irene gave me jumped out the window.
> As she walked, past events in her life crowded before her mind's eye.
> We came to the door of the meeting room and opened it. Inside, a few students were standing about, three or four to a group.

44g Do not mistake a restrictive appositive for a nonrestrictive one.

Right: According to Senator James Higginbottom, the economy is improving daily.

Few if any would put a comma after *Senator* in such a sentence. Yet all too often one comes across a sentence like this:

Wrong: The proceedings were opened by union leader, John Smith, with remarks attacking the government.

The comma after *leader* is incorrect, since it is only his name, *John Smith*, that clearly identifies him; the appositive is therefore *restrictive*.

Right: The proceedings were opened by the union's leader, John Smith, with remarks attacking the government.

In this version the definite article *the* and the possessive *union's* define—restrict—the man; the name itself, *John Smith*, is only incidental information and is therefore *nonrestrictive*.

Wrong: According to spokesman, James Higginbottom, the economy is improving daily.

Right: According to the spokesman, James Higginbottom, the economy is improving daily.

The definite article *the* makes all the difference, as again in the following:

Wrong: It was the stated belief of heavyweight champion, Muhammad Ali, that no one could beat him.

Right: It was the stated belief of the heavyweight champion, Muhammad Ali, that no one could beat him.

But even the presence or absence of the definite article is not always a sure test. Consider this sentence for example:

One of the best-known mysteries of the sea is that of the ship *Mary Celeste*, the disappearance of whose entire crew has never been satisfactorily explained.

Here the phrase *the ship* is insufficient identification; the proper name is needed, and is therefore restrictive.

This error most often occurs when a proper name *follows* a defining or characterizing phrase. The proper name in such instances is usually restrictive, and therefore not set off with commas. Be careful not to confuse such appositives with appositives that occur in the reverse order (and include the definite article); these are nonrestrictive and set off with commas:

James Higginbottom, the senator, said the economy was improving daily. Muhammad Ali, the heavyweight champion, often stated that he was unbeatable.

See also **37b**.

44h   Do not set off indirect quotations as if they were direct quotations:

no p: In his last chapter the author says, that civilization as we have come to know it is in jeopardy.

no p: If you ask Andrew he's sure to say, he doesn't want to go.

The commas in these two sentences are wrong because "the author" and "Andrew" are not being quoted directly; what they said is being reported indirectly. If Andrew is quoted directly, a comma before the quotation is correct:

If you ask Andrew he's sure to say, "I don't want to go."

See also **43a**.

44i   Do not put a semicolon in front of a mere phrase or subordinate clause. Use such a semicolon only where you *could*, if you chose, use a period instead.

Wrong: They cancelled the meeting; being disappointed at the low turnout.

Wrong: Only about a dozen people showed up; partly because there had not been enough publicity.

Those semicolons should be *commas*. Periods in those spots would turn what follows them into *fragments* (see **1y**); since a semicolon is also a heavy "stop," these in effect do the same thing. Since a semicolon signals that an *independent clause* is coming next, readers are distracted when only a phrase or a subordinate clause arrives. This error sometimes occurs when a student who is afraid of committing a comma splice errs in the other direction and overpunctuates. If this happens to you, devote some further study to the comma splice (**33e**) and to learning how to recognize an independent clause (see **1m-o**).

Similarly, do not put a semicolon between a subordinate clause and an independent clause.

Wrong: In my first few years of school, my formative years, when my hobby was still in its infancy; the sky was alive with wonder.

That semicolon too should be a comma. The presence of other commas earlier in the sentence does not mean that the later comma needs to be raised to a semicolon; there is no danger of misreading—as there sometimes is when a comma and a co-ordinating conjunction join two independent clauses (see **33b**).

44j   Do not use a colon after a syntactically incomplete construction; a colon is appropriate only after an independent clause.

Wrong: He preferred such foods as: potatoes, corn, and spaghetti.

Here the colon is misused, since "He preferred such foods as" is not a syntactically complete construction: *such as* needs a noun to be complete. Had it been extended to "He preferred such foods as these," it would have been complete, an independent clause, and a colon fol-

44j *unwanted colons*

lowing it would have been not only appropriate but necessary; without the addition of *these* or *the following*, no punctuation mark should be used before the list of foods. Here is another illustration of this common error:

> *Wrong:* His favourite pastimes are: fishing, hunting, swimming, and hiking.

Again, the colon should be removed, since the linking verb *are* clearly needs a complement for the construction to be complete. Another way to remember this principle: Don't use a colon after a *preposition* or after a form of the verb *be*.

44k Do not use a question mark at the end of indirect questions; questions that are not quoted verbatim should end with a period:

> I asked what we were having for dinner.
> She wanted to find out what had happened the year before.
> What he asked himself then was how he was going to explain it to his boss.

44-l Never put a comma or a semicolon or a colon together with a dash. Such combinations used to be common, but they are now avoided because they contribute little but clutter. Use whichever mark is appropriate.

Hyphens and *apostrophes* are dealt with in Chapter VI, on spelling. See **5lo-s** and **51v**, respectively.

Review Exercises: Chapter IV

(1) Correcting Punctuation
Correct any errors in punctuation in the following sentences. Where something else seems wrong or weak, feel free to improve that too, even if it doesn't affect the punctuation.

1. It is a question of careful preparation, attentive reading and review.
2. I feel, that for a number of important reasons, research into this field should be curtailed.
3. She accepts being an outsider for that is all she has known.
4. Many of his plays are about royalty, as in: *Richard II, Richard III*, and *Henry IV*.
5. In Shakespeare's play, *Hamlet*, there are many well-known scenes.
6. Claudius now sits on the throne and has married Hamlet's mother Gertrude.
7. With him too, she felt uncomfortable.
8. I did not like the boy named John because he was the teacher's pet.
9. The encounter that deepened his feelings more, occurred at age nine.
10. Therefore, Forster praises democracy as well for it allows variety and criticism.

11. This then, was the plan. Return to our campsite for the night, and tackle Black Tusk the next morning.
12. I joined in; haltingly at first and then more confidently.
13. As a person exercises the muscle of the heart becomes stronger, therefore, it can pump more blood while beating less.
14. Three or four horses were easy enough to count but entire herds of cows were beyond my capability.
15. The tip is manufactured from a rubbery substance; especially designed for erasing typographical errors.
16. It was after all, exactly what he had asked for.
17. Crisp memories of laughing eyes, loving smiles and peaceful easy feelings still linger.
18. The same word was used three times in the same paragraph; twice to describe different ideas altogether.
19. The other team had played valiantly, if not desperately till the final buzzer.
20. Eighteenth-century mathematicians unlike their counterparts in the seventeenth century, were able to develop both pure and applied mathematics. Leonard Euler, a notable genius in both these fields contributed invaluably to every branch of mathematics.
21. Another family tradition, that keeps me in mind of my background, is the food.
22. It began to rain, nevertheless, since they were on the sixteenth fairway they went ahead and finished the round.
23. When company spokesman, Sidney O'Malley, rose to speak someone began to giggle.
24. To me this indicates, that although he remembers the details of the events he describes, there is an enormous space of time, between them and the present, that makes them intangible.
25. The sounds of the poem are soft and never harsh which helps create the melancholy tone.
26. The bristles in my hairbrush are no longer uniform—some are missing and others stick out in all directions.
27. It is hard to appreciate freedom, if one has always lived with it.
28. Many things pleased me but some shocked me; one event in particular.
29. The title and the subtitle indicate the subject, and help us to understand what the essay is discussing.
30. My dictionary is my favourite book not because of its essential function: try to get along without one, but because of some of the extra features I've discovered in it.
31. I moved into Grandpa's home when I was a year old because of my mother's illness, and remained there by choice, until I was almost six.
32. No one can weigh his deeds but heaven, and we who know of his acts.
33. One moment I was running for my life but in the next, the ground gave way beneath me and I was falling through space. Upon hitting the bottom I thought resignedly; it has got me.
34. Watching the Canada-Russia hockey series was overall a rewarding experience. The one game however, which stands out most in my mind, is the eighth and final game. With the series all tied up, this was a crucial game; for both teams.
35. I don't think I had ever known anybody as a person before, only their exterior characteristics. That is I suppose one of the facts of one's childhood, superficiality reigns supreme. Someone to talk to and listen to, it was a novel experience for me and so it came as rather a shock when he left.

exercises

(2) Comparing punctuation

Here are some passages of prose written in the eighteenth century, when the conventions of punctuation were in some ways different from ours. How would you punctuate them if you had written them today? (You might also consider what other changes you would make.)

1. There are many accomplishments, which though they are comparatively trivial, and may be acquired by small abilities, are yet of great importance in our common intercourse with men. Of this kind is that general courtesy, which is called Good Breeding; a name, by which, as an artificial excellence, it is at once characterised and recommended.

   (The Adventurer, No. 87, 1753)

2. The philosophers of King Charles his reign were busy in finding out the art of flying. The famous Bishop Wilkins was so confident of success in it, that he says he does not question but in the next age it will be as usual to hear a man call for his wings when he is going a journey, as it is now to call for his boots. The humour so prevailed among the virtuosos of his reign, that they were actually making parties to go up to the moon together, and were more put to it in their thoughts how to meet with accommodations by the way, than how to get thither. Every one knows the story of the great Lady, who at the same time was building castles in the air for their reception.

   (The Guardian, No. 112, 1713)

3. By this original form, the usual station of the actors, in almost every scene, was advanced at least ten foot nearer to the audience, than they now can be; because, not only from the stage's being shortened, in front, but likewise from the additional interposition of those stage-boxes, the actors (in respect to the spectators, that fill them) are kept so much more backward from the main audience, than they used to be: But when the actors were in possession of the forwarder space, to advance upon, the voice was then more in the centre of the house, so that the most distant ear had scarce the least doubt, or difficulty in hearing what fell from the weakest utterance: All objects were thus drawn nearer to the sense; every painted scene was stronger; every grand scene and dance more extended; every rich, or fine-coloured habit had a more lively lustre: Nor was the minutest motion of a feature (properly changing with the passion, or humour it suited) ever lost, as they frequently must be in the obscurity of too great a distance: And how valuable an advantage the facility of hearing distinctly, is to every well-acted scene every common spectator is a judge.

   (An Apology for the Life of Colley Cibber, 1740)

4. My father had a small estate in Nottinghamshire; I was the third of five sons. He sent me to Emanuel-College in Cambridge, at fourteen years old, where I resided three years, and applied my self close to my studies: But the charge of maintaining me (although I had a very scanty allowance) being too great for a narrow fortune; I was bound apprentice to Mr. James Bates, an eminent surgeon in London, with whom I continued four years; and my father now and then sending me small sums of money, I laid them out in learning navigation, and other parts of mathematicks, useful to those who intend to travel, as I always believed it would be some time or other my fortune to do.

   (Jonathan Swift, *Gulliver's Travels*, 1726)

exercises

5. It is justly considered as the greatest excellency of art, to imitate nature; but it is necessary to distinguish those parts of nature, which are most proper for imitation: greater care is still required in representing life, which is so often discoloured by passion, or deformed by wickedness. If the world be promiscuously described, I cannot see of what use it can be to read the account; or why it may not be as safe to turn the eye immediately upon mankind, as upon a mirror which shows all that presents itself without discrimination.

(Samuel Johnson, *The Rambler*, No. 4, 1750)

(3) Using punctuation

Punctuate the following sentences as you think necessary. Consider possible alternatives, and be prepared to defend your choices. (For all but the last ten, periods are supplied; for those ten, the terminal punctuation itself is part of the exercise.)

1. When the meeting ended he went to a pub and got drunk.
2. Fred went home to bed as soon as the meeting was over.
3. There was still much to be done but he decided to call it a night.
4. In 1971 he moved to Halifax Nova Scotia and bought a small business.
5. He felt uneasy about the trip yet he knew he had to go along.
6. I took the book that I didn't like back to the library.
7. Mary Winnie and Cora came to the party together.
8. He had a broad engaging smile.
9. Having heard all she wanted Bridget left the meeting.
10. But once you've taken the first few steps the rest will naturally be easy.
11. The poem was short the novel was long the poem was good the novel better.
12. Perhaps we can still think of some way out of this mess.
13. But Canadians don't think that way they prefer to sit back and wait.
14. Last summer we visited Hastings the site of the battle won by William the Conqueror in 1066.
15. It is not good policy to start writing right away because your work will probably be weak in organization coherence and unity.
16. There are only three vegetables I can't tolerate turnips turnips and turnips.
17. The doctor a specialist in family practice made house calls all morning.
18. August 1914 was when the world went to war.
19. He had to finish the novel quickly or he wouldn't be ready for class.
20. We arrived we ate we departed and that's all there was to the evening.
21. You must plan your budget carefully in times of inflation.
22. He is the only man I know who wears a tie every day whatever the season.
23. His several hobbies were philately woodworking chess and fishing.
24. The two opponents settled the question amicably at the meeting and then went home to write nasty letters to each other.
25. I enjoyed both the novel and the poem but the novel which was an adventure story was much easier to read.
26. It was a splendid old stone house surrounded by well-landscaped lush green lawns and approached by a long sweeping gravel driveway.
27. This new machine looking like a caricature of a human being may yet prove beneficial.
28. It was to prove a very important day for Richard the embattled king he having to decide which course to pursue.
29. One August afternoon it was the hottest day of the year he perversely decided to play tennis.

exercises

30. He enjoyed the work of Melville Hemingway and Twain even more than that of such a talented successful entertaining novelist as Dickens.
31. I found many mistakes in the paper which was a mess from beginning to end.
32. Because of the vast distances the extreme climate rapidly rising costs and far from least important the rights and needs of native peoples the matter of northern development is a difficult problem but more and more society's demand for energy and other resources dictates that some kind of action be taken that the north be increasingly opened up to technological exploitation.
33. Before I was even half-way through the job my boss told me I could have the rest of the day off.
34. They sat there glowing with pride in their accomplishments.
35. I drove my car which was splashed all over with mud down to the carwash.
36. He found many mistakes in the paper which were quite serious.
37. It was a simple assignment for the student was asked to write only one page.
38. It was a long hot summer in fact it was so hot I got scarcely any work done.
39. To avoid error he proofread the paper carefully.
40. I kept my distance from Gustav feeling uneasy about his display of temper.
41. If winter is here can spring be far behind
42. As soon as the plane had landed I began to wonder would I be able to fly again without fear
43. Well can you beat that
44. Has anyone ever come up to you on the street and asked Where's the best place in town to eat
45. Later he thought of many things he could have done but at the moment of crisis only one way out occurred to him run like mad
46. Tell me Algernon whether you would write March 16 1962 or put it like this 16 March 1962
47. Wayne's tirade finished Anita said No one will be swayed by such behaviour
48. He said that he would try to calm down
49. I should think she remarked that you could see where your own best interests lie Can't you my dear
50. Then came the reply she'd been hoping for I'll do whatever you think is best

V

Manuscript Conventions and Other Mechanical Conventions of Writing

Manuscript Conventions

Format

ms

Certain conventions govern the form of a manuscript that is being prepared for submission. Unless directed otherwise, you should carefully adhere to the following principles:

1. Use white paper of good quality, 21 by 28 cm or $8\frac{1}{2}$ by 11 inches. Most instructors will ask you not to use erasable paper, since type, pencil, and ink all tend to smudge and blur on such paper. Do not submit work on paper torn out of a spiral notebook.
2. If you type your papers, use a good black ribbon, a regular (i.e., not italic) typeface, and keep the type clean. Use unruled paper and double-space your text. If you use a word-processor with a dot-matrix printer, check to see if your instructor will accept what it produces.
3. If you write your papers by hand, use medium- to wide-ruled paper and write on alternate lines. Use either black or blue-black ink. Never submit anything in pencil. Write legibly.
4. Use one side of the page only.
5. Leave generous margins, $3\frac{1}{2}$ to 4 cm ($1\frac{1}{2}$ inches) at the left and probably at the top, and $2\frac{1}{2}$ to 3 cm (1 inch) at the right and at the bottom.

6. Do not number the first page, or pages on which a new section begins (e.g., Notes or Bibilography), unless at bottom centre. Number all other pages consecutively with Arabic numerals in either the top right-hand corner or at the top centre. Do not adorn the numerals with periods, dashes, slashes, circles, or other gizmos.

7. Centre the title about 5 cm (2 inches) down from the top of the first page. Leave at least one or two extra lines between the title and the beginning of the essay. For a long essay, such as a research paper, which is so bulky that it cannot easily be folded, it is customary to include a separate title page on which—centred or a little above centre—are the title, your name, the date, the course number, and the instructor's name. If you use such a title page, do not repeat the title on the first page of the essay.

8. Capitalize the title correctly (see **47n**). Do not put the whole title in capital letters.

9. Do not underline your title or put it in quotation marks or put a period after it. If it includes the title of a poem, story, book, etc., or a ship's name, punctuate that part of it appropriately. Do not use the title of a published work by itself as your own title, though a work's title may be a part of your title. Here are some examples:

   > Techniques of Irony in Swift's "A Modest Proposal"
   > Thematic Imagery in *A Jest of God*
   > How Are the Mighty Fallen: The Sinking of the *Titanic*

10. Never begin a line with a comma, semicolon, period, question mark, exclamation point, or hyphen. These marks of punctuation are attached to the words they follow, and therefore must occur at the end of a line rather than at the beginning of a new line. Occasionally a dash or the three or four dots of an ellipsis will fall at a line break; these *can* be put at the beginning of a new line, but even with these it is preferable—for clarity and ease of reading—to place them at the end of a line rather than at the beginning of a new line.

11. If you type, leave two spaces after any terminal punctuation; use two hyphens together to make a dash, with no space before or after them; and leave spaces before and after each period of an ellipsis. (But see **43i**.)

12. Indent each paragraph five spaces (about 2 cm or an inch in handwritten papers). You need not leave extra space between paragraphs.

13. Be neat. Avoid messy erasures, blots, and strike-overs. If you make more than two or three emendations on a page, recopy the page. When you change or delete a word or short phrase, draw a single horizontal line through it and write the new word or phrase, if any, above it. If you wish to insert an additional word or short

phrase, place a caret (∧) *below* the line at the point of insertion and write the addition *above* the line. If you wish to start a new paragraph where you have not indented for one, put the symbol ¶ where you want the paragraph to begin. If you wish to cancel a paragraph indention, put "No ¶" in the left margin.

14. Endorse your paper on the outside (usually at the top of the right-hand side of the back of the last page when the paper is folded vertically) with your name, the course number, the date, and probably the number of the assignment and the instructor's name. (See number 7 above.)

15. If necessary, fasten the pages of an essay together with a paper clip. Never use a staple or a pin. Long essays are sometimes submitted in folders.

45b Syllabication and Word Division

syl div

1. You should seldom need to divide a word at the end of a line; no one expects the right-hand margin of typed or handwritten material to be very straight. Therefore keep breaks to a minimum. If you must divide a word at the end of a line—perhaps because it is an unusually long word—be sure to divide it only between syllables. (Obviously, only words of two or more syllables can be divided.) If you are in doubt about where a word may be divided, consult your dictionary. Place a hyphen at the end of the line and the remainder of the divided word at the beginning of the next line.

2. Never separate a syllable consisting of only one letter from the rest of the word; if it were at the end of the word you would gain nothing, since the hyphen would occupy a space. Further, a single letter at either the beginning or the end of a line is often difficult to read as part of the rest of the word. It is even worth trying to avoid setting off syllables of only two letters; especially, do not separate a final *ed* from the rest of the word, even if it is a genuinely separate syllable. Do not divide any word of less than five letters.

3. Always try to begin the second part of the divided word with a consonant rather than a vowel. It makes for much easier reading. For example, divide *radical* so that the new line will begin with the consonant *c* rather than the vowel *i*: *radi-cal*, not *rad-ical*.

4. Try to avoid dividing words that are already hyphenated. If you must divide such a word, divide it only where the hyphen already stands.

Exercise 45b: Syllabication

Divide the following words according to their syllables. Consult your dictionary afterwards to see if you were correct. Indicate those syllabic breaks that should not be used to divide a word at the end of a line.

1. accommodated	11. distinctly
2. apartment	12. Machiavellian
3. appointed	13. perspicacity
4. befuddled	14. philosophical
5. cannibalism	15. prevaricated
6. cigarette	16. sentenced
7. commercialization	17. suggestion
8. confused	18. tachometer
9. counterirritant	19. thoroughly
10. differentiating	20. verisimilitude

46 Abbreviations
abbr

Abbreviations are acceptable, even expected, in some special kinds of writing (technical and scientific writing, legal writing, business writing, memos, reports, reference works, bibliographies and footnotes, tables and charts, and often in journalistic writing); in ordinary writing, however, only a few kinds should appear.

46a Titles before proper names, with or without initials or given names:

Mr. Johnson, Mrs. L.W. Smith, Ms. Helene Greco, Dr. David Adams, St. John.

46b In informal writing, titles before proper names with initials or given names:

Prof. Roger Thomson (*but* Professor Thomson)
Sen. I.C. Power (*but* Senator Power)
Gen. John S. Hawkins (*but* General Hawkins)
Rev. Matthew Markle (or, more formally, the Reverend Matthew Markle, the Reverend Mr. Markle)

These and similar titles should be spelled out in formal writing.

46c Titles and degrees after proper names:

Timothy Johnson, Jr.
David Adams, M.D. (but *not* Dr. David Adams, M.D.)
A. Pullerman, D.D.S.
Joseph McGregor, Ph.D., F.R.S.C.

Note: Academic degrees not following a name may also be abbreviated:

Shirley is working toward her B.A.
Abdul is studying for his M.A. examinations.

46c *titles and degrees*

46d Standard words used with dates and numerals:

720 B.C., A.D. 231, the second century A.D., 7 a.m., 8:30 p.m., no. 17 (*or* No. 17)

Note that *A.D.* precedes a specific date whereas *B.C.* follows one.

46e Agencies and organizations commonly known by their initials:

UNESCO, SIU, CBC, RCMP, NASA, CP Air

See also **42a**.

46f Some scientific, technical, or other terms (usually of considerable length) commonly known by their initials:

BTU, DDT, DNA, ESP, FM, IPA, MLA, SST, TNT

See also **42a**.

46g Common Latin expressions used in English (in formal writing, it is preferable to spell out the English or, as with *versus*, the Latin equivalent):

i.e. (that is), e.g. (for example), cf. (compare), etc. (and so forth), vs. (*versus*), et al. (and others)

Notes:
(1) If you use the abbreviation *e.g.*, use it only to *introduce* the example or list of examples: *following* the example or list, it should be written out:

Some provinces—e.g., Alberta, Saskatchewan, and New Brunswick— felt that they had been poorly represented on the committee.
Some provinces—Alberta, Saskatchewan, and New Brunswick, for example—felt that they had been poorly represented on the committee.

Note also that if you introduce a list with *e.g.*, or *for example* or even *such as*, it is illogical to follow it with *etc.* or *and so forth*.

(2) Use a comma after *i.e.* (just as you would to indicate the pause if you had written out *that is*). And usually use one after *e.g.* (test for it by reading aloud to see if you would pause after saying "for example").

(3) The abbreviation *cf.* stands for the Latin *confer*, meaning *compare*. Do not use it, as so many carelessly do, to mean simply "see"; for that meaning the Latin *vide* (v.) would be correct.

Caution: Avoid using the abbreviation *etc.* lazily. Use it only when there are several items to follow and when they are obvious:

> Evergreen trees—cedars, pines, etc.—are common in northern latitudes.
> Learning the Greek alphabet—alpha, beta, gamma, delta, etc.—isn't really very difficult.

> *Wrong*: He considered several possible professions: accounting, teaching, farming, etc.

Further, if you do use *etc*, do not write *and etc.*, since *etc.* (*et cetera*) already means "*and* so forth."

46h Terms used in official titles being copied exactly:

> Johnson Bros., Ltd.; Ibbetson & Co.; Smith & Sons, Inc.; Harper & Row; *Quill & Quire*

Caution: Never use the ampersand (&) as a substitute for *and*; use it only when copying a title of a company or publication exactly, as above.

47 **Capitalization**
cap

All writers know that they should capitalize the first words of sentences and the pronoun *I*, but they are occasionally uncertain about some other uses of capitals. Here are the simple conventions governing capitalization.

Generally, capitalize proper nouns, abbreviations of proper nouns, and words derived from proper nouns, as follows:

47a Names and nicknames of real and fictional people:

> Lester B. Pearson, Barbara Ward, Bobby Orr, Rumplestiltskin

47b Names of real or fictional individual animals:

> Elsa, Rin Tin Tin, Lassie, King Kong, Dumbo, Washoe

47c Titles when they are part of a name:

> Professor Jones (*but* I see that Jones is your professor.)
> Captain John Smith (*but* John Smith was a captain.)
> Rabbi David Small (*but* Mr. Small was our rabbi.)

Note: Normally titles that follow a name are not capitalized unless they have in effect become a part of the name: Joe Doaks, the senator; Bull Halsey, the admiral; *but* William the Conqueror, Peter the Hermit,

47c titles in names

Smokey the Bear. Some titles of particular distinction are customarily capitalized even if the person is not named:

> The Prime Minister will tour the Maritimes next month.
> The Queen visited Canada to open the Olympic Games.

47d   Names designating family relationships when they are used as parts of proper names. When they are used in place of proper names, they are capitalized except when they follow a possessive:

> Uncle George (*but* I have an uncle named George.)
> There's my uncle, George. (*but* There's my Uncle George!)
> I told Father about it. (*but* My father knows about it.)
> I have always respected Grandmother. (*but* Juanita's grandmother is a splendid old lady.)

47e   Place names; Months, Days:

> Alberta, Asia, Buenos Aires, the Amazon, the Andes, the Sahara, Japan, Vancouver Island, Hudson Bay, Kejimkujik National Park, Lake Ladoga, Moose Jaw, Rivière-du-loup, the Suez Canal, Trafalgar Square, Banff, Mt. Etna, Yonge Street, Québec, Niagara Falls

Caution: Do not capitalize *north, east, south*, and *west* unless they are part of specific place names (North Dakota, West Vancouver, South America) or are used to designate specific geographical areas (the frozen North, the East Coast, the Deep South, the Wild West, the Far East). Capitalize the names of months and the days of the week, but not the seasons: spring, summer, autumn, fall, winter.

47f   Names of groups and organizations and of their members:

> Canadian, Australian, Scandinavian, South American, Irish, Yankee, Toronto Maple Leafs, Progressive Conservatives, Catholic, Lions, Teamsters, Alcoholics Anonymous

47g   Names of institutions:

> McGill University, Vancouver General Hospital, the Better Business Bureau, Lincoln Center, Le Reine Elizabeth

47h   Names of deities and other religious names and terms:

> God, the Holy Ghost, the Virgin Mary, the Bible, the Dead Sea Scrolls, the Koran, Vishnu, Taoism, Islam, the Talmud

Note: Some people capitalize pronouns referring to a deity; others prefer not to.

47i   Specific academic courses, but not the subjects themselves, except for languages:

> Philosophy 101, Fine Art 300
> an English course, a major in French
> a history course, an economics major, a degree in psychology

47j   Common nouns used as parts of proper nouns:

> the Ottawa River, the Rocky Mountains, Fourth Street, the Pacific Ocean, Capilano College, the Eiffel Tower, the Mojave Desert, Canterbury Cathedral

47k   Derivatives of proper nouns:

> Shakespearean, French Canadian, Confucianism, Haligonian, Celtic, Québecois, Christian, Miltonic, Vancouverite, Keynesian, Edwardian, Muscovite

Note: Some words derived from proper nouns—and some proper nouns themselves—have become so familiar, so commonly used, that they are no longer capitalized; for example: bible (in secular contexts), biblical, herculean, raglan, martial, quixotic, hamburger, frankfurter, french fries, champagne, burgundy, crapper, roman and italic, vulcanized, macadamized, galvanized, pasteurized, curie, volt, ampere, joule, gerrymander, denim, china, japanned, erotic, bloomers, jeroboam, jeremiad.

47-l   Abbreviations of proper nouns:

> NDP, CPR, TVA, CUPE, NATO, the BNA Act, P.E.I., B.C.

Note that abbreviations of agencies and organizations commonly known by their initials do not need periods (see **46e**), but that abbreviations of geographical entities such as provinces usually do. When in doubt, consult your dictionary. See also **42a**.

47m   The pronoun *I* and the vocative interjection *O*:

> O my people, what have I done unto thee? (Micah 6:3)

Do not capitalize the interjection *oh* unless it begins a sentence.

47n   In the title of any written work, including student essays, use a capital letter to begin the first word, the last word, and all other important words; leave uncapitalized only articles (*a, an, the*) and any conjunctions and prepositions that are less than five letters long (unless of course one of these is the first or last word in the title):

47n literary titles

A Jest of God	*How to Win at Chess*
All About Eve	*Of Thee I Sing*
In Which We Serve	*Such Is My Beloved*
Victory Through Air Power	*As for Me and My House*
As the World Wags On	*Roughing It in the Bush*

But be careful, for there can be exceptions: The relative pronoun *that* is usually not capitalized (*All's Well that Ends Well*), and in Ralph Ellison's "Tell It Like It Is, Baby," the preposition-cum-conjunction *like* demands to be capitalized.

Note: If the title includes a hyphenated word, capitalize the part after the hyphen if it is an important word:

> *The Scorched-Wood People*
> *Murder Among the Well-to-do*

Capitalize the first word of a subtitle, even if it is an article:

> *The Interior Landscape: The Literary Criticism of Marshall McLuhan*

47o   Always capitalize the first word of a major or minor sentence—of anything, that is, that concludes with terminal punctuation:

> Modern art. Now that's a controversial topic. Right?

47p   Also capitalize the first words of quotations that are intended as sentences or that are capitalized sentences in the original, but not fragments from other than the beginning of such sentences:

> When he said "Let me take the wheel for a while," I shuddered at the memory of what had happened the last time I had let him "take the wheel."

If explanatory matter interrupts a quoted sentence, do not begin its second part with a capital:

> "It was all I could do," she said, "to keep my head above water."

47q   Capitalize the first word of a sentence in parentheses only if it stands by itself, apart from other sentences; if it is incorporated within another sentence, it is neither capitalized nor ended with a period (though it could end with a question mark or exclamation point; see **40** and **42**):

> He did as he was told (there was really nothing else for him to do), and the tension was relieved. (But of course he would never admit to himself that he had been bested.)

47r   An incorporated sentence following a colon may be capitalized if it seems to stand as a separate statement, for example if it is itself long or otherwise requires emphasis; otherwise it is best left uncapitalized:

> There was one thing, he said, which we must never forget: No one has a right to a happiness that deprives someone else of deserved happiness.
>
> It was a splendid night: the sky was clear except for a few picturesque clouds, the moon was full, and even a few stars shone through. (This *could* be capitalized, if the writer wanted particular emphasis on the details.)
>
> It was no time for petty quarrels: everything depended on unanimity.

47s Although it is risky, and should not be done very often, writers who have good control of tone can on occasion capitalize a personified abstraction or a word or phrase to which they want to impart a special importance of one kind or another:

> It was no longer a matter of simply getting along adequately; now it was a question of Survival.
>
> Only when it begins to fade does Youth appear so valuable.
>
> The filching fingers of the monster Inflation reach everywhere.

Sometimes the slight emphasis of capitalization can be used for a humorous or ironic effect:

> Once he had popped The Question, she relented and let him catch her.
>
> He insisted on driving His Beautiful Car: everyone else preferred to walk the two blocks without benefit of jerks and jolts and carbon monoxide fumes.

On occasion, but very infrequently, you can capitalize whole words and phrases or even sentences for a special sort of graphic emphasis:

> When we reached the site, however, we were confronted by a sign warning us in no uncertain terms to KEEP OUT—TRESPASSERS WILL BE PROSECUTED.
>
> When he made the suggestion to the group he was answered by a resounding NO.

Clearly in such instances no further indications, such as quotation marks or underlining, are necessary.

48 **Titles**
title

Generally, titles of short works are enclosed in quotation marks; titles of longer works are italicized (see **49**). (For the other uses of italics, see **49**; for the capitalization of titles, see **47n** above.)

48a Put quotation marks around the titles of short stories, essays, short poems, chapters of books, and songs:

48a *titles of short works*

Leonard Cohen's "Suzanne" is both poem and song.
Poe's "The Cask of Amontillado" is one of his most famous stories.

48b Use italics (see **49**) for titles of written works published as units, such as books, magazines, journals, newspapers, and plays and movies:

Paradise Lost is Milton's greatest work.
Have you read Alice Munro's *Lives of Girls and Women?*
Saturday Night is a popular magazine.
The scholarly journal *Canadian Literature* is published quarterly.
I recommend that you see the Stratford production of *The Tempest*.
I prefer *The Globe and Mail* to the *Winnipeg Free Press*.

Note: If the name of the city is printed as a part of a newspaper's name on the front page, it should be italicized (including the definite article): *The Toronto Star*, but *The Province*, *The Times* of London. Sometimes the definite article which often is part of a newspaper's name is not capitalized or italicized: *The New York Times* or the *New York Times*. This is especially likely if the name of the city necessarily intervenes: *The Citizen*, but the Ottawa *Citizen*. Some writers prefer never to consider the city as a part of the paper's name: the New York *Times*; the Edmonton *Journal*. Whichever practice you adopt, be consistent.

48c Titles of musical compositions (other than single songs), paintings, and sculpture are also italicized:

Ravel's *Bolero*; Rembrandt's *The Night Watch*; Michelangelo's *David*

Caution: Be particularly careful with the definite article *the*: italicize and capitalize it only when it is actually part of the title: Margaret Laurence's *The Stone Angel*; Ethel Wilson's *Swamp Angel*; Pierre Boulle's *The Bridge on the River Kwai*; the *Partisan Review; The Encyclopaedia Britannica;* the *Atlas of Ancient Archaeology*. Occasionally the indefinite article, *a* or *an*, bears watching as well.

48d Remember, do not italicize the titles of parts of publications; put quotation marks around them:

The first chapter of Thoreau's *Walden* is called "Economy."
"Shakespeare" is one of the poems in Irving Layton's collection *Nail Polish*.

There are exceptions, however. For example, a book by Robertson Davies, *Four Favourite Plays*, contains *Eros at Breakfast*, *The Voice of* the People, *At the Gates of the Righteous*, and *Fortune, My Foe*, each of which as an individual play deserves to be italicized in its own right. Nevertheless, if you were to refer, for example in a footnote, to one of these plays as a part of this collection, you could enclose the title in quotation marks. Italicizing a title means that the work being referred to was published separately. Some works, however, for example Coleridge's *The Rime of the Ancient Mariner* and Conrad's *Heart of Darkness*, although originally published as parts of larger collections, are fairly long and have attained a reputation and importance as individual works. Consequently most (though not all) writers feel justified in dignifying them with italics rather than consigning them to the relatively lesser regions indicated by quotation marks. Correct punctuation of titles can get quite tricky, and you must be careful. Consider for example the following:

> Northrop Frye's "Conclusion" to the 1965 *Literary History of Canada* is reprinted in his 1971 collection, *The Bush Garden: Essays on the Canadian Imagination*, where it is called simply "Conclusion to a *Literary History of Canada*."

48f *titles within titles*

48e Another note on punctuating titles: If a book has a subtitle, it customarily appears below the title on the book's title page; usually there is no punctuation between title and subtitle. If you wish to include such a book's subtitle (as you would in a bibliographical entry), you must insert a *colon* between them, as we have done in the example above. (In this circumstance a single space following the colon is sufficient; the same is true for colons used in footnotes and bibliographical entries.)

48f As in the last example cited in **48d**, note than an essay title that includes a book title calls for italicizing part of what is enclosed in quotation marks. If a book title includes something that requires quotation marks, retain the quotation marks and italicize the whole thing:

> *From Fiction to Film: D.H. Lawrence's "The Rocking-Horse Winner"*

When a book title includes something that itself would be italicized, such as a ship's name, another book title, or the name of a magazine, that secondary title is either put in quotation marks:

> *The Cruise of the "Nona"*

or left in roman type (i.e., not underlined):

> *D.H. Lawrence and* Sons and Lovers: *Sources and Criticism*

Italics are a special kind of slanting type; in handwritten work or work typed on a standard typewriter, one represents italic type by <u>underlining</u>. The conventional uses of italics, other than for titles (see the preceding section), are as follows:

49a Italicize names of individual ships, planes, and the like:

> the *Golden Hind*, the *Erebus* and the *Terror*, the *St. Bonaventure*, the *Lusitania*, *The Spirit of St. Louis*, *Mariner IX*, the *Columbia*, the *Super Chief*

49b Italicize French and foreign words and phrases that are not yet sufficiently common to be entirely at home in English. English contains many terms that have come from other languages but that are no longer thought of as non-English and are therefore not italicized; for example: moccasin, wigwam, prairie, genre, tableau, bamboo, arroyo, corral, hara-kiri, chutzpah, spaghetti, goulash, hashish, eureka, litotes, hiatus, vacuum, and sic. There are also words which are sufficiently Anglicized not to require italicizing but which usually retain their original accents, umlauts, and the like: cliché, naïf, cañon, façade, Götterdämmerung, fête champêtre. But English also makes use of many terms that are still felt to be sufficiently non-English to need italicizing; for example: *ad hoc, ad nauseam, au courant, chez, coup d'état, joie de vivre, Lebensraum, outré, per se, raison d'être, savoir faire, tempus fugit, vade mecum, verboten, Weltanschauung.* Many such expressions are on their way to full acceptance into English. If you are at all unsure about a word, it is wise to consult a good up-to-date dictionary to find out if italics are necessary.

49c Italicize words, letters, and numerals referred to as such:

> The word *helicopter* is formed from Greek roots.
> There are two *r*'s in *embarrass*. (Note that only the *r* itself is italicized, and not the *s* which makes it plural.)
> The number *13* is considered unlucky even by many otherwise rational people.

49d Italicize words or phrases—or even whole sentences—that you want to emphasize, for example as they might be if read aloud:

> One thing he was now sure of: *that* was no way to go about it.
> Careful thought should lead one to the conclusion that *character*, not wealth or connections, will be most important in the long run.

If people try to tell you otherwise, *don't listen to them.*

Try to remember that *Fredericton*, not Saint John, is the capital of New Brunswick.

He gave up his ideas of fun and decided instead to finish his education. *And it was the most important decision of his life.*

As with any typographical device, this method of achieving emphasis is worth trying to avoid in ordinary writing, for no merely mechanical means of emphasizing something can be as sound and, ultimately, as effective as punctuation, word order, and syntax. Such an easy method will often produce only a transitory effect. Consider the differences between the following sentences:

Well, I felt just *terrible* when he told me that! (mere typographical effect, not helped by the exclamation point)

I felt terrible, just terrible, when he told me that. (repetition—a little better)

I can think of only one way to describe how I felt when he told me that: I felt terrible. (placement and punctuation—much better)

Note: On some typewriters you can switch to italic type, and some computer printers will let you use not only *italic* type but even **boldface** and other faces and sizes of type.

▄ 50 ▄ Numerals
num

In technical and scientific writing, numerals are of course appropriate; newspapers sometimes use them to save space. But in ordinary writing certain conventions limit the use of numerals to express numbers.

50a Generally, spell out numbers that can be expressed in one or two words; use numerals for numbers that would take more than two words:

four; thirty; eighty-three; one third; two hundred; seven thousand; 115; 385; 2120; three dollars; $3.48; five hundred dollars; $517

If you are writing about more than one number, say for purposes of comparison or giving statistics, numerals are usually preferable:

Enrollment dropped from 250 two years ago, to 200 last year, to only 90 this year.

Numerals are conventionally used for the following purposes:

50b For the time of day with *a.m.* or *p.m.*:   3 p.m. (*but* three o'clock)

50b time of day

50c For dates: November 11, 1918, *or* 11 November 1918

Note: *st, nd, rd,* and *th* can be used with numerals in dates, but only if the year is not given; also, the number may be written out:

May 2, 1951; May 2nd; the second of May; May second

The year is almost always represented by numerals, and centuries written out:

1900 was the last year of the nineteenth century, not the first year of the twentieth century.

50d For addresses:

2132 Fourth Avenue; 4771 128th Street; P.O. Box 91; Apartment 8

50e For technical and mathematical numbers, such as percentages and decimals:

31 percent; 31%; 37°C; 37 degrees Celsius; 2.54 centimetres; 2.54 cm; 78 rpm

50f For page numbers and other divisions of a written work, especially in documentation (including parenthetical references) (see **82, 83,** and **85**):

page 27, pp. 27, (pp. 9-13), pp. 33-38, line 13, lines 3 and 5, (lines 7-9), stanza 2, chapter 4, Chapter 4, Ch. 4, Chapter IV, section 3, Part 2, section III, Book IX, (IX, 120), 2 Samuel 22:3, II Samuel 19:1

(Note that books of the Bible are not italicized.)

50g A special form is used to refer to parts of a play:

Act IV, scene ii, line 57 *or* (IV.ii.57)

50h Commas have long been conventionally used to separate groups of three figures in long numbers: 3,172,450; 17,920. In the metric system, however, along with the rest of SI (Système Internationale, or International System of Units), such conventions are different. Under SI (so abbreviated in all languages) groups of three digits on either side of a decimal point are separated by spaces rather than commas; with four-digit numbers a space is optional:

3 172 450   3.1416 or 3.141 6   But: 3.141 59

This convention does not apply to addresses or amounts of money. For further information about SI consult the *Canadian Metric Practice Guide,* published by the Canadian Standards Association.

50i   **Caution**: Do not begin a sentence with a numeral. Either spell out the number or rewrite the sentence so that the number does not come first:

> Thirty to 40 percent goes for taxes. (Or rewrite to avoid the oddness: Taxes consume from 30 to 40 percent.)

> *Wrong:*   750 people showed up to watch the chess tournament.
> *Right:*   As many as 750 people came to watch the chess tournament.
> *Right:*   The chess tournament drew 750 interested spectators.

Dates are sometimes considered acceptable at the beginning of a sentence:

> 1976 was a presidential election year in the United States.

But even this usage is worth avoiding, since some people object to it. Begin a sentence with a date only if you want a particular emphasis on it and can get it in no other way or if any rewritten version of the sentence sounds impossibly awkward. See for example **50c**; but even there we could have written

> Remember that 1900 was the last year of the nineteenth century, not the first year of the twentieth century.

Ms Note: When typing the Arabic numeral *one*, do not use a capital *I*, for that produces a Roman numeral. If your machine has no numeral *1*, use lower-case *l*.

50i   no initial numerals

SPELLING

For some writers, spelling seems to be the most troublesome convention of all; for others, it presents little or no difficulty. But even confident writers must look up a word in the dictionary now and again to check its spelling. If you are a poor speller, the dictionary may well be in a sense the best friend you have.

Spelling is not something to be taken lightly, to be shrugged off as not having any significant effect on a writer's ability to communicate a desired meaning. If you want a reader to respect what you write, you must respect it yourself; sloppy spelling is visible evidence of a lack of respect. Furthermore, correct spelling is not merely a conventional courtesy to the reader: judges have thrown cases out of court because of a misspelled name or a missing hyphen or apostrophe.

Contrary to what you might think, English spelling is remarkably consistent, though it can at times be capricious, even chaotic; sometimes the same sound can be spelled in several ways (offer, fine, phone, cough; soap, sow, sew, so, beau, dough), or a single spelling element can be pronounced in several ways (cough, tough, dough, through, bough, fought; lot, tote, women, lost, tomb, fork, love). When such inconsistencies occur in longer and less familiar words, sometimes only a dictionary can help us. And remember, a dictionary does not offer *pre*scription but *de*scription: it is not commanding us to be correct, telling us what is "right" or "wrong," but simply recording as accurately as possible the conventions currently accepted by those who use the language—that is, by all of us.

The English language has changed a great deal over the centuries, and it is still changing. Old words pass out of use, new words are added, conventions of grammar change, pronunciations change—and spelling changes, but not very fast; dictionaries can do a fairly good job of recording what is conventional, and therefore acceptable, and therefore "correct," right now. Words that are in transition are usually recorded as having more than one "correct" meaning or pronunciation or spelling. The word *pejorative*, for example, has several acceptable pronunciations (lexicographers usually record them in what they consider to be the order of preference, with the most acceptable, or most common, first). Or consider the verb *dream*: its past tense can be either *dreamed* or *dreamt*. The past tense of *slide* has been *slid* since about the middle of the nineteenth century, before which it was *slided*; will the past tense of *glide* someday be "glid"? And consider *dove*: just a few years ago it was considered unacceptable, colloquial or dialectal at best, as the past tense of the verb *dive*; today it is at least as acceptable as the form *dived*. *Clue* is now the prevalent spelling, although for centuries it shared acceptability with *clew*. And so on.

In Canada we also have to contend with the influence of British and American spelling on ours. Some consider this a nuisance, but it can be thought of as a boon: we have greater choice than others. Broadly speaking, Canadian conventions—whether of spelling, punctuation, usage, pronunciation, or whatever—are closer to American conventions than to British, and where they are changing they are changing in the direction of American conventions. Broadcast and print media by and large have chosen to adopt the usually simpler and more phonetic American spellings and pronunciations, and our closer proximity to the United States is gradually influencing the population at large in the same direction. We still say "leftenant" instead of "lootenant" although we spell it *lieutenant*, but we say and spell *aluminum* rather than *aluminium*. The last letter of the alphabet is still called *zed* rather than *zee* by most of us, though this difference is fading. (Long ago the letter *z* was called *izzard*—so you can see how far we have come.) Most Canadians write *centre* and *theatre* rather than, as Americans do, *center* and *theater*; but "skedule" is replacing "shedule" as the pronunciation of *schedule*. We usually write *connection* rather than *connexion* (though the influence of the British form apparently confuses some people into misspelling it *connextion*). Endings in *our* (colour, honour, labour, etc.) exist alongside those in *or* (color, honor, labor, etc.); either spelling is conventional in Canada. (Oddly enough, Americans prefer *glamour* to *glamor*, as do the British; many Canadians prefer *glamor*.) The same is true of endings in *ise* or *ize*, though in Canada the *ize* forms are clearly preferred. The usefully distinct *cheque* (bank) is far more common than *check*, and *racquet* (tennis) seems to be holding out against *racket*; but *draught* is losing ground to *draft*, and *program* is rapidly replacing *programme*; *judgment* and *judgement* are probably about even. And so on. (Should you ever wish to make an adverb out of the adjective *supple*, you may be pleased to discover that Canadians, like Americans, prefer the form *supplely* rather than the potentially confusing British form *supply*.)

Where alternative spellings exist, either is correct. But as in other areas where alternatives are available, you should try to be consistent; that is, if you spell *honour* thus, then you should also write *humour* and *colour* and *labour*; if you choose the form *analyze*, then you will also choose *paralyze* and *modernize*; if you choose *centre*, you will also choose *lustre* and *fibre*. And if you do use the *our* ending, watch out for the trap: if you write *humour, colour, vapour, labour*, etc., then, when you add the suffixes *ous, ious, ate* or *ation*, and *ize* (or *ise*) to them, you must drop the *u* and write *humorous, coloration, vaporize, laborious*.

The point is, there is choice. In this book, for example, we have chosen to use the *our* rather than the *or* ending because we think it is still considered standard outside the popular media. And we have chosen the *ize* rather than the *ise* ending (where alternative possibilities exist) because we believe it to be the dominant form. If a particular form is clearly dominant or an acknowledged standard, we think it should be used: *catalogue, employee, furor*, and *syrup*, for example, are at present such forms. (We have included in the Spelling List at the end of this chapter some other words with alternative spellings that might occasionally be troublesome. The first form listed is at least slightly preferable.)

But such dilemmas, if they are dilemmas, are relatively infrequent. The real spelling difficulties, those shared by Canadian, British, and American writers, are of a different order.

51 Spelling Rules and Common Causes of Error

Many spelling errors result from carelessness or ignorance; self-discipline and a good dictionary are the only cures. Many other spelling errors, however, fall into clear categories. Weak spellers should familiarize themselves with the main rules and the main sources of spelling error.

51a *ie* or *ei*

The question of whether to use *ie* or *ei* plagues many writers. The old jingle should help: Use *i* before *e* except after *c*, or when sounded like *a* as in *neighbour* and *weigh*.

> *ie*: achieve, believe, chief, shriek, fiend, field, siege, wield
> *ei* after *c*: conceive, deceive, receive, perceive, ceiling
> *ei* when sounded like *a*: neighbour, sleigh, weigh, veil, eight

When the sound is neither that of long *e* (ē) or long *a* (ā), the spelling *ei* is usually used:

> foreign, heir, height, counterfeit, their, forfeit

But there are several exceptions, which can only be memorized:

> seize, weird, leisure, either, neither, sieve, financier, friend

When in doubt, consult your dictionary.

51b *cede, ceed,* or *sede*:

A simple act of memorizing will prevent confusion about these endings. The *sede* ending occurs in only one word: *supersede.* The *ceed* ending is used for only three words: *exceed, proceed,* and *succeed.* All other words ending in this sound use *cede:* accede, concede, intercede, precede, recede, secede.

51c **Final *e* before a suffix:**

A *suffix* is one or more syllables added on to the end of a *root* word to form a new word, usually changing its part of speech. For example:

root	suffix	new word
appear (v.)	ance	appearance (n.)
content (adj.)	ment	contentment (n.)
occasion (n.)	al	occasional (adj.)
occasional (adj.)	ly	occasionally (adv.)

When the root word ends in a silent (unpronounced) *e*, however, certain rules generally apply. If the suffix begins with a *vowel* (*a,e,i,o,*or *u*), the final *e* of the root is usually dropped:

desire + able = desirable	forgive + able = forgivable
sphere + ical = spherical	argue + ing = arguing
come + ing = coming	allure + ing = alluring
continue + ous = continuous	desire + ous = desirous
sense + ual = sensual	architecture + al = architectural

If a word ends with two *e*'s, they are both pronounced, and therefore not dropped:

> agree + ing = agreeing   flee + ing = fleeing

If the suffix begins with *a* or *e*, most words ending in *ce* or *ge* retain the final *e* in order to preserve the soft sound of the *c* (like *s* rather than *k*) or the *g* (like *j* rather than hard as in *gun*):

> notice + able = noticeable
> outrage + ous = outrageous

Note that the words *vengeance* and *gorgeous* also have such a silent *e*. (Similarly, words like *picnic* and *frolic,* which end with a hard *c,* must have a *k* added to preserve the hard sound before a suffix beginning with *e* or *i: picnicked, picknicking, frolicked, frolicking, politicking;* but *tactical, frolicsome.* Exception: *arced, arcing.*)

51c   e before suffix

If the suffix begins with a *consonant*, the final *e* of the root word is usually not dropped:

definite + ly = definitely   involve + ment = involvement
effective + ness = effectiveness mere + ly = merely
hoarse + ly = hoarsely   separate + ly = separately
immediate + ly = immediately   awe + some = awesome
immense + ly = immensely   woe + ful = woeful

Here there is a subgroup of words whose final silent *e*'s often are wrongly omitted before suffixes beginning with consonants. In these words, the *e* in question is essential to keep the sound of the preceding vowel long:

livelihood   hopelessness   loneliness   extremely
remoteness   severely   completely   tasteless

But again there are some important exceptions, so be very careful:

awe + ful = awful   argue + ment = argument
due + ly = duly   true + ly = truly

Note that in these exceptions no consonant intervenes between the long vowel and the final *e* (the *w* in *awe* is a semi-vowel, not a true consonant); if necessary, memorize this point.

51d   Final *y* after a consonant before a suffix

When the suffix is *ing*, the *y* is retained:

try + ing = trying   bully + ing = bullying

(**Note:** Words ending in *ie* change it to *y* before adding *ing*:

die + ing = dying.)

When the suffix begins with something other than *i*, the *y* is changed to *i*:

happy + er = happier   duty + ful = dutiful
fancy + ful = fanciful   angry + ly = angrily
happy + ness = happiness

Exceptions: shyly, shyness; slyer or slier, slyly or slily, flyer or flier.

Caution: Do not carelessly omit the *y* before *ing*: not *worring, but worrying*.

51e   Doubling of a final consonant before a suffix

Double the final consonant of the root if

(a)   that final consonant is preceded by a single vowel,

(b)   the root is a one-syllable word or a word accented on its last syllable, and

(c)   the suffix begins with a vowel.

One-syllable words:

fit + ed = fitted   fit + ing = fitting
                        fit + er = fitter

shop + ed = shopped   shop + ing = shopping
                        shop + er = shopper

bar + ed = barred   bar + ing = barring
hot + er = hotter   hot + est = hottest

Words accented on last syllable:

allot + ed = allotted   allot + ing = allotting
commit + ed = committed   commit + ing = committing
occur + ed = occurred   occur + ing = occurring
                           occur + ence = occurrence
propel + ed = propelled   propel + ing = propelling
                           propel + or = propellor

But note that when the addition of the suffix shifts the accent of the root word away from the last syllable, the final consonant is not doubled:

refer + ed = referred   refer + ing = referring   BUT *ref*erence
infer + ed = inferred   infer + ing = inferring   BUT *inf*erence
prefer + ed = preferred   prefer + ing = preferring   BUT *pref*erence

Do not double the final consonant if that consonant is preceded by another single consonant:

faint + ed = fainted   faint + er = fainter
sharp + er = sharper   sharp + en = sharpen

or if the final consonant is preceded by two vowels:

fail + ed = failed   fail + ing = failing
stoop + ed = stooped   stoop + ing = stooping

or if the root word is more than one syllable and *not* accented on its last syllable:

benefit + ed = benefited   ballot + ed = balloted
parallel + ed = paralleled paralleling   parallelism

Note: For other words ending in *l*, even when they are of two or more syllables and not accented on the final syllable, the final *l* is often doubled; for example: *labelled* or *labeled*; *traveller* or *traveler*. Either form is correct, though in Canada the preference is for the doubled *l*. (Some even double the *l* at the end of *parallel*, in spite of the awkwardly present double *ll* preceding it.) The word *kidnap* is a similar exception, for the obvious reason of pronunciation. Either *kidnapped* or *kidnaped* is correct (and *kidnapping* or *kidnaping*). Another is *worship*: either *worshipped* or *worshiped*, *worshipping* or *worshiping*. In both instances, the double final consonant is preferred.

The final consonant should not be doubled if the suffix does not begin with a vowel:

> commit + ment = commitment   hot + ly = hotly

51f   The suffix *ly*

When *ly* is added to an adjective already ending in a single *l*, that final *l* is retained, resulting in an *lly* ending for the new adverb; correct pronunciation of these and similar words will help prevent you from misspelling them.

> accidental + ly = accidentally   mental + ly = mentally
> incidental + ly = incidentally   natural + ly = naturally
> political + ly = politically   cool + ly = coolly

If the root already ends in a double *ll*, one *l* is of course dropped: full + ly = fully, chill + ly = chilly, droll + ly = drolly.

Note: Many adjectives ending in *ic* have alternative forms ending in *ical*. But even if they don't, nearly all add *ally*, not just *ly*, in becoming adverbs, as do nouns like *music*; again correct pronunciation will help avoid error:

> alphabetic, alphabetical, alphabetically
> basic, basically
> cyclic, cyclical, cyclically
> dramatic, dramatically
> drastic, drastically
> enthusiastic, enthusiastically
> scientific, scientifically
> symbolic, symbolical, symbolically

One exception is *publicly*. Can you think of any others?

51g   Prefixes

The more you know about how words are put together, the less trouble you will have with spelling. Many spelling errors, for example, occur because a writer does not realize that a given word consists of a root word with something stuck onto the front of it: a **prefix**. (*Pre* is from a Latin word meaning *before; fix* is a root, meaning *fasten* or *place*; the new word is *prefix*.) When a prefix ends with the same letter that the root begins with, the result is a double letter; be careful not to forget one of them:

ad + dress = address	mis + spell = misspell
com + motion = commotion	un + necessary = unnecessary

Similarly, one must be careful not to omit one of the doubled letters in certain compounds; for example:

beach + head = beachhead	room + mate = roommate
book + keeping = bookkeeping	

Many words have been formed by adding a prefix to a root whose first letter "pulls" the last letter of the prefix over, causing it to change, so that a double letter results. Writers unaware that a prefix is involved sometimes forget to double the consonant. The Latin prefix *ad*, meaning *to, toward, near*, is very commonly affected this way; for example, *ad* became *af* when it was added to the Latin *facere*, meaning *to do*; hence our word *affect* is spelled with two *f*'s. Here are some examples of this phenomenon occurring with *ad* and a few other prefixes:

ad	>	an	in annul, annihilate
		ap	in apprehend, apparatus, application
		ac	in access, accept, acquire, acquaint
		al	in allusion
com	>	con	in connect
		col	in collide
		cor	in correct, correspond
ob	>	op	in opposed
sub	>	suc	in success, succumb
		sup	in suppress

Note the structure of this frequently misspelled word: *accommodate*; both the *ac* and the *com* are prefixes, so the word must be spelled with both a double *c* (*cc*) and a double *m* (*mm*). Errors can also result from mistaking the prefix. The writer who spells *arouse* with a double *r* (*rr*) doesn't realize that the prefix in this instance is simply *a*, not *ad>ar*. And the writer who spells *apology* with a double *p* (*pp*) is unaware that the prefix here is *apo*, not *ad>ap* (here awareness that the root involved is the Greek *logos*, "speech," would have helped prevent the error). It is helpful to be familiar with as many prefixes as possible. Here is a list of words with their prefixes printed in capital letters; each word is followed by a common misspelling that could have been avoided had the writers known their prefixes:

51g *prefixes*

Right	Wrong	Right	Wrong
AFOREmentioned	aformentioned	MILLImetre	milimetre
BY-product	biproduct	MINIature	minature
CONTROversial	conterversial	PENinsula	penninsula
DEscribe	discribe	PERsuade	pursuade
DEstroy	distroy	PERvading	prevading
DIAlogue	diologue	PORtraying	protraying
DISappointed	dissappointed	PROfessor	proffessor
EXTRAordinary	extrordinary	Utopia	eutopia

51h   Suffixes

Suffixes too can give trouble. For example, if you add *ness* to a word already ending in *n*, that original *n* must be retained, resulting in a double *n* (*nn*):

    barren + ness = barrenness
    open + ness = openness
    stubborn + ness = stubbornness

This is true even when the final *n* is not pronounced:

    solemn + ness = solemnness

ful:

Remember that the correct suffix is *ful*, not *full*:

    spoonful, cupful, shovelful, bucketful, roomful, successful

51i   Troublesome Word-endings

Several groups of suffixes—here more conveniently thought of simply as word-endings—consistently plague bad spellers and sometimes confuse even good spellers. There are no rules governing them; pronunciation is seldom any help; one either knows them or does not. Whenever you are not absolutely sure of the correct spelling, consult your dictionary. The following examples will at least alert you to the potential trouble spots:

able, ably, ability; ible, ibly, ibility:

Many more words end in *able* than in *ible*, which should be a help; nevertheless, it is the *ible* endings that seem to cause the most trouble:

advisable	laudable	audible	irresistible
comparable	noticeable	deductible	negligible
debatable	quotable	eligible	plausible
desirable	respectable	flexible	responsible
immeasurable	syllable	forcible	tangible
indubitable	veritable	incredible	visible
inevitable		inexpressible	

ent, ently, ence, ency; ant, antly, ance, ancy:

apparent	inherent	appearance	flamboyant
consistent	persistence	attendance	irrelevant
coherent	permanent	blatant	maintenance
independent	resilient	brilliant	resistance
existence	tendency	concomitant	warrant
excellent		extravagant	

tial, tian, tiate; cial, cian, ciate:

confidential	influential	beneficial	mathematician
dietitian	martial	crucial	mortician
existential	spatial	emaciated	physician
expatiate	substantial	enunciate	politician

ce; se:

choice	presence	course	expense
evidence	pretence	dense	phrase
fence	voice	dispense	sparse

ative; itive:

affirmative	negative	additive	positive
imaginative	restorative	competitive	sensitive
informative		genitive	

51j Changes in Spelling of Roots

Some words require extra care because the spelling of their roots changes when they shift from one part of speech to another—sometimes because of a change in stress; for example:

clear, clarity	maintain, maintenance
curious, curiosity	prevail, prevalent
despair, desperate	pronounce, pronunciation
exclaim, exclamatory	repair, reparable
generous, generosity	repeat, repetition

inherit, heritage, BUT heredity, hereditary

51k Faulty Pronunciation

If you pronounce a word incorrectly, you may also spell it incorrectly. Try to acquire the habit of careful and correct pronunciation; sound words to yourself, exaggeratedly if necessary, even at the expense of temporarily slowing down your reading speed. Here are some correctly spelled words followed by common misspellings; notice that mispronunciation is the likely culprit. Check your dictionary for any pronunciations you are not sure of.

51k *faulty pronunciation*

Right	Wrong	Right	Wrong
academic	acedemic	insurgence	ensurgence
accelerate	exelerate	interpretation	interpertation,
accidentally	accidently		interpratation
analogy	anology	intimacy	intamacy
approximately	approximently	inviting	enviting
architectural	architectual	irrelevant	irrevelant
athlete,	athelete,	itinerary	itinery
athletics	atheletics	larynx	larnyx
authoritative	authoratative	lightning	lightening
barbiturate	barbituate	limpidly	lipidly
Britain	Britian	lustrous	lusterous
candidate	canidate	mathematics	mathamatics,
celebration	celabration		mathmatics
conference	confrence	negative	negitive
congratulate	congradulate	nuclear	nucular
controversial	contraversial	occasional	occational,
definitely	definately		occassional
deteriorating	detiorating	optimism	optomism
detrimental	dentremental	original	origional
dilapidated	delapitated	particular	peticular
diphthong	dipthong	peculiar	perculiar
disastrous	disasterous	permanently	perminently
disgruntled	disgrunted	phenomenon	phenomanon
disgust	discust	philosophical	philisophical
disillusioned	disallusioned	predilection	predeliction
eerie	errie	prevalent	prevelent
elaborate	elaberate	privilege	privelege
emperor	emporer	pronunciation	pronounciation
environment	enviorment,	quantity	quanity
	enviroment	repetitive	repeditive
epitomize	epitemize	reservoir	resevoir
escape	excape	significant	signifigant
especially	expecially	similar	similiar, simular
etcetera	excetra	strength	strenth
evident	evedent	subsidiary	subsidary
excerpt	exerpt	suffocate	sufficate
facsimiles	facsimalies	surprise	suprise, supprise
February	Febuary	temporarily	tempirarily
film	filum		tempararily
foliage	foilage	ultimatum	ultamatum
frailty	fraility	village	villiage
further	futher	villain	villian
government	goverment	visible	visable
governor	govenor	vulnerability	vulnerbility,
gravitation	gravatation		vunerability
height	heighth	where	were
hereditary	heriditary	whether	wether
hurriedly	hurridly	whines	wines
immersing	emersing	wondrous	wonderous

Sometimes changing the form of a word shifts its accent. For example, when the suffix *ical* is added to the word *technólogy*, the accent shifts to the third syllable: *technológical*; since the first *o* is no longer stressed, some writers change it, quite wrongly, to an *i* or an *a* (technilogical, technalogical). With such words, try to remember the spelling of the *root* word; it will almost always remain the same, even though its pronunciation may change when a suffix or a prefix is added.

Caution: Be careful not to omit the *d* or *ed* from such words as *used* and *supposed*, *old-fashioned* and *prejudiced*, which are often carelessly pronounced:

> I used to read a lot. (NOT use)
> She's a very old-fashioned girl. (NOT old-fashion)
> You were supposed to pick up a loaf of bread. (NOT suppose to)
> He seemed very prejudiced against Ontarians. (NOT prejudice against)

And don't write or copy so hastily that you omit whole syllables (usually near-duplications in sound). Write carefully—and proofread even more carefully, sounding the words to yourself. Here are some examples of "telescoped" words that occur repeatedly:

Right	*Wrong*	*Right*	*Wrong*
politician	politian	independent	indepent
remembrance	rembrance	convenience	convience
repetition	repition	inappropriate	inappriate
criticize	critize	institution	instution
examining	examing		

51-1 Confusion with Other Words
Don't let false analogies and similarities of sound lead you astray.

A careless writer who thinks of a word like:	may make the error of spelling another word WRONG, like this:	instead of spelling it the RIGHT way, like this:
young	amoung	among
breeze	cheeze	cheese
conform	conformation	confirmation
diet	diety	deity
desolate	desolute	dissolute
exalt	exaltant	exultant
democracy	hypocracy	hypocrisy
discrete	indiscrete	indiscreet
ideal	idealic	idyllic
air, fairy	ordinairy	ordinary
ledge, knowledge	priviledge	privilege
size	rize	rise
religious	sacreligious	sacrilegious
familiar	similiar	similar

51-1 *similar sounds*

stupid	stupifying	stupefying
summer	summerize	summarize
prize	surprize	surprise
tack	tacktics	tactics
rink, sink	zink	zinc

51m Homophones and Other Words Sometimes Confused

Some words are pronounced exactly like other words but mean different things and are spelled differently; these are called **homophones** (or **homonyms**). Be sure to distinguish such words from their sound-alikes. Here are some that have proved troublesome; look up in the dictionary any whose meanings you are not sure of, for this is a matter not just of spelling but of meaning as well (and see *Wrong Word*, 57).

aisle, isle
alter, altar
assent, ascent
bear, bare
birth, berth
board, bored
border, boarder
born, borne
break, brake
by, by-, bi-, buy, bye
callous, callus
canvas, canvass
capital, capitol
complement, compliment
cord, chord
council, counsel
course, coarse
desert (v.), dessert
die, dying; dye, dyeing
discreet, discrete
flair, flare
forgo, forego
forth, fourth
hail, hale
hanger, hangar
hear, here
heard, herd
hoard, horde
hole, whole
holy, holey, wholly
idle, idol, idyll
its, it's
led, lead

lesson, lessen
manner, manor
mantel, mantle
meat, meet, mete
naval, navel
paid, payed
past, passed
patience, patients
peddle, pedal
phase, faze
piece, peace
plain, plane
populous, populace
pray, prey
precedence, precedents
presence, presents
principle, principal
rain, reign, rein
right, write, rite
ring, wring
road, rode
roll, role
seen, scene
sight, site, cite
soul, sole
sow, sew; sown, sewn
stationary, stationery
steal, steel
straight, strait
surf, serf
there, their, they're
through, threw
to, too, two

vein, vain, vane
vice, vise
waste, waist
wave, waive

way, weigh
weak, week
whose, who's
your, you're

There are also words which, although not pronounced exactly alike, are yet so similar that they are often confused. Be careful to distinguish between such words as these (and again, look up in the dictionary any whose meanings you are not sure of):

accept, except
access, excess
adopt, adapt, adept
adverse, averse
advice, advise
affect, effect
allude, elude
angle, angel
anti-, ante-
bisect, dissect
bizarre, bazaar
breath, breathe
careen, career
cease, seize
choose, chose
censor, censure
climatic, climactic
conscious, conscience, conscientious
credible, creditable, credulous
custom, costume
diary, dairy
decent, descent, dissent
desert (n.), dessert
detract, distract
device, devise
discomfit, discomfort
elicit, illicit
emigrate, immigrate
eminent, imminent, immanent
ensure, insure
envelop, envelope
finely, finally
flaunt, flout

forbear, forebear
fortunate, fortuitous
founder, flounder
gantlet, gauntlet
genius, ingenious, ingenuous
Granada, Grenada
illusion, allusion, disillusion
impractical, impracticable
incident, incidence, instance
incredulous, incredible
ingenious, ingenuous
insight, incite
instant, instance
later, latter
lineage, linage
liniment, lineament
loathe, loath
loose, lose
mitigate, militate
moral, morale
persecute, prosecute
practical, practicable
predominate, predominant
proceed, precede
prophecy, prophesy
quite, quiet
rational, rationale
statue, statute
tack, tact
than, then
verses, *versus*
whether, wether
while, wile

51m *homophones*

Be careful also to distinguish between such words as the following, for although they sound the same, they function differently depending on whether they are spelled as one word or two:

already (adverb)	all ready (adverb plus adjective)
altogether (adverb)	all together (adverb plus adjective)
anyway (adverb)	any way (adjective plus noun)
awhile (adverb)	a while (article plus noun)
everyday (adjective)	every day (adjective plus noun)
maybe (adverb)	may be (verb)
someday (adverb)	some day (adjective plus noun)
sometime (adverb)	some time (adjective plus noun)

51n One Word or Two Words?

The following words, among others, are always spelled as one unhyphenated word; do not spell them as if they consisted of two or three separate or hyphenated words:

alongside	easygoing	nowadays	straightforward
background	lifetime	outshine	sunrise
buildup (n.)	nevertheless	setback	throughout
countryside	nonetheless	spotlight	wrongdoing

Note: *Cannot* should almost always be written as one word. Write it as two words only when you want special emphasis on the *not*, as in "No, Johnny, you can *not* go out and play!"

The following, on the other hand, should always be spelled as two words, unhyphenated:

a bit	as though	in order (to)
a few	at least	in spite (of)
after all	close by	much less
a lot	even though	no longer
a part (noun)	every time	(on the) other hand
all right (NOT alright)	in between	(in) other words
any more	in fact	time period
any time	in front	up to

When in doubt consult your dictionary. You may find, as with *insofar*, *in so far*, that either form is acceptable.

51o Hyphenation

To hyphenate or not to hyphenate? That is often the question. There are some firm rules; there are some sound guidelines; and there is a large territory where only common sense and a good dictionary can help you find your way. Since the conventions are constantly changing, sometimes rapidly, make a habit of checking your dictionary for current usage; at least then you can be consistent. (For hyphens to divide words at the end of a line, see *Syllabication and Word Division*, **45b**.)

Use hyphens in compound numbers from twenty-one to ninety-nine:

Forty-three people came.
He scored eighty-five out of a possible one hundred.

Use hyphens with fractions used as adjectives:

A two-thirds majority is required to defeat the amendment.

When a fraction is used as a noun, however, many writers do not use a hyphen:

Four fifths of the audience was asleep.
The correct amount to use is about one third of the whole.

Use hyphens with compounds indicating time, when these are written out:

seven-thirty, nine-fifteen

Use a hyphen between a pair of numbers (including hours and dates) which indicate a range, for example of pages or time:

You will find the information on pages 73-78.
The festival will be held June 20-26.

Note that the hyphen in these instances is equivalent to the word *to*. If, however, you use the word *from* to introduce the range, you should write out the word *to* instead of using a hyphen: "from June 20 to 26." Similarly, since you would not write "held between June 25 to July 2," neither should you write "held between June 25-July 2," but simply "held June 25-July 2."

Use hyphens with prefixes before proper nouns:

all-Canadian	pre-Christian
anti-Fascist	pro-Tory
ex-Prime Minister	pseudo-Pindaric
non-Communist	semi-Gothic
post-Elizabethan	Trans-Siberian Railroad
Pan-Slavic	un-English

But there are some long-established exceptions; for example:

transatlantic   transpacific   antichrist

Use hyphens with compounds beginning with the prefix *self*: self-made, self-deluded, self-pity, self-confidence, self-esteem, self-assured, etc. Only a few words beginning with *self* are written without a hyphen: selfhood, selfish, selfless, selfsame; in these words *self* is the root, not the prefix. Hyphens are conventionally used with certain other prefixes, such as *all*, *ex* (meaning *former*), and *quasi*: all-important, ex-premier, quasi-religious. (It is usually preferable to use *former* rather than *ex*.)

Hyphens are conventionally used with most, but not all, compounds beginning with *vice* and *by*: vice-consul, vice-chancellor, vice-president, vice-principal, vice-regent, etc., BUT viceregal, vicereine, viceroy; by-election, by-product, etc., BUT bygone, bystander, byword.

Hyphens are used with the suffixes *elect* and *designate*: mayor-elect, ambassador-designate.

Hyphens are used with *great* and *in-law* in compounds designating family relationships:

> mother-in-law, son-in-law, great-grandfather, great-aunt

Use hyphens to prevent a word's being mistaken for an entirely different word:

> He recounted what had happened after the ballots had been re-counted.
> If you're going to re-strain the juice, I'll restrain myself from drinking it now, seeds and all.
> Once at the resort after the bumpy ride, we sat down to re-sort our jumbled fishing gear.
> If you re-cover that chair before you sell it, you may be able to recover your investment.

Use hyphens to prevent awkward or confusing combinations of letters and sounds: anti-intellectual, photo-offset, re-echo, set-to, war-risk, doll-like.

Hyphens are sometimes necessary to prevent ambiguity:

> *Ambiguous:* The ad offered six week old kittens for sale.
> *Clear:* The ad offered six week-old kittens for sale.
> *Clear:* The ad offered six-week-old kittens for sale.

Another example:

> It will require two-hundred foot-pounds of energy to do the job.

Here, although *two hundred* would not normally be hyphenated, it is advisable in order to avoid the possible momentary misreading of *two hundred-foot*. And though one might refer to "forty odd dollars," one would be well advised to use a hyphen if referring to "forty-odd students." Here is another example:

> Some people think that what we need is a social evening out of benefits and responsibilities.

Simply hyphenating *evening-out* removes the possibility of misreading the sentence. (Using another word, such as *sharing* or *levelling*, would probably be even better.)

51p **Compound Nouns**

Some nouns composed of two or more words are conventionally hyphenated; for example: free-for-all, half-and-half, half-breed, maneater, merry-go-round, old-timer, runner-up, safe-conduct, shut-in, tam-o'-shanter, trade-in, well-being. But many nouns that one might think should be hyphenated are not, and others that may once have been hyphenated, or even two separate words, have become so familiar that they are no longer separated by either a space or a hyphen. Usage is constantly and rapidly changing, and even dictionaries do not always agree on what is standard at a given time. Here for example is how nine different dictionaries list the same words:

1. pre-eminence	sheep-dog	waste-paper
2. pre-eminence or preëminence	sheep dog	wastepaper or waste paper
3. preeminence or pre-eminence	sheep dog	wastepaper
4. preeminence pre-eminence, or preëminence	sheepdog or sheep dog	wastepaper
5. preeminence	sheep dog	wastepaper or waste paper
6. pre-eminence	sheep dog	wastepaper
7. pre-eminence, or preeminence, or preëminence	sheep dog, or sheepdog	waste paper
8. preeminence	sheepdog	wastepaper
9. preeminence, or pre-eminence	sheep dog	wastepaper, or waste paper

Here the dictionaries are cited in order of age, from the oldest (1) to the most recent (9). Though one would expect separate words to give way to hyphenated compounds, and hyphenated compounds to give way to solid forms, the pattern is far from consistent, as you see, even within a single dictionary. Some dictionaries still record such old-fashioned and outdated forms as *to-night* and *to-morrow* as alternatives; be sure you use the preferred and newer forms *tonight* and *tomorrow*. Clearly one should consult a dictionary that is both good and up-to-date, and use the form it lists first.

51q **Compound Modifiers**

When two or more words are used together in such a way that they act like a single adjective before a noun, they are usually hyphenated: a well-dressed man, greenish-gray eyes, middle-class values, a once-in-a-lifetime chance, a three-day-old strike. But note that many compound modifiers are already listed as hyphenated words in the dictionary. One dictionary, for example, lists these, among others: first-class, fly-by-night, good-looking, habit-forming, matter-of-fact, open-minded, right-hand, short-lived, tongue-tied, warm-blooded, wide-eyed. These compound modifiers—already hyphenated—will of course remain hyphenated even when they follow the nouns they modify:

> Her performance was first-class.
> The tone of the speech was very matter-of-fact.
> The blossoms on this plant are very short-lived.

If the compound includes an *ly* adverb, however, it is not hyphenated, even when it precedes the noun it modifies:

> He is a happily married man.
> The superbly wrought sculpture was the centre of attention.

Exercise 51pq: Checking hyphenation

What does your dictionary say about the following compounds? Should they be two separate words, hyphenated, or one solid word?

1. boy friend
2. dumb waiter
3. fish pole
4. foot candle
5. girl friend
6. half life
7. half moon
8. home stretch
9. nail set
10. pocket book
11. power boat
12. pre empt
13. run around
14. slip stream
15. south bound
16. stock pile
17. time out
18. wine skin
19. world weary
20. world wide

51r   When two prefixes are used with one root, a "suspension" hyphen is used—even if the prefix would not normally be hyphenated:

> The audience was about equally divided between pro- and anti-Liberals.
> You can either pre- or postdate the letter.
> You can choose between the three- and five-day excursions.

Note that some expressions can be spelled either as two separate words or as compounds, depending on what part of speech they are functioning as; for example:

> He works full time. (n.) He has a full-time job. (adj.)
> If you get too dizzy you may black out. (v.) You will then suffer a blackout. (n.)
> Call up the next group of trainees. (v.) The commander ordered a general call-up. (n.)

51s Verbs too are sometimes hyphenated. A dictionary will list most of the ones you might want to use; for example: baby-sit, pan-broil, pistol-whip, pole-vault, re-educate, second-guess, sight-read, soft-pedal, straight-arm, two-time.

Exercise 51o-s: Using hyphens

Insert hyphens wherever they are needed in the following sentences. Consult your dictionary if necessary.

1. His broad jump record was twenty three and three quarters feet.
2. I would expect that two thirds of the members will be uncooperative.
3. The speech had a distinctly antiAmerican tone, and one of selfcongratulation to boot.
4. The all Canadian team proved too much for even the exchampions.
5. My half sister showed me an old tintype picture of her greatgrandmother.
6. She had bluish grey eyes, but they went well with her light blue dress.
7. The fully developed outline will be on your desk by midmorning.
8. The three youths, though well built, looked to me a run of the mill sort.
9. Summertime was only a golden memory.
10. There will be a two month delay.
11. I watched an interesting documentary about an alien smuggling operation.
12. Enjoy our beautiful dining room or take it with you service in one minute or less.
13. In the small town where I grew up there was a once a month barndance.
14. Much contemporary art is designed to fit readily into the middle class living room or the corporate board room.
15. The average high school graduate doesn't have much hope of getting a good career job.

51t **Plurals**

Most nouns add *s* or *es* to the singular to indicate plural number:

one girl, two girls	one wish, two wishes
one cat, two cats	one church, two churches
one building, two buildings	one box, two boxes

Add *es* rather than just *s* if forming the plural makes an extra syllable, as in the three examples on the right. Sometimes the added *s* alone produces an extra syllable:

fireplaces   adages   cases   blazes   houses

Nouns ending in *o* preceded by a consonant form their plural with either *s* or *es*. Some of these nouns use either plural form, but you should use the one listed first in your dictionary. Here are a few examples:

altos	echoes	buffaloes or buffalos
solos	heroes	mottoes or mottos
chromos	potatoes	zeros or zeroes

51t *plurals*

If the final *o* is preceded by a vowel, usually only an *s* is added:

arpeggios   cameos   ratios   cuckoos   embryos

To form the plural of some nouns ending in a single *f* or an *fe*, change the ending to *ve* before adding *s*; for example:

knife, knives   life, lives   shelf, shelves
leaf, leaves   loaf, loaves   thief, thieves

But some simply add the *s*:

beliefs   gulfs   safes
griefs   poufs   still lifes

Most words ending in two *f*'s simply add an *s*:

cliffs   sheriffs   puffs

Some words ending in *f* have alternative acceptable plurals:

wharfs or wharves   scarfs or scarves   dwarfs or dwarves

The plural of *hoof* can be either *hoofs* or *hooves*. *Roofs* is at present the only acceptable plural of *roof*, but someday, perhaps in only a few years, "rooves" will also be acceptable; one already hears it being pronounced that way.

Note: The well-known athletic group called the *Maple Leafs* is obviously a special case, a proper noun that does not follow the rules governing common nouns.

Nouns ending in *y* preceded by a consonant change the *y* to *i* and add *es*:

one city, two cities
one family, two families
one country, two countries
one trophy, two trophies

Exception: Most *proper* nouns simply add *s*: There are two Marys and three Henrys in the group. Since 1949 there have been two Germanys. (But note that we always refer to the Rockies, and the Canary Islands are also known as the Canaries.) Nouns ending in *y* preceded by a vowel add *s* only:

bays   valleys   toys   guys   buoys

Plurals of Compounds
Generally, form the plurals of compounds simply by adding *s*:

backbenchers	man-eaters
forget-me-nots	merry-go-rounds
great-grandmothers	prime ministers
lieutenant-governors	second cousins
major generals	shut-ins

But when the first part of the compound is a noun and the rest is not, or if the first part is the more important of two nouns, then that word is the one made plural:

daughters-in-law	mayors-elect
governors general	passers-by
jacks-of-all-trades	poets laureate

But there are exceptions, and—as usual—usage is changing. Note for example these plural forms:

spoonfuls (*not* spoonsful; this is the pattern for all nouns ending in *ful*)
courts-martial *or* court martials

A few compounds conventionally pluralize both nouns; for example:

menservants
ups and downs

And a few compounds are the same in both singular and plural; for example:

crossroads, daddy-long-legs, fancy pants

Irregular Plurals

Some nouns are irregular in forming their plurals, but these are common and generally well known; for example:

one child, two children
one foot, two feet
one man, two men
one mouse, two mice

Some plural forms are the same as the singular, for example:

one deer, two deer
one series, two series
one sheep, two sheep

The plurals of words borrowed from other languages (mostly Latin and Greek) can pose a problem. Words used formally or technically tend to retain their original plural forms; words used more commonly tend to form their plurals according to regular English rules. Since many such words are in transition, you will probably encounter both plural forms. If you are in any doubt, use the preferred form listed in your dictionary. Here are some examples:

Some words that have tended to retain their original plurals:

alumna, alumnae	larva, larvae
alumnus, alumni	madame, mesdames
analysis, analyses	nucleus, nuclei
basis, bases	parenthesis, parentheses
crisis, crises	phenomenon, phenomena
criterion, criteria	stimulus, stimuli
hypothesis, hypotheses	synthesis, syntheses
kibbutz, kibbutzim	thesis, theses

Some words that are (apparently) in transition and have both forms of plurals (the choice often depending on the formality or technicality of the context):

antenna, antennae (insects), antennas (radios and the like)
apparatus, apparatus, apparatuses
appendix, appendices, appendixes
beau, beaux, beaus
cactus, cacti, cactuses
curriculum, curricula, curriculums
focus, foci, focuses
formula, formulae, formulas
index, indices, indexes
lacuna, lacunae, lacunas
memorandum, memoranda, memorandums
radius, radii, radiuses
referendum, referenda, referendums
syllabus, syllabi, syllabuses
symposium, symposia, symposiums
terminus, termini, terminuses
ultimatum, ultimata, ultimatums
vertebra, vertebrae, vertebras

Some words that now tend to follow regular English patterns in forming their plurals:

bureau, bureaus
campus, campuses
genius, geniuses (*genii* for mythological creatures)
stadium, stadiums

Note: *Data* is plural; the singular is *datum*. Similarly for *strata (stratum)*. *Kudos* is singular and should not be used as if it were plural. *Trivia* is plural and should not be used as if it were singular. *Bacteria* is plural and should not be used as if it were singular.

Media is the plural of *medium* and should not be used as if it were singular. (Note: *Mediums* is the correct plural for spiritualists who claim to communicate with the dead.)

Opinion, as well as usage, is divided on the spelling of the plurals of these and similar words. Most writers, for example, loathe *criterions* and *phenomenons*, preferring the original plural forms *criteria* and *phenomena*. On the other hand, they may not object to *data* as a singular noun. And *agenda*, originally the plural of *agendum*, is now simply a singular noun with its own plural, *agendas*.

Your dictionary should indicate any irregular plurals; if you are not sure of a word, look it up.

Note: If you are using or quoting French or foreign words that use such diacritical marks as the cedilla, the circumflex, the tilde, the umlaut, or acute or grave accents, be sure you write them accurately; for example:

façade, fête, cañon, Götterdämmerung, passé, à la mode

Exercise 51t: Forming plurals

Write out what you think is the correct plural form of each of the following nouns. When you have finished, check your dictionary to see if you were right.

1. aide-de-camp	16. mosquito
2. alley	17. museum
3. ambassador-designate	18. octopus
4. analysis	19. ox
5. bonus	20. plateau
6. bus	21. radius
7. cloverleaf	22. serf
8. embargo	23. society
9. fifth	24. solo
10. glass	25. speech
11. goose	26. staff
12. handful	27. territory
13. locus	28. town
14. mongoose	29. wife
15. moose	30. yokefellow

51u **Third-Person-Singular Verbs in the Present Tense**

The present-tense inflection of verbs in the third person singular is usually formed by following the same rules that govern the formation of the plurals of nouns. For example:

I lift. The fog lifts.
I run. He runs.

51u third-person-singular verbs

I hate. She hates.
I lurch. It lurches.
They wish. He wishes.
I carry. He carries.
I try. She tries.
I portray. She portrays.
I buy. He buys.
I brief him. She briefs me.

But be careful, for there can be exceptions:

I loaf. He loafs.
I wolf my food. He wolfs his food.

Exercise 51u: Inflecting verbs

Supply the present-tense, third-person-singular form of each of the following verbs.

1. atrophy		11. leaf	
2. buy		12. mouth	
3. chafe		13. rally	
4. choose		14. reach	
5. comb		15. relieve	
6. condone		16. revoke	
7. convey		17. search	
8. echo		18. ski	
9. go		19. swing	
10. grasp		20. tunnel	

51v Apostrophes

apos

The *only* time an apostrophe can be used to form a plural is when it is used with an *s* to form the plurals of numerals, symbols, letters, and words referred to as words:

She knew her ABC's at the age of four.
Study the three R's.
It happened in the 1870's.
Indent all ¶'s.
Accommodate is spelled with two *c*'s and two *m*'s.
There are four 7's in my telephone number.
There are too many *and*'s in that sentence.

Note that when a word, letter, or figure is italicized, the *s* for the plural is not.

Note: Some people prefer to form such plurals without the apostrophe: Rs, 7s, ¶s, 1870s, *and*s. But this practice can be confusing, especially with letters and words:

> How many *is* are there in Mississippi? (looks like "is")
> Too many *his*s can spoil a good paragraph. (likely to be misread at first).

It is clearer and easier always to use the apostrophe. (Whichever method you use, it is best, in order to avoid ambiguity, to form possessives of abbreviations with *of* rather than with apostrophes: the opinion of the MLA; the opinion of the MLA's; the opinion of the MLAs).

Use apostrophes to indicate omitted letters in contractions, and omitted (though obvious) numbers:

aren't (are not)	they're (they are)
can't (cannot)	won't (will not)
doesn't (does not)	wouldn't (would not)
don't (do not)	goin' home (going home)
isn't (is not)	back in '63
it's (it is)	the crash of '29
she's (she is)	the summer of '42

If an apostrophe is already present to indicate a plural, you may leave out the apostrophe that indicates omission:

> the 20's   the 60's

51w Possessives

apos

Some people neglect the simple mechanics of inflecting nouns for possessive case; such neglect can lead to confusion with the inflection for the plural. For correct and consistent usage, you should strictly follow these rules:

To indicate the possessive case of a noun—whether singular or plural—that does not end in *s*, add *'s*:

Emil's briefcase	a year's leave of absence
the girl's teacher	tomorrow's news
Alberta's capital city	children's books
the car's colour	the men's jobs
a day's work	the deer's hides

To form the possessive of compound nouns, use an apostrophe after the last noun:

> The Solicitor General's report is due tomorrow.
> Sally and Mike's dinner party was a huge success.

51w *possessives*

But be careful: if the nouns do not actually form a compound, each will need the apostrophe:

Sally's and Mike's lunches were markedly different.

To indicate the possessive case of most singular nouns ending in *s*, add *'s* to one-syllable words and also to words of more than one syllable for whose plural you would normally pronounce an extra syllable:

the *cross's* symbolic significance
the *class's* achievement as a whole
the *congress's* interminable debates

To indicate the possessive case of plural nouns ending in *s*, add an apostrophe only:

the *girls'* sweaters	the *Smiths'* cottage
the *cannons'* roar	the *Joneses'* garden

About some nouns, however, opinion is divided. Some writers feel that pronouncing an extra syllable would sound awkward, and therefore prefer to indicate the possessive case with only an apostrophe. Others feel that for consistency and clarity an *'s* should be added even to these words, in spite of the possibly awkward pronunciation:

Jesus's birth *or* Jesus' birth
Moses's miracles *or* Moses' miracles
Dickens's novels *or* Dickens' novels
Keats's poems *or* Keats' poems
Jones's lawnmower *or* Jones' lawnmower
Kansas's capital *or* Kansas' capital

Note that this problem seems to arise only with proper nouns, and often with those that end in two successive sibilants (*s* sounds.) Simply pronounce the word yourself and then decide how you should form its possessive case. The problem can often be avoided (as it probably would be in speech, in order to avoid ambiguity as well as awkward sound) by simply rephrasing; instead of inflecting the noun for possessive case, use it in a prepositional phrase beginning with *of*:

the novels of Dickens; the poems of Keats; the birth of Jesus; the price of success; the roar of the cannons; the roof of the house

(For information about prepositions and their objects, see **11**.)

Caution: Do not use apostrophes in possessive personal pronouns:

NOT her's, but *hers*
NOT it's, but *its*
NOT our's, but *ours*
NOT their's, but *theirs*
NOT your's, but *yours*

(See also **3a**.)

Possessives with 's or with *of*
Generally, use the *'s* inflection with the names of living creatures, an *of* phrase with the names of inanimate things:

> the girl's coat, Sherman's home town, the cat's tail
> the arm of the chair, the contents of the refrigerator, the surface of the desk

But this is not an inflexible rule. The *'s* form is common, for example, with nouns that refer to things that are or can be thought of as made up of people or animals or as extensions or parts of them:

> the team's strategy, the committee's decision, the company's representative, the government's policy, the city's bylaws, Canada's climate, the factory's output, the heart's affections, the law's delay, humanity's experience

or things that are "animate" in the sense that they are part of nature:

> the dawn's early light, the wind's velocity, the comet's tail, the sea's surface, the plant's roots, the sky's colour

or periods of time:

> today's paper, a day's work, a month's wages, winter's storms

Even beyond such uses the *'s* is not uncommon; sometimes there is a sense of personification, but not always:

> *Love's Labour's Lost*, at death's door, beauty's ensign, time's fool, the glass's edge, a razor's edge, freedom's holy light, ship's helm

If it seems natural and appropriate to you, then, don't be afraid to speak or write of a *car's engine*, a *book's contents*, a *rocket's trajectory*, a *poem's imagery*, and the like (but don't be surprised if a few people object to the practice). Conversely, for the sake of emphasis or rhythm you will occasionally want to use an *of*-phrase where *'s* would be normal; for example, *the jury's verdict* doesn't carry the punch of *the verdict of the jury*. You will also want to use an *of*-phrase to avoid ugly sounds (see the preceding paragraph, on "the novels of Dickens," etc.) and unwieldy constructions; for example, *the opinion of the Minister of Finance* is preferable to *the Minister of Finance's opinion*.

Double Possessives
Although some people object to them, there is nothing wrong with double possessives—showing possession with both an *of*-phrase and a possessive inflection. They are standard with possessive pronouns and can be used similarly with common and proper nouns:

> a favourite *of mine*, a friend *of hers*, a friend *of the family* or *of the family's*, a contemporary *of Shakespeare* or *of Shakespeare's*

51w possessives

And a sentence like "The story was based on an idea of Shakespeare" is at least potentially ambiguous, whereas "The story was based on an idea of Shakespeare's" is clear. But if you feel that this sort of construction is unlovely, you can usually manage to revise it to something like "on one of Shakespeare's ideas." And certainly avoid such double possessives with a *that*-construction: "His hat was just like that of Arthur's"; all would agree that that is unlovely.

Caution: Don't commit the careless and vulgar error of using an apostrophe before the final *s* of a verb ("It show's ignorance") or to form the plural of a proper name ("The Smith's should know better").

Exercise 51vw(1): Using apostrophes

Insert apostrophes where necessary in the following sentences.

1. I dont know whether this book is his or hers, but theres no doubt its a handsome one, and its value on todays market, what its worth now, must surely be greater than its value as a new book, way back in the 1930s.
2. Clearly he doesnt know whats going on; itll take him a weeks study to catch up.
3. Our reports so far ahead of theirs that shell have to work nights to make ends meet.
4. It isnt whom you know but what you know that in the end seals the deal.
5. Dianas guess is closer than Seans, but the jars full and accurate count of beans wont be verified till Mondays announcement.
6. The teachers comments about Guys paper pointed out its errors.
7. Its sometimes a full days work to write a good paragraph.
8. It doesnt matter who wins the game; its rather its quality that counts.
9. When the childrens shouting got too loud, the Joneses neighbours had to shut their windows, but Alice left hers open.
10. Their approach was by ones and twos, whereas ours was a matter of charging in all at once.

Exercise 51vw(2): Using apostrophes

In the following sentences, supply any missing apostrophes and correct any instances of their misuse.

1. Now we see wives who, by working and pooling their wages with their husbands, can purchase extra luxury items for the home and family.
2. Able people are often held back by societies structure.
3. The two main characters are each others foils.
4. He acted without a moments hesitation.
5. We will meet again in two days time.
6. Have you read H.G. Well's *The Time Machine*?
7. If it is to perform it's duties properly, the committees frame of reference needs to be made clearer.
8. You can buy boys and girls jeans in any good department store.
9. The Smith's came to dinner.
10. In the Middle Ages, Latin was the universal language of Europes educated classes.

51x **Spelling List**

In addition to the words listed and discussed in the preceding pages, many other words often cause spelling problems. Following is a list of frequently misspelled words. If you are at all weak in spelling, you should test yourself frequently on these words, as well as those discussed earlier. These lists and examples, however, are not exhaustive; it is therefore important that you keep your own list of misspelled words, especially recurrent ones, and that you practise spelling them correctly until you have mastered them.

absorption	beggar	consumer
accessible	beneficent	control
acclaim	botany	controlled
accumulate	buoyant	convenient
acknowledgment or	bureau	court
acknowledgement	burglar	courteous
acquaintance	buried	create
acquire	cafeteria	criticism
additional	calendar	crucifixion
advertise	Calvinist	curiosity
adviser	cameraderie	cylinder
or advisor	candidate	decorative
aesthetic or	cannibal	decrepit
esthetic	captain	defence or
affection	careful	defense
affidavit	carnival	defensive
aging	cartilage	delusion
allege	catalogue	desperate
alternately	category	develop
always	cemetery	devastation
amour	chagrin	diameter
analyze or analyse	challenge	dilemma
analogy	changeable	diminution
anaesthetic	chocolate	dining
anonymous	cinnamon	diphtheria
anticipated	clamour or	dispatch or
apartment	clamor	despatch
appal or	clothed	dissatisfied
appall	coincide	dissipate
approach	colossal	doctor
architect	committee	drunkenness
arctic	comprise	eclectic
arithmetic	comrade	ecstasy
article	concomitant	efficient
atmosphere	conqueror	electorate
audience	conscious	elegiac
automatically	consensus	eligible
auxiliary	conservative	embarrassment
axe or ax	consider	emancipation

emphasize
employee
emulate
encompass
encyclopedia
endeavour or
    endeavor
enforced
engraver
enterprise
epilogue
equip
equipment
equipped
erupt
euphonious
exalt
exaggerate
excel
exercise
exhausted
exhilarating
exuberant
facilities
fallacy
fascinating
fervour or
    fervor
filter
flippant
flourish
flyer or
    flier
focusses or
    focuses
foreign
foresee
fulfill
fundamentally
furor
gaiety
gauge
genealogy
gleam
goddess
gray or grey
grievous
guarantee
guard

harass
harmonious
height
heinous
heroine
hesitancy
hindrance
homogeneous
horseshoe
household
humorous
hygienist
hypocrisy
hypocrite
illegal
illegitimate
illiterate
imagery
imagination
imitate
immediate
impious
implementation
importance
impostor
improvise
inadequacy
indefinite
industrialization
inevitable
influence
injuries
innocent
inoculate
inquire
integrated
interrupt
intimate
intriguing
jealousy
jeweller or
    jeweler
judgment or
    judgement
knowledge
knowledgeable
laboratory
leeches

library
license or
    licence (v.)
licence or
    license (n.)
lieutenant
likelihood
lineage
liquefy
liqueur
liquor
luxury
magnificent
mammoth
manoeuvre or
    maneuver
manual
manufactured
marriage
marshal
mattress
meant
medieval
melancholy
mineralogy
minuscule
mischievous
molester
monologue
monotonous
mould or mold
museum
mustache or
    moustache
naive
necessary
nineteenth
nosey or nosy
nostrils
numerous
obstacle
occurred
occurrence
offence or
    offense
omniscient
oneself
operator
ostracize

parnalleled or
parallelled
paralyze or
paralyse
paraphernalia
parliament
partner
peculiar
peddler
perseverance
personality
personify
personnel
persuade
pharaoh
phony or
phoney
plagiarism
playwright
plough or
plow
poem
pollution
porous
positioning
possession
practicality
practice (n.)
practise or
practice (v.)
predecessors
prejudice
prestige
pretense or
pretence
procedure
proletariat
proscenium
psychiatry
psychology
pursue
putrefy
puzzled
pyjamas or
pajamas
quandary
quantity

quatrain
quizzically
rarefied
reality
recognize
recommend
reflection
religious
reminisce
repel
repetition
resemblance
rhythm
ridiculous
sacrifice
safety
scandal
sceptic or
skeptic
separate
sheik
shepherd
sheriff
shining
shiny
signifies
simile
sincerity
siphon
simultaneous
skiing
skillful or
skilful
smoulder or
smolder
solely
soliloquy
species
spectators
sponsor
storey or
story (floor)
straddle
strategy
stretched
styrofoam
subconsciously

subsequent
subtly
succinct
sulphur or
sulfur
superintendent
suspense
symbolic
symbolize
symmetry
synonymous
syrup
tariff
temperament
temperature
territory
theory
therein
threshold
tragedy
trailed
tranquillity or
tranquility
transferred
troubadour
tyranny
unavailing
undoubtedly
unmistakable
until
usefulness
vehicle
vilify
weary
whisky or
whiskey
willful or
wilful
wintry
wistfulness
woollen or
woolen
woolly
writing
written

51x spelling list

Review Exercise: Chapter VI

Below are 100 misspelled words. First spell them correctly, and then try to decide which rule each one violates or which classification of error each falls into. Remember, a given error could belong in more than one classification. (For convenience, the misspellings are divided into four groups of 25 each.)

51x *spelling list*

	A	*B*	*C*	*D*
1.	artisticly	surender	defered	exhorbitant
2.	hense	studing	vien	speach
3.	trailled	sofistication	marshmellows	bullit
4.	complextion	applys	polititian	interpretted
5.	incompatable	sentance	feasable	religous
6.	comparitive	procede	deliberatly	succomb
7.	dilemna	incidently	Elizabethian	primative
8.	exitment	excrutiating	fragrence	Heroshima
9.	inconcievable	mischievious	dilusion	backround
10.	disatisfaction	coherant	askes	ninty
11.	benifit	contemptable	proffessional	succeptible
12.	critisize	champian	reproachs	magestic
13.	indispensible	effecient	metaphore	inadvertantly
14.	unquardinated	repetative	devistated	successfull
15.	angery	familier	suspence	predjudice
16.	storys (tales)	exclaimation	denile	palacial
17.	menicing	striken	fourty	allys
18.	alure	absense	harmonous	accessable
19.	perfectable	repreive	foreigness	dependant
20.	prominant	monsterous	secretarys	fundemental
21.	grammer	dosent	opulant	permissable
22.	devide	concreate	representitive	listner
23.	substanciate	useable	realisticly	unforgiveable
24.	amature	reguarding	envelopped	finaly
25	tryed	heavilly	wonderous	neice

STYLE AND THE LARGER ELEMENTS OF COMPOSITION

It is next to impossible to define style. For simplicity and directness—two of the most important qualities of good style—Jonathan Swift's attempt is probably the best: "Proper words in proper places make the true definition of a style." In its broadest sense, **style** consists of everything that is not the *content* of what is being expressed. It is the *manner* as opposed to the *matter*: everything that is a part of the *way* something is said constitutes its style. Although we generally distinguish between style and content in order to facilitate discussion and analysis, the distinction is in some ways false, for the two are inseparably bound together; the way in which something is expressed inescapably becomes a part of what is being said. "I have a hangover" may seem to say essentially the same thing as "I'm feeling a bit fragile this morning," but the different *styles* of the statements create quite different effects. And it is the effect, finally, that counts, for the manner determines what the content means. The medium, then, if it is not the entire message, is at least a good part of it.

An important attribute of style is **tone**, which is usually defined as a writer's attitude toward both subject matter and audience. Tone in writing is analogous to tone in speech. We hear or describe someone as speaking in a sarcastic tone of voice, or as sounding angry, or jocular, or matter-of-fact. Writing, like speech, can "sound" ironic, conversational, intimate, morbid, tragic, frivolous, cold, impassioned, comic, coy, energetic, phlegmatic, detached, sneering, contemptuous, laudatory, condescending, and so forth. The tone of a piece of writing—whether an essay or only a sentence—largely determines the feeling or impression the writing creates.

The style of a piece of writing, including its tone, arises from such things as syntax and point of view and even punctuation. It is also largely determined by diction: choice of words, figurative language, and even sounds.

VII

DICTION

Diction—a writer's choice of words—is obviously near the heart of effective writing and of style. No amount of correct grammar and rhetorical expertise can compensate for poor diction. This chapter isolates the principal difficulties writers encounter in choosing and using words, and offers some suggestions for overcoming these difficulties.

Use your dictionary. Become familiar with it; find out how it works and discover the variety of information it has to offer. Good college or desk dictionaries do not merely list the spelling, syllabication, pronunciation, and meaning of words; they also offer advice on usage, idioms, and synonyms and antonyms to help you decide on the best word for a particular context; they list any irregularities in the principal parts of verbs and in the inflection of adjectives and adverbs; they supply etymologies (knowing a word's original form and meaning can sometimes help you decide on its appropriateness for your purpose); they even tell you whether a word or expression is considered slang, colloquial, informal, or archaic. Take advantage of the many resources of your dictionary.

52 Level

Use words appropriate to you, to your topic, and to the circumstances in which you are writing; that is, consider the occasion, your purpose, and your audience. Avoid any word or phrase that calls attention *to itself* rather than to the meaning you are trying to convey. Generally, avoid slang and colloquial or informal expressions at one extreme, and pretentious, overly formal language at the other. Of course there will be times when one or the other, or both, will be useful—for example to make a point in a particularly telling way, to achieve a humorous effect, or to make dialogue realistic. But it is usually preferable to adopt a straightforward, moderate style, a medium level of diction that neither crawls on its belly in the dirt nor struts about on stilts.

See also **12d**.

52a   Slang

Slang is diction that is at the opposite extreme from **formal**. It therefore follows that, although we all use it in our speech and in informal contexts, slang is seldom appropriate in a formal context. Nevertheless, there is nothing inherently wrong with slang; it is in fact a lively and vigorous part of our language. But partly because it is so lively and vigorous, it is often faddish; some slang words remain in vogue only a few weeks, some linger on for a few years, and new ones are constantly popping up to take the place of those going out of fashion. Much slang is so ephemeral that dictionaries cannot keep up with it. The adjective *strapped*, for example, meaning out of money, has been around at least since the beginning of this century; one present-day dictionary does not even list it, a second labels it *slang*, another calls it *informal* (i.e., colloquial), and yet another includes it but assigns no label, implying that it has entered the general vocabulary and become "respectable." A writer does well, therefore, to be careful—and conservative. The temptation to enliven one's writing with some pungent slang is often great, but too much spice can ruin the taste of something, especially something delicate—which in a way formal style is. In order to help you get the matter in perspective, here is a brief discussion of slang and a few examples culled from the thousands of slang terms that exist, or once existed.[1]

Clearly not all words which begin their lives as slang die out. Here are some which entered the language at least as long ago as the sixteenth and seventeenth centuries: *balderdash* has become not only standard but rather highfalutin; *budge, cocksure, to hedge, mob,* and *nincompoop*

---

[1]The information in the following pages comes from our own experience and observation, and from the following books, to which we direct those readers interested in pursuing the subject further: Eric Partridge, *A Dictionary of Slang and Unconventional English*, 8th ed. (New York: Macmillan, 1984), and *Slang To-day and Yesterday*, 3rd ed. (New York: Bonanza, n.d.); Harold Wentworth and Stuart Berg Flexner, *Dictionary of American Slang*, 2nd ed. (New York: Crowell, 1975); H.L. Mencken, *The American Language*, 4th ed. (New York: Knopf, 1936); Walter S. Avis, et al., eds., *A Dictionary of Canadianisms on Historical Principles* (Toronto: Gage, 1967); and several general dictionaries, principally *Funk & Wagnalls Standard College Dictionary*, Canadian edition (Toronto: Fitzhenry & Whiteside, 1976), *Gage Canadian Dictionary* (Toronto: Gage, 1983), and *The Houghton Mifflin Canadian Dictionary of the English Language* (Markham, Ont.: Houghton Mifflin Canada, 1980).

became standard long ago (i.e. in the eighteenth or nineteenth century); *blab* and *bolt* (depart quickly) became standard more recently; *bamboozle, to belt* (hit), *break the ice, chum,* and *clodhopper* are hovering between informal and standard; *brass* (impudence), *cocky, flame* (sweetheart), and *let on* (tell) are still considered informal (or colloquial; because many people confuse it with *dialectal,* some dictionaries no longer use the label *colloquial*); and *brass* (money) and *pinch* (steal) are still labelled slang. Many others have disappeared altogether; in fact, many more slang words die out than survive.

Here are some that arrived in the nineteenth century and that are still considered slang—insofar as they are at all current (how many of them do you even recognize?): *bats* or *batty, chin music, dough* (money), *frost* (failure), *gasser* (big success), *java, make the grade, perks* (perquisites), *Popsy-Wopsy* (a term of affectionate address), *shebang, stiff* (corpse), *sugar* (money).

Here are some other nineteenth-century slang terms that are still called slang; these, unlike the preceding group, are still fairly current (or do you not find them so?): *baloney, bang-up, beef, bender, bounced, flog, hang out, hold out, jug, kid* (fool), *lip, loony, pull, sack.*

Many nineteenth-century terms have become at least informal; for example: *backtalk, the blues, boom, boost, boss, break even, carry on, cave in, chip in, cram, dander, dig up, fix* (bribe, etc.), *freak* (but not *freak out,* which is recent slang), *game* (lame), *get the hang of, go the whole hog, hard up, has-been, in the clear, kid* (child), *rowdy, sleuth, smart aleck, splurge.* Others such as *get one's back up, go all out, landslide* (of an election), *loafer* (and the verb *loaf,* formed from it), *nerve* (courage), and *shadow* (follow secretly), have attained respectability.

And linguistic inventiveness has not flagged in the twentieth century: *bat* (spree), *bawl out, beat it, big shot, broad, canned music, frame, guts, have someone taped, main drag, neck, pep, scram, scrounge, wonky*—all these originated early in the century, are still slang, and are probably familiar to you. Other slang terms from the same period have become at least informal: *to batch, break, buddy, cagey, chump, cold feet, date, double-cross, flu, grad, grouch, nerve* (audacity), *on the level, road hog.* Still others that were once slang, such as *dude* and *major* (as a verb), have been accepted into standard English. But still others that were once popular have all but disappeared and would sound very out-of-place today: *applesauce, balloon juice, banana oil, bean* and *loaf* (head), *the berries, the heebie-jeebies.*

The 1920's were rich in slang, but who now would dream of using—except facetiously—such words as *flapper* or *frail* for a girl, or such expressions as *the bee's knees, the cat's pyjamas,* or *twenty-three skiddoo?*

Canadian slang is particularly rich in what it shares with or has borrowed from the United States, England, and Australia. It also has

52a *slang*

its own colourful terms, like *sodbuster, crowbar palace, high muckamuck.* But to someone neither a player nor a fan of hockey, such slang terms as *cream, deke,* and *rink rat* would be minimally meaningful.

Much slang begins as a kind of private language or lingo within a group or profession—among hoboes, thieves, circus people, actors, athletes, gamblers, sailors, students, and so on. Since much of the point of such lingoes is to keep outsiders from understanding, or simply to instill a feeling of being an insider, as soon as terms are picked up by others they are dropped by members of the group and replaced by new inventions—another reason for the short life-span of much slang. Nevertheless many slang terms come into general use from such specialized sources. From the world of crime, for example, come such terms as *bump off* and *knock off* and *rub out, hold up* and *stick up, racket, crook, bootlegger, hoodlum* (and from it *hood*), *copper* (and from it *cop*). From card playing come *pass the buck, four-flusher,* and *poker face.* Our language is full of nautical terms, among them such slangy ones as *on deck, hit the deck, bilge, chow, get spliced, pipe down,* and at least two for being drunk: *half-seas over* and *three sheets in* (or *to*) *the wind.*

Indeed, inebriety provides a good example of the vigour and colourfulness of much slang and also of the astonishing number of words for one thing. Here are several others—some new, some very old, and many still in use: *blotto, boiled* (also *fried* and *stewed*), *bombed, canned, crocked, lacquered, oiled* (or *well-oiled*), *ossified, pickled, pie-eyed* (or *pied*), *pifflicated* (or *spifflicated*), *plastered* (or *stuccoed*), *snoggered, snozzled* (or *sozzled*), *soused, squiffed, stinko, tanked, tiddly, tight, tipsy, woozy.* Note also *tie one on* and *get bent out of shape* (from *bender?*). And there are dozens, if not hundreds, more.

The transitoriness of much slang makes it risky to use in writing; a phrase that is *hot* (or *cool*) when you write it may sound stale and dated soon after. Occasionally a slang term will fade out to reappear later. *Snafu,* for example, military slang from the Second World War, was little if at all known to the next generation, but has recently enjoyed a considerable vogue among the young—and may (or may not) continue to do so; but an older reader encountering it in a new context would get associations the writer may not have intended.

Even more disconcerting is the way slang terms tend to shift their meanings or to have multiple meanings; to use slang is thus sometimes to risk complete misunderstanding. *Frazzled* is another slang word meaning "drunk," but it also has the standard meanings "frayed" and "tired, worn out." Yet another is *stoned,* but it is unlikely that in a contemporary context it would be taken to mean merely "drunk." Here are some other examples: *Chopper* used to refer to a machine gun, *mike* to a microscope, *sauce* to gasoline, *benny* to an overcoat, and *drag* to influence or to an unpopular girl. *Dude* used to apply specifically to a city-bred person or to a dandy. *Blab* used to mean "nonsense" or "camouflage talk," and a *sap* in the early nineteenth century was one who studied hard—perhaps the ironic source of its later meaning.

Fashions change, and it is all but impossible to keep up with them, however up-to-date one tries to be. *Coffin-nail* for a cigarette has been around since the nineteenth century; but for a while it was more common to ask for or offer a *fag* or a *weed*; later it was *cancer stick; dart* is a relatively recent arrival; and who knows what will be fashionable by the time you read this—or by next week, next month, or next year? Would anyone nowadays seriously consider calling something *corny* or *groovy*, or someone a *noodnick* or a *drip* or a *jerk*? *Bread* for money and *threads* for clothing, so *with it* a decade or so ago, are now obsolescent; *wheels* for a car appears to have more staying power, but though it may still seem fresh to some, others already find it stale. Slang, then, because it is often not as universally understood as "standard" English, may not convey the meaning you intend. Not only is it often confined to certain age-levels and groups, but it is also often regional. Consequently, rather than being pointed and vivid, in using slang you may only be confusing your reader.

But slang, because of its sharpness, vividness, and seeming timeliness, is always attractive. It can trap the unwary writer, and tempt even the wary, into sounding not only dated but also artificially chic and clever. Mixing even an occasional slang term with otherwise formal diction is always tricky, and nearly always damaging to a writer's effectiveness. Yet sometimes a slang term will seem the most economical way to say something, or even the only right way. Slang, therefore, is not to be avoided entirely; rather it is to be used only when it is the most appropriate means to a desired end—but used infrequently and with the utmost discretion. If tempted to write something slangy, then, think twice, or thrice—and consult not only a good dictionary but also your ear, your common sense, and your good taste.

Note: Remember, if you do decide to use a slang term, do not put quotation marks around it. (See **43g**.)

Exercise 52a: Thinking about slang

List as many slang terms as you can think of for each of the following. Which are current in your vocabulary? Which if any would you consider using in an essay? In a letter to a friend? In conversation with someone of your own sex? In conversation with someone of the opposite sex?

1. criminal (n.)	6. court (v.)	11. bright person
2. mad (adj.)	7. bore (n.)	12. boy
3. intoxicated	8. very good	13. girl
4. cheat (v.)	9. talk (v.)	14. beautiful
5. cheat (n.)	10. stupid person	15. ugly

52a *slang*

52b Informal, Colloquial
inf. colloq.

It is often difficult to distinguish between slang and **informal** usage. Even dictionaries cannot agree. Slang terms are in one sense simply extreme examples of the colloquial or informal. Nevertheless, there are many words and phrases that can be labelled informal; although not slang, they do not belong in formal writing. For example, unless you are intentionally aiming for a somewhat informal level, you should avoid such abbreviations as *prof, gent, rev;* you should also avoid contractions (*can't, isn't, don't, wouldn't,* etc.), although such contractions are normal in spoken English.

Here are some examples of other informal or colloquial usages that most writers think should be avoided in strictly formal writing:

Informal or Colloquial	*Acceptable equivalents*
absolutely	very; yes
a lot of, lots of, lots	much, many, a great deal of
and such	and so on, and things like that, and the like
anyplace, everyplace, noplace, someplace	anywhere, everywhere, nowhere, somewhere
around	about, approximately
awful	bad, ill, ugly, unpleasant, etc.
be sure and	be sure to
back of, in back of	behind
chance of + gerund (e.g., chance of getting)	chance + infinitive (chance to get)
enthused	was enthusiastic
expect (as in "I expect you want me to work overtime")	suppose, suspect, imagine
figure	think, believe, etc.
fix (verb or noun)	repair, prepare, etc; predicament, etc.
funny	odd, peculiar, strange, unusual
guess	believe, suppose, think
mean	bad, cruel, evil, etc.
most (as in "most everyone")	almost
nice	agreeable, attractive, pleasant, etc.
nowhere near	not nearly, not at all, not anywhere near
out loud	aloud
over with	ended, finished, done
phone	telephone
photo	photograph
plan on + gerund (e.g., plan on going)	plan + infinitive (plan to go)

quite, quite a bit, quite a few, quite a lot, etc.	somewhat, rather, many, a large amount, much, etc.
real, really (as intensive adverb)	very, greatly, surely, etc.
right away, right now	immediately
shape (good, bad, fine, etc.)	condition
show up	appear, arrive; prove better than, best (v.)
size up	judge, estimate the strength of, etc.
terrible, terribly (also as vague intensifiers)	unpleasant, uncomfortable, very, etc.
try and	try to
wait on	await, wait for
where (as in "I see where we're in for a storm")	that

In addition, many words have been so abused in movie and other advertising, used for gushy and exaggerated effect, that they can now seldom be used with precision in formal writing. For example:

fantastic, marvellous, stupendous, terrific, tremendous, wonderful

Exercise 52b: Using formal diction

Provide formal substitutes for each of the slang or informal terms below. Use your dictionary as necessary. Compose sentences for at least ten of the terms, using them in ways that you think would be acceptable in relatively formal writing.

1. bawl out
2. beef (n. and v.)
3. booze
4. bunk
5. cheapskate
6. chump
7. cinch (n.)
8. con (v.)
9. conniption
10. cook up
11. crackdown
12. crash pad
13. crummy
14. cuss (v. and n.)
15. cute
16. died with his boots on
17. ditch (v.)
18. dope out
19. down the tube
20. egged on
21. face the music
22. fall guy
23. gamp
24. highbrow
25. hoofed it
26. hoosegow
27. hunch
28. jerk
29. miss out
30. monkey business
31. on the spot
32. scram
33. scrounge
34. slapdash
35. slouch
36. smarmy
37. southpaw
38. square
39. stunner
40. truck (n.)

52b   informal, colloquial

52c "Fine Writing"

Unnecessarily formal or pretentious diction is called "fine writing"—a term of disapproval here. Efforts to impress readers with such writing almost always backfire. Do not write "It was felicitous that the canine in question was demonstrably more exuberant in emitting threatening sounds than in attempting to implement said threats by engaging in actual physical assault," when all you mean is "Luckily, the dog's bark was worse than his bite." Do not write "I deem it unjust on the part of the professor to have refused passage to my latest expositional effort solely on the grounds that my orthography was in his judgment deficient" when you could say, more directly and effectively, "I don't think the teacher should have failed my last essay just because of my bad spelling." These are exaggerated examples, of course, but they illustrate how important it is to be natural (within reason) and straightforward. Writers who over-reach themselves often use supposedly sophisticated and elegant terms incorrectly. The student who wrote "Riding majestically down the street on a magnificent float was the Festival Queen surrounded by all her courtesans" was striving for sophistication, but succeeded only in getting an undesired laugh from the reader who knew the correct meaning of *courtesans*.

Exercise 52c: Thinking about "big" words

For each of the following words, provide one or more equivalents that are less formal, more common or natural. Use your dictionary as necessary. How many of these words do you consider to be in your own vocabulary? Mark any that you think should *not* be avoided as overly formal or pretentious in a normal context.

1. ablutions	21. eleemosynary	41. penurious
2. assiduity	22. equitation	42. peregrinations
3. aviate	23. erstwhile	43. propinquity
4. bellicose	24. frangible	44. *raison d'être*
5. cachinnation	25. gustatory	45. rebarbative
6. cinereous	26. habiliments	46. refection
7. circumambient	27. hebdomadal	47. regurgitate
8. collation	28. imbibition	48. repast
9. colloquy	29. impudicity	49. rubicund
10. comminatory	30. jejune	50. salubrious
11. compotation	31. lubricity	51. sartorial
12. concatenation	32. lucubrations	52. serendipitous
13. confabulate	33. matutinal	53. sesquipedalian
14. conflagration	34. mentation	54. superincumbent
15. contumelious	35. objurgation	55. tenebrous
16. crepuscular	36. obloquy	56. transpontine
17. defenestration	37. oppugnant	57. vilipend
18. divagation	38. orthography	58. visage
19. doff	39. otiose	59. veridical
20. egress	40. pellucid	60. *Weltanschauung*

53 Figurative Language
fig

Strictly speaking, figurative language includes many "figures of speech," such as personification, synecdoche, metonymy, hyperbole (overstatement), litotes (understatement), and even paradox, irony, and symbolism. Generally, however, the term "figurative language" refers to metaphoric language, whose most common devices are the **metaphor** and the **simile**. A **simile** is an explicit comparison which is usually introduced by *like* or *as*:

> The river is *like* a snake winding across the plain.
> She was as carefree *as* a wild canary.

A **metaphor,** on the other hand, is an implicit comparison; the things being compared are assumed to be identical:

> The river *is* a snake winding across the plain.

Frequently a metaphor is condensed into a verb, an adjective, or an adverb. A condensed *verb* metaphor:

> The river *snakes* its way across the plain.

A condensed *adjective* metaphor:

> The *serpentine* river meanders across the plain.

A condensed *adverb* metaphor:

> The river winds *snakily* across the plain.

Figurative language is an important element of good style. Writing that lacks it will be relatively dry, flat, and dull. It is important to remember, however, that a good metaphor does not merely enhance style; it also clarifies meaning. That is, one should use a metaphor not simply for its own sake, but rather to convey an idea or concept in a clearer or more effective way. For example, to say that "the hillside was covered with a profusion of colourful flowers" is clear enough. But if one writes instead that "the hillside was a tapestry of spring blossoms," the metaphor not only enriches the style but also provides readers with an image (that of the tapestry) that helps them visualize the scene. In other words, an appropriate metaphor is another way of being more *concrete* (see the next section), the concreteness in this instance being a function of the explicit or implicit comparison embodied in the simile or metaphor.

53a Inappropriate Metaphors

But one must be careful not to force a metaphor upon a given expression merely to embellish one's style, for it will likely be inappropriate and call attention to itself rather than enhance the desired meaning. It will, to use a rather tired but still expressive simile, stick out like a sore thumb. For example, "the tide of emotion suddenly stopped" does not work, since tides do not stop; they ebb and flow. And a phrase like "bomb craters blossoming all over the landscape" may be evocative, but only if one intends the inherent discord. Writing something like "he ran like an ostrich in heat" may confuse the reader with inappropriate associations.

53b Overextended Metaphors

Another fault occurs when a writer becomes overly fond of a supposedly clever metaphor and extends it beyond the point where it can be of service, allowing it to take control of what is being said:

> When she came out of the surf her hair looked like limp spaghetti. A sauce of seaweed and sand, looking like spinach and grated cheese, had been carelessly applied, the red flower fastened in her tresses looked like a wayward piece of tomato, and globs of mud clung like meatballs to the pasty pasta of her face. The fork of my attention hovered hesitatingly over this odd dish. Clearly I would need more than one glass of the red wine of remembered beauty and affection to wash it all down.

This may all be very clever, but after the first sentence—the spaghetti image itself being somewhat questionable—one quickly loses sight of the original descriptive intention and becomes mired in all the associated metaphors and similes; in short, the reader is likely to feel fed up, and to turn to something less fattening and overseasoned. Don't extend a metaphor beyond its usefulness.

53c Dead Metaphors

One must also guard against dead metaphors and clichés (see **59e**). The language is full of such dead metaphors as the *leg* of a table, *branching out*, *flew* to the rescue, and the like, which are perfectly all right since we no longer think of them as metaphors. But moribund metaphors, not yet dead but with little metaphoric force left, can be dangerous. Such hackneyed phrases as *the ladder of success, making mountains out of molehills, nipped in the bud, flog a dead horse,* and *between the devil and the deep blue sea* are muddying and soporific instead of enlivening and clarifying.

Occasionally, however, a dead or trite metaphor can be revivified, consciously used in a fresh way. For example, the hackneyed phrase *bit off more than he could chew* was given a new life by the person who said of Henry James's writing that he "chewed more than he bit off." *Sound as a dollar* would these days be more appropriately rendered as "unsound as a dollar." Even a slangy phrase like *chew the fat* might be transformed and updated in a description of people sitting down to "chew the cholesterol." But be careful, for such attempts can misfire;

like an over-extended metaphor, they sometimes call attention to their own cleverness at the expense of the intended meaning.

53d Mixed Metaphors

Be particularly careful to avoid incongruously mixed metaphors. The person who wrote, of the Great Depression, that "what began as a zephyr soon blossomed into a giant," had lost control of metaphor. The following paragraph about Shakespeare's *Othello* was written by a student who obviously began with the good intention of using metaphors to help describe the almost unbelievable evil of Iago, but who soon became lost in a self-created maze of contradictions and incongruities:

> Iago has spun his web and like a spider he waits. His beautiful web of silk is so fragile and yet it captures the souls of its victims by gently luring them into his womb. Unsuspecting are those unfortunate creatures who sense the poisonous venom oozing through their veins. It has a tranquil effect, for it numbs the mind with its magical potion. The victims are transformed into pawns as they satisfy the queen's appetite and so they serve their purpose.

Here is a paragraph, again by a student, that not only successfully uses metaphor throughout to create its impression but that is also, in its entirety (note the title and the final clause), a single metaphor:

> At the Movies
>
> I remember once, as a kid, lying on my back watching clouds. Row upon row of factory-perfect models drifted along the assembly line. There went a nifty schooner, flag flying—and look, a snapping toy poodle with the most absurd cut! Next came chilly Greenland, with Labrador much too close for comfort. But the banana split was the best one of all. It reminded me how hungry I was, and how close to home. With a jump, I promised myself I'd catch the second feature on the next sunny day.

By all means, then, use figurative language. It can lend grace and charm and liveliness and—above all—clarity of meaning and greater effectiveness to your writing. But beware of its potential pitfalls: inappropriate, over-extended, or mixed metaphors.

54 Concrete and Abstract; Weak Generalizations

54a Concreteness and Specificity
conc

Concrete words denote tangible things, capable of being apprehended by our physical senses (*cars, trees, fire, walking, animals, seeing, buildings*). **Abstract** words denote intangible things, like ideas or qualities (*transportation, nature, destruction, movement, life, vision, architecture*). The more *concrete* your writing, the more your readers will respond to it the way you want them to, for it will provide handles for their imaginations to get hold of. If you write

Transportation is becoming a major problem in our city.

and leave it at that, readers *might* understand you, but you'd be taking a chance on their conjuring up the right kinds of images. But if you write, or add,

In the downtown core of our city there are far too many cars and far too few buses.

you know that your readers will understand exactly what you mean: in their minds they will see the traffic jams and overloaded buses.

Similarly, the less **general** and more **specific** your writing is, the clearer and more effective it will be. *General* and *specific* are relative terms: a general term designates a *class* (*modes of transportation*); a less general or more specific term designates one or more members of that class (*vehicles, ships, airplanes*); a still more specific term designates members of still smaller classes (*cars, trucks, trains, buses*); and so on, getting narrower and narrower, the classes and sub-classes getting smaller and smaller, until—if one wants or needs to go that far—one arrives at a single, unique item, a class of one. For example:

cars–imported cars–imported sports cars–Porsches–Porsche 911's–the particular Porsche 911, licence number XYZ-123, in someone's garage

Here are some more examples of terms on a spectrum moving from general to specific:

plant life–trees–evergreens–cedars, pines, firs, etc.
fire–forest fires–forest fires started by lightning–the huge fires of 1985
moved–walked–pranced, sidled, stumbled, staggered, swaggered, strode, etc.
creature–animal–dog–dachshund, St. Bernard, collie, etc.–my dachshund Prince
saw, looked–glimpsed, spied, stared, glared, etc.
structure–building–house–government house–24 Sussex Drive

Don't write "We experienced a hot day" when you could write more clearly "We sweltered all afternoon in the 35-degree heat" or "We enjoyed basking in the hot sun all afternoon." Don't write "I found him attractive" when you could write "I liked his handsome face and slim figure," or, better still, "I was enchanted by his curly blond hair and sharp blue eyes, his finely chiselled nose and determined chin, his muscular shoulders and arms." Do not write "He drove around the track very rapidly" when you could bring it alive by writing "He took

54a *concrete, specific*

every corner on two wheels and roared down the straightaways, shifting like a demon and never lifting his foot from the throttle."

The following passage makes sense, but its abstractness prevents it from being very memorable or effective:

> If one makes a purchase that a short time later proves to have been ill-advised due to the rapid deterioration of quality, then it is the opinion of this writer that one has every right to seek redress either by expressing one's displeasure to the individual who conducted the original transaction or, if it should prove necessary, by resorting to litigation.

Inexperienced writers often assume that this kind of language is good because it sounds formal and sophisticated. But notice how much more vivid the revised version is:

> If you buy a car on Thursday and the engine falls out of it on Saturday, I think you should shout "Hey!" to the dealer who sold it to you, and hale him into court if necessary to get back the good money you paid for what turned out to be a pile of junk.

Of course abstract and general terms are perfectly legitimate and often necessary, for one can scarcely present all ideas concretely. Nevertheless, try to be as concrete and specific as your subject will allow.

54b   Weak Generalizations
gen

The most common weakness of student writing is an overdependence on generalizations. Merely stating a generalization or assumption is not enough. To be clear and effective, a generalization must be illustrated and supported by specifics. The amount of support needed will vary, but two pieces of support are more than twice as effective as only one, and three pieces—often an optimum number to aim for—are probably twice as effective as two. "Women today are no longer content with their traditional roles in life." A reader who unquestioningly accepted such a general assertion would scarcely be a reader worth having, for the statement evokes all kinds of questions: it cries out for illustration, evidence, qualification: All women? In all countries? What "roles" in particular? Is such discontent really something new? And so on.

Here are two in-class essays on the same topic. Read the first one through:

> Travel can be a very broadening experience for people who go with the intention of having their eyes opened, which may often occur by unpleasant means. Culture shock can be a very unpleasant and hurtful experience to people who keep their eyes and minds closed to different attitudes or opinions. This problem of culture shock is an example of why people

should prepare for the unexpected and try to learn from difficult experiences, rather than keeping a closed mind which will cause them to come away with a grudge or hurt feelings.

Besides causing negative attitudes travel can also confirm the prejudices of people with narrow minds. For example, I once met an Englishman who had travelled around the world visiting the last vestiges of the British empire. He had even travelled to South Africa, and still come away with his colonialist attitudes.

Even if one goes to a country with an open mind, one may still come away with a superficial perception of that country. It takes time to get to know a country and understand its people. The time one spends in a country will thus greatly affect one's perception of that country.

Time is also needed before travelling begins, for people to read and learn about the area they will be going to. This background will enable them to look for things they might otherwise never see, and they will appreciate more the things they do discover. If one knows something about the architecture of a country before one visits it, one can plan one's trip to include visits to buildings of special interest.

Thus an open, well-prepared mind will benefit from the experiences of travel, but otherwise travel is likely to have a very negative, narrowing effect on people's minds.

Now, without looking back at the essay, ask yourself what it said. Chances are you will remember something about a well-travelled but still narrow-minded Englishman, and perhaps something about the advisability of knowing something about foreign architecture; for those are the only concrete items in the essay. (Think how much more vivid and therefore meaningful and memorable the point about architecture would have been had it included a reference to a specific landmark, such as the Leaning Tower of Pisa or the Taj Mahal or the Parthenon or St. Paul's Cathedral.)

Now read the second essay, noting as you read how much clearer its points are than the relatively unsupported generalizations of the first essay:

> Travel can be broadening. The knowledge gained in the areas of historical background, cultural diversity, and the range of personalities encountered in foreign lands gives us a more objective outlook on ourselves, on Canada and Canadian issues, and on our position as a cog in the great machine of civilization.

> The impact of history upon visitors to foreign lands is immense indeed. One cannot help but feel somewhat small when looking across valley upon valley of white crosses in France, coming face to face with the magnitude of death taking place in World Wars. Before long, one realizes that many of the events that took place years ago have an effect upon the way in which we live today. In some areas, scars such as the Berlin Wall remain, reminders to the visitor that the way he lives is not the same way people throughout the world live and that, indeed, many people live desperately

frustrating lives, clinging to the dreams and aspirations of their forefathers and hoping beyond hope that one day they will be able to live without the threat of starvation, imminence of disease, or suppression of freedom.

This is not to say that there are not pleasant aspects of history as well. Sixteenth-century cobblestone lanes, usually less than ten feet wide, still remain in many old English villages, surrounded by Tudor cottages, complete with thatched roofs, oil lamps, and sculpted wrought-iron fences. Standing in such an environment and thinking about the writings of masters like Shakespeare brings out a much deeper and richer taste than merely reading about them in a cold classroom at home. And places like this remind us of how our ancestors lived, making it easier to understand the customs and ideas of the past.

In going through different foreign lands, one cannot ignore the great cultural diversity. This is best illustrated by contrasting Fiestas in Spain and *Oktoberfest* in Munich with our own celebrations. Many countries, besides having different languages (and dialects of those languages), also have their own dress, holidays, and religious beliefs. This variety is often startling to the tourist, used to the general homogeneity of such things back here and often taking it for granted that what is standard for him is also the norm throughout much of the rest of the world.

There is also a wide range of social habits within a country. This is especially true of Britain, which still rigidly clings to its class system. A visitor from Canada may find it hard to understand such a system, not realizing that it is a centuries-old tradition; a son always does the same job as the father, whether knight or knave, and lives in the same place, and often dies there.

Above all, the differences among people from other countries are what leave a visitor with the most lasting impression. From the beggar in the slums of Casablanca, to the well-dressed German walking briskly in the streets of Hanover, to the British businessman sipping his beer in "the local" on Hyde Street, there are myriad personalities as one travels through foreign lands. When we look at the world from this perspective, realizing that we are *not* all the same, we are better equipped to understand many of the problems throughout the world.

Even the next-to-last paragraph, with its feeble topic sentence, is at least partly saved by the examples that follow—even though they aren't very specific. The first essay is not devoid of meaning, for generalizations do have content; but the similar meaning in the second is clearer, more forceful; readers will better remember what it said simply because their minds have something concrete and specific to hang on to.

(Note also the different ways the two writers conclude: the first tacks on a perfunctory short paragraph, simply summarizing and restating the thesis, whereas the second ends by tying up the final substantive paragraph with a single strong sentence—much the better way, especially for so short an essay.)

In the second paragraph of the sample research paper (**84**), the general statements of the first two sentences, the topic sentences, are backed up with several specific examples. Examine the rest of the sample research paper: Are any generalizations, assertions, or assumptions left unexplained or unsupported? If so, is such a generalization of a kind—for example a commonly accepted assumption—that doesn't need clarification or support? Or does its being left unsupported result in a weakness in the explanation or argument? Examine Sample Essays 1 through 5 (Chapter X), all on the same topic: Is there a noticeable difference in the amount and kind of detail their writers provide to support their generalizations? If so, is there any correlation between these differences and the effectiveness of the essays? The flabbiness of essay number 8 is largely a result of unsupported generalizations. Note also the amount and kind of evidence supplied in essay number 10, an argument; do you find any places where you think more evidence should have been provided?

It is also important to consider whether pieces of supporting evidence are matters of fact or of opinion. In an argument, for example, fact would clearly carry more weight than mere opinion. But are there other kinds of essays where opinion is sufficient? (Again, consider the sample essays.) And does it matter—especially in an argument—just whose opinion is being cited? (See the sample research paper, for example. See also **74**, on writing arguments.)

Exercise 54(1): Using specific diction

For each of the following words, supply several increasingly specific terms (see the examples in **54a**):

1. furniture
2. art
3. answered
4. said
5. food

6. drink (v.)
7. drink (n.)
8. winged thing
9. seat
10. entertainment

Now compose a paragraph that uses one of the general terms in its first sentence and then develops by using increasingly specific terms.

Exercise 54(2): Being concrete and specific

Rewrite this vague and abstract autobiographical paragraph. Try to make it sharp and vivid by supplying concrete and specific details wherever suitable.

> When I was still fairly young it became necessary for our large family to move from a small prairie town to a large city. At first we were all a little sad, but after a while we settled into our new environment. When

I had finished primary and secondary school, I enrolled in an institution of higher learning, and after pursuing my chosen course of studies for the required number of years I received my degree. With it in my possession, I began the search for suitable employment; however, for some time I met with no success, and I had to accept the help of others in order to get along. But finally I found the sort of thing I was looking for, and the people here seem to feel that I am the right person for the position, and even hint at rapid advancement. Consequently I look forward to a pleasant and rewarding career.

▇ 55 ▇   Connotation and Denotation

Be careful of connotation: a word may **denote** (literally mean) what you want it to, yet **connote** (suggest) something you do not want to include. For example, if you describe someone as "skinny" your reader will understand the meaning of "light in weight" but will also understand you to feel negative; if you in fact approve of the condition (and the person), you should use a word like "slim" or "slender," for though they *denote* much the same thing as "skinny," their *connotation* is favourable rather than unfavourable. The denotations of *childlike* and *childish* are the same, but again one is favourable and the other unfavourable. Consider the differences in the connotations of these words: stink, stench, smell, odour, aroma, fragrance. Another example: If you say that a man "harped" on a subject, you are implicitly criticizing him for doing so. If you say that he "insisted" on something, you are implying that you have a neutral attitude. If, however, you say that he "pleaded his case" or that he "repeatedly called attention to" the subject, you automatically suggest that you are on his side. As the old joke goes, "I am firm; you are stubborn; he is pig-headed": it's all a matter of the connotation of the words used.

Caution: Be careful when consulting a thesaurus or a dictionary of synonyms: never assume that simply because words are listed together they are necessarily synonymous. They can be subtly different not only in denotation but—and this is where the danger lies—in connotation as well. Always distinguish very carefully among supposed synonyms; never use a thesaurus without using a dictionary in conjunction with it. A thesaurus is an excellent vocabulary-building tool, but it should be used with extreme care, for it can all too easily trap the unwary into saying things they don't mean. As an example, consider the fact that many of the words in each group in the following exercise were listed in a thesaurus simply as synonyms.

Label each of the following words as having a favourable (f), unfavourable (u), or neutral (n) connotation. If you think some could be labelled more than one way, depending on context, be prepared to explain. Use your dictionary if necessary.

1. earthy ribald obscene dirty nasty off-colour blue risqué bawdy coarse spicy vulgar
2. ingenuous simple naive stupid innocent candid ignorant shallow inept unthinking green artless
3. chunky heavy plump fat obese stout overweight corpulent beefy hefty buxom portly
4. slight underweight bony trim slender skinny svelte lean spare scrawny gaunt spindly
5. lithe limber rubbery willowy loose limp flaccid supple lissome floppy sapless pliant
6. flimsy delicate feathery fragile frail feeble slight dainty puny lightweight effeminate wispy
7. cherubic angelic goody-goody demure sanctimonious strait-laced narrow prim pious pietistic canting saintly
8. slimy oily greasy slippery unctuous smooth diplomatic suave insinuating clever artful wily
9. clothes duds attire dress costume apparel outfit get-up raiment garb garments trappings
10. scatterbrained confused mixed-up puzzled fuzzy uncertain irresolute undecided bewildered perplexed addled flustered
11. giggly frivolous frolicsome silly irresponsible capricious dizzy giddy volatile impulsive
12. stark bold naked straightforward undisguised plain clear forthright gross candid flagrant bare
13. power strength force ability impact clout influence pull drag sway high-handedness weight
14. boldness cheek impudence arrogance assurance presumption nerve effrontery gall chutzpah insolence audacity
15. intellectual egghead brain genius smarty sage scholar brainworker highbrow pundit bookworm pedant

56   **Euphemism**
euph

Euphemisms are substitutes for words whose meanings are felt to be unpleasant and therefore in certain circumstances socially or psychologically undesirable. Because as time passes certain words take on a pejorative quality, we tend to substitute others which in turn will be replaced. Women's underwear, for example, can be delicately referred to in the best of circles as lingerie, underclothing, or underthings. In social settings we tend to ask for the location not of the toilet, which is what we are really after, but of the restroom, the bathroom, the washroom, the powder room, the john, or even the little boys' or little girls' room. (The word *toilet* was itself once a euphemism.) Hearty words describing various bodily functions, words which once were generally acceptable, have now been replaced with euphemisms like bowel movement, passing water, sexual intercourse, intimate relations. In most instances such usage is commendable as a reflection of the degree of refinement and sensibility characteristic of our state of civilization.

However, the process is often abused. Euphemisms may be used, for example, to unnecessarily gloss over some supposed unpleasantness, or even to deceive. Someone who sweeps floors and cleans washrooms is sometimes called a "sanitary engineer" instead of a "custodian" or "janitor." A person who was once known simply as a salesman or a clerk is now often called a "sales representative" or even a "sales engineer." And some bank tellers are now known as "customer service representatives." What was once faced squarely as depression is now, in an attempt to mitigate its implications, termed at worst a recession, or an economic downturn, or a mere "growth cycle slowdown." A government official who has patently lied admits only that he "misspoke" himself. Someone who runs a sleazy boarding house is likely to advertise the fact with a sign in the window inviting "paying guests."

Such euphemisms imply a degree of dignity or virtue that is not always justified by the facts. Calling pornography "mature entertainment" seriously distorts the meaning of both "mature" and "entertainment." And how many sponsors or television stations are honest enough to refer to their ads as commercial *interruptions?* They are commonly referred to as commercial *breaks*, as if they were something to look forward to, like a coffee break. And how many are even honest enough to call them "commercials" rather than "messages"?

Other euphemisms help us to avoid the unpleasant reality of death, which we call "passing away," or "loss"; the lifeless body, the cadaver or corpse, we find less offensive as "remains." Such usage may be acceptable in certain circumstances; it may enable one to avoid aggravating the pain and grief of the bereaved. But in other circumstances, direct, more precise diction is preferable.

Euphemisms that deceive are obviously undesirable. Other euphemisms may be acceptable if circumstances seem to justify them; one must exercise taste and judgment. But generally speaking, call a spade a spade.

Exercise 56: Avoiding euphemisms

Supply more straightforward equivalents for the following euphemisms and pretentious job-titles.

1. underdeveloped or developing countries
2. senior citizen

3. mortician
4. in the family way, expecting
5. realtor
6. underprivileged
7. social disease
8. impaired
9. lady of the night
10. untruth

57 ■ Wrong Word

ww

Any error in diction is a "wrong word," but there is a particular kind of incorrect word choice that one must guard against. Don't write *effect* when you mean *affect*. Don't use *infer* where the correct word is *imply*. (See the lists of often-confused words, **51-l** and **51m**, and the *Usage Checklist*, **60**.) But wrong words are not always the result of confusion between two similar words. People sometimes unthinkingly use words that do not convey the intended meaning or that will not work in the desired way. Here are some examples from student writing:

> *ww:* Late in the summer I met my best friend, which I hadn't seen since graduation.

The pronoun *which* is wrong; the pronoun *whom* is the correct one for a person (see **4d**).

> *ww:* Most men would have remembered spending several days in an open ship with little water and under the tropic sun as a terrible hardship, but Marlow recalls only that he felt he could "last forever, outlast the sea, the earth, and all men."

The word *ship* cannot be used to describe a small vessel like a rowboat or canoe; *boat* is the appropriate word here. *Boat* can be used to describe any size of water-going vessel, but *ship* is appropriate only for large ones.

> *ww:* Many miles of beach on the west coast of Vancouver Island are *absent of* rocks.

The wrong phrase came to the writer's mind: *devoid of* was the one wanted. (See also the next section, *Idiom*.)

See also **nsw** (no such word) in Chapter XI.

Exercise 57: Avoiding wrong words

Correct the wrong words in the following sentences.

1. The conference is intended to focus attention on the problems facing our effluent society.

2. Hamlet is filled with a desire to reek vengeance.
3. The representatives of the company claimed to be authoritarians on the subject.
4. Politicians try to maintain an impressionable image in the eyes of the public.
5. We tried to convince him that his fear was entirely imaginative.
6. Some shoppers stopped buying coffee because they found the price so absorbent.
7. The Premier of Alberta led his party to the best of his possibilities.
8. He was deciduously on the wrong track with that theory.
9. It was an incredulous display of manual dexterity.
10. The cat was very expansive, weighing over twenty pounds.

◼ 58 ◼ Idiom
id

A particular kind of incorrect word choice has to do with **idiom**. An idiom is an expression peculiar to a given language, one that may not make logical or grammatical sense but which is nevertheless customary, "the way it is said." The English expression "to sow one's wild oats," for example, if translated into another language, would not have its idiomatic meaning; but in French there is an equivalent expression, *jeter sa gourme*, which would make little sense if translated into English. Here are some peculiarly English turns of phrase: to have a go at, to be down in the dumps, to be at sixes and sevens, to feel one's oats. You will notice that these idioms have a colloquial flavour about them, or even sound like clichés; but other similarly untranslatable English idioms are a part of our everyday language and occur in formal writing as well; for example: to do oneself proud, to take after someone, to get along with someone.

Most errors in idiom result from using prepositions that are incorrect—unidiomatic—in combination with certain other words. For example, we get *in* or *into* a car, but we get *on* or *onto* a bus. One is usually angry *with* a person, but angry *at* a thing. One is fond *of* something or someone, but one has a fondness *for* something or someone. And so on. Errors in idiom are particularly likely to occur in the speech and writing of those whose native language is not English; they have to be especially careful. But experience has shown that being a native speaker of English is no guarantee that one's idioms will always be correct: one may have a tin ear for language, or never have encountered a particular usage, and therefore be prone to error. For example, even a native speaker of English could write something like this:

> *In* the beginning of the trilogy . . . . (should be *At*)

But when we use *beginning* to denote the start of a period of time and do not follow it with an identifying prepositional phrase, the preposition *in* is usually more idiomatic:

> *In* the beginning was the Word.
> *In* the beginning he worked enthusiastically.

But when a defining phrase is added, *at* or *from* is more idiomatic:

> *At* the beginning of his employment here he worked enthusiastically.
> It was clear *from* the beginning that he wouldn't survive.

Here, from student papers, are some other examples of errors in idiom:

> France was at that time a close ally *to* Sweden. (of)
> He took the liberty *to introduce* himself to the group. (of introducing)
> He was screaming *of* how dangerous it was for me to walk so near the edge of the cliff. (about)
> It is pleasant to live in the dorms and be in close proximity *of* everything on campus. (to)

One must also sometimes be careful about choosing between an infinitive and a prepositional gerund phrase. After some expressions either is acceptable; for example:

> He is afraid *to lose.* He is afraid *of losing.*
> They are hesitant *to attend.* They are hesitant *about attending.*
> They plan *to appeal.* They plan *on appealing.* (informal)

But some terms demand one or the other:

> They propose *to go.* They are prepared *to go.*
> They insist *on going.* They are insistent *on going.*

Yet sometimes when a word changes to a different part of speech, the kind of phrase that follows must also change:

> It was *advisable to forget* what they had seen. He reminded them of the *advisability of forgetting* what they had seen.
> They *desired to go.* They were *desirous of going.*
> It is *important to remember.* He spoke of the *importance of remembering.*

But it isn't always even that simple:

> He *intended to go.* He spoke of his *intention to go.* He had every *intention of going.*

And sometimes a *that*-clause is the only idiomatic possibility:

> I asked them *to come.* I recommended *that they come.*

Idiom is a matter of usage and is not something which logic or grammar can much help us with. Although most users of the language will automatically speak and write idiomatically, it nevertheless pays, as you read and listen, to be alert to the way things are expressed, for one needs continually to sharpen one's ear for the idioms of the language. One should maintain intimate familiarity with the spoken and written word, and know where to go for guidance when in doubt. A good dictionary can often help; for example, if one looks up *adhere*, one finds that it is to be used with *to*, so one would know not to write "adhere *on*" or "adhere *with*." And the writer of the first example in the above list could probably have inferred from a good dictionary that whereas one allies oneself, or is allied, *with* or *to* another, one is simply an ally *of* the other. Or, should you be worried about using the word *oblivious*, your dictionary will probably inform you that it can be followed by either *of* or *to*. (And see *agree* and *differ* in the *Usage Checklist* at the end of this chapter. Also see **id** in Chapter XI for more examples of idiomatic usage.)

Other references that help with idiom (and with other matters) are H.W. Fowler's *A Dictionary of Modern English Usage* (Second Edition, revised by Sir Ernest Gowers), which discusses usage in a most informative, interesting, and often amusing way; *The Oxford English Dictionary*, which always provides examples of words used in various contexts; and Theodore M. Bernstein's *The Careful Writer*, which lists many verbs requiring certain prepositions.

And you can always ask a friend whose ear you can trust.

Exercise 58: Correcting idioms

Correct the unidiomatic usages in the following sentences.

1. She has an unusual philosophy towards modern technology.
2. She was grieved of her lover's death.
3. Last summer I was bestowed with a scrawny, mangy mutt.
4. Desdemona had unquestioning faith of Iago's character.
5. The concrete imagery gives the reader a better grasp at the expressed emotion.
6. The analysis is weak because it lacks in specific details.
7. These actions were the cause for his downfall.
8. He describes the scene so clearly that he must be serious of what he's saying.
9. Higgins now walks around behind her and bellows out his indignation of her ignorance.
10. Most intriguing for the spectator are the reasons behind each character's preference in one person and not the other.
11. Recent findings on depression suggest that climate can influence one's mood.
12. He held strong beliefs against smoking and drinking.
13. My father demanded for me to go to university.
14. To hear a man standing in centre stage and holding a brick explain that he represents a wall is funny in the least.
15. Lovers and poets create dream worlds in which only they can inhabit.
16. It was often easier for a doctor to say someone had died from being bewitched than to admit ignorance to the cause of death.
17. Ironically, although Huck fails, Tom succeeds to free Jim.
18. She is curious of everything around her.
19. The generation gap is evident by their uneasiness of each other's boredom.
20. His helplessness to his predicament in life leads him to despair.

58 *idiom*

59 Wordiness, Jargon, and Associated Plagues

Any diction that decreases the precision, clarity, and effectiveness of expression is bad. Using too many words, or tired words, or fuzzy words, can only be harmful. In this section we discuss and illustrate several kinds of weakness in diction. We have placed them all under this one omnibus heading because they are related, sometimes even overlapping. For example, a phrase like "on the order of" could be labelled *wordy, trite, jargon.*

Not all the items listed in the following pages are so variously classifiable, but there is an inevitable family relationship among the several groupings—if only because one error frequently leads to, or is accompanied by, others. Considering them all together rather than separately should give you a better sense of the kinds of weakness they produce. No lists such as those that follow can be exhaustive, for new words and phrases are every day shoving their way into these categories. Some of those we list are notorious, others borderline; try to understand the principles, to get a feeling in your bones for the *kinds* of violations of good writing they represent. (If the reason for a given term's inclusion is not immediately apparent to you, the illustrations in the exercises may help to clarify the matter.)

59a Wordiness

w

The fewer words you use to make a point the better. Useless words (deadwood) clutter up a sentence; they dissipate its force, cloud its meaning, blunt its effectiveness. The student who wrote the following sentence, for example, used many words where few would have been better:

> *w:* What a person should try to do when communicating by writing is to make sure the meaning of what he is trying to say is clear.

Notice the gain in clarity and force when the sentence is revised:

> *revised:* A writer should strive to be clear.

Expletives

A common source of weakness and wordiness is expletive constructions (see 1k and 18f). There is nothing inherently wrong with them (there are many in this book—two already in this sentence), and they are natural and invaluable in enabling us all to form certain kinds of sentences the way we want to. Nevertheless they are so easy to use that writers—ourselves included—sometimes use them when a tighter and more direct form of expression would be preferable. If you can get rid of an expletive without creating awkwardness or losing desired emphasis, do it. Don't write

> *w:* There are several reasons why it is important to revise carefully.

when you can so easily get rid of the flab caused by the *there are* and *it is* structure:

> *revised:* Careful revision is important for several reasons.
> *revised:* For several reasons, careful revision is important.

> *w:* It is one of the rules in this dorm that you make your own bed.
> *revised:* One rule in this dorm requires you to make your own bed.
> *revised:* In this dorm you have to make your own bed.

> *w:* In this town there are over a hundred people on welfare.
> *revised:* Over a hundred people in this town are on welfare.

The saving in words may not always be much, but such changes can help strengthen your style.

See also Exercise 11a-c (2c), on getting rid of the clutter of an excess of prepositional phrases, and **6n** and **18f**, on the passive voice.

59b Repetition
rep

Another kind of wordiness results from unnecessary repetition, which often produces awkwardness as well. Here is a student's sentence:

> *rep:* Looking at the general appearance of the buildings, you can see that special consideration was given to the choice of colours for these buildings.

The sentence is wordy in general, but one could begin pruning by cutting out the needless repetition of *buildings*. Here is another example:

> *rep:* She is able to make the decision to leave Manawaka and to abide by her decision.

It might be argued that the repetition of *decision* aids emphasis, but "make the decision" could be shortened to "decide," or the final "her decision" could be changed to "it."

59c Redundancy
red

Another kind of wordiness is **redundancy**. ("Redundancy" can mean "excess" in general, but it is also used to designate the particular error known technically as "tautology.") Redundancy is also a kind of repetition, but of an idea rather than of a word. Something is redundant if it has already been expressed earlier in a sentence. In the preceding sentence, for example, the word *earlier* is redundant, since the idea of *earlier* is present in the word *already*: repeating it is illogical and, of course, wordy. (Double negatives are a kind of redundancy, and plainly illogical: *can't never, don't hardly, cannot but.*) To begin a sentence with "In my opinion, I think . . . " is already being redundant, for you could hardly do your thinking in anyone else's opinion. If you write that "Henry is a personal friend of mine," you are being redundant: Can a *friend* be other than *personal?* To speak of a "new innovation" is to be redundant, since the meaning of "new" is present in the word *innovation.* And the person who wrote, in a letter to a prospective employer, that "an interview would be mutually helpful to both of us," probably did not get the job. Here are some other frequently encountered phrases that are redundant because the idea of one word is present in the other as well:

advance planning	erode away
but nevertheless	necessary prerequisite
character trait	general consensus
climb up	low ebb
close scrutiny	mental attitude
consensus of opinion	more preferable
continue on	new record
contributing factor	other alternatives
enter into	revert back

One common kind of redundancy is called "doubling"—adding an unnecessary second word (usually an adjective) as if to make sure the meaning of the first is clear:

red: The report was brief and concise.

Either *brief* or *concise* alone would convey the meaning. Sometimes an insecure writer will go to even greater lengths:

red: The report was brief, concise, and to the point.

Further, people addicted to wordiness and jargon will prefer long words to short ones, and pretentious-sounding words to relatively simple ones. Try to be different: choose the shorter, the simpler, the more natural. In the following pairs of words, for example, the shorter forms are preferable:

analysis, analyzation	orient, orientate
connote, connotate	preventive, preventative
courage, courageousness	remedy, remediate
existential, existentialistic	symbolic, symbolical

(Many *ical* adjectives are giving way to the shorter *ic* forms; follow the trend.)

On rare occasions the longer form of such a word may be preferable for reasons of euphony or rhythm. And if in a particular context there were any possibility of mistaking the verb *orient* for the noun *orient* or *Orient* (for example in reading aloud), then of course *orientate* would be the better choice.

Exercise 59c: Cutting redundancy

Revise the following sentences to remove redundancy:

1. If enough food cannot be supplied for all the people in the world, man will have to deal with hunger, starvation, and wide-spread famine.
2. He is adventurous in that he likes a challenge and is willing to try new experiences, but he is not adventurous to the point of insanity, though.
3. Looking ahead into the future, the economist sees even worse conditions.
4. He approached the door with feelings of fear and dread.
5. The novel *Lord of the Flies* concerns a group of young children, all boys, who revert back to savagery.
6. If one doesn't thoroughly examine every part of the subject fully, one is almost sure to miss something that could be important.
7. Most people would rather flee away from danger than face it squarely.
8. Carol soon realized that she had to make a careful outline first, before she could expect an essay to be well organized.
9. She told him in exact and precise terms just what she thought of him.
10. The hangman in the story does not fit the stereotyped image of an executioner.

Exercise 59abc(1): Removing wordiness

Revise the following sentences to eliminate wordiness.

1. Time is a very powerful, strong image in this poem.
2. Davies attempts to divert attention away from himself by citing "them blacks" as the cause of the noises.
3. These were the very things that caused him his misery and his grief.
4. Advances in developments of modern technology greatly contribute to making the equipment necessary for computerization of machinery more and more feasible for potential users.
5. Since he has both positive and negative qualities of human nature, Othello is far from perfect and has many faults.
6. Her refusal to express her feelings caused her to store her problems within herself, which added to her visible instability.
7. Pope and Dryden shared that idea in common.
8. Another device used by the poet was one of repetition.
9. There were two hundred people outside the theatre, pressing against the ropes.
10. In the past six months I have been subjected to moving from two locations to other surroundings.

Exercise 59abc(2): Reducing wordiness by combining sentences

Often one can save many words by combining two or more drafted sentences into one. Try doing that with each of the following groups, from students' drafts; cut all the wordiness you can while you're at it.

1. Also, parents who wish to see a game live, but do not want to be disturbed by their children, have no choice except to leave them attended at home. In this case, the parents would have to hire a babysitter. As a result, the parents end up paying the babysitter as well as for the game.
2. In P.E. class she would punish the students who had the least athletic ability. An example of this would be the relays in P.E. class. The team that came in last in the relays would be punished by having to run after class.
3. There are a surprising number of lawyers and stockbrokers playing the game. This may be because these people must thrive on strategic planning to be in those professions in the first place. [And see **gr** in Chapter XI.]

59d   **Ready-made Phrases**

"Prefabricated" or formulaic phrases that leap to our minds whole are almost always wordy. They are obviously a kind of cliché, and many also sound like jargon. Following are some examples; if you find yourself using any of them or others like them, try to eliminate or shorten them (some shorter equivalents are given in parentheses):

a person who, one of those who
as of the moment
at the present time, at this time, at that time (now, then)
at the same time that (while)
by and large
by means of (by)
due to the fact that, because of the fact that, on account of the fact that, in view of the fact that, owing to the fact that (because)
during the course of, in the course of (during)
for the purpose of (for, to)
for the reason that, for the simple reason that (because)
in all likelihood (probably)
in all probability (probably)
in fact, in point of fact
in character, of a . . . character
in colour
in height (high)
in length (long)
in nature
in number
in reality
in shape
in size
in spite of the fact that (although)

in the case of
in the event that (if)
in the form of
in the light of (considering)
in the midst of (amid)
in the near future (soon)
in the not too distant future (soon)
in the neighbourhood of, in the vicinity of (about, near)
it is, there is, there are, there were
manner, in manner, in a . . . manner
on the part of
period of time (period, time)
personal, personally
previous to (before)
prior to (before)
the fact that
up until, up till (until, till)
use of, the use of, by the use of, through the use of
with the exception of (except for)
with the result that

Another danger of such phrases is that they sometimes get misused. A ready-made phrase like *point of view* is so solid an entity that a student unthinkingly tacked *of view* onto the word *point* and wrote, "My dentist made the point of view that candy is bad for our teeth." Two-part verbs (see **11d**) sometimes trip up writers in the same way: the verb *fill in* is correct for "Fill in this form," but not for "The pharmacist filled in the prescription"; just *filled* is correct there. Don't let your guard down (and see also the next section).

59e   Triteness, Clichés
trite

Trite or hackneyed expressions, clichés, are another form of wordiness: they are tired, worn out, all too familiar, and thus contribute little to a sentence. Since they are by definition prefabricated phrases, they are another kind of deadwood that should be pruned away. Some trite phrases are metaphors, once clever and fresh, but now so old and weary that the metaphorical sense is, for some people, entirely gone— which is why one sees such errors as "tow the line" instead of "toe the line," and "the dye is cast" instead of "the die is cast." Similarly, a student who weakly settled for the cliché "time immemorial" was trapped into confusing it with something else: "This is a problem with which international relations have been plagued since time in memoriam." Another carelessly asserted that a particular poet's message to us was that "we should make hay while the tide's in."

Some clichés are not only trite but redundant as well: *first and foremost, few and far between, over and above, each and every, one and only, to all intents and purposes, ways and means, various and sundry, all and sundry, part and parcel, in this day and age* (now, today), *in our world today* (now, today), *in our modern world today* (now, today), and so on.

Of course clichés serve a useful purpose, especially in speech, enabling one to fill in pauses and gaps in thinking and get on to the next point. Even in writing they can on occasion—simply because they are immediately recognizable, even familiar—be the best way of saying something. And there is no denying their usefulness for an occasional humorous effect. In all such instances, however, they should be used consciously. It is not so much that clichés are bad in themselves but that the thoughtless use of clichés is weak. Generally, then, avoid them. No list can be complete, but here are a few more examples to suggest the kinds of expressions to avoid:

a bolt from the blue	it goes without saying
a heart as big as all outdoors	it stands to reason
a matter of course	lock, stock, and barrel
all things being equal	last but not least
as a last resort	love at first sight
as a matter of fact	many and diverse
as the crow flies	moment of truth
beat a hasty retreat	needless to say
brown as a berry	nipped in the bud
busy as a bee	no way, shape, or form
by leaps and bounds	off the beaten track
by no manner of means	on the right track
by no means	one and the same
clear as crystal (or mud)	par for the course
conspicuous by its absence	pride and joy
cool as a cucumber	raining cats and dogs
corridors of power	rears its ugly head
doomed to disappointment	rude awakening
easier said than done	sadder but wiser
fast as greased lightning	seeing is believing
from dawn till dusk	sharp as a tack
gentle as a lamb	slowly but surely
good as gold	smart as a whip
if and when	strike while the iron is hot
in a manner of speaking	strong as an ox
in one ear and out the other	when all is said and done
in the long run	wrong side of the tracks

Watch out also for the almost automatic couplings that occur between some adjectives and nouns. One seldom hears of a circle that isn't a *vicious* circle, or a fog that isn't a *pea-soup* fog, or a tenement that isn't a *run-down* tenement. Mere insight is seldom enough: it must be labelled *penetrating* insight. Here are a few more examples:

acid test	hearty breakfast
ardent admirers	heated opposition
budding genius	knee-jerk reaction
bulging biceps	natty dresser
blushing bride	proud possessor
consummate artistry	sacred duty
devastating effect	severe stress
drastic action	tangible proof
festive occasion	vital role

Some of these are clichés in the making; most have fully arrived. And several of the same sort are redundant as well:

advance notice	foreseeable future
advance warning	just deserts
blazing inferno	perfectly clear
cozy (little) nook	serious concern
end result	serious crisis
final outcome	terrible tragedy
final result	total (complete) surprise

59f   Overuse of Nouns

The "noun disease" is another frequent source of deadwood; it is also a form of jargon. The focus of a sentence is its main verb; the verb activates it, moves it, makes it go. Too many nouns piled on one verb can slow a sentence down, especially if the verb is only *be* or some other verb with little or no action in it. Consider the following:

> The opinion of the judge in this case is of great significance to the outcome of the investigation and its effects upon the behaviour of all the members of our society in the future.

The verb *is* in this sentence must struggle to move the great load of nouns and prepositional phrases along to some kind of finish. One could easily improve the sentence by reducing the proportion of nouns to verbs and making the verbs more vigorous:

> The judges' decision will inevitably influence how people act.

A particularly virulent form of the noun disease appears in the piling up of *tion* nouns:

> The depredations of the conflagration resulted in the destruction of many habitations and also of the sanitation organization of the location; hence the necessitation of the introduction of activization procedures in relation to the implementation of emergency preparations for the amelioration of the situation.

This example is not as exaggerated as you might think. Here is a simpler version of this monstrosity:

> Since the fire destroyed not only many houses but also the water-treatment plant for the town, emergency procedures had to be quickly implemented.

The one verb of the original (*resulted*), a weak one at that, is here replaced by *destroyed and implemented*—some improvement, at least, especially since the two verbs have only one-third as much noun-baggage to carry. There is nothing inherently wrong with nouns ending in *tion*; the damage is done when they come in clusters.

Note: Avoid other unpleasant patterns of sound and rhythm as well, such as excessive alliteration or too regular a metrical pattern:

> At the top of the tree sat a bird on a branch.

or jarring repetitions of sound:

> They put strict restrictions on lending, which constricted the flow of funds.

or accidental rhyme:

> At that time he was in his prime; the way he later let himself go was a crime.

59g   Nouns Used as Adjectives

One particularly insidious form of the noun disease is the awkward and unnecessary use of nouns as if they were adjectives. Many English nouns have long functioned adjectivally, some even becoming so idiomatic as to form parts of compounds:

school board	schoolbook	schoolteacher
bathing suit	bath towel	bathtub
lunch hour	lunch box	lunchroom
fire alarm	fire engine	firewood
space heater	space travel	spacesuit
business school	business card	businessman

Using nouns in this way is correct and normal, but it can be carried too far. "Lounge chair" is clearly preferable to "chair for lounging," but just as clearly "medicine training" does not conform to the usages of English as well as "medical training" or "training in medicine," nor "poetry skills" as well as "poetic skill" or "skill in poetry." In these last two examples, since there is a clear adjectival form available (*medical, poetic*), the simple nouns need not and should not be so used. But increasingly in recent years speakers and writers—especially those in government or other official positions, in business, and in the social

59g nouns as adjectives

sciences—have settled for or even actively chosen such noun-noun combinations. As a result, our language is becoming cluttered with such cumbersome phrases as *learning situation, resource person, cost factors, cash position, area man, profit outlook, opinion sampling, communication skills, leadership role, role model,* and so on and on. Even worse is the piling up of several nouns, as in something like "the labour force participation rate" or "the Resource Management Personnel Training and Development Program."

Resist as much as possible the tendency to reduce the vigour of the English language to the flatness and awkwardness of such jargon. Do not speak, as we did a few sentences back, of people *in government positions,* but of those *in government* or *holding governmental office*; do not write, as a student did in a discussion of extracurricular activities, of their taking place "either in a school situation or a community-type situation"; don't talk of "emergency situations" or "crisis situations" but of *emergencies* and *crises.* And, obviously, try to avoid the word *situation* altogether.

59h   Jargon
jarg

Jargon in a narrow sense refers to terms peculiar to a specific discipline, such as psychology or chemistry or literary criticism, terms unlikely to be fully understood by an outsider; we prefer to use the word *jargon* in a broader sense, to refer to all the rubbish that tends to clutter contemporary expression. The private languages of particular disciplines or special groups are less dangerous to the general writer (and reader) than is the gobbledygook that so easily finds its way into the ears and minds and mouths and pens of most of us. As potential jargonauts, we must all be on guard against creeping sociologese and bureaucratese and the like, terms from other disciplines and from business and government that infiltrate layman's language. The unsophisticated, bombarded by such locutions, uncritically and even automatically use them in their own speech and writing; and so the disease spreads. If you write to communicate rather than merely to impress, you will avoid the pitfalls discussed and illustrated here; in that way, you will impress your readers in the best way.

Warning: *Context* can promote jargon. The more formal and restrained and impersonal you are trying to be, the more likely you are to slip into jargon, wordiness, passive voice, and other weak forms of expression. And if your subject happens to be from one of the social sciences, you need to be especially on guard against being trapped into using jargon unawares.

The following list is a sampling of words and phrases that are virtually guaranteed to decrease the quality of your expression, whether spoken or written. The trouble with some should be obvious; others are fuzzy, imprecise, unnecessarily abstract; and still others are objectionable mainly because they are overused, whether as true clichés or merely popular jargon. (We would succumb to the temptation to call some of these terms "buzz words" were this label itself not a voguish buzz word.)

59h *jargon*

access (verb)
affirmative, negative
along the lines of, along that line, in the line of
angle
area
aspect
at that point in time (then)
at this point in time (now)
background (especially as a verb)
basis, on the basis of, on a . . .
basis (see the *Checklist*, **60**)
bottom line
case
certain
circumstances
concept, conception
concerning, concerned
confrontation
connection, in connection with, in this (that) connection
considerable
considering, consideration, in consideration of
contact (especially as a verb)
cope
definitely
dialogue
escalate
eventuate
evidenced by
exactly
expertise
facet
factor
feedback
field
formulate

function
guidelines
hopefully (see the *Checklist*)
identify with
image
impact (especially as a verb)
implement (verb)
importantly
infrastructure
input, output
in relation to
instance
interface
in terms of (see the *Checklist*)
in the final analysis
involved
–ize verbs (finalize, concretize)
level
life-style
marginal
meaningful, meaningful dialogue
motivation
not at all (as an adverb: not at all well, not at all badly)
ongoing
on stream
parameters
personage
phase
picture, in the picture
position
posture
profile, low profile
realm
regarding, in regard to, with regard to
relate to
relevant

replicate	standpoint, vantage point, viewpoint
respect, respecting, in respect to, with respect to	point
	structure
scenario	time frame
sector	type, –type (see the *Checklist*)
self-image	viable
situated	–wise (see the *Checklist*)
situation	worthwhile (see the *Checklist*)

Of course many of these words are perfectly legitimate and can be used in quite normal and acceptable ways. But even such acceptable words can be used as jargon, and those in this list are among the most likely offenders. For example, why say "He replied in the affirmative" when "He said yes" would do? *Angle* is a good and useful word, but in such expressions as "looking at the problem from a different angle" it begins to become jargon. *Aspect* has precise meanings, but they are seldom honoured; the student who wrote the following sentence certainly did not know them, but grabbed thoughtlessly at an all too familiar word: "Due to money aspects, many high-school graduates would rather work than enter university." Here *aspects* has no real meaning at all (and see *due to* in the *Checklist*, **60**). A phrase like "For financial reasons" or "Because of a need for money" would be far better. Another student, analyzing a poem, fell into the jargon trap and wrote "The third quatrain develops the aspect of time." Attempting to revise the sentence the writer fell right back into the trap: "The third quatrain brings in the factor of time"; *factor* is nearly as bad here as *aspect*. Unless you use *case* to mean a box or container, a medical case, a legal case, a grammatical case, or in phrases like "in case of fire," you will be in danger of creating wordy jargon: "In most cases, students who worked hard got good grades." Why not "Most students who worked hard got good grades"? *Interface*, as a noun, has a precise technical meaning; but after social scientists adopted it for their purposes it began surfacing as jargon, used—even as a verb—by many who are evidently unaware of its meaning. *Realm* means a kingdom, and it can—or once could—be useful metaphorically in phrases like "the realm of poetry" or "the realm of ideas"; but it has long been so loosely and so widely applied that any thinking writer will avoid it except in its meaning of kingdom. The verb *relate to* does not properly mean "understand" or "empathize" or "interact with in a meaningful way." And so on. If you read and listen carefully you will frequently find the terms listed, and other words and phrases like them, being used in ways that are offenses against clear and concise and precise expression. A few other specific items from this list are dealt with at length in the *Checklist* below (**60**). And you will find more examples in the exercises.

59h *jargon*

Usage: A Checklist of Troublesome Words and Phrases

In the following pages we list words and phrases that have a history of being especially confusing or troublesome. Study the whole list carefully, perhaps marking for frequent review any entries that you recognize as personal problem spots. Like any such list, this one cannot hope to be exhaustive; in fact, we have tried to keep it short. As with the list of frequently misspelled words, you should keep a list of your own errors of this kind for special study. You can supplement the information and advice provided below by consulting your dictionary. See also the index and the lists and discussions under the following: *Often Confused Words* (**51-l** and **m**), *Slang* (**52a**), *Informal, Colloquial* (**52b**), *Wordiness* (**59a**), *Triteness, Clichés* (**59e**), *Nouns* (**59f** and **g**), and *Jargon* (**59h**).

above, below

Try to avoid stiff references to something preceding or following in your essay. Say, "for these (or those) reasons" rather than "for the above reasons." If you find yourself writing "as I said above" or "as I will explain below" and the like, you may well be the victim of your own poor organization; try revising your outline.

actually (See *very.*)

affect, effect

Try to avoid the common confusion between these words. *Affect* is a transitive verb meaning *to act upon* or *to influence*; *effect* is a noun meaning *result, consequence*:

He tried to *affect* the outcome, but all his efforts had no *effect*.

Note: The plural noun *effects* can also refer to items of movable property, as in "household effects." And *effect* can also be a verb, but a relatively uncommon one, meaning *to bring about, to cause*: "The fertilizer *effected* rapid growth." *Affect* can also be a noun; its occurrence, however, is very uncommon and technical. It means, in psychology, something tending to arouse emotion rather than thought.

afterward, afterwards (See *toward, towards.*)

aggravate

Frequently misused to mean *annoy, irritate*. Properly speaking, something can be *aggravated* only if it is already bad; *aggravate* means *make worse*:

His standing so long in the hot sun *aggravated* his headache.
The unexpectedly high tax bill *aggravated* the company's already serious financial condition.

agree to, agree with, agree on
Be careful to use the correct preposition with the verb *agree*. One agrees *to* a proposal or request or *to* do something; one agrees *with* another person on a question or opinion; a climate or certain foods agree *with* a person; one agrees *on* (or *about*) the terms or details of something settled after negotiation, or *on* a course of action.

alternate, alternative; alternately, alternatively
Some writers blur the useful distinction between these words. *Alternate* (adjective) means by turns, one following another, or every other one; *alternative* (adjective or noun) refers to one of a number of possible choices (usually two). Avoid using *alternate* when the sense has something to do with *choice*. The same distinction holds for the adverbial forms.

> The squares on the board are *alternately* red and black.
> In summer they could water their lawns only on *alternate* days.
> The judge had no *alternative*: he had to dismiss the charges.
> There is an *alternative* method, much simpler than the one you are using.
> He could meekly resign or, *alternatively*, he could take his case to a higher authority.

The confusion perhaps arises partly from the legitimate use of *alternate* as a noun meaning a substitute or stand-by:

> Each delegate to the convention had a designated *alternate*.

although, though
These words introduce adverbial phrases or clauses of concession. They mean the same thing, but *although* with its two syllables usually sounds smoother at the beginning of a sentence, where *though* sounds relatively abrupt; *though* is more commonly used to introduce a phrase or clause that follows an independent clause, but it can be slightly emphatic if used to open a sentence. The two words are not always interchangeable, however: *even though* is a two-word equivalent, but one cannot—or should not—say "even although"; some people find even the sound of "and although" unpleasant. As a substitute for *however* ("there was, though, nothing to be done"; "he didn't eat much, though"), *though* is considered informal or colloquial. See also *despite that*.

among, between (See *between, among*.)

amount, number

Use *number* only with countable things, *amount* only for something considered as a total or mass: a *number* of dollars, an *amount* of money; a large *number* of lumps of coal, a large *amount* of coal. *Number* can be either singular or plural, depending upon whether it refers to a collective *unit* or to a collection of distinct items; with the definite article it is usually singular, with the indefinite article, plural:

Singular: The *number* of unsolved crimes is appalling.
Plural: A large *number* of people object to his proposal.

See also *less, fewer,* and **7f.**

and/or

To be avoided if possible. It is better to say "We'll get there on foot or horseback, or both," than "We'll get there on foot and/or horseback."

anxious

Does not mean *eager*; use it only where there is real anxiety, even to the point of suffering; think of the German word *Angst*.

anyplace, someplace

Colloquial for *anywhere, somewhere.*

anyways, anywheres, everywheres, nowheres, somewheres

Dialectal errors for *anyway, anywhere, everywhere, nowhere, somewhere.*

apt (See *likely, liable, apt.*)

as

To prevent ambiguity, do not use *as* in such a way that it can mean either *while* or *because*:

ambig: *As* I was walking after dark I tripped over a sleeping dog.
ambig: *As* I turned the flame up too high the grease caught fire.
ambig: The car gathered speed quickly, *as* I pressed harder on the accelerator.

It is impossible to be sure whether the *as* in each of these means *while* or *because*. Many careful writers have banned *as* in the sense of *because* from their vocabularies; using it only in the sense of *while*, they are unlikely to commit an inadvertent ambiguity, for it is primarily when *as* is used to mean *because* (or *for* or *since*) that it leads to ambiguity. Watch out for another awkward use of *as*: In a sentence like "The book was considered *as* a threat to the authority of the church," the *as* should be omitted; not only is it unnecessary, but it also alters the essential meaning of the sentence. See also *like, as, as if, as though.*

as being

Don't follow with *being* when *as* alone is enough:

> He always thinks of himself *as* (not *as being*) the life of the party.
> She sees the deputy minister *as* (not *as being*) an incompetent wretch.

as far as . . . is (are) concerned, as far as . . . goes

This construction has a wordy, jargon-like air about it, but if you feel that you need to use it anyway, don't carelessly leave it unfinished, as in this example:

> *poor:*   *As far as* financing my education, I'm going to have to get a summer job.

This frequent error probably stems from a confusion of *as far as* with *as for.*

as such

Don't sloppily or pretentiously use this phrase as if it were equivalent to *thus* or *therefore*:

> *Wrong:*   My uncle wants to be well-liked. *As such*, he always gives expensive gifts.

In this phrase *as* is a preposition and *such* is a pronoun that requires a clear antecedent:

> My uncle is a generous *man*. As *such*, he always gives me an expensive Christmas present.

as to

A phrase worth avoiding; substitution or rephrasing will almost always improve matters.

> *Poor:*   He made several recommendations *as to* the best method of proceeding.
> *Better:*   He made several recommendations with respect to the best method of proceeding.
> *Still better:*   He recommended several methods of proceeding.
> *Poor:*   I was in doubt *as to* which road to take.
> *Better:*   I was in doubt about which road to take.
> *Still better:*   I was not sure which road to take.
>   I did not know which road to take.

As to at the beginning of a sentence may seem more tolerable, but even there it can sound awkward; try changing it to *As for.*

awaiting for
Awaiting does not require the preposition *for*; *waiting* does:

> I am *waiting for* the whistle to blow.
> I am *awaiting* the train's arrival.

awful, awfully
Colloquialisms when used as intensifiers ("They were awfully nice to us") or to mean *bad*. See *very* and **52b**.

bad, badly (See *good, bad, badly, well.*)

basis, on the basis of, on a . . . basis
Basis is a perfectly good word, but these prepositional phrases using it are worth avoiding, for they are almost always wordy jargon.

> She made her decision *on the basis of* the committee's report.

This can easily be improved:

> She based her decision on the committee's report.

Again:

> He selected the furniture *on the basis of* its shape and colour. (by? for? according to? because of?)

The other phrase is even worse: *on a daily basis* is jargon for *daily*; *on a yearly basis* is jargon for *annually*; *on a temporary basis* is jargon for *temporarily*; *We'll do this for a week on a trial basis* is jargon for *We'll try this for a week*; *on a regular basis* is jargon for *regularly*; *on a political basis* is jargon for *politically* or *for political reasons*; and so on *ad nauseam*. See also *in terms of*.

being that, being as, being as how
Illiterate substitutes for *because* or *since* to introduce a subordinate clause. *Seeing as (how)* is even worse. Avoid all of them. See also *as being*.

belabour, labour
To *labour* something, as in *labour a point*, means to work too hard at it—to overelaborate or overexplain or overdevelop it—and thus to spoil it, to detract from its effectiveness. Don't mistakenly use the verb *belabour* in such a context. To *belabour* something or some-one means to strike or beat it, as with a whip or a club, or with strong or abusive language.

below   (See *above, below.*)

beside, besides

Don't confuse these words. *Beside,* a preposition, means *next to*; *besides* as an adverb means *also, too, as well*:

She stood *beside* her car.
She knew she would have to pay the cost of repairs and the towing charges *besides.*

As a preposition, *besides* means *other than, in addition to*:

Besides the cost of repairs, she knew she would have to pay towing charges.
Besides this, what should I do?

between, among

Although even some good writers no longer strictly observe this rule, it is still usually best to use *between* only where two persons or things are involved, and *among* when there are more than two:

They divided the cost equally *among* the three of them.
There is almost no difference *between* the two products.

Don't let plurals trap you into error:

There were the predictable differences *between* (not *among*) Liberals and Conservatives during the debate.

—though at times there are also differences *among* Liberals or *among* Conservatives. And on occasion *between* can be the more appropriate choice even for groups of three or more, especially if the emphasis is on the individual persons or groups as overlapping pairs:

At the end there remained little bitterness *between* the four men.
It seems impossible to keep the peace *between* the nations of the world.

blame

As a verb *blame* should not be followed by *on,* for one does not blame *something on* someone, but rather blames *someone for* something. One can of course *put* the blame for something *on* someone.

bust, busted

Slang or illiterate for *burst* (principal parts *burst, burst, burst*), meaning *broken.*

but (See *can't hardly,* etc.)

can, may (could, might)

Opinion and usage are divided, but in formal contexts it is still advisable to use *can* to denote *ability, may* to denote *permission* or *possibility*:

usage **60**

"*May* I have some more soup, please?" "Are you sure you *can* eat another bowl?"

He knew that he *might* leave if he wished, but he *could* not make himself rise from his chair.

Things *may* turn out worse than you expect.

But *can* is frequently used in the sense of permission, especially in informal contexts and with questions and negatives (*Can I go? No, you cannot!*) or where the distinction between *ability* and *permission* is blurred (*Anyone with an invitation can get in*)—a blurring which, inherent in the concepts, is making the two words increasingly interchangeable.

can't hardly, etc.

Barely, hardly, scarcely, only, and *but* are considered negatives. Therefore do not use words like *can't* and *don't* and *couldn't* with them, for the result is an ungrammatical *double negative,* almost as bad as writing (or saying) *don't never* or *wasn't never.* Use instead the positive form of the verb: *I can hardly believe it. He could scarcely finish on time.*

centre around

An illogical phrase. The meaning of the word *centre* (or *focus*) demands a different preposition:

The discussion centred *on* the proposed amendment.

Or something can centre *in* or *at* something. One can of course say *revolved around, circled around,* and be quite logical.

compare to, compare with

Use *compare to* to liken one thing to another, to express a similarity:

Shall I compare thee *to* a summer's day?
He compared his job *to* that of a coolie.

Compare with means to examine for differences or similarities, or both:

He compared the sports car *with* the compact car to see which one was the best for him.
He compared favourably *with* the boyfriend she had had the previous year.
Compared *with* a desk job, farm work is more healthful by far.

(There is often an implication that, asked to compare *a* with *b*, you are being asked to look for similarities; that is true in the sense that you are expected to determine the extent of similarity, but one cannot easily do that without discovering and pointing out the differences as well.)

comprise, compose

Confusion often arises from these words and the concepts they express. *Comprise* means *consist of, contain, take in, include*:

> The city *comprises* several separate communities.
> His duties *comprise* opening and shutting the shop, keeping the shelves stocked at all times, and running errands.

Compose means *constitute, form, make up*:

> The seven small communities together *compose* (constitute, make up) the city.

Here it would be incorrect to use *comprise*. And never use *comprise* in the passive voice—*(be) comprised (of, by)*; use *composed*.

continual, continuous

Although these two words are very close to each other in meaning, there is an important distinction between them. *Continual* refers to something that happens frequently or even regularly but with interruptions; *continuous* refers to something that occurs constantly, without interruptions:

> Your *continual* harping on my faults has given me a *continuous* headache.
> The heckler *continually* tried to interrupt, but the speaker's voice went on in a *continuous* drone.

convince, persuade

These two words overlap in meaning, but they are not synonymous, though they are often used interchangeably. Both mean to cause someone to believe or do something, but with *convince* the emphasis is on the belief, with *persuade* on the action. The difference is reflected in idiom: you can either convince or persuade someone *of* something or *that* something is true; but you can also persuade someone *to* do something, whereas *convince* should not be followed by an infinitive. Further, *convince* implies appeal to reason, logic, hard facts; *persuade* implies appeal both to reason and to emotion, feelings. *Convince* also connotes an overcoming of objections, a change of mind. (Perhaps the distinction is blurred by the fact that changing one's mind is itself a sort of action.)

culminate

This verb is intransitive; don't use it with a direct object or in a passive construction:

> *Wrong:* He *culminated* his remarks with a strong blast at the opposition.
> *Wrong:* The building was *culminated* by a revolving restaurant and a television tower.

Instead, use it only intransitively, usually with the preposition *in*:

Our search *culminates* here.

His speech *culminated in* a strong blast at the opposition.

The building *culminated in* a revolving restaurant and a television tower.

data (See **51t.**)

decimate

Avoid using this in the hackneyed sense of causing great destruction and death. Strictly it means (or meant) to select and kill one out of every ten.

despite that

This phrase is similar in meaning to *but* or *nevertheless* or *however*:

The weather was poor. *Despite that*, we enjoyed our outing.

It could also be written *Despite that fact*, making the demonstrative *that* an adjective rather than a pronoun. The phrase, however, is *not* equivalent in meaning to *though* or *although*:

Wrong: *Despite that* the weather was poor, we enjoyed our outing.

Such usage is not idiomatic. To be used this way it would have to be expanded to the wordy *Despite the fact that* (or *In spite of the fact that*). Use *although* or *though* or *even though*.

different from, different than

From is the idiomatic preposition to use after *different*:

Your car is noticeably *different from* mine.

Than, however, is becoming increasingly common, especially when followed by a clause and when it results in fewer words:

The finished picture looks far *different than* I had intended.

But to avoid criticism and the label "colloquial," use the more acceptable construction with *from*:

The finished picture looks *different from* what I intended.

differ from, differ with

To differ *from* something or someone is to be unlike in some way; to differ *with* someone is to disagree, to quarrel:

He *differed from* his colleague in that he was less prone to *differ with* everyone on every issue.

disinterested

A much abused word, *disinterested* means *impartial, objective, free from personal bias.* Although often used sloppily as a synonym for *uninterested, not interested,* the distinction between the two should be retained:

> It is necessary to find a judge who is *disinterested* in the case, for he will then try it fairly; we assume that he will not also be uninterested in it, for then he would be bored by it.

due to

Rather than risk censure, use this only as a predicate adjective after a form of the verb *be*:

> The accident was *due to* bad weather.

Used to introduce an adverbial phrase at the beginning of a sentence, *due to* is considered awkward or incorrect; use *because of* or *on account of* instead:

> Because of (not *due to*) the bad weather, we had an accident.

As a substitute, *owing to* is little if any better.

each other, one another

In formal writing use *each other* for two, *one another* for more than two:

> The bride and groom kissed *each other*.
> The five boys traded hockey cards with *one another*.

effect (See *affect, effect.*)

either, neither

Use these indefinite pronouns only to refer to one or the other of *two* things, not more than two. And remember that *either* and *neither* are singular and take the singular form of a verb:

> *Either* of the two answers is all right.

For more than two, *any* or *any one* (two words) will usually suffice:

> *Any (one)* of the four proposals is acceptable.

emulate

Does not mean simply *imitate,* but rather *vie with, try to outdo.*

enormity

Often incorrectly used to mean *great size, enormousness,* this word actually means *outrageousness, heinousness,* or *atrocity*:

> In pronouncing sentence, the judge emphasized the *enormity* of the arsonist's crime.

equally as

Avoid this awkward redundancy by dropping one or the other of the two words. In expressions like the following, *as* is unnecessary:

> Her first novel was highly praised, and her second is *equally* (as) good.
> He may be a good jumper, but she can jump *equally* (as) high, if not higher.

In expressions like the following, *equally* is unnecessary:

> In a storm, one port is (equally) *as* good as another.
> His meat pies were (equally) *as* tasty as hers.

especially, specially

Especially means *particularly, unusually*; *specially* means *specifically, for a certain or special purpose*:

> We *especially* want Juan to come; we planned the party *specially* for him.
> It's *especially* cold today; I'm going to wear my *specially* made jacket.

essential (See *unique*, etc.)

ever

Not needed after *seldom* and *rarely*.

everywheres (See *anyways*, etc.)

farther, further

The distinction between these is frequently overlooked. Use *farther* and *farthest* to refer to actual physical distance, and *further* and *furthest* to refer figuratively to non-physical things like time and degree:

> To go any *farther* down the road is the *furthest* thing from my mind.
> Rather than delay any *further*, he chose the card *farthest* from him.

fatal, fatalistic (See *simple, simplistic.*)

feel(s)

Try to avoid using the word *feel* loosely when what you really mean is *think* or *believe*; *feel* is more appropriate to emotional or physical responses, *think* to intellectual ones:

> I *feel* the need of sustenance; I *think* I had better have something to eat.
> I *feel* that we shouldn't start tonight; I *think* the road may be dangerous.

fewer (See *less, fewer.*)

firstly, secondly, etc.

Drop the old-fashioned and unnecessary *ly*; say simply *first, second, third*, etc. Even if you decide to use *secondly*, *thirdly*, etc., which are acceptable, begin your series with *first*, not *firstly*.

following

It is a pretentious error to use *following* as a preposition meaning *after*: *Following the concert, we went home*. *Following* is a noun (*He had a large following*; *Study the following*) or an adjective (*Study the following rules*; *Following the hearse, we entered the cemetery*). It should not be used as a preposition to introduce an adverbial phrase.

former, latter

Use these only when referring to the first or the second of two things, and only when the reference is clear and unambiguous—that is, when it is to something immediately preceding. But, like *above* and *below*, they are worth avoiding if possible.

forward, forwards (See *toward, towards*.)

fulsome

Although frequently used as if it meant *full*, *abundant*, as in "fulsome praise," the word actually means *too full*, *excessive*, and therefore *disgusting*, *offensive*, *distasteful*, as in "fulsome flattery"; keep in mind that its meaning has been influenced by the word *foul* and you will likely not misuse it.

further (See *farther, further*.)

good, bad, badly, well

To avoid confusion and error with these words, simply remember that *good* and *bad* are adjectives, *badly* and *well* adverbs (except when *well* is an adjective meaning *healthy*). Troubles most often arise after linking verbs.

> Helena looks good. (She is attractive.)
> That suit looks bad on you. (It doesn't fit properly; do not use *badly* here.)
> Nathan acted bad. (He did naughty things.)
> Nathan acted badly. (His performance as Hamlet was terrible.)
> I feel good. (I am happy.)
> I feel bad. (I have a splitting headache.)
> Herman feels badly. (An unlikely statement; it would mean that he was feeling some object with his hands and doing it badly.)
> Sophia looks well. (She looks healthy, not sick.)
> This wine travels well. (It wasn't harmed by the long train journey.)
> That steak smells good. (I look forward to eating it.)
> Your dog doesn't smell well. (He is too old to hunt.)

See also **9b**.

half a(n), a half

Both are correct. Use whichever sounds smoother or more logical. (Is *half a loaf* better than *a half loaf*? Is *a half hour* more formal than *half an hour*?) But don't use *a half a(n)*; one article is enough.

hanged, hung

Use the past form *hanged* only when referring to an execution by hanging. For all other uses of the verb *hang*, the correct past form is *hung*.

hardly (See *can't hardly*, etc.)

he or she, his or her, he/she (See **4d**.)

healthy, healthful

Keep *healthy* as a word meaning *in a state of good health*, and use *healthful* to mean *contributing to good health*:

> To stay *healthy*, one should participate in a *healthful* sport like swimming.

herself, himself, myself, etc. (See **3h**.)

hopefully

Use this adverb only to modify a verb or an adjective (preferably a verbal one):

> "Will you lend me ten dollars?" I *asked hopefully*.
> *Smiling hopefully*, she began to untie the package.

Do not use it as a sentence modifier:

> *us:*   *Hopefully*, the sun will shine tomorrow.

If the sun does shine, it can scarcely "shine hopefully"—yet syntactically the adverb *hopefully* in this sentence wants to modify the verb *will shine*. Although many people use *hopefully* this way—indeed overuse it, especially in speech—it grates on the ears of most people who care about language. Instead of using *hopefully* as a sentence adverb, then, say *I hope* or *We hope* or *One hopes* or *It is to be hoped that*—whichever best suits your meaning. So corrupted is the word by sloppy misuse that even used correctly it can be misunderstood. Consider the following sentence:

> *Hopefully*, many people will come to the prize drawing.

This would probably be understood as expressing the sentiments of the organizer or whoever gets a cut of the admission price. A careful writer who meant otherwise would have phrased it differently:

Many people will come, full of hope, to the prize drawing.

Even if you are using it correctly, then, to mean *full of hope*, you have to be careful. Here are two more examples:

ambig: Stephen was outside somewhere, *hopefully* looking for an empty cab.

ambig: *Hopefully*, the coach has designated his best quarterback to handle the crucial plays.

Here simply moving the adverb will prevent misreading: *looking hopefully*; *has hopefully designated*.

in, into

In formal writing, *in* means *inside of* and *into* means *moving toward the inside of*:

He went *into* the dining room to see if she was there, but she was *in* the kitchen.

We moved *into* our new home *in* the suburbs last Saturday.

individual

Not a synonym for *person*. The word *individual* should be used only when the meaning *distinct from others* is present:

The *person* (not *individual*) you are referring to is my aunt.

He is very much an *individual* in his behaviour. (That is, he behaves like no one else.)

You are safer if you use it as an adjective rather than as a noun. But see also *person, persons*.

infer, imply

These two words give rise to frequent confusion and misuse; learn to distinguish between them and to use them correctly. A common error is to use *infer* where *imply* would be the correct word. *Imply* means *suggest, hint at, indicate indirectly*. *Infer*, however, does not mean the same thing. Rather it means *conclude by reasoning, deduce*. What one person *implies* in a statement, then, a listener can *infer* from it:

Her speech strongly *implied* that she could be trusted.

I *inferred* from her speech that she was trustworthy.

in terms of

This phrase is another example of contemporary clutter. Note that it is similar, sometimes even equivalent, to those other offenders, *on the basis of* (see *basis*) and *-wise*. Such locutions are like verbal tics, capable of leading to such inane utterances as this (by the governor of a drought-stricken state): "We're very scarce in terms of water." Do not write things like

> He tried to justify the price increase *in terms of* [on the basis of] the company's increased operating costs.
>
> *In terms of* experience [experience-wise], she was as qualified for the post as anyone else applying for it.
>
> *In terms of* fuel economy, this car is better than any other in its class.
>
> He first considered the problem *in terms of* the length of time it would take him to solve it.
>
> When they planned the assault, they were clearly thinking *in terms of* how to minimize property damage.

when the ideas could so easily be much better expressed:

> He tried to justify the increase in price by citing the company's increased operating costs.
>
> She was as experienced as anyone else applying for the post.
>
> This car has the best fuel economy of any in its class.
>
> First he thought about how long it would take him to solve the problem.
>
> When they planned the assault, they were clearly thinking about how to minimize property damage.

And note the further family resemblance of this phrase to others like *along the lines of, in connection with, in relation to, in [with] regard to, regarding, in [with] respect to,* and *from the standpoint [viewpoint] of. Perspective* and *approach* are two more terms often used in a similar way.

irregardless

Properly, there is no such word. The prefix *ir* (not) is redundant, since the suffix *less* already expresses the "not." The correct word is *regardless.* (The error evidently stems from confusion of *regardless* with *irrespective.*)

is when, is where

Incorrect because a *when* or *where* adverbial clause cannot properly follow the linking verb *is*; a predicate adjective or predicate noun is required as complement after a linking verb:

> *Wrong:* A double play *is when* two base runners are put out during one play.
>
> *Right:* In a double play, two base runners are put out during one play.
>
> *Right:* A double play occurs when two base runners are put out during one play.

(Since *occurs* is not a linking verb, the adverbial clause beginning with *when* is all right.)

60 usage

Note: This error is grammatically similar to that of *the reason . . . is because* (see **gr** in Chapter XI).

its, it's

Don't join the multitudes of the ignorant who can't keep these simple words straight. *Its* is the possessive form of *it*; *it's* is the contracted form of *it is*. Proofread carefully.

kind of, sort of

Do not use these as adverbs, as in *kind of tired, sort of strange*. Do not follow with an article, as in "I had a bad kind of an afternoon" or "She was a rather peculiar sort of a guide." Even when used legitimately, these phrases are frequently awkward and unnecessary. Why not "I had a bad afternoon" and "She was a rather peculiar guide"? See also *type*.

labour (See *belabour, labour*.)

lay (See *lie, lay*.)

less, fewer

Less should be used only in comparisons of things or amounts that are not being counted or considered as units; *fewer* refers to things that are countable:

fewer dollars, *less* money
fewer hours, *less* time
fewer shouts, *less* noise
fewer cars, *less* traffic
fewer bottles of beer, *less* beer

See also *amount, number*.

liable (See *likely, liable, apt*.)

lie, lay

If necessary, memorize the principal parts of these often misused verbs: *lie, lay, lain; lay, laid, laid. Lie* means *recline*, or *be situated*; *lay* means *put* or *place*; *lie* is intransitive; *lay* is transitive.

> I *lie* down now. I *lay* down yesterday. I *have lain* down several times today.
>
> I *lay* the book on the desk now. I *laid* the book on the desk yesterday. I *have laid* the book on the desk every morning for a week.

A particularly distressing error (because it makes its perpetrator sound illiterate) is the use of *laying* where *lying* is correct. How often have you heard a hockey commentator say "He's laying on the ice" (laying what? eggs?) when of course he should say "He's *lying* on the ice." Get them straight. (In the sense of "prevaricate" the principal parts of *lie* are *lie*, *lied*, *lied*.)

like, as, as if, as though

In the following sentence, *like* is a *preposition*:

Roger is dressed exactly *like* Ray.

But if *Ray* is given a verb, then he becomes the subject of a clause, and *like* is no longer functioning as a preposition:

Wrong: Roger is dressed exactly *like* Ray is.

Like now functions as a conjunction––which in good usage it cannot be. Always use *as*, a perfectly good conjunction, when a clause follows:

Roger is dressed exactly *as* Ray is.
The steak is rare, *as* a good steak should be.

In slightly different constructions, either *as if* or *as though* is the correct form to use in place of the pernicious *like*:

It looks *like* rain. (*not* It looks like it will rain.)
OR
It looks *as if* (or *as though*) it will rain.
He stood there *like* a bronze Apollo. (*not* He stood there like he was a bronze Apollo.)
OR
He stood there *as though* (or *as if*) he were a bronze Apollo.

But be careful that, in an effort to avoid this error, you don't overcompensate; don't shun *like* for *as* when what follows it is *not* a clause:

Wrong: Rover stood stiffly alert, pointing, head and tail down, *as* any well-trained dog.

Wrong: Nicklaus, just *as* last year's winner, sank a stunning birdie putt on the final hole.

In each of these the *as* should be changed to *like*.

likely, liable, apt

Likely means *probable, showing a tendency, suitable*:

A storm seems *likely*. He is *likely* to succeed. This is a *likely* spot.

Liable means *legally responsible, susceptible to something undesirable*:

He is *liable* for damages. She is *liable* to headaches.

Confusion most often arises when either word would seem appropriate:

> If he isn't careful, he is *liable* to fall off that ladder.

Although *likely* ("showing a tendency") would seem right here, *liable* is preferable, in its sense of *susceptible to something undesirable*. *Apt* is often used loosely as a synonym for both *likely* and *liable*, but it is best reserved for *habitual* tendency or inclination:

> Jimmy is *apt* to trip over his own feet.

literally, virtually, figuratively

Don't use these unthinkingly. *Literally* means *actually, really*. *Virtually* means *in effect, practically*. *Figuratively* means *metaphorically, not literally*. All too often *literally* and *virtually* are used to mean their exact opposites.

> She was *literally* swept off her feet. (Hardly! What the writer means is that the lady in question was *figuratively* or *virtually* swept off her feet.)
> They were caught in a *virtual* downpour. (It *was* a downpour! Who needs *virtual?*)

loan, lend

Some people still restrict *loan* to being a noun, but it is now generally accepted as a verb equivalent to *lend*.

mad

Only informally is *mad* a synonym for *angry*. Formal usage demands that *mad* be restricted to the meaning *insane*.

material, materialistic

Don't use *materialistic* when all you need is the adjective *material*. *Material* means *physical, composed of matter*, or *concerned with physical rather than spiritual or intellectual things*; it is often the sufficient word:

> His life is founded almost entirely on *material* values.

Materialistic is the adjectival form of the noun *materialist*, which in turn denotes one who believes in *materialism*, a philosophical doctrine holding that everything can be explained in terms of matter and physical laws. A *materialist* can also be one who is notably or questionably concerned with material as opposed to spiritual or intellectual things and values:

> He is very *materialistic* in his outlook on life.

Unless you intend the philosophical overtones, use the simpler *material*. There is an analogous tendency to use *relativistic* rather than *relative*, and *moralistic* rather than *moral*. Consult your dictionary. See also *real, realism, realist, realistic*.

may (See *can, may*.)

media (See **51t**.)

momentarily
Worth trying to keep as meaning *at the moment, at every moment*; do not use it to mean *in a moment, soon*. (See *presently*.)

muchly (See *thusly*.)

myself, herself, etc. (See **3h**.)

necessary (See *unique*, etc.)

nowheres (See *anyways*, etc.)

number (See *amount, number*.)

of
Unnecessary after the prepositions *off, inside, outside*, and often unnecessary after the pronoun *all*, especially when countable items are not involved:

He fell *off* (or *from*) the fence. (not *off of*)
He found himself *inside* a large crate. (not *inside of*)
As requested, she remained in the hall *outside* the room for five minutes.
   (not *outside of*)
We had *all* the time in the world. (*of* not necessary)   ˙
All of the members were present. (*of* acceptable but not necessary)

Of is needed after *all* before some pronouns, and usually helps before proper nouns:

Bring *all of* them. We travelled across *all of* Canada.

Note: In "He inspected the outside of the building," *outside* is a noun.

Don't make the mistake of unidiomatically using *of* after *remember*:

I *remembered* (not *remembered of*) all the things my mother had told me about the big city.

In addition, because of the way we speak, phrases like "would have," "should have," "might have," and so on often come out as contractions: "would've," "should've," "might've"; because of the way they *hear* such words, some people mistakenly assume that the *ve* is actually *of*, and then proceed to write "would of," "should of," "might of," etc. Avoid this illiterate error.

on

This preposition is sometimes awkwardly unidiomatic when used as a substitute for *about* or *of*:

id: She had no doubts *on* what to do next. (should be *about*)
id: I am calling my essay "A Study *on* the Effects of Automation." (should be *of*)

Another point: *On* sounds less stiff and formal than *upon*, though the two are often interchangeable. Sometimes you can choose according to whether a one- or a two-syllable word will best suit the rhythm of a sentence.

one another (See *each other, one another.*)

oral, verbal (See *verbal, oral.*)

owing to (See *due to.*)

partially, partly

Since *partially* also means *with prejudice or bias*, using it in the sense of *partly* could be ambiguous. (*His decision was partially arrived at.*) It is simpler and safer to use the shorter *partly*.

perfect (See *unique*, etc.)

person, persons

The word *person* is becoming tainted by overuse in such expressions as "If necessary, a person should complain to a higher authority." The currency of *person* and *persons* is evidently due to a growing wish to avoid using the potentially sexist *man* or *woman* or the generic pronoun *he*. Try instead to use the impersonal pronoun *one*, or even the second-person pronoun *you* (see **4d**). In the plural, use *persons* only when the number of people in a group is small, say two or three ("Two persons refused to sign the petition") or when you want to emphasize the presence of *individuals* in a group ("Those persons wishing to attend the party should sign up now")—but even then the demonstrative pronoun *those* alone will often serve better ("Those wishing to attend . . . "). Otherwise, use *people*. See also *individual*.

60 usage

persuade (See *convince, persuade.*)

plus (See **d** in Chapter XI.)

presently
   Presently should mean *in a short while, soon*; it should not be used to mean *now, at present, currently*. But this word is now so commonly misused that many writers try to avoid it altogether. Use the alternative terms and your meaning will be clear. Besides, *presently* now often sounds pretentious. See also *momentarily.*

put forth (See *set forth.*)

quote
   This is a verb. Used as a noun, instead of *quotation*, it is colloquial, as is *quotes* instead of *quotation marks.*

raise, rise
   Raise is transitive, requiring an object: *I raised my hand. He raises wheat. Rise* is intransitive, used without an object: *The temperature rises. I rise in the morning.* Learn the principal parts of these verbs: *raise, raised, raised; rise, rose, risen.*

real, realism, realist, realistic
   Be careful with these words; try to use them correctly. It pays to consult your dictionary in order to be sure. The student who wrote that "Huxley's novel is not about realistic people" was at best being ambiguous: does the word *realistic* here mean "lifelike," or "facing facts"? The one who wrote "He based his conclusions not on theory but on realistic observation" probably meant "observation of reality." See also *material, materialistic.*

real, really
   Real is not an adverb ("real different"); use *really* (see **9b**). But see also *very.*

reason is because (See **gr** in Chapter XI.)

reason why
   The *why* is often redundant, as in "We'll probably have rain tomorrow, and here's the reason why," and "The reason why I'm taking Spanish is that I want to travel in Latin America." Always check to see if you need the *why*; usually you won't.

relation, relationship

The longer word, *relationship*, is often used where it is not necessary; it is necessary only when speaking of family connections or where the desired meaning is analogous to that:

> What is the *relationship* between you two? (That is, how are you related to each other?) Are you sisters, cousins, or what?

Elsewhere the sense of the connection or state of being related is most often adequately expressed by the shorter word:

> I do not see any *relation* between your answer and the question I asked.
> The two countries have long enjoyed friendly *relations*.

rise, raise (See *raise, rise*.)

scarcely (See *can't hardly*, etc.)

seeing as how (See *being that, being as how*.)

sensual, sensuous

Sensuous means *pertaining to the senses, sensitive to beauty*, etc. *Sensual*, on the other hand, means *lewd, carnal, pertaining to the body and to the satisfaction of physical appetites*:

> Many Canadian poets, responding to the beauty of their natural environment, write *sensuous* poetry.
> The minister emphasized the spiritual quality of "The Song of Solomon" rather than its *sensual* features.

set, sit

Don't confuse these common verbs. *Set* (principal parts *set, set, set*) means *put, place, cause to sit*; it is transitive, requiring an object: *He set the glass on the counter.* *Sit* (principal parts *sit, sat, sat*) means *rest, occupy a seat, assume a sitting position*; it is intransitive: *The glass sits on the counter. May I sit in the easy chair?*

set forth

As an unwieldy, stiff substitute for *expressed* or *presented* or *stated*, this phrase is an attempt at sophistication that usually misfires. *Put forth* is similarly weak.

shall, will (See **6h/3**.)

simple, simplistic

Don't use *simplistic* when all you want is *simple*. *Simplistic* means *oversimplified, unrealistically simple*. Similarly, *fatalistic* does not mean the same as *fatal*.

since

Since can refer both to time ("Since April we haven't had any rain") and to cause ("Since you won't tell me, I'll have to figure it out for myself"). Don't use *since* in the sense of *because* when it could also be understood as referring to time:

> *ambig:* Since you went away, I've been sad and lonely.

sit, set (See *set, sit.*)

so . . . as

Prefer *so* or *so . . . as* with *negative* comparisons, *as* or *as . . . as* with *positive* comparisons:

> Barbara was almost *as* tall *as* he was, but she was not *so* heavy.
> He was not *so* light on his feet *as* he once was, but he was *as* strong *as* ever.

someplace (See *anyplace, someplace.*)

somewheres (See *anyways,* etc.)

sort of (See *kind of, sort of.*)

specially (See *especially, specially.*)

state

A stronger verb than *say*, *state* should be reserved for places where you want the heavier, more forceful meaning of *assert, declare, make a formal statement.*

substitute

One thing cannot be *substituted by* or *with* another; the correct verb there is *replace*:

> *Wrong:* The french fries were substituted by (or *with*) a tossed salad.
> *Wrong:* The term paper was substituted by (or *with*) three smaller reports.
> *Right:* The french fries were replaced by (or *with*) a tossed salad.
> *Right:* The term paper was replaced by (or *with*) three smaller reports.

Used correctly, *substitute* usually takes the preposition *for*:

> The waitress kindly substituted a tossed salad for the greasy french fries.
> This year you may substitute three short reports for the term paper.

Substitute can also be used intransitively:

> Because he is off his game this season, Randolph has only substituted.

sure, surely

Sure is not an adverb. See **9b**.

suspicion, suspect, suspicious

Suspicion is a noun; *suspect* is the verb (though it can also, if pronounced *sus'-pect*, be an adjective or a noun). Though *suspicious* can mean *arousing suspicion*, it is sometimes safer to reserve it for the person in whom the suspicions are aroused, using the adjectival sense of *suspect* for the object of those suspicions; otherwise ambiguity may result (unless the context makes everything clear):

> *ambig:* He was a very suspicious man.
> *clear:* I thought his actions suspect.
> *clear:* He was suspicious of everyone he met.
> *clear:* All of us were suspect in the eyes of the police.

tend, tends

This word is often no more than a mushy filler. Don't say "My French teacher tends to mark strictly" when what you mean is "My French teacher marks strictly."

though (See *although, though.*)

thusly

A pretentious-sounding error for *thus*, as is *muchly* for *much*.

too

Used as an intensifier, *too* is illogical; if an intensifier is necessary, use *very*:

> I don't like my cocoa *too* hot. (Well, of *course* you don't!)
> I don't like my cocoa *very* hot.
> She didn't care for the brown suit *too* much. (How *could* she care *too* much!)
> She didn't care for the brown suit *very* much.

You can usually omit the intensifier as unnecessary:

> She didn't much care for the brown suit.

See *very*.

toward, towards

These are interchangeable, but *toward* is usually preferred to *towards*, just as *afterward* is preferred to *afterwards*, and *forward* to *forwards*.

true facts, etc.

An attempt to be emphatic that backfires into illogic. If there are such things as "true facts" or "real facts," then what are "false facts" or "unreal facts"? Let the word *facts* mean what it is supposed to; trying to prop it up with *true* or *real* only makes a reader suspect it of being weak or insincere.

type, -type

Don't use *type* as an adjective or part of an adjective, as in "He is a very athletic type person." In any but a technical context, the word *type* almost always sounds like jargon, even when followed by the obligatory *of*. Without the *of* it is colloquial at best. In general writing, if you *can* substitute *kind of* for *type of*, do so—but even then check to make sure you really need it, for often it is unnecessary: He is an intelligent [kind of] man. As a hyphenated suffix, -*type* is similarly often unnecessary, as well as being one of the worst results of the impulse to turn nouns into adjectives: "This is a new-type vegetable slicer," or "He is a patriotic-type person." Avoid it. See also *kind of, sort of.*

unique, necessary, essential, perfect, empty, full, straight, wrong, round, square, etc.

These and other such adjectives cannot logically be compared. Since by definition something that is *unique* is the *only one of its kind*, then clearly one thing cannot be "more unique" than another, or even "very unique"; in other words, *unique* is *not* a synonym for *unusual*. Similarly with the others: one thing cannot be "more necessary" than another. Since *perfect* means *without flaw*, there cannot be degrees of perfection. A thing is either round or not round; one tennis ball cannot be *rounder* than another. And so on. (Note that we get around this semantic limitation by speaking of one thing as, for example, *more nearly perfect, more nearly round*, or *closer to round* than another.)

upon, on (See *on.*)

usage, use, utilize, utilization

Usage (noun) is most appropriate when you mean customary or habitual use (*British usage*; *the usages of the early Christians*) or a particular verbal expression being characterized in a particular way (*an ironic usage, an elegant usage*). Otherwise the shorter noun *use* will be correct. *Use* (verb) should suffice nearly all the time; *utilize,* which is often pretentiously employed instead, should carry the specific meaning *put to use, make use of, turn to practical or profitable account*. Similarly with the noun *utilization*: simply the noun *use* will usually be more appropriate. Phrases like *use of, the use of, by the use of*, and *through the use of* tend toward jargon and are almost always wordy.

verbal, oral

These are not synonyms. If you mean *spoken aloud*, then *oral* is the right word. *Verbal* regularly means *pertaining to words*, which could be either written or spoken. (In some special contexts *verbal* is customarily used to mean *oral* as opposed to written: *verbal contract, verbal agreement*. But for general writing keep the distinction between *verbal* and *oral* clear.)

very

Do not overuse *very* as a lame intensifier. So thoughtlessly does it get used that someone during an interview responded to a question with "We're not very absolutely clear about that yet." You will often find that where you have used *very* you could just as well have omitted it; sometimes it even detracts from the force of the word it modifies, or is a lazy, vague, or euphemistic substitute for a more precise adverb or adjective:

It was *very* sunny today. (magnificently sunny? torturously sunny?)
I was *very* tired. (exhausted?)
He was *very* intoxicated. (falling-down drunk?)
Her embarrassment was *very* obvious. (It was either obvious or it wasn't; drop *very*, or change it to something like *excruciatingly*.)

The same goes for *really* and *actually*.

Note: Before some past participles, it is idiomatic to use another word along with *very*:

You are *very much* mistaken if you think I'll agree without an argument.
Sharon is *very well* rehearsed for the role.

way, ways

Don't use *ways* to refer to distance; *way* is correct:

We were a long *way* from home.
They had only a little *way* to go.

well (See *good, bad, badly, well*.)

while

As a subordinating conjunction, *while* is fine as long as it is restricted to meanings having to do with time:

While I cut the lawn she raked up the grass clippings.
She played the piano *while* I prepared the dinner.

When it is not intended to refer to time it can be imprecise at best, ambiguous at worst:

While I agree with some of his reasons, I still think my proposal is better.

Here the meaning would be better served by *although*.

The Liberals want a new freeway, *while* the Conservatives favour some form of rapid transit.

Here the meaning would be better served by *whereas*.

The winning team guzzled champagne, *while* the losers sat and sulked.

Here either an *and* or a *but* would make a sharper statement.

will, shall (See **6h/3**.)

-wise

Do not add this suffix—in its sense of "with respect to" or "in terms of" or "so far as . . . is concerned"—to nouns, for it produces such jargonautical inanities as what a politician recently announced: "We've just had our best month ever, fund-raisingwise." Find a way to say what you want to say without stooping to jargon.

not: *Grammarwise*, Stephen is not doing well.
but: Stephen is not doing well with grammar.
not: *Insurance-wise*, I believe I am well enough protected.
but: I believe I have enough insurance.
not: This is the best car I've ever owned, *powerwise*.
but: This car has more power than any other I have owned.

See also *in terms of*.

worthwhile

Try to find a more precise and concrete way to express the desired meaning. "It was a very worthwhile experience" tells one very little (nor does the *very* succeed in propping up the weak *worthwhile*). Skip the vague statement; instead, describe or explain just what was so worthwhile about the experience. See also *Concreteness*, **54**.

60 usage

Review Exercise: Chapter VII

Correct the errors, strengthen the diction, and normalize the usage in the following sentences.

1. They discussed the role of the psychiatrist in athlete motivation.
2. They are a close-knit unit that functions on a collective basis.
3. Poetry during this time period did not pay very well.
4. Because this particular word occurs frequently throughout the course of the play, it achieves a certain importance.
5. In the winter even less tourist dollars are spent.
6. His striving to be a perfectionist was evident in his business.
7. The scientist grew his sample bacteria in a test-tube situation.
8. He was ignorant as to the proper use of the tools.
9. As is so often the case, one type of error leads to another.
10. This passage is a very essential one in the play.
11. His metaphors really bring out a sinister feeling which one feels while reading it.
12. Eliot sees his poetry as occupying a kind of niche in a long conveyor belt of accumulated knowledge and poetry.
13. She has him literally at her beckon call.
14. He found himself in a powerless situation.
15. I resolved to do my best in terms of making friends and working hard.
16. The hulls of the tankers were ripped open in a majority of cases, dumping countless barrels of oil into the ocean.
17. Hamlet spends the whole play trying to reach a situation where he can revenge his father's death.
18. This poem is concerned with the fact that one should grasp an opportunity quickly.
19. They try hard, but the answers they search always seem to elude them.
20. A grave problem concerned with overpopulation besides the food crisis is the inability for our civilized world to educate the people of underdeveloped countries.
21. As he gave me so much money I thanked him profusely.
22. The overall impression of the place was so overwhelming that within two weeks, I had decided to stay for an indefinite period of time, and make a decision concerning departure at a later date.
23. People in watching these shows or movies may develop a love for violence as a result of watching this type of program.
24. It seems like he is rather mad at her for daring to try and deceive him.
25. In Olympic sports nationalism is increasingly becoming a more important factor.
26. When he speaks, it is to reassure her; therefore he speaks gently and reassuringly.
27. In the following stanza Donne tries to make his wife proud of their relationship by comparing it to "dull sublunary lovers' love whose soul is sense."
28. Frodo continuously fretted about the Ring.
29. The author cites that in one of Macaulay's speeches on the First Reform Bill he said, "Reform, that you may preserve."
30. At the end of the story Hardin comes up with a baffling solution to which the reader knew nothing about until then.

exercises

31. We are all intensely involved in profiting on the expenses of other people.
32. The contribution of the coalition to the passage of the legislation was capitalized on by the opposition.
33. As to getting a job, in some cases it has been shown that being in the right place at the right time is all that is required.
34. These instructions are contingent to your acceptance.
35. She was anxiously awaiting for some response from the government.
36. One must judge the various proposals on an equal basis.
37. The ad claims that this tonic is doctor-recommended.
38. Iago is regarded by all as an honest, truthful man.
39. The character of Nicholas is recognizable to people who really exist in the world.
40. His heroic deeds were awarded with medals.
41. In Elizabethan time, love was the dominant theme of poetry.
42. There were artists which continued to study and produce classical works and there were artists which developed new ideas in their fields.
43. Mealtime is when many people in a residence hall assemble together.
44. After going only a hundred miles the ship was forced to return to its point of origination.
45. The chairman insisted that the company must be better organized if it was to make any profit.
46. The new program will cost in the realm of five million dollars.
47. He was advised to keep his feelings on a spiritual plain for a while yet.
48. The minister said that he would not want to be categorized with respect to a reply to that statement.
49. Prospective teachers are required to take a Written Expression Competency Examination.
50. There was a general consensus in the neighbourhood that ambulance service in the area was frequently inadequate regarding response time.

Omnibus Review Exercise

Most of the following sentences are from student papers; some are from published sources. Each sentence contains at least one error or weakness of a kind discussed in this book; many contain more than one. Practise your proofreading skills and your revising techniques. Label the sentences with the appropriate correction symbols, and revise them in order to get rid of their various errors and weaknesses.

1. I was playing my typical type of game.
2. There was a clear increase in strength of Protestant power, especially in England and Prussia who had benefitted from the treaty of Utrecht.
3. In today's world it is becoming increasingly more difficult to find relatively inexpensive ways to use your liesure time.
4. It was difficult being a foreigner and try to comprehend the obsession of the army in Israel.
5. The nature of his errors were not serious.
6. New-wise, there is not much under the sun.
7. As for ancient man, being civilized was of no concern to one who was battling the many forces of nature such as hunting wild animals for food and shelter from the weather.
8. My landlord, as did most of the people in the district, spoke both french and english.
9. The reason their cars don't live as long is because most people have no idea of how to properly look after their cars.

10. Sam, my dog, is no exception as she provides me with enjoyment, companionship and protection.
11. Our apartment was not more than a ten minute walk away from the Opera House and if I weren't going to a concert on a Saturday evening, I was going to an Opera.
12. For those who are not gifted they are happy there because they can see that others are like them.
13. He was charged of embezzling over ten thousand dollars.
14. Though this fork is small and lifeless, on close examination, it gives forth the impression of something powerful and threatening.
15. She fears being thought of as a fool by everyone.
16. The poem's strange theme states that one is better off dying at a young age rather than growing old.
17. Eliza is understandably nervous, for this is her first lesson and she is wearing different clothes as well as being in strange surroundings.
18. I had truly scarred her while she had only embarrassed me.
19. In 1681, architect Sir Christopher Wren was being as creative as ever, as he was working on the famous Tom Tower, at Christ Church, in Oxford, which he had designed and was building.
20. He is only in town on a once-in-a-while basis.
21. A hobby such as playing music in a band gives more than just enjoyment, it gives relaxation, self satisfaction, it is educational, and it is competitive.
22. He did not seem to care to the least of his reputation.
23. I spent the afternoons participating in workshops such as, the newspaper, theatre, choir, painting, gymnastics and folk dancing.
24. I felt a sudden needle like pain.
25. Based on her findings, she concluded that comedy was more healthful than tragedy.
26. It may take a long time for it is not an easy task.
27. There are many arguments with respect to the importance of a university education in today's society.
28. In this modern day and age it is not unusual to find people who are ignorantly unaware of the technology of how things in our society work.
29. She had so many assignments over the holiday that she felt bogged under.
30. The police act against violators of this minor law only on a complaint basis.
31. They substituted butter with margarine in the belief that it was healthier.
32. For the children's sake he hoped he could find some acceptable substitute to television.
33. The silver mentioned at the beginning and the end of the story not only symbolize freedom but they foreshadow a better future.
34. My grandfather was a very introspective-type individual.
35. He is one of those people, (and there are many of them) who does not understand economics.
36. In Margaret Laurence's *A Jest of God* there is a symbol used throughout the novel which represents what Rachel's life is like at the time.
37. He prepared a dish that was a feast not only for the eyes but a treat for the palate as well.
38. Failure to produce efficiently together with failure to reduce imports have had serious economic consequences.
39. He was told that if he persisted on complaining he would soon find himself without a job.
40. There's so many good things on the menu that it's difficult to make a choice.
41. The government permits the sale of surplus material abroad on an intermittent basis.

exercises

42. I hope you will forgive me pointing out certain weaknesses in your argument.
43. The potatoes smelled so badly that I had to throw them out.
44. The laws were made by the parlament and enforced by a police force, which is a similar system to the present.
45. The room was furnished with the new chrome and plastic furniture but it wasn't very attractive.
46. With an increasing number of cars on the road there is a greater demand for cars to respond efficiently in emergency situations.
47. A poorly maintained car uses much more oil and gas than it should. This is not only expensive, but with the energy crisis on, we need all the fuel we can save.
48. The English aristocracy, which was mainly comprised of wealthy landowners, did not however, in spite of their comfortable lifestyle, know the manners and etiquette that seemed to elevate the French aristocracy.
49. He promised that he would take me to the movies, in spite of how much work that he hasn't finished yet, but has to do.
50. The adventurer struggles with his inner conflict between society and adventure.
51. The two characters vainly try to enter each others world.
52. It is the story of one man's answer for the problem of dealing with modern violence.
53. The scene is short and practical needs demand a simple set. A set which can easily be taken down or rolled off quickly.
54. The feeling of excitment comes across by the imagery.
55. Don't look directly at the eclipse of the sun. If you do, you may risk eye damage.
56. Hamlet is still unsure of whether the ghost was real or not and if so, if it spoke the truth.
57. In ancient times the sun was worshipped as a diety and has always had a leading role in mythology.
58. Computer break-ins have become far too easy to do and the law is ineffective in dealing with this type of problem.
59. The general shape of this particular hockey stick is no different than any other.
60. Upon entering university, it's size and population create a sort of "awe" in the individual.
61. We were driving on a bumpy, dirt road.
62. By having Hamlet say "Now I am alone," the audience becomes aware of the fact that the actor is speaking his thoughts.
63. Ron Luciano is the funniest and most outspoken major-league umpire still alive.
64. Its very difficult for man to perceive his own shortcomings, its all too easy for them to see the weaknesses of others.
65. A major reason as to why religion played such an important role in Elizabethan England was because it was a main pastime that the extremely large working class could afford.
66. The poem explains that the two people didn't really spend enough time together in order to get to know one another like any father and son should.
67. He attempts to hold the high ground against the entire U.S. Army—believing that his old-time values is the only weapon he needs.
68. The sermon poured in softly. It was comforting and reassuring; like listening to my father snoring in the next room, or an opera in a foreign language.

69. Former Anglican minister and *Toronto Star* religious editor Tom Harpur, who covered the Pope's activities as a journalist for several years, spoke to an interviewer about his experience.
70. She said she was not in a position to judge the minister then she proceeded to do just that.
71. The reasons why the difficult-to-define quality of image play such an important role in Canada's political life is the subject of frequent studies.
72. The second term re-opened in January and I continued to go to the practice everyday after school.
73. The first step in shopping around for a computer to assist you with your particular business needs is to decide what kind of equipment you will need to meet the needs and size of your company.
74. So many people are obsessed with their weight that the diet industry, whether it be in the form of pills, meal substitutes or a new fad diet, has boomed.
75. He was too mannerly to talk about a subject that did not interest whomever was with him.
76. I would have operated the other tractor, but due to mechanical problems, it was shut down until the necessary repairs were made.
77. Trust is a very important aspect in media effectiveness.
78. The passing of summer into autumn had always been experienced with pleasure while at the same time realizing that winter, the season I dislike the most, would soon be a fact of life.
79. Some people neglect not only their own work, but behave in such a way as to cause everyone else in the office to neglect his.
80. My favourite sports though, are those that can be played indoors, irregardless of the weather.
81. Looking through the newspapers, the cost of food products are seen to be expensive.
82. There was a broad lawn between the entrance and the tower, which was planted with flowers and creepers against the walls.
83. The cry of a heron, the low chugging of a stalwart fishing boat, and the far off barking of a startled, indignant dog, all lulled me into a sense of well being.
84. Whale blubber which tastes badly to you and I is a rare delicacy to the northern native.
85. The audience also sees how upset Hamlet is of the recent marriage of his mother to his uncle.
86. To some people, such an idea is considered to be a step forward towards a better future.
87. Lunch on Saturdays were my favourite, as Mom had always made a special effort to make it more interesting.
88. "Well, Chester, what do you think?" asked the salesman—which struck me as being just too chummy, our not having been formally introduced.
89. The golf tee, simplistic as it may be, is well designed to effectively achieve its specific function.
90. My mother turned my brother and I out spick and span, shorts and suspenders, when she sent us off to school.
91. Although the ethnic backrounds of the settlers of both countries is basically the same, the influence of British traditions in Canada has allowed our government system to remain distinct from that of the United States.
92. Unfortunately, the director prefers to evoke his own vanished childhood than to explore the protagonist's moral and psychological dilemma.
93. Paranoia is a mental illness where the person believes that he is being

exercises

persecuted by others.

94. Maintenance of both the home and the garden, household duties, and small children require enormous amounts of energy from an individual.

95. These computers have large amounts of storage space, ranging from 64k to 128k of Random Access Memory, which gives it the power to handle the large programs so essential for modern business management.

96. This speech indicates how the character feels at the present situation.

97. He's ran that putt at least six feet past the hole.

98. Both have the same fate awaiting for them; namely death.

99. Fugitive slaves travelled on the underground railroad alone or in groups of up to thirty in one case.

100. When the police came they didn't arrive with lights flashing and sirens blaring; rather they stole into the grounds stealthily.

Here are ten more sentences, most slightly longer or more complicated than the others, that invite more drastic or thoroughgoing revision.

1. The fact that there are many people who I can relate to, adds to a sense of security for me because I feel that I am liked and I have a position with them in society, which enhances my self-identity.

2. Further implications for disaster in postponing the driving experience to a later age could be encountered in those people wishing to use the car as their primary means of transportation to work or a post-secondary institution.

3. The poem mentions statues, pictures, and stairways, all of these seem to enable the reader to picture Prufrock better and the people he associates with.

4. An older person has already made a lot of mistakes in their life and sharing their mistakes with new generations will keep from every generation having to start from a beginning.

5. I am still not sure whether or not I did the right thing about coming here but everyone thought it was, so here I am.

6. Some people may view Hamlet as a feeble, gutless young man who can't make up his mind about anything and this is what I believed at first. But by reading the play carefully and by observing Hamlet's actions this can't be true.

7. A hobby is often a nice way to relax or to just sit down and read a favourite novel or listen to some music, anything, just as long as it is relaxing.

8. I'm lucky to live in a great country, have a family who I love and am loved in return, have caring relations, acquaintances, and the opportunity to meet strangers who may someday be friends.

9. With no increase in salaries, increased teaching loads, and cutbacks in research facilities, faculty is starting to slip away. The university has already lost at least seven faculty members since January, and there are strong indications of many more to come.

10. By portraying the Queen as being blind to the situation of hate between Hamlet and the King, and the fact that she does not seem to even consider the fact that the King killed her previous husband, the audience's attitude toward the King is made even stronger.

VIII

ELEMENTS AND PRINCIPLES OF COMPOSITION

In earlier chapters we discuss the primary units of communication—sentences—and the fundamental elements of expression that make up sentences, namely words, phrases, and clauses. To be effective, a sentence must be unified and coherent, and its parts must be arranged so that its emphasis is clear (see **18**, **28**, and **31**). These principles apply also to the paragraph and to the essay as a whole. Just as words go together to make up sentences, so sentences go together to make up paragraphs, and paragraphs go together to make up larger units of communication: stories, chapters, or—our main concern here—essays.

In this chapter we discuss the principles of composition as they apply to paragraphs and essays, and we provide a step-by-step guide to the process of planning and writing an essay.

61   Kinds of Paragraphs

We classify paragraphs in two ways: (a) according to the function of a particular paragraph in its larger context, and (b) according to the kind of material it contains and the way that material is developed.

61a   Functions of Paragraphs: Substantive and Nonsubstantive

Some paragraphs are especially designed to begin or end an essay or to provide bridges or links between other paragraphs in the body of an essay. These are **introductory** paragraphs, **concluding** paragraphs, and **transitional** paragraphs. When they do no more than perform such functions, such paragraphs are called **nonsubstantive**. They perform important structural and rhetorical functions, but they do not contribute significantly to the ideas that make up the substance of the essay. All other paragraphs in an essay—those that carry the freight, so to speak—are **substantive** paragraphs.

Introductory and concluding paragraphs, and occasionally even transitional paragraphs, can also contribute to the development of a topic; when they do they are of course partly substantive; but their principal functions are to begin, end, and bridge. Often, in fact, the most effective beginnings and endings are not separate paragraphs but only a sentence or two, or even just part of a sentence, at the beginning or end of an otherwise substantive paragraph. (See **84**, the sample research paper, paragraphs 1 and 22, 5 and 14.)

61b   Kinds of Substantive Paragraphs: Methods of Development

Only substantive paragraphs can be classified according to the way their material is developed. There are several methods of development to choose from. The one or more you elect to use for any given paragraph (or whole essay) will largely be determined by the nature of your topic and by your audience and your purpose.

For example if you want your readers to *visualize* a scene that you found interesting, or entrancing, or frightening, or exhilarating, you will **describe** it with words and sentence structures that communicate your feelings.

If, however, you want to provide an *account* of the day on which you came across that scene, you will **narrate** a sequence of events.

Or you might want to focus on how you happened to be where you came upon the scene; you could then construct a paragraph working from *cause* to *effect* or, conversely, from *effect* back to *cause*.

If your purpose is to enable your readers to *understand why* you reacted to the scene as you did, you will explain the reasons; that is, you will again deal with **cause and effect**.

Or you might decide to try to *explain* the particular effects of the scene by **analyzing** it, examining its elements—colours, shapes, the quality of light, the arrangement of its parts.

If you want to show how the scene or experience is similar to or different from one or more other scenes or experiences familiar to you or your readers, you can try **comparing and contrasting** their features.

Or you might decide to illuminate your experience by drawing an extended comparison to some other experience familiar to your readers; you would then be using **analogy**—that is, finding enough points of similarity between two wholes to persuade a reader that the two wholes themselves are similar.

61c   **Expository Writing and the Methods of Development**

If you merely narrate an event, you will in effect be telling a story. But most often you will be asked—and will want—to write an **essay** that explains or argues something: that is, you will be doing what is called **expository** writing, writing which "exposes" ideas and meanings for one purpose or another. The methods of development listed above are among those most commonly used in expository writing, or *exposition*. Others are **definition, classification, process analysis,** and the use of **examples and illustrations** to explain or support a point.

Further, these methods of development are seldom mutually exclusive. Two or more such methods are often combined in a single paragraph (or in an essay as a whole). Even narration may be used in an expository essay: for example a "story" may serve as an example or illustration, or an anecdote may be used as an analogy, or a full-length narrative of personal experience may lead to an expository point. Narration itself almost always includes some description. When you are comparing or contrasting, you are also necessarily classifying and defining. And almost any method can be thought of as the supplying of **details** to clarify or back up an assertion made early in a paragraph or an essay. As long as you maintain the fundamental requirements of *unity* and *coherence* (see **63-69**), you can mix and combine these methods in any way that will be effective.

61d-j   **Examples of Paragraphs Using Different Methods of Development**

The following are examples of substantive paragraphs using several of the different methods of development listed above. Each was composed as a self-contained unit, but since they all deal with the same subject, you might want to consider how, with a little judicious editing to avoid repetition, and with the introduction of some transitions, such a collection of paragraphs could be arranged and combined to form a more extensive discussion of the subject than a single paragraph allows—to form, in other words, a full-fledged essay. (We have numbered the sentences of the following paragraphs in order to facilitate later references to them.)

61d   **Description**

(1) One evening last October, after a day of hiking in the area east of the Sechelt Inlet, a friend and I arrived at a vantage point and confronted a spectacular display of nature's magnificence. (2) Across the inlet the Sechelt Peninsula lay like a long thin body stretched out in repose, darkly delineated against the sky. (3) The sun, just sunk behind the forested tops of the hills, was playing colourful music on the clouds that streaked the western horizon, chords of intermingled green and white and salmon-red, with a highlight or two of purple. (4) At the foot of the hills, the

61d *description*

waters of the inlet were as smooth as glass, broodingly black in the deep shadows; but near our shore, ruffled by a light breeze, they still sparkled with dancing light. (5) To the north the eastern and western shores of the inlet converged at the Skookumchuk Narrows, and beyond that seeming fusion the mountains of the Coast Range rose in varying shades of blue, ridge after ridge, their contours softened by the fading light. (6) At the furthest point a row of snowy peaks defined the horizon. (7) Looking southward over Porpoise Bay at the foot of the inlet, we could see the first feeble electric twinkles, faint in the lingering twilight, from the nearby marina and, beyond it, the small town of Sechelt settling in for another evening. (8) In the silence so filled with beauty, gazing from one end of this vista to the other, I imagined that, like Wordsworth near Tintern Abbey, I could hear "the still, sad music of humanity."

61e Narration

(1) The view of the Sechelt Inlet that my friend and I experienced one evening last October was the spectacular climax to a long day filled with petty events. (2) We started from Gibsons on our bicycles about 6:30 a.m., and all went smoothly until we reached Davis Bay, where John's rear tire suffered a puncture. (3) It took us over an hour to put his bike back in working order, what with patching the tire, re-adjusting the brakes and gears, and getting the wheel centred and straight between the forks. (4) But eventually we hit the road again, and soon reached Sechelt. (5) We left our bikes at a gas-station and set off on foot, looking for the trail that our map said would take us to Claholm Lake. (6) We never did find it; for some reason it wasn't where it was supposed to be. (7) We soon tired of walking along the power-line and turned off on what looked like a logging road that headed west. (8) But after only a mile or so it petered out and left us floundering through a heavy underbrush of salmonberry and salal. (9) We kept heading west, toward the setting sun, knowing that eventually we would have to reach the ridge east of the inlet, but in that dense forest we still felt pretty lost. (10) The going was difficult, and the late-afternoon heat and a few buzzing flies and mosquitoes added to our discomfort. (11) I began to think we would never get out. (12) Darkness was already falling and we were feeling rather desperate when, suddenly, we found ourselves on an open bluff overlooking the inlet, and were rewarded with a scene of breathtaking beauty.

61f Cause and Effect: Narration

(1) If I hadn't gone to see my friend John one afternoon when I was feeling bored with life, I wouldn't have come across the most spectacular and moving scene I've ever experienced. (2) I found John studiously bent over a map of the southwest part of B.C. (3) He told me that he wanted to explore the wilderness east and north of Sechelt, and that he was going to have a try at it later that week. (4) He pointed to where the map showed a trail that took off from the power-line just north of the town and ended at Claholm Lake, near the top of Salmon Inlet. (5) I swear his eyes lighted

up from inside, and his rusty hair seemed to give off sparks. (6) "Why don't you come along?" (7) Without thinking, and responding as much to my own boredom as to his enthusiasm, I said "Why not!" (8) That's how I came to find myself, one evening last October, looking at a stunningly magnificent scene, one I'll never forget.

61g Cause and Effect: Explanation

(1) One day last October I was moved almost to tears when I suddenly came upon a natural scene of great beauty. (2) The experience made me wonder, afterward, why beauty sometimes affects people so profoundly. (3) One reason, I decided, is that when we respond to something surpassingly beautiful we sense for a moment that it embodies our hopes not only for ourselves but for everyone, the goal of all our endeavours. (4) True beauty—a rare enough thing in our lives—seems somehow to be an actualization of human hopes, a visual symbol of what we are all striving for. (5) But especially when one encounters it unexpectedly and yet has time to contemplate it, one sees not only its desirability but also its intangibility and impermanence, its remoteness, its essential unattainableness. (6) All this will no doubt strike you as odd and overblown unless you've experienced something like it yourself, but such an encounter does, somehow, include both pleasure and pain; it can provide one of the most intense emotional (some would say spiritual) experiences human beings are capable of. (7) I think Keats was right when he suggested that beauty's powerful effect on us is largely the result of our own subliminal realization that "in the very temple of Delight, / Veil'd Melancholy has her sovran shrine."

61h Cause and Effect: Analysis

(1) It is difficult to understand why we respond to beauty the way we do. (2) I do know, however, that I was profoundly moved by the majesty and peace and colour and silence and substance of the scene I came upon when I broke out of the bush one evening after a long and uncomfortable afternoon. (3) What I saw was a seemingly normal, postcard-like combination of mountain masses, still and gently moving waters, open sky, sunset colours, darkening shadows, and—far off—some flickering signs of human presence. (4) Yet something beyond mere postcard magic was working. (5) No doubt relief from the discomfort and worry of our afternoon's wanderings in a strange wilderness contributed to my reaction. (6) But when I thought about it later, I couldn't isolate any single element as the cause of my response, which was both ecstatic and melancholy. (7) I think that somehow, at that precise moment, "all the mighty world of eye, and ear" had come together and engaged all my senses at once: the soft, muted glow of the sunset on one side, the sombre shadows on the other; there the open sky, here the deep enfolding forest; to the right the shadings of blue creating their miles-long vista, to the left the shadows sparsely twinkling with faint lights. (8) Here too were the warm smell of fir and cedar recently baked by the sun, and the cool, crisp sea-air borne

up to us by the evening breeze; the almost palpable silence of the visible world and the pounding of my own heart; the black and silver rippling of the water; the vaulted sky above the solid earth—a chaos of contrasts that in some mysterious way was fused into a unity that worked its way into the depths of my sensibilities. (9) But however hard I try to understand and explain such an experience, I find myself falling back on the unscientific term "miracle" to account for my reaction to such beauty.

61i Comparison and Contrast

(1) If you've lived all your life on the prairies, as I have, you will find the scenery of the west coast startlingly different from what you're used to. (2) I know I was quite unprepared for the impact of a particular scene I came upon one evening last October when I was holidaying in B.C. (3) The elements—earth, air, water, and fire—were the same as those that constitute prairie landscapes, but their combination on the coast that day was like a different world, a world the plainsdweller never sees. (4) The main difference was that of the undulating surface of the earth and of the vegetation that covered it. (5) Instead of endless flatland, here were rank upon rank of mountains; in place of fields of waving green or golden wheat, here were vast forests of tall and stately hemlocks, firs, and cedars, and beneath the trees a thick, almost impenetrable undergrowth of salal, thimbleberries, blackberries, salmonberries, scrub alder, and devil's club. (6) Here the evening sun reflected off rippling water rather than off fields of grain. (7) Instead of a single seemingly limitless expanse of prairie, here we had sombre shadows enclosed by the bases of dark blue mountains rising out of the deep waters. (8) The horizon was not simply a straight line, but a line that followed the heights of the mountains and plunged into the clefts dividing them. (9) For anyone east of the ridge the sun had already set, but on the west side people could bask in its warmth for another hour; on the prairies the sun sets for all at the same time. (10) I am sure that these differences contributed to the profound effect that scene had on my prairie-nurtured sensibilities.

61j Analogy

(1) After spending a long, hot, mosquito-filled afternoon bulling my way through thorny stems and clutching tendrils of undergrowth in a darkly canopied forest, I reacted powerfully when I suddenly emerged onto an open bluff and was treated to a panoramic view of nature's splendour extending for miles to right and left. (2) Imagine Keats's "stout Cortez" slashing his way with his men through the steaming jungles of the Isthmus of Panama, struggling agonizingly through the dense unknown. (3) And then imagine, as Keats did, how it must have felt when at last the exhausted band reached the other side of the formidable barrier and looked out upon the seemingly limitless Pacific, and stood gazing, awed into silence and "a wild surmise." (4) If you can imagine that, you will understand something of how I felt when, on an admittedly less historic occasion, I stood gazing awe-struck at the view from that bluff above the Sechelt Inlet.

62   Definition of a Paragraph: Unity, Coherence, Emphasis

A paragraph may of course be a unit complete in itself—a short letter or memo, for example, or a one-paragraph "essay." But paragraphs are most often parts of larger wholes. Such paragraphs may be defined as follows: A paragraph is a sentence or a group of sentences, conventionally marked by indention, that performs a particular rhetorical function in an extended piece of writing. It may introduce, conclude, or connect (nonsubstantive); or it may develop one idea or one part of one idea (substantive). All paragraphs, but especially substantive paragraphs, in order to be effective, must have **unity, coherence,** and properly controlled **emphasis**.

63   Paragraph Unity

Note, in the definition above, the emphasis on *oneness*: one function, one idea, one part of one idea. An effective paragraph deals with one theme; its singleness of purpose engages readers' minds, focussing their attention on that theme. If you allow a paragraph to be disrupted by irrelevant digressions or unnecessary shifts in point of view or focus, readers will lose the thread of your discourse. You will confuse them—and lose them.

Consider the sample descriptive paragraph above (**61d**). The opening sentence announces both what the paragraph is going to talk about and the writer's attitude toward it: "a spectacular arrangement of nature's magnificence." This opening sentence arouses certain expectations; a reader expects to find an enthusiastic description of a natural scene. That is, the opening makes an implicit *promise* to the reader; to be unified, the rest of the paragraph must fulfill that promise.

And it does. Each sentence after the first provides some element of the natural scene. Sentences 2 and 3 present details of the view to the west, directly in front of the viewer: the land mass, the sunset sky. In sentence 4 the writer pulls back toward the east, mentioning first the dark water in the shadow of the land and then the lighted water nearer at hand. Sentence 5 shifts the eye northward, where we look up the inlet toward the mountains in the distance. And sentence 6 brings that view to a stop at the snowy peaks. In sentence 7 we turn (with the writer) to the south, where faint lights announce the presence of human creatures in the natural setting. Finally, in the concluding sentence the writer brings all the elements together with the reference to Wordsworth and the well-known phrase from "Tintern Abbey." The promise of the opening sentence has been fulfilled: the paragraph describes the scene, enthusiastically, and moves toward a climax focussing on the nature of the writer's reaction to the scene.

The paragraph has **unity** because every sentence in it contributes to its purpose and because nothing in it is irrelevant to that purpose. It is like a tidy, well-wrapped package that will reach its destination without coming apart.

64-69 Paragraph Coherence

64 Coherence: What It Is and How To Achieve It

But though our paragraph-package has a homogeneous substance—is unified because every sentence contributes to the development of its single theme or idea—it could still come apart if it didn't have another essential quality: **coherence.**

Coherence is sticking-togetherness. It is achieved by packing the contents of a paragraph carefully and by using strong enough paper and string to hold everything together.

You can achieve coherence in your writing by

(a) carefully organizing your material and
(b) using the mechanical devices that create structural cohesion.

65 Organization

A substantive paragraph must have a *beginning*, a *middle*, and an *ending*. As writer, you must make sure the beginning adequately introduces the theme, that the middle clearly and logically follows from and develops that statement of theme, and that the ending is a natural conclusion unobtrusively closing the discussion—and perhaps also, in a larger context, providing a hook for the next paragraph to link onto. (For example, the last sentence of the section on unity, above, points forward in the phrase "without coming apart" to the discussion of coherence in the next section. But see the **Caution** below, under **66b**.)

Good organization means rational order. In the sample descriptive paragraph discussed above, for example, the writer begins with a "promise" and then fulfills it by first describing what is in front at a distance, then what is closer, then what is to the right (moving toward the distance), then what is to the left (again moving toward the distance), and then concluding with a sentence that in a natural and all-embracing way takes into account what has gone before and gives it meaning. The order of presentation follows the logical movement of the writer's eye and mind.

■ 66 ■ The Beginning

■ 66a ■ Topic Sentences

Most substantive paragraphs open with an explicit statement of theme, called a **topic sentence**. (Purely nonsubstantive paragraphs do not have topic sentences, though often introductory, concluding, and even transitional paragraphs may have them, depending on the extent to which they are also serving as substantive paragraphs.)

■ 66b ■ Functions of Topic Sentences

A good opening topic sentence performs the specific function of announcing what the paragraph will be about. As we say earlier, it is in effect a *promise* that the rest of the paragraph must make good.

If the paragraph is part of a larger context, such as an essay, the topic sentence should also perform two other functions:

(a) It should refer explicitly to the overall subject of the essay and at least suggest the relation of the paragraph to that subject.
(b) It should provide a transition so that the new paragraph flows smoothly from the preceding paragraph.

Caution: It is sometimes possible, but almost always difficult and risky, to provide forward-looking material at the end of a paragraph. If such material occurs naturally, well and good; but do not struggle to get something transitional into the last sentence of a paragraph. The work of transition should be done by the first sentence of the next paragraph. Tampering with a paragraph's final sentence merely for transitional purposes usually destroys that paragraph's integrity and effectiveness.

■ 66c ■ Efficiency of Topic Sentences

A good opening topic sentence, like other sentences, should be efficient. Here is one that is not:

> The poet uses a great deal of imagery throughout the poem.

The sentence announces the topic—the poem's imagery—but promises nothing more than to show that the poem contains a lot of it. All the writer can do is make a long list of images. But that would not develop an idea; it would merely illustrate in a boring way what should be self-evident. The writer would have nothing to say, the reader nothing to think. Trying to revise this weak topic sentence, the student inserted the adjective *good* before *imagery*; now the paragraph must at least try to show that the abundant images are *good* ones (not so easy a task as the writer may have thought). But the focus is still largely on the quantity of imagery, which is not where the focus should be. What is most important is the imagery's function: What does the poet *do* with the imagery? A little thought might lead to a revision like this—a topic sentence that is *efficient*, that not only has more substance in itself but also suggests the approach the paragraph will take:

> The poem's imagery, most of it drawn from nature, helps to create not only the poem's mood but its theme as well.

The same essay also contained the following inefficient topic sentence:

> In the second stanza the poet continues to use images.

The feeble revision didn't help much:

> In the second stanza the poet continues to use excellent images to express his ideas.

Again, what is needed is something sharper, more specific—an assertion that provides a significant idea that can usefully be talked about, developed. For example:

> The imagery in the second stanza contrasts vividly with that of the first.

or

> In the second stanza images of death begin the process that leads to the poem's ironic conclusion.

A good opening topic sentence should be more than just a label on a box; it should itself be a significant part of the contents of the box. It pays to give close attention to the formulation of your topic sentences, for they can help you achieve both *unity* and *coherence* not only in individual paragraphs but also in an essay as a whole (see **72a**).

On the placement of topic sentences, see **67c**.
See also *A Note on Beginnings*, **73-l**.

67 The Middle

67a Coherence Through Orderly Development

A well-developed substantive paragraph fulfills the promise of its beginning. If for example you were writing a paragraph that began with the last example of a topic sentence above, you would have to explain "the process" and the irony of the poem's conclusion, and you would have to *show* (not merely assert) how images of death from the second stanza set that process in motion. To fulfill your promise effectively, then, you would have to decide how to organize your material, what *order* to present it in. Ask yourself, "What will I do first? What next?" and so on. You might decide, for example, first to describe the irony of the conclusion and then to analyze the images to show how they lead to that conclusion. Or you might decide to start by analyzing the death imagery and then proceed to answer some questions that you could ask yourself: What effect do the images create? How does that effect contribute to the way the poem proceeds? How does that process lead to the conclusion? In other words, you would be *choosing* a way of presenting your material; and the order you choose to follow should be one that makes sense: one idea should lead logically to another until you reach your goal. Then your paragraph will be coherent.

67b Patterns of Development

Orderly development often occurs automatically, of course, as one works through one's ideas in composing paragraphs and essays. But often, too—especially for relatively inexperienced writers—it pays to give some conscious thought to just how a particular paragraph (or essay) can best be shaped. The most common patterns of development writers use to make sure their paragraphs are orderly and coherent are the following:

> chronological
> spatial
> moving from general to specific or abstract to concrete (see **54** and Exercise 54[1])
> moving from specific to general or concrete to abstract
> moving from simple to complex, small to large, minor to major
> rising to a climax
> moving from negative to positive (or vice versa)
> moving from question to answer
> logical progression

Further, some of the *methods* of development discussed above (**61b-c**) themselves impose patterns on the arrangement of ideas in a paragraph. In addition to using narration, with its chronological order (perhaps including a flashback or two), or description, with its spatial order, one can move from cause to effect or from effect to cause, or from a statement about a whole to a division of it into its parts (analysis), or from a statement about one thing to a comparison of it with another thing.

Similarly, as with the methods of development, these patterns are not mutually exclusive. For example if you are moving from small to large or minor to major, you are likely also rising to a climax. Even if you are narrating, and therefore following a generally chronological order, you are probably also telling your story in such a way that the reader's interest will mount as you move through a sequence of events until you finally provide the climax.

Look once again at the sample paragraphs above; you can see several of these patterns of development operating in them:

Description (61d)

In this paragraph the writer uses a *spatial* organization, a natural movement from west (straight ahead, as the view was first seen) to north
(right) to south (left). The description also moves from *general* ("a
spectacular display of nature's magnificence") to *specific* (all the subsequent detailed descriptions of the elements that create the general
impression). And the writer also injects a dramatic note, rising from
the visual experience to an intellectual or spiritual *climax*. Note that
there is also a touch of *comparison*, or *analogy*, in the closing reference
to Wordsworth.

Narration (61e)

The paragraph begins with a sentence suggesting the entire time span
("a long day"), the substance of the narrative ("filled with petty events"),
and the nature of the conclusion ("spectacular climax"). The paragraph
then recounts the events in *chronological* sequence from early morning
until just after sunset. Along the way it injects some suspense and
other dramatic preparation (the hour's delay over the flat tire, the
unlocated trail, "floundering," "dense forest," "lost," "discomfort,"
"never get out") for the "climax" ("suddenly," "breathtaking"). The
paragraph thus also uses the pattern of *rising to a climax*.

Cause and Effect: Explanation (61g)

Here the writer is explaining something rather involved and abstract,
and is obviously trying to clarify it all by moving carefully from idea
to idea in a *logical progression*, a pattern partly made up here of a
movement from *question to answer*, both explicit ("wonder . . . why,"
"One reason") and implicit. The elements of the answer are linked
with words that indicate the progress of thought ("I decided," "True,"
"But," "no doubt," "I think"). And the ending, restating the answer
in a well-known and concentrated poetic utterance, makes the abstract
concrete by way of metaphor.

67c   A Note on the Placement of Topic Sentences

In the great majority of paragraphs, as in each of the examples above
(**61d-j**), the development fulfills the promise made in an opening topic
sentence. But occasionally, by conscious design, a topic sentence may
be placed at the end or even elsewhere in a paragraph. Sometimes
delaying a topic sentence can increase readers' interest by creating a
little mystery or suspense to get them to read on. And stating a topic
at the end of a paragraph takes advantage of that most emphatic position
(see **70**). Note for example our paragraph above labelled *Coherence
Through Orderly Development* (**67a**). The label of course identifies the
topic, which has two elements; but the paragraph itself refers only to
"development" until the end, where the short last sentence explicitly

ties it all to the idea of coherence. That *part* of the topic, in other words, we delayed until the end, or climax.

A paragraph's topic, then, though single, may consist of more than one part. Similarly, it may not get stated all in one sentence. In this paragraph and in the preceding paragraph, for example, note that not until the end of the *second* sentence is the topic fully clear. It is not uncommon for a paragraph to have a second topic sentence, one that partly restates the topic and partly leads into the body of the paragraph.

And—rarely—a paragraph's topic may not be stated at all, but only implied. Occasionally the focal idea of a paragraph is so clearly and strongly implied that it would seem an insult to the reader's intelligence to state it baldly. Another kind of paragraph without a topic sentence often occurs in narratives, or in essays where a strong narrative element is present: sometimes a strong topic sentence can effectively govern two or three paragraphs, though the succeeding paragraphs must begin in such a way that their continuing relation to the preceding paragraph is sufficiently clear—perhaps indicated by no more than an opening *Then* or *When*.

But don't strain for these unusual kinds of paragraph. If they occur in your writing naturally, they will probably be all right; but always check them carefully to make sure they're clear and effective. The topic-sentence-first paragraph is the most common because it is the most natural, clear, and effective. Rest satisfied with that kind unless you have good reason to depart from it.

68   The Ending

As you compose and revise your drafts, the endings of your paragraphs will often come naturally, without your having to think about them—but they are likely to do so only if you know, when you begin a paragraph, just where it is going; that is, your paragraphs will be unified and coherent, their endings implicit or even explicit in their beginnings. The concluding sentence, like all the others, should be an organic part of the whole paragraph (see the **Caution** under **66b**).

Examine the sample paragraphs (**61d-j**). Note that in each one the final sentence is a *summation* (*not* a mere *summary*) growing out of the substance of the paragraph, a sentence that brings the topic to a clear and natural finish in an unobtrusive way. Each final sentence rounds off its paragraph in such a way that readers get the feeling of a satisfying close.

If one of your paragraphs does not seem to be ending naturally, you may have to stop and think consciously about it. Here are a few pointers to help you do that:

1. A good ending may point back to the beginning, but it will not merely repeat it; if it repeats something, it will do so in order to put it in the new light made possible by the development of the paragraph.

2. Usually, avoid writing a separate final sentence merely for the sake of concluding a paragraph. Above all, don't begin such a sentence with a stiff, obtrusive "In conclusion," or "Thus we see that . . . ." Sometimes, indeed, the best way to end a paragraph is simply to let it stop, once its point is made. A too-explicit conclusion will often seem tacked-on, anticlimactic, destroying the effectiveness of an otherwise good paragraph. To maintain coherence, the ending of a paragraph should be as much a functional and organic part of the whole as is the tail of a whale.

3. Sometimes a slight stylistic shift is all that's necessary to mark a paragraph's ending, perhaps no more than an unusually short or long sentence. Note for example how the endings of sample paragraphs **61d** and **61g** incorporate quotations from poetry.

4. As a rule, it is poor tactics to end a paragraph with an indented and single-spaced quotation, or even a full sentence of quotation. Even though you carefully introduce such a quotation, if you leave it dangling at the end it will almost inevitably leave a "so what?" feeling in the reader's mind, or a feeling that you have abandoned your paragraph to someone else. Always complete such a paragraph with at least a brief comment that explains the quotation, justifies it, or re-emphasizes its main thrust. (See for example paragraph 21 of the sample research paper, **84**.)

69 Structural Coherence

Careful organization and development go a long way toward achieving coherence. But you will need to use other techniques, as well, in order to ensure this all-important requirement of good writing. These techniques are mechanical; they enable you to provide sentences with links to ensure a smooth flow of thought from one sentence to the next.

Composing a paragraph is like fashioning a wooden box or a cupboard. You cut your pieces to size, making sure they're square-cornered and that the joints fit together. You can then assemble the pieces and reveal the final product as a well-designed and functional unit. But its *coherence* isn't assured until you nail, screw, or glue the pieces together. In this section we discuss the ways of attaching the pieces (sentences) to each other so that the assembled parts make a solid whole. Or, to return to our earlier figure of speech, we're putting the wrapping paper and string on our parcel so that even the postal service would have to deliver it intact.

The main devices for structural coherence are parallelism, repetition, pronouns and demonstrative adjectives, and transitional words and phrases. Like the methods and patterns of development, these devices are not mutually exclusive. Two or more may work together in the same paragraph, sometimes even in the same words and phrases.

69a Parallelism

Parallel sentence structure is a simple and effective way to bind sentences together. Similar structural patterns in successive clauses and phrases work like a call and its echo, or echoes. But note that the echoes diminish in power as they get farther from the original. Parallelism, like any other device, should not be overdone, or like the fading echo it will cease to be effective.

Look again at the sample paragraphs. In sentences 5, 6, and 7 of paragraph **61i**, with some variations to avoid a too-monotonous repetition of words and patterns, the similar structures echo each other, giving an even flow to the passage:

> Instead of . . . here were
> in place of . . . here were
> Here . . . rather than
> Instead of . . . here we had

In paragraph **61h**, note in sentences 7 and 8 the parallel series of contrasted elements:

> glow . . . on one side, . . . shadows on the other
> there . . . here
> to the right . . . to the left
> the warm smell . . . and the cool, crisp sea-air
> the . . . silence . . . and the pounding
> the black and silver
> the vaulted sky above the solid earth

In paragraph **61j** there is an example of parallel imperative verbs in sentences 2 and 3:

> Imagine . . . And then imagine . . .

In the "Description" paragraph (**61d**) there is a subtler, quieter parallelism running from sentence 2 through sentence 8; each sentence opens with either a prepositional or a participial phrase:

> Across the inlet
> The sun, just sunk behind the forested top of the hills,

At the foot of the hills,
To the north
At the furthest point
Looking southward over Porpoise Bay at the foot of the inlet,
In the silence so filled with beauty, gazing from one end of this vista to
the other,

Note that for a little variety sentence 3 lets the brief subject—"The sun"—come first, and that some of the phrases are not followed by a comma. And note that the next-to-last sentence begins with a participial phrase followed by three prepositional phrases, and that the final sentence, for stylistic climax to match the thematic climax, begins with a balanced combination of prepositional and participial phrases.

69b Repetition

Like parallelism, repetition links sentences together by forcing the reader to recall what came before, not by the similarity of sentence structure but by the repetition of words and phrases used earlier. Obviously the caution against overdoing is most applicable here. Repetition properly controlled for rhetorical effect can be powerful (Winston Churchill's "We will fight them" speech, Martin Luther King's "I had a dream" speech), but repetition can also become boring evidence of a writer's limited vocabulary or lack of verbal ingenuity. Structure your repetitions carefully; don't put too many too close together. And generally use the device sparingly.

In **69a** we point out the repetition, along with parallelism, in paragraph **61j**; there also is the repetition of *Keats* in sentences 2 and 3. In **61d**, *Inlet* in 1 is repeated in 2, 4, 5, and 7 (this is not to overdo it: given the circumstances, it is more natural to repeat the word *inlet* than to strain the context by trying to vary it with such terms as *fjord*, *body of water*, *reach*, and *arm of the sea*, for such variety would only confuse the reader; such artificial straining is called "elegant variation"—variation for its own sake—and is to be avoided just as much as unnecessary, dull repetition); the word *music* in 3 is picked up in the quotation at the end. In **61f** *John* occurs in 1 and 2, *map* in 2 and 4, *scene* in 1 and 8, and *bored* in 1 is picked up by *boredom* in 7. In **61g** the important thematic word *beauty* occurs in 1, 2, 3 (*beautiful*), 4, and 7. And so on; you can trace other instances of repetition for yourself.

69c Pronouns and Demonstrative Adjectives

By driving the reader's thoughts back to something mentioned before, a pronoun or a demonstrative adjective clearly constructs a bridge within the paragraph between itself and its antecedent or referent. (It is also possible of course to create similar links *between* paragraphs, but be careful, first, that there is an unambiguous antecedent or referent, and second, that you are not too far beyond it. If you are far from it, or if more than one is possible, you risk confusing your readers rather than building coherence for them. Either way, straight repetition is preferable.)

In paragraph **61d**, sentence 1 mentions the speaker ("I") and "a friend"; thereafter, the pronouns *our* (4) and *we* (7) refer to those two people, and *I* returns in 8. In **61e**, as one might expect, the phrase "my friend and I" in the topic sentence is recalled in every sentence that follows in the form of the pronouns *we*, *our*, and *us*. Also in that paragraph, the three *it*'s in sentence 6 refer to the *trail* in 5, and the *it* of 8 refers to the *logging road* of 7. In **61f** the repeated *John* of 1 and 2 is referred to by *he* and *his* in 3, 4, 5, and 7. In **61g** sentence 5 uses *it* and *its* to avoid over-repetition of the noun *beauty*. And so on.

Using the demonstratives (*this*, *that*, *these*, *those*) as adjectives is a similar way of building coherence, and it can add emphasis as well. In **61h** the phrase *that precise moment* in sentence 7 underlines the only vaguely suggested *when* of sentence 2. In sentence 3 of **61i**, *that day* points back to the *one evening* of the preceding sentence, and *that scene* in the final sentence refers emphatically to the *scene* of sentence 2. And *that bluff* near the end of **61j**, pointing back to the *open bluff* of sentence 1, helps tie together the beginning and the ending of the paragraph. In **61g** the word *such* in sentence 6 also functions as a demonstrative adjective, adding emphasis to *such an encounter*.

We emphasize the use of demonstratives as *adjectives* rather than as *pronouns*. As adjectives they are clear and they can add emphasis. As pronouns they are not emphatic; rather they can be weak and ambiguous (see **5c** and **28**). There are several demonstrative pronouns in our sample paragraphs, but they are not ambiguous—and they do of course contribute to coherence. See for example *That* in **61f**, sentence 8; *this* in **61g**, sentence 6; and *that* in the last sentence of **61j**.

69d transitional terms

69d   Transitional Terms

Transition, another kind of bridge between one element and another, is provided by particular words and phrases that relate sentences and parts of sentences to each other. Such terms create a logical flow from one idea to another by indicating their relation. Obviously one must choose the right transitional signal for a particular spot in order to create successful coherence; the transition must fit logically into the context. Here are some of the more common and useful transitional words and phrases:

Terms showing addition of one point to another:

    and, also, besides, moreover, another, in addition, further

Terms showing similarity between ideas:

> similarly, likewise, equally, in other words, in the same way, again

Terms showing differences between ideas:

> but, yet, however, nevertheless, despite, in spite of, on the other hand, still, though, although, even though, whereas, on the contrary, in contrast, otherwise, conversely

Terms showing cause and effect or other logical relations:

> because, for, since, as a result, consequently, therefore, then, thus, of course, hence

Terms introducing examples or details:

> for example, for instance, namely, to illustrate, that is, in particular, specifically

Terms expressing emphasis:

> especially, mainly, primarily, chiefly, indeed, more important

Terms showing relations in time and space:

> at the same time, simultaneously, while, meanwhile, later, earlier, subsequently, then, before, behind, nearby, in the distance, farther away, to the left, here, there, next

These and other such words and phrases, occurring usually at or near the beginnings of sentences, are the glue that helps hold paragraphs together. But if the paragraph isn't unified to begin with, and if its parts haven't been made and arranged so as to fit with each other, then even these explicit transitional terms can't do much good. Further, don't overdo such terms. If some other kind of coherence is already present, it won't need propping up with one of these. If a writer feels so insecure about coherence as to add a transitional word or phrase slavishly to nearly every sentence, whether it needs one or not, the writing will be stiff and awkward: the box will look ugly because globs of excess glue show at the joints.

See also **12**, **28**, and **33h**.

Exercise 64-69: Recognizing coherence

Point out the various means by which coherence is established in the following paragraph.

> Unlike those many modern countries which rose to nationhood out of tragic bloodbaths, Canada was built by men and women expressing the best qualities of human nature. It was built by the courage and stamina of explorers and their stalwart crews of *coureurs de bois* who allowed nothing to inhibit them.

69d   transitional terms

It was built by the staunch pioneering spirit and energy of those men and women who literally hacked homes out of the wilderness. It was built by the faith and determination of people who willingly gave the best that was in them to be free. Although blood was shed in the process of creating this nation, it owes its being, principally, not to lives lost in its cause but to lives lived in its cause.

---

70 ■ Emphasis in Paragraphs

Just as in a sentence, so in a paragraph the most emphatic position is its ending and the second most emphatic position is its beginning (see **18**). That is why the opening or topic sentence is so important a part of a paragraph. And an ending, because of its emphatic position, can make or break a paragraph.

But just as important as placement are structure and diction. Parallelism and repetition both create emphasis. Independent clauses are more emphatic than subordinate clauses. Precise, concrete, and specific words are more emphatic than vague, abstract, and general ones. A "big" word will stand out among plainer terms; a slang expression or colloquialism will stand out in the midst of formal diction. A long sentence will stand out among several shorter ones; a short sentence will stand out among longer ones. If you keep these points in mind as you compose and revise your paragraphs, you will be able to allow emphasis to contribute significantly to the effectiveness of your writing.

71 ■ Length of Paragraphs

There is of course no arbitrary optimum length for a paragraph. The length of a particular paragraph will be determined by the requirements of the particular job it is doing. In narration or dialogue especially, one word may constitute a paragraph. In complex exposition or argument, a paragraph may go on for a page or more—though such long paragraphs are rare in modern writing. Most substantive paragraphs, however, consist of at least three or four sentences, and seldom more than nine or ten. Transitional paragraphs are usually short, often only one sentence. Introductory and concluding paragraphs will be of various lengths, depending on the complexity of the material and on the techniques of beginning and ending that the writer is using.

Sometimes, if a particular point deserves special emphasis, it can be put into a one-sentence paragraph—like this one.

Normally, then, the paragraphs that make up a more extensive piece of writing will vary in length. If you find that you are writing many longish paragraphs, you may be overdeveloping, piling more into a paragraph than its topic requires. Or you may be rambling, not weeding out irrelevant material. Or you may be destroying unity by making one paragraph discuss two or more topics that should be dealt with in separate paragraphs.

71a   The Importance of Adequate Development

But the more common failing among inexperienced writers is to settle for paragraphs that are too short to develop their topics sufficiently. The body of a paragraph must be long enough to develop a topic well; merely restating or summarizing the topic is not enough. If you find yourself writing many short paragraphs, you may not be adequately developing your main ideas. Or you may be endangering coherence by splintering your discussion into small parts: when you revise, check to see if two or more related short paragraphs can be integrated to form one substantial paragraph.

Simply ensure that each of your paragraphs is as long or as short as it needs to be. And whatever their length, make sure that your paragraphs actually go somewhere rather than just tread water.

71b   Variety

Try also to ensure that any extended piece of writing you do contains a variety of paragraph lengths: long, short, medium. A constant similarity of paragraph lengths can be almost as tedious for a reader as a constant similarity of sentence lengths (see **17**). For the same reason, you should also try to provide a variety of patterns and methods in your paragraphs. For example parallelism, however admirable a device, would become tiresome if it were the basic pattern in several successive paragraphs.

Review Exercises: Working with paragraphs

1. Compose topic sentences that will effectively begin paragraphs on *five* of the following:
   (a) To explain to a ten-year-old how an internal-combustion engine works
   (b) To describe to the police a traffic accident you witnessed
   (c) To tell a friend about your experience of seeing an accident happen
   (d) To introduce an essay on the history of engines from steam to jet
   (e) To recount an anecdote about one of your relatives in order to illustrate his or her character
   (f) To describe your dream-house
   (g) To analyze a particular short poem
   (h) To explain why you are attending college or university
   (i) To introduce a short essay about something important you learned on your last holiday abroad
   (j) To explain what beauty means to you

2. Write paragraphs developing *two* of the topic sentences you composed for Exercise 1.

3. (a) Identify and illustrate the patterns and methods of development you used in writing each of the paragraphs for Exercise 2.
   (b) How did you ensure that your paragraphs are unified?
   (c) Identify and illustrate the techniques you used to make your paragraphs coherent.
   (d) What did you intend to achieve with your final sentence for each paragraph? How did you do it? Are your endings effective? If not, work on them until they are and then return to answer these questions.

4. Consider the following paragraph carefully and answer the questions that follow it.

Various incidents and circumstances led to my being where I was last October when I saw the most beautiful view I've ever seen. Before I went to the west coast for a holiday, I'd never even seen salt water. But my friend John, whom I'd grown up with and gone to school with, had moved to Vancouver from Saskatoon the year before, and every time he wrote he urged me to come. He never sounded the least bit homesick for the prairies. He always sounded very persuasive about the attractions of B.C. I would have been glad to see him again, but I had to keep things going on the farm, since Dad was laid up with arthritis. Dad and Mom both agreed that I needed a holiday. When my sister's husband lost his job in the city, they came home to the farm. That was last September, and Phil offered to look after the place if I wanted to take a holiday. I phoned John to tell him I was coming, and arranged to stay with Aunt Nora in Burnaby. She'd lived there for fifteen years, and was delighted that I was finally coming for a visit. John was equally enthusiastic. Anyway, all that got me to the coast. I liked it well enough, but after a couple of weeks I began to feel bored. Maybe I was getting homesick. One afternoon John asked me to come with him on a hike in the wilderness near Sechelt, and I agreed. That's how I came to be standing on a bluff enjoying a magnificent sunset view across Sechelt Inlet.

(a) What is the topic sentence? Is it an effective one? Is there more than one?
(b) Does the paragraph fulfill the "promise" of the beginning? How, or how not?
(c) What makes or mars the coherence of the paragraph? Is it unified?
(d) What pattern(s) and method(s) of development does it use?
(e) Is this a good paragraph? Why, or why not?

5. Compose an essay using the sample paragraphs and the paragraph in Exercise 4 as your material. You may use as much of the language of these sources as you wish, but edit as necessary to avoid unwanted repetition. Decide on your theme or purpose, discard whatever is inappropriate to that purpose, and arrange the rest in a reasonable sequence. Make sure your essay has a good beginning, a well-developed middle, and an effective ending. Build transitions between your paragraphs.

6. Here are a dozen substantive paragraphs from essays written by students. They range in quality from good to poor. Analyze and evaluate each one

exercises

(you may wish to assign grades to them). Consider specifically each of the principles discussed in the text:

methods of development
unity
coherence (organization; placement and effectiveness of topic sentences; patterns of development; effectiveness of endings; devices of structural coherence)
emphasis
length and adequacy of development

and anything else you think relevant. For example, does each paragraph make a promise and then fulfill it? When you are through analyzing, evaluating, and criticizing, practise your own writing skills by revising at least the weaker paragraphs to get rid of their worst defects as paragraphs, and to make any other stylistic improvements you think are needed.

(a) Physical activity is good for people. It contributes greatly to a person's physical and mental well-being. The schedules of varsity teams are very demanding. The swim team has eleven practices a week, of which eight are mandatory—two a day, each an hour and a half in length. The workouts consist of approximately four thousand metres each. The program also consists of running, weight training, and flexibility exercises. Not only does this sort of exercise keep a person in good physical shape, but it also increases their mental awareness. Because you are up and active before classes begin, you are more mentally and physically awake than if you had just gotten out of bed.

(b) It was five generations ago when my paternal ancestors sailed over from Czechoslovakia to settle in the New World. My grandfather finds great joy in telling us about these early settlers. It seems they were very happy to establish themselves in this new "land of opportunities." They were able to purchase a large amount of good farming land near a lake in northern Ontario. Soon others came to settle nearby, and my great-great-grandparents were an integral part of this Canadian community. And Grandpa tells us that it was he and his brothers who built the hydroelectric dam to provide the electricity for this growing village. My grandmother taught in the local schoolhouse, and their children sold garden vegetables and worked as housekeepers for the growing number of Americans who were building summer houses by the lake. I think that the feeling of inferiority from having to work for these rich Americans reinforced my forebears' strong sense of Canadianism. These feelings have been passed on to my generation.

(c) Besides having stronger hearts, well-conditioned runners tend to have slender bodies. Running will only help you lose weight if the food consumption is controlled. Losing weight and maintaining your new weight at the appropriate level, however, depends on the proper balance between your intake of calories and your expenditure of energy.

(d) The storyteller makes use of animal metaphors to describe an individual's character by naming him after the animal whose stereotyped personality he possesses. The importance of living creatures in folk tales is twofold. First, the folk tale is used to teach the tribe's children the significance of individual species; and second, the use of animal names suggests a great deal about a character's personality.

exercises

(e) A cold, wet, west-coast winter's day. I was weary from cursing all day. I was wet and exasperated. My crew-truck had spent most of the day on a precarious tilt with two wheels down a bank (someone had tried to turn it around for me); I had it coaxed back onto the road just by quitting time. Now, at day's end, I wallowed in the warmth of its heater while waiting for the crew.

(f) In order to have control over his language, a writer must understand the denotation and connotation of words. This understanding becomes particularly important when two words are similar in meaning but are not truly synonymous. If such similar but not synonymous words are carelessly handled, the writer may grossly misuse them. This will have an adverse effect on the clarity of his work, and will probably mislead and confuse the reader. Misleading the reader is a pitfall to be avoided. This pitfall can only be avoided by the writer's understanding such words and using them carefully so as not to produce ambiguity.

(g) Although the words *ignorance* and *stupidity* are often used interchangeably, there is a difference between them. *Ignorance* is defined as lack of knowledge and *stupidity* is defined as lack of intelligence. To call a person ignorant implies that the person does not know all that is known or can be learned. To call a person stupid implies that the person lacks the ability to learn and know. The words are similar in that they both indicate a deficiency in knowledge or learning, but they differ in that one signifies a permanent condition and the other a condition that may be only temporary. Ignorant people can educate and inform themselves. Stupid people have a dullness of mind which it is difficult or impossible to change.

(h) I believe that Jean Piaget's research has clearly shown that games and rule-making contribute to child development. Children learn much about autonomy and democracy while testing the rules of games. In his early research he chose 1100 children along with the game of marbles to reach his conclusions. The choice of the game of marbles was a good one since it requires no referee and no adult supervision. It is played from early childhood to pre-teens. One six-year-old when asked who he thought had made the rules replied, "God, my father and the town council." At about eleven years children agree that they can change the rules themselves. Piaget has shown that the game of marbles provides a way for children to test the quality of rules and the necessity of rules.

(i) If you intend to go gold panning there are a certain number of items that should be included in your equipment. The most obvious is the gold pan. There are two types of gold pans. They are metal and plastic. Plastic pans are molded from tough space-age plastic. They are said to be better than metal pans because they don't rust and they are lighter. They also have small riffles formed in the plastic that effectively trap the gold. Metal pans are constructed from heavy gauge steel and vary in size from six to sixteen inches in diameter.

(j) Everything looks beautiful from the saddle of my horse, especially on a crisp fall day. Even the autumn sun as it glints through the fretwork of golden poplar trees that border the road. The track ahead is muddy and well-trampled by many horses' feet. I can hear the clatter of hooves on the concrete, then the soft sucking sound of the mud as we gain momentum and move out to begin our ride. After we gain considerable speed, it happens. That wondrous sensation when horse and rider

exercises

become one glorious moving body. I feel it now as my horse takes full rein while the blood surges and pounds in my ears and the wind frees my hair as it stings my face. Time ceases to exist here in a world of exhilarating revelation as I become giddy with pleasure. Tired, my horse slows down. The spell is broken. The sun has disappeared completely, and the wind is beginning to rise in bone-chilling forecast of the dreary winter days to come. I will be back again, soon.

(k) Many people are under the impression that the Driver Training Programs offered to sixteen- and seventeen-year-old students prepare them to be capable drivers. I found the program very useful, but then I was nearly eighteen when I received my licence. Some authorities on the subject believe that the programs give students a false sense of security—a very dangerous thing.

(l) Structurally, there are in the subject paragraph fourteen sentences of varying lengths; the shortest sentence, #12, has nine words, while the longest, #6, has fifty-two. The opening sentence contains twelve words, and from there on the sentences alternate from short to long through to the end of the paragraph. The paragraph ends, surprisingly, with another twelve-word sentence. The alternation or variance of sentence lengths helps to keep the paragraph interesting by keeping the rhythm varied and not letting tedious repetition set in.

72   Essays: Unity, Coherence, and Emphasis

The principles of composition apply with equal validity to the essay as a whole and to each of its parts: what holds true for the sentence and the paragraph also holds true for the essay as a whole.

72a   Unity

Like a sentence or a paragraph, an essay should be unified. That is, it should be about one subject, and everything in it should contribute to the elucidation of that subject. If your paragraphs themselves are coherent and unified, and if you make sure that the first sentence of each paragraph refers explicitly (or implicitly but unmistakably) to your overall subject (see **66b**), then your essay itself will be unified.

72b   Coherence

There should be coherence not only between words in sentences and between sentences in paragraphs, but also between the paragraphs in an essay. If you make sure that the beginning of each paragraph provides some kind of *transition* from the preceding paragraph, then your essay will be coherent. (Of course there must be an inherent connection between one paragraph and the next—a function of the *unity* of an essay—or not even explicit transitions will be effective.) The transitional words and phrases listed above (**69d**) and others like them are often useful for establishing the necessary connections between paragraphs. Or you can create the link by repeating a significant word or two from the preceding paragraph—usually from somewhere near its end—and sometimes you will strengthen the link by using a demonstrative adjective.

72c Emphasis

Just as in a sentence or a paragraph (see **18a** and **70**), the most emphatic position in an essay is its ending, and the second most emphatic position is its beginning. That is why it is important to be clear and to the point at the beginning of an essay, usually stating the thesis explicitly (see below, **73-I**), and why the ending of an essay should be forceful, not weakly dissipating the energy built up in the body of the essay. Don't, for example, conclude with mere flat repetition of the points you have just made. The last thing readers see is what will stick most vividly in their minds. For that reason essays often build to a climax, beginning with simple or less important points and ending with more important or complex ones.

Further, the length of a paragraph automatically suggests to a reader something about the importance of its contents. Although a short, sharp paragraph can be emphatic in its own way, generally a long paragraph will be devoted to a relatively important part of the subject; less important matters will be dealt with in shorter paragraphs. As you look over your work, check to make sure that you haven't given an important point short shrift—failed to develop it adequately— and also that you haven't rambled on at unnecessary length about a relatively minor point. The relative proportions of paragraphs should generally reflect the relative importance of the ideas they discuss.

73 The Steps of Planning and Writing an Essay

No effective essay can be a mere random assemblage of sentences and paragraphs. It must have a shape, a design, even if only a simple one. The minimum requirement is that it start somewhere and by an orderly process arrive somewhere else.

Try not to think of introductions and conclusions as "parts" of essays. In fact, in order to avoid the stiffness so often found in over-formal "Introductions" and "Conclusions," acquire the habit of calling them "Beginnings" and "Endings" instead, as we do in discussing the paragraph. You may then more easily avoid writing a stiff paragraph of "introduction" simply because you think it's called for, or starting a final paragraph with "In conclusion"; coming upon that phrase is like encountering a piece of bone sticking out through the skin.

It is the *body* of the essay that must be thought of as starting somewhere, proceeding through its development, and arriving some-

73 steps of composition

where else. How does one get from the zero of a blank mind to the desired finished product? By taking certain steps—for a piece of writing, like any other end product, is the result of a *process*. The steps that any writer must take, whether consciously or not, are these:

1. Finding a subject
2. Limiting the subject
3. Determining audience and purpose
4. Gathering data
5. Classifying and organizing the data
6. Writing the first draft
7. Revising
8. Preparing a final draft
9. Proofreading

Sometimes a step may be obviated; for example if you are assigned a specific topic, steps 1 and 2 will be already taken care of. Sometimes several parts of the process will be going on at the same time; for example there is often a good deal of interaction among the first five steps. Sometimes the order will be different; for example you may not be clear about your purpose until you have finished steps 4 and 5. And sometimes at a late stage, such as revising, you may have to go back and rethink something about your purpose, or dig up some new material, or even limit your topic further. But all the steps have to happen somehow, somewhere, somewhen, for a finished piece of writing to be produced.

And even though some of these steps often occur automatically, it is wise for any relatively inexperienced writer to follow them rigorously and self-consciously, particularly if the projected essay is long or complicated, like a term paper or a research paper.

73a Step 1: Finding a Subject

If a subject has not been assigned, you must find one for yourself. Some people think this is among the most difficult parts of writing an essay, but it needn't be, for subjects are all around us and inside us. A few minutes with a pencil and a sheet of paper, jotting down and playing around with any ideas that pop into your head, will usually lead you at least to a subject area if not to a specific subject. Or look around you and let your mind wander over whatever comes into your field of vision. Or scan the pages of a magazine or a newspaper to stimulate a train of thought; editorial pages and letters pages are usually full of interesting subjects to write about, perhaps to argue about. Or think about people: your immediate family and other relatives, your friends, or people you particularly dislike, or acquaintances with interesting cultures different from your own; or think about your hobbies or favourite sports, or about your academic pursuits, or about your travels, or simply about some of the little things you do every day and why you do them. The possibilities are almost endless.

Obviously, try to find a subject that interests you, one that you will enjoy writing about. Do not, in desperation, pick a subject that bores you—for then you will almost certainly bore your readers as well.

73b Step 2: Limiting the Subject

Once you have a subject, limit it: narrow it down so that you can develop it adequately within the length of essay you want or have been asked to write. More often than not, people start with subjects that are too big to handle except with broad generalizations. Seldom do they come up, right off the bat, with a topic like what people's tooth-brushing habits reveal about their character, or the dominant image cluster in a short story, or the inefficiency of the library building; they're more likely to start with some vague notions about personal hygiene, or how enjoyable that story was, or campus architecture. To save both time and energy, to avoid frustration, and to guarantee a better essay, be as merciless with yourself as necessary at this stage in narrowing your subject. If anything overdo it, for it's easier at a later stage to broaden than it is to cut.

For example, you might decide you want to write about animals, but "animals" is far too broad a category. "Domestic animals" or "wild animals" is narrower, but still too broad. "Farm animals," perhaps, or "farm animals I have known"? Better, but still too large, for where would you begin? How thorough could you be in a mere 500 or even 1000 words? When you find yourself narrowing your subject to something like "Homer, the spoiled pig on my uncle's farm" or "my pet dachshund, Rex" or "the experience of living next door to a noisy dog" or "why a cat makes a better pet than a dog" or "the day Dobbin kicked the barn door down"—then you can with some confidence look forward to developing your subject with sufficient thoroughness and specificity. (See also **54**.)

Exercise 73ab: Finding and limiting subjects

List ten broad subject areas that you have some interest in. Then, for each, specify two narrowed topics, (a) one that would be suitable for an essay of about 1500 words (six typed pages) and (b) one for an essay of about 500 words. (Since you'll almost surely think of more than two for each, list several if you wish.)

Examples:	Clothing.	(a) Campus fashions. How to dress for winter hiking.	(b) My closet. Ten uses for a pair of old socks.
	Nature.	(a) Why we need more parks. Water imagery in a sonnet.	(b) My pet cactus. How to build a simple bird-feeder.

73b limiting a subject

Step 3: Determining Audience and Purpose

Audience

When you write a personal letter you have a specific reader in mind. If you write a "Letter to the Editor" of your local newspaper, you have only a vague notion of your potential readership—namely anyone who reads that newspaper; but you will know where almost all of them live, and knowing only that much about them could still give you something to aim at in your letter. The more of a handle you can get on your audience, the better you can control your writing in order to make it effective for that audience. Always try to define or characterize your audience for a given piece of writing as precisely and specifically as possible.

Much of the writing you do for school may have only one reader: the teacher. But some assignments may ask you to address—or pretend to address—some specific audience. And sometimes teachers ask students to write "for an audience of your peers." In the absence of any other guideline, that's not a bad rule of thumb: write for your classmates, or perhaps for some imaginary student who will occupy your seat or live in your room next year. Sometimes teachers read out or distribute students' work to other students; even if they don't, when they read and criticize your work they may think of themselves as reading over your shoulder, so to speak, or as playing the role of editor.

Purpose

All writing has the broad purpose of communicating ideas. And in school you write for the special purpose of demonstrating your ability and your knowledge to your teacher. But you will be able to write more effective essays if you think of each one as having one of three primary rhetorical purposes: to *inform*, to *persuade*, or to *entertain*. Few essays, however, are so single-minded as to have only one of these purposes. For example a set of instructions may have as its primary purpose simply to inform readers how to do something, but it may also be trying to persuade them that this is the right or best way to do it. And in order to interest them more, it may well also be written entertainingly. An analysis of a poem may seem to be pure exposition, explaining how the poem works and what it means, but at least implicitly it will also be trying to persuade readers that this interpretation is the correct one. Almost any argument will include exposition, for readers can scarcely be persuaded about something unless they understand it. An entertaining or even whimsical piece may well have a satiric thrust or some kind of implicit "lesson." And so on. Usually one of the three purposes will dominate, but one or both of the others will often be present as well. The clearer your idea of just what you want to do in an essay, and why, and for whom, the better you will be able to make rhetorical choices that will be effective. (And see **74** below.)

It may even be a good idea to *write down*, as a memo to yourself, a detailed description or "profile" of your audience and as clear a statement of your purpose or purposes as you can come up with. If your ideas become clearer as the work proceeds, you can refine these statements. In any event, as you go through the process of writing, never take your mental eyes off your *audience* and your *purpose*.

Exercise 73c: Thinking about audience and purpose

Choose some fairly simple and personal subject (for example your typical day at school, the state of your finances, your best or worst class, how different university is from high school, why you need a computer, your athletic ambitions). Write two letters on the topic (300-500 words each) to two distinctly different kinds of people—for example different in age, background, education, philosophy of life. In an accompanying paragraph, briefly account for the differences between your two letters. Did your purpose change when you changed audiences?

73d **Step 4: Gathering Data**

One cannot, or should not, write in an information vacuum. A good essay must contain facts, details, particulars, not just vague generalizations and unsupported statements and opinions. Whatever your subject, you must gather material somewhere, by reading, talking to others, or—especially if the subject draws on your personal experience—simply reflecting on it. It is a good idea to collect as much information as you can, even two or three times as much as you can possibly use, for then you can *select* the best and discard the rest.

Brainstorming

If you're not doing formal research on a subject but are expected to get your material from your own knowledge and experience, you may at first think of yourself as hard-up for ideas. But you're not. Sit down with a pencil and a sheet of paper, write your subject in the centre or at the top, and begin jotting down ideas. Put down everything that comes into your head about it. Let your mind run fast and free; let free-association take its course. Don't bother with sentences, don't worry about spelling and the like, don't even pause to wonder whether the words and phrases are of any value. Just keep scribbling. It shouldn't be long before you've filled the sheet with possible ideas, questions, facts, details, names, examples. You may even need to use a second sheet.

Using Questions

Another way to generate material is to ask yourself questions about your subject and write down the answers. Start with the reporter's standard questions and go on from there with more of your own: Who? What? Where? When? Why? How? What is it? Who is associated with it? In what way? Where and when is it? What causes it? What does it cause? How does it work? What are its parts? What is it a part of? Is it part of a process? What does it look like? What colour is it? What is it like or unlike? (Invent some metaphors.) What is its opposite? What if it didn't exist? Is it good, or bad? Such questions and the answers you get to them will make you think of other questions, and so on, until before long you will have much more than enough potentially useful material.

You may even find yourself writing several sentences—beginning, that is, to *develop* your points—since some of the questions prompt certain kinds of responses. For example asking *What is it?* may lead you to begin defining your subject; *What is it like or unlike?* may lead you to begin comparing and contrasting it, classifying it, thinking of analogies for it; *What causes it?* and *What does it cause?* may lead you to begin exploring cause-and-effect relations; *What are its parts?* or *What is it made of?* could lead you to analyze your subject; *How does it work?* or *Is it part of a process?* may prompt you to analyze and explain a process.

Exercise 73d: Generating material

Use two of your narrowed topics from Exercise 73ab. Brainstorm them and bombard them with questions to see how much material you can generate. You might also want to try getting together with one or two friends or classmates and bouncing ideas and questions off each other.

73e Step 5: Classifying and Organizing the Data

Classifying

As you brainstorm a subject and jot down notes and answers about it, you will begin to see connections between one idea and another and start putting them in groups or drawing circles around them and lines and arrows between them. When you have finished gathering material, finish this job of classification. You should soon find yourself with several groups of related items, which means that you will have classified your material according to some principle which arose naturally from it. During this part of the process you will probably also have discarded the weaker or less relevant details, keeping only those which best suit the subject as it is now beginning to take shape.

For a tightly limited subject and a short essay, you may have only one group of details, but for an essay of even moderate length (750 words or more) you should have several groups. Always try to classify your material in such a way that you end up with at least *three* groups (or three main parts in the single group) and not more than *seven*: an essay with more than seven parts is likely to be unwieldy for both writer and reader, and an essay with only two parts risks breaking into those two parts and therefore not being smoothly unified and coherent.

Organizing
Now put the classified groups into some kind of order. Don't accept the first arrangement that comes to mind; consider as many different arrangements as the material will allow. (For the most common kinds of order, see the *Patterns of Development* listed under **67b**.) The point is that unless you consider all the possibilities, you may adopt one that is less than the best. It is important that you consciously decide on a scheme of arrangement, that you don't simply let things line up by chance, for whatever the order, your readers should feel that it is a necessary one rather than an accidental or arbitrary one. Ideally, the order you finally decide on should grow out of your material; the groups and their details should speak to you, as it were, demanding to be arranged in a particular way because it is the most effective way.

Exercise 73e: Classifying and organizing data

Go back to the material you generated for the two topics in Exercise 73d. Classify each mass into groups (between 3 and 7) of related items and arrange each set of groups into the best kind of order you can think of for them. In a few sentences, explain why you chose each particular order rather than some of the other possibilities. Try also to justify the order in terms of your audience and your purpose.

73f   The Thesis Statement and the Outline
The last part of the planning or "pre-writing" stage is the formulation of a **thesis statement** and the construction of an **outline**. During the first four steps you gradually increase your control over your proposed essay: you find and narrow a subject, you think about audience and purpose, you gather data and generate ideas, and you classify and arrange your material. At some point while you are doing all this—certainly by the time you finish it—you will formulate at least a tentative

73f thesis and outline

thesis, a statement that identifies your subject and points the way to what you want to say about it. This *thesis statement* or *thesis sentence* performs the same function for an outline that a *topic sentence* does for a paragraph. It leads off the outline, the ordered groups become *main headings* with Roman numerals (I, II, III, etc.), and the details that make up each group, if they aren't simply absorbed by the main heading, become subdivisions of it in various levels of *subheadings* (A, B, C, etc.; 1, 2, 3, etc.). Here is an example, a student's outline for a short essay:

> *Thesis Statement:* I see three main reasons for the increasing popularity of ceramics as a hobby.
>
> *Beginning:* With more time available, many people are taking up creative arts and crafts. Ceramics is becoming one of the more popular such hobbies. Why?

I. Relatively easy to learn
   A. No natural "artistic" ability needed
   B. Patience and determination needed

II. Practicality
   A. Useful household items
   B. Decorative items

III. Psychological benefits
   A. Outlet for creativity, imagination
   B. Self-satisfaction, accomplishment
   C. Escape from frustrations of daily grind

> *Ending:* Have you got a few new-found leisure hours each week? Maybe you too would enjoy pottering about with ceramics.

Note the proper mechanical layout of an outline: numerals and letters are followed by periods and a space or two; subheadings are indented at least two spaces past the beginning of the first word of a main heading. If further subdivision is necessary, here is the correct way to indicate the successive levels:

I.
II.
  A.
  B.
    1.
    2.
      a.
      b.
        (1.)
        (2.)
          (a.)
          (b.)

73g   The Importance of Outlining

Don't make the mistake of thinking that outlining is mere busy-work, a waste of time and effort. If you decide to outfox a teacher by drawing up a required outline *after* you've written an essay, then, indeed, you will be wasting your time and effort, for such an outline is unlikely to do you any good—unless it reveals some structural malformation in your essay and forces you to go back and rewrite it; but of course that means you've wasted time and effort. A conscientious outline drawn up *before* you write an essay will usually save you both time and effort. Writing the draft will be easier and smoother because it follows a plan: you know where you're going. Moreover, a good outline enables you to avoid such pitfalls as unnecessary repetition, digression, and awkward, illogical, or otherwise incoherent organization. It is much easier to do things right the first time than to go through laborious revisions trying to undo such errors—if you are even aware of the errors, for without an outline you might not know they are there. You should no more start writing an essay without a carefully prepared outline than you would take a trip into unfamiliar territory without a good map. An outline keeps the traveller from taking wrong turns, wandering in circles, or getting lost altogether.

Keep in mind too that an outline is not a straitjacket. If as you write and revise you think of a better way to organize a part of your essay, or if some part of the outline proves clumsy when you try to set it down in paragraphs, or if you suddenly think of some new material that should be included, by all means do what you think best and revise your outline accordingly. You may even need to refine your thesis statement in order to reflect changes in your ideas. The virtue of an outline in any such instance is that rather than drifting about rudderless, you are in complete control of any changes in course you make. Without an outline, you can be lured unaware into digressions and irrelevancies; but when you make changes in an outline, you can't help making them consciously and carefully—and you will also have a record of them if you want to recheck them later.

73h   Kinds of Outlines

Outlining of some kind is necessary for a good essay. The more complicated the essay, the more important the outline. A short, relatively simple essay can sometimes be outlined in your head or with a few informal jottings; but even a short essay is usually easier to write if you have made a formal outline first. The method of outlining you use may be your own choice or it may be dictated by your instructor or by the nature of an assignment. Some people like the *topic outline* with its brief headings and subheadings, as in the example above (**73f**). Sometimes a *paragraph outline* will work well, one that simply lists the topic sentences of the successive paragraphs that will eventually form the essay. But the one kind of outline that consistently recommends itself is the *sentence outline*, for it is virtually foolproof.

73i   Sentence Outlines

Every entry in a sentence outline is a complete major sentence. Because such a sentence necessarily expresses a completely formulated thought, it is impossible for you to fool yourself into thinking you have something to say about a topic when in fact you don't. For example imagine that you were writing an essay on various cuisines and, in a topic outline, put down the heading "Chinese food." If you have little or no experience of Chinese food, you might find when you sit down to write the essay that you have little or nothing to say about it. But if your outline is a sentence outline, you will be forced to make a statement about Chinese food; for example: "Although Chinese food sometimes seems strange to Western tastes, it never fails to be interesting." With even such a vague sentence as this before you, you can more easily begin supplying corroborative particulars to develop your idea; the very act of formulating the sentence guarantees that you have at least some ideas about whatever you put down.

Another virtue of a sentence outline is that it is, when properly handled, self-constructing. In any outline, the thesis statement should as it were set up or contain the main headings—either implicitly, as in the example in **73f**, or explicitly, as in the example below. In a sentence outline, the main headings and subheadings should work the same way. For example a main heading like "Although Chinese food sometimes seems strange to Western tastes, it never fails to be interesting" automatically predicts two subheadings: A. Chinese food sometimes seems strange to Western tastes. B. Chinese food never fails to be interesting. (Such partial repetition is natural to a good sentence outline. It may seem stiff and clumsy, but it fosters coherence and unity within each part of an essay and in an essay as a whole.)

As an illustration, here is a sentence outline written by a student:

Thesis Statement: Three major causes of the Russian Revolution were the Great War, poor working conditions, and the influence of political groups.

Beginning: No doubt many contributing factors helped bring about one of the twentieth century's major historical events, the Russian Revolution of 1917. In retrospect, however, three important ones seem to stand out.

I. The Russian Revolution was partly caused by the First World War's great destruction of life and by its hampering of industrial modernization.

A. The war caused widespread death and disillusionment.

B. The war impeded any steps by industry toward modernization.

II. Poor working conditions, both past and present, contributed to the Russian Revolution.

A. The poor working conditions that led to Bloody Sunday and the 1905 Revolution caused a resentment that was still smouldering in 1917.

B. Lack of reasonable concessions in working conditions, such as an eight-hour day, caused resentment among the working class.

III. The Russian Revolution was precipitated by the two-fold actions of influential political groups.

A. Political groups stirred up the working class, playing on their disaffection and resentment.

B. Political groups provided the leadership to co-ordinate the actions of the enraged masses.

Ending: (Perhaps summarize main events and point to some of the historic repercussions of it all. Has the rest of the world learned anything from its understanding of these events?)

See also the outline for the sample research essay, **84**.

73j Constructing Sentence Outlines

There are several rules to follow in putting together a good sentence outline.

First, make every item from the thesis statement down to the last sub-subheading a single complete major sentence.

Second, use only simple or complex sentences; do not use compound sentences. A compound sentence, by its very nature, could be split into two sentences, which means that two headings could be masquerading as a single one, and thus lead to awkward problems of organization. If you find yourself writing a compound sentence, such as "Chinese food sometimes seem strange to Western tastes, but it never fails to be interesting," try to rephrase it as a complex sentence. In this instance it is easy: "Although Chinese food . . . . " But if for some reason you can't turn a compound sentence into a simple or complex one, rethink the whole matter: some revision or reorganization is necessary. Further, although questions can be rhetorically effective in an essay, try to avoid interrogative sentences in an outline; they seldom lend themselves to the requirements of a tightly structured outline.

Third (and this holds true for any kind of outline), you must supply at least two subheadings if you supply any at all; a heading cannot be subdivided into only one thing. If under *I* you have an *A* then you must also have at least a *B*; if you have a *1* then you must also have at least a *2*; and so on with all subheadings. If you find yourself unable to go beyond one subheading, then it probably isn't a subdivision at all but an integral part of the main heading, and should be incorporated into it.

Fourth, the headings or subheadings at each level should be reasonably parallel with each other; that is, I, II, III, etc. should have about the same importance. The same is true of subheadings A, B, C, etc. under a given main heading, and of 1, 2, 3, etc. under each of these. One way to ensure this balance is to make the sentences at any given level syntactically parallel—that is, the same kind of sentences and sentence patterns. (A and B under I should be parallel, but an A and B under II or III need not be parallel with those under I, though they may well be.)

Fifth, seldom does an outline need to go beyond the first level of subheading. If an essay is unusually long or complicated, you may find it helpful or necessary to break things down to a second or even third level of subheading. But remember that headings and subheadings in an outline should mostly state ideas, propositions, generalizations; the supporting facts can be supplied in the essay-writing stage of composition. For example, if we had a subheading saying that "Though many people think of Mexican food as impossibly fiery, the heat can easily be reduced, making the tangy, earthy flavours capable of being enjoyed by anyone," the next step would almost have to be some specific instances to illustrate the point, examples that need not appear in the outline. If you find yourself including several levels of subheading, you may already be at the level of facts and details; although this is not necessarily wrong, it can be wasteful (you may find yourself thinking of different details when you actually begin writing), and can lure a writer into producing a mechanical-sounding essay.

Sixth (and this also applies to any kind of outline), don't label the first main heading of an outline "Introduction" or the last one "Conclusion." By definition, introductions and conclusions are not substantive parts of an essay. If you label them as such, you may be misled about what constitutes the actual *body* of your material. If at the outline stage you already have in mind a possible way to begin your essay, by all means jot it down in a sentence or two and label it "Beginning" or "Introduction." Then you can proceed to Roman numeral *I*, the first main heading. Similarly, after completing the outline of the body of the essay, you can summarize a possible "Ending" or "Conclusion." See for example the two sample outlines above.

73j   constructing outlines

Exercise 73f-j (1): Writing thesis statements and outlines

Return to the two topics you've been working with from Exercise 73ab through 73e. If you haven't already done so, formulate a thesis statement for each topic. Make each a single simple or complex sentence. Try to compose the sentences in such a way that each foreshadows the major divisions of the outline to come. Then construct the two outlines. Make at least one of them a sentence outline. Include a statement of audience and purpose with each outline.

Exercise 73f-j (2): Revising weak outlines

One of the most important functions of an outline is to let you see a graphic representation of a projected essay so that before you begin writing the essay you can catch and correct structural and other flaws (repetition, overlap, illogical organization, introductory material masquerading as part of the body, inadequate thesis statements, subheadings that aren't really subheadings, and so on). Here are ten outlines drafted by students for possible essays. Analyze them critically; pretend that they are your own and that you'll have to try to write essays based on them. Detect their flaws, both major and minor, and then try to revise each so that it could guide you through the draft of an essay. Do any of them seem simply unworkable, unsalvageable? If so, why?

(1) *Thesis Statement:* Natural greenery is necessary for recreation, to relieve monotony, to provide aesthetic value, and it is also an important life-sustainer.
   I. Natural greenery for recreation is necessary in that it is essential to enable us to have fields, playgrounds, and parks.
   II. To relieve monotony natural surroundings are important in that they take you away from the tensions of the city, away from all the cement-gray colour, and offer you an isolated island away from people.
   III. In all its beauty natural greenery may be looked upon as having aesthetic value in such things as parks, gardens, and scenery.
   IV. As a life-sustainer greenery is important in providing oxygen, vegetation, and materials for food and shelter.

(2) *Thesis Statement*: Reading is a creative exercise for the imagination.
   I. Reading forces people to visualize settings of stories.
   II. Reading forces people to visualize the appearance of characters.
   III. Some plots force people to imagine the endings of stories or to fill in missing parts of stories.
   IV. Science-fiction stories provide people with inspiration that allows their imaginations to wander.

(3) *Thesis Statement*: Why disadvantaged children have low achievement in school.
   I. Poverty's effects on physical growth.
   II. Little opportunity to learn appropriate roles right from infancy.
   III. Lack of linguistic stimulation.
   IV. Not enough help from society.

(4) *Thesis Statement*: Getting involved, meeting people, and travelling are a few benefits of playing high-school basketball.
   I. Playing basketball helps you to get more involved in your school.
   II. It is quite easy to meet people while on the basketball team.
   III. One of the main benefits is the chance to travel and see other schools.

exercises

(5) *Thesis Statement*: The effects of television on our lives.

   I. There are too many shows pertaining to sex and violence on television.

      A. Many shows on TV lead people to accept violence as a way of life.

      B. Children are left to formulate their own opinions on sex.

   II. Many people centre their entire lives on TV.

   III. Advertising on TV disillusions people.

      A. Most ads deceive people into buying things they don't need.

   IV. There are some good educational shows on TV.

(6) *Thesis Statement*: Stress is a problem in university that must be dealt with. Students should be aware of it and must learn to cope with it.

   I. Different types of stress and what causes them.

      A. Unhealthy: stress overload, too much work, not enough rest, bad nutrition.

      B. Healthy stress levels: small amounts of pressure, beneficial to some extent, help one learn and grow.

      C. Emotional: family problems, love problems, depression, loneliness, unable to concentrate.

      D. Physical: work too hard, overdoing it, too much pressure, health problems.

   II. Problems that arise with stress.

      A. Sustained stress: heart attacks, health problems.

      B. Common symptoms: ulcers, insomnia, irritability, sweaty or clammy hands, fidgetiness, higher pulse rate.

   III. Treatments: How to cope.

      A. Physical: relax, read, take up a hobby, watch TV, do something relaxing.

      B. Emotional: relax mind, meditation, exercise.

      C. Serious stress: psychotherapy, counseling, get mind away from problems.

(7) *Thesis Statement*: Cross-country is a sport which requires a lot of endurance, willpower, and speed.

   I. Cross-country is a sport which requires a lot of practice.

   II. One needs a lot of willpower and concentration in order to run a very long distance.

   III. The weather can influence the pace of the runner.

(8) *Thesis Statement*: Traditional religious beliefs play a major role in African life.

   I. The religions are based on animism, the belief that everything has a spirit.

      A. The spirits can have an effect on human life.

         1. The effect can be good.

         2. The effect can be bad.

      B. The spirits of dead ancestors are believed to have great influence on the living.

   II. Many tribes keep a witch doctor and a sorcerer in the village.

      A. The witch doctors and sorcerers protect the people from evil spirits.

      B. The witch doctors protect the land from evil spirits.

    III. Colourful religious ceremonies are performed.
        A. Dancing and feasting are performed to please the spirits.
        B. Dancing and feasting are performed to promote the welfare of the tribe.

(9) *Thesis Statement*: Raising a litter of six cairn terriers is a learning experience!
    I. The pre-whelp period is a time of preparation for both the bitch and her owner.
    II. The actual birth never fails to awaken a sense of wonder at the miracle of life.
    III. As the puppies grow, the work-load of their care increases.
    IV. Happy, healthy puppies are fun to have: in caring for them, one learns many things.

(10) I. Introduction: running has been around since the time of the caveman.
    II. Benefits
        A. Cardiovascular system
          1. Builds up the heart, reduces heart attacks
          2. Nausea, dizziness
          3. Increases stamina: muscles, breathing
          4. Pulse rate
        B. Psychological effects
          1. Reduce habits
            (a.) Decreases urge to smoke and drink
          2. Relieve tension; clears the head; expands consciousness
          3. Enjoying fresh air
          4. Sense of accomplishment
        C. Weight control
    III. Before and after a run: to avoid injuries, preparation is important, as is slow return to normal
        A. Warming up
        B. Cooling down (slow jogging, walking, mild calisthenics) to avoid dizziness, nausea, cramps
        C. Stretching exercises
    IV. Conclusion: running will continue, and grow in popularity.

When you have finished working on these outlines, go back and examine closely your own two outlines from the preceding exercise. Do you see any possible weak spots in them? If necessary, revise them.

    Can you think of some possible titles for these potential essays, including your own? Try.

Exercise 73f-j (3): Writing and using outlines

Construct outlines for proposed essays on three of the following:

1. The pros and cons of keeping dogs, cats, birds, fish, or other animals as pets.
2. The methods used by politicians to influence voters.
3. The state of freedom of speech in Canada.

4. How to cook your favourite dish.
5. Your favourite winter sport.
6. The importance of good manners.
7. The pros and cons of minority government.
8. "Why I plan to be a _____."
9. Last year's popular music.
10. How to be lazy.

Check your outlines carefully for any weaknesses, and revise them as necessary. Then choose the one you like best and proceed to write the essay. When you've finished, ask yourself if having the outline to follow made the writing easier than it would otherwise have been.

73k   **Step 6: Writing the First Draft**

With the outline before you, drafting the essay should be easy; some-times one feels that, with a good outline to follow, the only work left is supplying transitions between parts and paragraphs. But of course the point is that with the shape of the whole laid out one can concentrate on the real job of writing: finding the right words, generating the right kinds of sentences, and constructing good paragraphs.

Note: Sometimes a main heading and its subheadings from the outline will become a single paragraph in the essay; sometimes each subheading will become a paragraph; and so on. The nature and the density of your material will determine its treatment. For example, one could have a paragraph on the virtues of Chinese food and a paragraph on the deficiencies of Chinese food, or one could have one longer paragraph dealing with both. Another point: it may be possible to transfer the thesis statement to the essay unchanged, but more likely you will want to change it to fit the style of the essay; the requirements of the outline may well have demanded a stiffish statement that would be inappro-priate in the essay itself. See the sample research paper, **84**, commen-tary on paragraphs 1, 2, and 14.

73-l   **A Note on Beginnings**

Starting the actual writing of the essay can be a problem: most writers have had the experience of staring at a blank sheet of paper for an uncomfortable length of time, trying to think of a good way to begin. If you have no beginning in mind at this point, don't waste time trying to think of one. Plunge right into the body of the essay and write it as rapidly as you can. When the first draft is finished, you will of course know what you have written—and therefore you will know precisely what it is that needs to be introduced. You can then go back and do the necessary introducing with relative ease. In fact, writers who write their beginnings first frequently discover that they have to discard their original version and write a new one to fit the essay that finally took shape.

Just as it is not a good idea to begin a final paragraph with "In conclusion," so it is generally not good practice to open a first paragraph with something like "In this essay I will discuss" or "This essay is concerned with." Rather than beginning by informing readers of what you are going to say (and then concluding by reminding them of what you have said), begin your essay by saying something substantial and if possible attention-getting (and conclude it with something similarly sharp and definitive). Occasionally, however, when an essay is unusually long or complicated, it can be helpful to explain in advance, to provide readers with what amounts to a brief outline (just as it is then often necessary to provide some summary by way of conclusion).

However you begin, it is always necessary to identify your subject, and usually also to state your thesis, somewhere at or near the beginning—almost never later than the first paragraph. For example, even if your title is something like "Imagery in Donne's 'The Flea,' " you must still, preferably in your first sentence, mention both the author and the title of the poem. The title of your essay is not a part of its content; the essay must be able to stand on its own. Further, be as direct and smooth and economical as you can. Here are three ways in which such an essay could begin; note how differences in order, punctuation, and wording make each succeeding one better than the one before:

1. In the poem "The Flea," by John Donne, there is a great deal of imagery.
2. John Donne, in his poem "The Flea," uses imagery to . . .
3. The imagery in John Donne's "The Flea" . . .

Here is the beginning of an essay on one of Shakespeare's sonnets. The writer cannot seem to get the engine warmed up:

> William Shakespeare, famous English poet and writer of plays, has always been known for the way he uses imagery to convey the point he is making in a particular piece of work. Shakespeare's Sonnet 65 is no exception to this, and this is one of the better examples of his work that I have studied, for illustrating his use of imagery.
>
> The best example in the sonnet comes in lines four and six, where Shakespeare compares a "summer's honey breath" and a "wrackful siege of battering days."

Compare this with another student's beginning on the same topic:

> Shakespeare's Sonnet 65 expresses its meaning through imagery. The poet appeals to a person's knowledge of visible properties in nature in an attempt to explain invisible properties of love and time.

Rather than vacillating as the first writer has done, this writer has taken control of the material immediately. Even though no particular image has yet been mentioned, the second writer, in two crisp sentences, is far beyond where the first writer still is, though well into a second paragraph.

Here is another example of a weak beginning. That the writer was in difficulty is shown by the jargon, awkwardness, and poor usage in the first sentence, the cliché and the illogicality in the second sentence, and the vague reference and the wordy emptiness of the third:

> With all aspects considered, a person's graduating year from high school is a very unique experience. It is filled with a seemingly endless variety of memories, dreams, and emotions. I would imagine this is experienced by almost everyone and I most certainly am not an exception.

The writer's own revision proves that the difficulties were merely the result of floundering, trying too hard to make a beginning; had the beginning been written after the essay was complete, it might well have taken this form in the first place:

> There are few things in life that can match the significance of one's high-school graduation year. At least that is the way it seems soon after one completes it.

Exercise 73-1: Evaluating beginnings

Here are five beginnings from student essays; the last two are on the same topic and were written in class. Which ones are good and which ones are weak? Point out the contrasting characteristics that enable you to evaluate them relative to each other.

(1)   Five months of backpacking left me tired, dirty, and eager for a nice fresh bed. But my backpack and I would take just one more night train, to see and experience just one more city. One of Europe's best, they told me. And this thought was far more thrilling than taking a hot shower.
   West Berlin; a city on its own. . . .

(2)   Problems relating to a society affect all its inhabitants; hence, all its inhabitants must take part in curing society's ills. I find that society is plagued by problems such as degenerating slums, growing unemployment, and increasing racism. Cultural conflicts have been the root of most of our problems; thus, if the situation is to improve, some changes must occur.

(3)   For many people, their first thought after the ring of the alarm clock is of a steaming cup of coffee. Their stumble to the kitchen for this pick-me-up blends with their dreams. The sleepy eyes that measure out the fragrant brown granules flick open after their owners have savoured that first morning cup of coffee. After a strong cup of coffee, most people perform physical and mental tasks at the peak of their ability.
   The reason is caffeine.

(4)   The poem, "To an Athlete Dying Young," written by A. E. Housman,

structurally contains different periods of time in its stanzas. The different stanzas refer to different times. The rhythm of the poem is not uniform in beat. However, it has a consistent rhyme scheme. This poem is also an example of a dramatic monologue.

(5) "Quit while you're ahead" may be an old and worn-out saying, but it aptly applies to A. E. Housman's poem "To an Athlete Dying Young." In this dramatic monologue the speaker seizes upon this idea as a means of consoling the athlete, or those who mourn him. Beauty and victory are fleeting. Not only does the eternal passing of time always bring change, but once our "peak" has been reached, there is no place to go but down. Rather than growing old and watching new athletes break his records, the young athlete in the poem dies at an early age. His victory garland is preserved, "unwithered," by death.

73m-o The Final Steps

Earlier we referred to the product of rapid composition as a first draft—which of course is all it is. It is very unlikely that it can be considered a finished product. This means that there are three more steps to be taken before the essay should be considered finished.

73m Step 7: Revising

Revision (re-vision: literally "scrutinizing again") is an extremely important stage of writing, far too often neglected by inexperienced (or lazy) writers. Writers who care at all about the quality of their work revise a piece of writing at least two or three times. Many writers revise their work five or even ten or more times before they consider it finished. In fact, the process of revision could be said to be never-ending, for one can almost always find something to improve.

Revise carefully, slowly, with an eye to anything that could improve what you have written; don't aim just to correct errors made in haste, but also to improve diction, sentence structure, punctuation, coherence, paragraphing, and so on. Some writers find that going through an essay for only one thing at a time is effective—for example, going through it looking only at paragraphing, then going through it again looking only at sentences, then at punctuation, and then at diction, and so on. Weaker writers should discipline themselves to revise in this careful way, concentrating on one thing at a time. When you are revising, pretend that you are a hypercritical reader looking for weaknesses and errors. (In order to do this effectively, it helps to wait as long as possible between the writing and the revising—at least two or three days—so that you can look at your own work with some objectivity.)

You should find the *Omnibus Checklist* (Chapter XII) helpful during your revisions.

73m *revising*

73n Step 8: Preparing the Final Draft

When you are through revising a piece of writing, carefully prepare the final draft, the one that will be presented to your reader or readers. Once the work is out of your hands it's too late to change anything; make sure it's in good shape when it leaves your hands. It should be neat, and it should be in the appropriate format for the kind of writing it is. For most of your academic writing, follow carefully the *Manuscript Conventions* listed and discussed in **45**.

73o Step 9: Proofreading

Proofreading will have been taking place during revision, naturally; but when what you consider to be the final copy of your essay is ready, go over it again. Rarely will this final proofreading not prove worthwhile; despite earlier careful scrutiny, you will probably discover not only typographical errors but also hitherto unnoticed errors in spelling, punctuation, or grammar. Do your proofreading with exaggerated care. Read each sentence, as a sentence, slowly; but also read each word as a word; check each punctuation mark, and consider the possibility of adding some or removing some or changing some. Particularly when you proofread for spelling errors, do so as a separate process, and do it by starting at the end of the essay and reading word by word, backward; then you are unlikely to get so caught up in the flow of a sentence that you overlook an error.

When you have taken all these steps conscientiously and carefully, you should be able to submit your finished essay with pride and confidence.

74 Argument: Writing to Convince or Persuade

Good argumentative writing must adhere to the same principles of composition as other kinds of writing. And as we imply earlier (**73c**), other kinds of writing, especially exposition, often include an element of argumentation. But when your principal purpose is to convince or persuade—when you are writing what can be called *an argument*—there are several additional points and principles that you need to keep in mind. Here are some brief suggestions and some practical advice to help you write effective arguments. (See also *convince, persuade* in **60**.)

74a Subject

When you are focussing on your subject for an argumentative essay, keep in mind that there is no point in arguing about easily verifiable facts or generally accepted assumptions (2 + 2 = 4; the sky looks blue;

good nutrition promotes good health; oil is a nonrenewable energy source). One cannot argue about facts, only about what the facts mean. Liberals and Conservatives might well differ in the way they interpret election results, but not about the results themselves. But since an argument depends on logical reasoning, when you argue about opinions based on facts you will necessarily use factual data to support your contentions. A collection of unsupported opinions is not an argument but merely a series of assertions. Similarly, you cannot argue about matters of taste or personal preference. You can't argue that blue is a prettier colour than green; you can only assert that *you* find it prettier, perhaps because of some childhood association. The subject of an argument must be something that is supposedly *capable of verification*, though the fact that it is being argued about at all indicates that its verification is not easy.

74b   Audience

When your *purpose* is to convince or persuade, your knowledge of your *audience* and your constant awareness of that audience are more important than in any other kind of writing. Consider for example how differently you would have to handle your material and your tone depending on whether you were writing to an audience of (a) people who are basically sympathetic to your position, (b) people who are entirely neutral, or (c) people who are likely to be hostile to your position. Since the effectiveness of an argument depends partly on your gaining and maintaining the confidence of your readers, or at least getting them to listen to you willingly and with an open mind, it is vital that you avoid anything that might put them off. Know your audience. Are your readers largely men? women? elderly? young? well-educated? middle-class? business people? students? politically conservative? wealthy? poor? artistic? sports lovers? car owners? family oriented? animal lovers? and so on. The more you know about your potential readers, the better you will know both what kinds of things to avoid in order not to alienate them and what kinds of things to use in order to appeal to them, to attract them toward your position.

74c   Evidence

When you are gathering material for an argument, look especially for concrete, specific, precise, factual data that you can use to support your generalizations (see **54b**). The effectiveness of your argument will in part depend on the quality and the quantity of the *evidence* you provide both to support your position and to counter your opposition. For example try to find some statistics you can cite, or some expert you can quote (the appeal to authority), or some common experience or assumption about life that you can remind your readers of (the appeal to common sense). You may be able to make good use of your own experience or that of someone you know well. But be sure that the evidence you gather and use is both *reliable* and *relevant*. Don't cite a film star as an authority on a medical question; don't cite the results of an experiment that has been superseded by later experiments; don't discuss the styling and upholstery of a car if you're arguing about which car provides the most efficient transportation.

74d Organization

As with the other principles of composition, good organization is especially important in argument. Take extra pains when you are laying out your material. And be sure to construct—carefully—a detailed formal outline. Here are some specific points to keep in mind:

Emphasis

Usually you will want to save your strongest point or points for last, the most emphatic position. But since the beginning is also emphatic, don't open with a weak or minor point. Begin with strength; then deal with minor points and proceed to the end in the order of *climax*. (See **18, 70, 72c.**)

Thesis

In an argument, your thesis statement is in effect a *proposition* that you intend to support or attack; you want to prove or disprove it, at least to the satisfaction of your readers. For that reason, it usually appears at the beginning, just as a formal debate begins with a reading of the proposition to be debated. Occasionally, however, you can delay your statement of the thesis until at or near the end, letting a logical progression of reasoning lead up to it. But don't try for this dramatic effect unless you're sure it will work better than stating your proposition up front; for example, consider whether your readers might be put off, rather than drawn in, by being kept in the dark about what your proposition is.

Methods of Development

Arguments can make use of *any* of the methods of development: narration (an illustrative anecdote), description (a detailed description of something it is important for readers to understand clearly), comparison and contrast, analysis, and so on (see **61b** and **c**). But be careful with *analogy* (see **74h**): never use an analogy as the central pillar of an argumentative structure, for opponents can too easily break it down; use analogy, if at all, only as extra illustration or as one of several minor props. And do give strong consideration to *cause-and-effect* analysis (What caused it? What does it cause? What *will* it cause?), often a mainstay of argument: you argue for or against something because of what happens or will happen as a result of it.

Patterns of Development

Similarly, an argument can use any one or more of the common patterns of development (see **67b**). It is almost certain, for example, to follow a logical progression, to move from general to specific or from specific to general, and to rise to a climax. But there is one further pattern that often occurs in argument: like a formal debate, many arguments move back and forth between *pro* and *con*, between statements supporting your *pro*position and statements and *con*futations of your opponents' position (see **74f**, and sample essay 10 in Chapter X).

74e-h How to Argue: Reasoning Logically

74e Being Reasonable

Appeal to common sense; appeal to authority; above all, appeal to *reason*. Demonstrate your respect for your readers' intelligence by appealing to it; they are then more likely to respect you and your arguments. If you appeal to prejudices and baser instincts you may get through to a few, but no thoughtful reader will respond favourably to such tactics. Appeals to people's emotions (sympathy for the poor or sick, love of children, feelings of patriotism, fear of injury) can be effective *additions* to an appeal to reason, but they are not a valid substitute for it. By itself an appeal to emotion ("Those little mice and rabbits and monkeys are so cute! People shouldn't be allowed to experiment on them in medical laboratories.") is not an argument. Similarly, if you're conducting a reasoned argument you will usually want to adopt a *moderate tone*. Stridency and sarcasm may win points with readers who are already thoroughly in agreement with your position—but then you wouldn't be *arguing* so much as just showing off.

74f Including the Opposition

Be fair: bring into your argument any major opposing points. If you try to sway your readers by mentioning only what favours your side, they will lose faith in you because they will themselves think of counterarguments and conclude that you are unfairly suppressing unfavourable evidence. By raising opposing points and doing your best to refute them convincingly, you will not only strengthen the logic of your argument but also present yourself as a reasonable person, willing to concede that there is another side to the issue. Moreover, by in effect

74f including opposition

taking on the role of both sides in a debate, you can often impart a useful back-and-forth momentum to your argument, and you can see to it that after demolishing the opposition you end on one or more of your own strongest points.

74g Using Induction and Deduction

The two principal methods of reasoning, *induction* and *deduction*, occur both separately and in combination in argument. You should know how each works, and it sometimes helps to be aware of which one you are using at any given moment so that you can use it effectively and avoid its potential pitfalls.

Induction

Inductive reasoning argues from the particular to the general. It uses specific examples to support a general proposition. A team of chemists will argue that their new theory is correct by describing the results of several experiments which point to it. If you want to persuade people to vote for mayoral candidate A rather than B, you could point to several instances of A's actions on behalf of the city while on city council—and also perhaps point to several instances of B's harmful decisions. If you wanted to argue against a proposal to cut back on the athletic program at your school, you could cite the major ways in which the program benefits the school and its students; you could also interview other students to show that the majority agree with you.

Inductive reasoning cannot *prove* anything; it can establish only degrees of likelihood or probability. Obviously the number of examples affects the force of such arguments. If the chemists could point to only two successful experiments, their theory would remain weak; if they could cite a hundred consecutive successes, their argument would be convincing: there would be a strong likelihood that the experiment would work again if tried for the 101st time. But don't overdo it: if in a speech or a written argument you detailed fifty noble acts of candidate A and fifty ignoble ones of candidate B, you would probably bore or anger your audience and turn them against you and your proposition. You would do better to describe a few actions on each side and try to establish that those actions were *representative* or *typical* of the two candidates' official behaviour. Similarly, if you interviewed students about the athletic program, you would need to talk to enough of them for your sampling to be considered representative; if you polled only PE majors, you could hardly claim that their opinions were typical. And though the sampling would have to be large in order for the results to be convincing, it would be the total number that would carry weight—as on a petition—not the detailed opinions of each individual student.

In addition, you must be able to explain away any notable exceptions among your examples—possible opposition arguments. For example if one of their experiments failed miserably, the chemists would need to show perhaps that at that time their equipment was faulty, or that one of their ingredients had accidentally become adulterated. If candidate A had once voted to close a useful facility, you could try to show that financial exigency at that time left no choice, or that the facility, though generally perceived as beneficial, was in fact little used and therefore an unnecessary drain on the city's resources. If you explicitly acknowledge such exceptions and show that they are unimportant or atypical, they can't be used against you in the mind of a hostile reader.

Deduction

Deductive reasoning argues from the general to the particular. It begins with facts or generally accepted assumptions or principles and applies them to specific instances. For example we all know that oil and other fossil fuels are nonrenewable energy sources that will presumably someday be depleted; and we also know that the world's energy needs are increasing at an accelerating rate. Basing their argument on those two facts, people conclude that it is increasingly important for us to discover or develop alternative sources of energy. The standard way of representing this process of thinking is the *syllogism*, of which the following is a simple example:

> *Major premise:* All mammals are warm-blooded animals.
> *Minor premise:* Whales are mammals.
> *Conclusion:* Therefore whales are warm-blooded animals.

Syllogistic reasoning is a basic mode of thought, though commonly in everyday thinking and writing one of the premises is omitted as "understood"; for example if a student says, "This term paper is due tomorrow, so I'll have to finish it tonight," the assumed second premise ("I don't want to hand the paper in late") goes without saying.

Deductive reasoning, unlike inductive reasoning, can establish proof, but only if the premises are correct and you follow the rules. For example, if one of the premises is negative, the conclusion must be negative (*two* negative premises cannot lead to a conclusion). The term common to both premises—called the "middle" term (in the example, *mammals*)—cannot appear in the conclusion. Most important, if the conclusion is to be an absolute certainty, this "middle" term must in at least one of the premises be all-inclusive, universal, what is called "distributed"; that is, it must refer to all members of its class, usually with an absolute word like *all, every, no, none, always, never*.

74g *induction, deduction*

If instead it is qualified by a word like *some, most,* or *seldom,* the conclusion cannot be a certainty, only a probability:

> Most mammals are viviparous.
> Whales are mammals.
> Therefore whales are probably viviparous.

Here of course one could reason further that since whales are not among the oviparous exceptions (platypus, echidna), they are indeed viviparous. (If *both* premises include such qualifiers, they cannot lead to a conclusion.) Obviously, for a conclusion to amount to certainty both premises must be true, or accepted as true:

> No mammals can fly.
> Whales are mammals.
> Therefore whales cannot fly.

Here the conclusion is *valid* (the reasoning process follows the rules), but it is not *sound*, since the first premise with its categorical *no* excludes the bat, a flying mammal. Such a conclusion, even if true (as this one is), will be suspect because it is based on a false premise. If one argues that

> All mammals are four-legged animals.
> Whales are mammals.
> Therefore whales are four-legged animals.

the conclusion, however valid, is not only unsound but untrue. To be accurate, the first premise must refer to *some* or *many*; the conclusion would then have to be something like "whales *may* be four-legged animals." Here the absurdity is obvious. But it is not uncommon to hear something like "X must be a communist; after all, he believes in socialism." Here the absurdity may not appear so obvious, but in the syllogism underlying this reasoning the first premise would read, "Everyone who believes in socialism is a communist"; again, changing *everyone* to the correctly qualifying *some people* renders the conclusion unsound. Be careful whenever you find yourself using—or thinking— terms like *all* and *everyone* and *no one* and *must* ("Everyone benefits from exercise"; "All exams are unfair"; "[All] Scots are stingy"; "Lawyers are overpaid"; "No one cares about the elderly"; "Vitamin E must be good for you"): you may be constructing an implicit syllogism that won't stand up, one that your opponents can turn against you. Use such qualifiers as *most* and *some* and *sometimes* when necessary; you won't be able to establish absolute proof or certainty, but you may still have a persuasive argument.

Induction and deduction often work together. For example, when you cite instances from A's record, you use induction to establish the general proposition of your candidate's worthiness. But then you implicitly turn to deduction, using that generalization as the basis for a further conclusion: "Candidate A has done all these good things for our city in the past; therefore when elected mayor he or she will do similar good things." (Would the unstated second premise—"A person who behaved in a certain way in the past will continue to behave that way in the future"—require some qualification?)

74h Detecting and Avoiding Fallacies

If you are mounting a counter-argument, it often pays to look for flaws in your opponent's reasoning, such as hidden assumptions and invalid syllogisms. There are several other kinds of recognized—and recognizable—logical fallacies to look for, and of course to guard against in your own writing. Most of them amount to either avoiding evidence or distorting evidence, or both, and some are related to or overlap with others. Here are the main ones to watch for:

argumentum ad hominem

"Argument directed at the person." Trying to evade the issue by diverting attention to the person: "Byron lived an immoral life; therefore his poetry is bound to be bad." Byron's morality is irrelevant to a discussion of the aesthetic quality of his poetry. "My opponent is obviously not fit to be mayor; he never goes to church, and his daughter was arrested last year for shoplifting." Neither the candidate's failure to attend church nor his daughter's arrest—whether or not she was guilty—necessarily have any bearing on the candidate's qualifications for office. Such tactics, according to their degree of directness or nastiness, are referred to as *innuendo* or *name-calling* or *mud-slinging*. A similar tactic uses *guilt* (or *virtue*) *by association* in an attempt to get one thing's qualities to rub off on another, even though the connection may not be real or relevant. A brand of coffee is not necessarily any better because a famous actress is paid to say it is, nor a politician necessarily evil because he once had his picture taken with someone later convicted of a crime.

argumentum ad populum

"Argument directed at the people." Evading the issue by appealing to mass emotion. Like *argumentum ad hominem*, this technique uses appeals to prejudices, fears, and other feelings not—or not clearly—relevant to the issue. Often by using what are called "glittering generalities," it calls upon large and usually vague, unexamined popular feelings about religion, patriotism, home and family, tradition, and the like. One version of it, called the "bandwagon" approach, associates mass appeal with virtue: if so many people are doing this or thinking that or drinking this or wearing that, it must be good. Most people don't want to be thought of as not in the swim.

74h fallacies

red herring

A false or misleading issue dragged across the trail to throw the dogs off the scent. The new matter raised may be interesting, but if it is fundamentally irrelevant to the question being argued it is a red herring. *Ad hominem* points are red herrings, diverting the reader's or listener's attention from the main question by injecting the issue of personality.

hasty generalization

Jumping to a conclusion; arriving at a generalization for which there is insufficient evidence. For example, just because you and a friend didn't like the food you were served at a particular restaurant, you aren't justified in assuming that the restaurant is a bad one; maybe the regular chef was ill. But if you've had several such experiences at that restaurant, and can find other people who've consistently had similar ones, you'll be closer to establishing that those experiences were *typical* and therefore sufficient to generalize upon.

begging the question

Assuming as true something that needs to be proved: "The government should be voted out of office because the new tax they've just imposed is unfair to consumers." The unfairness of the tax needs to be established before it can be used as a premise. Similar to question-begging is *circular reasoning*, in which a reason given to support a proposition is little or no more than a disguised restatement of the proposition: "Her consistently good cooking is easy to explain: she's an expert at all things culinary." Or sometimes the circle of logic can have a greater circumference: "I'm convinced that my new computer is the best one I could have bought for my particular needs. The man who sold it to me assured me that it was, and if anyone in this town knows all about computers, surely he does. Would he feature this brand if he didn't know it to be the best?"

post hoc ergo propter hoc

"After this, therefore because of this." Oversimplifying the evidence by assuming that merely because one thing follows another, it must be caused by the other. It's true that thunder is caused by lightning, but the subsequent power failure may have been caused not by the lightning but by a tree's having been blown down across the power line. If you always wear your green socks during an exam because you think they bring you good luck, you are a victim of the *post hoc* fallacy. "As soon as the new administration took office, the price of gasoline went up"—but there could be a complex set or chain of causes, perhaps including oil companies' fear of possible new policies; or the price hike might have nothing to do with the new government, the timing being coincidental. Be careful not to oversimplify cause-and-effect relations.

either–or, also called "false dilemma"
Oversimplifying an issue by presenting it as consisting of only two choices when in fact it is more complex than that. Some questions do present two clear choices: one either gets up or stays in bed; either one has had German measles or one has not; either one votes in an election or one doesn't. But most issues are not matters simply of black or white; there is often a large gray area between the extremes. One doesn't have to vote for either A or B; one can perhaps find a third candidate, or one can stay home and not vote for anyone. "If you aren't for us, then you must be against us!" Not so. One could be neutral, impartial, uninterested, or committed to a third option. "If I don't pass this course, my life will be ruined." An obvious exaggeration. "If we don't accept and develop nuclear power, we're throwing away the country's future." There are other alternatives. "The administration at this school is either indifferent to students' needs or against students in general." Neither unpleasant alternative is likely to be true. This insidious pattern of thinking underlies a good deal of what we think of as prejudice, bigotry, narrowmindedness: "If you're not a Christian, then you're not really religious." "If you're not religious, you're un-patriotic." "The choice is between American democracy and Russian communism." Don't oversimplify; acknowledge the rich complexity of most issues.

exaggerating the trivial
Distorting the evidence by treating a minor point as if it were a major one. If the point is your own, discerning readers will infer that you lack substantial evidence and have had to fall back on weak arguments. If the point is an opposing one, they will infer that you can't refute major points and are trying to make yourself look good by demolishing easy targets. "We should all give more to charity because being gen-erous can give us a warm feeling inside"—worth mentioning perhaps, but not worth dwelling on. "Those who are against raising tuition point out that students are happier if they have a little pocket-money. Now let's examine this argument carefully . . . " No—better leave it alone. On the other hand, don't distort the evidence by trivializing opposition points that *are* important.

false or weak analogy
Oversimplifying the evidence by arguing that because two things are alike in some features, they are necessarily alike in one or more others as well. You can say that learning to ride a bicycle is like learning to

play the piano: once you learn, you seldom forget; but you would scarcely go on to argue that one should have a bicycle tuned periodically or that one should mount a tail-light on the piano for safety while playing at night. Analogies can provide interesting and concrete illustrations; by suggesting similarities they can help define or clarify or explain or emphasize something; see for example our analogies between constructing paragraphs and cabinetmaking (**69** and **69d**) and between an outline and a road map (**73g**). Analogies cannot produce proof; they can seldom produce even strong probability; but they can assist in the job of persuasion. We would not expect our analogy to convince you of the importance of an outline, but we hope that, by adding its concrete touch, we help you understand and perhaps accept our assertions. One fairly common argument claims that because city or provincial or other governments are in some respects similar to large business organizations, they need experienced and successful business people to run them. The more similarities you can point to, the stronger the argument. The trouble with this and other arguments from analogy, however, is that no matter how many specific similarities you can come up with, your opponents can usually keep ahead of you by citing an even greater number of specific and significant differences. Try it.

equivocation

Using a term in more than one sense; being ambiguous, whether accidentally or intentionally. "It is only natural for intelligent people to reject this idea. And as science tells us, natural law is the law of the universe; it is the law of truth, and must be obeyed." Aside from the cheap appeal to snobbery and self-esteem (we all like to think we are "intelligent," but just what *is* "intelligence"?) and the appeal to the prestige of "science" in the modern world (but just how infallible *is* science?) and the imposing but vague term *universe* and the glittering abstraction *truth*, do the two occurrences of the word *natural* jibe with each other? And is a natural *law* comparable to legislation passed by a government and enforced by the police and the courts? Don't be attracted by nebulous nonsense, and don't let the meanings of words shift as you move from one phrase or sentence to the next. Choose and use your words carefully.

non sequitur

"It does not follow." Any flaw in reasoning. When for whatever reason a conclusion does not logically follow from its premises or from the particular examples cited to support it, it is a *non sequitur*. The term would apply to any of the fallacies discussed above and also to such leaps of emotional logic as "She's an attractive woman; she'd make a good vice-president," and "I've put a great deal of time and effort into this project; the grade it gets should reflect that fact."

Exercise 74 (1): Detecting faulty reasoning

Point out the fallacious reasoning in the following. If an item fits one or more of the named fallacies, identify it.

1. She's a Liberal, so she's sure to use the taxpayers' money for all sorts of give-away programs, for that's what "liberal" means: generous.
2. Your advertisement says that you want someone with experience as a computer programmer. I've had a year's experience as a computer programmer, so I'm clearly the person you want for the job.
3. Since aspirin can be harmful to some people—or to anyone, if it is over-used—it should either be taken off the market or made available by prescription only.
4. He's bound to have an inferiority complex. Look how short he is!
5. Novels written by women often have women as protagonists. Since this novel has a woman as protagonist, it was probably written by a woman.
6. In the past my garage has kept my car running well, but this year they've hired a new mechanic and my car is always acting up. Obviously the new mechanic is incompetent.
7. Dogs make better pets than cats because when they wag their tails they're happy; cats flick their tails when they're angry.
8. This critic says Jane Austen's novels are second-rate, but since he's known to be a Marxist his judgment won't stand up.
9. If I am not elected, the world will come to an end.
10. Student opinion is overwhelmingly in favour of dropping the second-year English requirement. I took a poll among my fellow science-majors, and over 80% of them agreed.
11. The police are supposed to protect society from criminals. When they give me parking tickets they're not doing their job, for I'm not harming society and I'm certainly not a criminal.
12. This has been an unusually hot summer, no doubt as a result of the eruption of that Mexican volcano last year.
13. Movie stars live glamorous lives. They must be much happier than most other people.
14. This party is for higher tariffs and lower taxes, and so am I. That's why I am loyal to the party and always vote for its candidate.
15. People who live and work together constitute a social community, and in a democracy social communities should have a measure of self-government. Since the university is such a community, and since the vast majority of those participating in its life are students, it follows that students should have a major say in the running of the university.
16. Politicians are all a bunch of crooks. Look for example at _____ and _____. And don't forget _____.
17. Advertising is like fishing. Advertisers use something attractive for bait and reel out their lines to dangle the bait in front of us. They think of consumers as poor dumb fish, suckers who will swallow their stuff hook, line, and sinker. And there's a lesson for us in that: if you bite you'll get hurt, for there's always a nasty hook under the bait. The only way to protect yourself is to make sure you don't fall for any advertiser's pitch.

exercises

Exercise 74 (2): Analyzing arguments and recognizing persuasive techniques

(a) In an essay, analyze three or four current magazine advertisements for different kinds of products. Point out all the techniques of persuasion you can find in them. Do they appeal more to emotion than to reason? Are they guilty of any particular fallacies?

(b) Look over a week's worth of the editorial and letters pages of a local city or campus newspaper. Select and analyze three or four editorials or letters in order to reveal their argumentative techniques.

(c) Find a more extended piece of argumentative writing in a magazine with national circulation. Try to find one arguing about some issue of national importance. Analyze it as an argument. Consider its subject, its audience, its structure, its methods of reasoning, its possible weaknesses, and so on.

Exercise 74 (3): Including the opposition

In the following sentence outline for an argumentative essay, the student took little account of points the opposition might raise. Read through it carefully, listing as many opposition arguments as you can think of; then recast the outline so as to include those arguments. You can improve the outline in other ways as well. If you find the counter-arguments compelling, you may recast the thesis so that you are arguing for the other side. Include in the revised outline one or more sentences each for both a possible beginning and a possible ending of the essay. Think up a good title.

Thesis statement: In my opinion, it is better to watch sports events at home rather than in a stadium.

  I. By staying home, sports fans save money on tickets, transportation, and baby-sitters.
    A. The cost of watching a game at home is a mere fraction of the cost of a ticket to get into a stadium.
    B. Any kind of transportation is an additional cost to a sports fan who goes to a stadium.
      1. Cars require fuel and parking.
      2. Taxis are expensive.
      3. Buses are too slow.
    C. Parents who wish to see a game live must hire a babysitter.

  II. Television viewers have the comforts and conveniences of staying at home.
    A. They have easy access to relatively inexpensive refreshments and to washroom facilities.
    B. They can sit in an open and relaxed manner.
      1. Stadium seats are too compact and uncomfortable.
      2. Bad weather causes outdoor fans even more discomfort.
    C. When one is in a large crowd it is often difficult to concentrate on a game.

  III. Television offers its viewers the best coverage of any kind of game.
    A. Instant replays and close-ups clarify important events in a game.
    B. Sportscasters provide play-by-play coverage with informative commentary.
    C. Television keeps its viewers entertained during intermission periods.

Exercise 74 (4): Writing an argument

Carefully plan and write an argument of between 1000 and 1250 words on some local issue—perhaps something you found while working on part (b) of Exercise 74 (2). Take a position you sincerely believe in. Don't pick so large a topic that you can't deal with it fairly thoroughly. Be sure to take into account any major opposition arguments.

| 75 | **Writing In-Class Essays and Essay Examinations** |

Writing an essay in class or during an examination is just like writing an essay in your own room, in the library, or anywhere else—except that you have to do it faster: you don't have time to think at leisure and at length. Therefore you need to make the best use of the time you have. All the principles we discuss earlier in this chapter still hold, but here is some additional advice to help you work quickly and efficiently.

1. On an examination, *read the whole thing through* right away. If it has more than one part, budget your time. Before you start thinking and writing, decide just how much time you will need or can afford to spend on each part.

2. *Read* the topics or questions *carefully*. Don't, in haste, misread or misinterpret. Don't read wishfully, finding in a question what you *want* to find instead of what is actually there.

3. *Follow instructions*. If you're asked for an argument, *argue*. If a question asks you to *analyze* a poem, don't simply give your opinion or evaluation of it. If it asks you to *justify* or *defend* your opinions or conclusions, don't simply assert them. If it asks for *comparison and contrast*, don't spend overlong on just one side of the matter. If it asks you to *define* a term or concept, don't simply describe it or give an example of it, and don't ramble on about your feelings or impressions of it. And so on.

4. *Take time to plan*. Don't panic and begin writing immediately. *Think* for a few minutes. The more time you spend planning, the easier and surer the writing itself will be. Do a little quick brainstorming. Take the time to make at least a sketch outline, with a *thesis* or proposition and a list of main points and supporting details; you will then be less likely to wander off the topic or change your thesis as you proceed. It's often a good idea to limit yourself to three or four main points, or parts (in *addition*, that is, to a beginning and an ending).

5. *Get started*. Once you've drawn up your plan, start writing. If necessary, leave several lines or a page blank at the beginning and plunge right into your first point. Don't waste time trying to think of a beginning if one doesn't occur to you quickly; you can come back and fill it in later. Quite possibly you won't need to supply a separate "beginning" at all. In any event, *don't waffle*. Get to the point quickly and stay with it. Make your *thesis* clear early on—that may be all you

need by way of a beginning. Often you can pick up some key words or phrases from the question or topic and use them to help frame a thesis and get yourself going.

6. *Write carefully.* Whereas on a home essay you may well write your draft hurriedly and spend most of your time revising, here you have to do most of your revising as you go along (another reason it's important to have a *plan*; without one, you could, as you pause to tinker with a sentence, forget your thread of continuity, your line of argument). And you won't have time to do much revising; your first efforts at sentences will often have to do. Furthermore, unless you make an illegible mess, don't waste time recopying.

7. Aim for *quality*, not *quantity*. *More* is not necessarily *better*. Of course your essay must be of reasonable length, and sometimes a required minimum length will be specified. What is most important is that you adequately *develop* your subject by developing each of your main points. But don't try to impress by going on and on, for then you will likely ramble, lose control of your thesis and your organization, and commit writing errors because of haste.

8. *Be specific.* Provide examples, illustrations, evidence. By all means generalize, but *support* your generalizations with specific and concrete details.

9. *Conclude effectively.* Don't tack on a stiff conclusion, especially one that is nothing more than lame repetition. Try somehow to refer to or restate your thesis, and if necessary refer again to your three or four main points, but do so in a way that adds something new. Sometimes a single concluding sentence can make a good clincher, especially if it suggests or underscores some result or effect growing out of what your discussion has said.

10. *Proofread carefully.* Leave yourself enough time to look for the kinds of careless mistakes we all make when writing fast. Don't just run your eyes over your sentences, assuming that any errors will leap out at you, even though that may give you the illusion that you've checked your work. Read carefully. If you know that you're prone to certain kinds of errors, look specifically for them.

If you need to consult only one or two outside sources in order to write an essay—for example some critical comment on a literary work—it will be easy enough to keep track of your sources and the notes you take from them so that you can provide the necessary documentation (see *ack* and *doc* in Chapter XI). But when you are writing a full-fledged research paper, one depending predominantly on outside sources, the task of keeping things straight can be formidable. The following chapter outlines briefly the mechanical process of writing such a paper and points out the precautions one must take to work efficiently and accurately.

But first, just what is a "research" or "library" paper or essay? At one extreme, it can be simply the culmination of a fact-finding process: the writer locates information about a subject and presents it in a coherent report. At the other extreme, it can mean that the writer consults a number of outside sources, interprets and evaluates the information and arguments they offer, and then produces an essay which is a piece of original thinking; though it is based on or begins with the information gathered by research, it is nevertheless an expression of a new attitude toward the subject. Most research papers fall somewhere in between these two extremes. A particular assignment or occasion will usually call for a particular kind of result. But it is a good rule to try to make the resulting essay represent your independent thought as much as possible, however much it may be based on facts and ideas gathered from outside sources; when writing a research paper, always try to draw your own conclusions. The worst—and dullest—kind of "research paper" presents gathered data in a mechanical way; such a paper is merely a pastiche, a cut-and-paste job, which has involved the writer's own intelligence only in deciding what data to present and in what order.

A student who is assigned or chooses an unfamiliar research topic, and who explores that topic conscientiously, may eventually produce a dull report—nevertheless that student will have learned a good deal in the process. (Only a graduate student writing a dissertation is really expected to produce a substantial and original contribution to knowledge.) And in the process of exploring an unfamiliar subject and writing about it, a student will also learn a good deal about how to do research and present the results. For the undergraduate, or for any inexperienced writer, learning about *method* is very important. The chapter which follows is intended to make that learning easier than it might otherwise be. It also provides examples of footnotes, parenthetical documentation, and bibliography. Finally, there is a sample research essay which, with the accompanying comments provided, will repay your close attention as an illustration of the matters discussed in the body of the chapter.

IX

THE PROCESS OF WRITING A RESEARCH PAPER

An essay based on library research is still an essay: it should conform to the principles governing any good essay. But research essays also require writers to follow certain procedures which are not a part of writing other kinds of essays. This chapter outlines the process of writing a research essay; in it we isolate and discuss and illustrate the various steps and the details that you must keep in mind in order to do a good job with a minimum of time and effort. All the matters discussed below are important. They are not intended merely to show you things you *may* do, but rather to show you the kinds of things you *must* do in order to put together a good essay without wasting time and energy and without risking serious error. Some of these steps and details may seem almost absurdly mechanical, and some of them may look like unnecessary fiddling, but all of them are important, and all of them have proved useful to many writers.

Note: The system outlined below is of course not the only possible system, but it is a tested one. An instructor may wish you to follow a different system, for example to make out note or bibliography cards in a different way or to cross-reference material in a special way. Indeed, after some experience you may yourself devise or discover different or additional methods of safeguarding accuracy and increasing efficiency. No one system is sacrosanct: the important thing is to *have* a system. The alternative is likely to be confusion, error, and wasted effort.

76 The Library and Its Resources

Learn your way around your library: whether on a conducted tour or all on your own, explore its layout, its reference facilities, its other holdings, its catalogues, its whole system—in a word, its resources. Don't be afraid to ask the librarians for help when you need it. Once you feel reasonably at home in what may be a vast and complex building, you can begin to use the library as it is intended to be used.

76a The Catalogues

You will find different kinds of cataloguing systems in different libraries, or even in a single library. Many libraries have converted or are in the process of converting to a **microcatalogue** using some kind of microform (microprint, microcard, microfilm, microfiche) which you can read on machines in the catalogue area. If your library has not converted to a space- and time-saving microcatalogue system, or uses one only for material acquired after a certain date, you will be using a **card catalogue**, in which a library's holdings are listed on cards, one item to a card (an "item" may consist of several volumes), and kept in drawers or trays.

In either kind of system the listings are usually cross-referenced (found under more than one heading), in order to make it easier for you to find what you need. If you know only the author of a book, look in the section called the Author Catalogue; if you know the title, look in the Title Catalogue. These two are often combined in one Author-Title Catalogue. If you are not seeking a specific book but are interested in a particular subject, look in the Subject Catalogue. In some libraries, parts of the subject catalogue, such as the names of writers, are combined with the author and title catalogues. In a small library, all three catalogues may be entirely combined. Some libraries also have a Shelf Catalogue, in which the cards are arranged by **call numbers** and are therefore in the same order as the books on the shelves. Such a catalogue may also double as a location file, if the library has branches. There may also be a Serial List of periodicals (magazines, newspapers, journals) and other works that are published serially, in a continuing succession of installments.

76b Reference Books

A library's reference section contains many sources of information. Here is a sampling to suggest the kinds of reference books usually available and some of the standard or more useful items in each category. Of course not all libraries will have all these, and the lists are necessarily incomplete; find out for yourself what reference aids are in your library. Make your own voyage of discovery through the reference section: you may be astonished at the quantity and variety of information available to you.

Before you begin work on any particular project, it is a good idea to browse through some of the relevant reference sources in order to get an idea of what kind of information is available. In addition, as you explore you will find that often an article in an encyclopedia or a book on a given subject will itself include bibliographical information; by following such leads you can often save much of the time you might otherwise spend searching for sources.

Note: Since many reference books—especially dictionaries, encyclopedias, and the like—are frequently updated in revised editions or with supplements, we omit dates of publication. Simply find and use the latest edition available. For many indexes and the like, we give the year when coverage began; that is, "1900-" means "from 1900 to the present date." With these, even if you're working on a current topic, you should go back at least a few years in search of relevant material.

Catalogues, Bibliographical Aids, and Reference Guides (General)

Basic Reference Sources: An Introduction to Materials and Methods
Bibliographic Index: A Cumulative Bibliography of Bibliographies (1938-)
Bibliography of Canadian Bibliographies
Books in Print; Paperbound Books in Print; Subject Guide to Books in Print
Canadian Books in Print
Cumulative Book Index
Government of Canada Publications
Guide to Basic Reference Materials for Canadian Libraries
Guide to Reference Books
Guide to the Use of Books and Libraries
Microform Research Collections: A Guide
Monthly Catalog of United States Government Publications
National Union Catalog
Union List of Serials in Libraries of the United States and Canada; New Serial Titles
Vertical File Index (1935-)
A World Bibliography of Bibliographies

Dictionaries and Other Word-Books

Brewer's Dictionary of Phrase and Fable
A Dictionary of American English on Historical Principles
A Dictionary of American Idioms

Dictionary of American Slang
A Dictionary of Canadianisms on Historical Principles
A Dictionary of Contemporary American Usage
Dictionary of Foreign Phrases and Classical Quotations
Dictionary of Foreign Terms
A Dictionary of Modern English Usage
Dictionary of Newfoundland English
A Dictionary of Slang and Unconventional English
Dictionary of Word and Phrase Origins
Funk & Wagnalls New Standard Dictionary
Funk & Wagnalls Standard Handbook of Synonyms, Antonyms, and Prepositions
Gage Canadian Dictionary
The Houghton Mifflin Canadian Dictionary of the English Language
Illustrated Dictionary of Place Names: United States and Canada
Modern American Usage
Nouveau Petit Larousse Illustré
Origins: A Short Etymological Dictionary of Modern English
The Oxford Dictionary of English Etymology
The Oxford English Dictionary
The Random House Dictionary of the English Language
Roget's International Thesaurus
Roget's II: The New Thesaurus
Webster's Third New International Dictionary of the English Language

Quotations

Bartlett's *Familiar Quotations*
Colombo's Canadian Quotations
The Macmillan Book of Proverbs, Maxims, and Famous Phrases
The Oxford Dictionary of English Proverbs
The Oxford Dictionary of Quotations
The Quotable Woman, 1800-1980

Periodical and Other Indexes (General)

Alternative Press Index (1973-)
British Humanities Index (1962-)
The Canadian Essay and Literature Index (1973-)
Canadian Newspaper Index (1977-)
Canadian Periodical Index (1929-)
Comprehensive Index to English-Language Little Magazines
Current Contents
Dissertation Abstracts; Dissertation Abstracts International

Essay and General Literature Index (1900-)
French Periodical Index (1973-)
Guide to Indian Periodical Literature (1964-)
Index to the Times (London) (1906-)
Indian Press Index (1968-)
International Index to Periodicals (1907-1960)
 International Index (1960-1965)
  Social Sciences and Humanities Index (1965-1974)
  Social Sciences Index (1974-)
  Humanities Index (1974-)
Le Monde: Index Analytique (1967-) (covers from 1944)
The New York Times Index (1851-)
Poole's Index to Periodical Literature (1802-1906)
Readers' Guide to Periodical Literature (1900-)
Répertoire analytique d'articles de revues de Québec (1972-)
Ulrich's International Periodicals Directory
The Wall Street Journal Index (1958-)

Book Reviews (General)

American Reference Books Annual (1970-)
The Book Review Digest (1905-)
Book Review Index (1965-)
The Canadian Book Review Annual (1975-)
Current Book Review Citations (1977-)
New York Times Book Review Index (1896-)

Encyclopedias (General)

Academic American Encyclopedia
The Canadian Encyclopedia
Chambers's Encyclopaedia
Collier's Encyclopedia
Colombo's Canadian References
Encyclopedia Americana
The Encyclopaedia Britannica (Don't overlook the often useful 11th
 edition, 1910-1911.)
The New Columbia Encyclopedia

Collections of Facts and Opinions; Yearbooks; Atlases and Gazetteers

The American Annual (1923-)
The Annual Register: A Record of World Events (1758-)
Britannica Book of the Year (1938-)

76b *reference books*

Canada Gazetteer Atlas
Canada Year Book (1886-)
Canadian News Facts (1967-)
Columbia Lippincott Gazetteer of the World
Cultural Atlas of Africa
Editorials on File (1970-)
Europa Year Book (1926-1929); *Europa* (1930-)
Facts on File: A Weekly World News Digest (1940-)
Gallup Opinion Index (1965-)
Information Please Almanac (1947-)
The Macmillan Bible Atlas
National Geographic Atlas of the World
New International Year Book (1907-)
Statesman's Year Book (1864-)
The Times Atlas of the World
The World Almanac & Book of Facts (1868-)
The Year Book of World Affairs

Biography (General)

Biography Index (1946-)
Canadian Who's Who (1910-)
Chambers's Biographical Dictionary
Current Biography (1940-)
Dictionary of American Biography
Dictionary of Canadian Biography
Dictionary of National Biography (British)
The International Who's Who (1935-)
The McGraw-Hill Encyclopedia of World Biography
Webster's Biographical Dictionary
Who's Who (British) (1849-)
Who's Who in America (1899-)
Who's Who of American Women (1958-)

History, Geography, Politics

African Encyclopedia
Arctic Bibliography (1953-)
Australian Public Affairs Information Service: Subject Index to Current Literature (1945-)
The Cambridge Ancient History
The Cambridge History of Islam
The Cambridge Medieval History
Canadian Annual Review of Politics and Public Affairs (1971-)
China: An Annotated Bibliography of Bibliographies

China Facts and Figures Annual (1978-)
China Official Yearbook
The Concise Maori Handbook
A Current Bibliography on African Affairs (1962-)
Current Geographical Publications (1938-)
Cyclopaedia of India
Dictionary of American History
A Dictionary of British History
Dictionary of Political Analysis
Dictionary of Political Science and Law
Encyclopedia of Asian Civilizations
Encyclopedia of Newfoundland and Labrador
An Encyclopedia of World History
Everyman's Dictionary of Dates
Geographical Abstracts (1966-)
A Guide to Reference Materials on India
The Harper Dictionary of Modern Thought
Harper Encyclopedia of the Modern World
Harvard Guide to American History
Historical Abstracts (1955-)
Historic Documents (1972-)
Index to Book Reviews in Historical Periodicals (1973-)
International Bibliography of Historical Sciences (1926-)
International Political Science Abstracts (1951-)
The New Cambridge Modern History
The Oxford Classical Dictionary
The Oxford Companion to American History
Peace Research Abstracts Journal (1964-)
Political Handbook of the World (1927-)
Public Affairs Information Service Bulletin (1915-)
The Times Atlas of World History
Vietnam: A Guide to Reference Sources
Yearbook of the United Nations (1946-)

76b *reference books*

Science and Technology

Agricultural Index (1916-1964); *Biological and Agricultural Index* (1964-)
Applied Ecology Abstracts (1975-1979); *Ecology Abstracts* (1980-)
Bibliography of Current Computing Literature (1967-)
Biological Abstracts (1926-)
British Technology Index (1962-)
The Cambridge Encyclopaedia of Astronomy
The Cambridge Encyclopaedia of Earth Sciences
Chemical Abstracts (1907-)

Computer and Control Abstracts (1969-)
Computer Dictionary and Handbook
Computer Literature Index (1980-)
Computer Yearbook (1972-)
Concise Encyclopedia of the Sciences
Dictionary of Biology
Dictionary of Computers, Data Processing, and Telecommunications
A Dictionary of Genetics
A Dictionary of Geology
Dictionary of Scientific Biography
The Encyclopedia of Chemistry
Encyclopedia of Computer Science and Technology
The Encyclopedia of Oceanography
The Encyclopedia of Physics
The Encyclopedia of the Biological Sciences
The Engineering Index (1884-)
Environment Abstracts (1971-)
The Environment Index (1971-)
A Guide to the History of Science
Guide to the Literature of the Life Sciences
Harper Encyclopedia of Science
Index Medicus (1899-)
Industrial Arts Index (1913-1957); *Applied Science and Technology Index*
   (1958-)
International Encyclopedia of Chemical Science
McGraw-Hill Basic Bibliography of Science and Technology
McGraw-Hill Encyclopedia of Environmental Science
McGraw-Hill Encyclopedia of Science and Technology
Oxford Dictionary of Computing
The Penguin Dictionary of Science
Prentice-Hall Encyclopedia of Mathematics
Reference Sources in Science and Technology
Science Citation Index (1961-)
Science Reference Sources
Sourcebook on the Environment: A Guide to the Literature
Stein and Day International Medical Encyclopedia
Universal Encyclopedia of Mathematics
Van Nostrand's Scientific Encyclopedia
Who's Who in Ecology (1973-)
The Zoological Record (1864-)

Social Sciences; Education

Abstracts in Anthropology (1970-)
Canadian Education Index (1965-)

Contemporary Psychology (1956-)
Current Anthropology (1960-)
Current Index to Journals in Education (1969-)
Dictionary of Anthropology
Dictionary of Education
A Dictionary of Psychology
A Dictionary of Sociology
A Dictionary of the Social Sciences
The Education Index (1929-)
The Encyclopedia of Education
Encyclopedia of Educational Research
Encyclopedia of Human Behavior: Psychology, Psychiatry, and Mental Health
Encyclopedia of Psychology
Encyclopedia of Social Work
Encyclopedia of Sociology
Encyclopedia of the Social Sciences
The Harvard List of Books in Psychology
Indian Behavioural Sciences Abstracts (1970-)
International Bibliography of Social and Cultural Anthropology (1955-)
International Bibliography of Sociology (1951-)
International Encyclopedia of the Social Sciences
Psychological Abstracts (1927-)
Psychological Index (1894-1935)
A Reader's Guide to the Social Sciences
Royal Anthropological Institute Index to Current Periodicals (1963-)
Social Sciences Index (1974-)
Sociological Abstracts (1953-)
Sources of Information in the Social Sciences: A Guide to the Literature
Women's Studies: A Checklist of Bibliographies
Women Studies Bibliography

Economics and Business

Business Periodicals Index (1958-)
Canadian Business Index (1975-)
Cumulative Bibliography of Economic Books (1954-)
A Dictionary of Economics
Economic Abstracts (1953-)
Encyclopedia of Advertising
Encyclopedia of Banking and Finance
Encyclopedia of Economics
The Encyclopedia of Management
Everyman's Dictionary of Economics
Handbook of Modern Marketing

International Bibliography of Economics (1952-)
The McGraw-Hill Dictionary of Modern Economics
Survey of Economic and Social History in Canada (1976-)

Philosophy, Religion, Mythology, Folklore

Analytical Concordance to the Bible
The Anchor Bible
Bulfinch's Mythology
Catholic Periodical Index (1930-)
The Concise Encyclopedia of Western Philosophy and Philosophers
Cruden's Complete Concordance to the Old and New Testaments
The Dartmouth Bible
A Dictionary of Non-Christian Religions
Dictionary of Philosophy
Dictionary of the Bible
Dictionary of the History of Ideas
Encyclopedia Judaica
Encyclopedia of Bioethics
An Encyclopedia of Occultism
The Encyclopedia of Philosophy
An Encyclopedia of Religion
Encyclopedia of Religion and Ethics
Everyman's Dictionary of Non-Classical Mythology
Funk & Wagnalls Standard Dictionary of Folklore, Mythology, and Legend
The Golden Bough: A Study in Magic and Religion
A Handbook of Greek Mythology
Harper Bible Dictionary
Index to Jewish Periodicals (1963-)
International Standard Bible Encyclopedia
The Interpreter's Bible
Larousse World Mythology
The Mennonite Encyclopedia
Motif-Index of Folk-Literature
The Mythology of All Races
Nelson's Complete Concordance of the Revised Standard Version Bible
New Catholic Encyclopedia
A New Dictionary of Christian Theology
The New Standard Jewish Encyclopedia
The Oxford Dictionary of Saints
The Oxford Dictionary of the Christian Church
The Philosopher's Index (1967-)
A Reader's Guide to the Great Religions

Religion Index (1949-)
The Universal Jewish Encyclopedia

The Arts

Art Index (1929-)
Arts and Humanities Citation Index (1978-)
Biographical Dictionary of Musicians
Bryan's Dictionary of Painters and Engravers
The Concise Oxford Dictionary of Ballet
The Concise Oxford Dictionary of Music
Crowell's Handbook of World Opera
The Dance Encyclopedia
Dictionary of Contemporary Photography
A Dictionary of Symbols
The Encyclopedia of Dance and Ballet
The Encyclopedia of Jazz
Encyclopedia of Music in Canada
Encyclopedia of Painting
Encyclopedia of Pop, Rock, and Soul
Encyclopedia of the Opera
Encyclopedia of World Architecture
Encyclopedia of World Art
The Harvard Dictionary of Music
The International Cyclopedia of Music and Musicians
The Larousse Encyclopedia of Music
The Lives of the Painters
McGraw-Hill Dictionary of Art
The Music Index (1949-)
New Dictionary of Modern Sculpture
The New Grove Dictionary of Music and Musicians
The New Oxford History of Music
The Oxford Companion to Art
The Oxford Companion to Music
The Oxford Companion to the Decorative Arts
The Praeger Encyclopedia of Art

Drama, Film, Television

Annual Index to Motion Picture Credits
Bibliographic Guide to Theatre Arts (1975-)
Canada on Stage: Canadian Theatre Review Yearbook
The Complete Encyclopedia of Television Programs
Dictionary of Films
Dramatic Criticism Index

76b *reference books*

The Dramatic Index (1909-)
The Encyclopedia of World Theater
Film Canadiana (1969-)
A History of English Drama
International Encyclopedia of Film
International Index to Film Periodicals (1972-)
International Motion Picture Almanac
International Television Almanac (1956-)
The Macmillan Film Bibliography
Magill's Survey of Cinema
McGraw-Hill Encyclopedia of World Drama
Modern World Drama: An Encyclopedia
The New York Times Film Reviews (1913-)
The New York Times Theater Reviews (1920-)
The Oxford Companion to Film
The Oxford Companion to the Theatre
Play Index (1949-)
Radio and Television: A Selected, Annotated Bibliography
The Reader's Encyclopedia of World Drama
Television Drama Series Programming: A Comprehensive Chronicle (1959-)
TV Facts
Variety International Showbusiness Reference
The World Encyclopedia of Film

Literature and Language

Abstracts of English Studies (1958-)
Annual Bibliography of English Language and Literature (1920-)
A Bibliography of the English Language from the Invention of Printing to the Year 1800
Children's Book Review Index (1975-)
Children's Literature Abstracts (1973-)
Children's Literature: An Annotated Bibliography of the History and Criticism
Children's Literature Review
A Complete and Systematic Concordance to the Works of Shakespeare
Contemporary Authors (1962-)
Contemporary Literary Criticism (1973-)
Critical Writings on Commonwealth Literatures: A Selective Bibliography to 1970, with a List of Theses and Dissertations
Dictionary of Literary Biography
Encyclopedia of World Literature in the 20th Century
Fiction Catalog (1908-)
A Handbook to Literature
A History of the English Language

Index to Children's Poetry
Language and Language Behavior Abstracts (1967-)
Letters in Canada (1935-)
Linguistic Bibliography (1939-)
Literary History of Canada
A Literary History of England
Literary History of the United States
Magill's Bibliography of Literary Criticism
MLA International Bibliography of Books and Articles on the Modern Languages and Literatures (1922-)
The New Cambridge Bibliography of English Literature
Nineteenth-Century Literary Criticism
The Oxford Companion to American Literature
The Oxford Companion to Canadian Literature
The Oxford Companion to Children's Literature
The Oxford Companion to Classical Literature
The Oxford Companion to English Literature
The Oxford Companion to French Literature
The Oxford Companion to German Literature
The Oxford Companion to Spanish Literature
The Oxford History of English Literature
The Penguin Companion to American Literature
The Penguin Companion to Classical, Oriental, and African Literature
The Penguin Companion to English Literature
The Penguin Companion to European Literature
Princeton Encyclopedia of Poetry and Poetics
The Reader's Encyclopedia
A Reference Guide to English, American, and Canadian Literature
A Reference Guide to English Studies
A Research Guide to Science Fiction Studies
Selective Bibliography for the Study of English and American Literature
Short Story Index (1953-)
Something about the Author: Facts and Pictures about Contemporary Authors and Illustrators of Books for Young People (1971-)
Survey of Science Fiction Literature
Twentieth Century Authors
Twentieth-Century Literary Criticism
The Who's Who of Children's Literature
The World Encyclopedia of Comics
The Year's Work in English Studies (1919-)
The Year's Work in Modern Language Studies (1929-)

76b *reference books*

(**Note:** For a more extensive list, see "Major Reference Works" in *The Random House Dictionary of the English Language*, pp. 1906-13.)

■ 77 ■ Collecting Data: Sources

■ 77a ■ The Preliminary Bibliography

Once you have decided on or been assigned a subject, the first step in gathering information is to compile a **preliminary bibliography**. By consulting various sources (for example periodical indexes, essay indexes, general and particular bibliographies, encyclopedias, and of course the card catalogue or microcatalogue), make a list of possibly useful sources of information about your topic. Next, look in the appropriate catalogues to find out which items on your list are available in your library, and record the call number of each one (you will already have done this for items you first found in the catalogues).

■ 77b ■ Bibliography Cards

When you begin looking at the actual books and articles on your list, there are two things you should do.

First, as soon as you locate a book or article, make out a bibliography card for it. It is best to use the small eight-by-twelve-centimetre or three-by-five-inch index cards. Using cards enables you to keep track of material easily: you can keep them in handy alphabetical order, insert new cards as you find new sources, and put aside cards for sources you think are of no use to you. **Caution**: Do not throw away any of these cards, even if you think they will be useless to you, for at a later stage you may decide to use some of them after all. In fact, don't throw away anything: keep all your notes, jottings, scribblings, lists, and drafts, for they may prove useful later when you want to check back on something.

You will save time if you record the bibliographical information exactly as it will appear later in your bibliography (see **83e**). Make sure that you record this information accurately and completely: double-check spellings, dates, page numbers, and so on. And be sure to record the information from the book or article itself; don't simply copy it onto your card from your preliminary list. Only if your data come from the actual work itself can you be confident that they are accurate.

Note: Some writers prefer not to make a list but instead to enter each item on a card as soon as they come across it in a bibliography or other source. This does save one step, but if you choose to follow such a method, be careful: as soon as you come upon the actual book or article, check your card against it for accuracy, because bibliographies and other lists sometimes contain errors, for example in spelling or punctuation or even dates. One could argue, then, that copying the information from the actual source onto a card also saves a step.

Second, peruse the book or article to find out how useful it promises to be, and jot down, on the card, a quick note to yourself about its worth as a source. For example, note whether it is promising or appears to be of little or no use, or whether it looks good for a particular part of your project, or whether one part of it looks useful and the rest not. Be as specific as you can, for a glance at such a note may later save you the trouble of a return trip to the library. You may also want to write a label, called a **slug** (see **78c**), on each card, indicating what part of your subject it pertains to; this information too could save you extra trips. For the same reason, you might note on a card just how thorough your examination of the source was; that is, if you just glanced at it, you may want to return to it, but if you found it so interesting that you read it carefully and even took notes, then you will know that you need not return to it later. And, in case you do want to return to a source, save yourself time by recording the call number of each item; the lower left-hand corner of the card is a good place for this.

Here are three sample bibliography cards that go with the sample research paper later in this chapter. Note the arrangement and completeness of the bibliographical information, the slugs in the upper

Bowman, James S. "Public Opinion and the Environment: Post-Earth Day Attitudes Among College Students," *Environment and Behavior*, 9 (1977), 385-416.

III-Concl

HM 206 — includes 3 pages of
E 59   references!
B 5

Calef, Charles E. "Not out of the Woods." *Environment*, 18, No. 7 (Sept. 1976), 17-20, 25

III ?

TD — read through; made notes
A1   on proposed "energy
E58   plantation."

> McBoyle, G. R., and E. Sommerville, eds.
> *Canada's Natural Environment: Essays*
> *in Applied Geography.* Toronto:
> Methuen, 1976
>
> HC — title sounds limiting, but maybe
> 120 "geographers" have more to do with
> E5 it than I thought. Theberge on
> C34 parks looks promising, and
> 1976 Jackson on 'government action.

right-hand corners, the writer's notes to herself in the lower right, and the library call numbers in the lower left. (One card has no slug; its several essays applied so widely that the writer later made out separate cards for each one she used.)

78 Taking Notes

When you have compiled your preliminary bibliography and begun consulting the items it lists, you will also be taking some notes—a process that will accelerate as you go along, until your collection of bibliography cards is complete and you are only taking notes. Your preliminary research should be relatively casual, for you will still be exploring your subject, investigating and weighing its possibilities, and attempting to limit it (see **73b**) as much as necessary. You should now be able to construct a **preliminary outline** (see **73f–j**)—which of course will be subject to change as you go along.

At first you may be uncertain about the usefulness or relevance of some of the material you come across. Be generous with yourself: take many notes. If you toss aside a book that doesn't look useful now, you may discover later that you need it after all; it is better to spend a few minutes taking some careful notes than to spend an hour or two on a return trip to the library only to find that the book has been borrowed by someone else. Use it while you have your hands on it.

For your notes you will need a separate stack of index cards. If you use the same size card as you used for your bibliography, use a different colour so that you can easily distinguish between them. Or use the larger ten-by-fifteen-centimetre or four-by-six-inch cards, especially if your writing is large. On each **note card** you will include at least three things: the note itself, the exact source, and a label or slug indicating just what part of your subject the note pertains to.

78a   The Note Itself

1. *Include only one point on each card.* The reason for using cards in the first place is that it is easy to shuffle them around, to arrange them as you see fit at various stages. If you try to cram too much information onto one card, you will not be able to move it so easily; you may even have to recopy part of the material onto another card so that you can shift it to where you want it. Don't include two or three closely related points on one card unless you are certain that they will occur together in your essay.

2. *Be as brief as possible.* If for some reason your note must extend beyond one side of a card—if for example it is an unusually long summary or quotation—it can be continued on the back of the card. If this happens, be sure to write a large OVER in the bottom right-hand corner so that you cannot forget that there is more to the note than appears on the front side. Or, to be even safer, continue the note on another card. If it is ever necessary to use more than one card for a single note, be sure to repeat the listing of the source at the top of each card, and number the cards. For example, if a note extended to three cards, card one should say *1 of 3*, card two *2 of 3*, and the last card *3 of 3*.

3. *Distinguish carefully between direct quotation and paraphrase or summary* (see **81**). Generally, use as little direct quotation as possible, but when you feel that you must quote directly, be exaggeratedly careful: your quotation must accurately reproduce the original, including its punctuation, spelling, and even any peculiarities that you think might be incorrect (see item 10 below); do not "improve" or in any way alter what you are copying. In fact, it is a good idea to doublecheck your copying for absolute accuracy, at least once, immediately after doing it, and then to mark it as checked (a check mark, or double check mark, perhaps in red, at the right-hand edge will do). When you do quote directly, put exaggeratedly large quotation marks around the quotation so that you cannot possibly later mistake it for summary or paraphrase. This is particularly important when a note is part quotation and part summary or paraphrase: the oversize quotation marks will help keep you straight.

4. If a note consists of a combination of (a) summary or paraphrase or quotation and (b) your own interjected thoughts or explanations or opinions, enclose your own ideas in square brackets—or, to be even safer, in double square brackets [[ ]]; you might even want to initial them. This will prevent you from later assuming that the ideas and opinions came from your source rather than from you.

5. As much as possible, *express the material in your own words when taking notes.* The more you can digest and summarize information

78a   notes

at the note-taking stage, the less interpreting you will need to do later—and it will never be fresher in your mind than at the time when you are taking the note. If you fail to assimilate it then, you may well have to return to the source to find out just why you quoted it in the first place. It is all too easy to forget, over a period of days, weeks, or even months, just what the point was.

6. When you quote, or even paraphrase or summarize, do so from the original source if possible. Second-hand quotation may be not only inaccurate but misleading as well. Seek out the most authoritative source—the original—whenever possible, rather than accept somebody else's reading of it. Similarly, if more than one edition of a source-book exists, use the most authoritative or definitive one.

7. *Distinguish between facts and opinions.* If you are quoting or paraphrasing a supposed authority on a subject, be careful not to let yourself be unduly swayed. Rather than note that "aspirin is good for you," say that "Dr. Jones claims that aspirin is good for you." Rather than write that "the province is running out of natural resources," say that "the Premier believes, from the report given him by his investigating committee, that the province is running out of natural resources." The credibility of your own presentation may well depend on such matters. (See **84**, commentary on paragraph 3.)

8. When you are quoting (or even just summarizing or paraphrasing), *be careful with page numbers.* If a quotation runs over from one page to another in your source, be sure to indicate just where the change occurs, for you may later want to use only a part of the material, and you must know just which page that part came from in order to provide an accurate footnote. A simple method is to indicate the end of a page with one or two slashes (/ or //). (See **84**, commentary on paragraph 21.)

9. Whenever you insert explanatory material in a quotation, use square brackets (see **43j**).

10. When there is something in a quotation that is obviously wrong, whether a supposed fact, a spelling, or a point of grammar or punctuation, insert [sic] after it (see **43j**).

11. Whenever you omit something from a quotation, use three spaced periods (suspension points) to indicate ellipsis (see **43i**).

78b   The Source

In the upper left-hand corner of each note card, identify the source. Usually the last name of the author and a page number will suffice.

But if you are using more than one work by the same author, you must include at least a shortened title of the particular work from which the note comes. Indeed, it is a good idea always to include the title, for later in your note-gathering you may come across a second work by an author you are already using; with a title on each card, no confusion can possibly arise. If the note comes from more than one page, indicate the inclusive page numbers; the note itself will indicate just where the page changes (see **78a**, item 8). (Some people, when the bibliography is complete, number the bibliography cards, if only to make it easier to put them back in order if they are dropped or otherwise mixed up. But it is unwise to use merely this number to identify the source of a particular note. Be cautious: use the author's name and at least a short title.)

78c   The Slug

In the upper right-hand corner of each note card, write a *slug*, a word or brief phrase indicating just what part of your essay the note belongs in—and be as *specific* as possible: this slug will be helpful when it comes to organizing the cards before writing the essay. If you have prepared a good outline, a key word or two from its main headings and sub-headings will be the logical choice to use as a slug on a card. It may be advisable to write the slug in pencil, for you may discover later that you want to rework your outline or use a particular note in a different place.

Caution: Except for the slug, *use ink or type* everything on your note cards and your bibliography cards. Pencil writing can easily become smudged and illegible. You may want to write even the slug in ink; if you leave enough space on the card you can cross out the slug and write a new version below it. Further, guard against the natural impulse to invent private symbols and abbreviations; they may make the writing of notes easier at first, but over even a short time you can all too easily forget what your own code means. Except for standard abbreviations (but not even these in material you are quoting), write everything out in full. Similarly, if you do not type, be sure to write with exaggerated legibility.

78d   Cross-Referencing: Numbering the Cards

Depending on the complexity of your project, you may want to devise some system for cross-referencing closely related note cards, or even ones you think might later prove to be closely related. One way to do this is to number the cards, probably at top-centre, when you are through taking notes. Indeed, it is important, when the cards are all arranged, to number them consecutively; imagine how long it would take, should you drop a stack of a hundred or so cards, to put them

78d cross-referencing

back into the correct order without the aid of such numbers. Be sure that your cards are organized according to your outline, or that your outline has been changed to conform to the organization of your cards.

78e Recording Your Own Ideas

In addition to taking notes from other sources, preserve your own ideas, insights, and flashes of inspiration as you go along, however fragmentary or tentative they may seem at the time; they may well turn out to be valuable at a later stage. Even if you suddenly have so strong an idea about something that you feel sure you will remember it forever, write it down; otherwise there is a good chance you will forget it, for another strong idea may dislodge it just a few minutes later. As with regular notes, restrict these to one idea per card. Even though there will be no indication of source in the upper left-hand corner, take the extra precaution of initialling such a card, or of putting double square brackets around the note, so that you cannot possibly later wonder where it came from. And of course put an appropriate slug in the upper right-hand corner.

For sample note cards illustrating these points, see **84** below.

79 Writing the Essay

When your research is complete and all the note cards you intend to use are in the desired order, you are ready to begin the actual writing of the essay. If your note-taking has been efficient—that is, if you have kept quotation to a minimum, assimilating and interpreting and judging as much as possible as you went along, and if you have included among the cards a sufficient number containing only your own ideas—then the essay will almost write itself; you will need to do little more than supply the necessary transitions as you move from card to card and follow your outline. (Of course the usual process of revision and proofreading must follow the writing of the first draft, as described in the preceding chapter; see **73m–o**.)

79a Keeping Track of Notes in Your Drafts

As you write your first draft, proceeding from card to card, include in your text the information that will eventually become part of your documentation. That is, at the end of every quotation, paraphrase, summary, or direct reference, put at least the last name of the author and the relevant page number or numbers—and also a title, if you are using more than one work by the same author; you can abbreviate these, but be clear, so that no confusion can possibly arise later. If you plan to use footnotes, *do not insert footnote numbers at this stage*, for you may well find yourself re-arranging material, or adding new material where you did not originally plan to use it—either of which would necessitate completely renumbering the notes. To avoid this needless and tedious task, do not put numbers in yet. As you revise, copy the footnote information into each successive draft. It is also a good idea to put these data not just in single parentheses but in double or triple parentheses, or in red ink, so that you cannot possibly overlook any of them when you come to number them. When you are ready to prepare the final copy, number the footnotes consecutively throughout the draft.

If you are using a system of parenthetical documentation, the final form of your notes will be similar to or the same as these parenthetical notes in your drafts (see **85a–b**). If you are using the "number" system (see **85c**), you need only make sure that in successive drafts your parenthetical numbers accurately point to the works in your list of references; but since you may alter that list as you proceed, and then have to alter the numbers in your text accordingly, it would be prudent to stick to names and page numbers or dates until you prepare your final draft.

Note: Usually, footnotes are gathered together in a list at the end of an essay instead of being put at the bottom or "foot" of each page. Then they are of course not *foot*notes but rather "endnotes." Such a list should be labelled "Notes." However, to avoid confusion with the word *notes* as used for facts and ideas taken from sources and put on note cards, we here use the word *footnotes* to designate these items of documentation, wherever they may appear.

80 Acknowledgment of Sources
ack

The purpose of documentation is three-fold: first, it acknowledges a writer's indebtedness to particular sources; second, it lends weight to a writer's statements and arguments by citing authorities to support them, and also demonstrates the extent of a writer's investigation of a topic; third, it enables an interested reader to follow up by consulting cited sources, possibly to evaluate a particular source or to check the accuracy of a reference or quotation, should it appear questionable.

(For the forms of documentation, see **83** and **85**.)

80a "Common Knowledge"

It is not necessary to provide documentation for facts or ideas or quotations that are well known, or "common knowledge"—such as the fact that Shakespeare wrote *Hamlet*, or that Hamlet said "To be or not to be," or that Sir Isaac Newton formulated the law of gravity,

80a   common knowledge

or that the story of Adam and Eve is in the Bible, or that the moon is not made of green cheese. But if you are at all uncertain whether or not something is "common knowledge," play safe: it is far better to over-document and appear a little naive than to under-document and commit plagiarism.

One rule of thumb sometimes adopted is that if a piece of information appears in three or more different sources, it qualifies as "common knowledge" and need not be documented. For example, such facts as the elevation of Mt. Logan, or the population of Peterborough in a given year, or the date of the execution of Louis Riel, can be found in dozens of reference books. But it can be dangerous for a student, or any non-professional, to trust to such a guideline when dealing with other kinds of material. For example, there may be dozens of articles and books referring to or attempting to explain something like a quark, or the red shift, or discoveries at the Olduvai Gorge, or Freudian readings of "The Turn of the Screw," or deep structure in linguistic theory, or neo-Platonic ideas in Renaissance poetry, or the origin of the name *Canada*; nevertheless, it is unlikely that a relatively unsophisticated writer will be sufficiently conversant with such material to recognize and accept it as "common knowledge": if something is new to *you*, and if you have not thoroughly explored the available literature on the subject, it is far better to acknowledge a source than to try to brazen it out and slide something past the reader.

When the question of "common knowledge" arises, ask yourself: common to whom? Your readers will probably welcome the explicit documentation of something that they themselves do not realize is, to a few experts, "common knowledge." Besides, if at any point in your presentation you give your readers even the slightest cause to question your data, you will have lost their confidence. Be cautious: document anything about which you have the least doubt.

81   Quotation, Paraphrase, Summary, and Plagiarism

Quotation must always be exact, verbatim. **Paraphrase**, on the other hand, reproduces the content of the original, but in different words. Paraphrase is a useful technique because it enables writers to make use of source material while still using their own words and thus to avoid too much quotation. But a paraphrase, to be legitimate, may not use significant words and phrases from an original without quotation marks. A paraphrase will usually be a little shorter than the original, but it need not be. A **summary**, however, is by definition a condensation, a boiled-down version that expresses only the principal points of an original passage.

Direct quotation must be documented: a reader of a passage in quotation marks will expect to be told who and what is being quoted. But it is important to know and remember that *paraphrase and summary must also be fully documented.* Some writers make the serious error of thinking that only direct quotations need to be documented; failure to document summaries and paraphrases is **plagiarism**, a form of theft. When you paraphrase or summarize, you must acknowledge your debt to the original source. To illustrate, here is a paragraph, a direct quotation, from Rupert Brooke's *Letters from America*, followed by (a) legitimate paraphrase, (b) illegitimate paraphrase, (c) combination paraphrase and quotation, (d) summary, and (e) a comment on plagiarism.

> Such is Toronto. A brisk city of getting on for half a million inhabitants, the largest British city in Canada (in spite of the cheery Italian faces that pop up at you out of excavations in the street), liberally endowed with millionaires, not lacking its due share of destitution, misery, and slums. It is no mushroom city of the West, it has its history; but at the same time it has grown immensely of recent years. It is situated on the shores of a lovely lake; but you never see that, because the railways have occupied the entire lake front. So if, at evening, you try to find your way to the edge of the water, you are checked by a region of smoke, sheds, trucks, wharves, storehouses, "depôts," railway-lines, signals, and locomotives and trains that wander on the tracks up and down and across streets, pushing their way through the pedestrians, and tolling, as they go, in the American fashion, an immense melancholy bell, intent, apparently, on some private and incommunicable grief. Higher up are the business quarters, a few sky-scrapers in the American style without the modern American beauty, but one of which advertises itself as the highest in the British Empire; streets that seem less narrow than Montreal [sic], but not unrespectably wide; "the buildings are generally substantial and often handsome" (the too kindly Herr Baedeker). Beyond that the residential part, with quiet streets, gardens open to the road, shady verandahs, and homes, generally of wood, that are a deal more pleasant to see than the houses in a modern English town.[1]

[1] Rupert Brooke, *Letters from America* (London: Sidgwick and Jackson, 1916), pp. 80-81.

(For more information about quotations, especially about punctuating them, see **43**.)

81a Paraphrase

During his 1913 tour of the United States and Canada, Rupert Brooke sent back to England articles about his travels. In one of them he describes Toronto as a large city, predominantly British, containing both wealth and poverty. He says that it is relatively old, compared to the upstart new cities further west, but that nevertheless it has expanded a great deal in the last little while. He implies that its beautiful setting is spoiled for its citizens by the railways, which have taken over all the land near the lake, filling it with buildings and tracks and smell and noise. He also writes of the commercial part of the city, with its buildings which are tall (like American ones) but not very attractive (unlike American ones); one of them, he says, claims to be the tallest in the British Empire. (He pokes fun at Baedeker for being over-generous with his comments about the city's downtown architecture.) The streets he finds wider than those of Montreal, but not too wide. Finally he compares Toronto's pleasant residential areas favourably with those of similar English towns.[1]

This is legitimate paraphrase. Even though it uses several words from the original (*British, railways, tracks, American, British Empire, streets, residential, English town*[s]), they are a small part of the whole; more important, they are common words that it would be difficult to find reasonable substitutes for without distorting the sense. And, even more important, they are used in a way that is natural to the paraphraser's own style and context. For example, had the writer said "in the American style" or "the entire lake shore," the style (and words) would have been too much Brooke's. Paraphrase, however, does not consist in merely substituting one word for another, but rather in assimilating something and restating it in your own words and your own syntax.

The footnote number, even though it comes at the end of the paragraph, is clear because the paragraph begins by clearly identifying its overall subject and because the writer has carefully kept Brooke's point of view apparent throughout by including him in each independent clause (a technique which also establishes good coherence): *Rupert Brooke, he describes, He says, He implies, He also writes, he says, He pokes fun, he finds, he compares.*

81b   Illegitimate Paraphrase

An illegitimate paraphrase of Brooke's paragraph might begin like this:

Brooke describes Toronto as a *brisk* kind of city with nearly *half a million inhabitants*, with some *Italian faces popping up* among the British, and with both *millionaires* and *slums*. He deplores the fact that the *lake front* on which *it is situated* has been *entirely occupied by the railways*, who have turned it into *a region of smoke and storehouses* and the like, and *trains that wander back and forth, ringing their huge bells.*[1]

Even the footnote does not protect such a treatment from the accusation of plagiarism, for too many of the words and phrases and too much of the syntax are Brooke's own. The words and phrases that we have italicized are all "illegitimate": a flavourful word like *brisk*; the intact phrases *half a million inhabitants* and *Italian faces*; *popping up*, so little different from *pop up*; and so on. Changing *the railways have occupied the entire lake front* to the passive *the lake front . . . has been entirely occupied by the railways*, or *trains that wander up and down* to *trains that wander back and forth*, or *tolling . . . an immense . . . bell* to *ringing their huge bells,* does not make them the writer's: they still have the diction, syntax, and stylistic flavour of Brooke's original, and therefore constitute plagiarism. Had the writer put quotation marks around "brisk," "Italian faces . . . pop[ping] up," "millionaires" and "slums," "lake front," "it is situated," "occupied," "a region of smoke," "trains that wander," and "bell[s]," the passage would, to be sure, no longer be plagiarism—but it would still be illegitimate, or at least very poor, paraphrase, for if so substantial a part is to be left in Brooke's own words and syntax, the whole might as well have been quoted directly: the writer would have done little more than lightly "edit" the original.

81c Paraphrase and Quotation Mixed

A writer who felt that a pure paraphrase was too flat and abstract, who felt that some of Brooke's more striking words and phrases should be retained, might choose to mix some direct quotation into a paraphrase:

> In *Letters from America,* Rupert Brooke characterizes Toronto as "brisk," largely British, and as having the usual urban mixture of wealth and poverty. Unlike the "mushroom" cities farther west, he says, Toronto has a history, but he notes that much of its growth has nevertheless been recent. He notes, somewhat cynically, that the people are cut off from the beauty of the lake by the railways and all their "smoke, sheds, trucks, wharves, storehouses, 'depôts,' railway lines, signals, and locomotives and trains" going ding-ding all over the place.[1]

This time the context is very much the writer's own, but some of the flavour of Brooke's original has been retained through the direct quotation of a couple of judiciously chosen words and the cumulatively oppressive catalogue. The writer is clearly in control of the material, as the writer of the preceding example was not.

81d Summary

A summary, whose purpose is to substantially reduce the original, conveying its essential meaning in a sentence or two, might go like this:

> Brooke describes Toronto as large and wealthy, aesthetically marred by the railway yards along the lake, with wide-enough streets and tall but (in spite of Baedeker's half-hearted approval) generally unprepossessing buildings, and a residential area more attractive than comparable English ones.[1]

81e Plagiarism

Had one of the foregoing versions of the passage not mentioned Brooke, nor included quotation marks, nor been footnoted, it would have been guilty of outright *plagiarism,* passing off Brooke's words or ideas, or both, as the writer's own, whether intentionally or not. Do not, either

81e *plagiarism*

through design or through carelessness, commit plagiarism. If you have any doubts whatever about what does or does not constitute plagiarism, ask your instructor about it: it is too serious a matter to remain uncertain about.

See **ack** and **doc** in Chapter XI.

On Avoiding Plagiarism

Be careful when you study. For example, suppose you want to write an essay on a particular literary work. Do not rush off and read half a dozen critical essays on the work and then use their ideas in an essay without footnotes or parenthetical references, merely listing the secondary sources in a bibliography. Be scholarly: take careful notes as you read, identify the source of any ideas other than your own, and explicitly acknowledge those ideas as you use them in the essay. A "covering" bibliography may protect you from a charge of outright dishonesty, but it will not exonerate you of plagiarism if ideas from those sources appear in your essay without being acknowledged there. If you label your bibliography "Works Cited," you may more easily remember that you must explicitly cite or quote those works in the essay itself and provide footnotes or parenthetical references.

On the mechanics of handling quotations, see **43**.

Exercise 81: Paraphrasing and summarizing

Here are two more paragraphs from Rupert Brooke's *Letters from America*. For each, write (a) a paraphrase, (b) a paraphrase with some quotation mixed in, and (c) a summary.

1. Ottawa came as a relief after Montreal. There is no such sense of strain and tightness in the atmosphere. The British, if not greatly in the majority, are in the ascendancy; also, the city seems conscious of other than financial standards, and quietly, with dignity, aware of her own purpose. The Canadians, like the Americans, chose to have for their capital a city which did not lead in population or in wealth. This is particularly fortunate in Canada, an extremely individualistic country, whose inhabitants are only just beginning to be faintly conscious of their nationality. Here, at least, Canada is more than the Canadian. A man desiring to praise Ottawa would begin to do so without statistics of wealth and growth of population; and this can be said of no other city in Canada except Quebec. Not that there are not immense lumber-mills and the rest in Ottawa. But the Government farm, and the Parliament buildings, are more important. Also, although the "spoils" system obtains a good deal in this country, the nucleus of the Civil Service is much the same as in England; so there is an atmosphere of Civil Servants about Ottawa, an atmosphere of safeness and honour and massive buildings and well-shaded walks. After all, there is in the qualities of Civility and Service much beauty, of a kind which would adorn Canada. (pp. 54-55)

2. Winnipeg is the West. It is important and obvious that in Canada there are two or three (some say five) distinct Canadas. Even if you lump the French

and English together as one community in the East, there remains the gulf of the Great Lakes. The difference between East and West is possibly no greater than that between North and South England, or Bavaria and Prussia; but in this country, yet unconscious of itself, there is so much less to hold them together. The character of the land and the people differs; their interests, as it appears to them, are not the same. Winnipeg is a new city. In the archives at Ottawa is a picture of Winnipeg in 1870—Mainstreet, with a few shacks, and the prairie either end. Now her population is a hundred thousand, and she has the biggest this, that, and the other west of Toronto. A new city; a little more American than the other Canadian cities, but not unpleasantly so. The streets are wider, and full of a bustle which keeps clear of hustle. The people have something of the free swing of Americans, without the bumptiousness; a tempered democracy, a mitigated independence of bearing. The manners of Winnipeg, of the West, impress the stranger as better than those of the East, more friendly, more hearty, more certain to achieve graciousness, if not grace. There is, even, in the architecture of Winnipeg, a sort of *gauche* pride visible. It is hideous, of course, even more hideous than Toronto or Montreal; but cheerily and windily so. There is no scheme in the city, and no beauty, but it is at least preferable to Birmingham, less dingy, less directly depressing. It has no real slums, even though there is poverty and destitution. (pp. 102-03)

82 ■ Further Advice on Footnotes

82a ■ Partial Footnotes

In the notes you take, you needn't include the author's name, since it will be at the top of the card. But in your essay you may want to include the names of some of your sources.

Notice that the foregoing paraphrases and the summary (**81a–d**) begin by referring to Brooke explicitly. Version (a) uses his full name, as should be done the first time he is mentioned; subsequent references to him then need cite only his surname. Mentioning a source's name in this way is a convenient way of indicating the source and the point of view of a sentence or two, or even of a whole paragraph. When an author's name is given in the text, the footnote need supply only the rest of the information about the source. If the text supplies both the author and title, as in version (c), the footnote need not repeat them, though some writers prefer to repeat the title, for clarity. If for some reason you do not want to bring the author's name into your text (for example if you were surveying a variety of opinions about Toronto and did not want to clutter your text with all their authors' names) then your text might read in part like this:

> Toronto was once described as "brisk," large, and encumbered with railways and tall but ugly buildings.[1]

Your footnote would then of course have to be complete.

82b   Subsequent References (see also **83d** below)

When at some later point in an essay you cite something else from a source already referred to, the second or subsequent footnote should not repeat all of the information; the author's last name and the relevant page number suffice:

> ⁷ Brooke, p. 82.

If another footnote referring to the same source immediately precedes, then the form

> ⁸ Ibid., p. 80.

is acceptable, but current practice favours using the author's name instead of *ibid*. If you are using more than one work by the same author, such subsequent references must also include at least a short version of the title of the work being cited. In an essay on Brooke which was also discussing his works of poetry, for example, a footnote might look like this:

> ⁹ Brooke, *Letters*, p. 75.

82c   Major Sources; Parenthetical References

If you are writing an essay which refers exclusively or predominantly to one particular source, such as a novel or a play, you can reduce the number of footnotes by including all but the first reference in your text. When you first quote or refer to the work, provide a complete footnote, and add an explanatory note, something like this: "Subsequent references to this work will be included in the text." Then, in an essay discussing Brooke's views of Canada, your subsequent references would take this form:

> Brooke calls Toronto a "brisk city" (p. 80).

Note that any necessary punctuation comes after the parentheses. Supply a period or other necessary mark even if the quotation ends with a question mark or exclamation point. If, however, the quotation is a longer one set off by indenting and single spacing, the period comes *before* the parentheses and two spaces intervene:

> It is impossible to give [Toronto] anything but commendation. It is not squalid like Birmingham, or cramped like Canton, or scattered like Edmonton, or sham like Berlin, or hellish like New York, or tiresome like Nice. It is all right. (pp. 83-84)

Parenthetical references can also be used for more than one source, especially if the information is brief. If for example you had earlier identified Brooke and his work, a page number in parentheses would probably be preferable to a footnote giving only a page number. In order to reduce the number of footnotes even further, writers sometimes put authors' names and even titles in such parenthetical references. (See the sample research paper, **84**, for illustrations of parenthetical references.)

82d   Consolidated Footnotes

In order to minimize the number of footnotes, consolidate them whenever possible. Suppose for example that in one sentence, or even in one paragraph, you refer to or quote more than one source. Rather than provide a separate footnote for each, use one footnote at the end of the sentence or paragraph, listing all the sources, in the relevant order—but be particularly careful: use consolidated footnotes only when you can do so without confusing your reader about just what came from where. Use only one number to signal such a footnote; do not put [9, 10, 11] to refer to separate footnotes or to the parts of a consolidated footnote.

82e   Covering Footnotes

When your use of a source is not specific, use a single "covering" footnote to express general indebtedness to a particular source; for example:

> [1] In preparing this biographical sketch, I have used the system of classification recommended by Jacques Barzun and Henry F. Graff in *The Modern Researcher*, 3rd ed. (New York: Harcourt Brace Jovanovich, 1977), chapter 8.

> [1] I am indebted to Cleanth Brooks and Robert Penn Warren, *Understanding Poetry*, 4th ed. (New York: Holt, Rinehart and Winston, 1976), p. 202, for suggesting this approach to the poem.

The number that signals such a footnote sometimes occurs at the very end of an essay, but it is more logical to put it near the beginning. Some writers insert it after the title of an essay, but others think that looks odd. It can often conveniently and logically be placed at the end of the first sentence, or at the end of the first paragraph. And sometimes such a footnote is simply added to the first footnote supplied for any other reason.

82f   Discursive Footnotes

Occasionally a writer will want to add a comment to a footnote, or include some tangential information or discussion that would be out of place in the text. But such footnotes, since they temporarily distract the reader from the flow of the main text, should be kept to a minimum. Usually such a comment, if it is truly relevant, can be worked into the text.

82g   Placement of Footnote Numbers

Try to so arrange things that a number indicating a footnote occurs at the end of a sentence rather than somewhere near the beginning or the middle of it. But if it is necessary to quote or paraphrase something, and then to follow it in the same sentence with added facts or comments of your own, the number should immediately follow the citation, especially if there is any possibility that your comment could be mistaken for material from the source.

82h   Mechanics of Footnotes

Footnote numbers in the text are *superscript* numbers—*written above* the line about half a space, not on the same line or below it. No space precedes the number. Before the footnote itself, the number is also written slightly above the line, and a space follows it. The footnote number is not followed by a period, not enclosed in parentheses, and not circled. A footnote number follows all punctuation marks except the dash. Footnotes may be single-spaced, but always double-space between them. Leave a quadruple space between text and footnotes. Indent each footnote five spaces.

83   Documentation
doc

If documentation is to do its three-fold job (see **80**), it must be complete, accurate, and clear. Completeness and accuracy depend on your careful recording of the necessary information as you do your research and take notes. Clarity depends on the way you present that information to your reader. You will be clear only if your intended audience can follow your method of documentation. Therefore it is important that before you present a piece of research, you find out what method of documentation you need to use. There are four main methods:

(a) The *note* method, used until recently by most disciplines in the humanities, and still preferred in some disciplines and by many individual writers and instructors (see **83a–f**);

(b) the *name-page* method, recently recommended by the Modern Language Association of America (see **85a**);

(c) the *name-date* method, widely used in the social sciences (see **85b**);

(d) the *number* method, widely used in the physical sciences (see **85c**).

Which method you choose will depend on what discipline you are writing in and on the wishes of the instructor for whom you are writing.

But you should familiarize yourself with all of them, or at least with those you will most often find in your textbooks and in your research for various courses.

In the advice in sections **81** and **82** and in the examples below, we follow the old or traditional MLA style because for at least a few more years it is the one you are most likely to encounter in your reading for English and other courses in the humanities, and because it is still the one that people in the humanities are most familiar with and therefore the one most likely to be expected or at least accepted by many instructors; moreover, many people think that the fuller forms of footnotes or endnotes, with or without a bibliography, provide a clearer reference than do the brief parenthetical citations used in the other systems. However, after the sample research paper, we provide in **85a** an explanation and some examples of the new MLA system so that you can begin familiarizing yourself with it and use it if you want or are asked to; and in Chapter X, Sample Essay No. 16 is a research report using that system. In sections **85b** and **85c** we also provide brief descriptions and examples of the methods used in the social and physical sciences.

83a Footnotes and Bibliographical Entries: The Traditional Forms

The forms of documentation are simple: the pattern of a footnote or an entry in a bibliography is straightforward, constant, and sensible. However, many books and other sources include anomalies and complexities that can be puzzling when one tries to account for them in an item of documentation. If you encounter an instance not covered by any of the following examples, try to work it out by applying common sense and the general principles outlined below.

The basic pattern of a footnote is as follows: author's name in normal order, title of work, publication data in parentheses (city: publisher, year) and page number. For example:

[1] Colin M. Turnbull, The Mountain People (New York: Simon and Schuster, 1972), p. 167.

The corresponding bibliographical entry contains the same information and looks like this:

Turnbull, Colin M. The Mountain People. New York: Simon and Schuster, 1972.

The differences between the two are obvious and easy to remember: A footnote is meant to read like a sentence; therefore it gives the author's name in normal order, puts the publication data in parentheses to de-emphasize it, and is punctuated with commas. A bibliographical entry is in a relatively stiff and technical form, with reverse indention and author's last name first (so that entries can be listed alphabetically) and periods, rather than commas, between the parts. Similarly, a footnote gives only the information necessary to identify a citation; secondary information, such as subtitles, introductions by someone other than author or editor, and general editors of extended series, need not be included in footnotes. Such things must, however, be included in bibliographical entries, for a bibliography is a reference tool. In instances where no bibliography is to be provided, such information would have to be included in the footnotes. And sometimes—but only when there is a bibliography—footnotes do not even identify the publishers of cited works; but it is more common practice to include them in all footnotes.

Since many sources do not present a simple and straightforward set of facts to record, examine closely the following examples, which include the more common kinds of sources and some of the more common variations. When necessary, refer to these samples for models. (Bibliographical entries for these works are given in **83e**. See also the footnotes and bibliography in the sample research paper, **84**.)

Caution: Always take the information for a footnote or a bibliographical entry only from the title page of a book, and if necessary (for example the date of publication) from the reverse of the title page (the copyright page); do not take it from the book's cover or from the running title at the top of the book's pages. Similarly, for an article in a periodical, take the author and title from the actual article, not from the cover or a table of contents, for they sometimes use shortened or otherwise varied forms of names and titles.

83b · Sample Footnotes: First References

A book with one author:

[1] Robertson Davies, <u>One Half of Robertson Davies</u> (Toronto: Macmillan, 1977), p. 138.

[2] Lewis Thomas, <u>The Lives of a Cell</u> (New York: Viking, 1974), p. 111.

Note that no comma precedes the parentheses, and that each footnote ends with a period, just as a sentence would.

A revised edition:

[3] William Zinsser, <u>On Writing Well</u>, 2nd ed. (New York: Harper & Row, 1980), p. 158.

A book with two or three authors:

> [4] E. H. Carter and R. A. F. Mears, <u>A History of Britain</u>, 2nd ed. (Oxford: Clarendon Press, 1948), pp. 821–22.

Note that the abbreviation for the plural *pages* is *pp.*, not just *p.* Note also that only the last two digits of a three-digit page number are given to locate the end of a cited passage. This edition was reprinted in 1953, but the date of its first printing, 1948, is the one used, since the book was not revised but merely reprinted.

A work with more than three authors:

> [5] Raymond Breton et al., "The Impact of Ethnic Groups on Canadian Society: Research Issues," in <u>Identities: The Impact of Ethnicity on Canadian Society</u>, ed. Wsevolod Isajiw, Canadian Ethnic Studies Association series, Vol. 5 (Toronto: Peter Martin Associates, 1977), p. 193.

The subtitle and series editor are not mandatory in a footnote, but the subtitle at least is useful information and so was included. One could use "and others" instead of the Latin *et al.*

A collection of pieces by one author:

> [6] Leonard Cohen, <u>Selected Poems 1956–1968</u> (Toronto: McClelland and Stewart, 1968), p. 200.

A specific work in a collection of pieces by one author:

> [7] Peter C. Newman, "Noises from the Attic," in his <u>Home Country: People, Places, and Power Politics</u> (Toronto: McClelland and Stewart, 1973), pp. 229–31.

Again, the subtitle seemed useful. This book has an introduction by Hugh MacLennan, but that need be recorded only in the bibliography.

A book with one author and an editor:

> [8] Thomas Carlyle, <u>Reminiscences</u>, ed. James Anthony Froude (New York: Harper, 1881), p. 260.

An essay in a collection by several authors, with an editor:

> [9] Douglas Bush, "Stephen Leacock," in <u>The Canadian Imagination</u>, ed. David Staines (Cambridge, Mass.: Harvard Univ. Press, 1977), p. 143.

Note that such abbreviations as *Univ.* are acceptable. This book has a subtitle, but it need not appear here; it is included, however, in the bibliography. *Mass.* is added to the city's name to avoid confusion with Cambridge, England. Harvard University Press also has an office in London, England, but that need not be recorded here; Cambridge is listed first, and it is also the likely origin of the book used in Canada; if the publisher had also had an office in, say, Toronto, that would have been the logical city for a Canadian to include in the footnote. David Staines also wrote an introductory essay for this book, but that need not be noted either here or in the bibliography. However, should one wish to quote or refer to that introduction, one could use a footnote like this:

[10] David Staines, "Canada Observed," editor's Introd. to <u>The Canadian Imagination</u> (Cambridge, Mass.: Harvard Univ. Press, 1977), p. 15.

If the introductory matter were not titled but merely labelled, one would use Introd., Pref., or Foreword, neither italicized nor in quotation marks.

A story in an anthology:

[11] Katherine Mansfield, "The Fly," in <u>A 20th-Century Anthology</u>, ed. W. E. Messenger and W. H. New (Scarborough, Ont.: Prentice-Hall Canada, 1984), p. 84.

A piece reprinted in a collection of essays by several authors:

[12] Northrop Frye, "The Typology of <u>Paradise Regained</u>," Modern Philology, 53 (1956), 227-38; rpt. in <u>Milton: Modern Essays in Criticism</u>, ed. Arthur E. Barker (New York: Galaxy-Oxford Univ. Press, 1965), p. 436.

Anthologies and casebooks such as this have become common in recent years. Even though you are using such a collection, it is a courtesy to give the reader all the data you can pertaining to an essay's original publication; this information is customarily provided in the anthologies. This footnote also illustrates how to treat the name of a paperbound series; "Galaxy" books are published by Oxford. See also footnote 32 below.

A reprint of an earlier edition (often in paperback):

[13] Robertson Davies, <u>The Diary of Samuel Marchbanks</u> (1947; rpt. Toronto: Clarke, Irwin, 1966), p. 57.

[14] Harold Nicolson, <u>Some People</u> ([London], 1927; rpt. New York: Vintage, 1957), p. 72.

83b   sample footnotes

Here, since the book originally appeared in a different country, the city's name is included; it was not given in the paperback, however, but deduced from the original publisher's name; it is therefore enclosed in square brackets.

A book with more than three editors:

> 15 Alexander W. Allison et al., eds., The Norton Anthology of Poetry, rev. ed. (New York: Norton, 1975).

With no specific author or page number, this would be a citation of the whole book. Again, one can use the English "and others" instead of the Latin abbreviation *et al.* The abbreviation *rev. ed.* means "revised edition"; in this instance, the revised edition was not given a number (cf. footnotes 3 and 4 above).

An anonymous book, for example a reference work:

> 16 Dictionnaire des Gallicismes les Plus Usités (Paris: Payot, 1951), p. 120.

A translation:

> 17 Carlos Fuentes, Where the Air is Clear, trans. Sam Hileman (New York: Ivan Obolensky; Toronto: George J. McLeod, 1960), pp. 299-300.

Some books, like this one, are published simultaneously in different places by different publishers; when possible, include this information. (This does not apply when a book is published in different places by the same publisher; see footnote 9 above.) If the work of the translator were being discussed, his name would come first. And here obviously all three digits of the second page number must be included.

A book that is one of a series:

> 18 William Wycherley, The Plain Dealer, ed. Leo Hughes, Regents Restoration Drama Series (Lincoln: Univ. of Nebraska Press, 1967), p. 120.

The name of the general editor is reserved for the bibliography. It is customary to include the state or country of less well-known cities like Lincoln, but here it was unnecessary, since "Univ. of Nebraska Press" identifies the publisher's location clearly enough.

> 19 Paul Hiebert, Sarah Binks, New Canadian Library, No. 44 (1947; rpt. Toronto: McClelland and Stewart, 1964), p. 68.

83b sample footnotes

[20] I. A. Richards, "Literature for the Unlettered," in Uses of Literature, ed. Monroe Engel, Harvard English Studies, 4 (Cambridge, Mass.: Harvard Univ. Press, 1973), p. 212.

Such series are open-ended; sometimes, however, a number of works are published over a period of years, but are nevertheless part of a set that has or will come to a definite end. The next footnote illustrates such a work.

A book that is part of several volumes:

[21] Ian Jack, English Literature 1815-1832, Vol. X of The Oxford History of English Literature (Oxford: Oxford Univ. Press, 1963), p. 313.

If you refer generally to a multivolume work, use this form:

[22] Margot Asquith, An Autobiography, 2 vols. (New York: Doran, 1920).

If you refer to a specific place in one of the volumes, this form:

[23] Margot Asquith, An Autobiography (New York: Doran, 1920), II, 98-101.

This refers to pages 98-101 of the second volume of the two-volume set. Note that since the volume number is given, the abbreviations *pp.* and *vol.* are omitted; when both are present, one cannot be mistaken for the other. This work's two volumes were published simultaneously, in 1920. When referring to a multivolume set that was published over a number of years, one must use a slightly different form:

[24] Samuel Pepys, The Diary of Samuel Pepys, ed. Robert Latham and William Matthews, III (London: Bell, 1970), 214-15.

Note that, once again, since the volume number is included, *pp.* is omitted. Since the volumes were not published all at the same time, the volume number precedes the publishing data, and the year given is the publication date of that particular volume. If one wanted to refer to the work of the editors rather than to Pepys's work, their names would come first:

[25] Robert Latham and William Matthews, eds., The Diary of Samuel Pepys, VII (London: Bell, 1972), 277n.

The *277n.* means that the material quoted or referred to occurs in a footnote on page 277. A general reference to the whole set would look something like this:

> ²⁶ All quotations from Pepys are from <u>The Diary of Samuel Pepys</u>, ed. Robert Latham and William Matthews, 9 vols. (London: Bell, 1970-76). Subsequent references appear in the text.

With such a covering reference to a major source, further footnotes to it are unnecessary; instead, references can be included in your text following each quotation, like this: (III, 214-15).

A book with a corporate author:

> ²⁷ Fellowship of Australian Writers, <u>Australian Writers Speak: Literature and Life in Australia</u> (Sydney: Angus and Robertson, 1943), p. 27.

A government publication:

> ²⁸ Department of External Affairs, <u>Canada from Sea to Sea</u>, rev. ed. (Ottawa: Queen's Printer, 1963), p. 44.

An unpublished dissertation:

> ²⁹ Kenneth Hugh Mclean, "The Treatment of History in Canadian Fiction," Diss. York Univ. 1980, p. 10.

An article in an encyclopedia or similar reference work, signed or unsigned:

> ³⁰ P[eter] C[halmers] M[itchell], "Evolution," <u>Encyclopaedia Britannica</u>, 11th ed. (1910).

> ³¹ "Halifax," <u>The New Columbia Encyclopedia</u>, 1975 ed.

Since such articles are arranged alphabetically, no volume or page numbers need be given. The article on evolution is signed "P.C.M.," but the name for which the initials stand is listed at the front of the volume; as information supplied from outside the actual article, therefore, the added letters are placed in square brackets. Note the spelling of *Encyclopaedia Britannica*.

A work without complete publication data:

> ³² William Kirby, <u>The Golden Dog: A Romance of Old Quebec</u> (Toronto: Musson, n.d.), p. 128.

The abbreviation *n.d.* stands for "no date"; similarly, if the place of publication is not provided, put *n.p.* (no place) before the colon; if the publisher is not identified, put *n.p.* (no publisher) after the

83b sample footnotes

colon. If the pages of a work are not numbered, put *n. pag.* (no pagination) at the end of the footnote. If such missing information can be found, even if it is only the country of publication, it should be included in square brackets.

Quotation at second hand:

³³ Sir Charles Lyell, <u>Life, Letters, and Journals of Sir Charles Lyell</u>, ed. Mrs. Katherine Lyell (London: John Murray, 1881), II, 436, as quoted in Loren Eiseley, <u>Darwin's Century</u> (1958; rpt. Garden City, N.Y.: Anchor-Doubleday, 1961), p. 107.

If the data for the original source can be found, they should be included, as here. Note that it is all right to abbreviate the state (N.Y.), but not the city.

Reference to the Bible:

³⁴ Hebrews 13:8.

Books of the Bible are not italicized. Lower case Roman numerals can be used for the chapter, but Arabic are becoming more common.

Reference to a play:

³⁵ Shakespeare, <u>Othello</u> V.i.19-20.

Shakespeare's name was not given in the text; the first name of such a well-known author is unnecessary in a footnote. Note that, as with the Bible, no comma is needed following the title. The Roman numerals are still common for plays; upper case *V* indicates act five; lower case *i*, scene one; and 19-20, the quoted lines. A footnote such as this would be proper only if an earlier footnote or the text had indicated the edition being used.

A weekly or bi-weekly magazine:

³⁶ Norman Cousins, "The Mysterious Placebo: How Mind Helps Medicine Work," <u>Saturday Review</u>, 1 Oct. 1977, p. 10.

A monthly magazine:

³⁷ Veronica Thomas, "The Hutterites of Canada," <u>Gourmet</u>, Nov. 1976, p. 36.

This and many other magazines have volume and issue numbers; but unless one is referring to scholarly periodicals, these numbers need not be included; compare 41, 42, and 43 below.

A newspaper article:

> [38] "Budworm Spray Opponents Meet," Ottawa *Citize*
> 8 Dec. 1977, p. 20, col. 1.

The column number could be omitted. Sometimes writers include the particular edition of a newspaper. The definite article *The* is customarily omitted from the title of the newspaper (see also footnotes 39 and 44 below).

A newspaper editorial:

> [39] "Bodies and Minds at the New U of T," Editorial,
> Toronto *Globe and Mail*, 9 March 1978, p. 6, col. 2.

An interview:

> [40] Barbara Ward, Interviewed by Peter C. Newman in
> *Maclean's*, 17 May 1976, p. 4.

An article in a journal with continuous pagination throughout annual volumes:

> [41] Robert Cuff and J. L. Granatstein, "The Rise and
> Fall of Canadian-American Free Trade, 1947-8," *Canadian
> Historical Review*, 58 (1977), 473.

↳ Volume

Note that the volume number is given in Arabic numerals. The additional information—that this was in No. 4 of the 58th volume, and that it appeared in December—is not necessary. And though such journals usually have one or more listed editors, these editors' names are never included in footnotes or bibliographies.

An article in a journal with separate pagination for each issue:

> [42] Naim Kattan, "Space in the Canadian Novel of the
> West," *Ariel: A Review of International English Literature*,
> 4, No. 3 (1973), 105.

The separate pagination in each issue necessitates that the number of the issue be given. As in the preceding footnote, the presence of the volume number means that *p.* is not needed.

A signed review; a journal that numbers only issues:

> [43] Herbert Rosengarten, "Urbane Comedy," rev. of *Lady
> Oracle*, by Margaret Atwood, *Canadian Literature*, No. 72
> (Spring 1977), p. 85.

With no volume number, the abbreviation *p.* is required. The word *Spring*, like months for other journals, is not necessary, but it (or Summer, Fall, Winter) is often provided as a possible aid to the reader.

An unsigned review:

⁴⁴ The Dispossessed Americans," rev. of <u>Bury My Heart at Wounded Knee</u>, by Dee Brown, <u>Times Literary Supplement</u>, 21 July 1972, p. 830.

The fact that this weekly publication numbers its pages consecutively throughout a year, or that this is issue number 3673, is irrelevant.

83c   References to Other Kinds of Sources

References to such things as films, paintings, musical and dramatic performances, radio and television programs, and tapes and records are handled in similar ways. Common sense, along with the particular use you're making of the material, should dictate what information you need to include. Some examples:

A lecture:

⁴⁵ Professor Peter Piper, lecture in Philosophy 303, Capricorn University, 29 March 1984.

A personal interview:

⁴⁶ Personal interview with Earle Birney, 30 Sept. 1984.

A performance of a play:

⁴⁷ Harold Pinter, dir., <u>Butley</u>, by Simon Gray, with Alan Bates, Criterion Theatre, London, 21 Oct. 1971.

A film:

⁴⁸ John Huston, dir., <u>Beat the Devil</u>, writ. John Huston and Truman Capote, with Humphrey Bogart, Jennifer Jones, Gina Lollobrigida, Peter Lorre, and Robert Morley, United Artists, 1954.

(Try to provide at least title, distributor, and date; depending on the purpose of your citation, other information may be interesting and useful.)

A television program:

> [49] "Rumpole and the Old Boy Net," <u>Rumpole of the Bailey</u>, writ. John Mortimer, with Leo McKern, Mystery!, PBS, 1 Nov. 1984.

A recording:

> [50] Pete Seeger, <u>God Bless the Grass</u>, Columbia, CS 9232, n.d.

> [51] T. S. Eliot, "The Love Song of J. Alfred Prufrock," <u>T. S. Eliot Reading Poems and Choruses</u>, Caedmon, TC 1045, 1955.

A painting:

> [52] Jacques Louis David, <u>The Death of Socrates</u>, The Metropolitan Museum of Art, New York.

If you are working from a published photograph, include the necessary data; for example, after a comma or a semicolon instead of a period, note 52 could be continued this way:

> illustration 9 (David) in <u>The Romantic Rebellion: Romantic versus Classic Art</u>, by Kenneth Clark (New York: Harper & Row, 1973), p. 29.

A personal letter:

> [53] Letter received from A. F. Day, 1 April 1982.

Material from an information service, such as ERIC (Educational Resources Information Center); if separately published, include that information:

> [54] James Ross, <u>Dene Language Study</u>, Northwest Territories Dept. of Education, 1981 (ERIC ED 226 875), p. 2.

> [55] Lorne Laforge, <u>Second Language Teaching in the Canadian University</u>, Alberta Teachers Association, Edmonton, Modern Language Council, <u>Alberta Modern Language Journal</u>, 16 (Winter 1977-78), 10 (ERIC ED 149 616).

83d   Sample Footnotes: Second and Subsequent References

Second or subsequent references are short. Once a first and full footnote has identified a particular source, usually all that a second or later

83d sample footnotes

reference need contain is the author's last name and a page number; this is now the most common practice. It is better—and easier—not to bother with such Latin abbreviations as *op. cit.* and *loc. cit.*, although *ibid.* (short for *ibidem*, "in the same place") is still sometimes used. Following are sample footnotes illustrating subsequent references to some of the works listed in the full footnotes in **83b** above.

[56] Zinsser, p. 40.

[57] Carter and Mears, p. 719.

[58] Ibid., p. 725.

Here *Ibid.* means that this is another reference to Carter and Mears; if you use *ibid.*, remember that it refers only to the footnote immediately preceding. One could almost as easily have repeated the authors' names; then a reader would not have to look back at the preceding footnote to see what *ibid.* referred to. (Since *ibid.* is an abbreviation, it must be followed by a period; it is not necessary to italicize it in a footnote.)

[59] Breton et al., p. 194.

[60] Ibid.

Here *Ibid.*, without a page number, means that footnote 60 documents another reference to page 194 of the work of Breton et al.; a page number after *Ibid.* is not necessary if the reference is to the same page cited in the preceding footnote.

[61] Bush, p. 143.

This refers to the same work referred to in footnote 9. Should one wish to refer to a different essay from the same book, some information would have to be repeated to identify the source clearly for the reader:

[62] Margaret Atwood, "Canadian Monsters: Some Aspects of the Supernatural in Canadian Fiction," in Staines, ed., The Canadian Imagination, p. 103.

Subsequent references to this essay would then simply cite Atwood and a page number.

[63] Davies, Diary, p. 63.

Since two works by Davies are cited earlier (see footnotes 1 and 13), it is necessary to repeat the title of the one being referred to a second time. Note that a shortened version of the title is sufficient if it is clear.

[64] Davies, One Half, p. 117.

[65] Ibid., pp. 75–76.

Since *Ibid.* refers only to the immediately preceding footnote, the title need not be repeated.

> 66 Allison et al., eds., <u>The Norton Anthology of Poetry</u>, p. 308.

This form would be used if the name of the author and the title of a cited poem were included in the text. The first editor's name and page number alone would not make a very clear reference. In such an instance, also, the title of the anthology could come first; one could even omit the editor's name. If you did decide to use only the editor's last name and a page number for such a footnote, you would not include *ed.* or *eds.*

> 67 <u>Dictionnaire des Gallicismes</u>, p. 98.

The shortened title of an anonymous work is sufficient. Such a form would serve also for second references to the sources cited in footnotes 27 and 28.

> 68 Asquith, II, 149.

Even though the reference is to the same volume as in the earlier footnote (23), the volume number must be included.

> 69 Ibid., I, 84.

This refers again to Asquith's work, but to the first volume. Similarly, in a subsequent reference to a multivolume work whose volumes were published over several years (see footnotes 24-26), the volume number must be given:

> 70 Pepys, <u>Diary</u>, III, 120.

If, however, you cite a different volume from such a set, the date of publication of that newly cited volume must also be included:

> 71 Pepys, <u>Diary</u>, V (1971), p. 117.

The title alone of an unsigned encyclopedia entry is sufficient:

> 72 "Halifax."

Second and subsequent references to periodicals are handled similarly:

> 73 Cousins, p. 8.

> 74 "The Dispossessed Americans," p. 831.

83d *sample footnotes*

83e   Sample Bibliographical Entries

Following are sample bibliographical entries that correspond to the
sample footnotes in **83b** and **c**. As in an actual bibliography, the items
are listed in alphabetical order.

Allison, Alexander W., et al., eds. The Norton Anthology of Poetry. Rev. ed. New York: Norton, 1975.

Asquith, Margot. An Autobiography. 2 vols. New York:
Doran, 1920.

Atwood, Margaret. "Canadian Monsters: Some Aspects of the
Supernatural in Canadian Fiction." In The Canadian
Imagination: Dimensions of a Literary Culture. Ed.
David Staines. Cambridge, Mass.: Harvard Univ. Press,
1977, pp. 97-122.

Birney, Earle. Personal interview. 30 Sept. 1984.

"Bodies and Minds at the New U of T." Editorial. Toronto
Globe and Mail, 9 March 1978, p. 6, cols. 1-2.

Breton, Raymond, et al. "The Impact of Ethnic Groups on
Canadian Society: Research Issues." In Identities:
The Impact of Ethnicity on Canadian Society. Ed.
Wsevolod Isajiw. Canadian Ethnic Studies Association
series, Vol. 5. Toronto: Peter Martin Associates,
1977, pp. 191-213.

Brooke, Rupert. Letters from America. Pref. Henry James.
London: Sidgwick & Jackson, 1916.

"Budworm Spray Opponents Meet." Ottawa Citizen, 8 Dec.
1977, p. 20, cols. 1-2.

Bush, Douglas. "Stephen Leacock." In The Canadian Imagination: Dimensions of a Literary Culture. Ed. David
Staines. Cambridge, Mass.: Harvard Univ. Press, 1977,
pp. 123-51.

Carlyle, Thomas. Reminiscences. Ed. James Anthony Froude.
New York: Harper, 1881.

Carter, E. H., and R. A. F. Mears. A History of Britain.
2nd ed. Oxford: Clarendon Press, 1948.

Cohen, Leonard. Selected Poems 1956-1968. Toronto:
McClelland and Stewart, 1968.

Cousins, Norman. "The Mysterious Placebo: How Mind Helps
Medicine Work." Saturday Review, 1 Oct. 1977, pp.
8-16.

Cuff, Robert, and J. L. Granatstein. "The Rise and Fall of
Canadian-American Free Trade, 1947-8." Canadian
Historical Review, 58 (1977), 459-82.

David, Jacques Louis. The Death of Socrates. Metropolitan
Museum of Art, New York. Illustration 9 (David) in The
Romantic Rebellion: Romantic versus Classical Art. By
Kenneth Clark. New York: Harper & Row, 1973.

Davies, Robertson. <u>The Diary of Samuel Marchbanks</u>. 1947; rpt. Toronto: Clarke, Irwin, 1966.

-----. <u>One Half of Robertson Davies: Provocative Pronouncements on a Wide Range of Topics</u>. Toronto: Macmillan of Canada, 1977.

Day, A. F. Letter to author. 1 April 1982.

Department of External Affairs. <u>Canada from Sea to Sea</u>. Rev. ed. Ottawa: Queen's Printer, 1963.

<u>Dictionnaire des Gallicismes les Plus Usités</u>. Paris: Payot, 1951.

"The Dispossessed Americans." Rev. of <u>Bury My Heart at Wounded Knee</u>, by Dee Brown. <u>Times Literary Supplement</u>, 21 July 1972, pp. 829-31.

Eiseley, Loren. <u>Darwin's Century: Evolution and the Men Who Discovered It</u>. 1958; rpt. Garden City, N.Y.: Anchor-Doubleday, 1961.

Eliot, T. S. "The Love Song of J. Alfred Prufrock." <u>T. S. Eliot Reading Poems and Choruses</u>. Caedmon, TC 1045, 1955.

Fellowship of Australian Writers. <u>Australian Writers Speak: Literature and Life in Australia</u>. Sydney: Angus and Robertson, 1943.

Frye, Northrop. "The Typology of <u>Paradise Regained</u>." <u>Modern Philology</u>, 53 (1956), 227-38. Rpt. in <u>Milton: Modern Essays in Criticism</u>. Ed. Arthur E. Barker. New York: Galaxy-Oxford Univ. Press, 1965, pp. 429-46.

Fuentes, Carlos. <u>Where the Air is Clear</u>. Trans. Sam Hileman. New York: Ivan Obolensky; Toronto: George J. McLeod, 1960.

"Halifax." <u>The New Columbia Encyclopedia</u>. 1975 ed.

Hiebert, Paul. <u>Sarah Binks</u>. Introd. by A. Lloyd Wheeler. New Canadian Library, No. 44. Ed. Malcolm Ross. 1947; rpt. Toronto: McClelland and Stewart, 1964.

Huston, John, dir. <u>Beat the Devil</u>. Writ. John Huston and Truman Capote. With Humphrey Bogart, Jennifer Jones, Gina Lollobrigida, Peter Lorre, and Robert Morley. United Artists, 1954.

Jack, Ian. <u>English Literature 1815-1832</u>. Vol. X of <u>The Oxford History of English Literature</u>. Ed. John Buxton and Norman Davis. Oxford: Oxford Univ. Press, 1963.

Kattan, Naim. "Space in the Canadian Novel of the West." <u>Ariel: A Review of International English Literature</u>, 4, No. 3 (1973), 103-10.

Kirby, William. <u>The Golden Dog: A Romance of Old Quebec</u>. Toronto: Musson, n.d.

83e sample bibliography

Laforge, Lorne. Second Language Teaching in the Canadian
   University. Alberta Teachers Association, Edmonton. Modern
   Language Council. Alberta Modern Language Journal, 16
   (Winter 1977-78), 6-15. ERIC ED 149 616.

Mansfield, Katherine. "The Fly." In A 20th-Century Anthology:
   Essays, Stories, and Poems. Ed. W. E. Messenger and W. H.
   New. Scarborough, Ont.: Prentice-Hall Canada, 1984, pp. 82-85.

McLean, Kenneth Hugh. "The Treatment of History in Canadian
   Fiction." Diss. York Univ. 1980.

M[itchell], P[eter] C[halmers]. "Evolution." Encyclopaedia Britannica. 11th ed. (1910).

Newman, Peter C. "Noises from the Attic." In Home
   Country: People, Places, and Power Politics. Introd.
   Hugh MacLennan. Toronto: McClelland and Stewart,
   1973, pp. 229-31.

Nicolson, Harold. Some People. [London], 1927; rpt. New
   York: Vintage, 1957.

Pepys, Samuel. The Diary of Samuel Pepys. Ed. Robert
   Latham and William Matthews. 9 vols. London: Bell,
   1970-76.

Pinter, Harold, dir. Butley. By Simon Gray. With Alan Bates.
   Criterion Theatre, London. 21 Oct. 1971.

Piper, Prof. Peter. Lecture in Philosophy 303. Capricorn
   Univ. 29 March 1984.

Richards, I. A. "Literature for the Unlettered." In
   Uses of Literature. Ed. Monroe Engel. Harvard
   English Studies, 4. Cambridge, Mass.: Harvard Univ.
   Press, 1973, pp. 207-24.

Rosengarten, Herbert. "Urbane Comedy." Rev. of Lady
   Oracle, by Margaret Atwood. Canadian Literature,
   No. 72 (Spring 1977), pp. 84-87.

Ross, James. Dene Language Study. Northwest Territories Dept.
   of Education, 1981. ERIC ED 226 875.

"Rumpole and the Old Boy Net." Rumpole of the Bailey. Writ. John
   Mortimer. With Leo McKern. Mystery! PBS, 1 Nov. 1984.

Seeger, Pete. God Bless the Grass. Columbia, CS 9232, n.d.

Shakespeare, William. Othello. Ed. M. R. Ridley. The
   Arden Edition of the Works of William Shakespeare.
   London: Methuen, Arden Shakespeare Paperbacks, 1965.

Staines, David. "Canada Observed." Editor's Introd. to
   The Canadian Imagination: Dimensions of a Literary
   Culture. Cambridge, Mass.: Harvard Univ. Press,
   1977, pp. 1-21.

Thomas, Lewis. <u>The Lives of a Cell: Notes of a Biology Watcher</u>.
New York: Viking, 1974.

Thomas, Veronica. "The Hutterites of Canada." <u>Gourmet</u>,
Nov. 1976, pp. 32–36, 94–97, 102–06.

Ward, Barbara. Interviewed by Peter C. Newman. <u>Maclean's</u>,
17 May 1976, pp. 4–8.

Wycherley, William. <u>The Plain Dealer</u>. Ed. Leo Hughes.
Regents Restoration Drama Series. Ed. John Loftis.
Lincoln: Univ. of Nebraska Press, 1967.

Zinsser, William. <u>On Writing Well: An Informal Guide to Writing
Nonfiction</u>. 2nd ed. New York: Harper & Row, 1980.

83f Points to Remember About Bibliographical Entries

Mechanics: Author's or editor's last name comes first; if there is more than one author or editor, only the first one is reversed: Carter, E.H., and R.A.F. Mears. Complete title, and subtitle if any, are provided. Periods separate main parts, each followed by two typed spaces, and the entry ends with a period. Only one space follows a colon. The second and all subsequent lines of an entry are indented. Entries are listed alphabetically by authors' last names or by the first significant word (ignore *The, A,* and *An*) of the titles of unsigned works. When more than one work by an author is listed, those after the first begin with a long dash—that is, a row of anywhere from three to ten hyphens, amounting to "ditto"; see the entries for Davies. Bibliographical entries are not numbered. Like footnotes, bibliographical entries may be single-spaced, but leave double spaces between them.

A source such as the Bible need not be included in the bibliography, unless a writer is using one or more particular editions for a particular purpose, such as comparing translations or citing and discussing commentary.

Unlike in footnotes, page numbers for references are not given. But note that entries for essays and articles from larger works or from periodicals end with the inclusive page numbers—the first and the last—of each piece (and columns, for newspaper articles).

The name of a university press must be given in full, but other publishers' names are given in short but clear forms. That is, "Scribner's," not "Charles Scribner's Sons"; "Norton," not "W.W. Norton & Co., Inc."; "McClelland and Stewart," not "McClelland and Stewart Limited."

When only one or two pieces from a collection are cited, as with the entries for Breton, Frye, Newman, and Richards, those individual pieces are usually the ones listed in a bibliography. But when as many as three pieces from a collection are cited, as with the entries for

83f bibliography

Atwood, Bush, and Staines, a writer may wish simply to list the collection itself as a source, not listing the individual pieces in the bibliography at all:

> Staines, David, ed. <u>The Canadian Imagination: Dimensions</u>
> <u>of a Literary Culture</u>. Cambridge, Mass.: Harvard
> Univ. Press, 1977.

A bibliography, when it consists—as it usually does—of a list of sources actually cited in the text and footnotes, is customarily labelled "Works Cited" or "List of Works Cited." On occasion, one may wish to add a list of "Works Consulted." Sometimes a large bibliography is divided into sections, such as "Primary Sources" and "Secondary Sources," or "Books" and "Periodicals."

83g Some Abbreviations Commonly Used in Documentation

anon.	anonymous
c., ca.	(Latin *circa*) about
cf.	(Latin *confer*) compare
ch.; chs.	chapter; chapters
col.; cols.	column; columns
comp.; comps.	compiled by, compiler; compilers
dir.	director, directed by
diss.	dissertation
ed.; eds.	editor, edited by, edition; editors, editions
et al.	(Latin *et alii*) and others
fig.; figs.	figure; figures
ibid.	(Latin *ibidem*) in the same place
introd.	introduction, introduced by
l.; ll.	line; lines
ms.; mss.	manuscript; manuscripts
n.d.	no date of publication
n.; nn.	note (footnote); notes
no.; nos.	number; numbers
n.p.	no place of publication, no publisher
n. pag.	no pagination
p.; pp.	page; pages
passim	(Latin) throughout
pref.	preface, preface by
rev.	revision, revised, revised by, review
rpt.	reprint, reprinted by
st.; sts.	stanza; stanzas
supp.; supps.	supplement; supplements
trans.	translated by, translator
vol.; vols.	volume; volumes
writ.	writer, written by

83g abbreviations

84 Sample Research Paper with Comments

This sample essay was selected less because it is a model research paper—though it is clearly a good one—than because it conveniently illustrates many of the details discussed in the preceding pages. The combined essay and commentary will repay your close attention.

Title Page:
The information could all have been grouped in the upper part of the page, but the arrangement opposite, with only the title and author at the top and the rest lower down (all centred, of course), presents an attractive and balanced appearance.

The Environment: Ours to Do with What We Will

by

Janice Elnor

English 100

Professor Smith

April 7, 1978

Since a title page is used, the title itself is not repeated on the first page. Notice also that the first page is not numbered. If a first page or a page beginning a new section, such as outline, notes, or bibliography, is to be numbered at all, it should only be at the bottom centre. The outline page, then, could have been numbered at bottom centre with a small Roman numeral *i*. The title page is not counted as a page for numbering purposes, and pages containing preliminary material such as outlines and prefaces are not considered part of the regular pagination but are instead numbered, if at all, with small Roman numerals.

Note that on page 1 the text begins about a quarter of the way down, presenting a cleanly balanced beginning page—and one that is obviously a beginning page, even without a number.

Note that the outline goes only to the first level of subheading. An obvious 1, 2, and 3 could easily have been supplied under each A, B, and C; for example, under I-B could come

1. Industry pollutes.
2. Industry wastes energy.
3. Industry harms wilderness and wildlife.

But these are so obvious as to be unnecessary.

Organization and Emphasis:
Note that paragraph 2 of the essay corresponds to section 1-A of the outline. The three subjects (pollution, energy, and wilderness) are covered in one paragraph, as also in paragraphs 3 and 4. The writer had more data, but decided not to include them. When she reached part II, however, she began to break some of the material into separate paragraphs. And though III-A becomes two paragraphs (15 and 16) and III-B only one (17), at III-C the whole pattern changes: the individual's importance is represented by this section's turning into several paragraphs in which pollution, energy, and wilderness are all woven together. All of this corresponds to the writer's desired emphasis on the need for greater action (part III occupies the last half of the paper) and especially on the need for changed attitudes (part III-C occupies the last quarter of the paper). That is, the essay builds to a climax.

Part II-A of the outline is spread over two paragraphs (6 and 7). Part II-B is given three (8, 9, and 10), continuing the expansion and consequent emphasis on solutions after stating the problem. One result of this is shorter and less satisfactory paragraphs in part II; paragraph 8, for example, is shorter even than paragraph 5, which is merely transitional. By part III, however, the section given most space, the writer gets back to longer, more fully developed paragraphs.

Outline

Thesis Statement: Since man is responsible for environmental
damage, and though he is trying to help, he must change his
attitudes and work harder to save the environment and himself.
Beginning: "Environmentalism" is something new, though the
          problem is not: "The Problem Is People."
I. The problem: Man as government, industry, and individual
   causes environmental deterioration.
     A. Lacking foresight, governments cause pollution, the
        waste of energy, and damage to wilderness.
     B. Profit-oriented industry causes pollution, wastes
        energy, and destroys wilderness.
     C. Through laziness and carelessness, individuals cause
        pollution, waste energy, and damage wilderness.
II. Government, industry, and individuals are currently working
   to repair the damage and prevent further harm.
     A. Through legislation and example, governments help to
        control pollution and save energy and wilderness.
     B. Largely under compulsion, industry helps to cut
        pollution, save energy, and preserve wilderness.
     C. Alone and in groups, individuals work to cut pollution,
        save energy, and preserve wilderness.
III. Government, industry, and individuals must all do more if we
   and our environment are to be saved.
     A. Government must act to control pollution and to
        promote the saving of energy and wilderness.
     B. Industry must change its priorities to halt pollution,
        save energy, and preserve wilderness.
     C. People must change their attitudes to stop pollution,
        save energy, and halt the destruction of wilderness.
Ending: The essential for the future is changed attitudes. We
        and our environment are interdependent, and we must
        behave accordingly.

Paragraph 1: The first paragraph is partly introductory and partly substantive. From two opening sentences which state and substantiate the newness of our environmental awareness, the writer moves quickly and economically to introduce the three elements—pollution, energy, and wilderness—that run throughout the essay. The rest of the paragraph, while continuing to provide background and definition, also states and restates the part of the thesis covering man's responsibility.

(Continued on next page)

Footnote 2: This book was out of the library, but the writer felt that the title alone was too good to pass up. She of course had to trust the accuracy of a bibliographical listing and the card catalogue.

Footnote 3: This is a discursive footnote, though the material could have been included in the text. The documentary part at the end is enclosed in parentheses, which means that square brackets must replace the usual internal parentheses. The dots do not indicate ellipsis but are part of the title; typing them without spaces is a device used by some writers to indicate that they are in the source, not added by the writer. Compare this footnote with the original source and with the version that appeared on the relevant note card to see how the information was successively boiled down. The source:

> Ecosystems represent a standing crop of energy and minerals that are stored in plants, animals, and soils. It is this standing crop that is utilized by man. If the removal of the crop, either wholesale or selective, proceeds at a rate greater than the recuperating processes operating in the ecosystem, in the absence of artificial fertilization, then ecosystem degradation, or landscape pollution, is inevitable.

Edgell, p. 49. "ecosystem" - Introd. or I?
says that "Ecosystems" amount to "a
standing crop of energy and minerals that
are stored in plants, animals, and soils."
If man removes the "crop" "at a rate
greater than the recuperating processes" of the
"ecosystem can restore it," "in the absence
of artificial fertilization, then ecosystem
degradation or landscape pollution, is inevitable."
[Euse as part of definition of the 'problem'?]]

(1)   In recent years there has been rapidly growing concern about the environment. A 1975 encyclopedia contains an entry on "environmentalism," whereas its predecessor of 1963 does not.[1] We hear about the environment every day: pollution is bad, energy resources are being depleted, and the wilderness is dwindling. The problem is not new, as the title of a recent article points out: "Pollution Begins in Prehistory: The Problem Is People."[2] But as population and technology grow, the troubles multiply, until now we are in the midst of a crisis. And clearly it is a man-made crisis. Any time he moves a rock from one place to another, or cuts down a tree for fuel, or kills an animal for its pelt, man is altering a natural balance: He is interfering with an "ecosystem."[3] In <u>Pollution: Canada's</u>

---

[1] <u>The New Columbia Encyclopedia</u>, 1975; cf. <u>The Columbia Encyclopedia</u>, 3rd ed., 1963.

[2] T. Cuyler Young, in <u>Man in Nature</u>, ed. Louis D. Levine (Toronto: Royal Ontario Museum, 1975).

[3] M. C. R. Edgell, in "Landscape Pollution," defines an ecosystem as consisting of "energy and minerals that are stored in plants, animals, and soils" and describes environmental deterioration as the result of man using up the "crop" faster than it is able to regenerate without artificial help (in <u>Pollution: What It Is...What It Does...What Can Be Done About It</u>, ed. W. J. Maunder [Victoria: Evening Division, Univ. of Victoria, 1969], p. 49).

The final sentence also makes explicit the part of the thesis that serves as an organizing principle throughout the essay. The rest of the thesis is not stated here but left until the second and third parts begin. By naming Morgan and his book's title (which itself helps state part of the thesis), the writer implies that he is an important source. Morgan's statement could have been paraphrased, but the writer felt that his words were distinctive and that a direct quotation was appropriate here in the opening paragraph.

Footnote 4: Since the author's full name and the book's title are in the text, they are not repeated here. The name of the editor of the series is reserved for the bibliography.

Footnote 5: This covering footnote, expressing general indebtedness, appears at the end of the first paragraph; the tripartite division mentioned in the last sentence is part of what is being credited. The subtitle of the first book is omitted here. The work by Ferguson gave no city as the place of publication; rather than put *n.p.*, however, the writer chose to accept the library's tentative suggestion in the card catalogue— "[Vancouver?]"—and included this logical guess in square brackets in her footnote.

Footnote 6: This "See for example" footnote indicates that Bell is only one of several sources that discuss the matter. This form is less direct documentation of material from Bell than it is a way of informing readers that the subject is a common one and telling them at least one place where they can find out more about it, a method which here is preferable to simply assuming that a widely mentioned matter is "common knowledge." The book edited by Maunder is fully identified in footnote 3, but rather than just say "Maunder, pp. 87-101," the writer decided to use not only the name but also *ed.* and a short title because of the possible confusion which could arise later (see footnote 10). The page numbers given are inclusive, indicating that the whole article is relevant to the point being made.

Critical Challenge, Frank Morgan says that "When man mismanages
his environment, man pays, sometimes with his livelihood, always
with some part of his way of life."[4] Man alone is responsible
for environmental damage, whether he acts as an individual or
through the industries he creates and the governments he elects.[5]

(2) Governments, through lack of foresight, have contributed to
the deterioration of the environment. All levels of government
want growth, whether of a nation, a province, or a city, but in
the past they have given little thought to the ecological
implications of rapid growth. Municipal governments, for
example, responding to the needs of their citizens, have been
major polluters of water, land, and air because of poor planning
of sewage and garbage disposal systems.[6] We were asleep at the
energy switch as well. It took the Arabs and the oil crisis of
the 1970's to alert governments and everyone else to the need
for conserving our dwindling supplies of conventional fuels.
And wildlife and wilderness areas have suffered because govern-

[4] Shaping Canada's Environment, No. 4 (Toronto: Ryerson,
Maclean-Hunter, 1970), p. 2.

[5] Some of the parts and organization of this paper were
suggested to me--or rather my inclinations toward them were
strengthened--by C. I. Jackson, "Environmental Policy and
Environmental Planning in Canada," in Canada's Natural Environment, ed. G. R. McBoyle and E. Sommerville (Toronto: Methuen,
1976), and Cherry Ferguson, Efforts by the Citizen, Labatt
Breweries, and Government to Achieve Environmental Quality in
B. C. ([Vancouver]: Labatt Breweries, 1971).

[6] See for example M. A. M. Bell, "Waste Management and
Environmental Quality in Victoria, B. C.," in Maunder, ed.,
Pollution, pp. 87-101.

Paragraph 3: It is safe enough to say in the second sentence that "Industry is one of the two main sources" rather than to hedge with something like "is said to be" or "is claimed to be." Footnote 10 covers the second sentence. The third sentence clearly draws on the writer's own experience, the fourth sentence is transitional, and footnote 11 covers the specific citation of the fifth sentence. Since the point of view of each sentence is therefore clear, the reader does not wonder about sources and documentation. Note how in the sixth sentence the writer has turned a weakness, the scarcity of useful information, into a strength by tying a different kind of environmental damage, the killing of fish, to her point about wasted energy.

Footnote 7: The edited book was fully identified in footnote 5; here the abbreviation *eds.* is not needed. *Passim* indicates that the points referred to occur here and there throughout Kitchen's article; this is slightly different from what footnote 6 tells us about Bell's article.

Footnote 8: Here the writer cites three specific points as the sources for the information referred to; as you see in the paragraph, the information is more specific than that documented in footnotes 6 and 7.

Footnote 9: The first reference to this source requires a complete footnote, though the writer again decided that it was not necessary to include the book's subtitle in the footnote.

Footnote 10: This consolidated footnote, its parts separated by a semicolon, refers to the two main parts of the sentence. The writer could find no model for the first reference to Maunder's essay in his own edited book, which had already been referred to; applying her common sense, she came up with this form. Note that repeating *ed.* after the second instance of his name keeps his functions as author and editor distinct (see also footnotes 6, 14, 33, and 40). Note that since the title of Maunder's article ends with a question mark, no comma follows it (see also footnotes 27 and 38).

ments have not adequately controlled highways, subdivisions, and industrial developments, to name a few of the manifestations of progress which are replacing the natural environment.[7] Governments establish lovely parks, but exploitation of the land--for example urban development in Banff, logging in Pacific Rim, and also in Algonquin, where it has reduced the deer population-- continues, and is sometimes written into the agreement which created the park in the first place.[8] And defoliants sprayed on roadsides have, when carried further afield by unexpected winds, transformed green areas into virtual deserts.[9]

Government has also been at fault in failing to control industry, whose effects on the ecology are sometimes massive. Industry is one of the two main sources of water pollution (the other being municipal sewage systems), and several other sources of man-made pollution are industry related, such as smokestack emissions, demolition and construction operations, and manu- facturing processes in general.[10] No one who has seen the brownish foam floating on the Fraser River near Prince George,

[7] Cameron M. Kitchen, "Ecology and Urban Development: The Theory and Practice of Ecoplanning in Canada," in McBoyle and Sommerville, pp. 217-40, passim.

[8] John B. Theberge, "Ecological Planning in National Parks," in McBoyle and Sommerville, pp. 195, 201, 211.

[9] M. J. Dunbar, Environment and Good Sense (Montreal: McGill-Queen's Univ. Press, 1971), pp. 46-47.

[10] Morgan, p. 4; W. J. Maunder, "What is Pollution?" in Maunder, ed., Pollution, p. 2.

Paragraph 4: Footnote 14 could have been omitted; it would be hard to find many things more "common knowledge" than auto exhausts and littered streets. Nevertheless the writer did encounter a specific mention of these and decided that the point would be stronger if documented from an authority. The rest of the paragraph is in fact her own information, her own thinking, and can also be claimed to be

(Continued on next page)

Footnote 11: Commoner's book was out of the library; the writer therefore had to take Hohenemser's word for what it said in chapter 7. Since the words quoted in the text are Hohenemser's, not Commoner's, it would be wrong to say "quoted by Hohenemser"; the word *cited*, which can mean "quoted" but can also mean "mentioned," is correct. *Environment* is a monthly magazine, but since it has volume and issue numbers and is specialized, the writer decided to treat it like a learned journal. Note that when the volume number is given, no *p.* precedes the page number.

Footnote 12: The superscript number *12* could logically be placed after the word *fish*. But in line with the principle that footnote numbers should when possible come at the ends of sentences, that is where it is placed here; the final clause is reasonably clearly the writer's, and the form "See Morgan" also suggests that he is to be consulted for the evidence of dead fish, not the conclusion about wasted energy. It would not, however, be wrong to put the number after *fish*, for then the reference would be completely unambiguous; the footnote would then read simply "Morgan, pp. 6-7."

4

B. C., or breathed the air on a foggy morning in Duncan, can
doubt the influence of the pulp and paper industry on the local
environment. Wasted energy is another of industry's contributions to the general deterioration of the environment. The
"profit motive" even leads industry to install equipment that
is "less energy-efficient" than what it replaces.[11] Evidence
of energy-wasting practices is hard to find, but if heated water
around industrial plants is killing fish, then energy is being
wasted somewhere.[12] As for wilderness, though industry is not
often directly responsible for the destruction of wildlife,
indiscriminate logging and mining practices are detrimental to
animals' habitats and food sources.[13]

(4) Man in his private role also accounts for some of the
ecological problems he encounters. Automobile exhausts and
littered streets are two major kinds of pollution to which the
individual contributes.[14] Few people think about the beer bottle
they toss from their boat or the cigarette butt they drop on the
street, but such acts pollute the environment, and also suggest a
poor attitude toward the problem of the environment in general.

[11] Barry Commoner, The Poverty of Power (New York: Knopf,
1976), ch. 7, cited by Kurt H. Hohenemser, "Energy: Waste Not,
Want Not," Environment, 18, No. 7 (Sept. 1976), 4.

[12] See Morgan, pp. 6-7.

[13] Dunbar, p. 39.

[14] Maunder, p. 2.

common knowledge. The final sentence, however, would have been strengthened by some specific examples of endangered and extinct species, accompanied by documentation of authoritative sources.

Paragraph 5: This is a transitional paragraph, a bridge between sections I and II of the outline. The quotation from Ferguson is very convenient in that it reminds the reader of the three-part structure of each section. (It is also fairly obviously one of the reasons Ferguson is cited in footnote 5.) The parenthetical reference following the quotation is sufficient since the author of the already footnoted work is named. Note that the period comes after the parenthesis.

5

Individuals waste energy through laziness (driving short distances) and indifference (turning up the heat instead of putting on a sweater; leaving lights on in unused rooms). Man's "I can't be bothered" attitude reflects an egocentric desire to save personal time and effort at the expense of his surroundings. And egocentric man the "sportsman" and outdoorsman does his share of damage to the wilderness and its wildlife through carelessness and indiscriminate hunting and fishing, even to the extent of adding to the list of endangered and extinct species.

(5) The problem, then, is the destruction of the natural environment at the hands of man. What is man doing to repair the damage and to prevent further harm? Since man created the problem, it is only logical that he work to correct it. And as Cherry Ferguson says, "effective environmental quality management is the product of a co-operative effort involving the citizen, industry and government" (p. 1). Indeed, all three are now working to slow down most and to eliminate some of the environmental deterioration in Canada.

(6) Since 1966, the federal government has enacted legislation aimed at preventing and cleaning up pollution, conserving energy, and preserving parklands. The Canada Centre for Inland Waters was established in 1967, a research facility which provided much of the information necessary to start the cleanup of the Great Lakes. In 1970, the government created Environment Canada and drew up such pollution-oriented legislation as the Canada Water Act and the Clean Air Act. Canada participated actively in

Paragraph 6: Footnote 15 documents the single source for all the data in the paragraph up to that point. The next sentence, about Habitat, is from the writer's own experience; though sources could easily be found, they are unnecessary. Footnote 16 documents the information in the final sentence.

Paragraph 7: Footnote 17 documents the data in the first sentence, and 18 the data in the second sentence. The third sentence, however, is documented by a parenthetical reference, since the author is named and has already been documented in an earlier footnote (number 7). Identifying Kitchen as a geographer is perhaps marginally useful, but it might have been worth remarking that Morgan, a principal source, is news editor for a medical journal. Whenever possible, identify cited authorities as indeed having some authority.

Footnote 17: A first reference to a newspaper article. Note that the definite article is usually omitted from a newspaper's name. Like many newspapers, this one has sections (A, B, C, etc.) which must be included as part of the page number. Identifying the column number or numbers is not essential, but is nevertheless a courtesy to the reader.

6

international conferences dealing with man and his environment, such as the UN Conference on the Human Environment (Stockholm, 1972) and the Law of the Sea Conference (Caracas, 1974-75).[15] And Canada sponsored the Habitat conference in Vancouver in 1976. Provincial and municipal governments help by establishing pollution control boards which regulate industry and by being more conscientious about regional planning.[16]

(7)   In order to conserve energy, governments are considering rapid transit systems to replace private cars as the main method of everyday travel; they are encouraging research into new energy sources; and they are leading the way to active energy conservation, for example with the federal government's "Save 10" program and the B. C. Energy Commission's programs to reduce energy consumption.[17] Wildlife and wilderness areas are also getting more attention from town planners (greenbelts and parks), provincial governments (agricultural land and parks), and also the federal government, as in the operations of Parks Canada and the Canadian Wildlife Service.[18] And more care precedes development now: Cameron M. Kitchen, a geographer, analyzes three case studies-- of a subdivision, a zoo, and a highway by-pass, all in Ontario--

[15] Jackson, pp. 247-60.

[16] Morgan, p. 19.

[17] Michael Harcourt, "Where to Start Saving Energy," Vancouver Sun, 25 Nov. 1977, p. A6, cols. 5-6.

[18] Theberge, pp. 197-98, 208.

Paragraph 9: The writer decided that the first two sentences needed no documentation, since this fact is so widely known and discussed. Nevertheless, the reader might have appreciated a "see for example" footnote, especially about the more specific matter of solar energy. The fourth sentence is clearly the writer's own speculation. Here is how the information from Calef's article looked on a note card, with the writer's own idea enclosed in double square brackets:

> Calef, pp. 17, 18   Industry + energy   II B
>
> —reminds us that burning wood for fuel is really a "solar technology, depending only upon the inexhaustible radiant energy from the sun." (p. 17)
>
> — U. S. proposal of a huge "energy plantation" — ca. 144,000 acres of trees (p. 18)
>
> [[Wouldn't this work well in Canada, with all our trees ?!]]

Note that in order to change the singular "energy plantation" of the original into a plural for the purposes of her own sentence, the writer added an *s* in square brackets.

Footnote 21: Note how a comment can be added to a documenting footnote. Harcourt's point is relevant, but would, the writer felt, be obtrusive in her text. Note also the parenthetical documentation of Harcourt's remark, and its punctuation: the period follows the parenthesis.

7

as examples of the "pre-development ecology" or "ecoplanning"
which has been lacking in the past (pp. 221-37).

(8)   Industry, too, is becoming more conscious of the environment. Government and individuals have forced this awareness on
industry, but as time goes by, industry is taking more responsibility upon itself. Tax breaks and subsidies encourage industry
to install pollution control equipment—though some industries
do not think these incentives great enough. But some industries
are even sponsoring public-awareness programs and providing
money for research and planning.[19]

(9)   Industry's main efforts are directed at reducing energy
consumption and finding new sources of energy. Power companies
and others are working on alternatives and additions to hydro
power and fossil fuels; solar energy is a major example. In the
United States some people are proposing huge "energy plantation[s]"
of trees, claiming that burning wood is actually a "solar technology."[20] Such an idea might work well in Canada, with all
its woodlands. And scientists are even beginning to work on
nuclear fusion.[21] There is also research into recycling energy,
and the government offers tax breaks to industries installing

[19] Ferguson, p. 38 and passim.

[20] Charles E. Calef, "Not Out of the Woods," Environment,
18, No. 7 (Sept. 1976), 17-18.

[21] Dieter Hohenberger, "Is Fusion the Answer? It Wouldn't
Hurt to Ask," Maclean's, 3 April 1978, p. 70. Harcourt, however,
says that fusion "is at least 30 years off" (col. 3).

Paragraph 10: The final sentence is the writer's own idea. Here is how she recorded it on a note card, complete with double square brackets, at the moment it occurred to her:

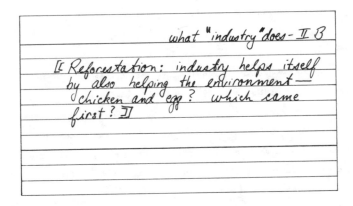

Footnote 22: As also in the preceding footnote, since Harcourt's entire article appears on one page, A6, there is no need to repeat the page number every time.

Footnote 23: Such a fragmentary sentence is permissible in this kind of footnote, though it could easily have begun with "See" or "Note" or "We have all seen" or the like.

8

heating equipment which can re-use energy.[22] Industry is even trying to educate the public in ways to conserve energy--with an emphasis, of course, on saving money.[23]

⑩ Although industry's interest in conserving wilderness and wildlife is largely government imposed, new restrictions on sites, methods, and tools are having the desired effects. Land developers are paying more attention to the ecology; consequently they produce better developments which are readily approved by local governments.[24] Industry is also helping to develop new methods that will, it is hoped, eliminate the need for chemical insecticides.[25] And reforestation is a prime example of how industry looks out for its own interests while helping to maintain natural ecological balance.

⑪ Public outcry and the work of citizens' groups are probably the most effective ways individuals can help to preserve their environment. The number of groups is rising, and though many problems have limited their success to date--poor facilities, low budgets, lack of active participation, poor communication with other groups as well as with government and industry--these

[22] Harcourt, col. 5.

[23] For example the frequent "public interest" TV spots, magazine ads, and even billboards by power companies, oil companies, and automobile manufacturers.

[24] Kitchen, p. 239.

[25] Dunbar, pp. 44-46.

Paragraph 11: The material in the last two sentences stems from the writer's own awareness and not from anything she read about these affairs in the sources. Nevertheless, one would think that she could without too much trouble have found one or two sources (for example in newspaper articles) in order to strengthen and document this point.

Paragraph 12: Unlike the points in the preceding paragraph about tankers and pipeline, those in this paragraph are obviously generally known. Sources for such data could be found, but documentation here would be superfluous.

Paragraph 13: Here is how the writer recorded on a note card one of the ideas that became a part of this paragraph:

> what "people" do - II C
>
> [[Individuals help by helping the experts — supporting, with contributions, such groups as Greenpeace and the Sierra Club.]]

Footnote 27: The writer chanced upon the review documented in this footnote when she was nearly through revising her essay, and felt that it would make a good discursive footnote to add depth and particularity to the paragraph's opening statement. The comment had to go into a footnote, she felt, for if put into the text it would destroy the already established flow and integrity of the paragraph.

9

problems are resolvable.[26] And there are more frequent public
hearings into potentially harmful projects. Plans for oil
tankers to dock at Kitimat, for example, and for a Mackenzie
Valley Pipeline, were met with public demands to know more
about their ecological implications.

(12)   Citizens' groups tend to concentrate on pollution and wildlife conservation, but the individual is also helping to conserve
energy. People are insulating their houses better, and buying
smaller cars; they are recycling glass and paper and metal; and
some refuse to buy such energy-hungry items as self-cleaning
ovens. Although some of these acts are economically motivated,
they nevertheless indicate changing attitudes.

(13)   The increase of public interest in outdoor activities such
as camping, hiking, climbing, and cross-country skiing has also
increased the individual's awareness of his environment.[27]
Interest in conserving wildlife and recreation areas is growing,
and with the aid of such groups as Greenpeace and the Sierra
Club, this interest is turning into action. Though the individual
may feel powerless to save a whale or preserve natural woodland,
his contributions help organizations that have the ability to

[26] Ferguson, p. 1.

[27] One indication of the growing interest in and respect
for the wilderness is the large number of books and articles
about it that are pouring out these days. See Diane Johnson,
"Ah, Wilderness!" rev. of The Last Cowboy, by Jane Kramer, and
Coming into the Country, by John McPhee, New York Review of
Books, 23 March 1978, pp. 3-6. Johnson discusses the phenomenon
and mentions several other works.

Paragraph 14: Note how this short transitional paragraph neatly sums up section II and then introduces section III with the appropriate part of the thesis.

Paragraph 15: The number for footnote 18 had to be placed early in the sentence, since only the opening clause derived from the source. Note also that the parenthetical reference to Morgan's book comes as soon as possible after his name rather than at the end of the sentence; this is the usual practice when the material is paraphrased or summarized rather than quoted (cf. the parenthetical references in paragraphs 5, 7, 11, 19, and 20, and in footnote 21).

Footnote 28: A first reference to an article in a scholarly journal with continuous pagination throughout the issues that make up each annual volume. The issue number is not necessary. Note the Arabic numeral for the volume number, and that no *p.* is included when the volume number is given.

10

accomplish something tangible.

(14)   Obviously some good results have been achieved, but man
cannot yet sit back on his laurels with a satisfied smile. As
industrialization and urbanization continue to grow, new environmental problems arise. The work must not only continue, therefore, but also be intensified if we are to preserve our quality
of life.

(15)   Government control over industries must be tightened. Since
voluntary controls have a way of not working,[28] there must be new
legislation which includes mandatory measures, such as limits on
the chemical contents of industrial discharges, and there must be
large fines for those who contravene the regulations. Governments must also try to make it attractive for industry to obey
the laws. By providing funds for research into new equipment
and alternative materials and methods, governments would be viewed
less as disrupters of the status quo than as active contributors
to a clean environment. Morgan (p. 3) advocates that environmental programs be under federal control but be carried out by
the provinces, and that they cover all the different kinds of
possible damage to the environment. But such programs can work
only if governments get together and agree to make them work.

(16)   Conservation also requires more attention from governments.
Not only should they set good examples; they also have a respon-

----

[28] Daniel J. Koenig, "Additional Research on Environmental
Activism," Environment and Behavior, 7 (1975), 475.

Paragraph 17: It would have been preferable to translate the obscure jargon of the quotation from Morgan into simpler, more comprehensible English. In contrast, the quotation from Novick on page 12, long enough to be indented and single-spaced, would be difficult to paraphrase effectively and is better left in the author's own words. Note that, for the sake of clarity, the writer herself inserted the year, in the obligatory square brackets. And note the four dots of the ellipsis at the end. Note also how the quotation is introduced with a complete sentence followed by a colon.

Footnote 29: Rather than cite a whole list of other sources, the writer merely calls attention to the fact that the subject of educating the public is a common one among her sources. She could probably have used a "see for example" footnote here, but perhaps felt that adding a comment would be stronger.

Footnote 31: A secondhand source. Identifying Pépin's position in this way adds authority to his ideas. If he were, say, a taxi driver, his thoughts on these matters would not carry so much weight.

11

sibility to educate the public.[29] By making people aware of
energy problems, government can lessen public resistance to
conservation measures; by imposing higher taxes on luxury items
such as big cars, government can discourage the use of energy-
draining extras; and by subsidizing improved insulation, government can encourage homeowners to save energy.[30] And educating
the public about the use and value of parkland and wilderness
areas is essential for effective land and animal conservation.

(17)   If education, legislation, and leadership are the key roles
for government, responsibility and unselfishness must increasingly
motivate industry. Most of the environmental problems created
by industry are the result of our profit-oriented system. One
expert proposes a plan that would require that we consider
"natural resources as economic assets. Their use should be
expressed in terms of an equation combining elements of cost-
profit and the individual-community--and all within a perspective
of relativity of both time and space."[31] Industry must
re-examine the relative values of profit and environmental
despoliation. Stopping pollution costs money, but pollution
itself can be expensive:

[29] Morgan, p. 133. Many other authorities also mention
this need.

[30] Harcourt, cols. 4-5.

[31] Pierre-Yves Pépin, of the Urban Institute of the
University of Montreal, as summarized by Morgan, p. 133.

Paragraph 18: The passage from Morgan on page 13 is much more quotable than that from Winham; Winham's is pedestrian and passive, whereas Morgan's has a distinctive rhetorical flavour that it would be a pity to lose by paraphrasing. All but perhaps the last few words of Winham's would better have been paraphrased. Note how the first quotation is introduced with a brief subordinate clause followed by a comma. The quotation begins with a capital *G* as it does in the source. Since the sentence following the block quotation continues with material from Winham and—which is important—repeats his name so that the point of view remains clear, no footnote number is needed at the end of the block quotation; it can wait until the end of the next sentence, when the writer is finished with Winham. The quotation

(Continued on next page)

Footnote 34: Since the author's full name (or as full as was available) is given in the text, it is not included in the footnote. Here is how the note card for this paraphrase looked:

Winham, p. 389   public opinion-IIIC

"Public attitudes are seldom the principal component of public policy, yet they are a factor which is weighed in the decisions of popularly elected leaders."

[∴ to lead into conclusion about the importance of people's attitudes toward their environment and their lives?]]

Footnotes must always begin on the page where the material they document occurs, and should if possible be completed on that page. Occasionally, however, as they do here, the exigencies of spacing and numbering require that a footnote be continued at the beginning of the footnotes on the next page. When this occurs, type or draw a line

(Continued on next page)

12

> Toward the end of June [1976], businessmen antici-
> pating heavy summer tourist trade in the famed
> Thousand Islands region of the Saint Lawrence
> Seaway were shocked to find themselves facing
> several months of shore cleanup in the wake of a
> barge grounding which released about 2.5 million
> gallons of toxic fuel oil into the seaway . . . .[32]

In the long run pollution may well cost more--not only in money, but also in health and happiness--than would steps taken now to prevent it.[33] It may cost more to install energy-recycling units, and it may be less efficient to operate in a location which does not interfere with wildlife, but industry must realize that its own survival hangs in the balance along with everyone else's.

(18) Industry is in a sense an unfortunate scapegoat, for it is after all a manifestation of man's desire for "progress" and material well-being. And government is equally unfortunate in that it is pulled in two directions. As G. Winham observes,

> Government officials today are pressed by the public
> to reduce environmental pollution. At the same time
> they are also expected to maintain high growth rates
> and to increase employment opportunities. Too often
> these demands are simply inconsistent.

Public opinion, as Winham notes, may not often be the primary influence, but it is an influence and can affect legislation.[34]

[32] Sheldon Novick, "Spectrum" (a monthly newsletter), Environment, 18, No. 7 (Sept. 1976), 22-23.

[33] See for example Maunder, pp. 5-8.

[34] "Attitudes on Pollution and Growth in Hamilton, or

from Morgan is also introduced with a short clause and a comma; this quotation, however, begins with a lower case *t* because it does not start at the beginning of a sentence in the source. Note that an opening ellipsis (. . .) is not necessary, since beginning with the lower case letter makes it clear that it is not from the beginning of a sentence. Note also that when a parenthetical reference follows a block quotation, it comes after the period rather than before it.

---

about one third of the way across the second page two or three spaces below the text, as here, to separate text from continued footnote. Otherwise, since the continued footnote does not begin with a raised number and a five-space indention, it could momentarily and confusingly be mistaken for part of the text. Notice the single quotation marks inside the usual double quotation marks.

Footnote 35: Strictly speaking, *The Gallup Poll of Canada* is the title of the annual bound volumes of reports; since it is given in the text, the writer does not repeat it in the footnote. She also decided that the Canadian Institute for Public Opinion was the corporate author rather than the publisher, and otherwise handled this difficult footnote with commendable common sense.

13

In any event, man's attitude is at the root of the problem, and must be modified if we are to be successful in our fight to preserve the environment. As Morgan concludes,

> the degree of national, international and even global commitment to control will depend finally on our own concern for the condition of the street on which we live, the river in which we fish and swim, the town in which we spend our time and money. (p. 133)

The Gallup Poll of Canada reported that on March 25, 1970, 91 percent of the people surveyed professed an awareness of pollution, and 69 percent of them regarded it as "very serious." A similar poll on February 26, 1975, showed 93 percent awareness-- but only 57 percent considered the problem very serious.[35] The decline in concern over five years may be attributable to improved environmental protection mechanisms, or it may be due to complacency. In any event, the initial furor of the late 1960's and early 1970's seems to be dying down, while oil spills and air pollution continue.

The media, once credited with increasing public awareness, have recently come under fire for misleading the public about environmental issues,[36] and it seems, of late, that only items

---

'There's an Awful Lot of Talk These Days About Ecology,'" Canadian Journal of Political Science, 5 (1972), 389.

[35] The Canadian Institute of Public Opinion, "Concern with Pollution Drops Among Canadians," Gallup Report of 26 Feb. 1975; cf. 25 March and 2 Dec. 1970.

[36] Jacqueline Cernot, quoted by Robert Wielaard, "News Media Augment Ignorance of Ecology, Ottawa Official Says," Winnipeg Free Press, 1 Dec. 1977, p. 6.

Paragraph 19: The writer inserted *sic* in square brackets in the quotation from Koenig lest she be accused of herself misspelling *despoliation*. This is strictly correct, since quotation is supposed to be verbatim. Most writers, however, would consider an error like this too minor to be concerned about, and would simply perform a silent correction as they transcribed the sentence. They would reserve *sic* for serious errors, such as errors of fact or stylistic errors that are obviously more than a slip. For example, note that we decided to include a *sic* in our long quotation from Rupert Brooke (see **81**); the correction—inserting "those of" before the word *Montreal*, or adding *'s* to it—was more than we felt we should do silently. If you are not sure which course to take, use *sic*; it is better to risk being thought a pedant than to be accused of tampering unduly with a quotation. Note that after the three dots of the ellipsis the writer has inserted a comma—inside the quotation mark—for the purpose of punctuating her own sentence. Note too how smoothly she has worked Koenig's words into the syntax of her own paraphrase. The parenthetical reference at the end clearly covers all the material from Koenig; a reference or footnote number after the first quotation as well is unnecessary since the paragraph obviously continues to draw on Koenig.

Paragraph 20: All the specific details of this paragraph are the writer's own. Note how neatly the paragraph is framed by the two sentences quoted from Harcourt, and how the first quotation is handled. Note also how the second sentence is a kind of second topic sentence (see **67c**).

Footnote 37: Here the writer, by means of a discursive and consolidated footnote, turns a point that could probably have been treated as common knowledge into something emphatic.

14

of great international interest (the Brittany oil spill, for
example) receive major coverage. As Daniel J. Koenig remarks,
"Individuals may be quickly aroused by sudden and visible
environmental despoilation [sic] in their immediate environment . . . ," but most people, he believes, remain passive
"until it is too late." People may be getting bored by all the
talk about the environment, but if they ignore it, matters will
only get worse. Koenig fears that if people continue to submit
passively, "the environmental rapists will quickly realize the
lack of genuine resistance to their advances," and continued
environmental destruction will be inevitable (pp. 473-74).

(20)   "The first thing Canadians should do," writes Michael Harcourt, "is recognize that they are the most wasteful, head-in-
the-sand nation on the face of the earth" (col. 3). Clearly,
people will have to accept "an associated reduction in the,
standard of living" if they really want to conserve energy.[37]
This may well mean smaller and fewer cars, less travel by jet,
fewer labour-saving but energy-consuming gadgets, more clothes
and less heat, and even a--perhaps welcome--decrease in the
amount of plastic in our lives. It also means higher prices
for manufactured goods, and probably higher taxes to support
government programs. The individual is also going to have to

----

[37] Hohenemser, p. 4. Most authorities agree on this
commonplace; see for example Winham, pp. 400-01, and James S.
Bowman, "Public Opinion and the Environment: Post-Earth Day
Attitudes Among College Students," <u>Environment and Behavior</u>,
9 (1977), 394-95.

Paragraph 21: Note how footnote 38 comes at the end of three sentences derived from the same source. Only one footnote is needed; do not make the mistake in such instances of providing three separate footnotes. The final clause before the number is clearly the writer's, and the number can come at the end of the sentence. Again with footnote 39 (next page), one footnote is sufficient, even though a reader cannot tell, without going to the source, just what part of the material comes from each of the three cited pages. Here is how one of the note cards from Bowman looked. Note that the writer was careful to write the hyphenated word *pro-environmental* all on one line; had *pro-* been written at the end of a line, she might have wondered later if the word was hyphenated in the source or merely in her note. Always be thus careful with hyphenated words in quoted notes:

Bowman, p. 393   III - C or (concl.)

" . . . student attitudes are decidedly pro-environmental."

In the long quotation from Loney on the next page, note that in the third ellipsis there is no space before the first of the four dots; this indicates that it is the period and that the ellipsis occurs at the beginning of the next sentence, which thus begins with a lower case *i*. Some writers would change it to a capital *I* in square brackets, to mark the beginning of a new sentence, but others feel that that would be awkward and unnecessary. The long quotation from Jackson (next page), as footnote 41 reveals, comes from two widely separated places in his article; the full line of dots indicates this unusually large ellipsis. Here is how the note card for the second part of the quotation looked:

(Continued on next page)

learn to enjoy his wilderness trips without the motor-home or
the trailer, to get back to tents and hiking so that green areas
may be spared the carnage of roads and artificially created
campsites. Such sacrifices are not great, though they may sound
somewhat less attractive than what we are used to. But unless
such changes take place, changes--for the worse--in our health
and the future quality of our lives are inevitable. As Harcourt
puts it, "We are all going to have to change our ways, either
wisely and voluntarily, or in a panic as an emergency reaction to
the crisis that looms a few years ahead" (col. 3).

(21)   We can only speculate about what will happen. One group of
American researchers concludes that since public concern about
pollution is a relatively "new phenomenon," it may turn out to
be no more than a "fad." They note that publicity in the media
had failed, in the town they surveyed, to stir up anti-pollution
sentiment. Yet they also remark that young people show more
concern than their elders, which offers some hope.[38] Indeed,
another sociologist suggests that students' attitudes may be the
most important ones because students did so much to bring
environmental matters to public attention with such affairs as
the Earth Day demonstrations in 1970, because they are less
likely than older and less-educated people to be bound by
tradition, and because they are likely to be the leaders of

---

[38] Marvin C. Sharma, Joseph E. Kivlin, and Frederick C.
Fliegel, "Environmental Pollution: Is There Enough Public
Concern to Lead to Action?" Environment and Behavior, 7 (1975),
467-68.

> *Jackson, pp. 260-61   the future, optimism; concl.*
>
> "... the concern in Canada and the rest of
> the world that // marked the late 1960's
> has left a permanent and substantial
> legacy. The sheer volume of legislative change
> during that period, combined with the
> creation of major departments of
> government concerned with environmental matters,
> should alone ensure that the momentum
> [OVER]

Observe that the double slash (//) indicates where the quotation went
from page 260 to page 261; had the writer carelessly omitted that mark
when taking the note, she would have had to make a trip to the library
to find out from the source—if it was still available—on just which
page or pages was the part she wanted to use. And note the important
OVER to remind her of the few further words on the back of the card.
Note that she lifted the phrase "the late 1960's" from earlier in the
passage and substituted it—in square brackets to indicate her editorial
tampering with the original—for the otherwise obscure "that period"
in the part quoted. Note also that whereas the preceding paragraph
ended effectively with a brief quotation, the writer here, knowing that
long quotations make poor paragraph endings, managed to follow it
with an expressive brief comment to end the paragraph effectively.
Identifying Loney as a municipal planner and Jackson as working in
a relevant federal ministry is good tactics, for it lends weight to their
statements. (See paragraph 7.)

Footnote 41: Jackson has been referred to before, but the writer wanted
to add the brief comment, and felt it would be silly to have both a
parenthetical reference and a discursive footnote at the same point
(although some writers do combine the two, putting the footnote number after the parenthesis).

tomorrow. He concludes from his survey that students are "decidedly pro-environmental" and that we need "to make the transition from a negative attitude to a positive one" in order to "actuate the widespread environmental concern that exists today."[39] T. W. Loney, a municipal planner, sees some hope:

> Public opinion . . . does change, and . . . cultural patterns today seem to be undergoing changes at an ever-accelerating rate. . . . if the causes and effects of pollution can be objectively measured and put before the people, they may be willing to support a much greater degree of control over, and investment in, the environment than is now generally accepted.[40]

And C. I. Jackson, of the Ministry of State for Urban Affairs, in Ottawa, is also guardedly optimistic:

> there seem to be adequate grounds for believing that Canadians, and their legislators and administrators, recognize the importance of environmental concerns and are prepared to give them adequate attention.
> . . . .
> The sheer volume of legislative change during [the late 1960's], combined with the creation of major departments of government concerned with environmental matters, should alone ensure that the momentum is maintained.[41]

Let us hope that this optimism is justified.

[39] Bowman, pp. 386-87, 393, 409.

[40] "Pollution and Planning in Victoria, B. C.," in Maunder, ed., Pollution, p. 86.

[41] Pp. 245, 261. Jackson insists that he is expressing his own views, not necessarily those of the government.

Paragraph 22: Notice how this finishing paragraph grows smoothly out of the point about changing people's attitudes that has recurred during the last half of the essay, especially toward the end. It therefore manages to sound not only like a conclusion but also like a logical substantive continuation of what has gone before.

Footnote 42: A quotation at second hand. Compare the handling of the additional comment here and in footnote 37 with the much weaker handling of a similar instance in footnote 29.

Footnote 44: Although this documents the same source as footnote 43, the two cannot be consolidated, because 44 must refer to Peterman citing Commoner, not to Peterman alone. For the same reason, although this is the only place in the essay where two successive references are to the same source, neither could one use an *ibid.* in footnote 44. Peterman gives no source other than Commoner's name; the writer therefore could not provide further information, since Commoner's books were out of the library.

17

(22)   Man as a whole is responsible for what has happened and is happening to our environment, and man as a whole must continue and increase his efforts if the damage is to be repaired, the environment--and ourselves--saved. As one student put it, "The basic key to helping the environment is to change people's attitudes."[42] If we can accept the philosophical fact that we are a part of nature, not separate from it; if we can bring ourselves to believe in "organism" rather than "dualism," we will not irreparably destroy our environment but rather use it intelligently.[43] "Everything," as Barry Commoner's "first law of ecology" puts it, "is connected to everything else."[44] People as individuals, as builders and users of industry, and as electors and members of governments, must work together in honouring this natural interdependence.

[42] Quoted by Bowman, p. 406. Many make this point: see for example I. Burton, "The Quality of the Environment," in Vegetation, Soils and Wildlife, ed. J. G. Nelson and M. J. Chambers (Toronto: Methuen, 1969), p. 360.

[43] William A. Peterman, "Nature: A Democracy of Trees," Environment, 18, No. 7 (Sept. 1976), 41.

[44] Cited by Peterman, p. 40.

The page on which a new section begins need not be numbered, but it can, as here, be numbered at bottom centre. The label "Works Cited" is usually preferable to the less precise "Bibliography." Note that a page beginning a new section has a wider margin at the top.

In bibliographical entries, as in footnotes, only one space follows a colon, whatever a writer's practice may be elsewhere. But note that the standard two spaces follow each period. Some people prefer to underline only the separate words of a title, claiming that one cannot italicize a space; to others this seems unnecessarily meticulous and choppy looking, and they feel, as well, that a continuous underlining gives a better graphic representation of the wholeness of a title.

Note that entries for articles in periodicals give inclusive page numbers—and inclusive column numbers for the newspaper article in the eighth entry. The page numbers in the third entry indicate that Calef's article concluded on a page that was not in consecutive sequence with its first pages, a common practice in some magazines.

The fourth entry is alphabetized according to "Canadian," the first significant word; the definite article "The" is ignored for the purposes of alphabetizing. The sixth item, an anonymous article in an encyclopedia, is alphabetized according to its title.

Although the third and tenth items are both from the same issue of the same journal, the complete data for that issue must be included in each entry.

The thirteenth entry, the last on the page, lists Maunder's edited book as a source; the individual essays from it—by Edgell, Loney, and Maunder himself—are not listed, since there are as many as three of them. *Maunder* is alphabetized before *McBoyle* (see next page), although some people, using the system adopted by telephone books, would put all *Mc*'s and *Mac*'s ahead of other names beginning with *M*.

Works Cited

Bowman, James S. "Public Opinion and the Environment: Post-Earth Day Attitudes Among College Students." Environment and Behavior, 9 (1977), 385-416.

Burton, I. "The Quality of the Environment." In Vegetation, Soils and Wildlife. Ed. J. G. Nelson and M. J. Chambers. Toronto: Methuen, 1969, pp. 347-60.

Calef, Charles E. "Not Out of the Woods." Environment, 18, No. 7 (Sept. 1976), 17-20, 25.

The Canadian Institute of Public Opinion. The Gallup Poll of Canada. 1970, 1975.

Dunbar, M. J. Environment and Good Sense: An Introduction to Environmental Damage and Control in Canada. Montreal: McGill-Queen's Univ. Press, 1971.

"Environmentalism." The New Columbia Encyclopedia. 1975 ed.

Ferguson, Cherry. Efforts by the Citizen, Labatt Breweries, and Government to Achieve Environmental Quality in B. C. [Vancouver]: Labatt Breweries, 1971.

Harcourt, Michael. "Where to Start Saving Energy." Vancouver Sun, 25 Nov. 1977, p. A6, cols. 1-6.

Hohenberger, Dieter. "Is Fusion the Answer? It Wouldn't Hurt to Ask." Maclean's, 3 April 1978, p. 70.

Hohenemser, Kurt H. "Energy: Waste Not, Want Not." Environment, 18, No. 7 (Sept. 1976), 3-5.

Johnson, Diane. "Ah, Wilderness!" Rev. of The Last Cowboy, by Jane Kramer, and Coming into the Country, by John McPhee. New York Review of Books, 23 March 1978, pp. 3-6.

Koenig, Daniel J. "Additional Research on Environmental Activism." Environment and Behavior, 7 (1975), 472-85.

Maunder, W. J., ed. Pollution: What It Is...What It Does... What Can Be Done About It. Victoria: Evening Division, Univ. of Victoria, 1969.

The first item on this page has two editors. Note that only the first editor's name is reversed, surname first, for the purpose of alphabetizing; the second name is written in normal order. As in the preceding entry, since as many as three articles from this book were cited (those by Jackson, Kitchen, and Theberge), the book itself is listed as a source and the individual articles are not.

In the second entry, the name of the editor of the series is included; it was not necessary in the footnote (number 4). It is unnecessary to record that Morgan's book includes an introduction by Forrester; had the introduction been by someone else, however—neither author nor editor, neither Morgan nor Forrester—his name would have had to be included, along with *Introd.* or *Introd. by.*

In the fifth entry on this page, note again that only the first of the three authors' names is reversed; the other two are written in normal order.

In the sixth entry, the fact that the "Ottawa official" is Jacqueline Cernot is not included; it was, however, necessary in the footnote (number 36) since Wielaard was quoting her. The column number or numbers for a newspaper article are not essential, though they are often included as a courtesy to the reader; the writer neglected to make a note of them for this article and so could not include the information here.

The final entry, though listing an item the writer never saw, must be included since she did directly cite its title. A work cited at second hand, such as Barry Commoner's in footnote 11, should not be included in a bibliography. The footnote (number 2) did not have to include the subtitle of Levine's book, but the bibliographical entry must.

Ms. note: Like footnotes (or notes collected at the end of an essay), bibliographical entries are often single-spaced, as here, with double spaces between them. If you or your instructor wish, however, they can be double-spaced throughout.

84 sample research paper

19

McBoyle, G. R., and E. Sommerville, eds. <u>Canada's Natural Environment: Essays in Applied Geography</u>. Toronto: Methuen, 1976.

Morgan, Frank. <u>Pollution: Canada's Critical Challenge</u>. Shaping Canada's Environment, No. 4. Ed. James Forrester. Toronto: Ryerson, Maclean-Hunter, 1970.

Novick, Sheldon. "Spectrum." <u>Environment</u>, 18, No. 7 (Sept. 1976), 21-24.

Peterman, William A. "Nature: A Democracy of Trees." <u>Environment</u>, 18, No. 7 (Sept. 1976), 38-41.

Sharma, Marvin C., Joseph E. Kivlin, and Frederick C. Fliegel. "Environmental Pollution: Is There Enough Public Concern to Lead to Action?" <u>Environment and Behavior</u>, 7 (1975), 455-71.

Wielaard, Robert. "News Media Augment Ignorance of Ecology, Ottawa Official Says." <u>Winnipeg Free Press</u>, 1 Dec. 1977, p. 6.

Winham, G. "Attitudes on Pollution and Growth in Hamilton, or 'There's an Awful Lot of Talk These Days About Ecology.'" <u>Canadian Journal of Political Science</u>, 5 (1972), 389-401.

Young, T. Cuyler. "Pollution Begins in Prehistory: The Problem Is People." In <u>Man in Nature: Historical Perspectives on Man in His Environment</u>. Ed. Louis D. Levine. Toronto: Royal Ontario Museum, 1975, pp. 9-26.

85   Alternative Systems of Documentation

85a   The Name-Page Method

The Modern Language Association of America now recommends the use of the name-page method instead of the traditional note method. In the new MLA handbook for students, the authors describe the principal and "most important" change this way: " . . . brief parenthetical citations in the text refer to a bibliography at the end of the research paper and thus eliminate the need for all but explanatory footnotes or endnotes."[1] In the new system, the statement we have just quoted would be documented as follows:

> In the new MLA Handbook for students, the authors describe the principal and "most important" change this way: " . . . brief parenthetical citations in the text refer to a bibliography at the end of the research paper and thus eliminate the need for all but explanatory footnotes or endnotes" (Gibaldi and Achtert 1).

No footnote or endnote is needed. The parenthetical reference includes the authors' surnames and the relevant page number, with no punctuation intervening; at the end of the paper there would be a standard bibliographical entry:

> Gibaldi, Joseph, and Walter S. Achtert. *MLA Handbook for Writers of Research Papers*. 2nd ed. New York: MLA, 1984.

The new system encourages the use of such short forms for publishers' names as "MLA" here, "Oxford UP" (for *Oxford Univ. Press*), "Prentice" (for *Prentice-Hall*), and "Simon" (for *Simon and Schuster*). But since clarity is a principal aim of documentation, you could, for example, use the abbreviation "Mod. Lang. Assn." if you thought your readers might not know what the initials "MLA" stand for, or more than just the first surname if you thought the truncated company name "Simon" might mislead them into assuming the publisher was the Canadian firm *Simon & Pierre*.

Such potential problems aside, however, the virtues of this method of citation are obvious: simplicity and efficiency. It does away with the possible distraction of readers' having to look at the foot of the page or the end of the paper for a documentary note. Some writers, however—especially when writing non-technical papers—feel that parenthetical references within the text are themselves obtrusive, distracting readers from the flow of their prose in a way that a simple superscript footnote number does not. But if you can manage, when quoting,

85   other systems

---

[1] Joseph Gibaldi and Walter S. Achtert, *MLA Handbook for Writers of Research Papers*, 2nd ed. (New York: The Modern Language Association of America, 1984), p. 1.

paraphrasing, or summarizing a source, to refer without awkwardness to the author or authors (and perhaps even the title) in your text, you need put only the page number in parentheses—and the reference is then no more obtrusive than a parenthetical page reference in the note system. For example:

> As Gibaldi and Achtert point out in the new *MLA Handbook for Writers of Research Papers*, "If . . . you include an author's name in a sentence, you need not repeat it in the parenthetical page citation that follows" (138).

If you refer to a whole work rather than to a specific page, by all means try to include the author's name in your text; then you'll need no parenthetical reference at all:

> In the new handbook Gibaldi and Achtert provide a multitude of sample references for both the name-page method and the note method.

Readers can find the documentary information under the authors' names in the list of "Works Cited" at the end.

As you can see from the examples above and from **82a**, some of the basic principles for parenthetical references are similar to those for footnotes. For example if a bibliography lists two or more works by the same author, a parenthetical citation must include at least a short version of the title of the one being cited. If a work is listed by title rather than by author, the citation must of course use that title. If you're citing a multivolume work, you must include the appropriate volume number. And so on. If **83e** above constituted a list of "Works Cited," here is how parenthetical references to some of them might appear in a text:

> One professional writer asserts that "Humor is the secret weapon of the nonfiction writer" (Zinsser 158).
>
> As William Zinsser says, "Humor is the secret weapon of the nonfiction writer" (158).
>
> Owen's attempts, the Tolpuddle Martyrs, and Chartism all failed, after which "English Trades Unionism . . . became less Socialist in character . . . ." (Carter and Mears 821-22).
>
> There are a number of ways to look at the influence ethnic groups have had in Canada (Breton et al.).
>
> Clearly the proximity of the United States affects how Canadians think about their country (Newman).
>
> Newman discusses some of the ways in which the proximity of the United States affects how Canadians think about their country.

Since the reference is to the whole article, and the author's name is included in the sentence, no parenthetical citation is necessary.

85a name-page method

Davies deplores the way cartoonists portray "personified Peace" (*Diary* 63).

Baugh discusses Renaissance and eighteenth-century attitudes, both *pro* and *con*, to foreign borrowings, or "inkhorn terms" (260-64, 346-48).

Note that when two page references occur in one citation, they are separated by a comma and a space.

As remarked by one woman who had met many kinds of people:

There is no contradiction I have not met with in men and women: the rarest combination is to find fundamental humbleness, freedom from self, intrepid courage and the power to love; when you come upon these, you may be sure that you are in the presence of greatness.   (Asquith 2: 100)

Note that two spaces follow the final period of a block quotation before the parenthetical reference is inserted. And note that the volume number is followed by a colon and a space.

According to a government booklet, the Canadian Shield covers "roughly half the country" (Department of External Affairs 44).

One Department of External Affairs booklet begins by pointing out the obvious: "Canada is a land of contrasts" (3).

Halifax "was intended originally to be a British naval stronghold" ("Halifax").

Since the encyclopedia from which the article comes is alphabetically arranged, no page number is necessary.

Charles Lyell once wrote in a letter that, in the matter of discoveries about evolution, "I had certainly prepared the way" (qtd. in Eiseley 63).

If the references are brief, you may include more than one source in a parenthetical citation; simply separate them with semicolons. Note 10 of the sample research paper above would appear as follows in a paper using the name-page system:

. . . and manufacturing processes in general (Morgan 4; Maunder 2).

If you have more than two or three items in a consolidated reference, or if a reference is otherwise bibliographically complicated and therefore likely to be obtrusive in your text, put it in a footnote or endnote.

Similarly, if you feel that a note must consist of or include some comment or explanation, such as in notes 3, 5, 21, 23, 27, 29, and 41 in the sample research paper, it should be a footnote or endnote rather than an obtrusive parenthetical reference. But in order to minimize the number of such notes, always try to include such comments in your text; if you cannot do so comfortably, you may decide that the material is not truly relevant after all and simply delete it. Here the discursive matter in notes 3, 21, 23, 27, 29, and 41 could fairly easily be incorporated; only the "covering" note 5 would have to remain a footnote or endnote.

"See" and "See for example" notes like 12 and 33 could be incorporated in the text with explicit references to Morgan and Maunder as examples, followed by parenthetical page numbers; or the names could be left in the parentheses along with a brief word or two: "(see Morgan 6-7)," "(see e.g. Maunder 5-8)."

The bibliography, or preferably the list of "Works Cited," must include an entry for each source you use in your paper. For example a bibliography for the sample research paper above would need to include not just the work edited by Maunder, but also the individual essays by Edgell, Bell, Loney, and Maunder himself, with cross-references to the whole volume; the entry for Bell would look like this, with inclusive page numbers for his essay:

```
Bell, M.A.M.  "Waste Management and Environmental Quality
     in Victoria, B.C."  Maunder 87-101.
```

The form of bibliographical entries in the name-page system is basically the same as that for the note system, but there are a few differences, such as where appropriate using a shortened form of a publisher's name, and omitting the abbreviations *p.* or *pp.* before page numbers. Recall the form for a reprint of an older edition:

> *note system:* Nicolson, Harold. <u>Some People</u>. [London], 1927; rpt. New York: Vintage, 1957.

In the new system it is listed as follows:

> *name-page system:* Nicolson, Harold. <u>Some People</u>. 1927. New York: Vintage, 1957.

In an entry for an article from a journal, use a colon after the year and list the inclusive page numbers without *pp.* Compare the forms for the two systems:

> *note system:* Rosengarten, Herbert. "Urbane Comedy." Rev. of <u>Lady Oracle</u>, by Margaret Atwood. <u>Canadian Literature</u>, No. 72 (Spring 1977), pp. 84-87.

> *name-page system:* Rosengarten, Herbert. "Urbane Comedy." Rev. of <u>Lady Oracle</u>, by Margaret Atwood. <u>Canadian Literature</u> 72 (1977): 84-87.

Note also that no comma follows the journal's title and that what is in this instance an *issue* number is treated the same way a volume number would be: as a plain Arabic numeral with no "No." or "Vol." preceding it.

The new MLA handbook considers the traditional note method of providing documentation an acceptable alternative to the name-page method, but if a bibliography is to accompany the footnotes or endnotes, it recommends these new forms for the entries. It also recommends that the notes themselves should be streamlined in similar ways: shortened publishers' names, no *p.* or *pp.*, no comma after the parentheses, a colon after the year of a periodical, and so on; here are some examples to compare with the older forms given in **83a**:

[3] William Zinsser, <u>On Writing Well</u>, 2nd ed. (New York: Harper, 1980) 158.

[9] Douglas Bush, "Stephen Leacock," <u>The Canadian Imagination</u> (Cambridge: Harvard UP, 1977) 143.

[23] Margot Asquith, <u>An Autobiography</u>, 2 vols. (New York: Doran, 1920) 2: 98–101.

[37] Veronica Thomas, "The Hutterites of Canada," <u>Gourmet</u> Nov. 1976: 36.

[41] Robert Cuff and J. L. Granatstein, "The Rise and Fall of Canadian-American Free Trade, 1947–8," <u>Canadian Historical Review</u> 58 (1977): 473.

If you know the traditional note method, you can easily adapt your documentation to these new forms.

Sample Essay No. 16 in Chapter X uses the name-page system. Examine the way the writer often refers to authors by name in his text, thereby keeping his parenthetical citations fairly unobtrusive; and note that he felt obliged to use one regular footnote. For further details and examples, consult the *MLA Handbook for Writers of Research Papers*.

85b   The Name-Date Method

This system is common in the social sciences (a representative guide is the *Publication Manual of the American Psychological Association*). It too uses parenthetical references in the text, but here the author's name is followed by the year, and the two are separated by a comma. If the sample research paper (**84**) had been written for a social science class, footnote 2 would have been replaced by a parenthetical reference in the text:

The problem is not new, as the title of a recent article points out: "Pollution Begins in Prehistory: The Problem Is People" (Young, 1975).

Since in the sciences reference is most often made to the argument or evidence presented by an entire article, page numbers are seldom necessary. Footnote 8, for example, would appear this way as a parenthetical reference:

> Governments . . . in the first place (Theberge, 1976).

But if the page of a citation is important, give its number after the date, with a comma and *p.* or *pp.* Footnote 9, for example, would appear this way:

> And defoliants . . . virtual deserts (Dunbar, 1971, pp. 46-47).

Footnote 38 would have appeared this way (note the use of an ampersand rather than *and*):

> Yet they also remark that young people show more concern than their elders, which offers some hope (Sharma, Kivlin, & Fliegel, 1975, pp. 467-468).

Note that all three digits of the second page number are included, unlike in the MLA style. Had the authors' names been mentioned in the text, they would not be repeated in the parentheses. In second and subsequent references, give only the first name and *et al.*; if there are more than five authors, even in the first reference use only the first surname followed by *et al.* Further, even first mentions of authors in the text itself customarily use only surnames; for example in the first paragraph of the sample research paper "Frank Morgan" would be simply "Morgan" and the year would immediately follow the name: "Morgan (1970)"; the relevant page number could come here, with the year, or by itself in parentheses after the quotation. If the bibliography includes two works by the same author and published in the same year, an *a* or *b* follows the year to indicate whether the citation is of the first or the second one listed.

As with the name-page system, the bibliography, here labelled "References," consists of a list of all works cited, alphabetized by author. But there are some differences in the format. The last two sources cited above, for example, would appear as follows:

```
Dunbar, M. J. (1971).  Environment and good sense: An
    introduction to environmental damage and control in
    Canada.  Montreal: McGill-Queen's University Press.

Sharma, M. C., Kivlin, J. E., & Fliegel, F. C.  (1975).
    Environmental pollution: Is there enough public
    concern to lead to action?  Environment and
    Behavior, 7, 455-471.
```

Note that

    (a) second and subsequent lines are indented only three spaces, rather than five;

    (b) only initials are used, not first names;

    (c) only the first word of a title and subtitle, and any proper nouns, are capitalized;

85b name-date method

(d) all authors' names are in reverse order;

(e) there are no quotation marks around the title of an article;

(f) a volume number is underlined;

(g) the year of publication goes after the name(s) of the author(s)—though in some versions of this method it goes at the end (for a book) or after the volume number (for a journal).

As with other systems, there are variations among different disciplines. For more information and examples, consult an appropriate style manual. And check with your instructor.

85c   The Number Method

Methods of documentation in the physical sciences vary more than those in the social sciences and the humanities. Most of them, however, use parenthetical references in the text that often consist simply of *numbers*—no names, dates, or pages—that refer to specific numbered items in the list of sources at the end. There the items may appear simply in the order in which they are referred to. For example, if the sample research paper had used this system, number 1 on the list would be "Environmentalism," number 2 Young, number 3 Edgell, number 4 Morgan, and so on. A repeated citation, such as in footnote 12, would simply repeat the number (4) for Morgan. Sometimes, however, the list is ordered and numbered alphabetically, but again a second or further citation of a source would simply repeat the relevant number.

And sometimes the numbers in the text will be superscript numbers rather than in parentheses; sometimes they will be in brackets rather than in parentheses; sometimes the parenthetical reference will include a page number or volume number, a date, or even an author's surname. In the bibliography, the place of publication usually follows the name of the publisher and a comma; some systems use quotation marks around book titles, or use no quotation marks or underlining, or omit titles of articles altogether, or put authors' names in capital letters, or put volume numbers in bold type (indicated by underlining with a wavy line); dates sometimes come early, sometimes late; sometimes endnotes stand in place of a list of references. And so on. The variations in method and format from one discipline to another, or even within one discipline, are so many that you should always find out what your instructor prefers, and if necessary consult an appropriate style manual, such as one of the following: *CBE Style Manual* (Council of Biology Editors), *Handbook for Authors of Papers in American Chemical Society Publications*, *A Manual for Authors of Mathematical Papers*, *Style Manual for Guidance in the Preparation of Papers* (American Institute of Physics).

SAMPLE ESSAYS, CORRECTION SYMBOLS, AND OMNIBUS CHECKLIST

SAMPLE STUDENT ESSAYS WITH COMMENTS AND GRADES

The sample essays which follow are actual essays written by students. Some were written in response to specific assignments; others were on freely chosen topics under some such general instruction as "Write a description" or "Write an argument." The essays vary in length, kind, and quality. The marginal comments may differ from those that other instructors would make, but we believe that they are generally accurate and fair. Similarly, the grades we have assigned may not be exactly what others would have given, but we think that they are reasonably accurate and that most instructors would agree with them. Since grading methods vary from institution to institution, here is how our letter grades would translate into other systems:

A	I	80-100%	Very Good to Excellent
B	II	65-79%	Fairly Good to Good
C	Pass	50-64%	Passably Weak to Fair
D	Fail	40-49%	Poor to Unsatisfactorily Weak
F		0-39%	Very Poor

Some comments on the individual essays

The first five essays were written in response to the same assignment and represent a range of quality. Essay 4, which we have failed with a D, could be considered a borderline case; for example, had it been written early in the academic year, it might have been awarded a C–. Similarly, essay number 1, had it been written late in the year, could be considered worth only an A–. Essay 5 is counted a very poor failure largely because of its style and mechanics; an instructor who wished to emphasize this might—especially if it were early in the year—decide to give it a "split" grade, such as C+/F, the C+ indicating the quality of content and the presumed promise of the writer, the F indicating the very careless performance. If the student in question improved in subsequent papers, the F component of the early grade could be effectively ignored in reckoning a final grade. Essay 6 is a brief description. Essay 7 might be considered borderline between A– and B+, but if one objectively gauges the actual performance rather than the strong potential demonstrated by the writer, the lower grade is accurate. Number 8, an essay in definition, is graded C, but a case could be made for giving it a C+, depending on variables such as the time of year and the student's past performance. Number 9, on the other hand, another attempt at definition, contains almost nothing to redeem its badness. Essay 10 is a straightforward and well-handled argument. Number 11 is also an argument, but of a special kind: it was written in response to a request for an argument using irony in the manner of Jonathan Swift's "A Modest Proposal." Since the student chose to commit deliberate errors as a part of the characterization of the speaker, those errors had to be labelled in the margin so that they would not be blamed on the student himself. Essays 12 through 16, unmarked and ungraded, are included for the purposes of practice and discussion. Number 16, basically an exercise in classification and definition, is a research report using the name-page method of documentation (see 85a).

Some teachers, rather than mark virtually all the errors and weaknesses in an essay, as we have done here, prefer to mark selectively so as not to smother a paper with symbols and comments and thereby possibly unduly discourage a student. Your instructor will inform you if such a method is being used—and if it is, you should make it your added responsibility to try to discover any further errors and weaknesses when an essay is returned to you. If your essay is to be resubmitted, your corrections and revisions of unmarked errors and weaknesses will make it an even better product, and will also impress your instructor.

(Essays 6, 10, 13, and 16 were written by second- and third-year university students for a course in intermediate composition; the rest were written by first-year students.)

Sample Essay No. 1

The Days of the Pioneers

Good opening ¶   The first Canadian was a hardy man from France.
He worked all day for bread. Today's Canadian works
half the day for cake. The pioneers worked to lay
the foundations. We work to add the playroom and
the bar.

     The <u>fermier</u> paid very little for his estate.
He built his home without blueprints. His prime
tools were the axe, the saw, and the hammer. When
the house was ready, he did not sit in his den and
read his newspaper. He had to clear the land so

that ∧ ∧he could <u>eat and feed his children</u>. *ambig. Rephrase to avoid cannibalism!*
     He got up at four in the morning, when it was
pitch black outside. No streetlights lit his
pathway to the out-buildings where his animals
were. He worked for three hours until breakfast.
His breakfast was not habit, but necessity. He ate
oatmeal, pancakes, and bacon, and drank coffee with
thick cream. His daily routine varied with the
season, not the time of the fiscal year. In spring, *p. necessary?*

p. necessary?   he cleared the land, then plowed and planted. He
helped his animals have their young. In summer he
cleared more land, and cultivated his crops. In
autumn he harvested. Winter brought some resting
time, but the <u>fermier</u> still had many chores to do.
     The man and his wife worked as a team on the

farm. Togetherness came naturally. They did not

have to strive for it. The children came, for

family planning was unheard of. They were made a

part of the working unit. They cleaned the chicken

coop, hoed the garden, and watched the inevitable

baby. The family <u>was</u> united, for <u>they</u> needed each

other. The nearest neighbor was often miles away.

co-ord.
Use ;

agr, shift

preferred sp.

Family loyalty was only one of the <u>fermier</u>'s

loyalties. He was a lover of his land, working

with it until he died. He remembered his mother

country, holding dear her language and customs. He

was loyal to his Church, loving the priest and

attending the masses.

Good
|| us. ✓

This man, this pioneer, experienced days of

discouragement, days when his crops failed, days

when his children died. He experienced days of

hardship, when the elements raged. But he had a

goal, a purpose, which was immediate and urgent.

He earned his bread. The Canadian of today does

not have this immediate goal, and his cake is

sometimes tasteless.

Good
|| us.

*A Your simple expression and crisp utterance, varied when
the need arises to prevent choppiness, give this essay
clarity, elegance, and charm. Very well done indeed.
Familiarize yourself with the meaning of the semicolon;
its use here would have added just that extra bit of
finesse. Some of the paragraphs are suspiciously
short, but each has unity and is sufficiently
developed. Very nice opening and closing image.*

Sample Essay No. 2

The Days of the Pioneers

As I read through well-thumbed history books about the great North American pioneers of a century ago, I often disregard the important names, dates *comma?* and places which must be memorized, and I read *unnecessary Q* between the lines, trying to imagine what the *are necessary?* ordinary, day-to-day life was like in those times. I think it could be favorably compared to our *sp.* present-day life, where we often become so involved *weak d. here* in the mad rush of living that we miss the real meaning, the essence of life.

In pioneer days life was simple. The one goal *inf. coord. conj.* everyone was working for was survival, so all *w.w.? toward?* activities were directed towards the achievement *Try co-ordinating with a semicolon.* of that goal. From the pre-dawn waking hours until the last chores were finished at night, the work was tedious and physically exhausting. But the pioneer knew that it had to be done in order for *d. (us)* his family to survive. As all activities were *logic? Can you be sure?* simple and elemental, the pioneer was not afflicted *w. comb?* by insomnia, ulcers, or migraine. These ailments are derived from the constant worry about success or failure, so were not familiar to the pioneer. *awk.* To him, life was reduced to its most simplest form: *gr. Check inflection for degree.*

2

lc   Success meant survival; failure, extinction.

As the pioneer worked hard, so too he played,
ate, and <u>slept with simple enthusiasm.</u> The secondary   *illog.* ‖

activities of eating and sleeping were considered

Funnee. word   <u>as</u> necessary parts of the plan of survival. The

pioneer reasoned that food and sleep were necessities   }   *log — is this really a matter for the mind?*

if he was to be able to continue working in order

to survive. According to <u>that belief</u> the foods   *ref.*

were simple, filling, and nourishing. Gourmet

dishes were unknown in those days and everyone's

health probably <u>profitted</u> from this ignorance.   *sp.*

Pleasures were simple and few in the days of the

pioneers, but they were always enjoyed enthusiastically.

The industrious pioneer usually tied pleasure in with

work, and such things as barn-raisings and quilting-

Perhaps, but hardly proven. Rather too sweeping for an effective ending | bees were made into social events.

The life of the pioneers was <u>hard and exhausting,</u>   *red?*

but, ultimately, it was more satisfying and rewarding

than our present life.

B   *Stylistically good, but your "most simplest" is "the most unkindest cut of all". Apart from that and the odd slip in idiom and diction, this is well executed. Consider the logic, however, at the places marked. The third paragraph contains some confusion and implicit contradiction. There is a tendency to wordiness throughout. As for substance, there is very little implicit comparison here of the kind the assignment asked for. Trying to do all the comparing in the last sentence of the first paragraph, and of the paper, doesn't work well.*

Sample Essay No. 3

The Days of the Pioneers

If the North American people of today were to suddenly go back in time, to the days of the   *p. unnecessary*
pioneers, they would find life very hard to endure. *w*
The pioneers did not have all the modern conveniences *log? only some?*
w. red   of today. They travelled in covered wagons, had to
hunt for their food, and slept outdoors with only a
canvas roof over their heads.

really?   They were constantly travelling. Because of *dev.; cl?*
weak ref. this they led very insecure and uncertain lives.
Education was limited because there were no schools, *vague; log. of cl?*
p.   and the children, at an early age were expected to
id. assist in the daily chores. Survival depended on
each person in the family doing his utmost in
whatever job he was expected to do.

ref. remote   They led very simple lives. There were no
motion pictures they could go to for entertainment,
rep. w. no laundromats to take the clothes to when there *f. p. ''*
were too many clothes to be washed at home, no
restaurants to go to when mother was too tired to
log?   cook dinner. Because they had no electricity, every- *misleading ''*
pas sp thing was done by manual labor. Since they worked
so hard and because there were no beauty parlors,
make-up, or face cream, the women grew haggard at *log*
an early age. The men also aged quickly because of

2

vague   the worries and hardships of life. The family   *coh*

cl?   worked together as a closely knit unit. The children

ref.   had no <u>outside</u> activities <u>outside</u> of the family,   *awk. rep.*

which kept them from seeing each other for days at

sp. X a time. <u>Because of this closeness,</u> there was no *coh, log -*

log. awk. juvenile deliquency or teen-age crime which is so *You've just said they didn't see each other for days at a time!*

ref. rampant today.

      The pioneer's sole worry was survival. He did

climactic order? not have to even think of such things as the atomic

bomb, politics and frustrations at the office. His *p, ambig*

id? time was <u>occupied by</u> protecting himself and his family

from Indians and wild animals, and providing enough

p, awk ‖ food to eat, and enough fuel to keep them warm.

(If) a person of today were to go back in time

to the days of the pioneers, (one) wonders (if) in spite *awk-log*

of the hardships, the simplicity of pioneer life *ss*

X ∧ would make him∧basically happier person than he is

in the modern world.

Why end on so vague a note? Why not discuss this and provide a positive conclusion?

C *Although you are reasonably careful with mechanics, and although you do bring in some contrasts, you fail to provide the vivid detail and close development that could make your commentary interesting. Is "face cream" and the like really worth bringing in? You do demonstrate some sense of form, but your handling of "facts" is often awkward and incorrect. There is also a strong flavour of clichés about much of the thinking and writing (e.g. "at an early age" applied to both children and women becomes a meaningless phrase). The ending is very weak. Illogicality and poor coherence plague this paper throughout. Be careful with loose reference of words like "this" and "which."*

Sample Essay No. 4

Reaching Maturity⊙ *no period*

The early pioneers were a hardy breed of people.
They had to be in order to survive the harsh and
dangerous life they lived. Their lot was not made
easy by modern technology. They didn't have urban
redevlopments and traffic control signals. Indeed,
in those times there was little traffic, and very
few roads for it to use anyway.

Life was more a calculated gamble. There was
more danger in the pioneer's life. There were no
police forces and men were more reliant on there own
strength, rather than on the strength of a society,
for their survival.

Sophistication and complex life had not yet
evolved. Life was of a simple nature unsullied by
modern mass production, eye shadow, freeways, con-
tinental suits, and split-level housing. We today
can not understand the appreciation of these people
of the past, of a log cabin; crude unpainted, warm
and secure. We would not appreciate a heavy homespun
shirt to keep a body warm.

The deep thick evergreen tree and sentinal
mountain peak were the dominant features of a man's
environment. He lived more with nature and did not
depend on a bloodless machine in a grey smoke-
vomiting factory for his existence. He was

Would there have made their lives easier?

× sp.

w

log? Is this an attempt at humour?

More than what?
Incomplete comparisons

sp !

what do these mean?
do these necessarily "sully" life?

log? where?
w, p. d.

one word?

The "of" phrases make awk. ||

p.

rephrase to make || with preceding sent.

p.v.

d? p.

sp.

What if he were home-steading in Saskatchewan?

2

Try for more vigour, conc.

comb.?

Is this what modern-man does do?

Is this specific comment appropriate here?

independent of the production line. The sky above
the pioneer was not grey with an oppressive industrial
waste. It was clear. A man produced his crops or
cut his timber for his own profit and for his own
survival. He did not push his buttons from eight
to five for E. P. Taylor's pocketbook.

The pioneer days were times of innocent infancy
of our civilization. Life's simplicity and man's
independence and self-reliance were the characteristics
of our nation's childhood.

air he breathed?

d. - fouled ? polluted

l an

Log. Did he have buttons?

awk. id?

Is this true?

Too exclusive.

Surely there were other characteristics?

D Your style here is unimpressive. Except for a few specific details, your essay has a "dead" feeling about it. You should try to find more effective ways to express your ideas. The points you raise are pertinent and could have been useful to you if you had developed them more fully with concrete detail and if you had expressed them in a more vigorous style. Watch idiom and wordiness. The incomplete comparisons, though implicitly clear, are nonetheless awkward as expressed. Weak logic and diction also damage the effect. The introduction and conclusion are both very poor. You have a reasonably good grasp of sentence structure, but in other respects your execution is very uneven.

Sample Essay No. 5

THE DAYS OF THE PIONEER FARMER — *MS: not all caps*

lc - passim   The Pioneers in Alberta led an exciting and
adventurous farming life as compared to the quiet
domesticated life the people lead now.   Inconveni-

log - Are   ences of farmers in Pioneer days seems unsurmountable *agr*
farmers not   *sp.*   *d?*
"domesticated"?   to us with all our conveniences.

weak, red   Although there are many aspects of this life, *ref? ambig.*
d
weak d, id   the farming life has the most vivid impression on
"makes"?   my imagination.

Starting in the spring when the crops must be   *al*
awk, dm   sowed, the farmer did not sit on a tractor (an) pull   *X*
PV shift   a seeder over his land; he hitched eight or twelve
horses to a seeder and walked every stretch of land, *id? means?*
d, us   as the horses did. (As) time was a precious period in *no meaning*
p.   seeding, he worked from dawn to dusk; unlike the   *Say what you*
mean.
sp - passim   present-day farmer.   The work went slowly; the
present day farmer can accomplish five times what   *Only?*   *cl*
the Pioneer farmer accomplished.   In the mid-day, *in the same*
time?
break the Pioneer had his dinner, but before he was
verb form?   eating he had to first go through the ritual of   *split ww?*
Are you sure?   unhitching, watering and feeding his eight(s) horses.   *P x*
After his meal the horses must be re-hitched, and   *PV shift,*
t
the slow work continued.   Present day farmers come
d?   in with the tractor, give it gas and grease, and in
agr   no time at all (he) is returned back to the field.   *vb form;*
red
Once the Pioneer had his seeding completed he had

page no.

Do present-
day farmers
do differently?   to wait till <u>summer</u>, <u>while</u> nature provided for his *weak d*

crops. If locusts should strike or choking <u>weed</u>   *plural?*

invade his fields he would be helpless in defending

ambig ref   them. It was not a matter of spraying his fields

ref   to insure <u>its</u> results. A dry year would mean a poor

yield; there was no irrigation to guarantee a

successful crop. If his crop survived the <u>trials</u>   *ambig.*

<u>of nature</u>, he had a harvest in August.

// two   August not only meant the harvest of his crop

also   but a spell of long hot days, if the weather <u>agreed</u>. *with what?*

X   Now by had he cut his crop, and with his hands he

this? coh? bound the sheaves. <u>A job which</u> <u>would take</u> the ₱ioneer *t?*

farmer from August to mid-October, takes the present *p.*

farmer four to six weeks.

Why not simply   Not only did the ₱ioneer farmer have to <u>cope</u>   *d*
"with nature"?
Are modern   with Nature's <u>trial</u> <u>but</u> also there <u>was a constant</u>   ⎰ *id*
farmers   ⎱ *meaning badly*
exempt from   <u>menace</u> of the Indians; a ridiculous thought of the   *garbled! Say*
such "natural"   farmer of today. He had to protect his crops from   *what you mean.*
problems?   fire set by the Indians or even protect himself from

harm. At nights it was maybe a matter of hustling

to the fort for protection within the high walls; *p*

X where as todays farmer relaxes in front of a tele- *sp (apos)*

vision set. It could be that todays farmer has the *sp (apos)*

conveniences but he certainly does not have the *p*

F   *sp*   <u>excitment</u> and adventure of the ₱ioneer.

I'm afraid this is entirely inadequate. You must carefully
review the conventions of punctuation and the elements of English
syntax; you must also make some attempt to master English
idiom. Consider your sentences before you write. Spelling errors
and other errors resulting from carelessness must be avoided.
When you are writing you should also be thinking. Many of
your details are good ones potentially, but so badly
handled that this essay must fail:

Sample Essay No. 6

My Special Place

Not far away is a special place I visit when
I want to feel quiet. From my park bench overlooking
the harbour, I see the flickering layout of North
Vancouver stretching from the cluster of lights on
the Grouse Nest to the reflections in the water.
Tug lights silently slip up the inlet and under the
span of lights known as Second Narrows Bridge. In
front of me, loading cranes stretch starward like
man-made redwood trees.

In this context sound patterns like alliteration are good.

Distantly, an engine grumbles as it pulls a line
of boxcars. Near me, a cat rustles through tangled
berry bushes. From behind, I hear the inconsistent
sound of leaves leaving their branches, sidestepping
down to the grass. Footsteps quicken on the sidewalk
as a dog erratically protests against a trespasser.

good // sentence rhythm

Intentional, I hope; effective.

nice fig

As I watch and listen, a cool mask of rain
lightly covers my face. This, and the cold, hard
bench slats persuade me to leave my special place.

good ref back to ¶ 1 (sight) and ¶ 2 (sound).

Excellent patterning throughout. Details well organized in each paragraph. A

This mistaken comma almost ruins the otherwise excellent effect you've created. Without that slip, this descriptive piece would have been virtually perfect.

Sample Essay No. 7

What _am_ I _doing_ here?   *MS - caps*

Years ago, two men were helping to build a cathedral.
A passerby stopped and asked: "What are you doing here?"
"I am just laying bricks," the first man grumbled. The
second replied, "I am building a monument to God's glory."

unnecessarily
drab, jargon-
like

In the present situation, the student is like the two
workers. When he asks himself the question, "What am I

P ℓ

doing here?", he may reply in one of two ways. His
answer depends on the range of his view of life.

an unnecessar-
ily vague
sentence and
unfortunately the

Probably better
not to start
a new ¶ here.

The student may be "just laying bricks." Plodding
through work without any connective thought or unifying
goal, he has only a short view of his efforts. He finds as
little satisfaction as the first worker, labouring without
plan or point at an aimless, backbreaking task. On the
other hand, the student may be building a memorial. He sees

next ¶ expands
on the vague-
ness rather
than on
something
specific. It
lacks
concreteness.

a point to his work beyond the confusion of courses, ex-

P - comma
would help.

periences and years. The student is laying a foundation
for his life. Looking beyond the immediate job, he is able
to see a goal, to recognize a purpose to his work.

The answer to "What am I doing here?" holds the key to
satisfying living. If the student, indeed any person,
recognizes _his own end_, he will not just be laying bricks;
he will be building a memorial. He will not merely be
existing; he will find satisfaction in getting nearer his
goal. He will know why he is here.

two different
and un-
fortunate
connotations
suggested by
this phrase besides the
meaning you intended.
"purpose"?

B+

You have chosen an interesting basis
for your discussion of this question. Well organized,
clear; good strong ending. Marred, however - mainly
by that central vagueness.

Sample Essay No. 8

Responsible Government

p. unnecessary   Here, in Canada, we enjoy the benefits of
responsible government. In responsible government
the cabinet, or governing body, is directly
responsible to the elected representatives of the   *in?*
ambig.   legislature, who, in turn, are responsible to their   *p. needed?*
plu?   elector, the people. Through this transfer of
comp: than   responsibility, a greater control can be exerted   *wo ambig.*
what?   on the machinery of government by the populace.

   In this country, we become more aware of the
workings of responsible government when a minority
sp   governement is in power. The term "minority govern-   *cast by or*
p.   ment," means that the combined votes of the opposi-   *for them?*
tion parties exceed the number of votes of the party   *ambig.*
in power. Then, if the legislature does not agree
with the cabinet and it is defeated, the prime   *ambig. ref.*
caps   minister is required to submit the question in
dispute to the people; that is, ∧call a general   *ss "he must"*
ref. vague   election. This clearly shows how the prime minister   *caps*
at best.   and his cabinet are directly responsible to the
weak &
conclusion.   legislature.

   There are many benefits of this system of
government. We, as citizens of Canada, are assured
of our control over the affairs of our country. No
W.W.?   leader can become authoritarian or radical because   *log p*
are these words
necessarily antithetical?

2

guaranteed? | he is always answerable for his actions. <u>Therefore,</u> *p. log.*
never self- | the governing body, the cabinet, <u>always</u> has the good
serving? | interests of the people in mind when planning and
executing governmental business. <u>They, themselves,</u> *p unnecessary*

Ms ⊃ were elected by the people⌐--⌐not appointed as the
cabinet is in the United States where the government

Ms ⊃ is only representative, not responsible <u>--</u> and so
must be directly concerned for the welfare of the
people.

p We have seen<u>,</u> how, in responsible government, *stiff*
conclusion
the great mass of people exert power over the chosen
ones who govern them and how these few<u>,</u> in turn <u>are</u> *p -2 commas*
or none.
responsible to them. In this system democracy <u>is</u> *weak*
<u>in</u> its most <u>complete</u> form.

meaning? What of Switzerland? ancient
Athens?

C

For the most part you form sentences well
and provide variety in structure. As for the
content here, you frequently express your
sentiments rather uncritically, and some-
times ambiguously. You need to work on
your punctuation.

Sample Essay No. 9

The Dignity of Man

The word? or the quality?

*p-ital
(passim)*

Dignity had its origin in a Latin word meaning

no p

worth. Nowadays this meaning is only occasionally

employed. But, if we could step outside this world

*"stand back
from"?
not very
clear*

and watch men playing out their lives in the passage

of time, we would use the original meaning to

*ref: all men?
some? certain?*

describe the stature of these men.

"How dignified he looks." The remark is often

d?

passed. Such an unconsequential statement may well

sp   *begs
the question
necessarily?*

sp

have lead to the modern corruption of the word

dignity. One might apply it to many Greek statues.

ref?

Identify it?

One of demosthanes immediately springs to mind.

*cap; sp
trite*

d-means?

There is a certain elevated stateliness about it,

ref-al?

which is neither elated nor despondent energetic

p

*al-can
qualities be
lofty or
immovable?*

nor lethargic. It possess all the loft immovable

xx

qualities of stone itself.

One might well ask why its neighbouring statue

of Socrates?

is so fat and ugly. True Socrates was an ugly man,

p

but his ideas and actions have transended time, In

sp

time the great orator Demosthanes is dwarfed by the

sp

sp

great phylosopher. Although I have seen a statue

*the one
referred to
above? or
another? all
very confusing
meaning?*

of Socrates, I must confess I think of him in my

minds eye as a tall slender figure who carries his

sp   *p*

majestic head high. Although I think I know the

difference academically, I am conditioned to reflect

2

on this dignified figure in the modern sense, in the
corrupted sense.

True worth then is what elevates a man in time. *ambig.*

log
cl { I avoid the word history because the light of human *ital.*
dignity has shone from many men without it ever
being recorded. I think of a relative of mine whose
contribution to other peoples lives has been tremen-   *sp (apos)*
d
Co-ordinate dous. To those who know her, in passing she is   *p misplaced*
with a simply a humble woman. To those who know her well
semicolon she is a saint.

Dignity may also be covered over by some querk   *sp*
of nature. It was this dignity in Hamlet which   *ref.*
caused his dying assailant to call him "noble
Hamlet. O   *×Q*

log &   So the dignity of a man is physically invisable   *sp*
Use the { and is sometimes perceivable. And we of this earth
right are therefore limited because we can only judge what   *log not*
conjunction) we can see.   *fully clear*

*F You are not defining the dignity of man. You deal
with only a part of it — a rather abstract and
difficult part — and you do not succeed in clarifying
your meaning precisely enough. The number and nature
of mechanical errors in this paper are appalling: it is
no courtesy to your reader to present him with
something so carelessly done as this. You have a high
potential, intellectually, for excellent work, but you
must learn to put your intellectual children into
neater, cleaner, more appropriate clothes.*

Sample Essay No. 10

Handle With Care   *could be l.c.*

Consider reversing order? Patent medicines and vitamins are bought in increasing quantities by people every day. They are placed on open shelves in stores to be bought without prescription by individuals who have little knowledge of what the chemical effects *awk. wo* will be on their bodies. Many of the drugs are potentially harmful; they should be removed from the *p unnecessary* shelves, and their sale more strictly controlled. To be sure, many of the drugs that are so readily available to consumers are helpful in relieving irritating conditions, and are not harmful if administered properly. But people have come to believe that many drugs on the shelves are not harmful at all. Certain medicines have become so commonly used that they are taken as panaceas and administered for any discomfort. The drug universally known under one brand name, "aspirin," is an obvious example. People take one, or two, or several aspirin tablets for headaches, stomach pains, insomnia, nervous and emotional upsets-- the whole range of disturbances--and many parents use aspirin to dose their children at the first sign of hyper- activity! These common cures are not safe when used in excess or when taken without being needed. Medicines are *w — "unnecessarily"* drugs, and when used incorrectly, drugs can be poison.

Of course one might say that the government cannot be expected to pass regulations protecting people from them-

2

comb? || ?   , that

selves. Individuals are expected to exercise their own
intelligence when using drugs. However, this reasoning   better
                                                          wo ?
assumes that the public is given information that will
help it to act wisely. Unfortunately, that is not so.
Most of the information received by society today is
transmitted through popular media. What the public hears
about patent medicines is conveyed via radio and television
in the form of advertising. Drug companies have launched
extensive campaigns designed to tell people how accessible
drugs are and how little they cost. The advertisements are
little more than popularity contests between brands. To
the consumer, what is the value of a film clip showing a   ~ ? (ok)
famous actor loading a shopping cart with fancy packages
picked off a shelf in a drug store? It is all very well
to be told that in a conveniently located store, the prices
are always "right," but that says nothing about the drugs.
The message is to buy.

Of course, some may say that instructions about dosage
are on the package of every medicine. Moreover, individual
drug companies often warn the public about misuse of their
products. But in an advertisement, the warning against
the detrimental effects of the drug is cleverly disguised.
For example, there are several medicines on sale that are
too strong for children's use. When one company says
(boasts) that its product is "not even recommended for
children," the message somehow gets mixed up. Adults are
made to feel that they are part of an exclusive class of

3

people who can, and therefore should, rush out and buy the
product. No one would rationally accept this line of
reasoning, but this kind of advertising appeals to the
emotions, and people think what they are made to feel.

Still, one must admit that many of these products are
helpful in controlling ailments or in maintaining proper
health, and that more stringent control of sales would
ambig ref cause prices to rise. This may be so, but after all,
medicines are used by many people who do not need them.
If these drugs—including vitamins—were less available
or cost more, people would find alternative, more natural
ways of maintaining good health. For instance, exercise
✓ can cure many ailments as quickly as aspirin; and regular *good p*
exercise is a better preventive medicine than regular *for emph.*
doses of patented, bottled cure-alls. Moreover, many
people would soon discover that the body functions very
well on a proper diet without daily vitamin supplements.
Indeed, the body is designed to assimilate what it needs
from good food. In this age of technology, people are
beginning to forget that the human race survived for
generations before nourishment was compressed into little
capsules, and the entire daily requirement swallowed with
a drink of water in one gulp.

I will concede that there are individuals who do need
to use these drugs or vitamins regularly, and other people
who need to use them occasionally. Nevertheless, there is
no good reason for the excessive use of medicine found in

4

today's society. People have mistakenly concluded that
if a drug can make one "better" when he is sick, then by
the same principle, that drug will improve his condition   *p*?
when he is not sick. ∧ What could possibly be "better"
than good health? Overdosing oneself with medicine is
not the way to find out. In fact, excessive <u>drug use</u>   *'use of drugs'*
will surely cause more harm than good. Drug companies
have had ample time to warn the public about the need to
take care when using their products. More stringent
methods are obviously required.

*"But" for
clearer con
and emph.*

A

*Good, clear, sharp presentation throughout. A few
weak or awkward spots will bear attention. The
overall argumentative structure is good, with
pros and cons appropriately balanced, but in a
couple of spots it's a little stiff; the
machinery clanks a bit. When you revise this
for resubmission, see if you can smooth the
jumps a little.*

*You might have saved a stronger point to
use as your final one, and you might have
offered a more specific recommendation.
Nevertheless, the conclusion is effective.*

Sample Essay No. 11

Guaranteed Satisfaction

In the past two years, violence in hockey has become a major concern of thousands of sports fans in North America. Myself being a sports fan, I too have witnessed the disgusting changes which have taken place in the professional and junior hockey ranks. I have spent hours deliberating over this problem and am happy to announce a sure-fire solution.

This solution will benefit all parties involved. It will definitely pick up the attendance at every game. We all know how quickly it has been falling lately, and surprisingly in a few cities which, until two years ago, always had sell out crowds. This increase in attendance *sp (hyphen)* will certainly put more money into the owners' bank accounts and consequently more money into the players'

frag   *X* wallets. Especially in our favourite player's wallets, the "goons," who are grossly underpaid while providing the fans with most of the entertainment. Sales in the concessions and the souvenir booths at the rink are bound to go up. The possibilities are endless. I cannot see any loopholes in my proposal which could, if properly carried out, turn hockey into the blooming business it once was, but this time on a scale at least three times as large.

First off, we must rid ourselves of some unnamed polititians across the nation, who have spoiled the game *p ?*

Consider the less awkward order: "the wallets of our favourite players..." because of the following appositive.

p v awk ref. try "my proposdl, a proposal which..."

MS —

sp (passim)

2

sp <u>attrocities</u> as creating a public disturbance, brutality,
by charging some of the league's best players with such
assault with a lethal weapon (hockey sticks), and even
manslaughter. After being pressed with such charges, these
players, and the teams they play for, have to think twice
before they touch, let alone slug, punch, kick <u>and</u> beat up *p*
a player on the opposite side. Thus the quality of the
game is destroyed. Who wants to watch a team <u>which</u> is *that would*
afraid to fight? I'm sure that with a bit of pushing and *be better*
kicking in the right places we could easily rid ourselves
of these cruel <u>polititians</u> who are out to destroy our fun.

Secondly, after the <u>polititians</u> are out of the way, we
must solve the problem of the players who will not fight.
Many players, whom I cannot blame, are still <u>leary</u> of fight- *sp* ?
ing after two years of government suppression. It is hard
to get back in the swing of things (arms, sticks, legs, etc.)
after two years of idleness. But I'm sure the owners will
id not put up much of a fight to the second part of my proposal.

The players would surely start fighting again if there
was a little cash up for grabs. If a cash bonus <u>was</u> awarded *subjunctive* ?
sp to players who were <u>profficient</u> in acts of violence or even
slang works
well here for the <u>guys</u> who tried hard to be, we would see plenty of
action at every game. The owners need not worry about losing
p money since the increased attendance would make up for it
three times over. We could easily urge the Hockey Night in
Canada crew to include a weekly series of fights for bet<u>ween</u> *hyphen*
period entertainment. It would be something like hockey
*t shouldn't this be
"Hockey Showdown"?*

3

P   showdown but with the toughest guys in the league.   A

trophy could be included in the year end hockey awards,   *sp (hyphen)*

mm ?   for toughest player in the league.   We could call it the

Goon Trophy or the Entertainer Award.   They both amount

to the same thing.   ✓

I am sure that everyone will agree that this proposal

can do nothing but improve our present–day hockey.   Our own   *hyphen*

ww   little hockey players will finally have idols which deserve

Good! The
"which" works   respect.   It will also open up many new jobs.   There will
nicely.

be a need for many new doctors and dentists (and they will

do good business), since there will always be a few players

on any team who are not quite tough enough.   Our labourers

will get their chance by building many new hospitals.   We

could call them Hockey Hospitals.   Bookies could make a

killing, taking thousands of bets on some bloody good fights.   ✓

Of course sponsors for the televised games could get a big

✓gr   chunk of extra business.   Like I said before, the list
nice touch   goes on and on.

id   I do not wish any credit endowed upon me for this

modest proposal.   A few of my friends forced me to write

it.   I am in the toothpaste business anyway and I don't

stand to make any money from this.   My friends guarantee

your satisfaction, though.

These friends are other sports fans who are only

B+   satisfied by brutality.

Good details, good intentional stylistic errors to help charac-
terize the speaker; the slang and other "defects" work well too.
But your misspellings and other errors betray you, I fear. It's
too bad so many careless little errors mar this otherwise
nice piece. The final sentence strikes me as anti-climactic,
and might better have been omitted. Watch your spelling
much more carefully. Learn about hyphens!

Sample Essay No. 12

Sonnet LXV, by William Shakespeare

Since brass, nor stone, nor earth, nor boundless sea,
But sad mortality o'ersways their power,
How with this rage shall beauty hold a plea,
Whose action is no stronger than a flower?
O! how shall summer's honey breath hold out
Against the wrackful siege of battering days,
When rocks impregnable are not so stout,
Nor gates of steel so strong, but Time decays?
O fearful meditation! where, alack,
Shall Time's best jewel from Time's chest be hid?
Or what strong hand can hold his swift foot back?
Or who his spoil of beauty can forbid?
   O! none, unless this miracle have might,
   That in black ink my love may still shine bright.

An Appreciation of Shakespeares' Sonnet 65.

Throughout this sonnet Shakespeare has the villain
as time; active enemy of youth, beauty and love. The
numerous metaphors telling us this are all conveyed by
the desperate voice of one speaker, and it is the
structure of the poem that helps to convey his despair.
He asks many rhetorical questions that get progressively
shorter as the sonnet continues, interjected with exclamations of his despair. The speaker begins three
of his questions with "O" or "Or" which stops us when
we are reading. We read it as an excited cry, which
it is. These crys, and the progressively shorter
sentences, make us more aware of what he is talking
about--time. We see his taste and get a sense of time

2

being continually over his shoulder--he must hurry to
his conclusion. This helps convey to us the despair
he feels about time's effects upon his love and youth.

The speaker uses mixed metaphors, but all of them
convey the idea that time is an active villain. Time
is the enemy that rages, decays and spoils. We see
time as strong and violent in the form of a battering
ram, and as a powerful rage that can even overpower
the earth and seas. And since Time wins all its battles
it is inevitable that it will eventually capture youth
and love.

Love is depicted as a passive flower whose only
defence against destruction is to stop us in our assault,
still with appreciation of its beauty. The action of
the flower and the action of beauty are one and the
same, they have no defence but to awe us.

Youth is depicted in the speaker's second lament
as being "summer's honey breath." As the critics René
Wellek and Austin Warren explain, this is again an image
of flowers in the summer, their scent being the breath
of their body--the earth. This is a somewhat different
idea but the fragile, transient and beautiful image of
youth is retained, they live as the inhabitant of a
fortress that is being specifically attacked by time.
Again the battle between the two is contrasted to that
between time and stones and steel--which are decayed
by time in spite of being strong and stout.

3

The speaker's next cry has time as the owner of a precious gem that has gone missing--and the gem is one that time wants back. Here the sense of battle is somewhat changed; youth is no longer seen as the enemy of time, but as the possession of time. Youth is the "spoils" in the battle, the possession over which the battle is waged, not the participant battling over something else. Youth is truly time's "best jewel" and although the speaker despairs at it being taken back he sees it as impossible to stop. This is as it should be, as youth without time is meaningless, and time without youth would be too ugly--and savage, as it is in this sonnet. The speaker's despair at being able to do nothing is given by the image of time striding on even though its foot is being clutched at by the strongest hands.

The couplet at the end begins with the cry of "O" again but immediately becomes quieter, slower and more deliberate. The last line is somewhat paradoxical; we know that the only thing of the bright shiny beauty of youth and love that will endure will be the black print of the poem praising it. Although they can shine brightly by themselves they will be gone, and the only way left for them to shine is through the words of the poem, which of course can not shine brightly, but only convey a small sense of their brilliance.

Sample Essay No. 13

Reflections on a Tourist Poster

Hey, lady! Yes, you--the one smiling up from the smokeless campfire on that poster advertising Canada's great outdoors. Did anyone ever tell you your eyes exactly match the lake water behind you? I guess everybody must, the colour is so remarkable. I never have seen a lake that colour; it's exactly the same aquamarine green that bath salts turn the water in my tub. Still, the fish must like it--I see you have four nice ones lined up in the pan beside your shiny aluminum coffee pot. Who caught those fish, anyway? Certainly not those two immaculate children playing games over on the lake shore; surely not your perfect husband, poised with his foot up on a convenient tree stump. He's too shiny-new! All polished teeth and polished boots, he looks like he just walked out of Eaton's catalogue. I wonder why I always look like I went swimming after the fish I try to catch. Well, it doesn't matter, really. I'll let you get back to your breakfast preparations and your plans for a perfectly marvelous day. I only stopped to ask you: Doesn't it ever rain where you are? Don't the campsites get overcrowded sometimes? Who are you really supposed to be?

Sample Essay No. 14

Wishing for a Dog

I don't own a dog but wish everytime I see one that
I did. My parents have a dog, so you could say, I suppose,
that I do part time. This occasional enjoyment is tanta-
lizing. You have to have owned and been close to a pet
of your own in order to understand.

A pet, especially a dog, has so much to offer by
just being itself. That is, if you are the kind of person
who is able to realize and appreciate this presence of
personality in an animal. Some cannot.

It is the most fabulous feeling to have your pet
greet you at the door and not quite know what to do with
himself because he's happy. A dog never holds back feeling
because of some silly hangup. Neither is he too busy nor
too tired to let you know he's glad your home.

Have you ever had a pet try to comfort you in sorrow?
Somehow they know what is going on, something is wrong.
Again their are no hangups stopping him from licking away
the tears or just staying by you when you need comforting.
These are afew of the reasons why I wish I could have a
fulltime dog of my own.

Sample Essay No. 15

A House But Not a Home

The house where I long ago spent three years of my life seems today, shrouded in a mist of greyness. This structure is not living as it once was; instead its life has gone and only its physical body remains. Spacious yards and wide, tree lined boulevards complement the beauty of its hilltop setting. The underlying beauty has remained until today, yet many subtle changes have occurred. Trees' limbs have grown rounder and the shade of the house's paint has become dull; perhaps caused by the exposure to thousands of hours of rain and fog. Eleven years ago children made a fort in a Mountain Ash tree. On the roof of the backyard garage they had a ship. Today only a stump remains of the tree and the garage silently serves the purpose that it was intended to do.

When the house was young an elderly man came through the community. He neatly painted the address numbers of the street's houses on the curb. When he came to our house he painted in brilliant white the numerals one nine seven five. He accepted only twenty-five cents for the job that he had done so carefully. Recently the numbers were repainted; the old man's work had become barely recognizable.

The house is now a stranger and not a home as it once was. The expanses of cold grey granite foundations and pale green walls are omens of the blank faces of strangers behind its closed doors. The numerous people who through the years have dwelled in the house must never have experienced the attraction to it that I did, eleven years ago.

Sample Essay No. 16

Symbolism in Communication

People communicate with each other in many different ways, but symbolism would seem to be the principal way, for language is itself a symbolic system. Alfred North Whitehead puts it bluntly: "A word is a symbol" (10). But language is so complex. S. I. Hayakawa says that "Of all forms of symbolism, language is the most highly developed, most subtle, and most complicated" (27). Most of us have enough trouble just reading, writing, and speaking our native tongue, let alone trying to figure out its fundamental nature and its complicated workings. But because communication is crucial in any society, understanding how we communicate is very important. In what follows, I have tried to piece together various ideas about language and symbolism that at least begin to make sense to me in order that I may make sense to you and perhaps get you, too, to think about the nature of symbolism. I have discovered, in the process, that although there is still a great deal of disagreement among the experts--philosophers, linguists, communications theorists, literary critics, semioticians (or semiologists), and so on--there has also, during recent decades, come to be a fair amount of consensus about what a symbol is and how it works. And that, in spite of my rather sweeping title, is where I want to focus.

My dictionary defines a symbol as "Something that represents something else by association, resemblance, or convention, especially, a material object used to represent something invisible," and as "A printed or written sign used to represent an operation, element, quantity, quality, or relation, as in mathematics or music." A flag

2

stands for a country and its principles, a rose for beauty; X stands for

the operation of multiplying, <u>Au</u> for the element gold. That's a start,

but there's more of interest to be said. In <u>Communications: The Transfer</u>

<u>of Meaning</u>, for example, Don Fabun distinguishes between audible symbols

such as words or exclamations, and visible symbols such as pictures,

objects, or written characters. He talks about human communication being

symbolic of an experience: the symbol used to relate an experience is not

the experience, but a new event. When we use or perceive symbols they are

events, not just objects (15-16). Fabun goes on to say that common

symbols have no meanings of their own; the person doing the communicating

has the meaning (19). To me this says that the interpretation of a symbol

depends on the background of the communicator. But according to Philip

Wheelwright, for a symbol to work there must also be a "fit interpreter,"

someone who knows how to understand its meaning. For example "The word

'dog' carries a definite meaning for those who know the English language,

and quite possibly no meaning at all for others" (8).

In <u>The Burning Fountain: A Study in the Language of Symbolism</u>,

Wheelwright is interested in what he calls "expressive" or "depth language"

as opposed to mere "literal language" (3-4, 73-101). Both are symbolic,

of course, since all words are symbols. But expressive language uses such

things as symbolism, metaphor, and analogy in a "poetic" way to refer to

things that are "real, but of a different order of being from that of

common familiarity" (5). Before he discusses such literary uses of

symbolism, however, he tries to define what a symbol is. Many basic

definitions are similar. For example, a symbol is "a thing that stands

for something else" (Lemon 72) or anything that "seems to represent or

3

stand for some reality other than itself" (Bevan 275). Wheelwright goes a little further. "A symbol," he says, "owes its symbolic character to the fact that it stands for something other than, or at least more than, what it immediately is" (6). Many authorities (e.g. Barnet, Burnam, and Burto 84) point out that the word <u>symbol</u> comes from the Greek <u>symballein</u>, "to throw together," or <u>symbolon</u>, "token," referring to one part of something that has been broken in two, and that therefore a symbol doesn't properly stand for "something else" but for something larger of which it is a part; for example a particular rose would be a single concrete instance of the entire abstract concept of beauty. This definition would exclude such things as plus signs and chemical "symbols" --and perhaps even words, for the word <u>rose</u> would then apparently be merely a "sign" standing for or pointing to a real or imagined rose which could in turn act as a symbol. I prefer Wheelwright's definition, for it seems to me more realistic to include both "something other than" and "or at least more than" as what symbols can stand for. Indeed, for Susanne K. Langer in her important 1942 book <u>Philosophy in a New Key: A Study in the Symbolism of Reason, Rite, and Art</u>, mathematical <u>symbols</u> are fundamental to our understanding of what symbolism is and how it works, for what such abstractions symbolize is not "data"--facts or objects--but "<u>concepts</u>," even fictitious ones such as "imaginary numbers" (14).

Nevertheless, distinguishing between <u>signs</u> and <u>symbols</u> is key to defining what a symbol is. Wheelwright (9-11) does this as he characterizes symbols further. First, he says, a symbol is not, like a traffic light, a "signal" directing us to do something. He quotes from

4

Langer, who says that a dog hearing a familiar name immediately expects
the person named to be present, or that if you say "dinner" the dog
expects to be fed; people, however, often use "signs" that don't refer to
anything in their immediate vicinity (24). "If I say: 'Napoleon,'"
notes Langer, "you do not bow to the conqueror of Europe as if I had
introduced him, but merely think of him" (48). Even animals, she says,
can use signs, for example in the well-known "conditioned reflex," and
"the use of signs is . . . . the beginning of intelligence" (22-23).
But "symbolism is the recognized key to that mental life which is
characteristically human and above the level of sheer animality" (21).
"Most of our words," she adds, "are not signs in the sense of signals.
They are used to talk <u>about</u> things, not to direct our eyes and ears and
noses toward them." And signs used in that way "are not <u>symptoms</u> of
things, but <u>symbols</u>" (24). We use signs--that is, symbols--not so much
for "practical" or "utilitarian" purposes as for their own sake, in order
to think about things, and in ritual and art (29-30).

Symbols, then, are signs; in fact they are a subclass of signs; but
signs are not necessarily symbols. For example, Wheelwright's second
point is that a symbol is not like a "natural sign," such as dark clouds
indicating a coming rainstorm. "A natural sign," he says, "is not used
with any purpose or intention of communicating; it works by causal
efficacy alone" (10). Smoke, for example, we commonly take to be a "sign"
of fire, but it doesn't "symbolize" fire (and see Langer 45-46).

According to Wheelwright, a symbol must also have "a certain
stability: it endures beyond one or two occasions." Thumbing the nose,
for example, he says is an established "symbol of contempt," whereas some

5

other gesture of contempt, a spontaneous one such as perhaps a sudden
snort, would not be a symbol. Nor would a landscape that triggered
memories of one's childhood be symbolic, he claims; it would merely be
"an associative stimulus" (11). But I think others might disagree with
him on this point. I don't see why something should be any less symbolic
just because it's a one-shot event. To use his own criterion of <u>intention</u>
(see 7), if I wrote a letter and purposely misspelled the recipient's
name to show my disrespect, wouldn't that be a symbolic act? If I did
it accidentally or out of ignorance it might convey a similar meaning,
but I suppose then it would be more a <u>sign</u> or <u>symptom</u> of my attitude
rather than a <u>symbol</u>. In any event, Wheelwright does say that if such
a gesture or scene or other experience were made part of a literary work,
it could be developed into a symbol. He mentions, among other examples,
Eliot's waste land and Proust's piece of cake dipped in tea (13). I would
think that a particular scene in a painting or a film could be made
similarly symbolic.

Consideration of symbolism in literature is (fortunately) beyond the
scope of this paper, although William York Tindall in <u>The Literary Symbol</u>
suggests many interesting lines of thought. For example he remarks that
"symbolism is the necessary condition of literature" (68) and also says
that any literary work as a whole is itself a symbol (4, 10; see also
Lemon 72). One point, however, that may (or may not) help us understand
symbolism is its relation to metaphor. Tindall quotes the poet Yeats:
"All poetic metaphors are symbols" (36); but he himself seems to stop
short of equating the two, claiming only that symbols are "founded on
analogy" and are therefore "related to metaphor" (12), and acknowledging

6

that as it becomes more suggestive rather than direct in its comparison, "metaphor approaches symbol" (64). In A Handbook to Literature, however, C. Hugh Holman distinguishes between the two more sharply: a metaphor, he says, "evokes an object in order to illustrate an idea or demonstrate a quality, whereas a symbol embodies the idea or the quality" (436). But then he wipes out this clear separation by referring to what W. M. Urban said: "The metaphor becomes a symbol when by means of it we embody an ideal content not otherwise expressible" (qtd. in Holman 436). M. H. Abrams, however, maintains the distinction by pointing to the fact that a metaphor (or simile) requires a "paired subject," as in Robert Burns's "O my love's like a red, red rose," whereas a symbol, as in William Blake's poem "The Sick Rose," lacks a "paired subject" (195-96); such a symbol, then, could be described as relatively "open-ended" in its signification (Liberman and Foster 115). I finally find myself preferring the looser way of approaching the matter, such as when Nelson Goodman says that metaphors are an "economical, practical, and creative . . . way of using symbols. In metaphor," he says, "symbols moonlight" (180).

But to get back to signs and symbols. According to John Fiske's Introduction to Communication Studies, Roland Barthes was the first to set up a system for analyzing signs and meaning. The key to his theory is a distinction between two kinds of signs. He says that signs have a denotative, "commonsense," or "obvious" meaning, but that they can also have a connotative meaning. For example, imagine two photos of the same street scene, one in cold and contrastive black and white, the other in warm colour and with a soft focus: the two pictures would denote the

7

same street, seen at the same time and from virtually the same angle, but in their <u>connotation</u> they would be far apart (90-91). In addition to connotation and what he calls "myth" ("a culture's way of thinking about something"), Barthes points to a third way that signs work, namely as symbols.[1] "An object becomes a symbol when it acquires through convention and use a meaning that enables it to stand for something else." For example there are status symbols (a Rolls Royce is more than just a car) and religious symbols (baptism is more than just getting dunked in the water) (Fiske 95). And we're back to part of my dictionary definition and to Wheelwright's criterion of "stability." Fiske (96-100) goes on to discuss metaphor, which I've looked at briefly, and metonymy, where a part stands for a whole—which sounds like one of the basic senses of symbolism. But I think this forest already has enough trees in it. Obviously authorities agree or disagree about definitions and classifications of signs and symbols and so on, depending, I suppose, on the degree to which they have developed their own theories. The list of terms and the questions about them go on and on (Is body-language symbolic? Is tone of voice symbolic?), and perhaps there are no firm answers on the horizon; but there are at least things to think about. For example we can think about literary symbolism, since poets, naturally, use "expressive" language as well as everyday, straightforward language. Poetry is therefore symbolic in a different way or to a different degree than is a memo or a recipe. But a scientific formula is also made

---

[1] Langer discusses denotation and connotation somewhat differently: for her both are symbolic functions, as opposed to mere "signification," since they involve "conception" (51-52).

8

up of symbols. And a phone book is full of symbols, for of course names
are symbols (see Wheelwright 16).

Symbolism, then, is more than just a literary device, something some
of us seem to think poets and other writers use just to make it difficult
for us to understand their poems and stories and novels. Symbols are
the essence of our lives as human beings. Wheelwright notes that "Langer
offers the highly suggestive hypothesis that man's basic need, the one
function that most truly distinguishes him from beasts, is the need for
symbolization, the need to form conceptions of things" (10; see Langer 32).
As she emphasizes, symbolization is "an act essential to thought, and prior
to it. Symbolization is the essential act of mind" (33). I agree with
Langer and Wheelwright. I have to. I look at the world around me and I
clearly see that we are unique in our will, if not our need, to think about
things, to understand why things are--to make symbols. And language is
our principal way of symbolizing. As Langer says, "Words are certainly
our most important instruments of expression, our most characteristic,
universal, and enviable tools in the conduct of life. Speech," she
says, "is the mark of humanity" (36).

I know that communication, person to person, works for me in many
ways I will never understand, and it will continue to work for me
whether I ever understand it or not. But if understanding symbolism
better can help us to communicate with one another more effectively,
further work is worth the effort. This ending, then, can for me be only
a beginning.

Works Cited

Abrams, M. H. A Glossary of Literary Terms. 4th ed. New York: Holt, 1981.

Barnet, Sylvan, Morton Berman, and William Burto. A Dictionary of Literary Terms. Boston: Little, 1960.

Bevan, Edwyn. Symbolism and Belief. 1938. Boston: Beacon, 1957.

Fabun, Don. Communications: The Transfer of Meaning. Rev. ed. Beverly Hills: Glencoe, 1968.

Fiske, John. Introduction to Communication Studies. London: Methuen, 1982.

Goodman, Nelson. "Metaphor as Moonlighting." On Metaphor. Ed. Sheldon Sacks. Chicago: U of Chicago P, 1979.

Hayakawa, S. I. Language in Thought and Action. New York: Harcourt, 1949.

Holman, C. Hugh. A Handbook to Literature. 4th ed. Indianapolis: Bobbs, 1980.

Langer, Susanne K. Philosophy in a New Key: A Study in the Symbolism of Reason, Rite, and Art. 1942. New York: NAL, 1948.

Lemon, Lee T. A Glossary for the Study of English. New York: Oxford UP, 1971.

Liberman, M. M., and Edward E. Foster. A Modern Lexicon of Literary Terms. Glenview, IL: Scott, 1968.

Tindall, William York. The Literary Symbol. 1955. Bloomington: Indiana UP, 1958.

Wheelwright, Philip. The Burning Fountain: A Study in the Language of Symbolism. Rev. ed. Bloomington: Indiana UP, 1968.

Whitehead, Alfred North. Symbolism: Its Meaning and Effect. New York: Macmillan, 1927.

9

THE CORRECTION
SYMBOLS EXPLAINED

This chapter provides an alphabetical list of the abbreviations commonly used to mark students' essays, and a short list of proofreader's marks and symbols that are also useful in such marking. In most instances, a correction symbol is followed by a brief explanation of its meaning and of the steps necessary to correct the error or weakness it indicates; usually one or more examples of the error are included, along with revisions. Probably no one instructor will use all the correction symbols listed here, and some instructors will use one or more that are not included. We have tried to include all the most common symbols and to provide cross-references for those that have more than one form. Some instructors, for example, will use *fs* (fused sentence) to indicate that egregious error; but since we believe the majority will refer to it as a *run-on* sentence, we have made the latter form the main entry and included *fs* only as a cross-reference. Inside the back cover you will find a complete list of all the symbols.

When you approach a marked paper for the purpose of revision, you will probably consult this chapter first. If the brief explanation you find here does not enable you to correct a specific error, then follow the cross-references to the fuller discussions elsewhere in the book. Only a few of the items listed below, such as *awk, nsw,* and *ss,* are not discussed specifically elsewhere in the book.

ab **Undesirable or Incorrect Abbreviation**
Generally, avoid abbreviations in formal writing. Avoid abbreviations like *e.g., viz., etc.*; use the more formal expressions *for example, namely, and so forth.* Sometimes an abbreviation has become so common that it is almost a sub-

stitute for the full words. *B.C.* and *U.S.A.* are obvious examples. We often speak or write of British Columbia as *B.C.* and of Prince Edward Island as *P.E.I.*, but never of Alberta as *Alta.* or of Ontario as *Ont.* Abbreviations like *B.C.* in writing are acceptable (but the name should be spelled in full the first time it appears), whereas *Alta.* and *Ont.* are not. If you are ever in doubt about a particular instance, it is wiser to avoid the abbreviation; the full word or words will never be inappropriate.

See **46** for more information about abbreviations.

ack **Acknowledgment of Sources**
Whenever you include in an essay *information, ideas,* or *wording* that you obtained from any other written source, you must acknowledge your indebtedness to that source in accordance with the conventions of documentation. Even information from lectures and conversations should be acknowledged.

   Failure to indicate indebtedness is **plagiarism**, or literary theft. Students guilty of plagiarism will be subject to severe penalties.

See **81e**; see also **doc** (*Documentation*).

ad **Adjectives and Adverbs Confused or Misused**
The most likely kind of error in this category is the use of either an adjective or an adverb where the other one should appear. For example:

   ad: He doesn't present his argument very *good*.

Here the adjective *good* should be replaced by the adverb *well*.

See **9b** and *good, bad, badly, well* in **60**.

agr **Agreement**
1. *Agreement between subject and verb:*
A finite verb must agree with its subject in number and person.

   agr: The falseness of the paper daffodils *were* to Vera like his
          words; they were "almost too sweet to bear."

The singular *falseness,* not the plural *daffodils,* is the subject; to agree in number, therefore, the first verb should be *was,* not *were.*

See **7**.

2. *Agreement between pronouns and their antecedents:*
A pronoun must agree in person and number with its antecedent, the word—usually preceding it—to which it refers.

> *agr:* When the teacher asked for volunteers, nobody in the
> class raised *their* hand.

The indefinite pronoun *nobody* is singular; to agree with it in number, the pronoun that refers to it must be changed from *their* to *his* (not *his or her* or *his/her*; if necessary, rephrase the sentence: "When the teacher asked for volunteers, not a single hand went up." See **4d**).

> *agr:* If one is to write a good report, *you* must take careful
> notes.

The subject pronoun *one* is third person; to agree with it in person, the second-person *you* must be changed to the third-person pronoun *he* or *one*.

See **4**; see also **26d–e**.

al Illogical or Incongruous Alignment of Elements
Revise to remove the illogicality. It may be a matter of faulty predication, predicating something illogical about a subject:

> *al:* His *job* as a schoolteacher *was* one *way* he could earn the
> community's respect.

A *job* is not a *way*. The error can be corrected by revising the sentence:

> *revised:* His job as a schoolteacher helped earn him the com-
> munity's respect.
> *revised:* One way he could earn the community's respect was
> by being a schoolteacher.

Other alignment errors also result from trying to make words behave in ways that their meanings do not permit:

> *al:* The general believed that acts such as cowardice and in-
> subordination should be severely punished.

But cowardice and insubordination are not *acts.*

> *revised:* The general believed that acts of cowardice and in-
> subordination should be severely punished.

See **30**; see also **log** (*Logic*), **comp** (*Incomplete Comparison*).

ambig Ambiguous
amb Ambiguity is a particular kind of lack of clarity, namely that which lets a reader understand something in two different ways. Although ambiguity is sometimes intentional, for ex-

ample in poetry where it can enrich the meaning, it has no place in expository prose, where it only confuses the reader and thus obscures the meaning.

> *ambig:* The Prime Minister was in favour of elimination of oil price controls and tax reductions.

Here co-ordination appears to link *price controls* and *tax reductions*; the meaning then would be that the Prime Minister wanted to eliminate tax reductions—a most unpopular and therefore unlikely political stand. The ambiguity can easily be removed by rearrangement or by changing the syntax:

> *clear:* The Prime Minister was in favour of tax reductions and the elimination of oil price controls.
> *clear:* The Prime Minister was in favour of reducing taxes and eliminating price controls.

In this second version, the parallel gerunds *reducing* and *eliminating* help enforce the intended meaning.

> *ambig:* George Delgarno, a teacher, wrote an essay on the educational system in England in 1680.

Was the essay written in 1680? Or was its subject "education in 1680"? It is impossible to tell, though the first is more likely. Simply putting *in 1680* before *wrote* or after *essay* would then make it clear.

See also **cl** (*Clarity*), **dm** (*Dangling Modifier*) and **24, mm** (*Misplaced Modifier*) and **23, fp** (*Faulty Parallelism*) and **27, p** (*Punctuation*) and Chapter IV, **ref** (*Faulty Reference*) and **5.**

apos   Apostrophe Missing or Misused

1. The apostrophe is used to indicate the possessive inflection of nouns.

> *apos:* She mended the girls dresses.

Here *girls* is obviously possessive, but in the absence of an apostrophe it is impossible to tell whether it is singular or plural: either *girl's* or *girls'* is necessary to make it clear.

2. The apostrophe is NOT used for the possessive case of personal pronouns.

> *Wrong:* her's, your's, their's

3. The apostrophe is used to indicate the omission of letters in contractions.

it's (it is)	we're (we are)
isn't (is not)	you're (you are)
hasn't (has not)	who's (who is)
haven't (have not)	we've (we have)

aren't (are not)   he'll (he will)
she's (she is)   you'll (you will)
he's (he is)   shouldn't (should not)
they're (they are)   wouldn't (would not)
won't (will not: an irregular contraction)

To omit such an apostrophe is to misspell the word.

4. Do not confuse a contraction with a possessive form.

Wrong: *Who's* book is this? (Whose)
Wrong: Is this where *your* going to sleep? (you're)

Note: Contractions are not usually desirable in formal writing. If you want a relatively informal tone, however, contractions are not only permissible but desirable.

See **51v** and **51w** for complete information on the apostrophe.

art **Article Missing or Misused**

art: At end of the story everyone is happy again.

Supply the missing *the* before *end*.

art: It was *an* humiliating experience.

Change *an* to *a*.

art: It was at this point in *the* life that he decided to reform.

Remove *the*, or change it to *his*.

See **8c**; see also **id** (*Idiom*) and **58**.

awk **Awkwardness**
k *Awk* (or *k*) is the symbol most teachers use when they know that there is something wrong with a sentence but are unable to put a finger on any particular error, or when the combination of several faults is unusually complicated. *Awk* could be translated as something like "Take this sentence into the shop for diagnosis and repairs." Awkwardness can stem from several causes. It can result from laziness or haste, from indiscriminately writing down the first thing that pops into one's head. It can occur because an unsophisticated writer uses as many words as possible—and the bigger the better—and thereby contorts the normal arrangements of English sentences, mistakenly thinking that such things will impress a reader; the truth is that the simple expression is frequently the most effective and even the most elegant expression. Awkwardness often results from clumsy use of the passive voice (see **6n**), or from poor punctuation, or from confused think-

ing. Here are some examples of awkward sentences from student essays, each followed by an attempt to straighten it out:

> *awk:* Caught up in this new way of life, I felt a closer existence to every thoughts of today.
>
> *revised:* Caught up in this new way of life, I felt myself to be more intimately involved in contemporary thought.
>
> *awk:* Now, as I began to get some feeling of confidence restored in me, I thought how silly my previous experience had been.
>
> *revised:* Now, as I regained confidence, I realized how foolish had been my response to the earlier experience.
>
> *awk:* I looked for a familiar face among that great sea of faces, but this was done in vain.

Here faulty idiom (*among* instead of *in*), the passive voice (*was done*), wordiness, and unnecessary co-ordination combined to produce a slovenly sentence.

> *revised:* I looked in vain for a friend in that great sea of faces.
>
> *awk:* Since Canada nowadays comprises many people of different origins, television provides an excellent means for different ethnic groups to communicate with ones of the same origin who do not reside closely or even to introduce their customs to others of different origins.
>
> *revised:* In Canada, whose far-flung population includes people of many different origins, television enables ethnic groups to communicate with their fellows elsewhere in the country and also to introduce their customs to others.
>
> *awk:* The essay is written in a way that he relates his beliefs to the reader, but does not force the reader to digest his beliefs.
>
> *revised:* He explains his beliefs although he does not expect the reader to share them.
>
> *awk:* The poem also gives a sense of lightness in the way it rhymes and in its metre.
>
> *revised:* The poem's rhymes and metre contribute to the light tone.
>
> *awk:* During the eighteenth century, chemistry became a real science instead of the previous alchemy.
>
> *revised:* In the eighteenth century chemistry became a real science, evolving out of and replacing the pseudo-science of alchemy.
>
> *awk:* In the poem, "To an Athlete Dying Young," by A.E. Housman, the speaker poses an argument of why the athlete benefited from dying young.
>
> *revised:* In A.E. Housman's poem "To an Athlete Dying Young," the speaker argues that it was fortunate for the athlete to die so young.

awk, k

ca   Case

The case of a pronoun depends on its function in its own clause or phrase. A pronoun that is a subject or a complement must be in the subjective case:

> *ca:*   Hans and *me* dug the ditch ourselves. (I)
> *ca:*   He's the one *whom* I predicted would win the race. (who)
> *ca:*   That is *her*. (she)

A pronoun that is an object of a verb or preposition must be in the objective case:

> *ca:*   They told Albert and *I* to leave. (me)
> *ca:*   It was up to Peggy and *I* to finish the job. (me)
> *ca:*   It doesn't matter *who* you take with you. (whom)

See **3e**. For information about the possessive case of nouns and pronouns see **2b**, **3a–d**, **8a**, and **51w**.

cap   Capitalization Needed or Faulty Capitalization

> *cap:*   Near Hudson bay in the Northwest Territories is the region known as the barrens.
> *corrected:*   Near Hudson Bay in the Northwest Territories is the region known as the Barrens.

See **47**; see also **lc** (*Lower Case*).

cl   Lack of Clarity

Like awkwardness, a lack of clarity can result from many causes. The parts of a sentence may fail to go together in a meaningful way, or the words chosen to express an idea may not do so adequately, or the writer may have had only a vague idea in the first place.

> *cl:*   There is also a general sense of irony in the plot or story behind the play.

What is a *general sense* as opposed to a *sense*? What is a *sense of irony* as opposed to *irony*? Why the choice of *plot or story*? And how is it that the plot (or story) is *behind* the play? It is impossible to know what the writer meant, but here is a clear sentence that uses the major features of the original: "There are ironic elements in the plot of the play."

> *cl:*   This blessing is intended to restore faith in God when things happen such as death which you don't understand and want to blame God for letting them happen.

This sentence could perhaps have been marked *awk* as well, but the muddiness of the thought and its expression seems to be its principal fault. Sorting it out and adding some logic as well as some careful syntax produce a clearer and more succinct version:

> This blessing is intended to restore faith in God, which may be lost when incomprehensible events like death make one question God's justice.

But here is an example of an unclear sentence that remains impenetrable; not even the context offered any help to understanding it:

> *cl:* Absurdist plays work on the situation in much greater detail than the dramatic level.

Here is another sentence that goes astray; one can only wonder what the intended meaning was:

> *cl:* He compares the athlete's achievements and victories to that of death.

Sometimes even punctuation is part of the trouble:

> *p:* Before I really had time to think they wanted me to report for work in the morning.

A comma after *think* makes it more likely that the sentence will be understood on the first reading rather than the second or third.

See also **ambig** (*Ambiguous*), **awk** (*Awkward*), **5**, and **23–31**.

cliché Cliché
See **trite** (*Trite, Worn-out, Hackneyed Expression*).

coh Not Coherent; Continuity Weak
Coherence is weak or faulty when there is insufficient transition between two sentences or two paragraphs. The first sentence of a paragraph, whether it is the topic sentence or not, should in some way provide a connection with the preceding paragraph. Similarly, sentences within paragraphs should flow smoothly from one to another. Here for example are two sentences which are not smoothly connected:

> Rachel is invited both to dine at Willard's and to go out with Calla. Despite her desire to accept one of the invitations she declines both of them because it is her mother's card night.

Granted that the idea of the invitations is present in both, the sentences nevertheless need something more by way of transition. Either a *But* to begin the second sentence or a

coh

however (between commas) after the word *invitations* would provide the necessary coherence.

See **64–69** and **72b**; see also **tr** (*Transition Weak or Lacking*), and *Sentence Coherence,* **31**.

colloq **Colloquialism**
See **inf** (*Informal, Colloquial*).

comb **Combine Sentences**
An instructor may write *coord* (Co-ordinate) or *sub* (Subordinate), or even *coord or sub* together, to indicate that some kind of improvement (economy, coherence, logic) could be gained by putting two (or more) sentences together. Sometimes, however, rather than specify which (*sub* or *coord*), or in instances where neither subordination nor co-ordination would be desirable, an instructor may write *comb*, meaning simply "Combine these two (or more) sentences in the way you think best." In the following, for example, which could have been marked *w* (Wordiness) as well, the improvement is great—and obvious:

> *w-comb:* The whiteness of the snow piled on their outstretched branches gave their green colour an extra richness. This added attractiveness seemed to enhance their beauty.
>
> *revised:* The whiteness of the snow piled on their outstretched branches gave their green colour an extra richness, enhancing their beauty.

See **coord** (*Co-ordinate*), **sub** (*Subordinate*), and Exercise 12c(2), Exercise 59abc(2), and **28**.

comp **Incomplete Comparison**
inc Revise to correct incomplete or illogical comparisons.

> *comp:* She is a better skater than any girl on the team.
> *revised:* She is a better skater than any *other* girl on the team.
>
> *comp:* Life in a small town is better than a big city.
> *revised:* Life in a small town is better than (*life*) *in* a big city.
>
> *comp:* I think tomato juice is as good, if not better, than orange juice.
> *revised:* I think tomato juice is as good *as*, if not better than, orange juice.
> *revised:* I think tomato juice is as good as orange juice, if not better.

colloq

> *comp:* Fresh vegetables have more vitamins.
> *revised:* Fresh vegetables have more vitamins than canned or frozen ones.

> *comp:* I like skiing more than David.
> *revised:* I like skiing more than David does.
> *revised:* I like skiing more than I like David.

Note that **ambig** (*Ambiguous*), **cl** (*Lack of Clarity*), or **log** (*Logic*) would be an appropriate mark for some of these sentences.

See **29** and **30**.

conc **Insufficient Concreteness**

Revise by increasing the concreteness of your diction. Replace abstract words and phrases with concrete ones, or expand upon abstract statements with specific and concrete details.

> *conc:* Seymour was a very *deep* person, known only to those who really loved him—his family.

The word *deep* here is suggestive, but too abstract to be very meaningful. *Deep* can mean several different things here (consult your dictionary); more information, especially in the form of concrete examples, would enable the reader to understand precisely what the writer meant to convey. Here are two sentences whose vague abstractness and illogical circularity (see **74h**) render them almost meaningless:

> *conc, log:* The author makes the setting so good that it is very convincing.
> *conc, log:* The characters are presented as fully described people.

Don't write empty sentences like those. Inject some specific, concrete content.

See **54**.

coord **Co-ordination Needed; Combine Sentences**

When two sentences are closely related, for example in expressing a contrast, it is usually preferable to combine them, using either punctuation or a co-ordinating conjunction or both.

> *coord:* Life in the North can be very challenging. Life in a large city offers more variety.
> *revised:* Life in the North can be very challenging, but life in a large city offers more variety.

Depending on context and desired emphasis, such sentences could also be joined with a semicolon, or one or the other could be subordinated with a beginning *though* or *whereas*.

See also **sub** *(Subordination)*, **comb** *(Combine)*, **cs** *(Comma Splice)*, **fc** *(Faulty Co-ordination)*, **coh** *(Coherence)*, and *Faulty Co-ordination,* **28**.

cs   Comma Splice

A comma splice results from putting a comma between in-dependent clauses that are not joined with a co-ordinating conjunction; "splicing" the clauses together with only a comma is not enough. More than one independent clause can of course exist in one sentence, but the clauses must be either properly joined with co-ordinating conjunctions or separated by the correct punctuation.

> *cs:*   The flight from Vancouver to Toronto takes only about four hours, it seems to last forever.

The comma between the two clauses is not enough. A semi-colon (or period) would be "correct," but a poor solution because the two clauses obviously are closely related. Here the desired contrast would best be emphasized either by using an appropriate co-ordinating conjunction:

> The flight from Vancouver to Toronto takes about four hours, but it seems to last forever.

or by using a subordinating conjunction to turn the first clause into a subordinate rather than an independent clause:

> Although the flight from Vancouver to Toronto takes only about four hours, it seems to last forever.

Here is another example:

> *cs:*   Contemporary Canadian poetry is, if nothing else, at least plentiful, it pours daily from a number of influential presses.

Here, since the second clause illustrates the notion expressed in the first, a co-ordinating conjunction would not be appro-priate. One could argue that *for* would do the connecting well enough, but a better way to handle this sentence would be to emphasize the syntactic integrity of the second clause by changing the comma to a semicolon:

> *revised:*   Contemporary Canadian poetry is, if nothing else, at least plentiful; it pours daily from a number of influ-ential presses.

In that sentence even a colon would work well (see **32c**). Here is an instance where a colon would be the preferred mark to replace the comma:

> *cs:*   Slavery took hold in the South for purely economic reasons, large numbers of workers were needed to attend to the large plantations.

Comma splices, then, can be corrected by replacing the offending comma with an appropriate mark—usually a semicolon, sometimes a colon, or even a period if you decide to turn the clauses into two separate sentences—or by showing the relation between the two clauses with a precise co-ordinating or subordinating conjunction. Or sometimes you can reduce one of the clauses to a modifying phrase:

> *cs:*   The poem gives us several clues to the poet's attitude toward death, one of these is the imagery.
>
> *revised:*   The poem gives us several clues to the poet's attitude toward death, one of these being the imagery.

See **33e**; see also **comb** (*Combine*), **coord** (*Co-ordination*), **fc** (*Faulty Co-ordination*), **sub** (*Subordination*), and Exercises 10(3), 10(4), and 11a-c(2)a.

d Faulty Diction

Errors in diction are often marked with one or another specific symbol, such as *ww* (wrong word), *nsw* (no such word), *inf* (informal or colloquial), or *id* (idiom). But sometimes a teacher will simply use *d*, implying either that the error does not fall into one of those particular categories or that the student is expected to find out just what specific kind of error it is. In either event, the first thing the writer should do is consult a dictionary; *d* could be said to stand for *dictionary*.

> *d:*   If we regard the poem in this way, the recurring images of the "unwatered," aimless, barren mind of modern man would be one of the musical themes, and the imagery of water *plus* its symbolism of replenishment would be another.

In this otherwise well-wrought sentence, the word *plus* creates a stylistic disturbance. *Plus* is normally a mathematical term; it is not a conjunction, nor appropriate to this context. The meaning of *plus* in expository rather than mathematical terms is conveyed by the conjunction *and*; the preposition *with* would also serve the meaning here.

Diction can also be poor by being weak or imprecise. In the following sentence, for example, the word *outlined* is inadequate for the job it is being asked to do:

> *d:*   The program should be *outlined* in such a way that learning can take place in the field as well as in the classroom.

A word like *designed, planned,* or *organized* would be better.

See Chapter VII. See also **inf** *(Informal, Colloquial),* **conc** *(Concreteness),* **id** *(Idiom),* **jarg** *(Jargon),* **nsw** *(No Such Word),* and **ww** *(Wrong Word).*

dev   Development Needed
This mark indicates that an idea, point, or subject needs to be further developed, expanded upon; revise by supplying details, examples, or illustrations, by defining or explaining, or by some other method. It most often applies to an inadequately developed paragraph.

See **54, 67,** and **71a.**

div   Word Division
See **syl** *(Syllabication).*

dm   Dangling Modifier
Correct a dangling modifier either by changing it so that it no longer dangles or by providing a logical noun or pronoun for it to modify.

> *dm:* Running too hurriedly around the corner of the building, a newsstand suddenly loomed in front of me.
>
> *corrected:* When I too hurriedly ran around the corner of the building, a newsstand suddenly loomed in front of me.
>
> *corrected:* Running too hurriedly around the corner of the building, I was suddenly confronted by a newsstand looming before me.

See **24.**

doc   Documentation
Observe the correct forms for your notes (whether at the foot of the page or collected at the end as "Notes") and your bibliography. In Chapter IX, "The Research Paper," you will find model footnotes and bibliographical entries (see **83** and **85**).

Even if you are not writing a full-fledged research paper, when you consult books or periodicals for information or for ideas or quotations which you use in writing an essay, you must provide documentation in the form of footnotes or parenthetical references. Your instructor may also want you to include a bibliography at the end of the essay in the form of an alphabetical list of all your sources.

See **ack** *(Acknowledgment of Sources)* and Chapter IX.

emph   Emphasis Weak or Unclear

Make the sentence or paragraph properly emphatic by re-arranging or by clarifying the relationship of its parts.

> *emph:*   The older generation of our society, like the younger, is also continually confronted with both beneficial and harmful advertisements which are effective on our society *in some way or other.*

This is a flabby sentence in general, but what little strength it has is almost entirely dissipated by the limp final prepositional phrase; simply removing it would somewhat sharpen the end of the sentence, which is its most emphatic part. But further improvement can be gained by sorting out and rearranging the sentence's content and cutting out the repetition and deadwood:

> *revised:*   All of society—not just the young but the older generation as well—is bombarded with advertising that can be beneficial as well as harmful.

This may not be the best version possible, but at least it has clear emphasis.

See **18**, **70**, and **72c**; see also *Faulty Co-ordination,* **28**.

euph   Euphemism

Avoid unnecessary euphemism ("good sounding," though not necessarily good in fact). Often directness and precision are preferable to even well-intended delicacy and vagueness. Is someone lacking money to buy enough food really made to feel better by being described as "disadvantaged" rather than "poor"? During a war the destruction and evacuation of whole communities are made to seem perfectly right and proper when the process is called "pacification." When you are tempted to use a euphemism to avoid an unpleasant reality (for example describing a person as "inebriated" or "in a state of intoxication" rather than "drunk"), consider the possible virtues of being direct and succinct instead.

See **56**.

fc   Faulty Co-ordination

Faulty co-ordination occurs when unrelated clauses are presented as co-ordinate, or when related clauses are linked by punctuation or co-ordinating conjunctions which fail to indicate the correct relation.

> *fc:*   Chaucer was born in 1340 and he was the greatest poet of medieval England.

The date of Chaucer's birth and the extent of his reputation are not related or equal in value as the co-ordinating conjunction *and* implies. The significant comment is contained in the second clause; the opening clause contains a minor fact which should be subordinate to the main statement.

> *revised:* Chaucer, who was born in 1340, was the greatest poet of medieval England.
> *revised:* Chaucer (1340-1400) was the greatest poet of medieval England.
> *fc:* He had worked all summer at handsome wages *and* he had earned enough to see him through the next year at university.

The two clauses are not separate statements, but related statements of which the latter is the more significant one. The opening clause should either be subordinated with the conjunction which precisely indicates the relation between the ideas in the sentence:

> *revised:* Since he had worked all summer at handsome wages, he had earned enough to see him through the next year at university.

or even be changed to a participial phrase:

> *revised:* Having worked all summer at handsome wages, he had earned enough to see him through the next year at university.

See **28**; see also **comb** (*Combine*), **coord** (*Co-ordination*), and **sub** (*Subordination*).

fig **Inappropriate or Confusing Figurative Language**
Revise to change or remove figurative language (similes, metaphors) that is inappropriate or mixed.

> *fig:* Physical Education provides a stepping stone on which students can learn what to do with their leisure time.

The image of a stepping stone adds nothing but oddity to this sentence. Some more appropriate figure may have been in the writer's mind, but the statement is probably better without the metaphor:

> *revised:* Physical Education offers students an opportunity to learn how to use their spare time.

Here is an example of a mixed metaphor:

> *fig:* Like a bolt from the blue the idea grabbed him, and it soon grew into one of his most prized pieces of mental furniture.

One of the troubles with clichés that are dead metaphors is that we often fail to visualize them; result: absurdity. The *bolt from the blue*, even if allowed, could scarcely *grab* anyone, nor could it grow (like a plant?) into a piece of furniture. The urge to be metaphorical backfired on the writer. Don't thoughtlessly juxtapose incongruous images.

See **53**.

fp **Faulty Parallelism**

// Revise by making co-ordinated elements grammatically parallel.

> *fp:* For me England brings back memories of pleasant walks in Cornwall on some windblown lea, looking out to sea dressed in warm woollen jerseys, and feeling a warmth brought about by being with my family in that place.

The preposition *of* here has three objects: *walks* is a normal noun whereas *looking* and *feeling* are verbal nouns (gerunds). Although they are all nouns, they are not strictly parallel. Repeating *of* before *looking* and *feeling* would improve the sentence, but it would be better to make the elements grammatically parallel:

> *revised:* For me England brings back pleasant memories of *walking* dressed in warm woollen jerseys in Cornwall on some windblown lea, *looking* out to sea, and *feeling* a warmth brought about by being with my family in that place.

(The phrase *dressed in warm woollen jerseys* seems more appropriate to the windblown lea than to looking out to sea.)

There is also the kind of error in which a parallel structure breaks down—or rather is not sufficiently built up. Consider the following sentence:

> *fp:* During my visit I had the chance to get involved with the children, help with the shopping and cooking—all of which helped make the experience enjoyable.

The implication of the sentence structure here is that we are going to be given more than two things (and the phrase *all of which* makes it sound as though we had been told more than we have been). That is, the implied parallel series after *to* is not fulfilled.

> *revised:* During my visit I had the chance to get involved with the children and to help with the shopping and the cooking; these activities helped make the experience enjoyable.

fp, //

Alternatively, at least a third element could be added to the abortive series.

See **27**.

frag **Unacceptable Fragment**
Word groups punctuated as sentences but which do not fulfill the requirements of sentences are usually unacceptable. The fragment is one of the most common and disrupting of these patterns. Fragmentary patterns either lack one or more of the essential sentence elements or are grammatically dependent upon a word or words in a preceding sentence.

> *frag:* Corbett was chosen to be the next attorney general. *He being clever and remarkably well versed in the law.*

The italicized group of words lacks a finite verb (*being* is a participle) and is therefore not a major sentence; yet it does not come across as an acceptable minor sentence. It is a fragment and should be part of the preceding sentence.

> *frag:* The convention was held at the Cornish Hotel. *Because it has a large banquet room which would accommodate us all.*

The italicized group of words is grammatically dependent upon the verb *was held* in the preceding sentence; it answers the question "why?" and is therefore an adverbial clause, and should not be written independently as a sentence.

In some fragmentary patterns both faults may occur:

> *frag:* I stayed home last weekend. *Having no money.*

The italicized group lacks both a subject and a finite verb and is grammatically dependent upon the pronoun "I."

> *frag:* Toll-roads would result in a general saving for everyone. *Lower sales taxes on automobiles and parts, and decreased levy on gasoline.*

The italicized fragment lacks a finite verb and is also in apposition to *general saving* in the preceding sentence.

Any word group which cannot stand by itself and communicate effectively is suspect. Avoid this serious error.

Note: Fragmentary patterns can sometimes be used effectively as a stylistic device by skilled writers. Unless you belong in that category, write complete sentences. If you deliberately use fragmentary patterns in essays, indicate in a marginal

frag

note that their presence is intentional. Your instructor can then tell you whether they succeed or fail, and why.

See **1y** and **20**.

fs **Fused Sentence**
See **run-on**.

gen **Inadequately Supported Generalization**
See **54b** and **conc** (*Insufficient Concreteness*).

gr **Error in Grammar**
Although several errors, such as *agr, dm, ref,* and *t,* fall into the category of grammatical error, instructors will sometimes simply mark an error *gr* either because it includes more than one kind of mistake or because they want a student to learn by discovering what the particular error is. An instructor may want to emphasize that an error like *The reason . . . is because* is not merely a matter of careless wording but an error in grammar: Since *is* is a linking verb, it can correctly be followed only by a complement that is either an adjective or a noun (see **6a, 1g, 1h**); but *because* introduces an adverbial modifier: the construction is therefore ungrammatical. There are, then, errors in grammar that are not in any of the specifically identified categories.

id **Faulty Idiom, Unidiomatic Usage**
Idiom refers to the forms of expression and the structures peculiar to a particular language. Idioms are not necessarily logical or explicable in grammatical terms. Correct marked errors by changing the unidiomatic usage to an idiomatic one. Errors in idiom most often occur with prepositions, as in the following examples:

> *id:* The extent of Creighton's influence *towards* our view of Canadian history is not fully appreciated.

Change *towards* to the idiomatic *on*.

> *id:* Iago has a reputation *of* honesty.

Change *of* to *for*.

See **58**; see also *Articles,* **8c**.

inc **Incomplete Comparison**
See **comp**.

inf **Inappropriate Informal or Colloquial Diction**
Replace the inappropriate word or words with something more formal.

> *inf:* He is the most *stuck-up* boy in the class. (*conceited, vain, egotistical, snobbish*)

See **52b.**

ital **Italics Needed or Incorrect**
Correct by italicizing or by removing unwanted italics. (In typed or handwritten material, italics are represented by <u>underlining</u>.)

> *ital:* "A Night to Remember" is about the sinking of the Titanic.
> *corrected:* *A Night to Remember* is about the sinking of the Titanic.

See **49**; see also *Titles,* **48.**

jarg **Jargon**
Revise to avoid unnecessary jargon.

> *jarg:* A truly professional-type player, he seemed able to judge every move from the standpoint of its bottom-line effect.
> *revised:* A true professional, he seemed able to judge the ultimate effect of every move he made.

See **59h.**

k **Awkward**
See **awk** (*Awkward*).

lc **Lower Case**
Change incorrect capital letter(s) to lower case.

> *lc:* You can now find Champagne made elsewhere than in France.
> *corrected:* You can now find champagne made elsewhere than in France.
> *lc:* I had always planned to get a University education.
> *corrected:* I had always planned to get a university education.

See **47.**

leg **Legibility, Illegible**
Re-do any messy or poor handwriting or struck-over typing that cannot be read clearly.

lev   **Inappropriate Level of Diction**
See **52**.

log   **Logic: Illogical as Phrased; Logicality of Reasoning Questioned**

Illogic underlies many different kinds of error and much weak writing and thinking. For fuller information, see **29** and **74e–h**. Nevertheless, **log** is frequently the mark used to indicate an error of logic arising out of the way something has been phrased. For example:

> *log:*   Insecurity *is* a characteristic basic to Davies's nature and it *becomes* a *consistent* weakness of his *throughout* the play.

If insecurity *is* a basic characteristic, it can scarcely *become* consistent in the course of the play. Similarly, it can scarcely *become* consistent *throughout* the play, since *throughout* logically contradicts the meaning of *become*. Here is another example:

> *log:*   In giving a precise definition of what this mental science is, Asimov is very vague.

The illogicality is obvious. At least three meanings are possible:

> *clear:*   Asimov fails to provide a precise definition of this mental science.
> *clear:*   Asimov's definition of this mental science is very vague.
> *clear:*   Asimov deals only vaguely with this mental science and makes no attempt to define it.

See also **29**, **al** (*Alignment*), **30**, and **74**.

mix   **Mixed Construction**

A shift from one pattern of syntax to another within a single sentence.

> *mix:*   The choice was between junk food that would be filling or a smaller but nourishing meal.

To revise, decide on one pattern or the other:

> *revised:*   The choice was *between* junk food that would be filling *and* a smaller but nourishing meal.
> *revised:*   We could choose *either* junk food that would be filling *or* a smaller but nourishing meal.

(In the last version, the word *either* could be omitted.)

See **25**.

mm **Misplaced Modifier**
Revise by moving the modifying word or phrase to the logical place in the sentence.

> *mm:* The solution is to make Demetrius view Helena as the object of his love *rather than Hermia*.
>
> *revised:* The solution is to make Demetrius view Helena rather than Hermia as the object of his love.
>
> *mm:* Sauron wished to be the Dark Lord of Middle-earth, and *almost* had enough power to succeed *twice*.
>
> *revised:* Sauron wished to be Dark Lord of Middle-earth, and twice had almost enough power to succeed.

See **23**; see also **wo** (*Word Order*).

ms **Improper Manuscript Form or Conventions**
A conscientious writer is careful to follow certain conventions pertaining to the form and presentation of a manuscript. These include such things as indenting paragraphs clearly, leaving two spaces after a period, not underlining one's own title, being consistent with punctuation marks, and leaving spaces between the dots of an ellipsis.

See Chapter V.

nsw **No Such Word**
Inventiveness and originality are commendable virtues in most instances, but they are inadequate substitutes for knowledge. When you need a particular word to do a special job, it is usually unnecessary to invent it; the English language is rich in vocabulary and is unlikely to let you down if you will take the trouble to look for the word you need. If you have any doubt about a word you've used, if it seems somewhat unusual or if it does not quite ring true, your dictionary can in a moment settle the question. A little extra care will enable you to avoid using such concoctions as these, all of which occurred in students' essays:

> ableness (ability)
> abolishment (abolition)
> afraidness (fear)
> artistism (artistry)
> condensated (condensed)
> cowardism, cowardness (cowardice)
> deteriorized (deteriorated)
> disgustion (disgust)
> enrichen (enrich)

mm

eternalty (eternity)
freedomship (freedom)
fruitition (fruition)
infidelous (unfaithful)
irregardless (regardless, irrespective)
nonchalantness (nonchalance)
prejudism (prejudice)
prophesize (prophesy)
scepticalism (scepticism)
superfluosity (superfluity, superfluousness)

num   Incorrect Use of Numerals
See **50** for the conventions governing the use of numerals.

org   Weak or Faulty Organization
Repetition, choppiness, lack of proportion or emphasis, haphazard order—all these and more can be signs of poor organization. It may be necessary to rethink your outline.

See **65** and **73e–j**.

p   Error in Punctuation
Punctuation marks are symbols that should be just as meaningful to readers as the symbols of speech (words) with which they are associated in writing. In speech, "punctuation" takes the form of inflections of voice, pauses, changes in pitch or intensity of utterance. In order to communicate meaningfully and clearly on paper, one must pay as much attention to finding the precise punctuation as one pays to the selection of one's words and structures. When you find *p* in the margin of your paper, refer to Chapter IV to find out not only *what* is wrong or weak, but also *why* it is so. Learning the nuances of punctuation is not easy. Although some of its conventions are arbitrary, good punctuation is to a considerable extent an expression of good taste and rhetorical understanding. Try to develop these qualities by learning the language of punctuation.

See Chapter IV, **32-44**.

para   Paragraphing
See **61-71**.

pas   Weak Passive Voice
This mark means that in the reader's opinion the sentence in question would be better served by a verb in the active voice than by one in the passive voice. (A verb in the passive

voice consists of some form of the verb *be* followed by a past participle; it converts the subject of a clause into the receiver of the action.)

> *pas:*   In these lines the comparison of himself and his lover to flies *is made.*
> *active:*   In these lines the speaker *compares* himself and his lover to flies.

> *pas:*   Davies always finds his fears *being played upon* by Mick.
> *active:*   Davies always finds that Mick *plays upon* his fears.
> *active:*   Mick always *plays upon* Davies's fears.

See **6n.**

passim   Latin for *throughout*; used to indicate that an error, such as the misspelling of a name, needs to be corrected throughout an essay.

pred   **Faulty Predication**
See **al** (*Alignment*) and **30.**

pv   **Point of View Inconsistent or Unclear; Shift in Perspective**
Revise to remove the awkward or illogical shift in tense, mood, or voice of verbs, or person or number of pronouns.

> *pv:*   One should never forget *your* snowshoes. (*one's*).
> *pv:*   It was four in the afternoon, beginning to get dark, and we *are* still only half-way down the mountain. (*were*)

See **26.**

Perspective can also seem to shift because of a lack of parallelism:

> *pv, fp:*   Ralph said that it was raining and he preferred to stay home.

If "he preferred to stay home" is meant as a part of what he said, then a second *that* is required after *and*; otherwise, *he preferred* could be taken as parallel to *Ralph said*. That is, without the second *that, he preferred* would be from the writer's point of view rather than Ralph's.

See **27a.**

q, Q   **Error in Handling of Quoted Material or Quotation Marks**
Sometimes this will refer to nothing more than the careless omission of quotation marks—usually at the end of a quo-

tation. But it could also refer to incorrect punctuation with quoted material, awkwardly introduced quoted material, and the like. If the error so marked is not an obvious one, you may have to consult the section on quotation to find out what is wrong.

See **43**.

red Redundancy

Redundancy can mean simply wordiness, but it is often used to refer specifically to the awkward and unnecessary repetition of the meaning of one word in another word. In the sentence "But he was not unfriendly though," the *But* and the *though* do the same job; one of them must go (obviously the *though*, since it is informal and also weakens the end of the sentence: see *although, though* in **60**, and **18c**). Here are two more examples:

> *red:* Throughout the entire story the tone is one of unrelieved gloom.

Since *throughout* means *all through, from beginning to end*, the word *entire* merely repeats what has already been said.

> *revised:* Throughout the story the tone is one of unrelieved gloom.

But this is still redundant, for if the tone is *unrelieved*, then it must be constant throughout the story. Hence further tightening is possible:

> *re-revised:* The story's tone is one of unrelieved gloom.

Again:

> *red:* Puck's playful pranks include tricks on housewives and village maids.

Here the writer's choice of the word *pranks* is accurate and effective, but since *pranks* are *frolicsome tricks*, the addition of the word *playful* is redundant and destroys the effectiveness.

> *revised:* Puck's pranks include tricks on housewives and village maids.

One might even want to try to get rid of the word *tricks*:

> Puck plays pranks on housewives and village maids.

See **59c**; see also **w** (*Wordiness*).

ref Weak or Faulty Pronoun Reference

Pronouns must clearly refer to their antecedents. The following sentence, for example, is muddled because it is not clear whom the pronouns refer to:

> *ref:* Because of all the attention which Seymour and Buddy gave to Franny and Zooey when *they* were young children, *they* never allowed *them* to develop *their* own ideas of life.

One can, by careful rereading, extract the sense of this sentence, but it is the writer's job to make clear sense, not the reader's to puzzle it out.

> *revised:* When Franny and Zooey were young, Seymour and Buddy gave *them* so much attention that the children were never able to develop their own ideas of life.

One clear pronoun instead of four confusing ones (and the redundant *young children* has been broken up, as well). Here is another example:

> *ref:* Merlin's power, quite naturally, is partially a result of his "Sight" and what are thought to be his magical powers. An example of *this* is given during the battle between King Ambrosius and the Saxons.

Clearly one must also be careful with demonstrative pronouns: here the reference of *this* is obscure. Probably in the writer's mind *this* somehow referred to the entire idea expressed in the first sentence. In other words, *this* has no precise antecedent, and the reference is therefore loose at best. A clearer and more precise version (clearing up the awkward parallelism and the passive voice as well) is possible:

> *revised:* Merlin's power derives from a combination of his Sight and his reputed magic. The battle between King Ambrosius and the Saxons provides an illustration of this fact.

Changing the demonstrative pronoun to a demonstrative adjective usually makes things clearer. But the passage is still clumsy and wordy. Try again, combining the sentences:

> *revised:* As the battle between King Ambrosius and the Saxons illustrates, Merlin's power derives from a combination of his Sight and his reputed magic.

Much tighter.

See **5**; see also **4**.

rep Weak, Awkward, or Unnecessary Repetition

This is another kind of wordiness that requires pruning. Although repetition is often useful for achieving emphasis and coherence, unnecessary repetition only encumbers.

> *rep:* The snow was falling heavily, but I didn't mind the snow, for I have always enjoyed the things one can do in the snow.

The repetition of *snow* at the end is all right, but the middle one must go; replace *the snow* with *it*, or with nothing at all. See **59b**.

run-on Run-on or Fused Sentence
fs Failure to put any punctuation between two independent clauses not joined by a co-ordinating conjunction results in a run-on sentence. Along with *comma splices* and *fragments*, *run-ons* are considered extremely serious errors. Since the run-on is often merely a careless slip, caused by writing too fast and not proofreading carefully, it should be easy to prevent.

> *run-on:* Vancouver is the most beautifully situated city in Canada it also has some ugly slums.

Like the comma splice, a run-on can be corrected by inserting a semicolon, by inserting a comma and a co-ordinating conjunction, or by subordinating one of the clauses and inserting a comma. One could also insert a period, making two sentences; this would be the best correction if indeed the error was merely careless omission of the period. In the present instance, however, one of the other methods would be better. For example:

> Vancouver is the most beautifully situated city in Canada; it also has some ugly slums.

This is correct, but weak in the same way that a period would be; a conjunctive adverb, however, will make the point of the contrast clear:

> Vancouver is the most beautifully situated city in Canada; however, it also has some ugly slums.

The other two ways of correcting a run-on work well here:

> Vancouver is the most beautifully situated city in Canada, but it also has some ugly slums.
> Although Vancouver is the most beautifully situated city in Canada, it also has some ugly slums.

See **22** and **33j**; see also **cs** (*Comma Splice*).

shift Shift in Perspective
See **pv** (*Point of View*).

sp   Spelling

When you make an error in spelling, do not simply try to guess how it should be corrected, for you are likely to get it wrong again. Instead, check the word in your dictionary, and take the opportunity to find out all that the dictionary tells you about the word, not only for the sake of learning something, but also because it will help fix the word in your mind and thus help you avoid misspelling it again. Then check Chapter VI to see if your error fits any of the categories discussed there; if so, study the principles involved. It is also important that you keep a list of all the words you misspell; review it often so that you will become thoroughly familiar with the correct spelling of those words.

See Chapter VI, **51**.

split   Unnecessary Split Infinitive
See **10b**.

ss   Sentence Structure or Sentence Sense

Sometimes an instructor will put *ss* (or only *s*) in the margin opposite a sentence to indicate that something is wrong with its sense or its structure, leaving it to the writer to discover what the problem is; it may for example be a grammatical error, or a faulty arrangement, or a lack of clarity. Or the sentence may be faulty in some way not covered by any of the more specific categories. If this mark appears often, you may need to review Chapters I and III, on sentences.

stet   Let it Stand (Latin)

This mark indicates that you were right the first time, that when you changed something, such as a punctuation mark or the spelling of a word, you should have left it the way it was. To correct, therefore, merely restore it to its original form. (Note that an instructor will be able to advise you of this only if you cancel a word or mark with a single line through it; if you blot out the original entirely, you may never find out that your first instinct was correct.)

sub   Subordination Needed; Combine Sentences

> *sub:*   Forster has also done a superb job in his use of examples. His examples are clear and precise.
> *revised:*   Forster has also done a superb job in his use of examples, which are clear and precise.

As two sentences this example was wordy. Even the revised

version could be made tighter.

> *better:*   Forster has also provided clear and precise examples.

See also **coord** (*Co-ordination*), **comb** (*Combine*), **fc** (*Faulty Co-ordination*), **coh** (*Coherence*), and **28**.

syl   Syllabication

This mark (or sometimes *div*, for *word division*) indicates that you have incorrectly or inappropriately broken a word at the end of a line. Consult your dictionary to find out where the syllable breaks occur in the word. If that is not the problem, then check *Syllabication and Word Division* to find out what you have done wrong.

See **45b**.

t   Error in Tense

> I often think back to the day, five years ago, when I bought my first horse. To many people this wouldn't be very
> *t:*   exciting, but I *have wanted* a horse for as long as I *can* remember.

Change the present perfect *have wanted* to the correct *had wanted*, which is past perfect, and *can* to *could*, which is past.

See **6g-i**.

title   Manuscript Conventions for Titles
See **48**.

tr   Transition Weak or Lacking

Provide some kind of transitional word or phrase, or improve upon an existing one, or otherwise improve the transition at the place indicated—which will be either between two paragraphs or between two sentences.

See **coh** (*Coherence*) and **69**.

trite   Trite, Worn-out, Hackneyed Expression

Remove unnecessary or weak clichés; if need be replace them with fresh diction or reword the sentence. Some clichés will simply be wordy and therefore wholly or partly expendable; others will have to be replaced with something fresher. The following example contains both kinds:

> *trite:*   It *goes without saying* that *over the years many and diverse* opinions have been held regarding the origin of the universe.

> *revised:*   Ever since people began thinking about it, astronomers and others have held many different opinions about the origin of the universe.

The passive voice of *have been held* was also contributing to the sluggishness of the sentence.

See **59e**.

u   Unity of Sentence, Paragraph, or Essay Is Weak
See **28, 63,** and **72a**.

us   Usage
A subcategory of *diction*, this refers specifically to the kind of advice given in the *Checklist of Troublesome Words and Phrases*.

See **60**.

var   Variety
Try to improve the variety of lengths, kinds, and patterns of your sentences (see **17**) or your paragraphs (see **71b**), or both.

vb   Verb Form
This abbreviation will mark an error in the form of a verb, for example an incorrect inflection or an incorrect principal part of an irregular verb.

See **6b-f**.

w   Wordiness
If your desire to reach a required word-count has been greater than your desire to achieve crisp, clear, effective communication, you may find this mark haunting the margins of an essay. Try to think of the words in each sentence as costing money, say a dollar apiece; perhaps that will make it easier to be economical. Mere economy, of course, is not a virtue; never sacrifice something necessary just to reduce the number of words. But don't use several words when one will not only do the same job but even do it better, and don't use words that do no real work at all. Here are some examples of squandered words:

> *w:*   In today's society, England has earned herself a name of respect with everyone in the world.
> *revised:*   England has earned universal respect. ($11.00 saved)

Again:

w: His words have a romantic quality to them.

The phrase *to them* does no work. In fact, its effect is negative because it destroys the emphatic crispness of the meaningful part of the sentence.

w: Hardy regarded poetry as his serious work, and wrote novels only in order to make enough money to live on.

revised: Hardy regarded poetry as his serious work, and wrote novels only to make a living. ($5.00 saved)

w: Othello's trust in Iago becomes evident during the first encounter that the reader observes between the two characters.

revised: Othello's trust in Iago becomes evident during their first encounter. ($8.00 saved)

w: The flash of lightning is representative of God's power.

revised: The flash of lightning represents God's power.

Only $2.00 saved, but the sentence is much more direct and vigorous.

See **59**; see also **red** (*Redundant*) and **rep** (*Repetition*).

wo **Word Order**

This mark means that you should examine the word order of a sentence to see how it can be improved. A misplaced modifier is one kind of faulty word order, but there are other kinds not so easily classified.

wo: She was naturally hurt by his indifference.

revised: Naturally she was hurt by his indifference.

The potential ambiguity could also have been removed by putting commas around *naturally*, but that would slow the sentence down unnecessarily.

wo: I will never forget the day July 17, 1975, when I began my first job.

revised: I will never forget July 17, 1975, the day I began my first job.

wo: The image created in the advertisement is what really makes us buy the product and not the product itself.

revised: The image created in the advertisement, not the product itself, is what makes us buy it.

This is not the only possible revision, of course, but it is the simplest, and the sentence is now clearer and less awkward.

wo: Only at the end was clearly revealed the broad scope of the poem and the intensity of the emotions involved.

There seems no justification for such awkward distortion of normal sentence order.

> *revised:* Only at the end were the poem's broad scope and the intensity of its emotions revealed.

Note: In a stated comparison using *similar to*, a noun modified by the adjective *similar* should precede, not follow it:

> *wo:* The film has a similar plot to that of Shakespeare's *The Tempest.*
>
> *revised:* The film has a plot similar to that of Shakespeare's *The Tempest.*

See **mm** *(Misplaced Modifier)* and **1s-t, 8d,** and **9d.**

ww **Wrong Word**
This category of diction error covers those mistakes which result from confusion about meaning or usage. For example:

> *ww:* England is a nation *who* has brought the past and the present together.

Who refers to persons, not things; usage demands *that* or *which* in this context (see **3d** and **37a**, Note).

> *ww:* He came to the meeting at the special *bequest* of the chairman.

A glance at the dictionary confirms that *bequest* cannot be the right word here; the writer probably confused it with *request* and *behest.*

See **57**; see also **51-l** and **51m.**

Here are a few other symbols often used in marking essays:

ℰ	Delete, omit
¶ ; no ¶	Paragraph; no paragraph (sometimes abbreviated *para*)
//	Parallelism; see *fp*
X	Obvious error (e.g., typographical)
∧	Something omitted? Insert
=/	Insert hyphen
?	Something questionable or unclear: Is this what you mean?
∿	Transpose
◡	Close up
#	Space; more space
✓	Something especially good

XII

OMNIBUS CHECKLIST FOR PLANNING, WRITING, AND REVISING

Here is a list of questions to ask yourself about any piece of writing before you consider it finished. If you can conscientiously answer all of these questions in the affirmative, your essay should be not just adequate, but good.

1. After planning the essay, ask yourself these questions:

Subject	Have I chosen an interesting *subject*? (**73a**)
	Have I sufficiently *limited* my subject? (**73b**)
Audience and Purpose	Have I thought about *audience* and *purpose*? Have I written down a statement of purpose and a profile of my audience? (**73c**)
Data	Have I collected or generated *more than enough material*? (**73d**)
Organization and Outline (**73e-j**)	Does my *thesis statement* state a proposition about the subject?
	Is each heading and subheading on my outline, including the T.S., a *single complex or simple sentence*?
	Have I *at least three and no more than about seven* main headings?
	Is the content of my T.S. *equal* to that of the main headings combined?

Is the content of each main heading and each sub-heading *equal* to that of any subheadings under it?

Are my main headings reasonably *parallel* to each other?

Are the items in each set of subheadings reasonably *parallel* to each other?

Does each set of parallel subheadings consist of *at least two and not more than about seven* parts?

Have I chosen a good *order* for the main parts?

Have I chosen a good *order* for each set of subparts?

2. After completing the essay, ask yourself these questions:

Title	Does the *title* of my essay clearly indicate the subject?
	Does the *title* have something to catch a reader's interest?
Structure	Does my *beginning* (introduction) in some way try to engage a reader's curiosity or interest?
	Have I kept the *introductory part* of my essay from becoming disproportionately long? (73-I)
	Have I clearly stated my *subject* (and perhaps my *thesis* as well) somewhere near the beginning of the essay? (73-I)
	Is my *ending* (conclusion) such as to convey a sense of completion? (72c, 75[9])
	Have I kept my *ending* (conclusion) short enough, not overdone it with unnecessary repetition and summary? (75[9])
Unity *Development* *Emphasis*	Is my essay *unified*? Do all its parts contribute, and have I avoided digression? (72a)
	Have I been sufficiently *particular*, and not left any generalizations unsupported? (54)
	Have I devoted an appropriate amount of space (*emphasis*) to each part? (72c)
Paragraphs	Does the first sentence of each paragraph (except perhaps the first, and last, and any patently transitional ones) *mention* the overall subject of the essay in some way? (66b, 72a)
	Does the first sentence of each paragraph (except the first) provide a clear *transition* from the preceding paragraph? (66b)

Does the first sentence of each substantive paragraph clearly state the *topic* of that paragraph—or, if it is not the first sentence, is the *topic sentence* effective where it is placed? (**66a, 67c**)

Is each substantive paragraph *long* enough to *develop* its topic adequately? (**71a**)

Does each paragraph *conclude* adequately, but not too self-consciously? (**68**)

Coherence   Do the sentences in each paragraph have sufficient *coherence* with each other? (**64-69**)

Is the *coherence* between sentences and between paragraphs *smooth*, or have I inserted unnecessary transitional devices? (**69**)

Sentences   Is each sentence (especially compound, complex, or longer ones) *coherent* within itself? (**31**)

Is each sentence clear and *emphatic* in making its point? (**18**)

Have I avoided monotony by using a variety of *kinds* and *lengths* of sentences? (**16, 17**)

Have I avoided the *passive voice* except where it is clearly necessary or desirable? (**6n, 18f**)

Diction   Have I used *words* whose meanings I am sure of, or checked the *dictionary* for any whose meanings I am not sure of? (Chapter VII)

Is my diction as *concrete* and *specific* as possible? (**54a**)

Have I avoided *unidiomatic* usages? (**58**)

Have I weeded out any unnecessary repetitions and other *wordiness*? (**59**)

Have I excluded *jargon* and unnecessary *clichés* and *euphemisms* from my diction? (**59d-h, 56**)

Have I avoided *slang* and *informal* diction—unless intentional—and also any *overformal* diction, or "fine writing"? (**52**)

Have I avoided inappropriate or confusing *figurative language*? (**53**)

Grammar   Are all my sentences *grammatically sound*—free of dangling modifiers, agreement errors, incorrect tenses and cases, and the like? (Chapters II and III)

Have I avoided *run-ons* and unacceptable *fragments* and *comma splices*? (**33j, 1y, 33e**)

revising, checklist

Punctuation
Spelling
Mechanics

Is the *punctuation* of each sentence correct and effective? (Reading aloud, with special attention to punctuation, can be helpful.) (Chapter IV)

Have I checked all my words—reading backwards if necessary—for possible *spelling* errors? (Chapter VI)

Have I carefully *proofread*, and corrected all careless and typographical errors? (**73o**)

Is my manuscript neat and legible, and does it conform to all the *manuscript conventions*? (Chapter V)

Have I introduced and handled all *quotations* properly? (**43**; Chapter IX)

Have I checked all *quotations* for accuracy? (**81**)

Acknowledg-
ment

Have I *acknowledged* everything that requires acknowledgment? (**80, 81**)

Have I checked my *documentation*, my notes and bibliography, for accuracy and correct form? (**83, 85**)

The Last Step

Have I read my essay aloud as a final check on how it sounds?

revising, checklist

INDEX